Types and Programming Languages

Types and Programming Languages

Benjamin C. Pierce

The MIT Press
Cambridge, Massachusetts
London, England

This book was set in Lucida Bright by the author using the LaTeX document preparation system.

Printed and bound in the United States of America.

Library of Congress Cataloging-in-Publication Data

Pierce, Benjamin C.
  Types and programming languages / Benjamin C. Pierce
      p.   cm.
  Includes bibliographical references and index.
  ISBN 978-0-262-16209-8 (hc. : alk. paper)
  1. Programming languages (Electronic computers). I. Title.

QA76.7 .P54   2002   6 - 17 - 14
005.13—dc21

                                                  2001044428

    10 9

Contents

Preface

The study of type systems—and of programming languages from a type-theoretic perspective—has become an energetic field with major applications in software engineering, language design, high-performance compiler implementation, and security. This text offers a comprehensive introduction to the fundamental definitions, results, and techniques in the area.

Audience

The book addresses two main audiences: graduate students and researchers specializing in programming languages and type theory, and graduate students and mature undergraduates from all areas of computer science who want an introduction to key concepts in the theory of programming languages. For the former group, the book supplies a thorough tour of the field, with sufficient depth to proceed directly to the research literature. For the latter, it provides extensive introductory material and a wealth of examples, exercises, and case studies. It can serve as the main text for both introductory graduate-level courses and advanced seminars in programming languages.

Goals

A primary aim is **coverage** of core topics, including basic operational semantics and associated proof techniques, the untyped lambda-calculus, simple type systems, universal and existential polymorphism, type reconstruction, subtyping, bounded quantification, recursive types, and type operators, with shorter discussions of numerous other topics.

A second main goal is **pragmatism**. The book concentrates on the use of type systems in programming languages, at the expense of some topics (such as denotational semantics) that probably would be included in a more mathematical text on typed lambda-calculi. The underlying computational substrate is a call-by-value lambda-calculus, which matches most present-day programming languages and extends easily to imperative constructs such as references and exceptions. For each language feature, the main concerns are the practical *motivations* for considering this feature, the techniques needed to prove *safety* of languages that include it, and the *implementation issues* that it raises—in particular, the design and analysis of typechecking algorithms.

A further goal is respect for the **diversity** of the field; the book covers numerous individual topics and several well-understood combinations but does not attempt to bring everything together into a single unified system. Unified presentations have been given for some subsets of the topics—for example, many varieties of "arrow types" can be elegantly and compactly treated in the uniform notation of *pure type systems*—but the field as a whole is still growing too rapidly to be fully systematized.

The book is designed for **ease of use**, both in courses and for self-study. Full solutions are provided for most of the exercises. Core definitions are organized into self-contained figures for easy reference. Dependencies between concepts and systems are made as explicit as possible. The text is supplemented with an extensive bibliography and index.

A final organizing principle is **honesty.** All the systems discussed in the book (except a few that are only mentioned in passing) are implemented. Each chapter is accompanied by a typechecker and interpreter that are used to check the examples mechanically. These implementations are available from the book's web site and can be used for programming exercises, experimenting with extensions, and larger class projects.

To achieve these goals, some other desirable properties have necessarily been sacrificed. The most important of these is **completeness** of coverage. Surveying the whole area of programming languages and type systems is probably impossible in one book—certainly in a textbook. The focus here is on careful development of core concepts; numerous pointers to the research literature are supplied as starting points for further study. A second non-goal is the practical **efficiency** of the typechecking algorithms: this is not a book on industrial-strength compiler or typechecker implementation.

Structure

Part I of the book discusses untyped systems. Basic concepts of abstract syntax, inductive definitions and proofs, inference rules, and operational semantics are introduced first in the setting of a very simple language of numbers and booleans, then repeated for the untyped lambda-calculus. Part II covers the simply typed lambda-calculus and a variety of basic language features such as products, sums, records, variants, references, and exceptions. A preliminary chapter on typed arithmetic expressions provides a gentle introduction to the key idea of type safety. An optional chapter develops a proof of normalization for the simply typed lambda-calculus using Tait's method. Part III addresses the fundamental mechanism of subtyping; it includes a detailed discussion of metatheory and two extended case studies. Part IV covers recursive types, in both the simple *iso-recursive* and the trickier *equi-recursive* formulations. The second of the two chapters in this part develops the metatheory of a system with equi-recursive types and subtyping in the mathematical framework of coinduction. Part V takes up polymorphism, with chapters on ML-style type reconstruction, the more powerful impredicative polymorphism of System F, existential quantification and its connections with abstract data types, and the combination of polymorphism and subtyping in systems with bounded quantification. Part VI deals with type operators. One chapter covers basic concepts; the next develops System F_ω and its metatheory; the next combines type operators and bounded quantification to yield System $F^\omega_{<:}$; the final chapter is a closing case study.

The major dependencies between chapters are outlined in Figure P-1. Gray arrows indicate that only part of a later chapter depends on an earlier one.

The treatment of each language feature discussed in the book follows a common pattern. Motivating examples are first; then formal definitions; then proofs of basic properties such as type safety; then (usually in a separate chapter) a deeper investigation of metatheory, leading to typechecking algorithms and their proofs of soundness, completeness, and termination; and finally (again in a separate chapter) the concrete realization of these algorithms as an OCaml (Objective Caml) program.

An important source of examples throughout the book is the analysis and design of features for object-oriented programming. Four case-study chapters develop different approaches in detail—a simple model of conventional imperative objects and classes (Chapter 18), a core calculus based on Java (Chapter 19), a more refined account of imperative objects using bounded quantification (Chapter 27), and a treatment of objects and classes in the purely functional setting of System $F^\omega_{<:}$, using existential types (Chapter 32).

To keep the book small enough to be covered in a one-semester advanced course—and light enough to be lifted by the average graduate student—it was necessary to exclude many interesting and important topics. Denotational and axiomatic approaches to semantics are omitted completely; there are already excellent books covering these approaches, and addressing them here would detract from this book's strongly pragmatic, implementation-oriented perspective. The rich connections between type systems and logic are suggested in a few places but not developed in detail; while important, these would take us too far afield. Many advanced features of programming lan-

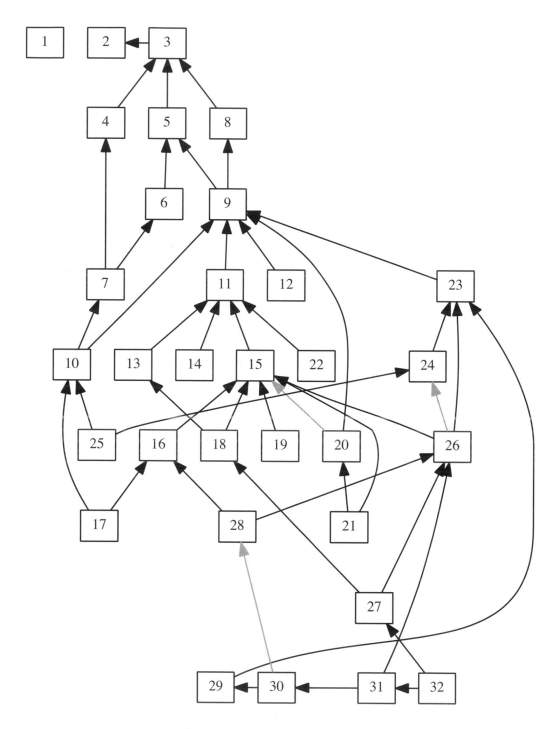

Figure P-1: Chapter dependencies

guages and type systems are mentioned only in passing, e.g, dependent types, intersection types, and the Curry-Howard correspondence; short sections on these topics provide starting points for further reading. Finally, except for a brief excursion into a Java-like core language (Chapter 19), the book focuses entirely on systems based on the lambda-calculus; however, the concepts and mechanisms developed in this setting can be transferred directly to related areas such as typed concurrent languages, typed assembly languages, and specialized object calculi.

Required Background

The text assumes no preparation in the theory of programming languages, but readers should start with a degree of mathematical maturity—in particular, rigorous undergraduate coursework in discrete mathematics, algorithms, and elementary logic.

Readers should be familiar with at least one higher-order functional programming language (Scheme, ML, Haskell, etc.), and with basic concepts of programming languages and compilers (abstract syntax, BNF grammars, evaluation, abstract machines, etc.). This material is available in many excellent undergraduate texts; I particularly like *Essentials of Programming Languages* by Friedman, Wand, and Haynes (2001) and *Programming Language Pragmatics* by Scott (1999). Experience with an object-oriented language such as Java (Arnold and Gosling, 1996) is useful in several chapters.

The chapters on concrete implementations of typecheckers present significant code fragments in OCaml (or Objective Caml), a popular dialect of ML. Prior knowledge of OCaml is helpful in these chapters, but not absolutely necessary; only a small part of the language is used, and features are explained at their first occurrence. These chapters constitute a distinct thread from the rest of the book and can be skipped completely if desired.

The best textbook on OCaml at the moment is Cousineau and Mauny's (1998). The tutorial materials packaged with the OCaml distribution (available at `http://caml.inria.fr` and `http://www.ocaml.org`) are also very readable.

Readers familiar with the other major dialect of ML, Standard ML, should have no trouble following the OCaml code fragments. Popular textbooks on Standard ML include those by Paulson (1996) and Ullman (1997).

Course Outlines

An intermediate or advanced graduate course should be able to cover most of the book in a semester. Figure P-2 gives a sample syllabus from an upper-level course for doctoral students at the University of Pennsylvania (two 90-minute lectures a week, assuming minimal prior preparation in programming language theory but moving quickly).

For an undergraduate or an introductory graduate course, there are a number of possible paths through the material. A course on *type systems in programming* would concentrate on the chapters that introduce various typing features and illustrate their uses and omit most of the metatheory and implementation chapters. Alternatively, a course on *basic theory and implementation of type systems* would progress through all the early chapters, probably skipping Chapter 12 (and perhaps 18 and 21) and sacrificing the more advanced material toward the end of the book. Shorter courses can also be constructed by selecting particular chapters of interest using the dependency diagram in Figure P-1.

The book is also suitable as the main text for a more general graduate course in theory of programming languages. Such a course might spend half to two-thirds of a semester working through the better part of the book and devote the rest to, say, a unit on the theory of concurrency based on Milner's pi-calculus book (1999), an introduction to Hoare Logic and axiomatic semantics (e.g. Winskel, 1993), or a survey of advanced language features such as continuations or module systems.

In a course where term projects play a major role, it may be desirable to postpone some of the theoretical material (e.g., normalization, and perhaps some of the chapters on metatheory) so that a broad range of examples can be covered before students choose project topics.

Exercises

Most chapters include extensive exercises—some designed for pencil and paper, some involving programming examples *in* the calculi under discussion, and some concerning extensions to the ML implementations *of* these calculi. The estimated difficulty of each exercise is indicated using the following scale:

⋆	Quick check	30 seconds to 5 minutes
⋆⋆	Easy	≤ 1 hour
⋆⋆⋆	Moderate	≤ 3 hours
⋆⋆⋆⋆	Challenging	> 3 hours

Exercises marked ⋆ are intended as real-time checks of important concepts. Readers are strongly encouraged to pause for each one of these before moving on to the material that follows. In each chapter, a roughly homework-assignment-sized set of exercises is labeled RECOMMENDED.

LECTURE	TOPIC	READING
1.	Course overview; history; administrivia	1, (2)
2.	Preliminaries: syntax, operational semantics	3, 4
3.	Introduction to the lambda-calculus	5.1, 5.2
4.	Formalizing the lambda-calculus	5.3, 6, 7
5.	Types; the simply typed lambda-calculus	8, 9, 10
6.	Simple extensions; derived forms	11
7.	More extensions	11
8.	Normalization	12
9.	References; exceptions	13, 14
10.	Subtyping	15
11.	Metatheory of subtyping	16, 17
12.	Imperative objects	18
13.	Featherweight Java	19
14.	Recursive types	20
15.	Metatheory of recursive types	21
16.	Metatheory of recursive types	21
17.	Type reconstruction	22
18.	Universal polymorphism	23
19.	Existential polymorphism; ADTs	24, (25)
20.	Bounded quantification	26, 27
21.	Metatheory of bounded quantification	28
22.	Type operators	29
23.	Metatheory of F_ω	30
24.	Higher-order subtyping	31
25.	Purely functional objects	32
26.	Overflow lecture	

Figure P-2: Sample syllabus for an advanced graduate course

Complete solutions to most of the exercises are provided in Appendix A. To save readers the frustration of searching for solutions to the few exercises for which solutions are not available, those exercises are marked ↛.

Typographic Conventions

Most chapters introduce the features of some type system in a discursive style, then define the system formally as a collection of inference rules in one or more figures. For easy reference, these definitions are usually presented in full, including not only the new rules for the features under discussion at the moment, but also the rest of the rules needed to constitute a complete calculus. The new parts are set on a gray background to make the "delta" from previous systems visually obvious.

An unusual feature of the book's production is that all the examples are mechanically typechecked during typesetting: a script goes through each chapter, extracts the examples, generates and compiles a custom typechecker containing the features under discussion, applies it to the examples, and inserts the checker's responses in the text. The system that does the hard parts of this, called *TinkerType,* was developed by Michael Levin and myself (2001). Funding for this research was provided by the National Science Foundation, through grants CCR-9701826, *Principled Foundations for Programming with Objects*, and CCR-9912352, *Modular Type Systems.*

Electronic Resources

A web site associated with this book can be found at the following URL:

    http://www.cis.upenn.edu/~bcpierce/tapl

Resources available on this site include errata for the text, suggestions for course projects, pointers to supplemental material contributed by readers, and a collection of implementations (typecheckers and simple interpreters) of the calculi covered in each chapter of the text.

These implementations offer an environment for experimenting with the examples in the book and testing solutions to exercises. They have also been polished for readability and modifiability and have been used successfully by students in my courses as the basis of both small implementation exercises and larger course projects. The implementations are written in OCaml. The OCaml compiler is available at no cost through http://caml.inria.fr and installs very easily on most platforms.

Readers should also be aware of the Types Forum, an email list covering all aspects of type systems and their applications. The list is moderated to ensure reasonably low volume and a high signal-to-noise ratio in announcements and discussions. Archives and subscription instructions can be found at http://www.cis.upenn.edu/~bcpierce/types.

Acknowledgments

Readers who find value in this book owe their biggest debt of gratitude to four mentors—Luca Cardelli, Bob Harper, Robin Milner, and John Reynolds—who taught me most of what I know about programming languages and types.

The rest I have learned mostly through collaborations; besides Luca, Bob, Robin, and John, my partners in these investigations have included Martín

Abadi, Gordon Plotkin, Randy Pollack, David N. Turner, Didier Rémy, Davide Sangiorgi, Adriana Compagnoni, Martin Hofmann, Giuseppe Castagna, Martin Steffen, Kim Bruce, Naoki Kobayashi, Haruo Hosoya, Atsushi Igarashi, Philip Wadler, Peter Buneman, Vladimir Gapeyev, Michael Levin, Peter Sewell, Jérôme Vouillon, and Eijiro Sumii. These collaborations are the foundation not only of my understanding, but also of my pleasure in the topic.

The structure and organization of this text have been improved by discussions on pedagogy with Thorsten Altenkirch, Bob Harper, and John Reynolds, and the text itself by corrections and comments from Jim Alexander, Penny Anderson, Josh Berdine, Tony Bonner, John Tang Boyland, Dave Clarke, Diego Dainese, Olivier Danvy, Matthew Davis, Vladimir Gapeyev, Bob Harper, Erik Hilsdale, Haruo Hosoya, Atsushi Igarashi, Robert Irwin, Takayasu Ito, Assaf Kfoury, Michael Levin, Vassily Litvinov, Pablo López Olivas, Dave MacQueen, Narciso Marti-Oliet, Philippe Meunier, Robin Milner, Matti Nykänen, Gordon Plotkin, John Prevost, Fermín Reig, Didier Rémy, John Reynolds, James Riely, Ohad Rodeh, Jürgen Schlegelmilch, Alan Schmitt, Andrew Schoonmaker, Olin Shivers, Perdita Stevens, Chris Stone, Eijiro Sumii, Val Tannen, Jérôme Vouillon, and Philip Wadler. (I apologize if I've inadvertently omitted anybody from this list.) Luca Cardelli, Roger Hindley, Dave MacQueen, John Reynolds, and Jonathan Seldin offered insiders' perspectives on some tangled historical points.

The participants in my graduate seminars at Indiana University in 1997 and 1998 and at the University of Pennsylvania in 1999 and 2000 soldiered through early versions of the manuscript; their reactions and comments gave me crucial guidance in shaping the book as you see it. Bob Prior and his team from The MIT Press expertly guided the manuscript through the many phases of the publication process. The book's design is based on LaTeX macros developed by Christopher Manning for The MIT Press.

Proofs of programs are too boring for the social process of mathematics to work. —*Richard DeMillo, Richard Lipton, and Alan Perlis, 1979*

... So don't rely on social processes for verification. —*David Dill, 1999*

Formal methods will never have a significant impact until they can be used by people that don't understand them. —*attributed to Tom Melham*

1 *Introduction*

1.1 Types in Computer Science

Modern software engineering recognizes a broad range of *formal methods* for helping ensure that a system behaves correctly with respect to some specification, implicit or explicit, of its desired behavior. On one end of the spectrum are powerful frameworks such as Hoare logic, algebraic specification languages, modal logics, and denotational semantics. These can be used to express very general correctness properties but are often cumbersome to use and demand a good deal of sophistication on the part of programmers. At the other end are techniques of much more modest power—modest enough that automatic checkers can be built into compilers, linkers, or program analyzers and thus be applied even by programmers unfamiliar with the underlying theories. One well-known instance of this sort of *lightweight formal methods* is *model checkers,* tools that search for errors in finite-state systems such as chip designs or communication protocols. Another that is growing in popularity is *run-time monitoring*, a collection of techniques that allow a system to detect, dynamically, when one of its components is not behaving according to specification. But by far the most popular and best established lightweight formal methods are *type systems*, the central focus of this book.

As with many terms shared by large communities, it is difficult to define "type system" in a way that covers its informal usage by programming language designers and implementors but is still specific enough to have any bite. One plausible definition is this:

> *A type system is a tractable syntactic method for proving the absence of certain program behaviors by classifying phrases according to the kinds of values they compute.*

A number of points deserve comment. First, this definition identifies type systems as tools for reasoning about *programs*. This wording reflects the orientation of this book toward the type systems found in programming languages. More generally, the term *type systems* (or *type theory*) refers to a much broader field of study in logic, mathematics, and philosophy. Type systems in this sense were first formalized in the early 1900s as ways of avoiding the logical paradoxes, such as Russell's (Russell, 1902), that threatened the foundations of mathematics. During the twentieth century, types have become standard tools in logic, especially in proof theory (see Gandy, 1976 and Hindley, 1997), and have permeated the language of philosophy and science. Major landmarks in this area include Russell's original *ramified theory of types* (Whitehead and Russell, 1910), Ramsey's *simple theory of types* (1925)—the basis of Church's simply typed lambda-calculus (1940)—Martin-Löf's *constructive type theory* (1973, 1984), and Berardi, Terlouw, and Barendregt's *pure type systems* (Berardi, 1988; Terlouw, 1989; Barendregt, 1992).

Even within computer science, there are two major branches to the study of type systems. The more practical, which concerns applications to programming languages, is the main focus of this book. The more abstract focuses on connections between various "pure typed lambda-calculi" and varieties of logic, via the *Curry-Howard correspondence* (§9.4). Similar concepts, notations, and techniques are used by both communities, but with some important differences in orientation. For example, research on typed lambda-calculi is usually concerned with systems in which every well-typed computation is guaranteed to terminate, whereas most programming languages sacrifice this property for the sake of features like recursive function definitions.

Another important element in the above definition is its emphasis on *classification* of terms—syntactic phrases—according to the properties of the values that they will compute when executed. A type system can be regarded as calculating a kind of *static* approximation to the run-time behaviors of the terms in a program. (Moreover, the types assigned to terms are generally calculated *compositionally,* with the type of an expression depending only on the types of its subexpressions.)

The word "static" is sometimes added explicitly—we speak of a "statically typed programming language," for example—to distinguish the sorts of compile-time analyses we are considering here from the *dynamic* or *latent typing* found in languages such as Scheme (Sussman and Steele, 1975; Kelsey, Clinger, and Rees, 1998; Dybvig, 1996), where run-time *type tags* are used to distinguish different kinds of structures in the heap. Terms like "dynamically typed" are arguably misnomers and should probably be replaced by "dynamically checked," but the usage is standard.

Being static, type systems are necessarily also *conservative:* they can categorically prove the *absence* of some bad program behaviors, but they cannot prove their presence, and hence they must also sometimes reject programs that actually behave well at run time. For example, a program like

```
if <complex test> then 5 else <type error>
```

will be rejected as ill-typed, even if it happens that the <complex test> will always evaluate to true, because a static analysis cannot determine that this is the case. The tension between conservativity and expressiveness is a fundamental fact of life in the design of type systems. The desire to allow more programs to be typed—by assigning more accurate types to their parts—is the main force driving research in the field.

A related point is that the relatively straightforward analyses embodied in most type systems are not capable of proscribing arbitrary undesired program behaviors; they can only guarantee that well-typed programs are free from *certain* kinds of misbehavior. For example, most type systems can check statically that the arguments to primitive arithmetic operations are always numbers, that the receiver object in a method invocation always provides the requested method, etc., but not that the second argument to the division operation is non-zero, or that array accesses are always within bounds.

The bad behaviors that can be eliminated by the type system in a given language are often called *run-time type errors*. It is important to keep in mind that this set of behaviors is a per-language choice: although there is substantial overlap between the behaviors considered to be run-time type errors in different languages, in principle each type system comes with a definition of the behaviors it aims to prevent. The *safety* (or *soundness*) of each type system must be judged with respect to its own set of run-time errors.

The sorts of bad behaviors detected by type analysis are not restricted to low-level faults like invoking non-existent methods: type systems are also used to enforce higher-level *modularity* properties and to protect the integrity of user-defined *abstractions*. Violations of information hiding, such as directly accessing the fields of a data value whose representation is supposed to be abstract, are run-time type errors in exactly the same way as, for example, treating an integer as a pointer and using it to crash the machine.

Typecheckers are typically built into compilers or linkers. This implies that they must be able to do their job *automatically*, with no manual intervention or interaction with the programmer—i.e., they must embody computationally *tractable* analyses. However, there is still plenty of room for requiring guidance from the programmer, in the form of explicit *type annotations* in programs. Usually, these annotations are kept fairly light, to make programs easier to write and read. But, in principle, a full proof that the program meets some arbitrary specification could be encoded in type annotations; in this case, the typechecker would effectively become a *proof* checker. Technologies like Extended Static Checking (Detlefs, Leino, Nelson, and Saxe, 1998) are working to settle this territory between type systems and full-scale program verification methods, implementing fully automatic checks for some broad classes of correctness properties that rely only on "reasonably light" program annotations to guide their work.

By the same token, we are most interested in methods that are not just automatable in principle, but that actually come with *efficient* algorithms for checking types. However, exactly what counts as efficient is a matter of debate. Even widely used type systems like that of ML (Damas and Milner, 1982) may exhibit huge typechecking times in pathological cases (Henglein and Mairson, 1991). There are even languages with typechecking or type reconstruction problems that are undecidable, but for which algorithms are available that halt quickly "in most cases of practical interest" (e.g. Pierce and Turner, 2000; Nadathur and Miller, 1988; Pfenning, 1994).

1.2   What Type Systems Are Good For

Detecting Errors

The most obvious benefit of static typechecking is that it allows early detection of some programming errors. Errors that are detected early can be fixed immediately, rather than lurking in the code to be discovered much later, when the programmer is in the middle of something else—or even after the program has been deployed. Moreover, errors can often be pinpointed more accurately during typechecking than at run time, when their effects may not become visible until some time after things begin to go wrong.

In practice, static typechecking exposes a surprisingly broad range of errors. Programmers working in richly typed languages often remark that their programs tend to "just work" once they pass the typechecker, much more often than they feel they have a right to expect. One possible explanation for this is that not only trivial mental slips (e.g., forgetting to convert a string to a number before taking its square root), but also deeper conceptual errors (e.g., neglecting a boundary condition in a complex case analysis, or confusing units in a scientific calculation), will often manifest as inconsistencies at the level of types. The strength of this effect depends on the expressiveness of the type system and on the programming task in question: programs that manipulate a variety of data structures (e.g., symbol processing applications such as compilers) offer more purchase for the typechecker than programs involving just a few simple types, such as numerical calculations in scientific applications (though, even here, refined type systems supporting *dimension analysis* [Kennedy, 1994] can be quite useful).

Obtaining maximum benefit from the type system generally involves some attention on the part of the programmer, as well as a willingness to make good use of the facilities provided by the language; for example, a complex program that encodes all its data structures as lists will not get as much help from the compiler as one that defines a different datatype or abstract type for each. Expressive type systems offer numerous "tricks" for encoding information about structure in terms of types.

For some sorts of programs, a typechecker can also be an invaluable *maintenance* tool. For example, a programmer who needs to change the definition of a complex data structure need not search by hand to find all the places in a large program where code involving this structure needs to be fixed. Once the declaration of the datatype has been changed, all of these sites become type-inconsistent, and they can be enumerated simply by running the compiler and examining the points where typechecking fails.

Abstraction

Another important way in which type systems support the programming process is by enforcing disciplined programming. In particular, in the context of large-scale software composition, type systems form the backbone of the *module languages* used to package and tie together the components of large systems. Types show up in the interfaces of modules (and related structures such as classes); indeed, an interface itself can be viewed as "the type of a module," providing a summary of the facilities provided by the module—a kind of partial contract between implementors and users.

Structuring large systems in terms of modules with clear interfaces leads to a more abstract style of design, where interfaces are designed and discussed independently from their eventual implementations. More abstract thinking about interfaces generally leads to better design.

Documentation

Types are also useful when *reading* programs. The type declarations in procedure headers and module interfaces constitute a form of documentation, giving useful hints about behavior. Moreover, unlike descriptions embedded in comments, this form of documentation cannot become outdated, since it is checked during every run of the compiler. This role of types is particularly important in module signatures.

Language Safety

The term "safe language" is, unfortunately, even more contentious than "type system." Although people generally feel they know one when they see it, their notions of exactly what constitutes language safety are strongly influenced by the language community to which they belong. Informally, though, safe languages can be defined as ones that make it impossible to shoot yourself in the foot while programming.

Refining this intuition a little, we could say that *a safe language is one that protects its own abstractions.* Every high-level language provides abstractions of machine services. Safety refers to the language's ability to guarantee the integrity of these abstractions and of higher-level abstractions introduced by the programmer using the definitional facilities of the language. For example, a language may provide arrays, with access and update operations, as an abstraction of the underlying memory. A programmer using this language then expects that an array can be changed only by using the update operation on it explicitly—and not, for example, by writing past the end of some other data structure. Similarly, one expects that lexically scoped variables can be accessed only from within their scopes, that the call stack truly behaves like a stack, etc. In a safe language, such abstractions can be used *abstractly;* in an unsafe language, they cannot: in order to completely understand how a program may (mis)behave, it is necessary to keep in mind all sorts of low-level details such as the layout of data structures in memory and the order in which they will be allocated by the compiler. In the limit, programs in unsafe languages may disrupt not only their own data structures but even those of the run-time system; the results in this case can be completely arbitrary.

Language safety is not the same thing as static type safety. Language safety can be *achieved* by static checking, but also by run-time checks that trap nonsensical operations just at the moment when they are attempted and stop the program or raise an exception. For example, Scheme is a safe language, even though it has no static type system.

Conversely, unsafe languages often provide "best effort" static type checkers that help programmers eliminate at least the most obvious sorts of slips, but such languages do not qualify as type-safe either, according to our definition, since they are generally not capable of offering any sort of *guarantees* that well-typed programs are well behaved—typecheckers for these languages can suggest the presence of run-time type errors (which is certainly better than nothing) but not prove their absence.

	Statically checked	Dynamically checked
Safe	ML, Haskell, Java, etc.	Lisp, Scheme, Perl, Postscript, etc.
Unsafe	C, C++, etc.	

The emptiness of the bottom-right entry in the preceding table is explained by the fact that, once facilities are in place for enforcing the safety of *most* operations at run time, there is little additional cost to checking *all* operations. (Actually, there are a few dynamically checked languages, e.g., some dialects of Basic for microcomputers with minimal operating systems, that do offer low-level primitives for reading and writing arbitrary memory locations, which can be misused to destroy the integrity of the run-time system.)

Run-time safety is not normally achievable by static typing alone. For example, *all* of the languages listed as safe in the table above actually perform *array-bounds checking* dynamically.[1] Similarly, statically checked languages sometimes choose to provide operations (e.g., the down-cast operator in Java—see §15.5) whose typechecking rules are actually unsound—language safety is obtained by checking each use of such a construct dynamically.

Language safety is seldom absolute. Safe languages often offer programmers "escape hatches," such as foreign function calls to code written in other, possibly unsafe, languages. Indeed, such escape hatches are sometimes provided in a controlled form within the language itself—`Obj.magic` in OCaml (Leroy, 2000), `Unsafe.cast` in the New Jersey implementation of Standard ML, etc. Modula-3 (Cardelli et al., 1989; Nelson, 1991) and C♯ (Wille, 2000) go yet further, offering an "unsafe sublanguage" intended for implementing low-level run-time facilities such as garbage collectors. The special features of this sublanguage may be used only in modules explicitly marked `unsafe`.

Cardelli (1996) articulates a somewhat different perspective on language safety, distinguishing between so-called *trapped* and *untrapped* run-time errors. A trapped error causes a computation to stop immediately (or to raise an exception that can be handled cleanly within the program), while untrapped errors may allow the computation to continue (at least for a while). An example of an untrapped error might be accessing data beyond the end of an array in a language like C. A safe language, in this view, is one that prevents untrapped errors at run time.

Yet another point of view focuses on portability; it can be expressed by the slogan, "A safe language is completely defined by its programmer's manual." Let the *definition* of a language be the set of things the programmer needs to understand in order to predict the behavior of every program in the language. Then the manual for a language like C does not constitute a definition, since the behavior of some programs (e.g., ones involving unchecked array

---

1. Static elimination of array-bounds checking is a long-standing goal for type system designers. In principle, the necessary mechanisms (based on *dependent types*—see §30.5) are well understood, but packaging them in a form that balances expressive power, predictability and tractability of typechecking, and complexity of program annotations remains a significant challenge. Some recent advances in the area are described by Xi and Pfenning (1998, 1999).

accesses or pointer arithmetic) cannot be predicted without knowing the details of how a particular C compiler lays out structures in memory, etc., and the same program may have quite different behaviors when executed by different compilers. By contrast, the manuals for Java, Scheme, and ML specify (with varying degrees of rigor) the exact behavior of all programs in the language. A well-typed program will yield the same results under any correct implementation of these languages.

Efficiency

The first type systems in computer science, beginning in the 1950s in languages such as Fortran (Backus, 1981), were introduced to improve the efficiency of numerical calculations by distinguishing between integer-valued arithmetic expressions and real-valued ones; this allowed the compiler to use different representations and generate appropriate machine instructions for primitive operations. In safe languages, further efficiency improvements are gained by eliminating many of the dynamic checks that would be needed to guarantee safety (by proving statically that they will always be satisfied). Today, most high-performance compilers rely heavily on information gathered by the typechecker during optimization and code-generation phases. Even compilers for languages without type systems *per se* work hard to recover approximations to this typing information.

Efficiency improvements relying on type information can come from some surprising places. For example, it has recently been shown that not only code generation decisions but also pointer representation in parallel scientific programs can be improved using the information generated by type analysis. The Titanium language (Yelick et al., 1998) uses type inference techniques to analyze the scopes of pointers and is able to make measurably better decisions on this basis than programmers explicitly hand-tuning their programs. The ML Kit Compiler uses a powerful *region inference* algorithm (Gifford, Jouvelot, Lucassen, and Sheldon, 1987; Jouvelot and Gifford, 1991; Talpin and Jouvelot, 1992; Tofte and Talpin, 1994, 1997; Tofte and Birkedal, 1998) to replace most (in some programs, all) of the need for garbage collection by stack-based memory management.

Further Applications

Beyond their traditional uses in programming and language design, type systems are now being applied in many more specific ways in computer science and related disciplines. We sketch just a few here.

An increasingly important application area for type systems is computer and network security. Static typing lies at the core of the security model of Java and of the JINI "plug and play" architecture for network devices (Arnold et al., 1999), for example, and is a critical enabling technology for Proof-Carrying Code (Necula and Lee, 1996, 1998; Necula, 1997). At the same time, many fundamental ideas developed in the security community are being re-explored in the context of programming languages, where they often appear as type analyses (e.g., Abadi, Banerjee, Heintze, and Riecke, 1999; Abadi, 1999; Leroy and Rouaix, 1998; etc.). Conversely, there is growing interest in applying programming language theory directly to problems in the security domain (e.g., Abadi, 1999; Sumii and Pierce, 2001).

Typechecking and inference algorithms can be found in many program analysis tools other than compilers. For example, AnnoDomini, a Year 2000 conversion utility for Cobol programs, is based on an ML-style type inference engine (Eidorff et al., 1999). Type inference techniques have also been used in tools for alias analysis (O'Callahan and Jackson, 1997) and exception analysis (Leroy and Pessaux, 2000).

In automated theorem proving, type systems—usually very powerful ones based on dependent types—are used to represent logical propositions and proofs. Several popular proof assistants, including Nuprl (Constable et al., 1986), Lego (Luo and Pollack, 1992; Pollack, 1994), Coq (Barras et al., 1997), and Alf (Magnusson and Nordström, 1994), are based directly on type theory. Constable (1998) and Pfenning (1999) discuss the history of these systems.

Interest in type systems is also on the increase in the database community, with the explosion of "web metadata" in the form of Document Type Definitions (XML 1998) and other kinds of schemas (such as the new XML-Schema standard [XS 2000]) for describing structured data in XML. New languages for querying and manipulating XML provide powerful static type systems based directly on these schema languages (Hosoya and Pierce, 2000; Hosoya, Vouillon, and Pierce, 2001; Hosoya and Pierce, 2001; Relax, 2000; Shields, 2001).

A quite different application of type systems appears in the field of computational linguistics, where typed lambda-calculi form the basis for formalisms such as *categorial grammar* (van Benthem, 1995; van Benthem and Meulen, 1997; Ranta, 1995; etc.).

1.3 Type Systems and Language Design

Retrofitting a type system onto a language not designed with typechecking in mind can be tricky; ideally, language design should go hand-in-hand with type system design.

One reason for this is that languages without type systems—even safe, dynamically checked languages—tend to offer features or encourage programming idioms that make typechecking difficult or infeasible. Indeed, in typed languages the type system itself is often taken as the foundation of the design and the organizing principle in light of which every other aspect of the design is considered.

Another factor is that the concrete syntax of typed languages tends to be more complicated than that of untyped languages, since type annotations must be taken into account. It is easier to do a good job of designing a clean and comprehensible syntax when all the issues can be addressed together.

The assertion that types should be an integral part of a programming language is separate from the question of where the programmer must physically write down type annotations and where they can instead be inferred by the compiler. A well-designed statically typed language will never require huge amounts of type information to be explicitly and tediously maintained by the programmer. There is some disagreement, though, about how much explicit type information is too much. The designers of languages in the ML family have worked hard to keep annotations to a bare minimum, using type inference methods to recover the necessary information. Languages in the C family, including Java, have chosen a somewhat more verbose style.

1.4   Capsule History

In computer science, the earliest type systems were used to make very simple distinctions between integer and floating point representations of numbers (e.g., in Fortran). In the late 1950s and early 1960s, this classification was extended to structured data (arrays of records, etc.) and higher-order functions. In the 1970s, a number of even richer concepts (parametric polymorphism, abstract data types, module systems, and subtyping) were introduced, and type systems emerged as a field in its own right. At the same time, computer scientists began to be aware of the connections between the type systems found in programming languages and those studied in mathematical logic, leading to a rich interplay that continues to the present.

Figure 1-1 presents a brief (and scandalously incomplete!) chronology of some high points in the history of type systems in computer science. Related developments in logic are included, in italics, to show the importance of this field's contributions. Citations in the right-hand column can be found in the bibliography.

1870s	*origins of formal logic*	Frege (1879)
1900s	*formalization of mathematics*	Whitehead and Russell (1910)
1930s	*untyped lambda-calculus*	Church (1941)
1940s	*simply typed lambda-calculus*	Church (1940), Curry and Feys (1958)
1950s	Fortran	Backus (1981)
	Algol-60	Naur et al. (1963)
1960s	*Automath project*	de Bruijn (1980)
	Simula	Birtwistle et al. (1979)
	Curry-Howard correspondence	Howard (1980)
	Algol-68	(van Wijngaarden et al., 1975)
1970s	Pascal	Wirth (1971)
	Martin-Löf type theory	Martin-Löf (1973, 1982)
	System F, F^ω	Girard (1972)
	polymorphic lambda-calculus	Reynolds (1974)
	CLU	Liskov et al. (1981)
	polymorphic type inference	Milner (1978), Damas and Milner (1982)
	ML	Gordon, Milner, and Wadsworth (1979)
	intersection types	Coppo and Dezani (1978)
		Coppo, Dezani, and Sallé (1979), Pottinger (1980)
1980s	NuPRL project	Constable et al. (1986)
	subtyping	Reynolds (1980), Cardelli (1984), Mitchell (1984a)
	ADTs as existential types	Mitchell and Plotkin (1988)
	calculus of constructions	Coquand (1985), Coquand and Huet (1988)
	linear logic	Girard (1987) , Girard et al. (1989)
	bounded quantification	Cardelli and Wegner (1985)
		Curien and Ghelli (1992), Cardelli et al. (1994)
	Edinburgh Logical Framework	Harper, Honsell, and Plotkin (1992)
	Forsythe	Reynolds (1988)
	pure type systems	Terlouw (1989), Berardi (1988), Barendregt (1991)
	dependent types and modularity	Burstall and Lampson (1984), MacQueen (1986)
	Quest	Cardelli (1991)
	effect systems	Gifford et al. (1987), Talpin and Jouvelot (1992)
	row variables; extensible records	Wand (1987), Rémy (1989)
		Cardelli and Mitchell (1991)
1990s	higher-order subtyping	Cardelli (1990), Cardelli and Longo (1991)
	typed intermediate languages	Tarditi, Morrisett, et al. (1996)
	object calculus	Abadi and Cardelli (1996)
	translucent types and modularity	Harper and Lillibridge (1994), Leroy (1994)
	typed assembly language	Morrisett et al. (1998)

Figure 1-1: Capsule history of types in computer science and logic

1.5   Related Reading

While this book attempts to be self contained, it is far from comprehensive; the area is too large, and can be approached from too many angles, to do it justice in one book. This section lists a few other good entry points.

Handbook articles by Cardelli (1996) and Mitchell (1990b) offer quick introductions to the area. Barendregt's article (1992) is for the more mathematically inclined. Mitchell's massive textbook on *Foundations for Programming Languages* (1996) covers basic lambda-calculus, a range of type systems, and many aspects of semantics. The focus is on semantic rather than implementation issues. Reynolds's *Theories of Programming Languages* (1998b), a graduate-level survey of the theory of programming languages, includes beautiful expositions of polymorphism, subtyping, and intersection types. *The Structure of Typed Programming Languages,* by Schmidt (1994), develops core concepts of type systems in the context of language design, including several chapters on conventional imperative languages. Hindley's monograph *Basic Simple Type Theory* (1997) is a wonderful compendium of results about the simply typed lambda-calculus and closely related systems. Its coverage is deep rather than broad.

Abadi and Cardelli's *A Theory of Objects* (1996) develops much of the same material as the present book, de-emphasizing implementation aspects and concentrating instead on the application of these ideas in a foundation treatment of object-oriented programming. Kim Bruce's *Foundations of Object-Oriented Languages: Types and Semantics* (2002) covers similar ground. Introductory material on object-oriented type systems can also be found in Palsberg and Schwartzbach (1994) and Castagna (1997).

Semantic foundations for both untyped and typed languages are covered in depth in the textbooks of Gunter (1992), Winskel (1993), and Mitchell (1996). Operational semantics is also covered in detail by Hennessy (1990). Foundations for the semantics of types in the mathematical framework of *category theory* can also be found in many sources, including the books by Jacobs (1999), Asperti and Longo (1991), and Crole (1994); a brief primer can be found in *Basic Category Theory for Computer Scientists* (Pierce, 1991a).

Girard, Lafont, and Taylor's *Proofs and Types* (1989) treats logical aspects of type systems (the Curry-Howard correspondence, etc.). It also includes a description of System F from its creator, and an appendix introducing linear logic. Connections between types and logic are further explored in Pfenning's *Computation and Deduction* (2001). Thompson's *Type Theory and Functional Programming* (1991) and Turner's *Constructive Foundations for Functional Languages* (1991) focus on connections between functional programming (in the "pure functional programming" sense of Haskell or Miranda) and constructive type theory, viewed from a logical perspective. A number of relevant topics from proof theory are developed in Goubault-Larrecq and Mackie's *Proof Theory and Automated Deduction* (1997). The history of types in logic and philosophy is described in more detail in articles by Constable (1998), Wadler (2000), Huet (1990), and Pfenning (1999), in Laan's doctoral thesis (1997), and in books by Grattan-Guinness (2001) and Sommaruga (2000).

It turns out that a fair amount of careful analysis is required to avoid false and embarrassing claims of type soundness for programming languages. As a consequence, the classification, description, and study of type systems has emerged as a formal discipline. —Luca Cardelli (1996)

2 *Mathematical Preliminaries*

Before getting started, we need to establish some common notation and state a few basic mathematical facts. Most readers should just skim this chapter and refer back to it as necessary.

2.1 Sets, Relations, and Functions

2.1.1 DEFINITION: We use standard notation for sets: curly braces for listing the elements of a set explicitly ($\{\ldots\}$) or showing how to construct one set from another by "comprehension" ($\{x \in S \mid \ldots\}$), $\varnothing$ for the empty set, and $S \setminus T$ for the set difference of S and T (the set of elements of S that are not also elements of T). The size of a set S is written $|S|$. The powerset of S, i.e., the set of all the subsets of S, is written $\mathcal{P}(S)$. □

2.1.2 DEFINITION: The set $\{0, 1, 2, 3, 4, 5, \ldots\}$ of *natural numbers* is denoted by the symbol $\mathbb{N}$. A set is said to be *countable* if its elements can be placed in one-to-one correspondence with the natural numbers. □

2.1.3 DEFINITION: An *n*-place *relation* on a collection of sets $S_1, S_2, \ldots, S_n$ is a set $R \subseteq S_1 \times S_2 \times \ldots \times S_n$ of tuples of elements from S_1 through S_n. We say that the elements $s_1 \in S_1$ through $s_n \in S_n$ are *related by R* if $(s_1, \ldots, s_n)$ is an element of R. □

2.1.4 DEFINITION: A one-place relation on a set S is called a *predicate* on S. We say that P is true of an element $s \in S$ if $s \in P$. To emphasize this intuition, we often write $P(s)$ instead of $s \in P$, regarding P as a function mapping elements of S to truth values. □

2.1.5 DEFINITION: A two-place relation R on sets S and T is called a *binary relation*. We often write $s\ R\ t$ instead of $(s, t) \in R$. When S and T are the same set U, we say that R is a binary relation on U. □

2.1.6   DEFINITION: For readability, three- or more place relations are often written using a "mixfix" concrete syntax, where the elements in the relation are separated by a sequence of symbols that jointly constitute the name of the relation. For example, for the typing relation for the simply typed lambda-calculus in Chapter 9, we write $\Gamma \vdash \mathsf{s} : \mathsf{T}$ to mean "the triple $(\Gamma, \mathsf{s}, \mathsf{T})$ is in the typing relation."   □

2.1.7   DEFINITION: The *domain* of a relation R on sets S and T, written $dom(R)$, is the set of elements $s \in S$ such that $(s, t) \in R$ for some t. The *codomain* or *range* of R, written $range(R)$, is the set of elements $t \in T$ such that $(s, t) \in R$ for some s.   □

2.1.8   DEFINITION: A relation R on sets S and T is called a *partial function* from S to T if, whenever $(s, t_1) \in R$ and $(s, t_2) \in R$, we have $t_1 = t_2$. If, in addition, $dom(R) = S$, then R is called a *total function* (or just *function*) from S to T. □

2.1.9   DEFINITION: A partial function R from S to T is said to be *defined* on an argument $s \in S$ if $s \in dom(R)$, and undefined otherwise. We write $f(x) \uparrow$, or $f(x) = \uparrow$, to mean "f is undefined on x," and $f(x)\downarrow$" to mean "f is defined on x."

In some of the implementation chapters, we will also need to define functions that may *fail* on some inputs (see, e.g., Figure 22-2). It is important to distinguish failure (which is a legitimate, observable result) from divergence; a function that may fail can be either partial (i.e., it may also diverge) or total (it must always return a result or explicitly fail)—indeed, we will often be interested in proving totality. We write $f(x) = fail$ when f returns a failure result on the input x.

Formally, a function from S to T that may also fail is actually a function from S to $T \cup \{fail\}$, where we assume that *fail* does not belong to T.   □

2.1.10   DEFINITION: Suppose R is a binary relation on a set S and P is a predicate on S. We say that P is *preserved by* R if whenever we have $s \mathrel{R} s'$ and $P(s)$, we also have $P(s')$.   □

2.2   Ordered Sets

2.2.1   DEFINITION: A binary relation R on a set S is *reflexive* if R relates every element of S to itself—that is, $s \mathrel{R} s$ (or $(s, s) \in R$) for all $s \in S$. R is *symmetric* if $s \mathrel{R} t$ implies $t \mathrel{R} s$, for all s and t in S. R is *transitive* if $s \mathrel{R} t$ and $t \mathrel{R} u$ together imply $s \mathrel{R} u$. R is *antisymmetric* if $s \mathrel{R} t$ and $t \mathrel{R} s$ together imply that $s = t$.   □

2.2.2   DEFINITION: A reflexive and transitive relation R on a set S is called a *pre-order* on S. (When we speak of "a preordered set S," we always have in mind some particular preorder R on S.) Preorders are usually written using symbols like $\leq$ or $\sqsubseteq$. We write $s < t$ ("s is *strictly less than* t") to mean $s \leq t \wedge s \neq t$.

     A preorder (on a set S) that is also antisymmetric is called a *partial order* on S. A partial order $\leq$ is called a *total order* if it also has the property that, for each s and t in S, either $s \leq t$ or $t \leq s$.   □

2.2.3   DEFINITION: Suppose that $\leq$ is a partial order on a set S and s and t are elements of S. An element $j \in S$ is said to be a *join* (or *least upper bound*) of s and t if

1. $s \leq j$ and $t \leq j$, and

2. for any element $k \in S$ with $s \leq k$ and $t \leq k$, we have $j \leq k$.

Similarly, an element $m \in S$ is said to be a *meet* (or *greatest lower bound*) of s and t if

1. $m \leq s$ and $m \leq t$, and

2. for any element $n \in S$ with $n \leq s$ and $n \leq t$, we have $n \leq m$.   □

2.2.4   DEFINITION: A reflexive, transitive, and symmetric relation on a set S is called an *equivalence* on S.   □

2.2.5   DEFINITION: Suppose R is a binary relation on a set S. The *reflexive closure* of R is the smallest reflexive relation R' that contains R. ("Smallest" in the sense that if R'' is some other reflexive relation that contains all the pairs in R, then we have $R' \subseteq R''$.) Similarly, the *transitive closure* of R is the smallest transitive relation R' that contains R. The transitive closure of R is often written R^+. The *reflexive and transitive closure* of R is the smallest reflexive and transitive relation that contains R. It is often written R^*.   □

2.2.6   EXERCISE [★★ ⇀]: Suppose we are given a relation R on a set S. Define the relation R' as follows:

$$R' = R \cup \{(s,s) \mid s \in S\}.$$

That is, R' contains all the pairs in R plus all pairs of the form (s,s). Show that R' is the reflexive closure of R.   □

2.2.7   EXERCISE [★★, ⇀]: Here is a more constructive definition of the transitive closure of a relation R. First, we define the following sequence of sets of pairs:

$$
\begin{aligned}
R_0 &= R \\
R_{i+1} &= R_i \cup \{(s,u) \mid \text{for some } t,\, (s,t) \in R_i \text{ and } (t,u) \in R_i\}
\end{aligned}
$$

That is, we construct each R_{i+1} by adding to R_i all the pairs that can be obtained by "one step of transitivity" from pairs already in R_i. Finally, define the relation R^+ as the union of all the R_i:

$$R^+ = \bigcup_i R_i$$

Show that this R^+ is really the transitive closure of R—i.e., that it satisfies the conditions given in Definition 2.2.5.   □

2.2.8   EXERCISE [★★, ↛]: Suppose R is a binary relation on a set S and P is a predicate on S that is preserved by R. Show that P is also preserved by R^*.   □

2.2.9   DEFINITION: Suppose we have a preorder $\leq$ on a set S. A *decreasing chain* in $\leq$ is a sequence $s_1, s_2, s_3, \ldots$ of elements of S such that each member of the sequence is strictly less than its predecessor: $s_{i+1} < s_i$ for every i. (Chains can be either finite or infinite, but we are more interested in infinite ones, as in the next definition.)   □

2.2.10   DEFINITION: Suppose we have a set S with a preorder $\leq$. We say that $\leq$ is *well founded* if it contains no infinite decreasing chains. For example, the usual order on the natural numbers, with $0 < 1 < 2 < 3 < \ldots$ is well founded, but the same order on the integers, $\ldots < -3 < -2 < -1 < 0 < 1 < 2 < 3 < \ldots$ is not. We sometimes omit mentioning $\leq$ explicitly and simply speak of S as a *well-founded set*.   □

2.3   Sequences

2.3.1   DEFINITION: A *sequence* is written by listing its elements, separated by commas. We use comma as both the "cons" operation for adding an element to either end of a sequence and as the "append" operation on sequences. For example, if a is the sequence $3, 2, 1$ and b is the sequence $5, 6$, then $0, a$ denotes the sequence $0, 3, 2, 1$, while $a, 0$ denotes $3, 2, 1, 0$ and b, a denotes $5, 6, 3, 2, 1$. (The use of comma for both "cons" and "append" operations leads to no confusion, as long as we do not need to talk about sequences of sequences.) The sequence of numbers from 1 to n is abbreviated $1..n$ (with just two dots). We write $|a|$ for the length of the sequence a. The empty sequence is written either as • or as a blank. One sequence is said to be a *permutation* of another if it contains exactly the same elements, possibly in a different order.   □

2.4 Induction

Proofs by induction are ubiquitous in the theory of programming languages, as in most of computer science. Many of these proofs are based on one of the following principles.

2.4.1   AXIOM [PRINCIPLE OF ORDINARY INDUCTION ON NATURAL NUMBERS]:
Suppose that P is a predicate on the natural numbers. Then:

> If $P(0)$
> and, for all i, $P(i)$ implies $P(i + 1)$,
> then $P(n)$ holds for all n. □

2.4.2   AXIOM [PRINCIPLE OF COMPLETE INDUCTION ON NATURAL NUMBERS]:
Suppose that P is a predicate on the natural numbers. Then:

> If, for each natural number n,
>> given $P(i)$ for all $i < n$
>> we can show $P(n)$,
> then $P(n)$ holds for all n. □

2.4.3   DEFINITION: The *lexicographic order* (or "dictionary order") on pairs of natural numbers is defined as follows: $(m, n) \leq (m', n')$ iff either $m < m'$ or else $m = m'$ and $n \leq n'$. □

2.4.4   AXIOM [PRINCIPLE OF LEXICOGRAPHIC INDUCTION]: Suppose that P is a predicate on pairs of natural numbers.

> If, for each pair (m, n) of natural numbers,
>> given $P(m', n')$ for all $(m', n') < (m, n)$
>> we can show $P(m, n)$,
> then $P(m, n)$ holds for all m, n. □

The lexicograpic induction principle is the basis for proofs by *nested induction*, where some case of an inductive proof proceeds "by an inner induction." It can be generalized to lexicographic induction on triples of numbers, 4-tuples, etc. (Induction on pairs is fairly common; on triples it is occasionally useful; beyond triples it is rare.)

Theorem 3.3.4 in Chapter 3 will introduce yet another format for proofs by induction, called *structural induction*, that is particularly useful for proofs about tree structures such as terms or typing derivations. The mathematical foundations of inductive reasoning will be considered in more detail in Chapter 21, where we will see that all these specific induction principles are instances of a single deeper idea.

2.5   Background Reading

If the material summarized in this chapter is unfamiliar, you may want to start with some background reading. There are many sources for this, but Winskel's book (1993) is a particularly good choice for intuitions about induction. The beginning of Davey and Priestley (1990) has an excellent review of ordered sets. Halmos (1987) is a good introduction to basic set theory.

A proof is a repeatable experiment in persuasion.   —*Jim Horning*

PART I

Untyped Systems

3 *Untyped Arithmetic Expressions*

To talk rigorously about type systems and their properties, we need to start by dealing formally with some more basic aspects of programming languages. In particular, we need clear, precise, and mathematically tractable tools for expressing and reasoning about the syntax and semantics of programs.

This chapter and the next develop the required tools for a small language of numbers and booleans. This language is so trivial as to be almost beneath consideration, but it serves as a straightforward vehicle for the introduction of several fundamental concepts—abstract syntax, inductive definitions and proofs, evaluation, and the modeling of run-time errors. Chapters 5 through 7 elaborate the same story for a much more powerful language, the untyped lambda-calculus, where we must also deal with name binding and substitution. Looking further ahead, Chapter 8 commences the study of type systems proper, returning to the simple language of the present chapter and using it to introduce basic concepts of static typing. Chapter 9 extends these concepts to the lambda-calculus.

3.1 Introduction

The language used in this chapter contains just a handful of syntactic forms: the boolean constants `true` and `false`, conditional expressions, the numeric constant 0, the arithmetic operators `succ` (successor) and `pred` (predecessor), and a testing operation `iszero` that returns `true` when it is applied to 0 and `false` when it is applied to some other number. These forms can be summarized compactly by the following grammar.

The system studied in this chapter is the untyped calculus of booleans and numbers (Figure 3-2, on page 41). The associated OCaml implementation, called `arith` in the web repository, is described in Chapter 4. Instructions for downloading and building this checker can be found at `http://www.cis.upenn.edu/~bcpierce/tapl`.

t ::=		*terms:*
	`true`	*constant true*
	`false`	*constant false*
	`if t then t else t`	*conditional*
	`0`	*constant zero*
	`succ t`	*successor*
	`pred t`	*predecessor*
	`iszero t`	*zero test*

The conventions used in this grammar (and throughout the book) are close to those of standard BNF (cf. Aho, Sethi, and Ullman, 1986). The first line (t ::=) declares that we are defining the set of *terms,* and that we are going to use the letter t to range over terms. Each line that follows gives one alternative syntactic form for terms. At every point where the symbol t appears, we may substitute any term. The italicized phrases on the right are just comments.

The symbol t in the right-hand sides of the rules of this grammar is called a *metavariable.* It is a variable in the sense that it is a place-holder for some particular term, and "meta" in the sense that it is not a variable of the *object language*—the simple programming language whose syntax we are currently describing—but rather of the *metalanguage*—the notation in which the description is given. (In fact, the present object language doesn't even have variables; we'll introduce them in Chapter 5.) The prefix *meta-* comes from *meta-mathematics*, the subfield of logic whose subject matter is the mathematical properties of systems for mathematical and logical reasoning (which includes programming languages). This field also gives us the term *metatheory*, meaning the collection of true statements that we can make about some particular logical system (or programming language)—and, by extension, the study of such statements. Thus, phrases like "metatheory of subtyping" in this book can be understood as, "the formal study of the properties of systems with subtyping."

Throughout the book, we use the metavariable t, as well as nearby letters such as s, u, and r and variants such as t_1 and s′, to stand for terms of whatever object language we are discussing at the moment; other letters will be introduced as we go along, standing for expressions drawn from other syntactic categories. A complete summary of metavariable conventions can be found in Appendix B.

For the moment, the words *term* and *expression* are used interchangeably. Starting in Chapter 8, when we begin discussing calculi with additional syntactic categories such as *types*, we will use *expression* for all sorts of syntactic phrases (including term expressions, type expressions, kind expressions, etc.), reserving *term* for the more specialized sense of phrases representing computations (i.e., phrases that can be substituted for the metavariable t).

A program in the present language is just a term built from the forms given by the grammar above. Here are some examples of programs, along with the results of evaluating them. For brevity, we use standard arabic numerals for numbers, which are represented formally as nested applications of succ to 0. For example, succ(succ(succ(0))) is written as 3.

```
if false then 0 else 1;
```

▸ 1

```
iszero (pred (succ 0));
```

▸ true

Throughout the book, the symbol ▸ is used to display the results of evaluating examples. (For brevity, results will be elided when they are obvious or unimportant.) During typesetting, examples are automatically processed by the implementation corresponding to the formal system under discussion (arith here); the displayed responses are the implementation's actual output.

In examples, compound arguments to succ, pred, and iszero are enclosed in parentheses for readability.[1] Parentheses are not mentioned in the grammar of terms, which defines only their *abstract syntax*. Of course, the presence or absence of parentheses makes little difference in the extremely simple language that we are dealing with at the moment: parentheses are usually used to resolve ambiguities in the grammar, but this grammar does not have any ambiguities—each sequence of tokens can be parsed as a term in at most one way. We will return to the discussion of parentheses and abstract syntax in Chapter 5 (p. 52).

The results of evaluation are terms of a particularly simple form: they will always be either boolean constants or numbers (nested applications of zero or more instances of succ to 0). Such terms are called *values,* and they will play a special role in our formalization of the evaluation order of terms.

Notice that the syntax of terms permits the formation of some dubious-looking terms like succ true and if 0 then 0 else 0. We shall have more to say about such terms later—indeed, in a sense they are precisely what makes this tiny language interesting for our purposes, since they are examples of the sorts of nonsensical programs we will want a type system to exclude.

---

1. In fact, the implementation used to process the examples in this chapter (called arith on the book's web site) actually *requires* parentheses around compound arguments to succ, pred, and iszero, even though they can be parsed unambiguously without parentheses. This is for consistency with later calculi, which use similar-looking syntax for function application.

3.2   Syntax

There are several equivalent ways of defining the syntax of our language. We have already seen one in the grammar on page 24. This grammar is actually just a compact notation for the following inductive definition:

3.2.1   DEFINITION [TERMS, INDUCTIVELY]: The set of *terms* is the smallest set $\mathcal{T}$ such that

1. $\{\texttt{true}, \texttt{false}, \texttt{0}\} \subseteq \mathcal{T}$;

2. if $\texttt{t}_1 \in \mathcal{T}$, then $\{\texttt{succ t}_1, \texttt{pred t}_1, \texttt{iszero t}_1\} \subseteq \mathcal{T}$;

3. if $\texttt{t}_1 \in \mathcal{T}$, $\texttt{t}_2 \in \mathcal{T}$, and $\texttt{t}_3 \in \mathcal{T}$, then $\texttt{if t}_1 \texttt{ then t}_2 \texttt{ else t}_3 \in \mathcal{T}$.   □

Since inductive definitions are ubiquitous in the study of programming languages, it is worth pausing for a moment to examine this one in detail. The first clause tells us three simple expressions that are in $\mathcal{T}$. The second and third clauses give us rules by which we can judge that certain compound expressions are in $\mathcal{T}$. Finally, the word "smallest" tells us that $\mathcal{T}$ has no elements besides the ones required by these three clauses.

Like the grammar on page 24, this definition says nothing about the use of parentheses to mark compound subterms. Formally, what's really going on is that we are defining $\mathcal{T}$ as a set of *trees,* not as a set of strings. The use of parentheses in examples is just a way of clarifying the relation between the linearized form of terms that we write on the page and the real underlying tree form.

A different shorthand for the same inductive definition of terms employs the two-dimensional *inference rule* format commonly used in "natural deduction style" presentations of logical systems:

3.2.2   DEFINITION [TERMS, BY INFERENCE RULES]: The set of terms is defined by the following rules:

$$\texttt{true} \in \mathcal{T} \qquad\qquad \texttt{false} \in \mathcal{T} \qquad\qquad \texttt{0} \in \mathcal{T}$$

$$\frac{\texttt{t}_1 \in \mathcal{T}}{\texttt{succ t}_1 \in \mathcal{T}} \qquad\qquad \frac{\texttt{t}_1 \in \mathcal{T}}{\texttt{pred t}_1 \in \mathcal{T}} \qquad\qquad \frac{\texttt{t}_1 \in \mathcal{T}}{\texttt{iszero t}_1 \in \mathcal{T}}$$

$$\frac{\texttt{t}_1 \in \mathcal{T} \qquad \texttt{t}_2 \in \mathcal{T} \qquad \texttt{t}_3 \in \mathcal{T}}{\texttt{if t}_1 \texttt{ then t}_2 \texttt{ else t}_3 \in \mathcal{T}} \qquad\qquad □$$

The first three rules here restate the first clause of Definition 3.2.1; the next four capture clauses (2) and (3). Each rule is read, "If we have established the statements in the premise(s) listed above the line, then we may derive the conclusion below the line." The fact that $\mathcal{T}$ is the *smallest* set satisfying these rules is often (as here) not stated explicitly.

Two points of terminology deserve mention. First, rules with no premises (like the first three above) are often called *axioms*. In this book, the term *inference rule* is used generically to include both axioms and "proper rules" with one or more premises. Axioms are usually written with no bar, since there is nothing to go above it. Second, to be completely pedantic, what we are calling "inference rules" are actually *rule schemas*, since their premises and conclusions may include metavariables. Formally, each schema represents the infinite set of *concrete rules* that can be obtained by replacing each metavariable consistently by all phrases from the appropriate syntactic category—i.e., in the rules above, replacing each t by every possible term.

Finally, here is yet another definition of the same set of terms in a slightly different, more "concrete" style that gives an explicit procedure for *generating* the elements of $\mathcal{T}$.

3.2.3   DEFINITION [TERMS, CONCRETELY]:   For each natural number i, define a set S_i as follows:

$$
\begin{aligned}
S_0 &= \varnothing \\
S_{i+1} &= \quad \{\text{true}, \text{false}, 0\} \\
&\cup \quad \{\text{succ } t_1, \text{pred } t_1, \text{iszero } t_1 \mid t_1 \in S_i\} \\
&\cup \quad \{\text{if } t_1 \text{ then } t_2 \text{ else } t_3 \mid t_1, t_2, t_3 \in S_i\}.
\end{aligned}
$$

Finally, let

$$
S = \bigcup_i S_i.
$$

S_0 is empty; S_1 contains just the constants; S_2 contains the constants plus the phrases that can be built with constants and just one succ, pred, iszero, or if; S_3 contains these and all phrases that can be built using succ, pred, iszero, and if on phrases in S_2; and so on. S collects together all the phrases that can be built in this way—i.e., all phrases built by some finite number of arithmetic and conditional operators, beginning with just constants.   □

3.2.4   EXERCISE [★★]:   How many elements does S_3 have?   □

3.2.5   EXERCISE [★★]:   Show that the sets S_i are *cumulative*—that is, that for each i we have $S_i \subseteq S_{i+1}$.   □

The definitions we have seen characterize the same set of terms from different directions: Definitions 3.2.1 and 3.2.2 simply *characterize* the set as the smallest set satisfying certain "closure properties"; Definition 3.2.3 shows how to actually *construct* the set as the limit of a sequence.

To finish off the discussion, let us verify that these two views actually define the same set. We'll do the proof in quite a bit of detail, to show how all the pieces fit together.

3.2.6   PROPOSITION: $\mathcal{T} = S$.   □

Proof: $\mathcal{T}$ was defined as the smallest set satisfying certain conditions. So it suffices to show (a) that S satisfies these conditions, and (b) that any set satisfying the conditions has S as a subset (i.e., that S is the *smallest* set satisfying the conditions).

For part (a), we must check that each of the three conditions in Definition 3.2.1 holds of S. First, since $S_1 = \{\texttt{true}, \texttt{false}, \texttt{0}\}$, it is clear that the constants are in S. Second, if $\texttt{t}_1 \in S$, then (since $S = \bigcup_i S_i$) there must be some i such that $\texttt{t}_1 \in S_i$. But then, by the definition of S_{i+1}, we must have $\texttt{succ } \texttt{t}_1 \in S_{i+1}$, hence $\texttt{succ } \texttt{t}_1 \in S$; similarly, we see that $\texttt{pred } \texttt{t}_1 \in S$ and $\texttt{iszero } \texttt{t}_1 \in S$. Third, if $\texttt{t}_1 \in S$, $\texttt{t}_2 \in S$, and $\texttt{t}_3 \in S$, then $\texttt{if } \texttt{t}_1 \texttt{ then } \texttt{t}_2 \texttt{ else } \texttt{t}_3 \in S$, by a similar argument.

For part (b), suppose that some set S' satisfies the three conditions in Definition 3.2.1. We will argue, by complete induction on i, that every $S_i \subseteq S'$, from which it clearly follows that $S \subseteq S'$.

Suppose that $S_j \subseteq S'$ for all $j < i$; we must show that $S_i \subseteq S'$. Since the definition of S_i has two clauses (for $i = 0$ and $i > 0$), there are two cases to consider. If $i = 0$, then $S_i = \varnothing$; but $\varnothing \subseteq S'$ trivially. Otherwise, $i = j + 1$ for some j. Let $\texttt{t}$ be some element of S_{j+1}. Since S_{j+1} is defined as the union of three smaller sets, $\texttt{t}$ must come from one of these sets; there are three possibilities to consider. (1) If $\texttt{t}$ is a constant, then $\texttt{t} \in S'$ by condition 1. (2) If $\texttt{t}$ has the form $\texttt{succ } \texttt{t}_1$, $\texttt{pred } \texttt{t}_1$, or $\texttt{iszero } \texttt{t}_1$, for some $\texttt{t}_1 \in S_j$, then, by the induction hypothesis, $\texttt{t}_1 \in S'$, and so, by condition (2), $\texttt{t} \in S'$. (3) If $\texttt{t}$ has the form $\texttt{if } \texttt{t}_1 \texttt{ then } \texttt{t}_2 \texttt{ else } \texttt{t}_3$, for some $\texttt{t}_1, \texttt{t}_2, \texttt{t}_3 \in S_i$, then again, by the induction hypothesis, $\texttt{t}_1$, $\texttt{t}_2$, and $\texttt{t}_3$ are all in S', and, by condition 3, so is $\texttt{t}$.

Thus, we have shown that each $S_i \subseteq S'$. By the definition of S as the union of all the S_i, this gives $S \subseteq S'$, completing the argument.   □

It is worth noting that this proof goes by *complete* induction on the natural numbers, not the more familiar "base case / induction case" form. For each i, we suppose that the desired predicate holds for all numbers strictly less than i and prove that it then holds for i as well. In essence, *every* step here is an induction step; the only thing that is special about the case where $i = 0$ is that the set of smaller values of i, for which we can invoke the induction hypothesis, happens to be empty. The same remark will apply to most induction proofs we will see throughout the book—particularly proofs by "structural induction."

3.3 Induction on Terms

The explicit characterization of the set of terms $\mathcal{T}$ in Proposition 3.2.6 justifies an important principle for reasoning about its elements. If $t \in \mathcal{T}$, then one of three things must be true about t: (1) t is a constant, or (2) t has the form succ t_1, pred t_1, or iszero t_1 for some *smaller* term t_1, or (3) t has the form if t_1 then t_2 else t_3 for some *smaller* terms t_1, t_2, and t_3. We can put this observation to work in two ways: we can give *inductive definitions* of functions over the set of terms, and we can give *inductive proofs* of properties of terms. For example, here is a simple inductive definition of a function mapping each term t to the set of constants used in t.

3.3.1 DEFINITION: The set of constants appearing in a term t, written *Consts*(t), is defined as follows:

Consts(true)	=	{true}
Consts(false)	=	{false}
Consts(0)	=	{0}
Consts(succ t_1)	=	*Consts*(t_1)
Consts(pred t_1)	=	*Consts*(t_1)
Consts(iszero t_1)	=	*Consts*(t_1)
Consts(if t_1 then t_2 else t_3)	=	*Consts*(t_1) $\cup$ *Consts*(t_2) $\cup$ *Consts*(t_3) □

Another property of terms that can be calculated by an inductive definition is their size.

3.3.2 DEFINITION: The *size* of a term t, written *size*(t), is defined as follows:

size(true)	=	1
size(false)	=	1
size(0)	=	1
size(succ t_1)	=	*size*(t_1) $+ 1$
size(pred t_1)	=	*size*(t_1) $+ 1$
size(iszero t_1)	=	*size*(t_1) $+ 1$
size(if t_1 then t_2 else t_3)	=	*size*(t_1) $+$ *size*(t_2) $+$ *size*(t_3) $+ 1$

That is, the size of t is the number of nodes in its abstract syntax tree. Similarly, the *depth* of a term t, written *depth*(t), is defined as follows:

$$
\begin{array}{lcl}
depth(\texttt{true}) & = & 1 \\
depth(\texttt{false}) & = & 1 \\
depth(\texttt{0}) & = & 1 \\
depth(\texttt{succ } \texttt{t}_1) & = & depth(\texttt{t}_1) + 1 \\
depth(\texttt{pred } \texttt{t}_1) & = & depth(\texttt{t}_1) + 1 \\
depth(\texttt{iszero } \texttt{t}_1) & = & depth(\texttt{t}_1) + 1 \\
depth(\texttt{if } \texttt{t}_1 \texttt{ then } \texttt{t}_2 \texttt{ else } \texttt{t}_3) & = & \max(depth(\texttt{t}_1), depth(\texttt{t}_2), depth(\texttt{t}_3)) + 1
\end{array}
$$

Equivalently, $depth(\texttt{t})$ is the smallest i such that $\texttt{t} \in S_i$ according to Definition 3.2.3. $\square$

Here is an inductive proof of a simple fact relating the number of constants in a term to its size. (The property in itself is entirely obvious, of course. What's interesting is the form of the inductive proof, which we'll see repeated many times as we go along.)

3.3.3   LEMMA: The number of distinct constants in a term $\texttt{t}$ is no greater than the size of $\texttt{t}$ (i.e., $|Consts(\texttt{t})| \leq size(\texttt{t})$). $\square$

Proof: By induction on the depth of $\texttt{t}$. Assuming the desired property for all terms smaller than $\texttt{t}$, we must prove it for $\texttt{t}$ itself. There are three cases to consider:

Case: $\texttt{t}$ is a constant

Immediate: $|Consts(\texttt{t})| = |\{\texttt{t}\}| = 1 = size(\texttt{t})$.

Case: $\texttt{t} = \texttt{succ } \texttt{t}_1$, $\texttt{pred } \texttt{t}_1$, or $\texttt{iszero } \texttt{t}_1$

By the induction hypothesis, $|Consts(\texttt{t}_1)| \leq size(\texttt{t}_1)$. We now calculate as follows: $|Consts(\texttt{t})| = |Consts(\texttt{t}_1)| \leq size(\texttt{t}_1) < size(\texttt{t})$.

Case: $\texttt{t} = \texttt{if } \texttt{t}_1 \texttt{ then } \texttt{t}_2 \texttt{ else } \texttt{t}_3$

By the induction hypothesis, $|Consts(\texttt{t}_1)| \leq size(\texttt{t}_1)$, $|Consts(\texttt{t}_2)| \leq size(\texttt{t}_2)$, and $|Consts(\texttt{t}_3)| \leq size(\texttt{t}_3)$. We now calculate as follows:

$$
\begin{array}{lcl}
|Consts(\texttt{t})| & = & |Consts(\texttt{t}_1) \cup Consts(\texttt{t}_2) \cup Consts(\texttt{t}_3)| \\
& \leq & |Consts(\texttt{t}_1)| + |Consts(\texttt{t}_2)| + |Consts(\texttt{t}_3)| \\
& \leq & size(\texttt{t}_1) + size(\texttt{t}_2) + size(\texttt{t}_3) \\
& < & size(\texttt{t}).
\end{array}
$$
                                                                                                                            $\square$

The form of this proof can be clarified by restating it as a general reasoning principle. For good measure, we include two similar principles that are often used in proofs about terms.

3.3.4   Theorem [Principles of induction on terms]: Suppose P is a predicate on terms.

> *Induction on depth:*
>
> > If, for each term s,
> >> given $P(r)$ for all r such that $depth(r) < depth(s)$
> >> we can show $P(s)$,
> > then $P(s)$ holds for all s.

> *Induction on size:*
>
> > If, for each term s,
> >> given $P(r)$ for all r such that $size(r) < size(s)$
> >> we can show $P(s)$,
> > then $P(s)$ holds for all s.

> *Structural induction:*
>
> > If, for each term s,
> >> given $P(r)$ for all immediate subterms r of s
> >> we can show $P(s)$,
> > then $P(s)$ holds for all s.   □

Proof: Exercise (★★).   □

Induction on depth or size of terms is analogous to complete induction on natural numbers (2.4.2). Ordinary structural induction corresponds to the ordinary natural number induction principle (2.4.1) where the induction step requires that $P(n + 1)$ be established from just the assumption $P(n)$.

Like the different styles of natural-number induction, the choice of one term induction principle over another is determined by which one leads to a simpler structure for the proof at hand—formally, they are inter-derivable. For simple proofs, it generally makes little difference whether we argue by induction on size, depth, or structure. As a matter of style, it is common practice to use structural induction wherever possible, since it works on terms directly, avoiding the detour via numbers.

Most proofs by induction on terms have a similar structure. At each step of the induction, we are given a term t for which we are to show some property P, assuming that P holds for all subterms (or all smaller terms). We do this by separately considering each of the possible forms that t could have (true, false, conditional, 0, etc.), arguing in each case that P must hold for any t of this form. Since the only parts of this structure that vary from one inductive proof to another are the details of the arguments for the individual cases, it is common practice to elide the unvarying parts and write the proof as follows.

Proof: By induction on t.

Case: t = true

... show $P(\text{true})$ ...

Case: t = false

... show $P(\text{false})$ ...

Case: t = if t_1 then t_2 else t_3

... show $P(\text{if } t_1 \text{ then } t_2 \text{ else } t_3)$, using $P(t_1)$, $P(t_2)$, and $P(t_3)$ ...

(And similarly for the other syntactic forms.)   □

For many inductive arguments (including the proof of 3.3.3), it is not really worth writing even this much detail: in the base cases (for terms t with no subterms) $P(t)$ is immediate, while in the inductive cases $P(t)$ is obtained by applying the induction hypothesis to the subterms of t and combining the results in some completely obvious way. It is actually *easier* for the reader simply to regenerate the proof on the fly (by examining the grammar while keeping the induction hypothesis in mind) than to check a written-out argument. In such cases, simply writing "by induction on t" constitutes a perfectly acceptable proof.

3.4   Semantic Styles

Having formulated the syntax of our language rigorously, we next need a similarly precise definition of how terms are evaluated—i.e., the *semantics* of the language. There are three basic approaches to formalizing semantics:

1. *Operational semantics* specifies the behavior of a programming language by defining a simple *abstract machine* for it. This machine is "abstract" in the sense that it uses the terms of the language as its machine code, rather than some low-level microprocessor instruction set. For simple languages, a *state* of the machine is just a term, and the machine's behavior is defined by a *transition function* that, for each state, either gives the next state by performing a step of simplification on the term or declares that the machine has halted. The *meaning* of a term t can be taken to be the final state that the machine reaches when started with t as its initial state.[2]

---

2. Strictly speaking, what we are describing here is the so-called *small-step* style of operational semantics, sometimes called *structural operational semantics* (Plotkin, 1981). Exercise 3.5.17 introduces an alternate *big-step* style, sometimes called *natural semantics* (Kahn, 1987), in which a single transition of the abstract machine evaluates a term to its final result.

It is sometimes useful to give two or more different operational semantics for a single language—some more abstract, with machine states that look similar to the terms that the programmer writes, others closer to the structures manipulated by an actual interpreter or compiler for the language. Proving that the behaviors of these different machines correspond in some suitable sense when executing the same program amounts to proving the correctness of an implementation of the language.

2. *Denotational semantics* takes a more abstract view of meaning: instead of just a sequence of machine states, the meaning of a term is taken to be some mathematical object, such as a number or a function. Giving denotational semantics for a language consists of finding a collection of *semantic domains* and then defining an *interpretation function* mapping terms into elements of these domains. The search for appropriate semantic domains for modeling various language features has given rise to a rich and elegant research area known as *domain theory*.

One major advantage of denotational semantics is that it abstracts from the gritty details of evaluation and highlights the essential concepts of the language. Also, the properties of the chosen collection of semantic domains can be used to derive powerful laws for reasoning about program behaviors—laws for proving that two programs have exactly the same behavior, for example, or that a program's behavior satisfies some specification. Finally, from the properties of the chosen collection of semantic domains, it is often immediately evident that various (desirable or undesirable) things are impossible in a language.

3. *Axiomatic semantics* takes a more direct approach to these laws: instead of first defining the behaviors of programs (by giving some operational or denotational semantics) and then deriving laws from this definition, axiomatic methods take the laws *themselves* as the definition of the language. The meaning of a term is just what can be proved about it.

The beauty of axiomatic methods is that they focus attention on the process of reasoning about programs. It is this line of thought that has given computer science such powerful ideas as *invariants*.

During the '60s and '70s, operational semantics was generally regarded as inferior to the other two styles—useful for quick and dirty definitions of language features, but inelegant and mathematically weak. But in the '80s, the more abstract methods began to encounter increasingly thorny technical problems,[3] and the simplicity and flexibility of operational methods came

---

3. The *bête noire* of denotational semantics turned out to be the treatment of nondeterminism and concurrency; for axiomatic semantics, it was procedures.

$\mathbb{B}$ *(untyped)*

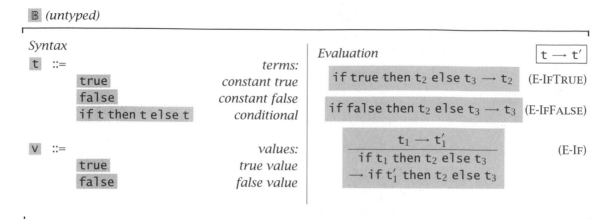

Syntax

$t ::=$ *terms:*

       `true`   *constant true*

       `false`   *constant false*

       `if t then t else t`   *conditional*

$v ::=$ *values:*

       `true`   *true value*

       `false`   *false value*

Evaluation $\boxed{t \longrightarrow t'}$

$$\text{if true then } t_2 \text{ else } t_3 \longrightarrow t_2 \qquad \text{(E-IFTRUE)}$$

$$\text{if false then } t_2 \text{ else } t_3 \longrightarrow t_3 \qquad \text{(E-IFFALSE)}$$

$$\frac{t_1 \longrightarrow t_1'}{\begin{array}{c}\text{if } t_1 \text{ then } t_2 \text{ else } t_3 \\ \longrightarrow \text{if } t_1' \text{ then } t_2 \text{ else } t_3\end{array}} \qquad \text{(E-IF)}$$

Figure 3-1: Booleans (B)

to seem more and more attractive by comparison—especially in the light of new developments in the area by a number of researchers, beginning with Plotkin's Structural Operational Semantics (1981), Kahn's Natural Semantics (1987), and Milner's work on CCS (1980; 1989; 1999), which introduced more elegant formalisms and showed how many of the powerful mathematical techniques developed in the context of denotational semantics could be transferred to an operational setting. Operational semantics has become an energetic research area in its own right and is often the method of choice for defining programming languages and studying their properties. It is used exclusively in this book.

3.5   Evaluation

Leaving numbers aside for the moment, let us begin with the operational semantics of just boolean expressions. Figure 3-1 summarizes the definition. We now examine its parts in detail.

The left-hand column of Figure 3-1 is a grammar defining two sets of expressions. The first is just a repetition (for convenience) of the syntax of terms. The second defines a subset of terms, called *values,* that are possible final results of evaluation. Here, the values are just the constants `true` and `false`. The metavariable v is used throughout the book to stand for values.

The right-hand column defines an *evaluation relation*[4] on terms, written

---

4. Some experts prefer to use the term *reduction* for this relation, reserving *evaluation* for the "big-step" variant described in Exercise 3.5.17, which maps terms directly to their final values.

t $\longrightarrow$ t′ and pronounced "t evaluates to t′ in one step." The intuition is that, if t is the state of the abstract machine at a given moment, then the machine can make a step of computation and change its state to t′. This relation is defined by three inference rules (or, if you prefer, two axioms and a rule, since the first two have no premises).

The first rule, E-IfTrue, says that, if the term being evaluated is a conditional whose guard is literally the constant true, then the machine can throw away the conditional expression and leave the then part, t_2, as the new state of the machine (i.e., the next term to be evaluated). Similarly, E-IfFalse says that a conditional whose guard is literally false evaluates in one step to its else branch, t_3. The E- in the names of these rules is a reminder that they are part of the evaluation relation; rules for other relations will have different prefixes.

The third evaluation rule, E-If, is more interesting. It says that, if the guard t_1 evaluates to t_1', then the whole conditional if t_1 then t_2 else t_3 evaluates to if t_1' then t_2 else t_3. In terms of abstract machines, a machine in state if t_1 then t_2 else t_3 can take a step to state if t_1' then t_2 else t_3 if *another* machine whose state is just t_1 can take a step to state t_1'.

What these rules do *not* say is just as important as what they do say. The constants true and false do not evaluate to anything, since they do not appear as the left-hand sides of any of the rules. Moreover, there is no rule allowing the evaluation of a then- or else-subexpression of an if before evaluating the if itself: for example, the term

    if true then (if false then false else false) else true

does not evaluate to if true then false else true. Our only choice is to evaluate the outer conditional first, using E-If. This interplay between the rules determines a particular *evaluation strategy* for conditionals, corresponding to the familiar order of evaluation in common programming languages: to evaluate a conditional, we must first evaluate its guard; if the guard is itself a conditional, we must first evaluate *its* guard; and so on. The E-IfTrue and E-IfFalse rules tell us what to do when we reach the end of this process and find ourselves with a conditional whose guard is already fully evaluated. In a sense, E-IfTrue and E-IfFalse do the real work of evaluation, while E-If helps determine where the work is to be done. The different character of the rules is sometimes emphasized by referring to E-IfTrue and E-IfFalse as *computation rules* and E-If as a *congruence rule*.

To be a bit more precise about these intuitions, we can define the evaluation relation formally as follows.

3.5.1   DEFINITION: An *instance* of an inference rule is obtained by consistently replacing each metavariable by the same term in the rule's conclusion and all
its premises (if any).   □

For example,

> if true then true else (if false then false else false) ⟶ true

is an instance of E-IFTRUE, where both occurrences of t_2 have been replaced
by true and t_3 has been replaced by if false then false else false.

3.5.2   DEFINITION: A rule is *satisfied* by a relation if, for each instance of the rule,
either the conclusion is in the relation or one of the premises is not.   □

3.5.3   DEFINITION: The *one-step evaluation* relation ⟶ is the smallest binary relation on terms satisfying the three rules in Figure 3-1. When the pair (t, t') is
in the evaluation relation, we say that "the evaluation *statement* (or *judgment*)
$t \longrightarrow t'$ is *derivable*."   □

The force of the word "smallest" here is that a statement $t \longrightarrow t'$ is derivable iff it is justified by the rules: either it is an instance of one of the axioms
E-IFTRUE and E-IFFALSE, or else it is the conclusion of an instance of rule E-IF
whose premise is derivable. The derivability of a given statement can be justified by exhibiting a *derivation tree* whose leaves are labeled with instances
of E-IFTRUE or E-IFFALSE and whose internal nodes are labeled with instances
of E-IF. For example, if we abbreviate

$$s \overset{\text{def}}{=} \text{if true then false else false}$$
$$t \overset{\text{def}}{=} \text{if s then true else true}$$
$$u \overset{\text{def}}{=} \text{if false then true else true}$$

to avoid running off the edge of the page, then the derivability of the statement

> if t then false else false ⟶ if u then false else false

is witnessed by the following derivation tree:

$$\cfrac{\cfrac{\cfrac{\qquad}{\text{s} \longrightarrow \text{false}} \text{ E-IFTRUE}}{\text{t} \longrightarrow \text{u}} \text{ E-IF}}{\text{if t then false else false} \longrightarrow \text{if u then false else false}} \text{ E-IF}$$

Calling this structure a tree may seem a bit strange, since it doesn't contain
any branches. Indeed, the derivation trees witnessing evaluation statements

will always have this slender form: since no evaluation rule has more than one premise, there is no way to construct a branching derivation tree. The terminology will make more sense when we consider derivations for other inductively defined relations, such as typing, where some of the rules do have multiple premises.

The fact that an evaluation statement $t \longrightarrow t'$ is derivable iff there is a derivation tree with $t \longrightarrow t'$ as the label at its root is often useful when reasoning about properties of the evaluation relation. In particular, it leads directly to a proof technique called *induction on derivations*. The proof of the following theorem illustrates this technique.

3.5.4   THEOREM [DETERMINACY OF ONE-STEP EVALUATION]: If $t \longrightarrow t'$ and $t \longrightarrow t''$, then $t' = t''$. □

Proof: By induction on a derivation of $t \longrightarrow t'$. At each step of the induction, we assume the desired result for all smaller derivations, and proceed by a case analysis of the evaluation rule used at the root of the derivation. (Notice that the induction here is not on the length of an evaluation sequence: we are looking just at a single step of evaluation. We could just as well say that we are performing induction on the structure of t, since the structure of an "evaluation derivation" directly follows the structure of the term being reduced. Alternatively, we could just as well perform the induction on the derivation of $t \longrightarrow t''$ instead.)

If the last rule used in the derivation of $t \longrightarrow t'$ is E-IFTRUE, then we know that t has the form if t_1 then t_2 else t_3, where t_1 = true. But now it is obvious that the last rule in the derivation of $t \longrightarrow t''$ cannot be E-IFFALSE, since we cannot have both t_1 = true and t_1 = false. Moreover, the last rule in the second derivation cannot be E-IF either, since the premise of this rule demands that $t_1 \longrightarrow t_1'$ for some t_1', but we have already observed that true does not evaluate to anything. So the last rule in the second derivation can only be E-IFTRUE, and it immediately follows that $t' = t''$.

Similarly, if the last rule used in the derivation of $t \longrightarrow t'$ is E-IFFALSE, then the last rule in the derivation of $t \longrightarrow t''$ must be the same and the result is immediate.

Finally, if the last rule used in the derivation of $t \longrightarrow t'$ is E-IF, then the form of this rule tells us that t has the form if t_1 then t_2 else t_3, where $t_1 \longrightarrow t_1'$ for some t_1'. By the same reasoning as above, the last rule in the derivation of $t \longrightarrow t''$ can only be E-IF, which tells us that t has the form if t_1 then t_2 else t_3 (which we already know) and that $t_1 \longrightarrow t_1''$ for some t_1''. But now the induction hypothesis applies (since the derivations of $t_1 \longrightarrow t_1'$ and $t_1 \longrightarrow t_1''$ are subderivations of the original derivations of $t \longrightarrow t'$ and

$t \longrightarrow t''$), yielding $t'_1 = t''_1$. This tells us that $t' = $ if t'_1 then t_2 else $t_3 = $ if t''_1 then t_2 else $t_3 = t''$, as required. $\square$

3.5.5   EXERCISE [⋆]: Spell out the induction principle used in the preceding proof, in the style of Theorem 3.3.4. $\square$

Our one-step evaluation relation shows how an abstract machine moves from one state to the next while evaluating a given term. But as programmers we are just as interested in the final results of evaluation—i.e., in states from which the machine *cannot* take a step.

3.5.6   DEFINITION: A term t is in *normal form* if no evaluation rule applies to it—i.e., if there is no t' such that $t \longrightarrow t'$. (We sometimes say "t is a normal form" as shorthand for "t is a term in normal form.") $\square$

We have already observed that `true` and `false` are normal forms in the present system (since all the evaluation rules have left-hand sides whose outermost constructor is an `if`, there is obviously no way to instantiate any of the rules so that its left-hand side becomes `true` or `false`). We can rephrase this observation in more general terms as a fact about values:

3.5.7   THEOREM: Every value is in normal form. $\square$

When we enrich the system with arithmetic expressions (and, in later chapters, other constructs), we will always arrange that Theorem 3.5.7 remains valid: being in normal form is part of what it *is* to be a value (i.e., a fully evaluated result), and any language definition in which this is not the case is simply broken.

In the present system, the converse of Theorem 3.5.7 is also true: every normal form is a value. This will not be the case in general; in fact, normal forms that are not values play a critical role in our analysis of *run-time errors,* as we shall see when we get to arithmetic expressions later in this section.

3.5.8   THEOREM: If t is in normal form, then t is a value. $\square$

Proof: Suppose that t is not a value. It is easy to show, by structural induction on t, that it is not a normal form.

Since t is not a value, it must have the form if t_1 then t_2 else t_3 for some t_1, t_2, and t_3. Consider the possible forms of t_1.

If $t_1 = $ `true`, then clearly t is not a normal form, since it matches the left-hand side of E-IFTRUE. Similarly if $t_1 = $ `false`.

If t_1 is neither `true` nor `false`, then it is not a value. The induction hypothesis then applies, telling us that t_1 is not a normal form—that is, that there is some t'_1 such that $t_1 \longrightarrow t'_1$. But this means we can use E-IF to derive $t \longrightarrow $ if t'_1 then t_2 else t_3, so t is not a normal form either. $\square$

It is sometimes convenient to be able to view many steps of evaluation as one big state transition. We do this by defining a multi-step evaluation relation that relates a term to all of the terms that can be derived from it by zero or more single steps of evaluation.

3.5.9 DEFINITION: The *multi-step evaluation* relation $\longrightarrow^*$ is the reflexive, transitive closure of one-step evaluation. That is, it is the smallest relation such that (1) if $t \longrightarrow t'$ then $t \longrightarrow^* t'$, (2) $t \longrightarrow^* t$ for all t, and (3) if $t \longrightarrow^* t'$ and $t' \longrightarrow^* t''$, then $t \longrightarrow^* t''$. □

3.5.10 EXERCISE [⋆]: Rephrase Definition 3.5.9 as a set of inference rules. □

Having an explicit notation for multi-step evaluation makes it easy to state facts like the following:

3.5.11 THEOREM [UNIQUENESS OF NORMAL FORMS]: If $t \longrightarrow^* u$ and $t \longrightarrow^* u'$, where u and u' are both normal forms, then $u = u'$. □

Proof: Corollary of the determinacy of single-step evaluation (3.5.4). □

The last property of evaluation that we consider before turning our attention to arithmetic expressions is the fact that *every* term can be evaluated to a value. Clearly, this is another property that need not hold in richer languages with features like recursive function definitions. Even in situations where it does hold, its proof is generally much more subtle than the one we are about to see. In Chapter 12 we will return to this point, showing how a type system can be used as the backbone of a termination proof for certain languages.

Most termination proofs in computer science have the same basic form:[5] First, we choose some well-founded set S and give a function f mapping "machine states" (here, terms) into S. Next, we show that, whenever a machine state t can take a step to another state t', we have $f(t') < f(t)$. We now observe that an infinite sequence of evaluation steps beginning from t can be mapped, via f, into an infinite decreasing chain of elements of S. Since S is well founded, there can be no such infinite decreasing chain, and hence no infinite evaluation sequence. The function f is often called a *termination measure* for the evaluation relation.

3.5.12 THEOREM [TERMINATION OF EVALUATION]: For every term t there is some normal form t' such that $t \longrightarrow^* t'$. □

Proof: Just observe that each evaluation step reduces the size of the term and that size is a termination measure because the usual order on the natural numbers is well founded. □

---

5. In Chapter 12 we will see a termination proof with a somewhat more complex structure.

3.5.13   EXERCISE [RECOMMENDED, ★★]:

1. Suppose we add a new rule

$$\text{if true then } t_2 \text{ else } t_3 \longrightarrow t_3 \qquad\qquad (\text{E-FUNNY1})$$

   to the ones in Figure 3-1. Which of the above theorems (3.5.4, 3.5.7, 3.5.8, 3.5.11, and 3.5.12) remain valid?

2. Suppose instead that we add this rule:

$$\frac{t_2 \longrightarrow t_2'}{\text{if } t_1 \text{ then } t_2 \text{ else } t_3 \longrightarrow \text{if } t_1 \text{ then } t_2' \text{ else } t_3} \qquad (\text{E-FUNNY2})$$

   Now which of the above theorems remain valid? Do any of the proofs need to change?   □

Our next job is to extend the definition of evaluation to arithmetic expressions. Figure 3-2 summarizes the new parts of the definition. (The notation in the upper-right corner of 3-2 reminds us to regard this figure as an extension of 3-1, not a free-standing language in its own right.)

Again, the definition of terms is just a repetition of the syntax we saw in §3.1. The definition of values is a little more interesting, since it requires introducing a new syntactic category of *numeric values*. The intuition is that the final result of evaluating an arithmetic expression can be a number, where a number is either 0 or the successor of a number (but not the successor of an arbitrary value: we will want to say that succ(true) is an error, not a value).

The evaluation rules in the right-hand column of Figure 3-2 follow the same pattern as we saw in Figure 3-1. There are four computation rules (E-PREDZERO, E-PREDSUCC, E-ISZEROZERO, and E-ISZEROSUCC) showing how the operators pred and iszero behave when applied to numbers, and three congruence rules (E-SUCC, E-PRED, and E-ISZERO) that direct evaluation into the "first" subterm of a compound term.

Strictly speaking, we should now repeat Definition 3.5.3 ("the one-step evaluation relation on arithmetic expressions is the smallest relation satisfying all instances of the rules in Figures 3-1 *and* 3-2...."). To avoid wasting space on this kind of boilerplate, it is common practice to take the inference rules as constituting the definition of the relation all by themselves, leaving "the smallest relation containing all instances..." as understood.

The syntactic category of numeric values (nv) plays an important role in these rules. In E-PREDSUCC, for example, the fact that the left-hand side is pred (succ nv_1) (rather than pred (succ t_1), for example) means that this rule cannot be used to evaluate pred (succ (pred 0)) to pred 0, since this

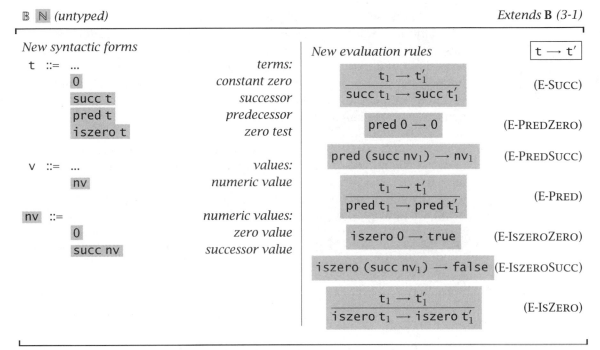

Figure 3-2: Arithmetic expressions (NB)

would require instantiating the metavariable nv_1 with pred 0, which is not a numeric value. Instead, the unique next step in the evaluation of the term pred (succ (pred 0)) has the following derivation tree:

$$\cfrac{\cfrac{\rule{2cm}{0.4pt}}{\text{pred } 0 \longrightarrow 0} \text{ E-PredZero}}{\cfrac{\text{succ (pred 0)} \longrightarrow \text{succ 0}}{\text{pred (succ (pred 0))} \longrightarrow \text{pred (succ 0)}} \text{ E-Pred}} \text{ E-Succ}$$

3.5.14 EXERCISE [★★]: Show that Theorem 3.5.4 is also valid for the evaluation relation on arithmetic expressions: if $t \longrightarrow t'$ and $t \longrightarrow t''$, then $t' = t''$. □

Formalizing the operational semantics of a language forces us to specify the behavior of *all* terms, including, in the case at hand, terms like pred 0 and succ false. Under the rules in Figure 3-2, the predecessor of 0 is defined to be 0. The successor of false, on the other hand, is not defined to evaluate to anything (i.e., it is a normal form). We call such terms *stuck*.

3.5.15 DEFINITION: A closed term is *stuck* if it is in normal form but not a value. □

"Stuckness" gives us a simple notion of *run-time error* for our simple machine. Intuitively, it characterizes the situations where the operational semantics does not know what to do because the program has reached a "meaningless state." In a more concrete implementation of the language, these states might correspond to machine failures of various kinds: segmentation faults, execution of illegal instructions, etc. Here, we collapse all these kinds of bad behavior into the single concept of "stuck state."

3.5.16   EXERCISE [RECOMMENDED, ★★★]: A different way of formalizing meaningless states of the abstract machine is to introduce a new term called wrong and augment the operational semantics with rules that explicitly generate wrong in all the situations where the present semantics gets stuck. To do this in detail, we introduce two new syntactic categories

badnat ::=	*non-numeric normal forms:*
wrong	*run-time error*
true	*constant true*
false	*constant false*
badbool ::=	*non-boolean normal forms:*
wrong	*run-time error*
nv	*numeric value*

and we augment the evaluation relation with the following rules:

$$\text{if badbool then } t_1 \text{ else } t_2 \longrightarrow \text{wrong} \qquad \text{(E-IF-WRONG)}$$

$$\text{succ badnat} \longrightarrow \text{wrong} \qquad \text{(E-SUCC-WRONG)}$$

$$\text{pred badnat} \longrightarrow \text{wrong} \qquad \text{(E-PRED-WRONG)}$$

$$\text{iszero badnat} \longrightarrow \text{wrong} \qquad \text{(E-ISZERO-WRONG)}$$

Show that these two treatments of run-time errors agree by (1) finding a precise way of stating the intuition that "the two treatments agree," and (2) proving it. As is often the case when proving things about programming languages, the tricky part here is formulating a precise statement to be proved—the proof itself should be straightforward.   □

3.5.17   EXERCISE [RECOMMENDED, ★★★]: Two styles of operational semantics are in common use. The one used in this book is called the *small-step* style, because the definition of the evaluation relation shows how individual steps of computation are used to rewrite a term, bit by bit, until it eventually becomes a value. On top of this, we define a multi-step evaluation relation that allows us to talk about terms evaluating (in many steps) to values. An alternative style, called *big-step* semantics (or sometimes *natural semantics*), directly formulates the notion of "this term evaluates to that final value," written $t \Downarrow v$. The big-step evaluation rules for our language of boolean and arithmetic expressions look like this:

$$v \Downarrow v \qquad\qquad\qquad \text{(B-Value)}$$

$$\frac{t_1 \Downarrow \text{true} \qquad t_2 \Downarrow v_2}{\text{if } t_1 \text{ then } t_2 \text{ else } t_3 \Downarrow v_2} \qquad\qquad \text{(B-IfTrue)}$$

$$\frac{t_1 \Downarrow \text{false} \qquad t_3 \Downarrow v_3}{\text{if } t_1 \text{ then } t_2 \text{ else } t_3 \Downarrow v_3} \qquad\qquad \text{(B-IfFalse)}$$

$$\frac{t_1 \Downarrow nv_1}{\text{succ } t_1 \Downarrow \text{succ } nv_1} \qquad\qquad \text{(B-Succ)}$$

$$\frac{t_1 \Downarrow 0}{\text{pred } t_1 \Downarrow 0} \qquad\qquad \text{(B-PredZero)}$$

$$\frac{t_1 \Downarrow \text{succ } nv_1}{\text{pred } t_1 \Downarrow nv_1} \qquad\qquad \text{(B-PredSucc)}$$

$$\frac{t_1 \Downarrow 0}{\text{iszero } t_1 \Downarrow \text{true}} \qquad\qquad \text{(B-IszeroZero)}$$

$$\frac{t_1 \Downarrow \text{succ } nv_1}{\text{iszero } t_1 \Downarrow \text{false}} \qquad\qquad \text{(B-IszeroSucc)}$$

Show that the small-step and big-step semantics for this language coincide, i.e. $t \longrightarrow^* v$ iff $t \Downarrow v$. □

3.5.18 EXERCISE [★★ ↛]: Suppose we want to change the evaluation strategy of our language so that the `then` and `else` branches of an `if` expression are evaluated (in that order) *before* the guard is evaluated. Show how the evaluation rules need to change to achieve this effect. □

3.6 Notes

The ideas of abstract and concrete syntax, parsing, etc., are explained in dozens of textbooks on compilers. Inductive definitions, systems of inference rules, and proofs by induction are covered in more detail by Winskel (1993) and Hennessy (1990).

The style of operational semantics that we are using here goes back to a technical report by Plotkin (1981). The big-step style (Exercise 3.5.17) was developed by Kahn (1987). See Astesiano (1991) and Hennessy (1990) for more detailed developments.

Structural induction was introduced to computer science by Burstall (1969).

Q: Why bother doing proofs about programming languages? They are almost always boring if the definitions are right.
A: The definitions are almost always wrong.   —*Anonymous*

4 *An ML Implementation of Arithmetic Expressions*

Working with formal definitions such as those in the previous chapter is often easier when the intuitions behind the definitions are "grounded" by a connection to a concrete implementation. We describe here the key components of an implementation of our language of booleans and arithmetic expressions. (Readers who do not intend to work with the implementations of the type-checkers described later can skip this chapter and all later chapters with the phrase "ML Implementation" in their titles.)

The code presented here (and in the implementation sections throughout the book) is written in a popular language from the ML family (Gordon, Milner, and Wadsworth, 1979) called *Objective Caml,* or *OCaml* for short (Leroy, 2000; Cousineau and Mauny, 1998). Only a small subset of the full OCaml language is used; it should be easy to translate the examples here into most other languages. The most important requirements are automatic storage management (garbage collection) and easy facilities for defining recursive functions by pattern matching over structured data types. Other functional languages such as Standard ML (Milner, Tofte, Harper, and MacQueen, 1997), Haskell (Hudak et al., 1992; Thompson, 1999), and Scheme (Kelsey, Clinger, and Rees, 1998; Dybvig, 1996) (with some pattern-matching extension) are fine choices. Languages with garbage collection but without pattern matching, such as Java (Arnold and Gosling, 1996) and pure Scheme, are somewhat heavy for the sorts of programming we'll be doing. Languages with neither, such as C (Kernighan and Ritchie, 1988), are even less suitable.[1]

The code in this chapter can be found in the `arith` implementation in the web repository, `http://www.cis.upenn.edu/~bcpierce/tapl`, along with instructions on downloading and building the implementations.

1. Of course, tastes in languages vary and good programmers can use whatever tools come to hand to get the job done; you are free to use whatever language you prefer. But be warned: doing manual storage management (in particular) for the sorts of symbol processing needed by a typechecker is a tedious and error-prone business.

4.1   Syntax

Our first job is to define a type of OCaml values representing terms. OCaml's datatype definition mechanism makes this easy: the following declaration is a straightforward transliteration of the grammar on page 24.

```
type term =
    TmTrue of info
  | TmFalse of info
  | TmIf of info * term * term * term
  | TmZero of info
  | TmSucc of info * term
  | TmPred of info * term
  | TmIsZero of info * term
```

The constructors `TmTrue` to `TmIsZero` name the different sorts of nodes in the abstract syntax trees of type `term`; the type following `of` in each case specifies the number of subtrees that will be attached to that type of node.

Each abstract syntax tree node is annotated with a value of type `info`, which describes where (what character position in which source file) the node originated. This information is created by the parser when it scans the input file, and it is used by printing functions to indicate to the user where an error occurred. For purposes of understanding the basic algorithms of evaluation, typechecking, etc., this information could just as well be omitted; it is included here only so that readers who wish to experiment with the implementations themselves will see the code in exactly the same form as discussed in the book.

In the definition of the evaluation relation, we'll need to check whether a term is a numeric value:

```
let rec isnumericval t = match t with
    TmZero(_) → true
  | TmSucc(_,t1) → isnumericval t1
  | _ → false
```

This is a typical example of recursive definition by pattern matching in OCaml: `isnumericval` is defined as the function that, when applied to `TmZero`, returns true; when applied to `TmSucc` with subtree `t1` makes a recursive call to check whether `t1` is a numeric value; and when applied to any other term returns `false`. The underscores in some of the patterns are "don't care" entries that match anything in the term at that point; they are used in the first two clauses to ignore the `info` annotations and in the final clause to match any `term` whatsoever. The `rec` keyword tells the compiler that this is a recursive function definition—i.e., that the reference to `isnumericval` in its body refs to the function now being defined, rather than to some earlier binding with the same name.

Note that the ML code in the above definition has been "prettified" in some small ways during typesetting, both for ease of reading and for consistency with the lambda-calculus examples. For instance, we use a real arrow symbol (→) instead of the two-character sequence ->. A complete list of these prettifications can be found on the book's web site.

The function that checks whether a term is a value is similar:

```
let rec isval t = match t with
    TmTrue(_)  → true
  | TmFalse(_) → true
  | t when isnumericval t  → true
  | _ → false
```

The third clause is a "conditional pattern": it matches any term t, but only so long as the boolean expression isnumericval t yields true.

4.2 Evaluation

The implementation of the evaluation relation closely follows the single-step evaluation rules in Figures 3-1 and 3-2. As we have seen, these rules define a *partial* function that, when applied to a term that is not yet a value, yields the next step of evaluation for that term. When applied to a value, the result of the evaluation function yields no result. To translate the evaluation rules into OCaml, we need to make a decision about how to handle this case. One straightforward approach is to write the single-step evaluation function eval1 so that it raises an exception when none of the evaluation rules apply to the term that it is given. (Another possibility would be to make the single-step evaluator return a term option indicating whether it was successful and, if so, giving the resulting term; this would also work fine, but would require a little more bookkeeping.) We begin by defining the exception to be raised when no evaluation rule applies:

```
exception NoRuleApplies
```

Now we can write the single-step evaluator itself.

```
let rec eval1 t = match t with
    TmIf(_,TmTrue(_),t2,t3) →
      t2
  | TmIf(_,TmFalse(_),t2,t3) →
      t3
  | TmIf(fi,t1,t2,t3) →
```

```
        let t1' = eval1 t1 in
        TmIf(fi, t1', t2, t3)
  | TmSucc(fi,t1) →
        let t1' = eval1 t1 in
        TmSucc(fi, t1')
  | TmPred(_,TmZero(_)) →
        TmZero(dummyinfo)
  | TmPred(_,TmSucc(_,nv1)) when (isnumericval nv1) →
        nv1
  | TmPred(fi,t1) →
        let t1' = eval1 t1 in
        TmPred(fi, t1')
  | TmIsZero(_,TmZero(_)) →
        TmTrue(dummyinfo)
  | TmIsZero(_,TmSucc(_,nv1)) when (isnumericval nv1) →
        TmFalse(dummyinfo)
  | TmIsZero(fi,t1) →
        let t1' = eval1 t1 in
        TmIsZero(fi, t1')
  | _ →
        raise NoRuleApplies
```

Note that there are several places where we are constructing terms from scratch rather than reorganizing existing terms. Since these new terms do not exist in the user's original source file, their `info` annotations are not useful. The constant `dummyinfo` is used as the `info` annotation in such terms. The variable name `fi` (for "file information") is consistently used to match `info` annotations in patterns.

Another point to notice in the definition of `eval1` is the use of explicit `when` clauses in patterns to capture the effect of metavariable names like `v` and `nv` in the presentation of the evaluation relation in Figures 3-1 and 3-2. In the clause for evaluating `TmPred(_,TmSucc(_,nv1))`, for example, the semantics of OCaml patterns will allow `nv1` to match any term whatsoever, which is not what we want; adding `when (isnumericval nv1)` restricts the rule so that it can fire only when the term matched by `nv1` is actually a numeric value. (We could, if we wanted, rewrite the original inference rules in the same style as the ML patterns, turning the implicit constraints arising from metavariable names into explicit side conditions on the rules

$$\frac{t_1 \text{ is a numeric value}}{\text{pred (succ } t_1) \longrightarrow t_1} \qquad \text{(E-PredSucc)}$$

at some cost in compactness and readability.)

Finally, the `eval` function takes a term and finds its normal form by repeatedly calling `eval1`. Whenever `eval1` returns a new term t', we make a recursive call to `eval` to continue evaluating from t'. When `eval1` finally reaches a point where no rule applies, it raises the exception `NoRuleApplies`, causing `eval` to break out of the loop and return the final term in the sequence.[2]

```
let rec eval t =
  try let t' = eval1 t
      in eval t'
  with NoRuleApplies → t
```

Obviously, this simple evaluator is tuned for easy comparison with the mathematical definition of evaluation, not for finding normal forms as quickly as possible. A somewhat more efficient algorithm can be obtained by starting instead from the "big-step" evaluation rules in Exercise 4.2.2.

4.2.2   EXERCISE [RECOMMENDED, ★★★ ↠]: Change the definition of the `eval` function in the `arith` implementation to the big-step style introduced in Exercise 3.5.17.   □

4.3   The Rest of the Story

Of course, there are many parts to an interpreter or compiler—even a very simple one—besides those we have discussed explicitly here. In reality, terms to be evaluated start out as sequences of characters in files. They must be read from the file system, processed into streams of tokens by a lexical analyzer, and further processed into abstract syntax trees by a parser, before they can actually be evaluated by the functions that we have seen. Furthermore, after evaluation, the results need to be printed out.

$$\boxed{\text{file I/O}} \xrightarrow{\textit{chars}} \boxed{\text{lexing}} \xrightarrow{\textit{tokens}} \boxed{\text{parsing}} \xrightarrow{\textit{terms}} \boxed{\text{evaluation}} \xrightarrow{\textit{values}} \boxed{\text{printing}}$$

Interested readers are encouraged to have a look at the on-line OCaml code for the whole interpreter.

---

2. We write `eval` this way for the sake of simplicity, but putting a `try` handler in a recursive loop is not actually very good style in ML.

4.2.1   EXERCISE [★★]: Why not? What is a better way to write `eval`?   □

5 *The Untyped Lambda-Calculus*

This chapter reviews the definition and some basic properties of the *untyped* or *pure lambda-calculus,* the underlying "computational substrate" for most of the type systems described in the rest of the book.

In the mid 1960s, Peter Landin observed that a complex programming language can be understood by formulating it as a tiny core calculus capturing the language's essential mechanisms, together with a collection of convenient *derived forms* whose behavior is understood by translating them into the core (Landin 1964, 1965, 1966; also see Tennent 1981). The core language used by Landin was the *lambda-calculus,* a formal system invented in the 1920s by Alonzo Church (1936, 1941), in which all computation is reduced to the basic operations of function definition and application. Following Landin's insight, as well as the pioneering work of John McCarthy on Lisp (1959, 1981), the lambda-calculus has seen widespread use in the specification of programming language features, in language design and implementation, and in the study of type systems. Its importance arises from the fact that it can be viewed simultaneously as a simple programming language *in which* computations can be described and as a mathematical object *about which* rigorous statements can be proved.

The lambda-calculus is just one of a large number of core calculi that have been used for similar purposes. The *pi-calculus* of Milner, Parrow, and Walker (1992, 1991) has become a popular core language for defining the semantics of message-based concurrent languages, while Abadi and Cardelli's *object calculus* (1996) distills the core features of object-oriented languages. Most of the concepts and techniques that we will develop for the lambda-calculus can be transferred quite directly to these other calculi. One case study along these lines is developed in Chapter 19.

The examples in this chapter are terms of the pure untyped lambda-calculus, λ (Figure 5-3), or of the lambda-calculus extended with booleans and arithmetic operations, λNB (3-2). The associated OCaml implementation is fulluntyped.

The lambda-calculus can be enriched in a variety of ways. First, it is often convenient to add special concrete syntax for features like numbers, tuples, records, etc., whose behavior can already be simulated in the core language. More interestingly, we can add more complex features such as mutable reference cells or nonlocal exception handling, which can be modeled in the core language only by using rather heavy translations. Such extensions lead eventually to languages such as ML (Gordon, Milner, and Wadsworth, 1979; Milner, Tofte, and Harper, 1990; Weis, Aponte, Laville, Mauny, and Suárez, 1989; Milner, Tofte, Harper, and MacQueen, 1997), Haskell (Hudak et al., 1992), or Scheme (Sussman and Steele, 1975; Kelsey, Clinger, and Rees, 1998). As we shall see in later chapters, extensions to the core language often involve extensions to the type system as well.

5.1   Basics

Procedural (or functional) abstraction is a key feature of essentially all programming languages. Instead of writing the same calculation over and over, we write a procedure or function that performs the calculation generically, in terms of one or more named parameters, and then instantiate this function as needed, providing values for the parameters in each case. For example, it is second nature for a programmer to take a long and repetitive expression like

```
(5*4*3*2*1) + (7*6*5*4*3*2*1) - (3*2*1)
```

and rewrite it as `factorial(5) + factorial(7) - factorial(3)`, where:

```
factorial(n)  =  if n=0 then 1 else n * factorial(n-1).
```

For each nonnegative number n, instantiating the function `factorial` with the argument n yields the factorial of n as result. If we write "λn. ..." as a shorthand for "the function that, for each n, yields...," we can restate the definition of `factorial` as:

```
factorial  =  λn. if n=0 then 1 else n * factorial(n-1)
```

Then `factorial(0)` means "the function (λn. if n=0 then 1 else ...) applied to the argument 0," that is, "the value that results when the argument variable n in the function body (λn. if n=0 then 1 else ...) is replaced by 0," that is, "if 0=0 then 1 else ...," that is, 1.

The *lambda-calculus* (or λ-calculus) embodies this kind of function definition and application in the purest possible form. In the lambda-calculus *everything* is a function: the arguments accepted by functions are themselves functions and the result returned by a function is another function.

The syntax of the lambda-calculus comprises just three sorts of terms.[1] A variable x by itself is a term; the abstraction of a variable x from a term t_1, written $\lambda x.t_1$, is a term; and the application of a term t_1 to another term t_2, written $t_1\ t_2$, is a term. These ways of forming terms are summarized in the following grammar.

t	::=		*terms:*
	x		*variable*
	$\lambda x.t$		*abstraction*
	t t		*application*

The subsections that follow explore some fine points of this definition.

Abstract and Concrete Syntax

When discussing the syntax of programming languages, it is useful to distinguish two levels[2] of structure. The *concrete syntax* (or *surface syntax*) of the language refers to the strings of characters that programmers directly read and write. *Abstract syntax* is a much simpler internal representation of programs as labeled trees (called *abstract syntax trees* or *ASTs*). The tree representation renders the structure of terms immediately obvious, making it a natural fit for the complex manipulations involved in both rigorous language definitions (and proofs about them) and the internals of compilers and interpreters.

The transformation from concrete to abstract syntax takes place in two stages. First, a *lexical analyzer* (or *lexer*) converts the string of characters written by the programmer into a sequence of *tokens*—identifiers, keywords, constants, punctuation, etc. The lexer removes comments and deals with issues such as whitespace and capitalization conventions, and formats for numeric and string constants. Next, a *parser* transforms this sequence of tokens into an abstract syntax tree. During parsing, various conventions such as operator *precedence* and *associativity* reduce the need to clutter surface programs with parentheses to explicitly indicate the structure of compound expressions. For example, * binds more tightly than +, so the parser interprets the unparen-

---

1. The phrase *lambda-term* is used to refer to arbitrary terms in the lambda-calculus. Lambda-terms beginning with a λ are often called *lambda-abstractions*.

2. Definitions of full-blown languages sometimes use even more levels. For example, following Landin, it is often useful to define the behaviors of some languages constructs as derived forms, by translating them into combinations of other, more basic, features. The restricted sublanguage containing just these core features is then called the *internal language* (or *IL*), while the full language including all derived forms is called the *external language* (*EL*). The transformation from EL to IL is (at least conceptually) performed in a separate pass, following parsing. Derived forms are discussed in Section 11.3.

thesized expression 1+2*3 as the abstract syntax tree to the left below rather than the one to the right:

The focus of attention in this book is on abstract, not concrete, syntax. Grammars like the one for lambda-terms above should be understood as describing legal tree structures, not strings of tokens or characters. Of course, when we write terms in examples, definitions, theorems, and proofs, we will need to express them in a concrete, linear notation, but we always have their underlying abstract syntax trees in mind.

To save writing too many parentheses, we adopt two conventions when writing lambda-terms in linear form. First, application associates to the left— that is, s t u stands for the same tree as (s t) u:

Second, the bodies of abstractions are taken to extend as far to the right as possible, so that, for example, λx. λy. x y x stands for the same tree as λx. (λy. ((x y) x)):

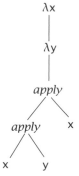

Variables and Metavariables

Another subtlety in the syntax definition above concerns the use of metavariables. We will continue to use the metavariable t (as well as s, and u, with or without subscripts) to stand for an arbitrary term.[3] Similarly, x (as well as y and z) stands for an arbitrary variable. Note, here, that x is a metavariable ranging over variables! To make matters worse, the set of short names is limited, and we will also want to use x, y, etc. as object-language variables. In such cases, however, the context will always make it clear which is which. For example, in a sentence like "The term λx. λy. x y has the form λz.s, where z = x and s = λy. x y," the names z and s are metavariables, whereas x and y are object-language variables.

Scope

A final point we must address about the syntax of the lambda-calculus is the *scopes* of variables.

An occurrence of the variable x is said to be *bound* when it occurs in the body t of an abstraction λx.t. (More precisely, it is bound by *this* abstraction. Equivalently, we can say that λx is a *binder* whose scope is t.) An occurrence of x is *free* if it appears in a position where it is not bound by an enclosing abstraction on x. For example, the occurrences of x in x y and λy. x y are free, while the ones in λx.x and λz. λx. λy. x (y z) are bound. In (λx.x) x, the first occurrence of x is bound and the second is free.

A term with no free variables is said to be *closed;* closed terms are also called *combinators*. The simplest combinator, called the *identity function,*

    id = λx.x;

does nothing but return its argument.

Operational Semantics

In its pure form, the lambda-calculus has no built-in constants or primitive operators—no numbers, arithmetic operations, conditionals, records, loops, sequencing, I/O, etc. The sole means by which terms "compute" is the application of functions to arguments (which themselves are functions). Each step in the computation consists of rewriting an application whose left-hand component is an abstraction, by substituting the right-hand component for the bound variable in the abstraction's body. Graphically, we write

$$(\lambda x.\ t_{12})\ t_2 \longrightarrow [x \mapsto t_2]t_{12},$$

where $[x \mapsto t_2]t_{12}$ means "the term obtained by replacing all free occurrences of x in t_{12} by t_2." For example, the term (λx.x) y evaluates to y and

---

3. Naturally, in this chapter, t ranges over lambda-terms, not arithmetic expressions. Throughout the book, t will always range over the terms of calculus under discussion at the moment. A footnote on the first page of each chapter specifies which system this is.

the term $(\lambda x.\ x\ (\lambda x.x))\ (u\ r)$ evaluates to $u\ r\ (\lambda x.x)$. Following Church, a term of the form $(\lambda x.\ t_{12})\ t_2$ is called a *redex* ("reducible expression"), and the operation of rewriting a redex according to the above rule is called *beta-reduction.*

Several different evaluation strategies for the lambda-calculus have been studied over the years by programming language designers and theorists. Each strategy defines which redex or redexes in a term can fire on the next step of evaluation.[4]

- Under *full beta-reduction,* any redex may be reduced at any time. At each step we pick some redex, anywhere inside the term we are evaluating, and reduce it. For example, consider the term

    $$(\lambda x.x)\ ((\lambda x.x)\ (\lambda z.\ (\lambda x.x)\ z)),$$

    which we can write more readably as id (id (λz. id z)). This term contains three redexes:

    > id (id (λz. id z))
    > id (id (λz. id z))
    > id (id (λz. id z))

    Under full beta-reduction, we might choose, for example, to begin with the innermost redex, then do the one in the middle, then the outermost:

    >   id (id (λz. id z))
    > $\longrightarrow$ id (id (λz.z))
    > $\longrightarrow$ id (λz.z)
    > $\longrightarrow$ λz.z
    > $\nrightarrow$

- Under the *normal order* strategy, the leftmost, outermost redex is always reduced first. Under this strategy, the term above would be reduced as follows:

    >   id (id (λz. id z))
    > $\longrightarrow$ id (λz. id z)
    > $\longrightarrow$ λz. id z
    > $\longrightarrow$ λz.z
    > $\nrightarrow$

---

4. Some people use the terms "reduction" and "evaluation" synonymously. Others use "evaluation" only for strategies that involve some notion of "value" and "reduction" otherwise.

Under this strategy (and the ones below), the evaluation relation is actually a partial function: each term t evaluates in one step to at most one term t′.

- The *call by name* strategy is yet more restrictive, allowing no reductions inside abstractions. Starting from the same term, we would perform the first two reductions as under normal-order, but then stop before the last and regard λz. id z as a normal form:

$$
\begin{aligned}
& \text{id } \underline{(\text{id } (\lambda z.\ \text{id } z))} \\
\longrightarrow\ & \underline{\text{id } (\lambda z.\ \text{id } z)} \\
\longrightarrow\ & \lambda z.\ \text{id } z \\
\nrightarrow\ &
\end{aligned}
$$

Variants of call by name have been used in some well-known programming languages, notably Algol-60 (Naur et al., 1963) and Haskell (Hudak et al., 1992). Haskell actually uses an optimized version known as *call by need* (Wadsworth, 1971; Ariola et al., 1995) that, instead of re-evaluating an argument each time it is used, overwrites all occurrences of the argument with its value the first time it is evaluated, avoiding the need for subsequent re-evaluation. This strategy demands that we maintain some sharing in the run-time representation of terms—in effect, it is a reduction relation on abstract syntax *graphs,* rather than syntax trees.

- Most languages use a *call by value* strategy, in which only outermost redexes are reduced *and* where a redex is reduced only when its right-hand side has already been reduced to a *value*—a term that is finished computing and cannot be reduced any further.[5] Under this strategy, our example term reduces as follows:

$$
\begin{aligned}
& \text{id } \underline{(\text{id } (\lambda z.\ \text{id } z))} \\
\longrightarrow\ & \underline{\text{id } (\lambda z.\ \text{id } z)} \\
\longrightarrow\ & \lambda z.\ \text{id } z \\
\nrightarrow\ &
\end{aligned}
$$

The call-by-value strategy is *strict*, in the sense that the arguments to functions are always evaluated, whether or not they are used by the body of the function. In contrast, *non-strict* (or *lazy*) strategies such as call-by-name and call-by-need evaluate only the arguments that are actually used.

---

5. In the present bare-bones calculus, the only values are lambda-abstractions. Richer calculi will include other values: numeric and boolean constants, strings, tuples of values, records of values, lists of values, etc.

The choice of evaluation strategy actually makes little difference when discussing type systems. The issues that motivate various typing features, and the techniques used to address them, are much the same for all the strategies. In this book, we use call by value, both because it is found in most well-known languages and because it is the easiest to enrich with features such as exceptions (Chapter 14) and references (Chapter 13).

5.2 Programming in the Lambda-Calculus

The lambda-calculus is much more powerful than its tiny definition might suggest. In this section, we develop a number of standard examples of programming in the lambda-calculus. These examples are not intended to suggest that the lambda-calculus should be taken as a full-blown programming language in its own right—all widely used high-level languages provide clearer and more efficient ways of accomplishing the same tasks—but rather are intended as warm-up exercises to get the feel of the system.

Multiple Arguments

To begin, observe that the lambda-calculus provides no built-in support for multi-argument functions. Of course, this would not be hard to add, but it is even easier to achieve the same effect using *higher-order functions* that yield functions as results. Suppose that s is a term involving two free variables x and y and that we want to write a function f that, for each pair (v,w) of arguments, yields the result of substituting v for x and w for y in s. Instead of writing f = λ(x,y).s, as we might in a richer programming language, we write f = λx.λy.s. That is, f is a function that, given a value v for x, yields a function that, given a value w for y, yields the desired result. We then apply f to its arguments one at a time, writing f v w (i.e., (f v) w), which reduces to ((λy.[x ↦ v]s) w) and thence to [y ↦ w][x ↦ v]s. This transformation of multi-argument functions into higher-order functions is called *currying* in honor of Haskell Curry, a contemporary of Church.

Church Booleans

Another language feature that can easily be encoded in the lambda-calculus is boolean values and conditionals. Define the terms tru and fls as follows:

```
tru = λt. λf. t;
fls = λt. λf. f;
```

(The abbreviated spellings of these names are intended to help avoid confusion with the primitive boolean constants `true` and `false` from Chapter 3.)

The terms `tru` and `fls` can be viewed as *representing* the boolean values "true" and "false," in the sense that we can use these terms to perform the operation of testing the truth of a boolean value. In particular, we can use application to define a combinator `test` with the property that `test b v w` reduces to `v` when `b` is `tru` and reduces to `w` when `b` is `fls`.

```
test = λl. λm. λn. l m n;
```

The `test` combinator does not actually do much: `test b v w` just reduces to `b v w`. In effect, the boolean `b` itself is the conditional: it takes two arguments and chooses the first (if it is `tru`) or the second (if it is `fls`). For example, the term `test tru v w` reduces as follows:

	test tru v w	
=	(λl. λm. λn. l m n) tru v w	by definition
⟶	(λm. λn. tru m n) v w	reducing the underlined redex
⟶	(λn. tru v n) w	reducing the underlined redex
⟶	tru v w	reducing the underlined redex
=	(λt.λf.t) v w	by definition
⟶	(λf. v) w	reducing the underlined redex
⟶	v	reducing the underlined redex

We can also define boolean operators like logical conjunction as functions:

```
and = λb. λc. b c fls;
```

That is, `and` is a function that, given two boolean values `b` and `c`, returns `c` if `b` is `tru` and `fls` if `b` is `fls`; thus `and b c` yields `tru` if both `b` and `c` are `tru` and `fls` if either `b` or `c` is `fls`.

```
and tru tru;
```

▶ (λt. λf. t)

```
and tru fls;
```

▶ (λt. λf. f)

5.2.1   EXERCISE [★]: Define logical `or` and `not` functions.   □

Pairs

Using booleans, we can encode pairs of values as terms.

```
pair = λf.λs.λb. b f s;
fst = λp. p tru;
snd = λp. p fls;
```

That is, pair v w is a function that, when applied to a boolean value b, applies b to v and w. By the definition of booleans, this application yields v if b is tru and w if b is fls, so the first and second projection functions fst and snd can be implemented simply by supplying the appropriate boolean. To check that fst (pair v w) $\longrightarrow^*$ v, calculate as follows:

	fst (pair v w)	
=	fst ((λf. λs. λb. b f s) v w)	by definition
$\longrightarrow$	fst ((λs. λb. b v s) w)	reducing the underlined redex
$\longrightarrow$	fst (λb. b v w)	reducing the underlined redex
=	(λp. p tru) (λb. b v w)	by definition
$\longrightarrow$	(λb. b v w) tru	reducing the underlined redex
$\longrightarrow$	tru v w	reducing the underlined redex
$\longrightarrow^*$	v	as before.

Church Numerals

Representing numbers by lambda-terms is only slightly more intricate than what we have just seen. Define the *Church numerals* c_0, c_1, c_2, etc., as follows:

```
c₀ = λs. λz. z;
c₁ = λs. λz. s z;
c₂ = λs. λz. s (s z);
c₃ = λs. λz. s (s (s z));
etc.
```

That is, each number n is represented by a combinator c_n that takes two arguments, s and z (for "successor" and "zero"), and applies s, n times, to z. As with booleans and pairs, this encoding makes numbers into active entities: the number n is represented by a function that does something n times—a kind of active unary numeral.

(The reader may already have observed that c_0 and fls are actually the same term. Similar "puns" are common in assembly languages, where the same pattern of bits may represent many different values—an int, a float, an address, four characters, etc.—depending on how it is interpreted, and in low-level languages such as C, which also identifies 0 and `false`.)

We can define the successor function on Church numerals as follows:

```
scc = λn. λs. λz. s (n s z);
```

The term `scc` is a combinator that takes a Church numeral `n` and returns another Church numeral—that is, it yields a function that takes arguments `s` and `z` and applies `s` repeatedly to `z`. We get the right number of applications of `s` to `z` by first passing `s` and `z` as arguments to `n`, and then explicitly applying `s` one more time to the result.

5.2.2   EXERCISE [★★]: Find another way to define the successor function on Church numerals. □

Similarly, addition of Church numerals can be performed by a term `plus` that takes two Church numerals, `m` and `n`, as arguments, and yields another Church numeral—i.e., a function—that accepts arguments `s` and `z`, applies `s` iterated `n` times to `z` (by passing `s` and `z` as arguments to `n`), and then applies `s` iterated `m` more times to the result:

```
plus = λm. λn. λs. λz. m s (n s z);
```

The implementation of multiplication uses another trick: since `plus` takes its arguments one at a time, applying it to just one argument `n` yields the function that adds `n` to whatever argument it is given. Passing this function as the first argument to `m` and c_0 as the second argument means "apply the function that adds `n` to its argument, iterated `m` times, to zero," i.e., "add together `m` copies of `n`."

```
times = λm. λn. m (plus n) c₀;
```

5.2.3   EXERCISE [★★]: Is it possible to define multiplication on Church numerals without using `plus`? □

5.2.4   EXERCISE [RECOMMENDED, ★★]: Define a term for raising one number to the power of another. □

To test whether a Church numeral is zero, we must find some appropriate pair of arguments that will give us back this information—specifically, we must apply our numeral to a pair of terms `zz` and `ss` such that applying `ss` to `zz` one or more times yields `fls`, while not applying it at all yields `tru`. Clearly, we should take `zz` to be just `tru`. For `ss`, we use a function that throws away its argument and always returns `fls`:

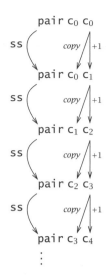

Figure 5-1: The predecessor function's "inner loop"

```
iszro = λm. m (λx. fls) tru;

iszro c₁;
```
▶ (λt. λf. f)
```
iszro (times c₀ c₂);
```
▶ (λt. λf. t)

Surprisingly, subtraction using Church numerals is quite a bit more difficult than addition. It can be done using the following rather tricky "predecessor function," which, given c_0 as argument, returns c_0 and, given c_{i+1}, returns c_i:

```
zz = pair c₀ c₀;
ss = λp. pair (snd p) (plus c₁ (snd p));
prd = λm. fst (m ss zz);
```

This definition works by using m as a function to apply m copies of the function ss to the starting value zz. Each copy of ss takes a pair of numerals pair c_i c_j as its argument and yields pair c_j c_{j+1} as its result (see Figure 5-1). So applying ss, m times, to pair c_0 c_0 yields pair c_0 c_0 when $m = 0$ and pair c_{m-1} c_m when m is positive. In both cases, the predecessor of m is found in the first component.

5.2.5   EXERCISE [★★]: Use prd to define a subtraction function.   □

5.2.6   EXERCISE [★★]: Approximately how many steps of evaluation (as a function of *n*) are required to calculate prd c*n*?   □

5.2.7   EXERCISE [★★]: Write a function equal that tests two numbers for equality and returns a Church boolean. For example,

> equal c₃ c₃;

▸ (λt. λf. t)

> equal c₃ c₂;

▸ (λt. λf. f)   □

Other common datatypes like lists, trees, arrays, and variant records can be encoded using similar techniques.

5.2.8   EXERCISE [RECOMMENDED, ★★★]: A list can be represented in the lambda-calculus by its fold function. (OCaml's name for this function is fold_left; it is also sometimes called reduce .) For example, the list [x,y,z] becomes a function that takes two arguments c and n and returns c x (c y (c z n))). What would the representation of nil be? Write a function cons that takes an element h and a list (that is, a fold function) t and returns a similar representation of the list formed by prepending h to t. Write isnil and head functions, each taking a list parameter. Finally, write a tail function for this representation of lists (this is quite a bit harder and requires a trick analogous to the one used to define prd for numbers).   □

Enriching the Calculus

We have seen that booleans, numbers, and the operations on them can be encoded in the pure lambda-calculus. Indeed, strictly speaking, we can do all the programming we ever need to without going outside of the pure system. However, when working with examples it is often convenient to include the primitive booleans and numbers (and possibly other data types) as well. When we need to be clear about precisely which system we are working in, we will use the symbol λ for the pure lambda-calculus as defined in Figure 5-3 and λNB for the enriched system with booleans and arithmetic expressions from Figures 3-1 and 3-2.

In λNB, we actually have two different implementations of booleans and two of numbers to choose from when writing programs: the real ones and the encodings we've developed in this chapter. Of course, it is easy to convert back and forth between the two. To turn a Church boolean into a primitive boolean, we apply it to true and false:

```
realbool = λb. b true false;
```

To go the other direction, we use an if expression:

```
churchbool = λb. if b then tru else fls;
```

We can build these conversions into higher-level operations. Here is an equality function on Church numerals that returns a real boolean:

```
realeq = λm. λn. (equal m n) true false;
```

In the same way, we can convert a Church numeral into the corresponding primitive number by applying it to succ and 0:

```
realnat = λm. m (λx. succ x) 0;
```

We cannot apply m to succ directly, because succ by itself does not make syntactic sense: the way we defined the syntax of arithmetic expressions, succ must always be applied to something. We work around this by packaging succ inside a little function that does nothing but return the succ of its argument.

The reasons that primitive booleans and numbers come in handy for examples have to do primarily with evaluation order. For instance, consider the term scc c_1. From the discussion above, we might expect that this term should evaluate to the Church numeral c_2. In fact, it does not:

```
scc c₁;
```

▶ (λs. λz. s ((λs'. λz'. s' z') s z))

This term contains a redex that, if we were to reduce it, would bring us (in two steps) to c_2, but the rules of call-by-value evaluation do not allow us to reduce it yet, since it is under a lambda-abstraction.

There is no fundamental problem here: the term that results from evaluation of scc c_1 is obviously *behaviorally equivalent* to c_2, in the sense that applying it to any pair of arguments v and w will yield the same result as applying c_2 to v and w. Still, the leftover computation makes it a bit difficult to check that our scc function is behaving the way we expect it to. For more complicated arithmetic calculations, the difficulty is even worse. For example, times c_2 c_2 evaluates not to c_4 but to the following monstrosity:

```
times c₂ c₂;
```

▶ (λs.
    λz.
      (λs'. λz'. s' (s' z')) s
      ((λs'.
```
```

```
        λz'.
          (λs". λz". s" (s" z")) s'
          ((λs". λz".z") s' z'))
      s
      z))
```

One way to check that this term behaves like c_4 is to test them for equality:

```
    equal c₄ (times c₂ c₂);
```

▶ (λt. λf. t)

But it is more direct to take `times` c_2 c_2 and convert it to a primitive number:

```
    realnat (times c₂ c₂);
```

▶ 4

The conversion has the effect of supplying the two extra arguments that `times` c_2 c_2 is waiting for, forcing all of the latent computation in its body.

Recursion

Recall that a term that cannot take a step under the evaluation relation is called a *normal form*. Interestingly, some terms cannot be evaluated to a normal form. For example, the *divergent* combinator

```
    omega = (λx. x x) (λx. x x);
```

contains just one redex, and reducing this redex yields exactly `omega` again! Terms with no normal form are said to *diverge*.

The `omega` combinator has a useful generalization called the *fixed-point combinator*,[6] which can be used to help define recursive functions such as `factorial`.[7]

```
    fix = λf. (λx. f (λy. x x y)) (λx. f (λy. x x y));
```

Like `omega`, the `fix` combinator has an intricate, repetitive structure; it is difficult to understand just by reading its definition. Probably the best way of getting some intuition about its behavior is to watch how it works on a specific example.[8] Suppose we want to write a recursive function definition

---

6. It is often called the *call-by-value Y-combinator*. Plotkin (1975) called it Z.
7. Note that the simpler call-by-name fixed point combinator
    Y = λf. (λx. f (x x)) (λx. f (x x))
is useless in a call-by-value setting, since the expression Y g diverges, for any g.
8. It is also possible to derive the definition of `fix` from first principles (e.g., Friedman and Felleisen, 1996, Chapter 9), but such derivations are also fairly intricate.

of the form h = ⟨*body containing* h⟩—i.e., we want to write a definition where the term on the right-hand side of the = uses the very function that we are defining, as in the definition of `factorial` on page 52. The intention is that the recursive definition should be "unrolled" at the point where it occurs; for example, the definition of `factorial` would intuitively be

```
if n=0 then 1
else n * (if n-1=0 then 1
          else (n-1) * (if (n-2)=0 then 1
                        else (n-2) * ...))
```

or, in terms of Church numerals:

```
if realeq n c₀ then c₁
else times n (if realeq (prd n) c₀ then c₁
              else times (prd n)
                         (if realeq (prd (prd n)) c₀ then c₁
                          else times (prd (prd n)) ...))
```

This effect can be achieved using the `fix` combinator by first defining g = λf.⟨*body containing* f⟩ and then h = `fix` g. For example, we can define the factorial function by

```
g = λfct. λn. if realeq n c₀ then c₁ else (times n (fct (prd n)));
factorial = fix g;
```

Figure 5-2 shows what happens to the term `factorial` c_3 during evaluation. The key fact that makes this calculation work is that fct n —→* g fct n. That is, fct is a kind of "self-replicator" that, when applied to an argument, supplies *itself* and n as arguments to g. Wherever the first argument to g appears in the body of g, we will get another copy of fct, which, when applied to an argument, will again pass itself and that argument to g, etc. Each time we make a recursive call using fct, we unroll one more copy of the body of g and equip it with new copies of fct that are ready to do the unrolling again.

5.2.9   EXERCISE [⋆]: Why did we use a primitive `if` in the definition of g, instead of the Church-boolean `test` function on Church booleans? Show how to define the `factorial` function in terms of `test` rather than `if`.   □

5.2.10   EXERCISE [⋆⋆]: Define a function `churchnat` that converts a primitive natural number into the corresponding Church numeral.   □

5.2.11   EXERCISE [RECOMMENDED, ⋆⋆]: Use `fix` and the encoding of lists from Exercise 5.2.8 to write a function that sums lists of Church numerals.   □

```
        factorial c₃
  =     fix g c₃
  ⟶    h h c₃
        where h = λx. g (λy. x x y)
  ⟶    g fct c₃
        where fct = λy. h h y
  ⟶    (λn. if realeq n c₀
              then c₁
              else times n (fct (prd n)))
            c₃
  ⟶    if realeq c₃ c₀
          then c₁
          else times c₃ (fct (prd c₃))
  ⟶*   times c₃ (fct (prd c₃))
  ⟶*   times c₃ (fct c₂′)
        where c₂′ is behaviorally equivalent to c₂
  ⟶*   times c₃ (g fct c₂′)
  ⟶*   times c₃ (times c₂′ (g fct c₁′)).
        where c₁′ is behaviorally equivalent to c₁
        (by repeating the same calculation for g fct c₂′)
  ⟶*   times c₃ (times c₂′ (times c₁′ (g fct c₀′))).
        where c₀′ is behaviorally equivalent to c₀
        (similarly)
  ⟶*   times c₃ (times c₂′ (times c₁′ (if realeq c₀′ c₀ then c₁
                                         else ...)))
  ⟶*   times c₃ (times c₂′ (times c₁′ c₁))
  ⟶*   c₆′
        where c₆′ is behaviorally equivalent to c₆.
```

Figure 5-2: Evaluation of `factorial c₃`

Representation

Before leaving our examples behind and proceeding to the formal definition
of the lambda-calculus, we should pause for one final question: What, exactly,
does it mean to say that the Church numerals *represent* ordinary numbers?

To answer, we first need to remind ourselves of what the ordinary numbers
are. There are many (equivalent) ways to define them; the one we have chosen
here (in Figure 3-2) is to give:

- a constant 0,

- an operation iszero mapping numbers to booleans, and

- two operations, succ and pred, mapping numbers to numbers.

The behavior of the arithmetic operations is defined by the evaluation rules in Figure 3-2. These rules tell us, for example, that 3 is the successor of 2, and that iszero 0 is true.

The Church encoding of numbers represents each of these elements as a lambda-term (i.e., a function):

- The term c_0 represents the number 0.

  As we saw on page 64, there are also "non-canonical representations" of numbers as terms. For example, λs. λz. (λx. x) z, which is behaviorally equivalent to c_0, also represents 0.

- The terms scc and prd represent the arithmetic operations succ and pred, in the sense that, if t is a representation of the number n, then scc t evaluates to a representation of $n + 1$ and prd t evaluates to a representation of $n - 1$ (or of 0, if n is 0).

- The term iszro represents the operation iszero, in the sense that, if t is a representation of 0, then iszro t evaluates to true,[9] and if t represents any number other than 0, then iszro t evaluates to false.

Putting all this together, suppose we have a whole program that does some complicated calculation with numbers to yield a boolean result. If we replace all the numbers and arithmetic operations with lambda-terms representing them and evaluate the program, we will get the same result. Thus, in terms of their effects on the overall results of programs, there is no observable difference between the real numbers and their Church-numeral representation.

5.3   Formalities

For the rest of the chapter, we consider the syntax and operational semantics of the lambda-calculus in more detail. Most of the structure we need is closely analogous to what we saw in Chapter 3 (to avoid repeating that structure verbatim, we address here just the pure lambda-calculus, unadorned with booleans or numbers). However, the operation of substituting a term for a variable involves some surprising subtleties.

---

9. Strictly speaking, as we defined it, iszro t evaluates to a *representation of* true as another term, but let's elide that distinction to simplify the present discussion. An analogous story can be given to explain in what sense the Church booleans represent the real ones.

Syntax

As in Chapter 3, the abstract grammar defining terms (on page 53) should be read as shorthand for an inductively defined set of abstract syntax trees.

5.3.1 DEFINITION [TERMS]: Let $\mathcal{V}$ be a countable set of variable names. The set of terms is the smallest set $\mathcal{T}$ such that

1. $x \in \mathcal{T}$ for every $x \in \mathcal{V}$;

2. if $t_1 \in \mathcal{T}$ and $x \in \mathcal{V}$, then $\lambda x.t_1 \in \mathcal{T}$;

3. if $t_1 \in \mathcal{T}$ and $t_2 \in \mathcal{T}$, then $t_1\ t_2 \in \mathcal{T}$. □

The *size* of a term t can be defined exactly as we did for arithmetic expressions in Definition 3.3.2. More interestingly, we can give a simple inductive definition of the set of variables appearing free in a lambda-term.

5.3.2 DEFINITION: The set of *free variables* of a term t, written $FV(t)$, is defined as follows:

$$
\begin{aligned}
FV(x) &= \{x\} \\
FV(\lambda x.t_1) &= FV(t_1) \setminus \{x\} \\
FV(t_1\ t_2) &= FV(t_1) \cup FV(t_2)
\end{aligned}
$$

□

5.3.3 EXERCISE [★★]: Give a careful proof that $|FV(t)| \leq size(t)$ for every term t. □

Substitution

The operation of substitution turns out to be quite tricky, when examined in detail. In this book, we will actually use two different definitions, each optimized for a different purpose. The first, introduced in this section, is compact and intuitive, and works well for examples and in mathematical definitions and proofs. The second, developed in Chapter 6, is notationally heavier, depending on an alternative "de Bruijn presentation" of terms in which named variables are replaced by numeric indices, but is more convenient for the concrete ML implementations discussed in later chapters.

It is instructive to arrive at a definition of substitution via a couple of wrong attempts. First, let's try the most naive possible recursive definition. (Formally, we are defining a function $[x \mapsto s]$ by induction over its argument t.)

$$
\begin{aligned}
[x \mapsto s]x &= s \\
[x \mapsto s]y &= y && \text{if } x \neq y \\
[x \mapsto s](\lambda y.t_1) &= \lambda y.\ [x \mapsto s]t_1 \\
[x \mapsto s](t_1\ t_2) &= ([x \mapsto s]t_1)\ ([x \mapsto s]t_2)
\end{aligned}
$$

This definition works fine for most examples. For instance, it gives

$$[x \mapsto (\lambda z.\ z\ w)](\lambda y.x) = \lambda y.\lambda z.\ z\ w,$$

which matches our intuitions about how substitution should behave. However, if we are unlucky with our choice of bound variable names, the definition breaks down. For example:

$$[x \mapsto y](\lambda x.x) = \lambda x.y$$

This conflicts with the basic intuition about functional abstractions that *the names of bound variables do not matter*—the identity function is exactly the same whether we write it $\lambda x.x$ or $\lambda y.y$ or $\lambda franz.franz$. If these do not behave exactly the same under substitution, then they will not behave the same under reduction either, which seems wrong.

Clearly, the first mistake that we've made in the naive definition of substitution is that we have not distinguished between *free* occurrences of a variable x in a term t (which should get replaced during substitution) and *bound* ones, which should not. When we reach an abstraction binding the name x inside of t, the substitution operation should stop. This leads to the next attempt:

$$
\begin{aligned}
[x \mapsto s]x &= s \\
[x \mapsto s]y &= y &&\text{if } y \neq x \\
[x \mapsto s](\lambda y.t_1) &= \begin{cases} \lambda y.\ t_1 & \text{if } y = x \\ \lambda y.\ [x \mapsto s]t_1 & \text{if } y \neq x \end{cases} \\
[x \mapsto s](t_1\ t_2) &= ([x \mapsto s]t_1)\ ([x \mapsto s]t_2)
\end{aligned}
$$

This is better, but still not quite right. For example, consider what happens when we substitute the term z for the variable x in the term $\lambda z.x$:

$$[x \mapsto z](\lambda z.x) = \lambda z.z$$

This time, we have made essentially the opposite mistake: we've turned the constant function $\lambda z.x$ into the identity function! Again, this occurred only because we happened to choose z as the name of the bound variable in the constant function, so something is clearly still wrong.

This phenomenon of free variables in a term s becoming bound when s is naively substituted into a term t is called *variable capture*. To avoid it, we need to make sure that the bound variable names of t are kept distinct from the free variable names of s. A substitution operation that does this correctly is called *capture-avoiding substitution*. (This is almost always what is meant by the unqualified term "substitution.") We can achieve the desired effect by adding another side condition to the second clause of the abstraction case:

$$
\begin{array}{lll}
[x \mapsto s]x & = & s \\
[x \mapsto s]y & = & y \qquad\qquad\qquad\qquad\qquad \text{if } y \neq x \\
[x \mapsto s](\lambda y.t_1) & = & \begin{cases} \lambda y.\ t_1 & \text{if } y = x \\ \lambda y.\ [x \mapsto s]t_1 & \text{if } y \neq x \text{ and } y \notin FV(s) \end{cases} \\
[x \mapsto s](t_1\ t_2) & = & ([x \mapsto s]t_1)\ ([x \mapsto s]t_2)
\end{array}
$$

Now we are almost there: this definition of substitution does the right thing *when it does anything at all*. The problem now is that our last fix has changed substitution into a partial operation. For example, the new definition does not give any result at all for $[x \mapsto y\ z](\lambda y.\ x\ y)$: the bound variable y of the term being substituted into is not equal to x, but it does appear free in $(y\ z)$, so none of the clauses of the definition apply.

One common fix for this last problem in the type systems and lambda-calculus literature is to work with terms "up to renaming of bound variables." (Church used the term *alpha-conversion* for the operation of consistently renaming a bound variable in a term. This terminology is still common—we could just as well say that we are working with terms "up to alpha-conversion.")

5.3.4   CONVENTION: Terms that differ only in the names of bound variables are interchangeable in all contexts.   □

What this means in practice is that the name of any λ-bound variable can be changed to another name (consistently making the same change in the body of the λ), at any point where this is convenient. For example, if we want to calculate $[x \mapsto y\ z](\lambda y.\ x\ y)$, we first rewrite $(\lambda y.\ x\ y)$ as, say, $(\lambda w.\ x\ w)$. We then calculate $[x \mapsto y\ z](\lambda w.\ x\ w)$, giving $(\lambda w.\ y\ z\ w)$.

This convention renders the substitution operation "as good as total," since whenever we find ourselves about to apply it to arguments for which it is undefined, we can rename as necessary, so that the side conditions are satisfied. Indeed, having adopted this convention, we can formulate the definition of substitution a little more tersely. The first clause for abstractions can be dropped, since we can always assume (renaming if necessary) that the bound variable y is different from both x and the free variables of s. This yields the final form of the definition.

5.3.5   DEFINITION [SUBSTITUTION]:

$$
\begin{array}{lll}
[x \mapsto s]x & = & s \\
[x \mapsto s]y & = & y \qquad\qquad\qquad\quad\ \text{if } y \neq x \\
[x \mapsto s](\lambda y.t_1) & = & \lambda y.\ [x \mapsto s]t_1 \qquad \text{if } y \neq x \text{ and } y \notin FV(s) \\
[x \mapsto s](t_1\ t_2) & = & [x \mapsto s]t_1\ [x \mapsto s]t_2
\end{array}
$$

                                                                                       □

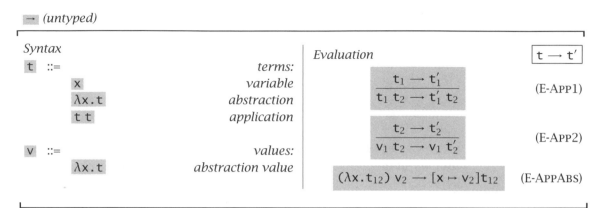

Figure 5-3: Untyped lambda-calculus (λ)

Operational Semantics

The operational semantics of lambda-terms is summarized in Figure 5-3. The set of values here is more interesting than we saw in the case of arithmetic expressions. Since (call-by-value) evaluation stops when it reaches a lambda, values can be arbitrary lambda-terms.

The evaluation relation appears in the right-hand column of the figure. As in evaluation for arithmetic expressions, there are two sorts of rules: the *computation* rule E-APPABS and the *congruence* rules E-APP1 and E-APP2.

Notice how the choice of metavariables in these rules helps control the order of evaluation. Since v_2 ranges only over values, the left-hand side of rule E-APPABS can match any application whose right-hand side is a value. Similarly, rule E-APP1 applies to any application whose left-hand side is *not* a value, since t_1 can match any term whatsoever, but the premise further requires that t_1 can take a step. E-APP2, on the other hand, cannot fire until the left-hand side *is* a value so that it can be bound to the value-metavariable v. Taken together, these rules completely determine the order of evaluation for an application $t_1 \, t_2$: we first use E-APP1 to reduce t_1 to a value, then use E-APP2 to reduce t_2 to a value, and finally use E-APPABS to perform the application itself.

5.3.6   EXERCISE [★★]: Adapt these rules to describe the other three strategies for evaluation—full beta-reduction, normal-order, and lazy evaluation.   □

Note that, in the pure lambda-calculus, lambda-abstractions are the only possible values, so if we reach a state where E-APP1 has succeeded in reducing t_1 to a value, then this value must be a lambda-abstraction. This observation fails, of course, when we add other constructs such as primitive booleans to the language, since these introduce forms of values other than abstractions.

5.3.7 EXERCISE [★★ ↦]: Exercise 3.5.16 gave an alternative presentation of the operational semantics of booleans and arithmetic expressions in which stuck terms are defined to evaluate to a special constant wrong. Extend this semantics to λNB. □

5.3.8 EXERCISE [★★]: Exercise 4.2.2 introduced a "big-step" style of evaluation for arithmetic expressions, where the basic evaluation relation is "term t evaluates to final result v." Show how to formulate the evaluation rules for lambda-terms in the big-step style. □

5.4 Notes

The untyped lambda-calculus was developed by Church and his co-workers in the 1920s and '30s (Church, 1941). The standard text for all aspects of the untyped lambda-calculus is Barendregt (1984); Hindley and Seldin (1986) is less comprehensive, but more accessible. Barendregt's article (1990) in the *Handbook of Theoretical Computer Science* is a compact survey. Material on lambda-calculus can also be found in many textbooks on functional programming languages (e.g. Abelson and Sussman, 1985; Friedman, Wand, and Haynes, 2001; Peyton Jones and Lester, 1992) and programming language semantics (e.g. Schmidt, 1986; Gunter, 1992; Winskel, 1993; Mitchell, 1996). A systematic method for encoding a wide variety of data structures as lambda-terms can be found in Böhm and Berarducci (1985).

Despite its name, Curry denied inventing the idea of currying. It is commonly credited to Schönfinkel (1924), but the underlying idea was familiar to a number of 19th-century mathematicians, including Frege and Cantor.

There may, indeed, be other applications of the system than its use as a logic.
—Alonzo Church, 1932

6 *Nameless Representation of Terms*

In the previous chapter, we worked with terms "up to renaming of bound variables," introducing a general convention that bound variables can be renamed, at any moment, to enable substitution or because a new name is more convenient for some other reason. In effect, the "spelling" of a bound variable name is whatever we want it to be. This convention works well for discussing basic concepts and for presenting proofs cleanly, but for building an implementation we need to choose a single representation for each term; in particular, we must decide how occurrences of variables are to be represented. There is more than one way to do this:

1. We can represent variables symbolically, as we have done so far, but replace the convention about implicit renaming of bound variables with an operation that explicitly replaces bound variables with "fresh" names during substitution as necessary to avoid capture.

2. We can represent variables symbolically, but introduce a general condition that the names of all bound variables must all be different from each other and from any free variables we may use. This convention (sometimes called the *Barendregt convention*) is more stringent than ours, since it does not allow renaming "on the fly" at arbitrary moments. However, it is not stable under substitution (or beta-reduction): since substitution involves copying the term being substituted, it is easy to construct examples where the result of substitution is a term in which some λ-abstractions have the same bound variable name. This implies that each evaluation step involving substitution must be followed by a step of renaming to restore the invariant.

3. We can devise some "canonical" representation of variables and terms that does not require renaming.

The system studied in this chapter is the pure untyped lambda-calculus, λ (Figure 5-3). The associated OCaml implementation is `fulluntyped`.

4. We can avoid substitution altogether by introducing mechanisms such as *explicit substitutions* (Abadi, Cardelli, Curien, and Lévy, 1991a).

5. We can avoid *variables* altogether by working in a language based directly on combinators, such as *combinatory logic* (Curry and Feys, 1958; Barendregt, 1984)—a variant of the lambda-calculus based on combinators instead of procedural abstraction—or Backus' functional language FP (1978).

Each scheme has its proponents, and choosing between them is somewhat a matter of taste (in serious compiler implementations, there are also performance considerations, but these do not concern us here). We choose the third, which, in our experience, scales better when we come to some of the more complex implementations later in the book. The main reason for this is that it tends to fail catastrophically rather than subtly when it is implemented wrong, allowing mistakes to be detected and corrected sooner rather than later. Bugs in implementations using named variables, by contrast, have been known to manifest months or years after they are introduced. Our formulation uses a well-known technique due to Nicolas de Bruijn (1972).

6.1   Terms and Contexts

De Bruijn's idea was that we can represent terms more straightforwardly—if less readably—by making variable occurrences *point directly to* their binders, rather than referring to them by name. This can be accomplished by replacing named variables by natural numbers, where the number k stands for "the variable bound by the k'th enclosing λ." For example, the ordinary term λx.x corresponds to the *nameless term* $\lambda.0$, while λx.λy. x (y x) corresponds to $\lambda.\lambda.\ 1\ (0\ 1)$. Nameless terms are also sometimes called *de Bruijn terms,* and the numeric variables in them are called *de Bruijn indices*.[1] Compiler writers use the term "static distances" for the same concept.

6.1.1   EXERCISE [⋆]: For each of the following combinators

```
c₀ = λs. λz. z;
c₂ = λs. λz. s (s z);
plus = λm. λn. λs. λz. m s (n z s);
fix = λf. (λx. f (λy. (x x) y)) (λx. f (λy. (x x) y));
foo = (λx. (λx. x)) (λx. x);
```

write down the corresponding nameless term.   ☐

---

1. Note on pronunciation: the nearest English approximation to the second syllable in "de Bruijn" is "brown," not "broyn."

Formally, we define the syntax of nameless terms almost exactly like the syntax of ordinary terms (5.3.1). The only difference is that we need to keep careful track of how many free variables each term may contain. That is, we distinguish the sets of terms with no free variables (called the 0-*terms*), terms with at most one free variable (1-*terms*), and so on.

6.1.2   DEFINITION [TERMS]: Let $\mathcal{T}$ be the smallest family of sets $\{\mathcal{T}_0, \mathcal{T}_1, \mathcal{T}_2, \ldots\}$ such that

1. $k \in \mathcal{T}_n$ whenever $0 \le k < n$;

2. if $t_1 \in \mathcal{T}_n$ and $n > 0$, then $\lambda.t_1 \in \mathcal{T}_{n-1}$;

3. if $t_1 \in \mathcal{T}_n$ and $t_2 \in \mathcal{T}_n$, then $(t_1\ t_2) \in \mathcal{T}_n$.

(Note that this is a standard inductive definition, except that what we are defining is a *family* of sets indexed by numbers, rather than a single set.) The elements of each $\mathcal{T}_n$ are called *n*-terms.   □

The elements of $\mathcal{T}_n$ are terms with *at most n* free variables, numbered between 0 and $n - 1$: a given element of $\mathcal{T}_n$ need not have free variables with all these numbers, or indeed any free variables at all. When t is closed, for example, it will be an element of $\mathcal{T}_n$ for every *n*.

Note that each (closed) ordinary term has just one de Bruijn representation, and that two ordinary terms are equivalent modulo renaming of bound variables iff they have the same de Bruijn representation.

To deal with terms containing free variables, we need the idea of a *naming context*. For example, suppose we want to represent λx. y x as a nameless term. We know what to do with x, but we cannot see the binder for y, so it is not clear how "far away" it might be and we do not know what number to assign to it. The solution is to choose, once and for all, an assignment (called a naming context) of de Bruijn indices to free variables, and use this assignment consistently when we need to choose numbers for free variables. For example, suppose that we choose to work under the following naming context:

$$\Gamma \quad = \quad \begin{array}{l} x \mapsto 4 \\ y \mapsto 3 \\ z \mapsto 2 \\ a \mapsto 1 \\ b \mapsto 0 \end{array}$$

Then x (y z) would be represented as 4 (3 2), while λw. y w would be represented as λ. 4 0 and λw.λa.x as λ.λ.6.

Since the order in which the variables appear in Γ determines their numerical indices, we can write it compactly as a sequence.

6.1.3   DEFINITION: Suppose x_0 through x_n are variable names from $\mathcal{V}$. The naming context $\Gamma = x_n, x_{n-1}, \ldots x_1, x_0$ assigns to each x_i the de Bruijn index i. Note that the rightmost variable in the sequence is given the index 0; this matches the way we count λ binders—from right to left—when converting a named term to nameless form. We write $dom(\Gamma)$ for the set $\{x_n, \ldots, x_0\}$ of variable names mentioned in Γ.   □

6.1.4   EXERCISE [★★★ ↠]: Give an alternative construction of the sets of n-terms in the style of Definition 3.2.3, and show (as we did in Proposition 3.2.6) that it is equivalent to the one above.   □

6.1.5   EXERCISE [RECOMMENDED, ★★★]:

1. Define a function $removenames_\Gamma(t)$ that takes a naming context Γ and an ordinary term t (with $FV(t) \subseteq dom(\Gamma)$) and yields the corresponding nameless term.

2. Define a function $restorenames_\Gamma(t)$ that takes a nameless term t and a naming context Γ and produces an ordinary term. (To do this, you will need to "make up" names for the variables bound by abstractions in t. You may assume that the names in Γ are pairwise distinct and that the set $\mathcal{V}$ of variable names is ordered, so that it makes sense to say "choose the first variable name that is not already in $dom(\Gamma)$.")

   This pair of functions should have the property that

   $$removenames_\Gamma(restorenames_\Gamma(t)) = t$$

   for any nameless term t, and similarly

   $$restorenames_\Gamma(removenames_\Gamma(t)) = t,$$

   up to renaming of bound variables, for any ordinary term t.   □

Strictly speaking, it does not make sense to speak of "some $t \in \mathcal{T}$"—we always need to specify how many free variables t might have. In practice, though, we will usually have some fixed naming context Γ in mind; we will then abuse the notation slightly and write $t \in \mathcal{T}$ to mean $t \in \mathcal{T}_n$, where n is the length of Γ.

6.2   Shifting and Substitution

Our next job is defining a substitution operation ($[k \mapsto s]t$) on nameless terms. To to this, we need one auxiliary operation, called "shifting," which renumbers the indices of the free variables in a term.

When a substitution goes under a λ-abstraction, as in $[1 \mapsto \mathsf{s}](\lambda.2)$ (i.e., $[\mathsf{x} \mapsto \mathsf{s}](\lambda\mathsf{y}.\mathsf{x})$, assuming that 1 is the index of x in the outer context), the context in which the substitution is taking place becomes one variable longer than the original; we need to increment the indices of the free variables in s so that they keep referring to the same names in the new context as they did before. But we need to do this carefully: we can't just shift every variable index in s up by one, because this could also shift *bound* variables within s. For example, if $\mathsf{s} = 2\ (\lambda.0)$ (i.e., $\mathsf{s} = \mathsf{z}\ (\lambda\mathsf{w}.\mathsf{w})$, assuming 2 is the index of z in the outer context), we need to shift the 2 but not the 0. The shifting function below takes a "cutoff" parameter c that controls which variables should be shifted. It starts off at 0 (meaning all variables should be shifted) and gets incremented by one every time the shifting function goes through a binder. So, when calculating $\uparrow_c^d(\mathsf{t})$, we know that the term t comes from inside c-many binders in the original argument to $\uparrow^d$. Therefore all identifiers $k < c$ in t are bound in the original argument and should not be shifted, while identifiers $k \geq c$ in t are free and should be shifted.

6.2.1   DEFINITION [SHIFTING]: The d-place shift of a term t above cutoff c, written $\uparrow_c^d(\mathsf{t})$, is defined as follows:

$$
\begin{aligned}
\uparrow_c^d(\mathsf{k}) &= \begin{cases} \mathsf{k} & \text{if } k < c \\ \mathsf{k} + d & \text{if } k \geq c \end{cases} \\
\uparrow_c^d(\lambda.\mathsf{t_1}) &= \lambda.\ \uparrow_{c+1}^d(\mathsf{t_1}) \\
\uparrow_c^d(\mathsf{t_1}\ \mathsf{t_2}) &= \uparrow_c^d(\mathsf{t_1})\ \uparrow_c^d(\mathsf{t_2})
\end{aligned}
$$

We write $\uparrow^d(\mathsf{t})$ for $\uparrow_0^d(\mathsf{t})$.   □

6.2.2   EXERCISE [⋆]:

1. What is $\uparrow^2(\lambda.\lambda.\ 1\ (0\ 2))$?

2. What is $\uparrow^2(\lambda.\ 0\ 1\ (\lambda.\ 0\ 1\ 2))$?   □

6.2.3   EXERCISE [⋆⋆ ↛]: Show that if t is an n-term, then $\uparrow_c^d(\mathsf{t})$ is an $(n+d)$-term. □

Now we are ready to define the substitution operator $[\mathsf{j} \mapsto \mathsf{s}]\mathsf{t}$. When we use substitution, we will usually be interested in substituting for the *last* variable in the context (i.e., $\mathsf{j} = 0$), since that is the case we need in order to define the operation of beta-reduction. However, to substitute for variable 0 in a term that happens to be a λ-abstraction, we need to be able to substitute for the variable number numbered 1 in its body. Thus, the definition of substitution must work on an arbitrary variable.

6.2.4   DEFINITION [SUBSTITUTION]: The substitution of a term s for variable number j in a term t, written $[j \mapsto s]t$, is defined as follows:

$$
\begin{array}{lcl}
[j \mapsto s]k & = & \begin{cases} s & \text{if } k = j \\ k & \text{otherwise} \end{cases} \\
[j \mapsto s](\lambda.t_1) & = & \lambda.\ [j{+}1 \mapsto \uparrow^1(s)]t_1 \\
[j \mapsto s](t_1\ t_2) & = & ([j \mapsto s]t_1\ [j \mapsto s]t_2)
\end{array}
$$
□

6.2.5   EXERCISE [⋆]: Convert the following uses of substitution to nameless form, assuming the global context is Γ = a,b, and calculate their results using the above definition. Do the answers correspond to the original definition of substitution on ordinary terms from §5.3?

   1. $[b \mapsto a]\ (b\ (\lambda x.\lambda y.b))$

   2. $[b \mapsto a\ (\lambda z.a)]\ (b\ (\lambda x.b))$

   3. $[b \mapsto a]\ (\lambda b.\ b\ a)$

   4. $[b \mapsto a]\ (\lambda a.\ b\ a)$
□

6.2.6   EXERCISE [⋆⋆ ↛]: Show that if s and t are *n*-terms and $j \le n$, then $[j \mapsto s]t$ is an *n*-term.
□

6.2.7   EXERCISE [⋆ ↛]: Take a sheet of paper and, without looking at the definitions of substitution and shifting above, regenerate them.
□

6.2.8   EXERCISE [RECOMMENDED, ⋆⋆⋆]: The definition of substitution on nameless terms should agree with our informal definition of substitution on ordinary terms. (1) What theorem needs to be proved to justify this correspondence rigorously? (2) Prove it.
□

6.3   Evaluation

To define the evaluation relation on nameless terms, the only thing we need to change (because it is the only place where variable names are mentioned) is the beta-reduction rule, which must now use our new nameless substitution operation.

   The only slightly subtle point is that reducing a redex "uses up" the bound variable: when we reduce $((\lambda x.t_{12})\ v_2)$ to $[x \mapsto v_2]t_{12}$, the bound variable x disappears in the process. Thus, we will need to renumber the variables of the result of substitution to take into account the fact that x is no longer part of the context. For example:

$$(\lambda.1\ 0\ 2)\ (\lambda.0) \longrightarrow 0\ (\lambda.0)\ 1 \qquad (\text{not } 1\ (\lambda.0)\ 2).$$

Similarly, we need to shift the variables in v_2 up by one before substituting into t_{12}, since t_{12} is defined in a larger context than v_2. Taking these points into account, the beta-reduction rule looks like this:

$$(\lambda.t_{12})\ v_2 \;\;\longrightarrow\;\; \uparrow^{-1}([0 \mapsto \uparrow^1(v_2)]t_{12}) \qquad\qquad (\text{E-AppAbs})$$

The other rules are identical to what we had before (Figure 5-3).

6.3.1   EXERCISE [⋆]: Should we be worried that the negative shift in this rule might create ill-formed terms containing negative indices?   □

6.3.2   EXERCISE [⋆⋆⋆]: De Bruijn's original article actually contained two different proposals for nameless representations of terms: the deBruijn *indices* presented here, which number lambda-binders "from the inside out," and *de Bruijn levels,* which number binders "from the outside in." For example, the term $\lambda x.\ (\lambda y.\ x\ y)\ x$ is represented using deBruijn indices as $\lambda.\ (\lambda.\ 1\ 0)\ 0$ and using deBruijn levels as $\lambda.\ (\lambda.\ 0\ 1)\ 0$. Define this variant precisely and show that the representations of a term using indices and levels are isomorphic (i.e., each can be recovered uniquely from the other).   □

7 An ML Implementation of the Lambda-Calculus

In this chapter we construct an interpreter for the untyped lambda-calculus, based on the interpreter for arithmetic expressions in Chapter 4 and on the treatment of variable binding and substitution in Chapter 6.

An executable evaluator for untyped lambda-terms can be obtained by a straightforward translation of the foregoing definitions into OCaml. As in Chapter 4, we show just the core algorithms, ignoring issues of lexical analysis, parsing, printing, and so forth.

7.1 Terms and Contexts

We can obtain a datatype representing abstract syntax trees for terms by directly transliterating Definition 6.1.2:

```
type term =
    TmVar of int
  | TmAbs of term
  | TmApp of term * term
```

The representation of a variable is a number—its de Bruijn index. The representation of an abstraction carries just a subterm for the abstraction's body. An application carries the two subterms being applied.

The definition actually used in our implementation, however, will carry a little bit more information. First, as before, it is useful to annotate every term with an element of the type `info` recording the file position where that term was originally found, so that error printing routines can direct the user (or even the user's text editor, automatically) to the precise point where the error occurred.

The system studied in most of this chapter is the pure untyped lambda-calculus (Figure 5-3). The associated implementation is `untyped`. The `fulluntyped` implementation includes extensions such as numbers and booleans.

```
type term =
    TmVar of info * int
  | TmAbs of info * term
  | TmApp of info * term * term
```

Second, for purposes of debugging, it is helpful to carry an extra number on each variable node, as a consistency check. The convention will be that this second number will always contain the *total length* of the context in which the variable occurs.

```
type term =
    TmVar of info * int * int
  | TmAbs of info * term
  | TmApp of info * term * term
```

Whenever a variable is printed, we will verify that this number corresponds to the actual size of the current context; if it does not, then a shift operation has been forgotten someplace.

One last refinement also concerns printing. Although terms are represented internally using de Bruijn indices, this is obviously not how they should be presented to the user: we should convert from the ordinary representation to nameless terms during parsing, and convert back to ordinary form during printing. There is nothing very hard about this, but we should not do it completely naively (for example, generating completely fresh symbols for the names of variables), since then the names of the bound variables in the terms that are printed would have nothing to do with the names in the original program. This can be fixed by annotating each abstraction with a string to be used as a hint for the name of the bound variable.

```
type term =
    TmVar of info * int * int
  | TmAbs of info * string * term
  | TmApp of info * term * term
```

The basic operations on terms (substitution in particular) do not do anything fancy with these strings: they are simply carried along in their original form, with no checks for name clashes, capture, etc. When the printing routine needs to generate a fresh name for a bound variable, it tries first to use the supplied hint; if this turns out to clash with a name already used in the current context, it tries similar names, adding primes until it finds one that is not currently being used. This ensures that the printed term will be similar to what the user expects, modulo a few primes.

The printing routine itself looks like this:

```
let rec printtm ctx t = match t with
    TmAbs(fi,x,t1) →
      let (ctx',x') = pickfreshname ctx x in
      pr "(lambda "; pr x'; pr ". "; printtm ctx' t1; pr ")"
  | TmApp(fi, t1, t2) →
      pr "("; printtm ctx t1; pr " "; printtm ctx t2; pr ")"
  | TmVar(fi,x,n) →
      if ctxlength ctx = n then
        pr (index2name fi ctx x)
      else
        pr "[bad index]"
```

It uses the datatype `context`,

```
type context = (string * binding) list
```

which is just a list of strings and associated `binding`s. For the moment, the bindings themselves are completely trivial

```
type binding = NameBind
```

carrying no interesting information. Later on (in Chapter 10), we'll introduce other clauses of the `binding` type that will keep track of the type assumptions associated with variables and other similar information.

The printing function also relies on several lower-level functions: `pr` sends a string to the standard output stream; `ctxlength` returns the length of a context; `index2name` looks up the string name of a variable from its index. The most interesting one is `pickfreshname`, which takes a context `ctx` and a string hint `x`, finds a name `x'` similar to `x` such that `x'` is not already listed in `ctx`, adds `x'` to `ctx` to form a new context `ctx'`, and returns both `ctx'` and `x'` as a pair.

The actual printing function found in the `untyped` implementation on the book's web site is somewhat more complicated than this one, taking into account two additional issues. First, it leaves out as many parentheses as possible, following the conventions that application associates to the left and the bodies of abstractions extend as far to the right as possible. Second, it generates formatting instructions for a low-level *pretty printing* module (the OCaml `Format` library) that makes decisions about line breaking and indentation.

7.2 Shifting and Substitution

The definition of shifting (6.2.1) can be translated almost symbol for symbol into OCaml.

```
let termShift d t =
  let rec walk c t = match t with
    TmVar(fi,x,n) → if x>=c then TmVar(fi,x+d,n+d)
                    else TmVar(fi,x,n+d)
  | TmAbs(fi,x,t1) → TmAbs(fi, x, walk (c+1) t1)
  | TmApp(fi,t1,t2) → TmApp(fi, walk c t1, walk c t2)
  in walk 0 t
```

The internal shifting $\uparrow^d_c$(t) is here represented by a call to the inner function walk c t. Since d never changes, there is no need to pass it along to each call to walk: we just use the outer binding of d when we need it in the variable case of walk. The top-level shift $\uparrow^d$(t) is represented by termShift d t. (Note that termShift itself is not marked recursive, since all it does is call walk once.)

Similarly, the substitution function comes almost directly from Definition 6.2.4:

```
let termSubst j s t =
  let rec walk c t = match t with
    TmVar(fi,x,n) → if x=j+c then termShift c s else TmVar(fi,x,n)
  | TmAbs(fi,x,t1) → TmAbs(fi, x, walk (c+1) t1)
  | TmApp(fi,t1,t2) → TmApp(fi, walk c t1, walk c t2)
  in walk 0 t
```

The substitution [j ↦ s]t of term s for the variable numbered j in term t is written as termSubst j s t here. The only difference from the original definition of substitution is that here we do all the shifting of s at once, in the TmVar case, rather than shifting s up by one every time we go through a binder. This means that the argument j is the same in every call to walk, and we can omit it from the inner definition.

The reader may note that the definitions of termShift and termSubst are very similar, differing only in the action that is taken when a variable is reached. The untyped implementation available from the book's web site exploits this observation to express both shifting and substitution operations as special cases of a more general function called tmmap. Given a term t and a function onvar, the result of tmmap onvar t is a term of the same shape as t in which every variable has been replaced by the result of calling onvar on that variable. This notational trick saves quite a bit of tedious repetition in some of the larger calculi; §25.2 explains it in more detail.

In the operational semantics of the lambda-calculus, the only place where substitution is used is in the beta-reduction rule. As we noted before, this rule actually performs several operations: the term being substituted for the bound variable is first shifted up by one, then the substitution is made, and then the whole result is shifted down by one to account for the fact that the bound variable has been used up. The following definition encapsulates this sequence of steps:

```
let termSubstTop s t =
  termShift (-1) (termSubst 0 (termShift 1 s) t)
```

7.3 Evaluation

As in Chapter 3, the evaluation function depends on an auxiliary predicate isval:

```
let rec isval ctx t = match t with
    TmAbs(_,_,_) → true
  | _ → false
```

The single-step evaluation function is a direct transcription of the evaluation rules, except that we pass a context ctx along with the term. This argument is not used in the present eval1 function, but it is needed by some of the more complex evaluators later on.

```
let rec eval1 ctx t = match t with
    TmApp(fi,TmAbs(_,x,t12),v2) when isval ctx v2 →
      termSubstTop v2 t12
  | TmApp(fi,v1,t2) when isval ctx v1 →
      let t2' = eval1 ctx t2 in
      TmApp(fi, v1, t2')
  | TmApp(fi,t1,t2) →
      let t1' = eval1 ctx t1 in
      TmApp(fi, t1', t2)
  | _ →
      raise NoRuleApplies
```

The multi-step evaluation function is the same as before, except for the ctx argument:

```
let rec eval ctx t =
  try let t' = eval1 ctx t
      in eval ctx t'
  with NoRuleApplies → t
```

7.3.1 EXERCISE [RECOMMENDED, ★★★ ↩]: Change this implementation to use the "big-step" style of evaluation introduced in Exercise 5.3.8.   □

7.4   Notes

The treatment of substitution presented in this chapter, though sufficient for our purposes in this book, is far from the final word on the subject. In particular, the beta-reduction rule in our evaluator "eagerly" substitutes the argument value for the bound variable in the function's body. Interpreters (and compilers) for functional languages that are tuned for speed instead of simplicity use a different strategy: instead of actually performing the substitution, we simply record an association between the bound variable name and the argument value in an auxiliary data structure called the *environment,* which is carried along with the term being evaluated. When we reach a variable, we look up its value in the current environment. This strategy can be modeled by regarding the environment as a kind of *explicit substitution*—i.e., by moving the mechanism of substitution from the meta-language into the object language, making it a part of the *syntax* of the terms manipulated by the evaluator, rather than an external operation on terms. Explicit substitutions were first studied by Abadi, Cardelli, Curien, and Lévy (1991a) and have since become an active research area.

Just because you've implemented something doesn't mean you understand it.
—Brian Cantwell Smith

PART II

Simple Types

8 *Typed Arithmetic Expressions*

In Chapter 3, we used a simple language of boolean and arithmetic expressions to introduce basic tools for the precise description of syntax and evaluation. We now return to this simple language and augment it with static types. Again, the type system itself is nearly trivial, but it provides a setting in which to introduce concepts that will recur throughout the book.

8.1 Types

Recall the syntax for arithmetic expressions:

t ::=		terms:
	true	constant true
	false	constant false
	if t then t else t	conditional
	0	constant zero
	succ t	successor
	pred t	predecessor
	iszero t	zero test

We saw in Chapter 3 that evaluating a term can either result in a value...

v ::=		values:
	true	true value
	false	false value
	nv	numeric value

nv ::=		numeric values:
	0	zero value
	succ nv	successor value

The system studied in this chapter is the typed calculus of booleans and numbers (Figure 8-2). The corresponding OCaml implementation is tyarith.

or else get *stuck* at some stage, by reaching a term like `pred false`, for which no evaluation rule applies.

Stuck terms correspond to meaningless or erroneous programs. We would therefore like to be able to tell, without actually evaluating a term, that its evaluation will definitely *not* get stuck. To do this, we need to be able to distinguish between terms whose result will be a numeric value (since these are the only ones that should appear as arguments to `pred`, `succ`, and `iszero`) and terms whose result will be a boolean (since only these should appear as the guard of a conditional). We introduce two *types,* `Nat` and `Bool`, for classifying terms in this way. The metavariables S, T, U, etc. will be used throughout the book to range over types.

Saying that "a term t has type T" (or "t belongs to T," or "t is an element of T") means that t "obviously" evaluates to a value of the appropriate form— where by "obviously" we mean that we can see this *statically,* without doing any evaluation of t. For example, the term `if true then false else true` has type `Bool`, while `pred (succ (pred (succ 0)))` has type `Nat`. However, our analysis of the types of terms will be *conservative,* making use only of static information. This means that we will not be able to conclude that terms like `if (iszero 0) then 0 else false` or even `if true then 0 else false` have any type at all, even though their evaluation does not, in fact, get stuck.

8.2   The Typing Relation

The typing relation for arithmetic expressions, written[1] "t : T", is defined by a set of inference rules assigning types to terms, summarized in Figures 8-1 and 8-2. As in Chapter 3, we give the rules for booleans and those for numbers in two different figures, since later on we will sometimes want to refer to them separately.

The rules T-True and T-False in Figure 8-1 assign the type `Bool` to the boolean constants `true` and `false`. Rule T-If assigns a type to a conditional expression based on the types of its subexpressions: the guard t_1 must evaluate to a boolean, while t_2 and t_3 must both evaluate to values of the *same* type. The two uses of the single metavariable T express the constraint that the result of the `if` is the type of the `then`- and `else`- branches, and that this may be any type (either `Nat` or `Bool` or, when we get to calculi with more interesting sets of types, any other type).

The rules for numbers in Figure 8-2 have a similar form. T-IsZero gives the type `Nat` to the constant 0. T-Succ gives a term of the form `succ` t_1 the type `Nat`, as long as t_1 has type `Nat`. Likewise, T-Pred and T-IsZero say that `pred`

---

1. The symbol ∈ is often used instead of :.

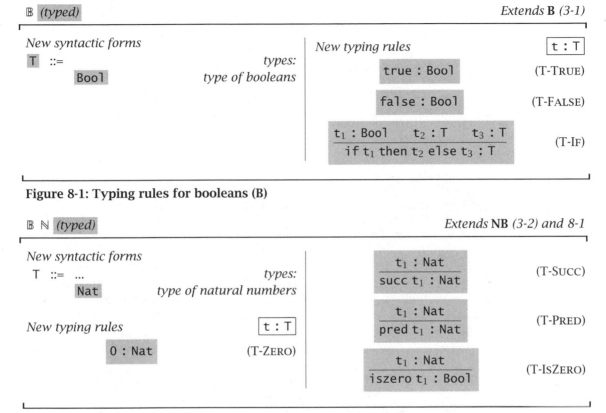

Figure 8-1: Typing rules for booleans (B)

Figure 8-2: Typing rules for numbers (NB)

yields a Nat when its argument has type Nat and iszero yields a Bool when its argument has type Nat.

8.2.1   DEFINITION: Formally, the *typing relation* for arithmetic expressions is the smallest binary relation between terms and types satisfying all instances of the rules in Figures 8-1 and 8-2. A term t is *typable* (or *well typed*) if there is some T such that t : T.   □

   When reasoning about the typing relation, we will often make statements like "If a term of the form succ t_1 has any type at all, then it has type Nat." The following lemma gives us a compendium of basic statements of this form, each following immediately from the shape of the corresponding typing rule.

8.2.2   LEMMA [INVERSION OF THE TYPING RELATION]:

1. If `true` : R, then R = Bool.

2. If `false` : R, then R = Bool.

3. If `if` t_1 `then` t_2 `else` t_3 : R, then t_1 : Bool, t_2 : R, and t_3 : R.

4. If `0` : R, then R = Nat.

5. If `succ` t_1 : R, then R = Nat and t_1 : Nat.

6. If `pred` t_1 : R, then R = Nat and t_1 : Nat.

7. If `iszero` t_1 : R, then R = Bool and t_1 : Nat.   □

Proof: Immediate from the definition of the typing relation.   □

The inversion lemma is sometimes called the *generation lemma* for the typing relation, since, given a valid typing statement, it shows how a proof of this statement could have been generated. The inversion lemma leads directly to a recursive algorithm for calculating the types of terms, since it tells us, for a term of each syntactic form, how to calculate its type (if it has one) from the types of its subterms. We will return to this point in detail in Chapter 9.

8.2.3   EXERCISE [★ ↠]: Prove that every subterm of a well-typed term is well typed. □

In §3.5 we introduced the concept of evaluation derivations. Similarly, a *typing derivation* is a tree of instances of the typing rules. Each pair (t, T) in the typing relation is justified by a typing derivation with conclusion t : T. For example, here is the derivation tree for the typing statement "`if iszero 0 then 0 else pred 0 : Nat`":

$$
\cfrac{
\cfrac{\cfrac{}{\texttt{0 : Nat}}\text{ T-ZERO}}{\texttt{iszero 0 : Bool}}\text{ T-ISZERO}
\quad
\cfrac{}{\texttt{0 : Nat}}\text{ T-ZERO}
\quad
\cfrac{\cfrac{}{\texttt{0 : Nat}}\text{ T-ZERO}}{\texttt{pred 0 : Nat}}\text{ T-PRED}
}{\texttt{if iszero 0 then 0 else pred 0 : Nat}}\text{ T-IF}
$$

In other words, *statements* are formal assertions about the typing of programs, *typing rules* are implications between statements, and *derivations* are deductions based on typing rules.

8.2.4   THEOREM [UNIQUENESS OF TYPES]: Each term t has at most one type. That is, if t is typable, then its type is unique. Moreover, there is just one derivation of this typing built from the inference rules in Figures 8-1 and 8-2.   □

Proof: Straightforward structural induction on t, using the appropriate clause of the inversion lemma (plus the induction hypothesis) for each case.   □

In the simple type system we are dealing with in this chapter, every term has a single type (if it has any type at all), and there is always just one derivation tree witnessing this fact. Later on—e.g., when we get to type systems with subtyping in Chapter 15—both of these properties will be relaxed: a single term may have many types, and there may in general be many ways of deriving the statement that a given term has a given type.

Properties of the typing relation will often be proved by induction on derivation trees, just as properties of the evaluation relation are typically proved by induction on evaluation derivations. We will see many examples of induction on typing derivations, beginning in the next section.

8.3   Safety = Progress + Preservation

The most basic property of this type system or any other is *safety* (also called *soundness*): well-typed terms do not "go wrong." We have already chosen how to formalize what it means for a term to go wrong: it means reaching a "stuck state" (Definition 3.5.15) that is not designated as a final value but where the evaluation rules do not tell us what to do next. What we want to know, then, is that well-typed terms do not get stuck. We show this in two steps, commonly known as the *progress* and *preservation* theorems.[2]

Progress: A well-typed term is not stuck (either it is a value or it can take a step according to the evaluation rules).

Preservation: If a well-typed term takes a step of evaluation, then the resulting term is also well typed.[3]

These properties together tell us that a well-typed term can never reach a stuck state during evaluation.

For the proof of the progress theorem, it is convenient to record a couple of facts about the possible shapes of the *canonical forms* of types Bool and Nat (i.e., the well-typed values of these types).

---

2. The slogan "safety is progress plus preservation" (using a canonical forms lemma) was articulated by Harper; a variant was proposed by Wright and Felleisen (1994).

3. In most of the type systems we will consider, evaluation preserves not only well-typedness but the exact types of terms. In some systems, however, types can change during evaluation. For example, in systems with subtyping (Chapter 15), types can become smaller (more informative) during evaluation.

8.3.1   LEMMA [CANONICAL FORMS]: 1. If v is a value of type Bool, then v is either
        true or false.

2. If v is a value of type Nat, then v is a numeric value according to the
grammar in Figure 3-2.   □

Proof: For part (1), according to the grammar in Figures 3-1 and 3-2, values
in this language can have four forms: true, false, 0, and succ nv, where nv
is a numeric value. The first two cases give us the desired result immediately.
The last two cannot occur, since we assumed that v has type Bool and cases 4
and 5 of the inversion lemma tell us that 0 and succ nv can have only type
Nat, not Bool. Part (2) is similar.   □

8.3.2   THEOREM [PROGRESS]: Suppose t is a well-typed term (that is, t : T for some
        T). Then either t is a value or else there is some t′ with t ⟶ t′.   □

Proof: By induction on a derivation of t : T. The T-TRUE, T-FALSE, and
T-ISZERO cases are immediate, since t in these cases is a value. For the other
cases, we argue as follows.

Case T-IF: t = if t_1 then t_2 else t_3
                 t_1 : Bool t_2 : T t_3 : T

By the induction hypothesis, either t_1 is a value or else there is some t_1' such
that $t_1 \longrightarrow t_1'$. If t_1 is a value, then the canonical forms lemma (8.3.1) assures
us that it must be either true or false, in which case either E-IFTRUE or
E-IFFALSE applies to t. On the other hand, if $t_1 \longrightarrow t_1'$, then, by E-IF, t ⟶
if t_1' then t_2 else t_3.

Case T-SUCC: t = succ t_1 t_1 : Nat

By the induction hypothesis, either t_1 is a value or else there is some t_1' such
that $t_1 \longrightarrow t_1'$. If t_1 is a value, then, by the canonical forms lemma, it must be
a numeric value, in which case so is t. On the other hand, if $t_1 \longrightarrow t_1'$, then,
by E-SUCC, succ $t_1 \longrightarrow$ succ t_1'.

Case T-PRED: t = pred t_1 t_1 : Nat

By the induction hypothesis, either t_1 is a value or else there is some t_1' such
that $t_1 \longrightarrow t_1'$. If t_1 is a value, then, by the canonical forms lemma, it must be
a numeric value, i.e., either 0 or succ nv_1 for some nv_1, and one of the rules
E-PREDZERO or E-PREDSUCC applies to t. On the other hand, if $t_1 \longrightarrow t_1'$, then,
by E-PRED, pred $t_1 \longrightarrow$ pred t_1'.

Case T-ISZERO: t = iszero t_1 t_1 : Nat
Similar.   □

The proof that types are preserved by evaluation is also quite straightforward for this system.

8.3.3 THEOREM [PRESERVATION]: If $t : T$ and $t \longrightarrow t'$, then $t' : T$. □

Proof: By induction on a derivation of $t : T$. At each step of the induction, we assume that the desired property holds for all subderivations (i.e., that if $s : S$ and $s \longrightarrow s'$, then $s' : S$, whenever $s : S$ is proved by a subderivation of the present one) and proceed by case analysis on the final rule in the derivation. (We show only a subset of the cases; the others are similar.)

Case T-TRUE: $t = \text{true}$ $T = \text{Bool}$

If the last rule in the derivation is T-TRUE, then we know from the form of this rule that t must be the constant `true` and T must be `Bool`. But then t is a value, so it cannot be the case that $t \longrightarrow t'$ for any t', and the requirements of the theorem are vacuously satisfied.

Case T-IF: $t = \text{if } t_1 \text{ then } t_2 \text{ else } t_3$ $t_1 : \text{Bool}$ $t_2 : T$ $t_3 : T$

If the last rule in the derivation is T-IF, then we know from the form of this rule that t must have the form $\text{if } t_1 \text{ then } t_2 \text{ else } t_3$, for some t_1, t_2, and t_3. We must also have subderivations with conclusions $t_1 : \text{Bool}$, $t_2 : T$, and $t_3 : T$. Now, looking at the evaluation rules with `if` on the left-hand side (Figure 3-1), we find that there are three rules by which $t \longrightarrow t'$ can be derived: E-IFTRUE, E-IFFALSE, and E-IF. We consider each case separately (omitting the E-IFFALSE case, which is similar to E-IFTRUE).

Subcase E-IFTRUE: $t_1 = \text{true}$ $t' = t_2$

If $t \longrightarrow t'$ is derived using E-IFTRUE, then from the form of this rule we see that t_1 must be `true` and the resulting term t' is the second subexpression t_2. This means we are finished, since we know (by the assumptions of the T-IF case) that $t_2 : T$, which is what we need.

Subcase E-IF: $t_1 \longrightarrow t_1'$ $t' = \text{if } t_1' \text{ then } t_2 \text{ else } t_3$

From the assumptions of the T-IF case, we have a subderivation of the original typing derivation whose conclusion is $t_1 : \text{Bool}$. We can apply the induction hypothesis to this subderivation, obtaining $t_1' : \text{Bool}$. Combining this with the facts (from the assumptions of the T-IF case) that $t_2 : T$ and $t_3 : T$, we can apply rule T-IF to conclude that $\text{if } t_1' \text{ then } t_2 \text{ else } t_3 : T$, that is $t' : T$.

Case T-ZERO: $t = 0$ $T = \text{Nat}$

Can't happen (for the same reasons as T-TRUE above).

Case T-SUCC: $t = \text{succ } t_1$ $T = \text{Nat}$ $t_1 : \text{Nat}$

By inspecting the evaluation rules in Figure 3-2, we see that there is just one rule, E-SUCC, that can be used to derive $t \longrightarrow t'$. The form of this rule tells us that $t_1 \longrightarrow t_1'$. Since we also know t_1 : Nat, we can apply the induction hypothesis to obtain t_1' : Nat, from which we obtain succ t_1' : Nat, i.e., t' : T, by applying rule T-Succ.   □

8.3.4   EXERCISE [★★ ↦]: Restructure this proof so that it goes by induction on evaluation derivations rather than typing derivations.   □

The preservation theorem is often called *subject reduction* (or *subject evaluation*)—the intuition being that a typing statement t : T can be thought of as a sentence, "t has type T." The term t is the subject of this sentence, and the subject reduction property then says that the truth of the sentence is preserved under reduction of the subject.

Unlike uniqueness of types, which holds in some type systems and not in others, progress and preservation will be basic requirements for all of the type systems that we consider.[4]

8.3.5   EXERCISE [★]: The evaluation rule E-PREDZERO (Figure 3-2) is a bit counterintuitive: we might feel that it makes more sense for the predecessor of zero to be undefined, rather than being defined to be zero. Can we achieve this simply by removing the rule from the definition of single-step evaluation?   □

8.3.6   EXERCISE [★★, RECOMMENDED]: Having seen the subject reduction property, it is reasonable to wonder whether the opposite property—subject *expansion*—also holds. Is it always the case that, if $t \longrightarrow t'$ and t' : T, then t : T? If so, prove it. If not, give a counterexample.   □

8.3.7   EXERCISE [RECOMMENDED, ★★]: Suppose our evaluation relation is defined in the big-step style, as in Exercise 3.5.17. How should the intuitive property of type safety be formalized?   □

8.3.8   EXERCISE [RECOMMENDED, ★★]: Suppose our evaluation relation is augmented with rules for reducing nonsensical terms to an explicit wrong state, as in Exercise 3.5.16. Now how should type safety be formalized?   □

> *The road from untyped to typed universes has been followed many times, in many different fields, and largely for the same reasons.*
> *—Luca Cardelli and Peter Wegner (1985)*

---

4. There *are* languages where these properties do not hold, but which can nevertheless be considered to be type-safe. For example, if we formalize the operational semantics of Java in a small-step style (Flatt, Krishnamurthi, and Felleisen, 1998a; Igarashi, Pierce, and Wadler, 1999), type preservation in the form we have given it here fails (see Chapter 19 for details). However, this should be considered an artifact of the formalization, rather than a defect in the language itself, since it disappears, for example, in a big-step presentation of the semantics.

9 *Simply Typed Lambda-Calculus*

This chapter introduces the most elementary member of the family of typed languages that we shall be studying for the rest of the book: the simply typed lambda-calculus of Church (1940) and Curry (1958).

9.1 Function Types

In Chapter 8, we introduced a simple static type system for arithmetic expressions with two types: Bool, classifying terms whose evaluation yields a boolean, and Nat, classifying terms whose evaluation yields a number. The "ill-typed" terms not belonging to either of these types include all the terms that reach stuck states during evaluation (e.g., if 0 then 1 else 2) as well as some terms that actually behave fine during evaluation, but for which our static classification is too conservative (like if true then 0 else false).

Suppose we want to construct a similar type system for a language combining booleans (for the sake of brevity, we'll ignore numbers in this chapter) with the primitives of the pure lambda-calculus. That is, we want to introduce typing rules for variables, abstractions, and applications that (a) maintain type safety—i.e., satisfy the type preservation and progress theorems, 8.3.2 and 8.3.3—and (b) are not too conservative—i.e., they should assign types to most of the programs we actually care about writing.

Of course, since the pure lambda-calculus is Turing complete, there is no hope of giving an *exact* type analysis for these primitives. For example, there is no way of reliably determining whether a program like

```
if <long and tricky computation> then true else (λx.x)
```

yields a boolean or a function without actually running the long and tricky computation and seeing whether it yields true or false. But, in general, the

The system studied in this chapter is the simply typed lambda-calculus (Figure 9-1) with booleans (8-1). The associated OCaml implementation is fullsimple.

long and tricky computation might even diverge, and any typechecker that tries to predict its outcome precisely will then diverge as well.

To extend the type system for booleans to include functions, we clearly need to add a type classifying terms whose evaluation results in a function. As a first approximation, let's call this type →. If we add a typing rule

$$\lambda x.t : \rightarrow$$

giving every λ-abstraction the type →, we can classify both simple terms like λx.x and compound terms like if true then (λx.true) else (λx.λy.y) as yielding functions.

But this rough analysis is clearly too conservative: functions like λx.true and λx.λy.y are lumped together in the same type →, ignoring the fact that applying the first to true yields a boolean, while applying the second to true yields another function. In general, in order to give a useful type to the result of an application, we need to know more about the left-hand side than just that it is a function: we need to know what type the function returns. Moreover, in order to be sure that the function will behave correctly when it is called, we need to keep track of what type of arguments it expects. To keep track of this information, we replace the bare type → by an infinite family of types of the form $T_1 \rightarrow T_2$, each classifying functions that expect arguments of type T_1 and return results of type T_2.

9.1.1   DEFINITION: The set of *simple types* over the type Bool is generated by the following grammar:

T ::=	*types:*
T→T	*type of functions*
Bool	*type of booleans*

The *type constructor* → is right-associative—that is, the expression $T_1 \rightarrow T_2 \rightarrow T_3$ stands for $T_1 \rightarrow (T_2 \rightarrow T_3)$.   □

For example Bool→Bool is the type of functions mapping boolean arguments to boolean results. (Bool→Bool)→(Bool→Bool)—or, equivalently, (Bool→Bool)→Bool→Bool—is the type of functions that take boolean-to-boolean functions as arguments and return them as results.

9.2   The Typing Relation

In order to assign a type to an abstraction like λx.t, we need to calculate what will happen when the abstraction is applied to some argument. The next question that arises is: how do we know what type of arguments to expect? There are two possible responses: either we can simply annotate the λ-abstraction with the intended type of its arguments, or else we can analyze the body of the abstraction to see how the argument is used and try to deduce, from this, what type it should have. For now, we choose the first alternative. Instead of just $\lambda x.t$, we will write $\lambda x:T_1.t_2$, where the annotation on the bound variable tells us to assume that the argument will be of type T_1.

In general, languages in which type annotations in terms are used to help guide the typechecker are called *explicitly typed*. Languages in which we ask the typechecker to *infer* or *reconstruct* this information are called *implicitly typed*. (In the λ-calculus literature, the term *type-assignment systems* is also used.) Most of this book will concentrate on explicitly typed languages; implicit typing is explored in Chapter 22.

Once we know the type of the argument to the abstraction, it is clear that the type of the function's result will be just the type of the body t_2, where occurrences of x in t_2 are assumed to denote terms of type T_1. This intuition is captured by the following typing rule:

$$\frac{x:T_1 \vdash t_2 : T_2}{\vdash \lambda x:T_1.t_2 : T_1 \rightarrow T_2} \qquad \text{(T-Abs)}$$

Since terms may contain nested λ-abstractions, we will need, in general, to talk about several such assumptions. This changes the typing relation from a two-place relation, $t : T$, to a three-place relation, $\Gamma \vdash t : T$, where Γ is a set of assumptions about the types of the free variables in t.

Formally, a *typing context* (also called a *type environment*) Γ is a sequence of variables and their types, and the "comma" operator extends Γ by adding a new binding on the right. The empty context is sometimes written $\varnothing$, but usually we just omit it, writing $\vdash t : T$ for "The closed term t has type T under the empty set of assumptions."

To avoid confusion between the new binding and any bindings that may already appear in Γ, we require that the name x be chosen so that it is distinct from the variables bound by Γ. Since our convention is that variables bound by λ-abstractions may be renamed whenever convenient, this condition can always be satisfied by renaming the bound variable if necessary. Γ can thus be thought of as a finite function from variables to their types. Following this intuition, we write $dom(\Gamma)$ for the set of variables bound by Γ.

The rule for typing abstractions has the general form

$$\frac{\Gamma, x:T_1 \vdash t_2 : T_2}{\Gamma \vdash \lambda x:T_1.t_2 : T_1 \rightarrow T_2} \qquad \text{(T-Abs)}$$

where the premise adds one more assumption to those in the conclusion.

The typing rule for variables also follows immediately from this discussion: a variable has whatever type we are currently assuming it to have.

$$\frac{\text{x:T} \in \Gamma}{\Gamma \vdash \text{x} : \text{T}} \qquad\qquad (\text{T-Var})$$

The premise x:T $\in \Gamma$ is read "The type assumed for x in Γ is T."

Finally, we need a typing rule for applications.

$$\frac{\Gamma \vdash t_1 : T_{11}{\rightarrow}T_{12} \qquad \Gamma \vdash t_2 : T_{11}}{\Gamma \vdash t_1\ t_2 : T_{12}} \qquad\qquad (\text{T-App})$$

If t_1 evaluates to a function mapping arguments in T_{11} to results in T_{12} (under the assumption that the values represented by its free variables have the types assumed for them in Γ), and if t_2 evaluates to a result in T_{11}, then the result of applying t_1 to t_2 will be a value of type T_{12}.

The typing rules for the boolean constants and conditional expressions are the same as before (Figure 8-1). Note, though, that the metavariable T in the rule for conditionals

$$\frac{\Gamma \vdash t_1 : \text{Bool} \qquad \Gamma \vdash t_2 : T \qquad \Gamma \vdash t_3 : T}{\Gamma \vdash \text{if } t_1 \text{ then } t_2 \text{ else } t_3 : T} \qquad\qquad (\text{T-If})$$

can now be instantiated to any function type, allowing us to type conditionals whose branches are functions:[1]

```
if true then (λx:Bool. x) else (λx:Bool. not x);
▶ (λx:Bool. x) : Bool → Bool
```

These typing rules are summarized in Figure 9-1 (along with the syntax and evaluation rules, for the sake of completeness). The highlighted regions in the figure indicate material that is new with respect to the untyped lambda-calculus—both new rules and new bits added to old rules. As we did with booleans and numbers, we have split the definition of the full calculus into two pieces: the *pure* simply typed lambda-calculus with no base types at all, shown in this figure, and a separate set of rules for booleans, which we have already seen in Figure 8-1 (we must add a context Γ to every typing statement in that figure, of course).

We often use the symbol $\lambda_{\rightarrow}$ to refer to the simply typed lambda-calculus (we use the same symbol for systems with different sets of base types).

9.2.1   EXERCISE [⋆]: The pure simply typed lambda-calculus with no base types is actually *degenerate,* in the sense that it has no well-typed terms at all. Why? □

Instances of the typing rules for $\lambda_{\rightarrow}$ can be combined into *derivation trees,* just as we did for typed arithmetic expressions. For example, here is a derivation demonstrating that the term (λx:Bool.x) true has type Bool in the empty context.

---

1. Examples showing sample interactions with an implementation will display both results and their types from now on (when they are obvious, they will be sometimes be elided).

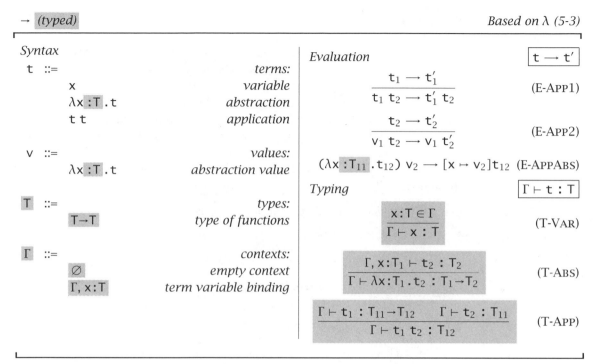

→ *(typed)*   *Based on λ (5-3)*

Syntax

t ::=   terms:
      x   variable
      λx:T.t   abstraction
      t t   application

v ::=   values:
      λx:T.t   abstraction value

T ::=   types:
      T→T   type of functions

Γ ::=   contexts:
      ∅   empty context
      Γ,x:T   term variable binding

Evaluation $\boxed{t \longrightarrow t'}$

$$\frac{t_1 \longrightarrow t_1'}{t_1\ t_2 \longrightarrow t_1'\ t_2} \qquad (\text{E-App1})$$

$$\frac{t_2 \longrightarrow t_2'}{v_1\ t_2 \longrightarrow v_1\ t_2'} \qquad (\text{E-App2})$$

$$(\lambda x{:}T_{11}.t_{12})\ v_2 \longrightarrow [x \mapsto v_2]t_{12} \quad (\text{E-AppAbs})$$

Typing $\boxed{\Gamma \vdash t : T}$

$$\frac{x{:}T \in \Gamma}{\Gamma \vdash x : T} \qquad (\text{T-Var})$$

$$\frac{\Gamma, x{:}T_1 \vdash t_2 : T_2}{\Gamma \vdash \lambda x{:}T_1.t_2 : T_1{\to}T_2} \qquad (\text{T-Abs})$$

$$\frac{\Gamma \vdash t_1 : T_{11}{\to}T_{12} \qquad \Gamma \vdash t_2 : T_{11}}{\Gamma \vdash t_1\ t_2 : T_{12}} \qquad (\text{T-App})$$

Figure 9-1: Pure simply typed lambda-calculus ($\lambda_\to$)

$$\cfrac{\cfrac{\text{x:Bool} \in \text{x:Bool}}{\text{x:Bool} \vdash \text{x : Bool}}\ {}^{\text{T-Var}}}{\cfrac{\vdash \lambda\text{x:Bool.x : Bool}{\to}\text{Bool}}{} \quad \cfrac{}{\vdash \text{true : Bool}}\ {}^{\text{T-True}}}{\vdash (\lambda\text{x:Bool.x) true : Bool}}\ {}^{\text{T-App}}$$

9.2.2   EXERCISE [★ →]: Show (by drawing derivation trees) that the following terms have the indicated types:

1. f:Bool→Bool ⊢ f (if false then true else false) : Bool

2. f:Bool→Bool ⊢ λx:Bool. f (if x then false else x) : Bool→Bool   □

9.2.3   EXERCISE [★]: Find a context Γ under which the term f x y has type Bool. Can you give a simple description of the set of *all* such contexts?   □

9.3   Properties of Typing

As in Chapter 8, we need to develop a few basic lemmas before we can prove type safety. Most of these are similar to what we saw before—we just need to add contexts to the typing relation and add clauses to each proof for λ-abstractions, applications, and variables. The only significant new requirement is a *substitution lemma* for the typing relation (Lemma 9.3.8).

First off, an *inversion lemma* records a collection of observations about how typing derivations are built: the clause for each syntactic form tells us "if a term of this form is well typed, then its subterms must have types of these forms..."

9.3.1   LEMMA [INVERSION OF THE TYPING RELATION]:

1. If $\Gamma \vdash x : R$, then $x:R \in \Gamma$.

2. If $\Gamma \vdash \lambda x{:}T_1.\ t_2 : R$, then $R = T_1 \rightarrow R_2$ for some R_2 with $\Gamma, x{:}T_1 \vdash t_2 : R_2$.

3. If $\Gamma \vdash t_1\ t_2 : R$, then there is some type T_{11} such that $\Gamma \vdash t_1 : T_{11} \rightarrow R$ and $\Gamma \vdash t_2 : T_{11}$.

4. If $\Gamma \vdash \mathtt{true} : R$, then $R = \mathtt{Bool}$.

5. If $\Gamma \vdash \mathtt{false} : R$, then $R = \mathtt{Bool}$.

6. If $\Gamma \vdash \mathtt{if}\ t_1\ \mathtt{then}\ t_2\ \mathtt{else}\ t_3 : R$, then $\Gamma \vdash t_1 : \mathtt{Bool}$ and $\Gamma \vdash t_2, t_3 : R$. $\square$

Proof: Immediate from the definition of the typing relation. $\square$

9.3.2   EXERCISE [RECOMMENDED, ★★★]: Is there any context Γ and type T such that $\Gamma \vdash x\ x : T$? If so, give Γ and T and show a typing derivation for $\Gamma \vdash x\ x : T$; if not, prove it. $\square$

In §9.2, we chose an explicitly typed presentation of the calculus to simplify the job of typechecking. This involved adding type annotations to bound variables in function abstractions, but nowhere else. In what sense is this "enough"? One answer is provided by the "uniqueness of types" theorem, which tells us that well-typed terms are in one-to-one correspondence with their typing derivations: the typing derivation can be recovered uniquely from the term (and, of course, vice versa). In fact, the correspondence is so straightforward that, in a sense, there is little difference between the term and the derivation.

9.3.3   THEOREM [UNIQUENESS OF TYPES]: In a given typing context Γ, a term t (with free variables all in the domain of Γ) has at most one type. That is, if a term is typable, then its type is unique. Moreover, there is just one derivation of this typing built from the inference rules that generate the typing relation. $\square$

Proof: Exercise. The proof is actually so direct that there is almost nothing to say; but writing out some of the details is good practice in "setting up" proofs about the typing relation. □

For many of the type systems that we will see later in the book, this simple correspondence between terms and derivations will not hold: a single term will be assigned many types, and each of these will be justified by many typing derivations. In these systems, there will often be significant work involved in showing that typing derivations can be recovered effectively from terms.

Next, a canonical forms lemma tells us the possible shapes of values of various types.

9.3.4   LEMMA [CANONICAL FORMS]:

1. If v is a value of type Bool, then v is either true or false.

2. If v is a value of type $T_1 \rightarrow T_2$, then $v = \lambda x : T_1 . t_2$. □

Proof: Straightforward. (Similar to the proof of the canonical forms lemma for arithmetic expressions, 8.3.1.) □

Using the canonical forms lemma, we can prove a progress theorem analogous to Theorem 8.3.2. The statement of the theorem needs one small change: we are interested only in *closed* terms, with no free variables. For open terms, the progress theorem actually fails: a term like f true is a normal form, but not a value. However, this failure does not represent a defect in the language, since complete programs—which are the terms we actually care about evaluating—are always closed.

9.3.5   THEOREM [PROGRESS]: Suppose t is a closed, well-typed term (that is, $\vdash t : T$ for some T). Then either t is a value or else there is some t' with $t \rightarrow t'$. □

Proof: Straightforward induction on typing derivations. The cases for boolean constants and conditions are exactly the same as in the proof of progress for typed arithmetic expressions (8.3.2). The variable case cannot occur (because t is closed). The abstraction case is immediate, since abstractions are values.

The only interesting case is the one for application, where $t = t_1\ t_2$ with $\vdash t_1 : T_{11} \rightarrow T_{12}$ and $\vdash t_2 : T_{11}$. By the induction hypothesis, either t_1 is a value or else it can make a step of evaluation, and likewise t_2. If t_1 can take a step, then rule E-APP1 applies to t. If t_1 is a value and t_2 can take a step, then rule E-APP2 applies. Finally, if both t_1 and t_2 are values, then the canonical forms lemma tells us that t_1 has the form $\lambda x : T_{11} . t_{12}$, and so rule E-APPABS applies to t. □

Our next job is to prove that evaluation preserves types. We begin by stating a couple of "structural lemmas" for the typing relation. These are not particularly interesting in themselves, but will permit us to perform some useful manipulations of typing derivations in later proofs.

The first structural lemma tells us that we may permute the elements of a context, as convenient, without changing the set of typing statements that can be derived under it. Recall (from page 101) that all the bindings in a context must have distinct names, and that, whenever we add a binding to a context, we tacitly assume that the bound name is different from all the names already bound (using Convention 5.3.4 to rename the new one if needed).

9.3.6   LEMMA [PERMUTATION]: If $\Gamma \vdash t : T$ and Δ is a permutation of Γ, then $\Delta \vdash t : T$. Moreover, the latter derivation has the same depth as the former.   □

Proof: Straightforward induction on typing derivations.   □

9.3.7   LEMMA [WEAKENING]: If $\Gamma \vdash t : T$ and $x \notin dom(\Gamma)$, then $\Gamma, x{:}S \vdash t : T$. Moreover, the latter derivation has the same depth as the former.   □

Proof: Straightforward induction on typing derivations.   □

Using these technical lemmas, we can prove a crucial property of the typing relation: that well-typedness is preserved when variables are substituted with terms of appropriate types. Similar lemmas play such a ubiquitous role in the safety proofs of programming languages that it is often called just "the substitution lemma."

9.3.8   LEMMA [PRESERVATION OF TYPES UNDER SUBSTITUTION]: If $\Gamma, x{:}S \vdash t : T$ and $\Gamma \vdash s : S$, then $\Gamma \vdash [x \mapsto s]t : T$.   □

Proof: By induction on a derivation of the statement $\Gamma, x{:}S \vdash t : T$. For a given derivation, we proceed by cases on the final typing rule used in the proof.[2]   The most interesting cases are the ones for variables and abstractions.

Case T-VAR: $t = z$
                   with $z{:}T \in (\Gamma, x{:}S)$

There are two sub-cases to consider, depending on whether z is x or another variable. If $z = x$, then $[x \mapsto s]z = s$. The required result is then $\Gamma \vdash s : S$, which is among the assumptions of the lemma. Otherwise, $[x \mapsto s]z = z$, and the desired result is immediate.

---

2. Or, equivalently, by cases on the possible shapes of t, since for each syntactic constructor there is exactly one typing rule.

Case T-ABS: $t = \lambda y : T_2 . t_1$
               $T = T_2 {\rightarrow} T_1$
               $\Gamma, x{:}S, y{:}T_2 \vdash t_1 : T_1$

By convention 5.3.4, we may assume $x \neq y$ and $y \notin FV(s)$. Using permutation on the given subderivation, we obtain $\Gamma, y{:}T_2, x{:}S \vdash t_1 : T_1$. Using weakening on the other given derivation ($\Gamma \vdash s : S$), we obtain $\Gamma, y{:}T_2 \vdash s : S$. Now, by the induction hypothesis, $\Gamma, y{:}T_2 \vdash [x \mapsto s]t_1 : T_1$. By T-ABS, $\Gamma \vdash \lambda y{:}T_2. [x \mapsto s]t_1 : T_2 {\rightarrow} T_1$. But this is precisely the needed result, since, by the definition of substitution, $[x \mapsto s]t = \lambda y{:}T_2. [x \mapsto s]t_1$.

Case T-APP: $t = t_1\ t_2$
               $\Gamma, x{:}S \vdash t_1 : T_2 {\rightarrow} T_1$
               $\Gamma, x{:}S \vdash t_2 : T_2$
               $T = T_1$

By the induction hypothesis, $\Gamma \vdash [x \mapsto s]t_1 : T_2 {\rightarrow} T_1$ and $\Gamma \vdash [x \mapsto s]t_2 : T_2$. By T-APP, $\Gamma \vdash [x \mapsto s]t_1\ [x \mapsto s]t_2 : T$, i.e., $\Gamma \vdash [x \mapsto s](t_1\ t_2) : T$.

Case T-TRUE: $t = \mathtt{true}$
                $T = \mathtt{Bool}$

Then $[x \mapsto s]t = \mathtt{true}$, and the desired result, $\Gamma \vdash [x \mapsto s]t : T$, is immediate.

Case T-FALSE: $t = \mathtt{false}$
                $T = \mathtt{Bool}$

Similar.

Case T-IF: $t = \mathtt{if}\ t_1\ \mathtt{then}\ t_2\ \mathtt{else}\ t_3$
              $\Gamma, x{:}S \vdash t_1 : \mathtt{Bool}$
              $\Gamma, x{:}S \vdash t_2 : T$
              $\Gamma, x{:}S \vdash t_3 : T$

Three uses of the induction hypothesis yield

$\Gamma \vdash [x \mapsto s]t_1 : \mathtt{Bool}$
$\Gamma \vdash [x \mapsto s]t_2 : T$
$\Gamma \vdash [x \mapsto s]t_3 : T,$

from which the result follows by T-IF.   □

Using the substitution lemma, we can prove the other half of the type safety property—that evaluation preserves well-typedness.

9.3.9   THEOREM [PRESERVATION]: If $\Gamma \vdash t : T$ and $t \longrightarrow t'$, then $\Gamma \vdash t' : T$.   □

Proof: EXERCISE [RECOMMENDED, ★★★]. The structure is very similar to the proof of the type preservation theorem for arithmetic expressions (8.3.3), except for the use of the substitution lemma.   □

9.3.10   EXERCISE [RECOMMENDED, ★★]: In Exercise 8.3.6 we investigated the *subject expansion* property for our simple calculus of typed arithmetic expressions. Does it hold for the "functional part" of the simply typed lambda-calculus? That is, suppose t does not contain any conditional expressions. Do t ⟶ t′ and Γ ⊢ t′ : T imply Γ ⊢ t : T?   □

9.4   The Curry-Howard Correspondence

The "→" type constructor comes with typing rules of two kinds:

1. an *introduction rule* (T-ABS) describing how elements of the type can be *created,* and

2. an *elimination rule* (T-APP) describing how elements of the type can be *used.*

When an introduction form (λ) is an immediate subterm of an elimination form (application), the result is a redex—an opportunity for computation.

The terminology of introduction and elimination forms is frequently useful in discussing type systems. When we come to more complex systems later in the book, we'll see a similar pattern of linked introduction and elimination rules for each type constructor we consider.

9.4.1   EXERCISE [★]: Which of the rules for the type Bool in Figure 8-1 are introduction rules and which are elimination rules? What about the rules for Nat in Figure 8-2?   □

The introduction/elimination terminology arises from a connection between type theory and logic known as the *Curry-Howard correspondence* or *Curry-Howard isomorphism* (Curry and Feys, 1958; Howard, 1980). Briefly, the idea is that, in constructive logics, a proof of a proposition P consists of concrete *evidence* for P.[3] What Curry and Howard noticed was that such evidence has a strongly computational feel. For example, a proof of a proposition $P \supset Q$ can be viewed as a mechanical procedure that, given a proof of P, constructs a proof of Q—or, if you like, a proof of Q *abstracted on* a proof of P. Similarly, a proof of $P \wedge Q$ consists of a proof of P together with a proof of Q. This observation gives rise to the following correspondence:

---

3. The characteristic difference between classical and constructive logics is the omission from the latter of proof rules like the law of the *excluded middle,* which says that, for every proposition Q, either Q holds or $\neg Q$ does. To prove $Q \vee \neg Q$ in a constructive logic, we must provide evidence either for Q or for $\neg Q$.

LOGIC	PROGRAMMING LANGUAGES
propositions	types
proposition $P \supset Q$	type P→Q
proposition $P \wedge Q$	type P×Q (see §11.6)
proof of proposition P	term t of type P
proposition P is provable	type P is inhabited (by some term)

On this view, a term of the simply typed lambda-calculus is a proof of a logical proposition corresponding to its type. Computation—reduction of lambda-terms—corresponds to the logical operation of proof simplification by *cut elimination*. The Curry-Howard correspondence is also called the *propositions as types* analogy. Thorough discussions of this correspondence can be found in many places, including Girard, Lafont, and Taylor (1989), Gallier (1993), Sørensen and Urzyczyn (1998), Pfenning (2001), Goubault-Larrecq and Mackie (1997), and Simmons (2000).

The beauty of the Curry-Howard correspondence is that it is not limited to a particular type system and one related logic—on the contrary, it can be extended to a huge variety of type systems and logics. For example, System F (Chapter 23), whose parametric polymorphism involves quantification over types, corresponds precisely to a second-order constructive logic, which permits quantification over propositions. System F_ω (Chapter 30) corresponds to a higher-order logic. Indeed, the correspondence has often been exploited to transfer new developments between the fields. Thus, Girard's *linear logic* (1987) gives rise to the idea of *linear type systems* (Wadler, 1990, Wadler, 1991, Turner, Wadler, and Mossin, 1995, Hodas, 1992, Mackie, 1994, Chirimar, Gunter, and Riecke, 1996, Kobayashi, Pierce, and Turner, 1996, and many others), while *modal logics* have been used to help design frameworks for *partial evaluation* and *run-time code generation* (see Davies and Pfenning, 1996, Wickline, Lee, Pfenning, and Davies, 1998, and other sources cited there).

9.5   Erasure and Typability

In Figure 9-1, we defined the evaluation relation directly on simply typed terms. Although type annotations play no role in evaluation—we don't do any sort of run-time checking to ensure that functions are applied to arguments of appropriate types—we do carry along these annotations inside of terms as we evaluate them.

Most compilers for full-scale programming languages actually avoid carrying annotations at run time: they are used during typechecking (and during code generation, in more sophisticated compilers), but do not appear in the compiled form of the program. In effect, programs are converted back to an untyped form before they are evaluated. This style of semantics can be formalized using an *erasure* function mapping simply typed terms into the corresponding untyped terms.

9.5.1   DEFINITION: The *erasure* of a simply typed term t is defined as follows:

$$
\begin{aligned}
\mathit{erase}(\mathsf{x}) &= \mathsf{x} \\
\mathit{erase}(\lambda \mathsf{x}\!:\!\mathsf{T}_1.\ \mathsf{t}_2) &= \lambda \mathsf{x}.\ \mathit{erase}(\mathsf{t}_2) \\
\mathit{erase}(\mathsf{t}_1\ \mathsf{t}_2) &= \mathit{erase}(\mathsf{t}_1)\ \mathit{erase}(\mathsf{t}_2)
\end{aligned}
$$ □

Of course, we expect that the two ways of presenting the semantics of the simply typed calculus actually coincide: it doesn't really matter whether we evaluate a typed term directly, or whether we erase it and evaluate the underlying untyped term. This expectation is formalized by the following theorem, summarized by the slogan "evaluation commutes with erasure" in the sense that these operations can be performed in either order—we reach the same term by evaluating and then erasing as we do by erasing and then evaluating:

9.5.2   THEOREM:

1. If $t \longrightarrow t'$ under the typed evaluation relation, then $\mathit{erase}(t) \longrightarrow \mathit{erase}(t')$.

2. If $\mathit{erase}(t) \longrightarrow m'$ under the typed evaluation relation, then there is a simply typed term t' such that $t \longrightarrow t'$ and $\mathit{erase}(t') = m'$.   □

Proof: Straightforward induction on evaluation derivations.   □

Since the "compilation" we are considering here is so straightforward, Theorem 9.5.2 is obvious to the point of triviality. For more interesting languages and more interesting compilers, however, it becomes a quite important property: it tells us that a "high-level" semantics, expressed directly in terms of the language that the programmer writes, coincides with an alternative, lower-level evaluation strategy actually used by an implementation of the language.

Another interesting question arising from the erasure function is: Given an untyped lambda-term m, can we find a simply typed term t that erases to m?

9.5.3   DEFINITION: A term m in the untyped lambda-calculus is said to be *typable* in $\lambda_\rightarrow$ if there are some simply typed term t, type T, and context Γ such that $\mathit{erase}(t) = m$ and $\Gamma \vdash t : T$.   □

We will return to this point in more detail in Chapter 22, when we consider the closely related topic of *type reconstruction* for $\lambda_\rightarrow$.

9.6   Curry-Style vs. Church-Style

We have seen two different styles in which the semantics of the simply typed lambda-calculus can be formulated: as an evaluation relation defined directly on the syntax of the simply typed calculus, or as a compilation to an untyped calculus plus an evaluation relation on untyped terms. An important commonality of the two styles is that, in both, it makes sense to talk about the behavior of a term t, whether or not t is actually well typed. This form of language definition is often called *Curry-style*. We first define the terms, then define a semantics showing how they behave, then give a type system that rejects some terms whose behaviors we don't like. Semantics is prior to typing.

A rather different way of organizing a language definition is to define terms, then identify the well-typed terms, then give semantics just to these. In these so-called *Church-style* systems, typing is prior to semantics: we never even ask the question "what is the behavior of an ill-typed term?" Indeed, strictly speaking, what we actually evaluate in Church-style systems is typing *derivations,* not terms. (See §15.6 for an example of this.)

Historically, implicitly typed presentations of lambda-calculi are often given in the Curry style, while Church-style presentations are common only for explicitly typed systems. This has led to some confusion of terminology: "Church-style" is sometimes used when describing an explicitly typed *syntax* and "Curry-style" for implicitly typed.

9.7   Notes

The simply typed lambda-calculus is studied in Hindley and Seldin (1986), and in even greater detail in Hindley's monograph (1997).

Well-typed programs cannot "go wrong."   —*Robin Milner (1978)*

10 *An ML Implementation of Simple Types*

The concrete realization of $\lambda_\rightarrow$ as an ML program follows the same lines as our implementation of the untyped lambda-calculus in Chapter 7. The main addition is a function `typeof` for calculating the type of a given term in a given context. Before we get to it, though, we need a little low-level machinery for manipulating contexts.

10.1 Contexts

Recall from Chapter 7 (p. 85) that a `context` is just a list of pairs of variable names and `bindings`:

```
type context = (string * binding) list
```

In Chapter 7, we used contexts just for converting between named and nameless forms of terms during parsing and printing. For this, we needed to know just the names of the variables; the `binding` type was defined as a trivial one-constructor datatype carrying no information at all:

```
type binding = NameBind
```

To implement the typechecker, we will need to use the context to carry typing assumptions about variables. We support this by adding a new constructor called `VarBind` to the `binding` type:

```
type binding =
    NameBind
  | VarBind of ty
```

The implementation described here corresponds to the simply typed lambda-calculus (Figure 9-1) with booleans (8-1). The code in this chapter can be found in the `simplebool` implementation in the web repository.

Each VarBind constructor carries a typing assumption for the corresponding variable. We keep the old NameBind constructor in addition to VarBind, for the convenience of the printing and parsing functions, which don't care about typing assumptions. (A different implementation strategy would be to define two completely different context types—one for parsing and printing and another for typechecking.)

The typeof function uses a function addbinding to extend a context ctx with a new variable binding (x,bind); since contexts are represented as lists, addbinding is essentially just cons:

```
let addbinding ctx x bind = (x,bind)::ctx
```

Conversely, we use the function getTypeFromContext to extract the typing assumption associated with a particular variable i in a context ctx (the file information fi is used for printing an error message if i is out of range):

```
let getTypeFromContext fi ctx i =
  match getbinding fi ctx i with
      VarBind(tyT) → tyT
   | _ → error fi
      ("getTypeFromContext: Wrong kind of binding for variable "
       ∧ (index2name fi ctx i))
```

The match provides some internal consistency checking: under normal circumstances, getTypeFromContext should always be called with a context where the ith binding is in fact a VarBind. In later chapters, though, we will add other forms of bindings (in particular, bindings for *type variables*), and it is possible that getTypeFromContext will get called with the wrong kind of variable. In this case, it uses the low-level error function to print a message, passing it an info so that it can report the file position where the error occurred.

```
val error : info → string → 'a
```

The result type of the error function is the variable type 'a, which can be instantiated to any ML type (this makes sense because it is never going to return anyway: it prints a message and halts the program). Here, we need to assume that the result of error is a ty, since that is what the other branch of the match returns.

Note that we look up typing assumptions by *index,* since terms are represented internally in nameless form, with variables represented as numerical indices. The getbinding function simply looks up the ith binding in the given context:

```
val getbinding : info → context → int → binding
```

Its definition can be found in the `simplebool` implementation on the book's web site.

10.2 Terms and Types

The syntax of types is transcribed directly into an ML datatype from the abstract syntax in Figures 8-1 and 9-1.

```
type ty =
    TyArr of ty * ty
  | TyBool
```

The representation of terms is the same as we used for the untyped lambda-calculus (p. 84), just adding a type annotation to the `TmAbs` clause.

```
type term =
    TmVar of info * int * int
  | TmAbs of info * string * ty * term
  | TmApp of info * term * term
  | TmTrue of info
  | TmFalse of info
  | TmIf of info * term * term * term
```

10.3 Typechecking

The typechecking function `typeof` can be viewed as a direct translation of the typing rules for $\lambda_\rightarrow$ (Figures 8-1 and 9-1), or, more accurately, as a transcription of the inversion lemma (9.3.1). The second view is more accurate because it is the inversion lemma that tells us, for every syntactic form, exactly what conditions must hold in order for a term of this form to be well typed. The typing rules tell us that terms of certain forms are well typed under certain conditions, but by looking at an individual typing rule, we can never conclude that some term is *not* well typed, since it is always possible that another rule could be used to type this term. (At the moment, this may appear to be a difference without a distinction, since the inversion lemma follows so directly from the typing rules. The difference becomes important, though, in later systems where proving the inversion lemma requires more work than in $\lambda_\rightarrow$.)

```
let rec typeof ctx t =
  match t with
    TmVar(fi,i,_) → getTypeFromContext fi ctx i
  | TmAbs(fi,x,tyT1,t2) →
```

```
      let ctx' = addbinding ctx x (VarBind(tyT1)) in
      let tyT2 = typeof ctx' t2 in
      TyArr(tyT1, tyT2)
  | TmApp(fi,t1,t2) →
      let tyT1 = typeof ctx t1 in
      let tyT2 = typeof ctx t2 in
      (match tyT1 with
          TyArr(tyT11,tyT12) →
            if (=) tyT2 tyT11 then tyT12
            else error fi "parameter type mismatch"
        | _ → error fi "arrow type expected")
  | TmTrue(fi) →
      TyBool
  | TmFalse(fi) →
      TyBool
  | TmIf(fi,t1,t2,t3) →
     if (=) (typeof ctx t1) TyBool then
       let tyT2 = typeof ctx t2 in
       if (=) tyT2 (typeof ctx t3) then tyT2
       else error fi "arms of conditional have different types"
     else error fi "guard of conditional not a boolean"
```

A couple of details of the OCaml language are worth mentioning here. First, the OCaml equality operator = is written in parentheses because we are using it in prefix position, rather than its normal infix position, to facilitate comparison with later versions of typeof where the operation of comparing types will need to be something more refined than simple equality. Second, the equality operator computes a *structural* equality on compound values, not a *pointer* equality. That is, the expression

```
let t  = TmApp(t1,t2) in
let t' = TmApp(t1,t2) in
(=) t t'
```

is guaranteed to yield true, even though the two instances of TmApp bound to t and t′ are allocated at different times and live at different addresses in memory.

11 *Simple Extensions*

The simply typed lambda-calculus has enough structure to make its theoretical properties interesting, but it is not yet much of a programming language. In this chapter, we begin to close the gap with more familiar languages by introducing a number of familiar features that have straightforward treatments at the level of typing. An important theme throughout the chapter is the concept of *derived forms*.

11.1 Base Types

Every programming language provides a variety of *base types*—sets of simple, unstructured values such as numbers, booleans, or characters—plus appropriate primitive operations for manipulating these values. We have already examined natural numbers and booleans in detail; as many other base types as the language designer wants can be added in exactly the same way.

Besides `Bool` and `Nat`, we will occasionally use the base types `String` (with elements like `"hello"`) and `Float` (with elements like `3.14159`) to spice up the examples in the rest of the book.

For theoretical purposes, it is often useful to abstract away from the details of particular base types and their operations, and instead simply suppose that our language comes equipped with some set $\mathcal{A}$ of *uninterpreted* or *unknown* base types, with no primitive operations on them at all. This is accomplished simply by including the elements of $\mathcal{A}$ (ranged over by the metavariable A) in the set of types, as shown in Figure 11-1. We use the letter $\mathcal{A}$ for base types, rather than $\mathcal{B}$, to avoid confusion with the symbol $\mathbb{B}$, which we have used to indicate the presence of booleans in a given system. $\mathcal{A}$ can be thought of as standing for *atomic types*—another name that is often used for base types, because they have no internal structure as far as the type system

---

The systems studied in this chapter are various extensions of the pure typed lambda-calculus (Figure 9-1). The associated OCaml implementation, `fullsimple`, includes all the extensions.

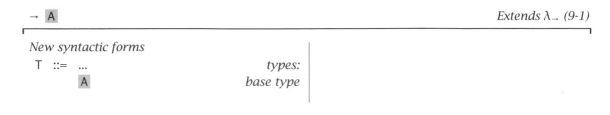

Figure 11-1: Uninterpreted base types

is concerned. We will use A, B, C, etc. as the names of base types. Note that, as we did before with variables and type variables, we are using A both as a base type and as a metavariable ranging over base types, relying on context to tell us which is intended in a particular instance.

Is an uninterpreted type useless? Not at all. Although we have no way of naming its elements directly, we can still bind variables that range over the elements of a base type. For example, the function[1]

    λx:A. x;

▸ <fun> : A → A

is the identity function on the elements of A, whatever these may be. Likewise,

    λx:B. x;

▸ <fun> : B → B

is the identity function on B, while

    λf:A→A. λx:A. f(f(x));

▸ <fun> : (A→A) → A → A

is a function that repeats two times the behavior of some given function f on an argument x.

11.2   The Unit Type

Another useful base type, found especially in languages in the ML family, is the singleton type Unit described in Figure 11-2. In contrast to the uninterpreted base types of the previous section, this type is interpreted in the

---

1. From now on, we will save space by eliding the bodies of λ-abstractions—writing them as just <fun>—when we display the results of evaluation.

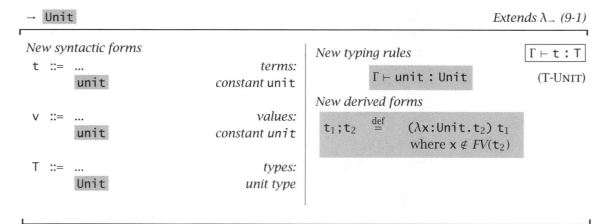

Figure 11-2: Unit type

simplest possible way: we explicitly introduce a single element—the term constant unit (written with a small u)—and a typing rule making unit an element of Unit. We also add unit to the set of possible result values of computations—indeed, unit is the *only* possible result of evaluating an expression of type Unit.

Even in a purely functional language, the type Unit is not completely without interest,[2] but its main application is in languages with side effects, such as assignments to reference cells—a topic we will return to in Chapter 13. In such languages, it is often the side effect, not the result, of an expression that we care about; Unit is an appropriate result type for such expressions.

This use of Unit is similar to the role of the void type in languages like C and Java. The name void suggests a connection with the empty type Bot (cf. §15.4), but the usage of void is actually closer to our Unit.

11.3   Derived Forms: Sequencing and Wildcards

In languages with side effects, it is often useful to evaluate two or more expressions in sequence. The *sequencing notation* $t_1;t_2$ has the effect of evaluating t_1, throwing away its trivial result, and going on to evaluate t_2.

---

2. The reader may enjoy the following little puzzle:

11.2.1   EXERCISE [★★★]: Is there a way of constructing a sequence of terms $t_1, t_2, \ldots$, in the simply typed lambda-calculus with *only* the base type Unit, such that, for each n, the term t_n has size at most $O(n)$ but requires at least $O(2^n)$ steps of evaluation to reach a normal form?   □

There are actually two different ways to formalize sequencing. One is to follow the same pattern we have used for other syntactic forms: add $t_1;t_2$ as a new alternative in the syntax of terms, and then add two evaluation rules

$$\frac{t_1 \longrightarrow t_1'}{t_1;t_2 \longrightarrow t_1';t_2} \qquad\qquad \text{(E-SEQ)}$$

$$\text{unit};t_2 \longrightarrow t_2 \qquad\qquad \text{(E-SEQNEXT)}$$

and a typing rule

$$\frac{\Gamma \vdash t_1 : \text{Unit} \qquad \Gamma \vdash t_2 : T_2}{\Gamma \vdash t_1;t_2 : T_2} \qquad\qquad \text{(T-SEQ)}$$

capturing the intended behavior of ;.

An alternative way of formalizing sequencing is simply to regard $t_1;t_2$ as an *abbreviation* for the term $(\lambda x{:}\text{Unit}.t_2)\ t_1$, where the variable x is chosen *fresh*—i.e., different from all the free variables of t_2.

It is intuitively fairly clear that these two presentations of sequencing add up to the same thing as far as the programmer is concerned: the high-level typing and evaluation rules for sequencing can be *derived* from the abbreviation of $t_1;t_2$ as $(\lambda x{:}\text{Unit}.t_2)\ t_1$. This intuitive correspondence is captured more formally by arguing that typing and evaluation both "commute" with the expansion of the abbreviation.

11.3.1   THEOREM [SEQUENCING IS A DERIVED FORM]: Write λ^E ("*E*" for *external language*) for the simply typed lambda-calculus with the Unit type, the sequencing construct, and the rules E-SEQ, E-SEQNEXT, and T-SEQ, and λ^I ("*I*" for *internal language*) for the simply typed lambda-calculus with Unit only. Let $e \in \lambda^E \rightarrow \lambda^I$ be the *elaboration function* that translates from the external to the internal language by replacing every occurrence of $t_1;t_2$ with $(\lambda x{:}\text{Unit}.t_2)\ t_1$, where x is chosen fresh in each case. Now, for each term t of λ^E, we have

- $t \longrightarrow_E t'$ iff $e(t) \longrightarrow_I e(t')$

- $\Gamma \vdash^E t : T$ iff $\Gamma \vdash^I e(t) : T$

where the evaluation and typing relations of λ^E and λ^I are annotated with *E* and *I*, respectively, to show which is which.   □

Proof: Each direction of each "iff" proceeds by straightforward induction on the structure of t.   □

Theorem 11.3.1 justifies our use of the term *derived form,* since it shows that the typing and evaluation behavior of the sequencing construct can be derived from those of the more fundamental operations of abstraction and application. The advantage of introducing features like sequencing as derived forms rather than as full-fledged language constructs is that we can extend the surface syntax (i.e., the language that the programmer actually uses to write programs) without adding any complexity to the internal language about which theorems such as type safety must be proved. This method of factoring the descriptions of language features can already be found in the Algol 60 report (Naur et al., 1963), and it is heavily used in many more recent language definitions, notably the Definition of Standard ML (Milner, Tofte, and Harper, 1990; Milner, Tofte, Harper, and MacQueen, 1997).

Derived forms are often called *syntactic sugar,* following Landin. Replacing a derived form with its lower-level definition is called *desugaring.*

Another derived form that will be useful in examples later on is the "wildcard" convention for variable binders. It often happens (for example, in terms created by desugaring sequencing) that we want to write a "dummy" lambda-abstraction in which the parameter variable is not actually used in the body of the abstraction. In such cases, it is annoying to have to explicitly choose a name for the bound variable; instead, we would like to replace it by a *wildcard binder,* written _. That is, we will write λ_:S.t to abbreviate λx:S.t, where x is some variable not occurring in t.

11.3.2 EXERCISE [★]: Give typing and evaluation rules for wildcard abstractions, and prove that they can be derived from the abbreviation stated above. □

11.4 Ascription

Another simple feature that will frequently come in handy later is the ability to explicitly *ascribe* a particular type to a given term (i.e., to record in the text of the program an assertion that this term has this type). We write "t as T" for "the term t, to which we ascribe the type T." The typing rule T-ASCRIBE for this construct (cf. Figure 11-3) simply verifies that the ascribed type T is, indeed, the type of t. The evaluation rule E-ASCRIBE is equally straightforward: it just throws away the ascription, leaving t free to evaluate as usual.

There are a number of situations where ascription can be useful in programming. One common one is *documentation.* It can sometimes become difficult for a reader to keep track of the types of the subexpressions of a large compound expression. Judicious use of ascription can make such programs much easier to follow. Similarly, in a particularly complex expression, it may not even be clear to the *writer* what the types of all the subexpressions are. Sprinkling in a few ascriptions is a good way of clarifying the programmer's

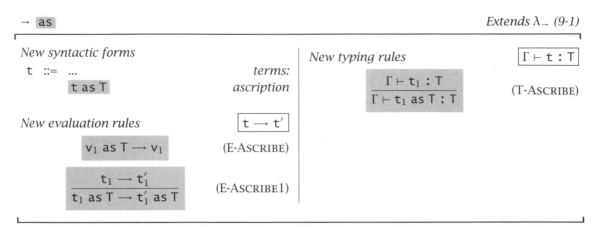

Figure 11-3: Ascription

thinking. Indeed, ascription is sometimes a valuable aid in pinpointing the source of puzzling type errors.

Another use of ascription is for controlling the *printing* of complex types. The typecheckers used to check the examples shown in this book—and the accompanying OCaml implementations whose names begin with the prefix `full`—provide a simple mechanism for introducing abbreviations for long or complex type expressions. (The abbreviation mechanism is omitted from the other implementations to make them easier to read and modify.) For example, the declaration

```
UU = Unit→Unit;
```

makes UU an abbreviation for `Unit→Unit` in what follows. Wherever UU is seen, `Unit→Unit` is understood. We can write, for example:

```
(λf:UU. f unit) (λx:Unit. x);
```

During type-checking, these abbreviations are expanded automatically as necessary. Conversely, the typecheckers attempt to collapse abbreviations whenever possible. (Specifically, each time they calculate the type of a subterm, they check whether this type exactly matches any of the currently defined abbreviations, and if so replace the type by the abbreviation.) This normally gives reasonable results, but occasionally we may want a type to print differently, either because the simple matching strategy causes the typechecker to miss an opportunity to collapse an abbreviation (for example, in systems where the fields of record types can be permuted, it will not recognize that `{a:Bool,b:Nat}` is interchangeable with `{b:Nat,a:Bool}`), or because we want the type to print differently for some other reason. For example, in

```
λf:Unit→Unit. f;
```

▶ `<fun>` : (Unit→Unit) → UU

the abbreviation UU is collapsed in the result of the function, but not in its argument. If we want the type to print as UU→UU, we can either change the type annotation on the abstraction

```
λf:UU. f;
```

▶ `<fun>` : UU → UU

or else add an ascription to the whole abstraction:

```
(λf:Unit→Unit. f) as UU→UU;
```

▶ `<fun>` : UU → UU

When the typechecker processes an ascription t as T, it expands any abbreviations in T while checking that t has type T, but then yields T itself, exactly as written, as the type of the ascription. This use of ascription to control the printing of types is somewhat particular to the way the implementations in this book have been engineered. In a full-blown programming language, mechanisms for abbreviation and type printing will either be unnecessary (as in Java, for example, where by construction all types are represented by short names—cf. Chapter 19) or else much more tightly integrated into the language (as in OCaml—cf. Rémy and Vouillon, 1998; Vouillon, 2000).

A final use of ascription that will be discussed in more detail in §15.5 is as a mechanism for *abstraction*. In systems where a given term t may have many different types (for example, systems with subtyping), ascription can be used to "hide" some of these types by telling the typechecker to treat t as if it had only a smaller set of types. The relation between ascription and *casting* is also discussed in §15.5.

11.4.1 EXERCISE [RECOMMENDED, ★★]: (1) Show how to formulate ascription as a derived form. Prove that the "official" typing and evaluation rules given here correspond to your definition in a suitable sense. (2) Suppose that, instead of the pair of evaluation rules E-ASCRIBE and E-ASCRIBE1, we had given an "eager" rule

$$t_1 \text{ as } T \longrightarrow t_1 \qquad \text{(E-ASCRIBEEAGER)}$$

that throws away an ascription as soon as it is reached. Can ascription still be considered as a derived form?   □

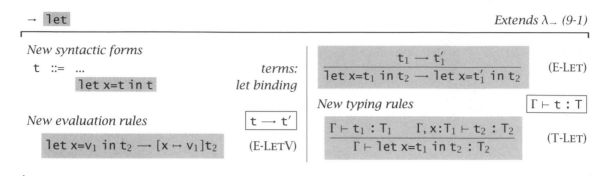

Figure 11-4: Let binding

11.5   Let Bindings

When writing a complex expression, it is often useful—both for avoiding repetition and for increasing readability—to give names to some of its subexpressions. Most languages provide one or more ways of doing this. In ML, for example, we write let x=t_1 in t_2 to mean "evaluate the expression t_1 and bind the name x to the resulting value while evaluating t_2."

Our let-binder (summarized in Figure 11-4) follows ML's in choosing a call-by-value evaluation order, where the let-bound term must be fully evaluated before evaluation of the let-body can begin. The typing rule T-LET tells us that the type of a let can be calculated by calculating the type of the let-bound term, extending the context with a binding with this type, and in this enriched context calculating the type of the body, which is then the type of the whole let expression.

11.5.1   EXERCISE [RECOMMENDED, ★★★]: The letexercise typechecker (available at the book's web site) is an incomplete implementation of let expressions: basic parsing and printing functions are provided, but the clauses for TmLet are missing from the eval1 and typeof functions (in their place, you'll find dummy clauses that match everything and crash the program with an assertion failure). Finish it.   □

Can let also be defined as a derived form? Yes, as Landin showed; but the details are slightly more subtle than what we did for sequencing and ascription. Naively, it is clear that we can use a combination of abstraction and application to achieve the effect of a let-binding:

$$\text{let } x=t_1 \text{ in } t_2 \quad \overset{\text{def}}{=} \quad (\lambda x{:}T_1.t_2) \ t_1$$

But notice that the right-hand side of this abbreviation includes the type annotation T_1, which does not appear on the left-hand side. That is, if we imagine derived forms as being desugared during the parsing phase of some compiler, then we need to ask how the parser is supposed to know that it should generate T_1 as the type annotation on the λ in the desugared internal-language term.

The answer, of course, is that this information comes from the typechecker! We discover the needed type annotation simply by calculating the type of t_1. More formally, what this tells us is that the let constructor is a slightly different sort of derived form than the ones we have seen up till now: we should regard it not as a desugaring transformation on terms, but as a transformation on *typing derivations* (or, if you prefer, on terms decorated by the typechecker with the results of its analysis) that maps a derivation involving let

$$
\frac{
\begin{array}{cc}
\vdots & \vdots \\
\overline{\Gamma \vdash t_1 : T_1} & \overline{\Gamma, x{:}T_1 \vdash t_2 : T_2}
\end{array}
}{\Gamma \vdash \text{let } x{=}t_1 \text{ in } t_2 : T_2} \text{T-LET}
$$

to one using abstraction and application:

$$
\frac{
\dfrac{
\dfrac{\vdots}{\Gamma, x{:}T_1 \vdash t_2 : T_2}
}{\Gamma \vdash \lambda x{:}T_1.t_2 : T_1{\rightarrow}T_2} \text{T-ABS} \qquad
\dfrac{\vdots}{\Gamma \vdash t_1 : T_1} \text{T-APP}
}{\Gamma \vdash (\lambda x{:}T_1.t_2)\ t_1 : T_2}
$$

Thus, let is "a little less derived" than the other derived forms we have seen: we can derive its evaluation behavior by desugaring it, but its typing behavior must be built into the internal language.

In Chapter 22 we will see another reason not to treat let as a derived form: in languages with Hindley-Milner (i.e., unification-based) polymorphism, the let construct is treated specially by the typechecker, which uses it for *generalizing* polymorphic definitions to obtain typings that cannot be emulated using ordinary λ-abstraction and application.

11.5.2   EXERCISE [$\star\star$]: Another way of defining let as a derived form might be to desugar it by "executing" it immediately—i.e., to regard let $x{=}t_1$ in t_2 as an abbreviation for the substituted body $[x \mapsto t_1]t_2$. Is this a good idea?   □

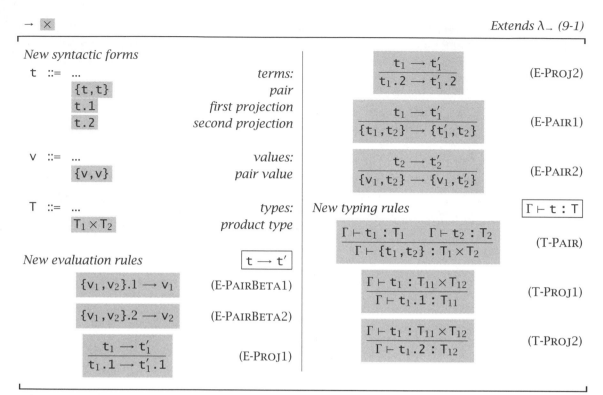

Figure 11-5: Pairs

11.6   Pairs

Most programming languages provide a variety of ways of building compound data structures. The simplest of these is *pairs,* or more generally *tuples,* of values. We treat pairs in this section, then do the more general cases of tuples and labeled records in §11.7 and §11.8.[3]

The formalization of pairs is almost too simple to be worth discussing—by this point in the book, it should be about as easy to read the rules in Figure 11-5 as to wade through a description in English conveying the same information. However, let's look briefly at the various parts of the definition to emphasize the common pattern.

Adding pairs to the simply typed lambda-calculus involves adding two new forms of term—pairing, written $\{t_1, t_2\}$, and projection, written $t.1$ for the

_____
3. The `fullsimple` implementation does not actually provide the pairing syntax described here, since tuples are more general anyway.

first projection from t and t.2 for the second projection—plus one new type constructor, $T_1 \times T_2$, called the *product* (or sometimes the *cartesian product*) of T_1 and T_2. Pairs are written with curly braces[4] to emphasize the connection to records in the §11.8.

For evaluation, we need several new rules specifying how pairs and projection behave. E-PAIRBETA1 and E-PAIRBETA2 specify that, when a fully evaluated pair meets a first or second projection, the result is the appropriate component. E-PROJ1 and E-PROJ2 allow reduction to proceed under projections, when the term being projected from has not yet been fully evaluated. E-PAIR1 and E-PAIR2 evaluate the parts of pairs: first the left part, and then—when a value appears on the left—the right part.

The ordering arising from the use of the metavariables v and t in these rules enforces a left-to-right evaluation strategy for pairs. For example, the compound term

```
{pred 4, if true then false else false}.1
```

evaluates (only) as follows:

```
      {pred 4, if true then false else false}.1
  ⟶   {3, if true then false else false}.1
  ⟶   {3, false}.1
  ⟶   3
```

We also need to add a new clause to the definition of values, specifying that $\{v_1, v_2\}$ is a value. The fact that the components of a pair value must themselves be values ensures that a pair passed as an argument to a function will be fully evaluated before the function body starts executing. For example:

```
      (λx:Nat×Nat. x.2) {pred 4, pred 5}
  ⟶   (λx:Nat×Nat. x.2) {3, pred 5}
  ⟶   (λx:Nat×Nat. x.2) {3,4}
  ⟶   {3,4}.2
  ⟶   4
```

The typing rules for pairs and projections are straightforward. The introduction rule, T-PAIR, says that $\{t_1, t_2\}$ has type $T_1 \times T_2$ if t_1 has type T_1 and t_2 has type T_2. Conversely, the elimination rules T-PROJ1 and T-PROJ2 tell us that, if t_1 has a product type $T_{11} \times T_{12}$ (i.e., if it will evaluate to a pair), then the types of the projections from this pair are T_{11} and T_{12}.

---

4. The curly brace notation is a little unfortunate for pairs and tuples, since it suggests the standard mathematical notation for sets. It is more common, both in popular languages like ML and in the research literature, to enclose pairs and tuples in parentheses. Other notations such as square or angle brackets are also used.

→ {}   *Extends* $\lambda_\rightarrow$ *(9-1)*

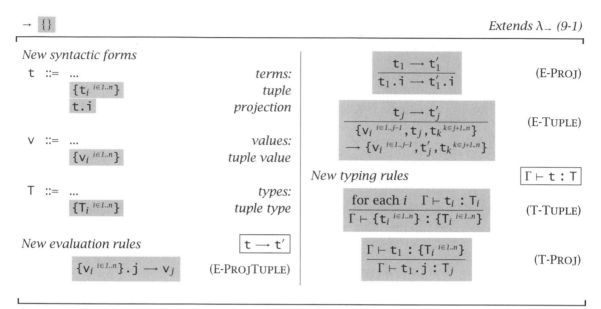

New syntactic forms

t ::= ...   *terms:*
     $\{t_i{}^{i\in 1..n}\}$ *tuple*
     t.i   *projection*

v ::= ...   *values:*
     $\{v_i{}^{i\in 1..n}\}$ *tuple value*

T ::= ...   *types:*
     $\{T_i{}^{i\in 1..n}\}$ *tuple type*

New evaluation rules $\boxed{t \longrightarrow t'}$

$$\{v_i{}^{i\in 1..n}\}.j \longrightarrow v_j \qquad \text{(E-PROJTUPLE)}$$

$$\frac{t_1 \longrightarrow t_1'}{t_1.i \longrightarrow t_1'.i} \qquad \text{(E-PROJ)}$$

$$\frac{t_j \longrightarrow t_j'}{\{v_i{}^{i\in 1..j-1}, t_j, t_k{}^{k\in j+1..n}\} \longrightarrow \{v_i{}^{i\in 1..j-1}, t_j', t_k{}^{k\in j+1..n}\}} \qquad \text{(E-TUPLE)}$$

New typing rules $\boxed{\Gamma \vdash t : T}$

$$\frac{\text{for each } i \quad \Gamma \vdash t_i : T_i}{\Gamma \vdash \{t_i{}^{i\in 1..n}\} : \{T_i{}^{i\in 1..n}\}} \qquad \text{(T-TUPLE)}$$

$$\frac{\Gamma \vdash t_1 : \{T_i{}^{i\in 1..n}\}}{\Gamma \vdash t_1.j : T_j} \qquad \text{(T-PROJ)}$$

Figure 11-6: Tuples

11.7   Tuples

It is easy to generalize the binary products of the previous section to *n*-ary products, often called *tuples*. For example, {1,2,true} is a 3-tuple containing two numbers and a boolean. Its type is written {Nat,Nat,Bool}.

The only cost of this generalization is that, to formalize the system, we need to invent notations for uniformly describing structures of arbitrary arity; such notations are always a bit problematic, as there is some inevitable tension between rigor and readability. We write $\{t_i{}^{i\in 1..n}\}$ for a tuple of *n* terms, t_1 through t_n, and $\{T_i{}^{i\in 1..n}\}$ for its type. Note that *n* here is allowed to be 0; in this case, the range *1..n* is empty and $\{t_i{}^{i\in 1..n}\}$ is {}, the empty tuple. Also, note the difference between a bare value like 5 and a one-element tuple like {5}: the only operation we may legally perform on the latter is projecting its first component.

Figure 11-6 formalizes tuples. The definition is similar to the definition of products (Figure 11-5), except that each rule for pairing has been generalized to the *n*-ary case, and each pair of rules for first and second projections has become a single rule for an arbitrary projection from a tuple. The only rule that deserves special comment is E-TUPLE, which combines and generalizes the rules E-PAIR1 and E-PAIR2 from Figure 11-5. In English, it says that, if we

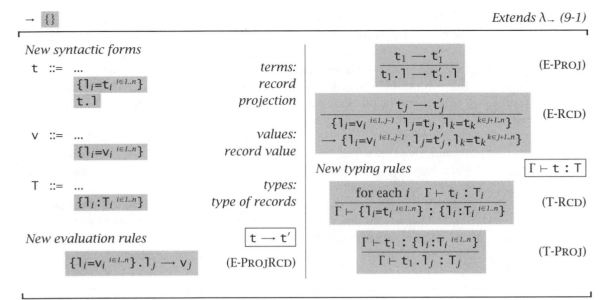

Figure 11-7: Records

have a tuple in which all the fields to the left of field j have already been reduced to values, then that field can be evaluated one step, from t_j to t'_j. Again, the use of metavariables enforces a left-to-right evaluation strategy.

11.8   Records

The generalization from n-ary tuples to labeled records is equally straightforward. We simply annotate each field t_i with a *label* l_i drawn from some predetermined set $\mathcal{L}$. For example, {x=5} and {partno=5524,cost=30.27} are both record values; their types are {x:Nat} and {partno:Nat,cost:Float}. We require that all the labels in a given record term or type be distinct.

The rules for records are given in Figure 11-7. The only one worth noting is E-PROJRCD, where we rely on a slightly informal convention. The rule is meant to be understood as follows: If $\{l_i{=}v_i{}^{i\in1..n}\}$ is a record and l_j is the label of its jth field, then $\{l_i{=}v_i{}^{i\in1..n}\}.l_j$ evaluates in one step to the jth value, v_j. This convention (and the similar one that we used in E-PROJTUPLE) could be eliminated by rephrasing the rule in a more explicit form; however, the cost in terms of readability would be fairly high.

11.8.1   EXERCISE [⋆ ↛]: Write E-PROJRCD more explicitly, for comparison.   □

Note that the same "feature symbol," {}, appears in the list of features on the upper-left corner of the definitions of both tuples and products. Indeed, we can obtain tuples as a special case of records, simply by allowing the set of labels to include both alphabetic identifiers and natural numbers. Then when the ith field of a record has the label i, we omit the label. For example, we regard {Bool,Nat,Bool} as an abbreviation for {1:Bool,2:Nat,3:Bool}. (This convention actually allows us to mix named and positional fields, writing {a:Bool,Nat,c:Bool} as an abbreviation for {a:Bool,2:Nat,c:Bool}, though this is probably not very useful in practice.) In fact, many languages keep tuples and records notationally distinct for a more pragmatic reason: they are implemented differently by the compiler.

Programming languages differ in their treatment of the order of record fields. In many languages, the order of fields in both record values and record types has no affect on meaning—i.e., the terms {partno=5524,cost=30.27} and {cost=30.27,partno=5524} have the same meaning and the same type, which may be written either {partno:Nat,cost:Float} or {cost:Float, partno:Nat}. Our presentation chooses the other alternative: {partno=5524, cost=30.27} and {cost=30.27,partno=5524} are *different* record values, with types {partno:Nat,cost:Float} and {cost:Float, partno:Nat}, respectively. In Chapter 15, we will adopt a more liberal view of ordering, introducing a subtype relation in which the types {partno:Nat,cost:Float} and {cost:Float,partno:Nat} are *equivalent*—each is a subtype of the other— so that terms of one type can be used in any context where the other type is expected. (In the presence of subtyping, the choice between ordered and unordered records has important effects on performance; these are discussed further in §15.6. Once we have decided on unordered records, though, the choice of whether to consider records as unordered from the beginning or to take the fields primitively as ordered and then give rules that allow the ordering to be ignored is purely a question of taste. We adopt the latter approach here because it allows us to discuss both variants.)

11.8.2 EXERCISE [★★★]: In our presentation of records, the projection operation is used to extract the fields of a record one at a time. Many high-level programming languages provide an alternative *pattern matching* syntax that extracts all the fields at the same time, allowing some programs to be expressed much more concisely. Patterns can also typically be nested, allowing parts to be extracted easily from complex nested data structures.

We can add a simple form of pattern matching to an untyped lambda calculus with records by adding a new syntactic category of *patterns,* plus one new case (for the pattern matching construct itself) to the syntax of terms. (See Figure 11-8.)

$\rightarrow \{\}$ `let` `p` *(untyped)*   *Extends 11-7 and 11-4*

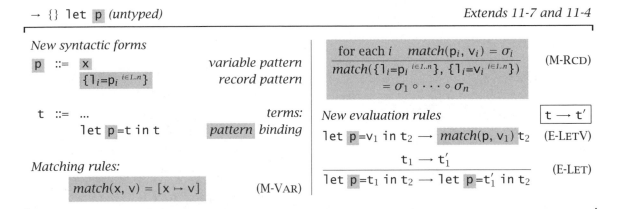

New syntactic forms

p ::=
  x   *variable pattern*
  $\{l_i\texttt{=}p_i^{\ i\in 1..n}\}$ *record pattern*

t ::= ...   *terms:*
  `let` p`=`t `in` t   *pattern binding*

Matching rules:

$$match(x, v) = [x \mapsto v] \qquad \text{(M-VAR)}$$

$$\frac{\text{for each } i \quad match(p_i, v_i) = \sigma_i}{match(\{l_i\texttt{=}p_i^{\ i\in 1..n}\}, \{l_i\texttt{=}v_i^{\ i\in 1..n}\})} \quad \text{(M-RCD)}$$
$$= \sigma_1 \circ \cdots \circ \sigma_n$$

New evaluation rules $t \longrightarrow t'$

`let` p`=`v_1 `in` t_2 $\longrightarrow$ $match(p, v_1)\, t_2$ (E-LETV)

$$\frac{t_1 \longrightarrow t_1'}{\texttt{let } p\texttt{=}t_1 \texttt{ in } t_2 \longrightarrow \texttt{let } p\texttt{=}t_1' \texttt{ in } t_2} \quad \text{(E-LET)}$$

Figure 11-8: (Untyped) record patterns

The computation rule for pattern matching generalizes the let-binding rule from Figure 11-4. It relies on an auxiliary "matching" function that, given a pattern p and a value v, either fails (indicating that v does not match p) or else yields a substitution that maps variables appearing in p to the corresponding parts of v. For example, $match(\{x,y\}, \{5,true\})$ yields the substitution $[x \mapsto 5, y \mapsto true]$ and $match(x, \{5,true\})$ yields $[x \mapsto \{5,true\}]$, while $match(\{x\}, \{5,true\})$ fails. E-LETV uses $match$ to calculate an appropriate substitution for the variables in p.

The $match$ function itself is defined by a separate set of inference rules. The rule M-VAR says that a variable pattern always succeeds, returning a substitution mapping the variable to the whole value being matched against. The rule M-RCD says that, to match a record pattern $\{l_i\texttt{=}p_i^{\ i\in 1..n}\}$ against a record value $\{l_i\texttt{=}v_i^{\ i\in 1..n}\}$ (of the same length, with the same labels), we individually match each sub-pattern p_i against the corresponding value v_i to obtain a substitution σ_i, and build the final result substitution by composing all these substitutions. (We require that no variable should appear more than once in a pattern, so this composition of substitutions is just their union.)

Show how to add types to this system.

1. Give typing rules for the new constructs (making any changes to the syntax you feel are necessary in the process).

2. Sketch a proof of type preservation and progress for the whole calculus. (You do not need to show full proofs—just the statements of the required lemmas in the correct order.)   □

→ +   *Extends* λ→ *(9-1)*

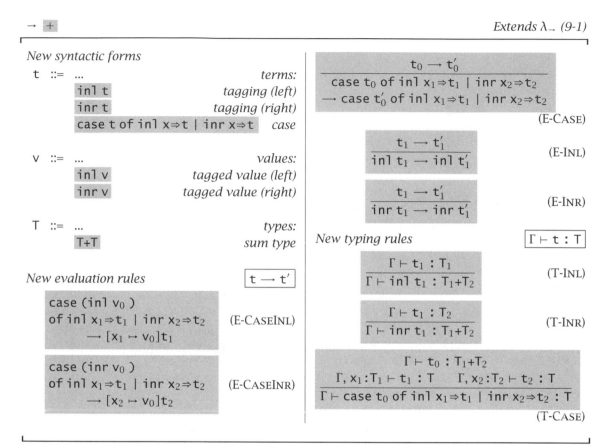

New syntactic forms

t ::= ...   *terms:*
    inl t   *tagging (left)*
    inr t   *tagging (right)*
    case t of inl x⇒t | inr x⇒t   *case*

v ::= ...   *values:*
    inl v   *tagged value (left)*
    inr v   *tagged value (right)*

T ::= ...   *types:*
    T+T   *sum type*

New evaluation rules $t \longrightarrow t'$

$$\text{case (inl } v_0\,) \text{ of inl } x_1 {\Rightarrow} t_1 \mid \text{inr } x_2 {\Rightarrow} t_2 \longrightarrow [x_1 \mapsto v_0] t_1 \quad \text{(E-CASEINL)}$$

$$\text{case (inr } v_0\,) \text{ of inl } x_1 {\Rightarrow} t_1 \mid \text{inr } x_2 {\Rightarrow} t_2 \longrightarrow [x_2 \mapsto v_0] t_2 \quad \text{(E-CASEINR)}$$

$$\frac{t_0 \longrightarrow t_0'}{\text{case } t_0 \text{ of inl } x_1 {\Rightarrow} t_1 \mid \text{inr } x_2 {\Rightarrow} t_2 \longrightarrow \text{case } t_0' \text{ of inl } x_1 {\Rightarrow} t_1 \mid \text{inr } x_2 {\Rightarrow} t_2} \quad \text{(E-CASE)}$$

$$\frac{t_1 \longrightarrow t_1'}{\text{inl } t_1 \longrightarrow \text{inl } t_1'} \quad \text{(E-INL)}$$

$$\frac{t_1 \longrightarrow t_1'}{\text{inr } t_1 \longrightarrow \text{inr } t_1'} \quad \text{(E-INR)}$$

New typing rules $\Gamma \vdash t : T$

$$\frac{\Gamma \vdash t_1 : T_1}{\Gamma \vdash \text{inl } t_1 : T_1{+}T_2} \quad \text{(T-INL)}$$

$$\frac{\Gamma \vdash t_1 : T_2}{\Gamma \vdash \text{inr } t_1 : T_1{+}T_2} \quad \text{(T-INR)}$$

$$\frac{\Gamma \vdash t_0 : T_1{+}T_2 \quad \Gamma, x_1{:}T_1 \vdash t_1 : T \quad \Gamma, x_2{:}T_2 \vdash t_2 : T}{\Gamma \vdash \text{case } t_0 \text{ of inl } x_1 {\Rightarrow} t_1 \mid \text{inr } x_2 {\Rightarrow} t_2 : T} \quad \text{(T-CASE)}$$

Figure 11-9: Sums

11.9   Sums

Many programs need to deal with *heterogeneous* collections of values. For example, a node in a binary tree can be either a leaf or an interior node with two children; similarly, a list cell can be either nil or a cons cell carrying a head and a tail,[5] a node of an abstract syntax tree in a compiler can represent a variable, an abstraction, an application, etc. The type-theoretic mechanism that supports this kind of programming is *variant types*.

Before introducing variants in full generality (in §11.10), let us consider the

---

5. These examples, like most real-world uses of variant types, also involve *recursive types*—the tail of a list is itself a list, etc. We will return to recursive types in Chapter 20.

simpler case of binary *sum types*. A sum type describes a set of values drawn from exactly two given types. For example, suppose we are using the types

```
PhysicalAddr = {firstlast:String, addr:String};
VirtualAddr  = {name:String, email:String};
```

to represent different sorts of address-book records. If we want to manipulate both sorts of records uniformly (e.g., if we want to make a list containing records of both kinds), we can introduce the sum type[6]

```
Addr = PhysicalAddr + VirtualAddr;
```

each of whose elements is either a `PhysicalAddr` or a `VirtualAddr`.

We create elements of this type by *tagging* elements of the component types `PhysicalAddr` and `VirtualAddr`. For example, if `pa` is a `PhysicalAddr`, then `inl pa` is an `Addr`. (The names of the tags `inl` and `inr` arise from thinking of them as functions

```
inl : PhysicalAddr → PhysicalAddr+VirtualAddr
inr : VirtualAddr → PhysicalAddr+VirtualAddr
```

that "inject" elements of `PhysicalAddr` or `VirtualAddr` into the left and right components of the sum type `Addr`. Note, though, that they are *not* treated as functions in our presentation.)

In general, the elements of a type T_1+T_2 consist of the elements of T_1, tagged with the token `inl`, plus the elements of T_2, tagged with `inr`.

To *use* elements of sum types, we introduce a `case` construct that allows us to distinguish whether a given value comes from the left or right branch of a sum. For example, we can extract a name from an `Addr` like this:

```
getName = λa:Addr.
  case a of
    inl x ⇒ x.firstlast
  | inr y ⇒ y.name;
```

When the parameter `a` is a `PhysicalAddr` tagged with `inl`, the case expression will take the first branch, binding the variable `x` to the `PhysicalAddr`; the body of the first branch then extracts the `firstlast` field from `x` and returns it. Similarly, if `a` is a `VirtualAddr` value tagged with `inr`, the second branch will be chosen and the `name` field of the `VirtualAddr` returned. Thus, the type of the whole `getName` function is `Addr→String`.

The foregoing intuitions are formalized in Figure 11-9. To the syntax of terms, we add the left and right injections and the `case` construct; to types,

---

6. The `fullsimple` implementation does not actually support the constructs for binary sums that we are describing here—just the more general case of variants described below.

we add the sum constructor. For evaluation, we add two "beta-reduction" rules for the case construct—one for the case where its first subterm has been reduced to a value v_0 tagged with inl, the other for a value v_0 tagged with inr; in each case, we select the appropriate body and substitute v_0 for the bound variable. The other evaluation rules perform evaluation in the first subterm of case and under the inl and inr tags.

The typing rules for tagging are straightforward: to show that inl t_1 has a sum type T_1+T_2, it suffices to show that t_1 belongs to the left summand, T_1, and similarly for inr. For the case construct, we first check that the first subterm has a sum type T_1+T_2, then check that the bodies t_1 and t_2 of the two branches have the same result type T, assuming that their bound variables x_1 and x_2 have types T_1 and T_2, respectively; the result of the whole case is then T. Following our conventions from previous definitions, Figure 11-9 does not state explicitly that the scopes of the variables x_1 and x_2 are the bodies t_1 and t_2 of the branches, but this fact can be read off from the way the contexts are extended in the typing rule T-CASE.

11.9.1   EXERCISE [★★]: Note the similarity between the typing rule for case and the rule for if in Figure 8-1: if can be regarded as a sort of degenerate form of case where no information is passed to the branches. Formalize this intuition by defining true, false, and if as derived forms using sums and Unit.   □

Sums and Uniqueness of Types

Most of the properties of the typing relation of pure λ_- (cf. §9.3) extend to the system with sums, but one important one fails: the Uniqueness of Types theorem (9.3.3). The difficulty arises from the tagging constructs inl and inr. The typing rule T-INL, for example, says that, once we have shown that t_1 is an element of T_1, we can derive that inl t_1 is an element of T_1+T_2 for *any* type T_2. For example, we can derive both inl 5 : Nat+Nat and inl 5 : Nat+Bool (and infinitely many other types). The failure of uniqueness of types means that we cannot build a typechecking algorithm simply by "reading the rules from bottom to top," as we have done for all the features we have seen so far. At this point, we have various options:

1. We can complicate the typechecking algorithm so that it somehow "guesses" a value for T_2. Concretely, we hold T_2 indeterminate at this point and try to discover later what its value should have been. Such techniques will be explored in detail when we consider type reconstruction (Chapter 22).

2. We can refine the language of types to allow *all* possible values for T_2 to somehow be represented uniformly. This option will be explored when we discuss subtyping (Chapter 15).

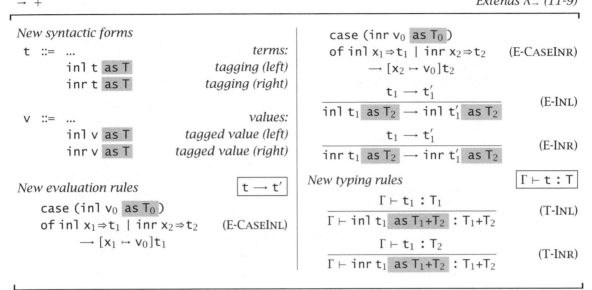

Figure 11-10: Sums (with unique typing)

3. We can demand that the programmer provide an explicit *annotation* to indicate which type T_2 is intended. This alternative is the simplest—and it is not actually as impractical as it might at first appear, since, in full-scale language designs, these explicit annotations can often be "piggybacked" on other language constructs and so made essentially invisible (we'll come back to this point in the following section). We take this option for now.

Figure 11-10 shows the needed extensions, relative to Figure 11-9. Instead of writing just inl t or inr t, we write inl t as T or inr t as T, where T specifies the whole sum type to which we want the injected element to belong. The typing rules T-INL and T-INR use the declared sum type as the type of the injection, after checking that the injected term really belongs to the appropriate branch of the sum. (To avoid writing T_1+T_2 repeatedly in the rules, the syntax rules allow any type T to appear as an annotation on an injection. The typing rules ensure that the annotation will always be a sum type, if the injection is well typed.) The syntax for type annotations is meant to suggest the ascription construct from §11.4: in effect these annotations can be viewed as syntactically required ascriptions.

$\rightarrow$ $<>$ *Extends* $\lambda_\rightarrow$ *(9-1)*

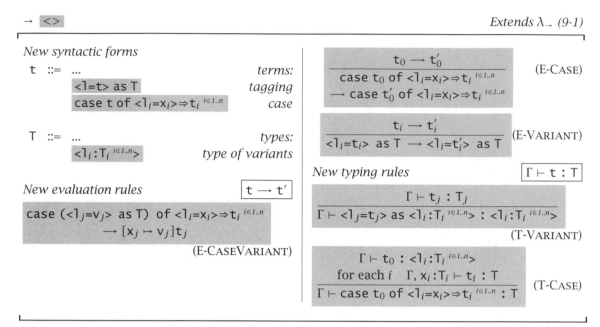

New syntactic forms

$$t ::= ...$$ *terms:*
$$<l=t> \text{ as } T$$ *tagging*
$$\text{case } t \text{ of } <l_i=x_i>\Rightarrow t_i{}^{i\in 1..n}$$ *case*

$$T ::= ...$$ *types:*
$$<l_i:T_i{}^{i\in 1..n}>$$ *type of variants*

New evaluation rules $\boxed{t \longrightarrow t'}$

$$\text{case } (<l_j=v_j> \text{ as } T) \text{ of } <l_i=x_i>\Rightarrow t_i{}^{i\in 1..n}$$
$$\longrightarrow [x_j \mapsto v_j]t_j$$

(E-CASEVARIANT)

$$\frac{t_0 \longrightarrow t_0'}{\text{case } t_0 \text{ of } <l_i=x_i>\Rightarrow t_i{}^{i\in 1..n} \longrightarrow \text{case } t_0' \text{ of } <l_i=x_i>\Rightarrow t_i{}^{i\in 1..n}}$$ (E-CASE)

$$\frac{t_i \longrightarrow t_i'}{<l_i=t_i> \text{ as } T \longrightarrow <l_i=t_i'> \text{ as } T}$$ (E-VARIANT)

New typing rules $\boxed{\Gamma \vdash t : T}$

$$\frac{\Gamma \vdash t_j : T_j}{\Gamma \vdash <l_j=t_j> \text{ as } <l_i:T_i{}^{i\in 1..n}> : <l_i:T_i{}^{i\in 1..n}>}$$ (T-VARIANT)

$$\frac{\Gamma \vdash t_0 : <l_i:T_i{}^{i\in 1..n}> \quad \text{for each } i \quad \Gamma, x_i:T_i \vdash t_i : T}{\Gamma \vdash \text{case } t_0 \text{ of } <l_i=x_i>\Rightarrow t_i{}^{i\in 1..n} : T}$$ (T-CASE)

Figure 11-11: Variants

11.10   Variants

Binary sums generalize to labeled *variants* just as products generalize to labeled records. Instead of T_1+T_2, we write $<l_1:T_1, l_2:T_2>$, where l_1 and l_2 are field labels. Instead of inl t as T_1+T_2, we write $<l_1=t>$ as $<l_1:T_1, l_2:T_2>$. And instead of labeling the branches of the case with inl and inr, we use the same labels as the corresponding sum type. With these generalizations, the getAddr example from the previous section becomes:

```
Addr = <physical:PhysicalAddr, virtual:VirtualAddr>;
a = <physical=pa> as Addr;
```
▸ a : Addr

```
getName = λa:Addr.
  case a of
    <physical=x> ⇒ x.firstlast
  | <virtual=y> ⇒ y.name;
```
▸ getName : Addr → String

The formal definition of variants is given in Figure 11-11. Note that, as with records in §11.8, the order of labels in a variant type is significant here.

Options

One very useful idiom involving variants is *optional values*. For example, an element of the type

```
OptionalNat = <none:Unit, some:Nat>;
```

is either the trivial `unit` value with the tag `none` or else a number with the tag `some`—in other words, the type `OptionalNat` is isomorphic to `Nat` extended with an additional distinguished value `none`. For example, the type

```
Table = Nat→OptionalNat;
```

represents finite mappings from numbers to numbers: the domain of such a mapping is the set of inputs for which the result is <some=n> for some n. The empty table

```
emptyTable = λn:Nat. <none=unit> as OptionalNat;
```

▶ `emptyTable : Table`

is a constant function that returns `none` for every input. The constructor

```
extendTable =
  λt:Table. λm:Nat. λv:Nat.
    λn:Nat.
      if equal n m then <some=v> as OptionalNat
      else t n;
```

▶ `extendTable : Table → Nat → Nat → Table`

takes a table and adds (or overwrites) an entry mapping the input `m` to the output <some=v>. (The `equal` function is defined in the solution to Exercise 11.11.1 on page 510.)

We can use the result that we get back from a `Table` lookup by wrapping a `case` around it. For example, if `t` is our table and we want to look up its entry for 5, we might write

```
x = case t(5) of
      <none=u> ⇒ 999
    | <some=v> ⇒ v;
```

providing 999 as the default value of `x` in case `t` is undefined on 5.

Many languages provide built-in support for options. OCaml, for example, predefines a type constructor `option`, and many functions in typical OCaml programs yield options. Also, the `null` value in languages like C, C++, and Java is actually an option in disguise. A variable of type `T` in these languages (where `T` is a "reference type"—i.e., something allocated in the heap) can actually contain either the special value `null` or else a pointer to a `T` value. That is, the type of such a variable is really `Ref(Option(T))`, where `Option(T) = <none:Unit,some:T>`. Chapter 13 discusses the `Ref` constructor in detail.

Enumerations

Two "degenerate cases" of variant types are useful enough to deserve special mention: enumerated types and single-field variants.

An *enumerated type* (or *enumeration*) is a variant type in which the field type associated with each label is `Unit`. For example, a type representing the days of the working week might be defined as:

```
Weekday = <monday:Unit, tuesday:Unit, wednesday:Unit,
              thursday:Unit, friday:Unit>;
```

The elements of this type are terms like `<monday=unit> as Weekday`. Indeed, since the type `Unit` has only `unit` as a member, the type `Weekday` is inhabited by precisely five values, corresponding one-for-one with the days of the week. The `case` construct can be used to define computations on enumerations.

```
nextBusinessDay = λw:Weekday.
  case w of <monday=x>    ⇒ <tuesday=unit> as Weekday
          | <tuesday=x>   ⇒ <wednesday=unit> as Weekday
          | <wednesday=x> ⇒ <thursday=unit> as Weekday
          | <thursday=x>  ⇒ <friday=unit> as Weekday
          | <friday=x>    ⇒ <monday=unit> as Weekday;
```

Obviously, the concrete syntax we are using here is not well tuned for making such programs easy to write or read. Some languages (beginning with Pascal) provide special syntax for declaring and using enumerations. Others—such as ML, cf. page 141—make enumerations a special case of the variants.

Single-Field Variants

The other interesting special case is variant types with just a single label `l`:

```
V = <l:T>;
```

Such a type might not seem very useful at first glance: after all, the elements of `V` will be in one-to-one correspondence with the elements of the field type `T`, since every member of `V` has precisely the form `<l=t>` for some `t : T`. What's important, though, is that the usual operations on `T` *cannot* be applied to elements of `V` without first unpackaging them: a `V` cannot be accidentally mistaken for a `T`.

For example, suppose we are writing a program to do financial calculations in multiple currencies. Such a program might include functions for converting between dollars and euros. If both are represented as Floats, then these functions might look like this:

```
dollars2euros = λd:Float. timesfloat d 1.1325;
```

▶ dollars2euros : Float → Float

```
euros2dollars = λe:Float. timesfloat e 0.883;
```

▶ euros2dollars : Float → Float

(where timesfloat : Float→Float→Float multiplies floating-point numbers). If we then start with a dollar amount

```
mybankbalance = 39.50;
```

we can convert it to euros and then back to dollars like this:

```
euros2dollars (dollars2euros mybankbalance);
```

▶ 39.49990125 : Float

All this makes perfect sense. But we can just as easily perform manipulations that make no sense at all. For example, we can convert my bank balance to euros twice:

```
dollars2euros (dollars2euros mybankbalance);
```

▶ 50.660971875 : Float

Since all our amounts are represented simply as floats, there is no way that the type system can help prevent this sort of nonsense. However, if we define dollars and euros as different variant types (whose underlying representations are floats)

```
DollarAmount = <dollars:Float>;
EuroAmount = <euros:Float>;
```

then we can define safe versions of the conversion functions that will only accept amounts in the correct currency:

```
dollars2euros =
  λd:DollarAmount.
    case d of <dollars=x> ⇒
      <euros = timesfloat x 1.1325> as EuroAmount;
```

▶ dollars2euros : DollarAmount → EuroAmount

```
    euros2dollars =
      λe:EuroAmount.
        case e of <euros=x> ⇒
          <dollars = timesfloat x 0.883> as DollarAmount;
```

▸ euros2dollars : EuroAmount → DollarAmount

Now the typechecker can track the currencies used in our calculations and
remind us how to interpret the final results:

```
    mybankbalance = <dollars=39.50> as DollarAmount;
    euros2dollars (dollars2euros mybankbalance);
```

▸ <dollars=39.49990125> as DollarAmount : DollarAmount

Moreover, if we write a nonsensical double-conversion, the types will fail to
match and our program will (correctly) be rejected:

```
    dollars2euros (dollars2euros mybankbalance);
```

▸ Error: parameter type mismatch

Variants vs. Datatypes

A variant type T of the form $<l_i:T_i{}^{i\in 1..n}>$ is roughly analogous to the ML
datatype defined by:[7]

```
    type T = l₁ of T₁
           | l₂ of T₂
           | ...
           | lₙ of Tₙ
```

But there are several differences worth noticing.

1. One trivial but potentially confusing point is that the capitalization conventions for identifiers that we are assuming here are different from those
   of OCaml. In OCaml, types must begin with lowercase letters and datatype
   constructors (labels, in our terminology) with capital letters, so, strictly
   speaking, the datatype declaration above should be written like this:

   ```
       type t = L₁ of t₁ | ... | Lₙ of tₙ
   ```

---

7. This section uses OCaml's concrete syntax for datatypes, for consistency with implementation chapters elsewhere in the book, but they originated in early dialects of ML and can be
found, in essentially the same form, in Standard ML as well as in ML relatives such as Haskell.
Datatypes and pattern matching are arguably one of the most useful advantages of these
languages for day to day programming.

To avoid confusion between terms t and types T, we'll ignore OCaml's conventions for the rest of this discussion and use ours instead.

2. The most interesting difference is that OCaml does *not* require a type annotation when a constructor l_i is used to inject an element of T_i into the datatype T: we simply write $l_i(t)$. The way OCaml gets away with this (and retains unique typing) is that the datatype T must be *declared* before it can be used. Moreover, the labels in T cannot be used by any other datatype declared in the same scope. So, when the typechecker sees $l_i(t)$, it knows that the annotation can only be T. In effect, the annotation is "hidden" in the label itself.

   This trick eliminates a lot of silly annotations, but it does lead to a certain amount of grumbling among users, since it means that labels cannot be shared between different datatypes—at least, not within the same module. In Chapter 15 we will see another way of omitting annotations that avoids this drawback.

3. Another convenient trick used by OCaml is that, when the type associated with a label in a datatype definition is just Unit, it can be omitted altogether. This permits enumerations to be defined by writing

   ```
   type Weekday = monday | tuesday | wednesday | thursday | friday
   ```

   for example, rather than:

   ```
   type Weekday = monday of Unit
               | tuesday of Unit
               | wednesday of Unit
               | thursday of Unit
               | friday of Unit
   ```

   Similarly, the label monday all by itself (rather than monday applied to the trivial value unit) is considered to be a value of type Weekday.

4. Finally, OCaml datatypes actually bundle variant types together with several additional features that we will be examining, individually, in later chapters.

   • A datatype definition may be *recursive*—i.e., the type being defined is allowed to appear in the body of the definition. For example, in the standard definition of lists of Nats, the value tagged with cons is a pair whose second element is a NatList.

   ```
   type NatList = nil
               | cons of Nat * NatList
   ```

- An OCaml datatype can be *parameterized* on a type variable, as in the general definition of the List datatype:

```
type 'a List = nil
             | cons of 'a * 'a List
```

Type-theoretically, List can be viewed as a kind of function—called a *type operator*—that maps each choice of 'a to a concrete datatype... Nat to NatList, etc. Type operators are the subject of Chapter 29.

Variants as Disjoint Unions

Sum and variant types are sometimes called *disjoint unions*. The type T_1+T_2 is a "union" of T_1 and T_2 in the sense that its elements include all the elements from T_1 and T_2. This union is disjoint because the sets of elements of T_1 or T_2 are tagged with inl or inr, respectively, before they are combined, so that it is always clear whether a given element of the union comes from T_1 or T_2. The phrase *union type* is also used to refer to *untagged* (non-disjoint) union types, described in §15.7.

Type Dynamic

Even in statically typed languages, there is often the need to deal with data whose type cannot be determined at compile time. This occurs in particular when the lifetime of the data spans multiple machines or many runs of the compiler—when, for example, the data is stored in an external file system or database, or communicated across a network. To handle such situations safely, many languages offer facilities for inspecting the types of values at run time.

One attractive way of accomplishing this is to add a type Dynamic whose values are pairs of a value v and a type tag T where v has type T. Instances of Dynamic are built with an explicit tagging construct and inspected with a type safe typecase construct. In effect, Dynamic can be thought of as an infinite disjoint union, whose labels are types. See Gordon (circa 1980), Mycroft (1983), Abadi, Cardelli, Pierce, and Plotkin (1991b), Leroy and Mauny (1991), Abadi, Cardelli, Pierce, and Rémy (1995), and Henglein (1994).

11.11 General Recursion

Another facility found in most programming languages is the ability to define recursive functions. We have seen (Chapter 5, p. 65) that, in the untyped lambda-calculus, such functions can be defined with the aid of the `fix` combinator.

Recursive functions can be defined in a typed setting in a similar way. For example, here is a function `iseven` that returns `true` when called with an even argument and `false` otherwise:

```
ff = λie:Nat→Bool.
       λx:Nat.
         if iszero x then true
         else if iszero (pred x) then false
         else ie (pred (pred x));
```

▸ `ff : (Nat→Bool) → Nat → Bool`

  `iseven = fix ff;`

▸ `iseven : Nat → Bool`

  `iseven 7;`

▸ `false : Bool`

The intuition is that the higher-order function `ff` passed to `fix` is a *generator* for the `iseven` function: if `ff` is applied to a function `ie` that approximates the desired behavior of `iseven` up to some number *n* (that is, a function that returns correct results on inputs less than or equal to *n*), then it returns a better approximation to `iseven`—a function that returns correct results for inputs up to *n* + 2. Applying `fix` to this generator returns its fixed point—a function that gives the desired behavior for all inputs *n*.

However, there is one important difference from the untyped setting: `fix` itself cannot be defined in the simply typed lambda-calculus. Indeed, we will see in Chapter 12 that *no* expression that can lead to non-terminating computations can be typed using only simple types.[8] So, instead of defining `fix` as a term in the language, we simply add it as a new primitive, with evaluation rules mimicking the behavior of the untyped `fix` combinator and a typing rule that captures its intended uses. These rules are written out in Figure 11-12. (The `letrec` abbreviation will be discussed below.)

The simply typed lambda-calculus with numbers and `fix` has long been a favorite experimental subject for programming language researchers, since it is the simplest language in which a range of subtle semantic phenomena such as *full abstraction* (Plotkin, 1977, Hyland and Ong, 2000, Abramsky, Jagadeesan, and Malacaria, 2000) arise. It is often called *PCF*.

---

8. In later chapters—Chapter 13 and Chapter 20—we will see some extensions of simple types that recover the power to define `fix` within the system.

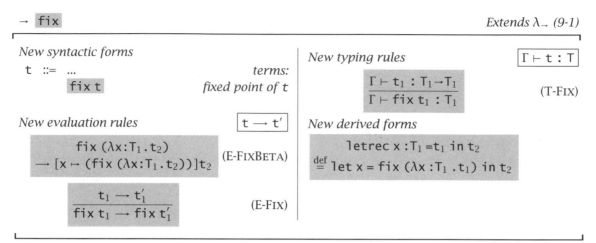

Figure 11-12: General recursion

11.11.1   EXERCISE [★★]: Define `equal`, `plus`, `times`, and `factorial` using `fix`.   □

The `fix` construct is typically used to build functions (as fixed points of functions from functions to functions), but it is worth noticing that the type T in rule T-FIX is not restricted to function types. This extra power is sometimes handy. For example, it allows us to define a *record* of mutually recursive functions as the fixed point of a function on records (of functions). The following implementation of `iseven` uses an auxiliary function `isodd`; the two functions are defined as fields of a record, where the definition of this record is abstracted on a record `ieio` whose components are used to make recursive calls from the bodies of the `iseven` and `isodd` fields.

```
ff = λieio:{iseven:Nat→Bool, isodd:Nat→Bool}.
       {iseven = λx:Nat.
                     if iszero x then true
                     else ieio.isodd (pred x),
        isodd = λx:Nat.
                     if iszero x then false
                     else ieio.iseven (pred x)};
```

▸ ff : {iseven:Nat→Bool,isodd:Nat→Bool} →
        {iseven:Nat→Bool, isodd:Nat→Bool}

Forming the fixed point of the function `ff` gives us a record of two functions

```
r = fix ff;
```

▸ r : {iseven:Nat→Bool, isodd:Nat→Bool}

and projecting the first of these gives us the iseven function itself:

```
iseven = r.iseven;
```

▸ iseven : Nat → Bool

```
iseven 7;
```

▸ false : Bool

The ability to form the fixed point of a function of type T→T for any T has some surprising consequences. In particular, it implies that *every* type is inhabited by some term. To see this, observe that, for every type T, we can define a function diverge$_T$ as follows:

```
diverge_T = λ_:Unit. fix (λx:T.x);
```

▸ diverge$_T$: Unit → T

Whenever diverge$_T$ is applied to a unit argument, we get a non-terminating evaluation sequence in which E-FixBeta is applied over and over, always yielding the same term. That is, for every type T, the term diverge$_T$ unit is an *undefined element* of T.

One final refinement that we may consider is introducing more convenient concrete syntax for the common case where what we want to do is to bind a variable to the result of a recursive definition. In most high-level languages, the first definition of iseven above would be written something like this:

```
letrec iseven : Nat→Bool =
  λx:Nat.
    if iszero x then true
    else if iszero (pred x) then false
    else iseven (pred (pred x))
in
  iseven 7;
```

▸ false : Bool

The recursive binding construct letrec is easily defined as a derived form:

$$\text{letrec } x{:}T_1{=}t_1 \text{ in } t_2 \quad \overset{\text{def}}{=} \quad \text{let } x = \text{fix } (\lambda x{:}T_1.t_1) \text{ in } t_2$$

11.11.2   EXERCISE [⋆]: Rewrite your definitions of plus, times, and factorial from Exercise 11.11.1 using letrec instead of fix.   □

Further information on fixed point operators can be found in Klop (1980) and Winskel (1993).

11.12 Lists

The typing features we have seen can be classified into *base types* like Bool
and Unit, and *type constructors* like → and × that build new types from
old ones. Another useful type constructor is List. For every type T, the type
List T describes finite-length lists whose elements are drawn from T.

Figure 11-13 summarizes the syntax, semantics, and typing rules for lists.
Except for syntactic differences (List T instead of T list, etc.) and the explicit type annotations on all the syntactic forms in our presentation,[9] these
lists are essentially identical to those found in ML and other functional languages. The empty list (with elements of type T) is written nil[T]. The list
formed by adding a new element t_1 (of type T) to the front of a list t_2 is written cons[T] t_1 t_2. The head and tail of a list t are written head[T] t and
tail[T] t. The boolean predicate isnil[T] t yields true iff t is empty.[10]

11.12.1   EXERCISE [★★★]: Verify that the progress and preservation theorems hold for
the simply typed lambda-calculus with booleans and lists.   □

11.12.2   EXERCISE [★★]: The presentation of lists here includes many type annotations
that are not really needed, in the sense that the typing rules can easily derive
the annotations from context. (These annotations are intended to ease comparison with the encoding of lists in §23.4.) Can *all* the type annotations be
deleted?   □

---

9. Most of these explicit annotations could actually be omitted (EXERCISE [★, ↛]: which cannot);
.

10. We adopt the "head/tail/isnil presentation" of lists here for simplicity. From the perspective of language design, it is arguably better to treat lists as a datatype and use case
expressions for destructing them, since more programming errors can be caught as type errors
this way.

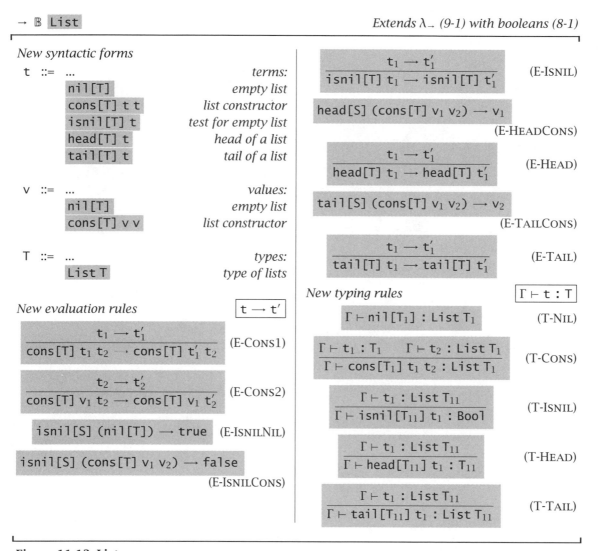

Figure 11-13: Lists

12 *Normalization*

In this chapter, we consider another fundamental theoretical property of the pure simply typed lambda-calculus: the fact that the evaluation of a well-typed program is guaranteed to halt in a finite number of steps—i.e., every well-typed term is *normalizable*.

Unlike the type-safety properties we have considered so far, the normalization property does not extend to full-blown programming languages, because these languages nearly always extend the simply typed lambda-calculus with constructs such as general recursion (§11.11) or recursive types (Chapter 20) that can be used to write nonterminating programs. However, the issue of normalization will reappear at the level of *types* when we discuss the metatheory of System F_ω in §30-3: in this system, the language of types effectively contains a copy of the simply typed lambda-calculus, and the termination of the typechecking algorithm will hinge on the fact that a "normalization" operation on type expressions is guaranteed to terminate.

Another reason for studying normalization proofs is that they are some of the most beautiful—and mind-blowing—mathematics to be found in the type theory literature, often (as here) involving the fundamental proof technique of *logical relations*.

Some readers may prefer to skip this chapter on a first reading; doing so will not cause any problems in later chapters. (A full table of chapter dependencies appears on page xvi.)

12.1 Normalization for Simple Types

The calculus we shall consider here is the simply typed lambda-calculus over a single base type A. Normalization for this calculus is not entirely trivial to prove, since each reduction of a term can duplicate redexes in subterms.

The language studied in this chapter is the simply typed lambda-calculus (Figure 9-1) with a single base type A (11-1).

12.1.1   EXERCISE [⋆]: Where do we fail if we attempt to prove normalization by a straightforward induction on the size of a well-typed term?   □

The key issue here (as in many proofs by induction) is finding a strong enough induction hypothesis. To this end, we begin by defining, for each type T, a set R_T of closed terms of type T. We regard these sets as predicates and write $R_T(t)$ for $t \in R_T$.[1]

12.1.2   DEFINITION:

- $R_A(t)$ iff t halts.

- $R_{T_1 \to T_2}(t)$ iff t halts and, whenever $R_{T_1}(s)$, we have $R_{T_2}(t\ s)$.   □

This definition gives us the strengthened induction hypothesis that we need. Our primary goal is to show that all *programs*—i.e., all closed terms of base type—halt. But closed terms of base type can contain subterms of functional type, so we need to know something about these as well. Moreover, it is not enough to know that these subterms halt, because the application of a normalized function to a normalized argument involves a substitution, which may enable more evaluation steps. So we need a stronger condition for terms of functional type: not only should they halt themselves, but, when applied to halting arguments, they should yield halting results.

The form of Definition 12.1.2 is characteristic of the *logical relations* proof technique. (Since we are just dealing with unary relations here, we should more properly say *logical predicates*.) If we want to prove some property *P* of all closed terms of type A, we proceed by proving, by induction on types, that all terms of type A *possess* property *P*, all terms of type A→A *preserve* property *P*, all terms of type (A→A)→(A→A) *preserve the property of preserving* property *P*, and so on. We do this by defining a family of predicates, indexed by types. For the base type A, the predicate is just *P*. For functional types, it says that the function should map values satisfying the predicate at the input type to values satisfying the predicate at the output type.

We use this definition to carry out the proof of normalization in two steps. First, we observe that every element of every set R_T is normalizable. Then we show that every well-typed term of type T is an element of R_T.

The first step is immediate from the definition of R_T:

12.1.3   LEMMA: If $R_T(t)$, then t halts.   □

The second step is broken into two lemmas. First, we remark that membership in R_T is invariant under evaluation.

---

1. The sets R_T are sometimes called *saturated sets* or *reducibility candidates*.

12.1.4   LEMMA: If $t : T$ and $t \longrightarrow t'$, then $R_T(t)$ iff $R_T(t')$.   □

Proof: By induction on the structure of the type T. Note, first, that it is clear that t halts iff t′ does. If T = A, there is nothing more to show. Suppose, on the other hand, that $T = T_1 \rightarrow T_2$ for some T_1 and T_2. For the "only if" direction ($\Longrightarrow$) suppose that $R_T(t)$ and that $R_{T_1}(s)$ for some arbitrary $s : T_1$. By definition we have $R_{T_2}(t\ s)$. But $t\ s \longrightarrow t'\ s$, from which the induction hypothesis for type T_2 gives us $R_{T_2}(t'\ s)$. Since this holds for an arbitrary s, the definition of R_T gives us $R_T(t')$. The argument for the "if" direction ($\Longleftarrow$) is analogous.   □

Next, we want to show that every term of type T belongs to R_T. Here, the induction will be on typing derivations (it would be surprising to see a proof about well-typed terms that did not somewhere involve induction on typing derivations!). The only technical difficulty here is in dealing with the λ-abstraction case. Since we are arguing by induction, the demonstration that a term $\lambda x : T_1 . t_2$ belongs to $R_{T_1 \rightarrow T_2}$ should involve applying the induction hypothesis to show that t_2 belongs to R_{T_2}. But R_{T_2} is defined to be a set of *closed* terms, while t_2 may contain x free, so this does not make sense.

This problem is resolved by using a standard trick to suitably generalize the induction hypothesis: instead of proving a statement involving a closed term, we generalize it to cover all closed *instances* of an open term t.

12.1.5   LEMMA: If $x_1 : T_1, \ldots, x_n : T_n \vdash t : T$ and $v_1 \ldots, v_n$ are closed values of types $T_1 \ldots T_n$ with $R_{T_i}(v_i)$ for each i, then $R_T([x_1 \mapsto v_1] \cdots [x_n \mapsto v_n]t)$.   □

Proof: By induction on a derivation of $x_1 : T_1, \ldots, x_n : T_n \vdash t : T$. (The most interesting case is the one for abstraction.)

Case T-VAR: $t = x_i$ $T = T_i$

Immediate.

Case T-ABS: $t = \lambda x : S_1 . s_2$ $x_1 : T_1, \ldots, x_n : T_n, x : S_1 \vdash s_2 : S_2$
$T = S_1 \rightarrow S_2$

Obviously, $[x_1 \mapsto v_1] \cdots [x_n \mapsto v_n]t$ evaluates to a value, since it is a value already. What remains to show is that $R_{S_2}(([x_1 \mapsto v_1] \cdots [x_n \mapsto v_n]t)\ s)$ for any $s : S_1$ such that $R_{S_1}(s)$. So suppose s is such a term. By Lemma 12.1.3, we have $s \longrightarrow^* v$ for some v. By Lemma 12.1.4, $R_{S_1}(v)$. Now, by the induction hypothesis, $R_{S_2}([x_1 \mapsto v_1] \cdots [x_n \mapsto v_n][x \mapsto v]s_2)$. But

$$(\lambda x : S_1 . [x_1 \mapsto v_1] \cdots [x_n \mapsto v_n]s_2)\ s$$
$$\longrightarrow^* [x_1 \mapsto v_1] \cdots [x_n \mapsto v_n][x \mapsto v]s_2,$$

from which Lemma 12.1.4 gives us

$$R_{S_2}((\lambda x : S_1 . [x_1 \mapsto v_1] \cdots [x_n \mapsto v_n]s_2)\ s),$$

that is, $R_{S_2}((([x_1 \mapsto v_1] \cdots [x_n \mapsto v_n](\lambda x : S_1 . s_2))\ s)$. Since s was chosen arbitrarily, the definition of $R_{S_1 \to S_2}$ gives us

$$R_{S_1 \to S_2}([x_1 \mapsto v_1] \cdots [x_n \mapsto v_n](\lambda x : S_1 . s_2)).$$

Case T-App: $t = t_1\ t_2$
$\quad\quad\quad\quad x_1 : T_1, \ldots, x_n : T_n \vdash t_1 : T_{11} \to T_{12}$
$\quad\quad\quad\quad x_1 : T_1, \ldots, x_n : T_n \vdash t_2 : T_{11}$
$\quad\quad\quad\quad T = T_{12}$

The induction hypothesis gives us $R_{T_{11} \to T_{12}}([x_1 \mapsto v_1] \cdots [x_n \mapsto v_n]t_1)$ and $R_{T_{11}}([x_1 \mapsto v_1] \cdots [x_n \mapsto v_n]t_2)$. By the definition of $R_{T_{11} \to T_{12}}$,

$$R_{T_{12}}(([x_1 \mapsto v_1] \cdots [x_n \mapsto v_n]t_1)\ ([x_1 \mapsto v_1] \cdots [x_n \mapsto v_n]t_2)),$$

i.e., $R_{T_{12}}([x_1 \mapsto v_1] \cdots [x_n \mapsto v_n](t_1\ t_2)),$.   □

We now obtain the normalization property as a corollary, simply by taking the term t to be closed in Lemma 12.1.5 and then recalling that all the elements of R_T are normalizing, for every T.

12.1.6   THEOREM [NORMALIZATION]: If $\vdash t : T$, then t is normalizable.   □

Proof: $R_T(t)$ by Lemma 12.1.5; t is therefore normalizable by Lemma 12.1.3. □

12.1.7   EXERCISE [RECOMMENDED, ★★★]: Extend the proof technique from this chapter to show that the simply typed lambda-calculus remains normalizing when extended with booleans (Figure 3-1) and products (Figure 11-5).   □

12.2   Notes

Normalization properties are most commonly formulated in the theoretical literature as *strong normalization* for calculi with full (non-deterministic) beta-reduction. The standard proof method was invented by Tait (1967), generalized to System F (cf. Chapter 23) by Girard (1972, 1989), and later simplified by Tait (1975). The presentation used here is an adaptation of Tait's method to the call-by-value setting, due to Martin Hofmann (private communication). The classical references on the logical relations proof technique are Howard (1973), Tait (1967), Friedman (1975), Plotkin (1973, 1980), and Statman (1982, 1985a, 1985b). It is also discussed in many texts on semantics, for example those by Mitchell (1996) and Gunter (1992).

Tait's strong normalization proof corresponds exactly to an algorithm for evaluating simply typed terms, known as *normalization by evaluation* or *type-directed partial evaluation* (Berger, 1993; Danvy, 1998); also see Berger and Schwichtenberg (1991), Filinski (1999), Filinski (2001), Reynolds (1998a).

13 *References*

So far, we have considered a variety of *pure* language features, including functional abstraction, basic types such as numbers and booleans, and structured types such as records and variants. These features form the backbone of most programming languages—including purely functional languages such as Haskell, "mostly functional" languages such as ML, imperative languages such as C, and object-oriented languages such as Java.

Most practical programming languages also include various *impure* features that cannot be described in the simple semantic framework we have used so far. In particular, besides just yielding results, evaluation of terms in these languages may assign to mutable variables (reference cells, arrays, mutable record fields, etc.), perform input and output to files, displays, or network connections, make non-local transfers of control via exceptions, jumps, or continuations, engage in inter-process synchronization and communication, and so on. In the literature on programming languages, such "side effects" of computation are more generally referred to as *computational effects*.

In this chapter, we'll see how one sort of computational effect—mutable references—can be added to the calculi we have studied. The main extension will be dealing explicitly with a *store* (or *heap*). This extension is straightforward to define; the most interesting part is the refinement we need to make to the statement of the type preservation theorem (13.5.3). We consider another kind of effect—exceptions and non-local transfer of control—in Chapter 14.

13.1 Introduction

Nearly every programming language[1] provides some form of *assignment* operation that changes the contents of a previously allocated piece of storage.

The system studied in this chapter is the simply typed lambda-calculus with `Unit` and references (Figure 13-1). The associated OCaml implementation is `fullref`.

1. Even "purely functional" languages such as Haskell, via extensions such as *monads*.

In some languages—notably ML and its relatives—the mechanisms for name-binding and those for assignment are kept separate. We can have a variable x whose value is the number 5, or a variable y whose value is a *reference* (or *pointer*) to a mutable cell whose current contents is 5, and the difference is visible to the programmer. We can add x to another number, but not assign to it. We can use y directly to assign a new value to the cell that it points to (by writing y:=84), but we cannot use it directly as an argument to plus. Instead, we must explicitly *dereference* it, writing !y to obtain its current contents. In most other languages—in particular, in all members of the C family, including Java—every variable name refers to a mutable cell, and the operation of dereferencing a variable to obtain its current contents is implicit.[2]

For purposes of formal study, it is useful to keep these mechanisms separate;[3] our development in this chapter will closely follow ML's model. Applying the lessons learned here to C-like languages is a straightforward matter of collapsing some distinctions and rendering certain operations such as dereferencing implicit instead of explicit.

Basics

The basic operations on references are *allocation, dereferencing,* and *assignment.* To allocate a reference, we use the ref operator, providing an initial value for the new cell.

```
r = ref 5;
```

▶ r : Ref Nat

The response from the typechecker indicates that the value of r is a reference to a cell that will always contain a number. To read the current value of this cell, we use the dereferencing operator !.

```
!r;
```

▶ 5 : Nat

To change the value stored in the cell, we use the assignment operator.

---

2. Strictly speaking, most variables of type T in C or Java should actually be thought of as pointers to cells holding values of type Option(T), reflecting the fact that the contents of a variable can be either a proper value or the special value null.

3. There are also good arguments that this separation is desirable from the perspective of language design. Making the use of mutable cells an explicit choice rather than the default encourages a mostly functional programming style where references are used sparingly; this practice tends to make programs significantly easier to write, maintain, and reason about, especially in the presence of features like concurrency.

```
r := 7;
```

▸ unit : Unit

(The result of the assignment is the trivial unit value; see §11.2.) If we dereference r again, we see the updated value.

```
!r;
```

▸ 7 : Nat

Side Effects and Sequencing

The fact that the result of an assignment expression is the trivial value unit
fits nicely with the *sequencing* notation defined in §11.3, allowing us to write

```
(r:=succ(!r); !r);
```

▸ 8 : Nat

instead of the equivalent, but more cumbersome,

```
(λ_:Unit. !r) (r := succ(!r));
```

▸ 9 : Nat

to evaluate two expressions in order and return the value of the second. Restricting the type of the first expression to Unit helps the typechecker to
catch some silly errors by permitting us to throw away the first value only if
it is really guaranteed to be trivial.

Notice that, if the second expression is also an assignment, then the type
of the whole sequence will be Unit, so we can validly place it to the left of
another ; to build longer sequences of assignments:

```
(r:=succ(!r); r:=succ(!r); r:=succ(!r); r:=succ(!r); !r);
```

▸ 13 : Nat

References and Aliasing

It is important to bear in mind the difference between the *reference* that is
bound to r and the *cell* in the store that is pointed to by this reference.

If we make a copy of r, for example by binding its value to another variable
s,

   s = r;

▸ s : Ref Nat

what gets copied is only the reference (the *arrow* in the diagram), not the cell:

We can verify this by assigning a new value into s

   s := 82;

▸ unit : Unit

and reading it out via r:

   !r;

▸ 82 : Nat

The references r and s are said to be *aliases* for the same cell.

13.1.1   EXERCISE [⋆]: Draw a similar diagram showing the effects of evaluating the
expressions a = {ref 0, ref 0} and b = (λx:Ref Nat. {x,x}) (ref 0).   □

Shared State

The possibility of aliasing can make programs with references quite tricky
to reason about. For example, the expression (r:=1; r:=!s), which assigns
1 to r and then immediately overwrites it with s's current value, has exactly
the same effect as the single assignment r:=!s, *unless* we write it in a context
where r and s are aliases for the same cell.

   Of course, aliasing is also a large part of what makes references useful. In
particular, it allows us to set up "implicit communication channels"—shared
state—between different parts of a program. For example, suppose we define
a reference cell and two functions that manipulate its contents:

   c = ref 0;

▸ c : Ref Nat

```
incc = λx:Unit. (c := succ (!c); !c);
```

▸ incc : Unit → Nat

```
decc = λx:Unit. (c := pred (!c); !c);
```

▸ decc : Unit → Nat

Calling incc

```
incc unit;
```

▸ 1 : Nat

results in changes to c that can be observed by calling decc:

```
decc unit;
```

▸ 0 : Nat

If we package incc and decc together into a record

```
o = {i = incc, d = decc};
```

▸ o : {i:Unit→Nat, d:Unit→Nat}

then we can pass this whole structure around as a unit and use its components to perform incrementing and decrementing operations on the shared piece of state in c. In effect, we have constructed a simple kind of *object*. This idea is developed in detail in Chapter 18.

References to Compound Types

A reference cell need not contain just a number: the primitives above allow us to create references to values of any type, including functions. For example, we can use references to functions to give a (not very efficient) implementation of arrays of numbers, as follows. Write NatArray for the type Ref (Nat→Nat).

```
NatArray = Ref (Nat→Nat);
```

To build a new array, we allocate a reference cell and fill it with a function that, when given an index, always returns 0.

```
newarray = λ_:Unit. ref (λn:Nat.0);
```

▸ newarray : Unit → NatArray

To look up an element of an array, we simply apply the function to the desired index.

```
lookup = λa:NatArray. λn:Nat. (!a) n;
▶ lookup : NatArray → Nat → Nat
```

The interesting part of the encoding is the `update` function. It takes an array, an index, and a new value to be stored at that index, and does its job by creating (and storing in the reference) a new function that, when it is asked for the value at this very index, returns the new value that was given to `update`, and on all other indices passes the lookup to the function that was previously stored in the reference.

```
update = λa:NatArray. λm:Nat. λv:Nat.
            let oldf = !a in
            a := (λn:Nat. if equal m n then v else oldf n);
▶ update : NatArray → Nat → Nat → Unit
```

13.1.2   EXERCISE [★★]: If we defined `update` more compactly like this

```
update = λa:NatArray. λm:Nat. λv:Nat.
            a := (λn:Nat. if equal m n then v else (!a) n);
```

would it behave the same?   □

References to values containing other references can also be very useful, allowing us to define data structures such as mutable lists and trees. (Such structures generally also involve *recursive types,* which we introduce in Chapter 20.)

Garbage Collection

A last issue that we should mention before we move on formalizing references is storage *de*allocation. We have not provided any primitives for freeing reference cells when they are no longer needed. Instead, like many modern languages (including ML and Java) we rely on the run-time system to perform *garbage collection,* collecting and reusing cells that can no longer be reached by the program. This is *not* just a question of taste in language design: it is extremely difficult to achieve type safety in the presence of an explicit deallocation operation. The reason for this is the familiar *dangling reference* problem: we allocate a cell holding a number, save a reference to it in some data structure, use it for a while, then deallocate it and allocate a new cell holding a boolean, possibly reusing the same storage. Now we can have two names for the same storage cell—one with type `Ref Nat` and the other with type `Ref Bool`.

13.1.3   EXERCISE [★★]: Show how this can lead to a violation of type safety.   □

13.2   Typing

The typing rules for ref, :=, and ! follow straightforwardly from the behaviors we have given them.

$$\frac{\Gamma \vdash t_1 : T_1}{\Gamma \vdash \text{ref } t_1 : \text{Ref } T_1} \qquad (\text{T-Ref})$$

$$\frac{\Gamma \vdash t_1 : \text{Ref } T_1}{\Gamma \vdash \text{!}t_1 : T_1} \qquad (\text{T-Deref})$$

$$\frac{\Gamma \vdash t_1 : \text{Ref } T_1 \qquad \Gamma \vdash t_2 : T_1}{\Gamma \vdash t_1\text{:=}t_2 : \text{Unit}} \qquad (\text{T-Assign})$$

13.3   Evaluation

A more subtle aspect of the treatment of references appears when we consider how to formalize their operational behavior. One way to see why is to ask, "What should be the *values* of type Ref T?" The crucial observation that we need to take into account is that evaluating a ref operator should *do* something—namely, allocate some storage—and the result of the operation should be a reference to this storage.

What, then, is a reference?

The run-time store in most programming language implementations is essentially just a big array of bytes. The run-time system keeps track of which parts of this array are currently in use; when we need to allocate a new reference cell, we allocate a large enough segment from the free region of the store (4 bytes for integer cells, 8 bytes for cells storing Floats, etc.), mark it as being used, and return the index (typically, a 32- or 64-bit integer) of the start of the newly allocated region. These indices are references.

For present purposes, there is no need to be quite so concrete. We can think of the store as an array of *values,* rather than an array of bytes, abstracting away from the different sizes of the run-time representations of different values. Furthermore, we can abstract away from the fact that references (i.e., indexes into this array) are numbers. We take references to be elements of some uninterpreted set $\mathcal{L}$ of *store locations,* and take the store to be simply a partial function from locations l to values. We use the metavariable μ to range over stores. A reference, then, is a location—an abstract index into the store. We'll use the word *location* instead of *reference* or *pointer* from now on to emphasize this abstract quality.[4]

---

4. Treating locations abstractly in this way will prevent us from modeling the *pointer arith-*

Next, we need to extend our operational semantics to take stores into account. Since the result of evaluating an expression will in general depend on the contents of the store in which it is evaluated, the evaluation rules should take not just a term but also a store as argument. Furthermore, since the evaluation of a term may cause side effects on the store that may affect the evaluation of other terms in the future, the evaluation rules need to return a new store. Thus, the shape of the single-step evaluation relation changes from $t \longrightarrow t'$ to $t \mid \mu \longrightarrow t' \mid \mu'$, where μ and μ' are the starting and ending states of the store. In effect, we have enriched our notion of *abstract machines,* so that a machine state is not just a program counter (represented as a term), but a program counter plus the current contents of the store.

To carry through this change, we first need to augment all of our existing evaluation rules with stores:

$$(\lambda x{:}T_{11}.t_{12})\ v_2 \mid \mu \longrightarrow [x \mapsto v_2]t_{12} \mid \mu \qquad \text{(E-AppAbs)}$$

$$\frac{t_1 \mid \mu \longrightarrow t_1' \mid \mu'}{t_1\ t_2 \mid \mu \longrightarrow t_1'\ t_2 \mid \mu'} \qquad \text{(E-App1)}$$

$$\frac{t_2 \mid \mu \longrightarrow t_2' \mid \mu'}{v_1\ t_2 \mid \mu \longrightarrow v_1\ t_2' \mid \mu'} \qquad \text{(E-App2)}$$

Note that the first rule here returns the store μ unchanged: function application, in itself, has no side effects. The other two rules simply propagate side effects from premise to conclusion.

Next, we make a small addition to the *syntax* of our terms. The result of evaluating a `ref` expression will be a fresh location, so we need to include locations in the set of things that can be results of evaluation—i.e., in the set of values:

v ::=		*values:*
	$\lambda x{:}T.t$	*abstraction value*
	`unit`	*unit value*
	l	*store location*

Since all values are also terms, this means that the set of terms should include locations.

---

metic found in low-level languages such as C. This limitation is intentional. While pointer arithmetic is occasionally very useful (especially for implementing low-level components of run-time systems, such as garbage collectors), it cannot be tracked by most type systems: knowing that location n in the store contains a `Float` doesn't tell us anything useful about the type of location $n + 4$. In C, pointer arithmetic is a notorious source of type safety violations.

t	::=		*terms:*
	x		*variable*
	λx:T.t		*abstraction*
	t t		*application*
	unit		*constant* unit
	ref t		*reference creation*
	!t		*dereference*
	t:=t		*assignment*
	l		*store location*

Of course, making this extension to the syntax of terms does not mean that we intend *programmers* to write terms involving explicit, concrete locations: such terms will arise only as intermediate results of evaluation. In effect, the term language in this chapter should be thought of as formalizing an *intermediate language,* some of whose features are not made available to programmers directly.

In terms of this expanded syntax, we can state evaluation rules for the new constructs that manipulate locations and the store. First, to evaluate a dereferencing expression $!t_1$, we must first reduce t_1 until it becomes a value:

$$\frac{t_1 \mid \mu \longrightarrow t_1' \mid \mu'}{!t_1 \mid \mu \longrightarrow !t_1' \mid \mu'} \qquad \text{(E-DEREF)}$$

Once t_1 has finished reducing, we should have an expression of the form $!l$, where l is some location. A term that attempts to dereference any other sort of value, such as a function or unit, is erroneous. The evaluation rules simply get stuck in this case. The type safety properties in §13.5 assure us that well-typed terms will never misbehave in this way.

$$\frac{\mu(l) = v}{!l \mid \mu \longrightarrow v \mid \mu} \qquad \text{(E-DEREFLOC)}$$

Next, to evaluate an assignment expression $t_1:=t_2$, we must first evaluate t_1 until it becomes a value (i.e., a location),

$$\frac{t_1 \mid \mu \longrightarrow t_1' \mid \mu'}{t_1:=t_2 \mid \mu \longrightarrow t_1':=t_2 \mid \mu'} \qquad \text{(E-ASSIGN1)}$$

and then evaluate t_2 until it becomes a value (of any sort):

$$\frac{t_2 \mid \mu \longrightarrow t_2' \mid \mu'}{v_1:=t_2 \mid \mu \longrightarrow v_1:=t_2' \mid \mu'} \qquad \text{(E-ASSIGN2)}$$

Once we have finished with t_1 and t_2, we have an expression of the form $l:=v_2$, which we execute by updating the store to make location l contain v_2:

$$l:=v_2 \mid \mu \longrightarrow \text{unit} \mid [l \mapsto v_2]\mu \qquad \text{(E-ASSIGN)}$$

(The notation $[l \mapsto v_2]\mu$ here means "the store that maps l to v_2 and maps all other locations to the same thing as μ." Note that the term resulting from this evaluation step is just unit; the interesting result is the updated store.)

Finally, to evaluate an expression of the form ref t_1, we first evaluate t_1 until it becomes a value:

$$\frac{t_1 \mid \mu \longrightarrow t_1' \mid \mu'}{\text{ref } t_1 \mid \mu \longrightarrow \text{ref } t_1' \mid \mu'} \qquad \text{(E-REF)}$$

Then, to evaluate the ref itself, we choose a fresh location l (i.e., a location that is not already part of the domain of μ) and yield a new store that extends μ with the new binding $l \mapsto v_1$.

$$\frac{l \notin dom(\mu)}{\text{ref } v_1 \mid \mu \longrightarrow l \mid (\mu, l \mapsto v_1)} \qquad \text{(E-REFV)}$$

The term resulting from this step is the name l of the newly allocated location.

Note that these evaluation rules do not perform any kind of garbage collection: we simply allow the store to keep growing without bound as evaluation proceeds. This does not affect the correctness of the results of evaluation (after all, the definition of "garbage" is precisely parts of the store that are no longer reachable and so cannot play any further role in evaluation), but it means that a naive implementation of our evaluator will sometimes run out of memory where a more sophisticated evaluator would be able to continue by reusing locations whose contents have become garbage.

13.3.1   EXERCISE [★★★]: How might our evaluation rules be refined to model garbage collection? What theorem would we then need to prove, to argue that this refinement is correct?   □

13.4   Store Typings

Having extended our syntax and evaluation rules to accommodate references, our last job is to write down typing rules for the new constructs—and, of course, to check that they are sound. Naturally, the key question is, "What is the type of a location?"

When we evaluate a term containing concrete locations, the type of the result depends on the contents of the store that we start with. For example, if we evaluate the term $!l_2$ in the store $(l_1 \mapsto \text{unit}, l_2 \mapsto \text{unit})$, the result is unit; if we evaluate the same term in the store $(l_1 \mapsto \text{unit}, l_2 \mapsto \lambda x{:}\text{Unit}.x)$, the result is $\lambda x{:}\text{Unit}.x$. With respect to the former store, the location l_2 has type Unit, and with respect to the latter it has type Unit→Unit. This observation leads us immediately to a first attempt at a typing rule for locations:

$$\frac{\Gamma \vdash \mu(l) : \mathsf{T}_1}{\Gamma \vdash l : \mathsf{Ref}\,\mathsf{T}_1}$$

That is, to find the type of a location l, we look up the current contents of l in the store and calculate the type T_1 of the contents. The type of the location is then $\mathsf{Ref}\,\mathsf{T}_1$.

Having begun in this way, we need to go a little further to reach a consistent state. In effect, by making the type of a term depend on the store, we have changed the typing relation from a three-place relation (between contexts, terms, and types) to a four-place relation (between contexts, *stores,* terms, and types). Since the store is, intuitively, part of the context in which we calculate the type of a term, let's write this four-place relation with the store to the left of the turnstile: $\Gamma \mid \mu \vdash \mathsf{t} : \mathsf{T}$. Our rule for typing references now has the form

$$\frac{\Gamma \mid \mu \vdash \mu(l) : \mathsf{T}_1}{\Gamma \mid \mu \vdash l : \mathsf{Ref}\,\mathsf{T}_1}$$

and all the rest of the typing rules in the system are extended similarly with stores. The other rules do not need to do anything interesting with their stores—just pass them from premise to conclusion.

However, there are two problems with this rule. First, typechecking is rather inefficient, since calculating the type of a location l involves calculating the type of the current contents v of l. If l appears many times in a term t, we will re-calculate the type of v many times in the course of constructing a typing derivation for t. Worse, if v itself contains locations, then we will have to recalculate *their* types each time they appear. For example, if the store contains

$(l_1 \mapsto \lambda\mathsf{x{:}Nat.}\ 999,$
$l_2 \mapsto \lambda\mathsf{x{:}Nat.}\ (!l_1)\ \mathsf{x},$
$l_3 \mapsto \lambda\mathsf{x{:}Nat.}\ (!l_2)\ \mathsf{x},$
$l_4 \mapsto \lambda\mathsf{x{:}Nat.}\ (!l_3)\ \mathsf{x},$
$l_5 \mapsto \lambda\mathsf{x{:}Nat.}\ (!l_4)\ \mathsf{x}),$

then calculating the type of l_5 involves calculating those of l_4, l_3, l_2, and l_1.

Second, the proposed typing rule for locations may not allow us to derive anything at all, if the store contains a *cycle*. For example, there is no finite typing derivation for the location l_2 with respect to the store

$(l_1 \mapsto \lambda\mathsf{x{:}Nat.}\ (!l_2)\ \mathsf{x},$
$l_2 \mapsto \lambda\mathsf{x{:}Nat.}\ (!l_1)\ \mathsf{x}),$

since calculating a type for l_2 requires finding the type of l_1, which in turn involves l_1, etc. Cyclic reference structures do arise in practice (e.g., they can

be used for building doubly linked lists), and we would like our type system
to be able to deal with them.

13.4.1   EXERCISE [⋆]: Can you find a term whose evaluation will create this particular
cyclic store?   □

Both of these problems arise from the fact that our proposed typing rule
for locations requires us to recalculate the type of a location every time we
mention it in a term. But this, intuitively, should not be necessary. After all,
when a location is first created, we know the type of the initial value that
we are storing into it. Moreover, although we may later store other values
into this location, those other values will always have the same type as the
initial one. In other words, we always have in mind a single, definite type for
every location in the store, which is fixed when the location is allocated. These
intended types can be collected together as a *store typing*—a finite function
mapping locations to types. We'll use the metavariable Σ to range over such
functions.

Suppose we are *given* a store typing Σ describing the store μ in which some
term t will be evaluated. Then we can use Σ to calculate the type of the result
of t without ever looking directly at μ. For example, if Σ is ($l_1 \mapsto$ Unit, $l_2 \mapsto$
Unit→Unit), then we may immediately infer that $!l_2$ has type Unit→Unit.
More generally, the typing rule for locations can be reformulated in terms of
store typings like this:

$$\frac{\Sigma(l) = \mathsf{T}_1}{\Gamma \mid \Sigma \vdash l : \mathsf{Ref}\,\mathsf{T}_1} \qquad\qquad \text{(T-Loc)}$$

Typing is again a four-place relation, but it is parameterized on a store *typing*
rather than a concrete store. The rest of the typing rules are analogously
augmented with store typings.

Of course, these typing rules will accurately predict the results of evaluation only if the concrete store used during evaluation actually conforms to the
store typing that we assume for purposes of typechecking. This proviso exactly parallels the situation with free variables in all the calculi we have seen
up to this point: the substitution lemma (9.3.8) promises us that, if $\Gamma \vdash t : \mathsf{T}$,
then we can replace the free variables in t with values of the types listed in
Γ to obtain a closed term of type T, which, by the type preservation theorem
(9.3.9) will evaluate to a final result of type T if it yields any result at all. We
will see in §13.5 how to formalize an analogous intuition for stores and store
typings.

Finally, note that, for purposes of typechecking the terms that programmers actually write, we do not need to do anything tricky to guess what store
typing we should use. As we remarked above, concrete location constants

arise only in terms that are the intermediate results of evaluation; they are not in the language that programmers write. Thus, we can simply typecheck the programmer's terms with respect to the *empty* store typing. As evaluation proceeds and new locations are created, we will always be able to see how to extend the store typing by looking at the type of the initial values being placed in newly allocated cells; this intuition is formalized in the statement of the type preservation theorem below (13.5.3).

Now that we have dealt with locations, the typing rules for the other new syntactic forms are quite straightforward. When we create a reference to a value of type T_1, the reference itself has type $Ref\ T_1$.

$$\frac{\Gamma \mid \Sigma \vdash t_1 : T_1}{\Gamma \mid \Sigma \vdash ref\ t_1 : Ref\ T_1} \qquad \text{(T-REF)}$$

Notice that we do not need to extend the store typing here, since the *name* of the new location will not be determined until run time, while Σ records only the association between already-allocated storage cells and their types.

Conversely, if t_1 evaluates to a location of type $Ref\ T_{11}$, then dereferencing t_1 is guaranteed to yield a value of type T_{11}.

$$\frac{\Gamma \mid \Sigma \vdash t_1 : Ref\ T_{11}}{\Gamma \mid \Sigma \vdash !t_1 : T_{11}} \qquad \text{(T-DEREF)}$$

Finally, if t_1 denotes a cell of type $Ref\ T_{11}$, then we can store t_2 into this cell as long as the type of t_2 is also T_{11}:

$$\frac{\Gamma \mid \Sigma \vdash t_1 : Ref\ T_{11} \qquad \Gamma \mid \Sigma \vdash t_2 : T_{11}}{\Gamma \mid \Sigma \vdash t_1 := t_2 : Unit} \qquad \text{(T-ASSIGN)}$$

Figure 13-1 summarizes the typing rules (and the syntax and evaluation rules, for easy reference) for the simply typed lambda-calculus with references.

13.5 Safety

Our final job in this chapter is to check that standard type safety properties continue to hold for the calculus with references. The progress theorem ("well-typed terms are not stuck") can be stated and proved almost as before (cf. 13.5.7); we just need to add a few straightforward cases to the proof, dealing with the new constructs. The preservation theorem is a bit more interesting, so let's look at it first.

Since we have extended both the evaluation relation (with initial and final stores) and the typing relation (with a store typing), we need to change the statement of preservation to include these parameters. Clearly, though, we

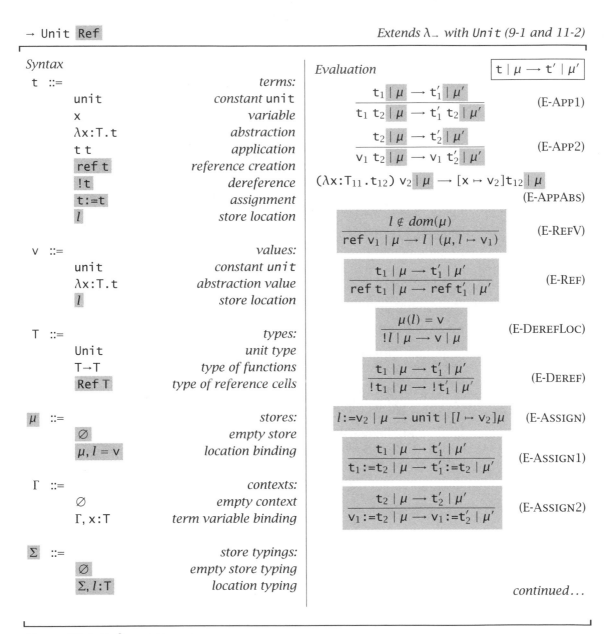

→ Unit Ref   *Extends λ→ with Unit (9-1 and 11-2)*

Syntax

t ::=   *terms:*
        unit   *constant* unit
        x   *variable*
        λx:T.t   *abstraction*
        t t   *application*
        ref t   *reference creation*
        !t   *dereference*
        t:=t   *assignment*
        l *store location*

v ::=   *values:*
        unit   *constant* unit
        λx:T.t   *abstraction value*
        l *store location*

T ::=   *types:*
        Unit   *unit type*
        T→T   *type of functions*
        Ref T   *type of reference cells*

μ ::=   *stores:*
        $\varnothing$ *empty store*
        $\mu, l = v$ *location binding*

Γ ::=   *contexts:*
        $\varnothing$ *empty context*
        Γ, x:T   *term variable binding*

Σ ::=   *store typings:*
        $\varnothing$ *empty store typing*
        Σ, l:T   *location typing*

Evaluation $\boxed{t \mid \mu \rightarrow t' \mid \mu'}$

$$\frac{t_1 \mid \mu \rightarrow t_1' \mid \mu'}{t_1\ t_2 \mid \mu \rightarrow t_1'\ t_2 \mid \mu'} \quad \text{(E-APP1)}$$

$$\frac{t_2 \mid \mu \rightarrow t_2' \mid \mu'}{v_1\ t_2 \mid \mu \rightarrow v_1\ t_2' \mid \mu'} \quad \text{(E-APP2)}$$

$$(\lambda x{:}T_{11}.t_{12})\ v_2 \mid \mu \rightarrow [x \mapsto v_2]t_{12} \mid \mu$$
$$\text{(E-APPABS)}$$

$$\frac{l \notin dom(\mu)}{\text{ref}\ v_1 \mid \mu \rightarrow l \mid (\mu, l \mapsto v_1)} \quad \text{(E-REFV)}$$

$$\frac{t_1 \mid \mu \rightarrow t_1' \mid \mu'}{\text{ref}\ t_1 \mid \mu \rightarrow \text{ref}\ t_1' \mid \mu'} \quad \text{(E-REF)}$$

$$\frac{\mu(l) = v}{!l \mid \mu \rightarrow v \mid \mu} \quad \text{(E-DEREFLOC)}$$

$$\frac{t_1 \mid \mu \rightarrow t_1' \mid \mu'}{!t_1 \mid \mu \rightarrow !t_1' \mid \mu'} \quad \text{(E-DEREF)}$$

$$l{:=}v_2 \mid \mu \rightarrow \text{unit} \mid [l \mapsto v_2]\mu \quad \text{(E-ASSIGN)}$$

$$\frac{t_1 \mid \mu \rightarrow t_1' \mid \mu'}{t_1{:=}t_2 \mid \mu \rightarrow t_1'{:=}t_2 \mid \mu'} \quad \text{(E-ASSIGN1)}$$

$$\frac{t_2 \mid \mu \rightarrow t_2' \mid \mu'}{v_1{:=}t_2 \mid \mu \rightarrow v_1{:=}t_2' \mid \mu'} \quad \text{(E-ASSIGN2)}$$

continued...

Figure 13-1: References

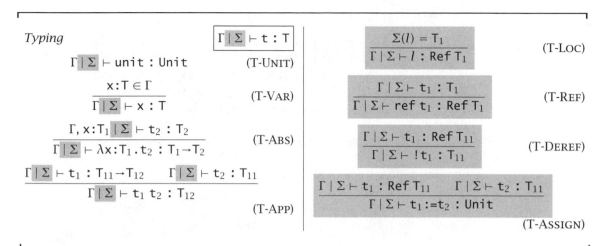

Typing $\boxed{\Gamma \mid \Sigma \vdash t : T}$

$$\Gamma \mid \Sigma \vdash \text{unit} : \text{Unit} \qquad \text{(T-UNIT)}$$

$$\frac{x{:}T \in \Gamma}{\Gamma \mid \Sigma \vdash x : T} \qquad \text{(T-VAR)}$$

$$\frac{\Gamma, x{:}T_1 \mid \Sigma \vdash t_2 : T_2}{\Gamma \mid \Sigma \vdash \lambda x{:}T_1.t_2 : T_1 {\rightarrow} T_2} \qquad \text{(T-ABS)}$$

$$\frac{\Gamma \mid \Sigma \vdash t_1 : T_{11}{\rightarrow}T_{12} \qquad \Gamma \mid \Sigma \vdash t_2 : T_{11}}{\Gamma \mid \Sigma \vdash t_1\, t_2 : T_{12}} \qquad \text{(T-APP)}$$

$$\frac{\Sigma(l) = T_1}{\Gamma \mid \Sigma \vdash l : \text{Ref } T_1} \qquad \text{(T-LOC)}$$

$$\frac{\Gamma \mid \Sigma \vdash t_1 : T_1}{\Gamma \mid \Sigma \vdash \text{ref } t_1 : \text{Ref } T_1} \qquad \text{(T-REF)}$$

$$\frac{\Gamma \mid \Sigma \vdash t_1 : \text{Ref } T_{11}}{\Gamma \mid \Sigma \vdash\, !t_1 : T_{11}} \qquad \text{(T-DEREF)}$$

$$\frac{\Gamma \mid \Sigma \vdash t_1 : \text{Ref } T_{11} \qquad \Gamma \mid \Sigma \vdash t_2 : T_{11}}{\Gamma \mid \Sigma \vdash t_1 := t_2 : \text{Unit}} \qquad \text{(T-ASSIGN)}$$

Figure 13-1: References (continued)

cannot just add stores and store typings without saying anything about how they are related.

If $\Gamma \mid \Sigma \vdash t : T$ and $t \mid \mu \longrightarrow t' \mid \mu'$, then $\Gamma \mid \Sigma \vdash t' : T$.   (*Wrong!*)

If we typecheck with respect to some set of assumptions about the types of the values in the store and then evaluate with respect to a store that violates these assumptions, the result will be disaster. The following requirement expresses the constraint we need.

13.5.1   DEFINITION: A store μ is said to be *well typed* with respect to a typing context Γ and a store typing Σ, written $\Gamma \mid \Sigma \vdash \mu$, if $dom(\mu) = dom(\Sigma)$ and $\Gamma \mid \Sigma \vdash \mu(l) : \Sigma(l)$ for every $l \in dom(\mu)$.   □

Intuitively, a store μ is consistent with a store typing Σ if every value in the store has the type predicted by the store typing.

13.5.2   EXERCISE [★★]: Can you find a context Γ, a store μ, and two different store typings Σ_1 and Σ_2 such that both $\Gamma \mid \Sigma_1 \vdash \mu$ and $\Gamma \mid \Sigma_2 \vdash \mu$?   □

We can now state something closer to the desired preservation property:

If

$$\Gamma \mid \Sigma \vdash t : T$$
$$t \mid \mu \longrightarrow t' \mid \mu'$$
$$\Gamma \mid \Sigma \vdash \mu$$

then $\Gamma \mid \Sigma \vdash t' : T.$ (*Less wrong.*)

This statement is fine for all of the evaluation rules except the allocation rule E-REFV. The problem is that this rule yields a store with a larger domain than the initial store, which falsifies the conclusion of the above statement: if μ' includes a binding for a fresh location l, then l cannot be in the domain of Σ, and it will not be the case that t' (which definitely mentions l) is typable under Σ.

Evidently, since the store can increase in size during evaluation, we need to allow the store typing to grow as well. This leads us to the final (correct) statement of the type preservation property:

13.5.3   THEOREM [PRESERVATION]: If

$$\Gamma \mid \Sigma \vdash t : T$$
$$\Gamma \mid \Sigma \vdash \mu$$
$$t \mid \mu \longrightarrow t' \mid \mu'$$

then, for some $\Sigma' \supseteq \Sigma$,

$$\Gamma \mid \Sigma' \vdash t' : T$$
$$\Gamma \mid \Sigma' \vdash \mu'. \qquad\qquad \square$$

Note that the preservation theorem merely asserts that there is *some* store typing $\Sigma' \supseteq \Sigma$ (i.e., agreeing with Σ on the values of all the old locations) such that the new term t' is well typed with respect to Σ'; it does not tell us exactly what Σ' is. It is intuitively clear, of course, that Σ' is either Σ or else it is exactly $(\Sigma, l \mapsto T_1)$, where l is a newly allocated location (the new element of the domain of μ') and T_1 is the type of the initial value bound to l in the extended store $(\mu, l \mapsto v_1)$, but stating this explicitly would complicate the statement of the theorem without actually making it any more useful: the weaker version above is already in the right form (because its conclusion implies its hypothesis) to "turn the crank" repeatedly and conclude that every *sequence* of evaluation steps preserves well-typedness. Combining this with the progress property, we obtain the usual guarantee that "well-typed programs never go wrong."

To prove preservation, we need a few technical lemmas. The first is an easy extension of the standard substitution lemma (9.3.8).

13.5.4   LEMMA [SUBSTITUTION]: If $\Gamma, x:S \mid \Sigma \vdash t : T$ and $\Gamma \mid \Sigma \vdash s : S$, then $\Gamma \mid \Sigma \vdash [x \mapsto s]t : T.$ $\square$

Proof: Just like Lemma 9.3.8. $\square$

The next lemma states that replacing the contents of a cell in the store with a new value of appropriate type does not change the overall type of the store.

13.5.5   LEMMA: If

$$\Gamma \mid \Sigma \vdash \mu$$
$$\Sigma(l) = \mathsf{T}$$
$$\Gamma \mid \Sigma \vdash \mathsf{v} : \mathsf{T}$$

then $\Gamma \mid \Sigma \vdash [l \mapsto \mathsf{v}]\mu$. □

Proof: Immediate from the definition of $\Gamma \mid \Sigma \vdash \mu$. □

Finally, we need a kind of weakening lemma for stores, stating that, if a store is extended with a new location, the extended store still allows us to assign types to all the same terms as the original.

13.5.6   LEMMA: If $\Gamma \mid \Sigma \vdash \mathsf{t} : \mathsf{T}$ and $\Sigma' \supseteq \Sigma$, then $\Gamma \mid \Sigma' \vdash \mathsf{t} : \mathsf{T}$. □

Proof: Easy induction. □

Now we can prove the main preservation theorem.

Proof of 13.5.3: Straightforward induction on evaluation derivations, using the lemmas above and the inversion property of the typing rules (a straightforward extension of 9.3.1). □

The statement of the progress theorem (9.3.5) must also be extended to take stores and store typings into account:

13.5.7   THEOREM [PROGRESS]: Suppose t is a closed, well-typed term (that is, $\varnothing \mid \Sigma \vdash \mathsf{t} : \mathsf{T}$ for some T and Σ). Then either t is a value or else, for any store μ such that $\varnothing \mid \Sigma \vdash \mu$, there is some term t' and store μ' with $\mathsf{t} \mid \mu \longrightarrow \mathsf{t}' \mid \mu'$. □

Proof: Straightforward induction on typing derivations, following the pattern of 9.3.5. (The canonical forms lemma, 9.3.4, needs two additional cases stating that all values of type Ref T are locations and similarly for Unit.) □

13.5.8   EXERCISE [RECOMMENDED, ★★★]: Is the evaluation relation in this chapter normalizing on well-typed terms? If so, prove it. If not, write a well-typed factorial function in the present calculus (extended with numbers and booleans). □

13.6   Notes

The presentation in this chapter is adapted from a treatment by Harper (1994, 1996). An account in a similar style is given by Wright and Felleisen (1994).

The combination of references (or other computational effects) with ML-style polymorphic type inference raises some quite subtle problems (cf. §22.7) and has received a good deal of attention in the research literature. See Tofte (1990), Hoang et al. (1993), Jouvelot and Gifford (1991), Talpin and Jouvelot (1992), Leroy and Weis (1991), Wright (1992), Harper (1994, 1996), and the references cited there.

Static prediction of possible aliasing is a long-standing problem both in compiler implementation (where it is called *alias analysis*) and in programming language theory. An influential early attempt by Reynolds (1978, 1989) coined the term *syntactic control of interference*. These ideas have recently seen a burst of new activity—see O'Hearn et al. (1995) and Smith et al. (2000). More general reasoning techniques for aliasing are discussed in Reynolds (1981) and Ishtiaq and O'Hearn (2001) and other references cited there.

A comprehensive discussion of garbage collection can be found in Jones and Lins (1996). A more semantic treatment is given by Morrisett et al. (1995).

> *Find out the cause of this effect,*
> *Or rather say, the cause of this defect,*
> *For this effect defective comes by cause.*   —*Hamlet II, ii, 101*

> *The finger pointing at the moon is not the moon.*   —*Buddhist saying*

14 *Exceptions*

In Chapter 13 we saw how to extend the simple operational semantics of the pure simply typed lambda-calculus with mutable references and considered the effect of this extension on the typing rules and type safety proofs. In this chapter, we treat another extension to our original computational model: raising and handling exceptions.

Real-world programming is full of situations where a function needs to signal to its caller that it is unable to perform its task for some reason—because some calculation would involve a division by zero or an arithmetic overflow, a lookup key is missing from a dictionary, an array index went out of bounds, a file could not be found or opened, some disastrous event occurred such as the system running out of memory or the user killing the process, etc.

Some of these exceptional conditions can be signaled by making the function return a variant (or option), as we saw in §11.10. But in situations where the exceptional conditions are truly *exceptional*, we may not want to force every caller of our function to deal with the possibility that they may occur. Instead, we may prefer that an exceptional condition causes a direct transfer of control to an *exception handler* defined at some higher-level in the program—or indeed (if the exceptional condition is rare enough or if there is nothing that the caller can do anyway to recover from it) simply aborts the program. We first consider the latter case (§14.1), where an exception is a whole-program abort, then add a mechanism for trapping and recovering from exceptions (§14.2), and finally refine both of these mechanisms to allow extra programmer-specified data to be passed between exception sites and handlers (§14.3).

The systems studied in this chapter are the simply typed lambda-calculus (Figure 9-1) extended with various primitives for exceptions and exception handling (Figures 14-1 and 14-2). The OCaml implementation of the first extension is fullerror. The language with exceptions carrying values (Figure 14-3) is not implemented.

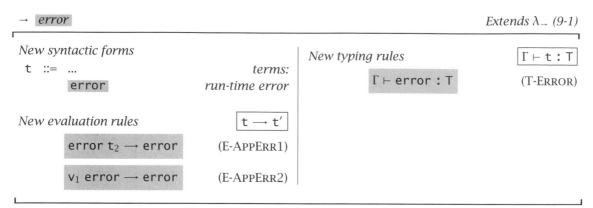

Figure 14-1: Errors

14.1   Raising Exceptions

Let us start by enriching the simply typed lambda-calculus with the simplest possible mechanism for signaling exceptions: a term `error` that, when evaluated, completely aborts evaluation of the term in which it appears. Figure 14-1 details the needed extensions.

The main design decision in writing the rules for `error` is how to formalize "abnormal termination" in our operational semantics. We adopt the simple expedient of letting `error` itself be the result of a program that aborts. The rules E-APPERR1 and E-APPERR2 capture this behavior. E-APPERR1 says that, if we encounter the term `error` while trying to reduce the left-hand side of an application to a value, we should immediately yield `error` as the result of the application. Similarly, E-APPERR2 says that, if we encounter an `error` while we are working on reducing the argument of an application to a value, we should abandon work on the application and immediately yield `error`.

Observe that we have *not* included `error` in the syntax of values—only the syntax of terms. This guarantees that there will never be an overlap between the left-hand sides of the E-APPABS and E-APPERR2 rules—i.e., there is no ambiguity as to whether we should evaluate the term

        (λx:Nat.0) error

by performing the application (yielding 0 as result) or aborting: only the latter is possible. Similarly, the fact that we used the metavariable v_1 (rather than t_1, ranging over arbitrary terms) in E-APPERR2 forces the evaluator to wait until the left-hand side of an application is reduced to a value before aborting it, even if the right-hand side is error. Thus, a term like

    (fix (λx:Nat.x)) error

will diverge instead of aborting. These conditions ensure that the evaluation relation remains deterministic.

The typing rule T-ERROR is also interesting. Since we may want to raise an exception in any context, the term error form is allowed to have any type whatsoever. In

    (λx:Bool.x) error;

it has type Bool. In

    (λx:Bool.x) (error true);

it has type Bool→Bool.

This flexibility in error's type raises some difficulties in implementing a typechecking algorithm, since it breaks the property that every typable term in the language has a unique type (Theorem 9.3.3). This can be dealt with in various ways. In a language with subtyping, we can assign error the minimal type Bot (see §15.4), which can be *promoted* to any other type as necessary. In a language with parametric polymorphism (see Chapter 23), we can give error the polymorphic type ∀X.X, which can be *instantiated* to any other type. Both of these tricks allow infinitely many possible types for error to be represented compactly by a single type.

14.1.1 EXERCISE [⋆]: Wouldn't it be simpler just to require the programmer to annotate error with its intended type in each context where it is used?   □

The type preservation property for the language with exceptions is the same as always: if a term has type T and we let it evaluate one step, the result still has type T. The progress property, however, needs to be refined a little. In its original form, it said that a well-typed program must evaluate to a value (or diverge). But now we have introduced a non-value normal form, error, which can certainly be the result of evaluating a well-typed program. We need to restate progress to allow for this.

14.1.2 THEOREM [PROGRESS]: Suppose t is a closed, well-typed normal form. Then either t is a value or t = error.   □

14.2 Handling Exceptions

The evaluation rules for error can be thought of as "unwinding the call stack," discarding pending function calls until the error has propagated all

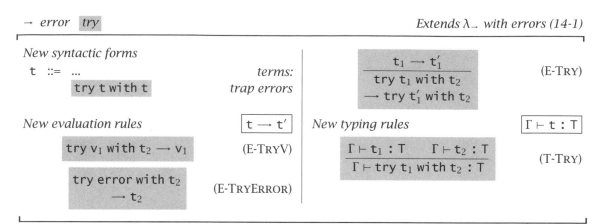

$\rightarrow$ *error* try   *Extends* $\lambda_\rightarrow$ *with errors (14-1)*

New syntactic forms

t ::= ...   *terms:*

    try t with t   *trap errors*

New evaluation rules $\boxed{t \rightarrow t'}$

    try v_1 with $t_2 \rightarrow v_1$ (E-TRYV)

    try error with t_2

        $\rightarrow t_2$ (E-TRYERROR)

$$\frac{t_1 \rightarrow t_1'}{\text{try } t_1 \text{ with } t_2 \rightarrow \text{try } t_1' \text{ with } t_2}$$ (E-TRY)

New typing rules $\boxed{\Gamma \vdash t : T}$

$$\frac{\Gamma \vdash t_1 : T \qquad \Gamma \vdash t_2 : T}{\Gamma \vdash \text{try } t_1 \text{ with } t_2 : T}$$ (T-TRY)

Figure 14-2: Error handling

the way to the top level. In real implementations of languages with exceptions, this is exactly what happens: the call stack consists of a set of *activation records,* one for each active function call; raising an exception causes activation records to be popped off the call stack until it becomes empty.

In most languages with exceptions, it is also possible to install *exception handlers* in the call stack. When an exception is raised, activation records are popped off the call stack until an exception handler is encountered, and evaluation then proceeds with this handler. In other words, the exception functions as a non-local transfer of control, whose target is the most recently installed exception handler (i.e., the nearest one on the call stack).

Our formulation of exception handlers, summarized in Figure 14-2, is similar to both ML and Java. The expression try t_1 with t_2 means "return the result of evaluating t_1, unless it aborts, in which case evaluate the handler t_2 instead." The evaluation rule E-TRYV says that, when t_1 has been reduced to a value v_1, we may throw away the try, since we know now that it will not be needed. E-TRYERROR, on the other hand, says that, if evaluating t_1 results in error, then we should replace the try with t_2 and continue evaluating from there. E-TRY tells us that, until t_1 has been reduced to either a value or error, we should just keep working on it and leave t_2 alone.

The typing rule for try follows directly from its operational semantics. The result of the whole try can be either the result of the main body t_1 or else the result of the handler t_2; we simply need to require that these have the same type T, which is also the type of the try.

The type safety property and its proof remain essentially unchanged from the previous section.

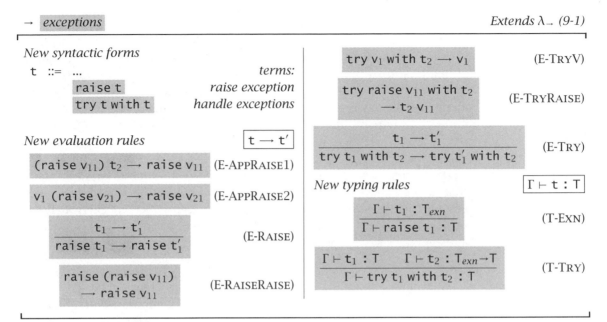

New syntactic forms

$$t ::= ... \qquad terms:$$
$$\text{raise } t \qquad raise\ exception$$
$$\text{try } t \text{ with } t \qquad handle\ exceptions$$

New evaluation rules $t \longrightarrow t'$

$$(\text{raise } v_{11})\ t_2 \longrightarrow \text{raise } v_{11} \qquad (\text{E-AppRaise1})$$

$$v_1\ (\text{raise } v_{21}) \longrightarrow \text{raise } v_{21} \qquad (\text{E-AppRaise2})$$

$$\frac{t_1 \longrightarrow t_1'}{\text{raise } t_1 \longrightarrow \text{raise } t_1'} \qquad (\text{E-Raise})$$

$$\text{raise (raise } v_{11}) \longrightarrow \text{raise } v_{11} \qquad (\text{E-RaiseRaise})$$

$$\text{try } v_1 \text{ with } t_2 \longrightarrow v_1 \qquad (\text{E-TryV})$$

$$\text{try raise } v_{11} \text{ with } t_2 \longrightarrow t_2\ v_{11} \qquad (\text{E-TryRaise})$$

$$\frac{t_1 \longrightarrow t_1'}{\text{try } t_1 \text{ with } t_2 \longrightarrow \text{try } t_1' \text{ with } t_2} \qquad (\text{E-Try})$$

New typing rules $\Gamma \vdash t : T$

$$\frac{\Gamma \vdash t_1 : T_{exn}}{\Gamma \vdash \text{raise } t_1 : T} \qquad (\text{T-Exn})$$

$$\frac{\Gamma \vdash t_1 : T \qquad \Gamma \vdash t_2 : T_{exn} \rightarrow T}{\Gamma \vdash \text{try } t_1 \text{ with } t_2 : T} \qquad (\text{T-Try})$$

Figure 14-3: Exceptions carrying values

14.3 Exceptions Carrying Values

The mechanisms introduced in §14.1 and §14.2 allow a function to signal to its caller that "something unusual happened." It is generally useful to send back some extra information about *which* unusual thing has happened, since the action that the handler needs to take—either to recover and try again or to present a comprehensible error message to the user—may depend on this information.

Figure 14-3 shows how our basic exception handling constructs can be enriched so that each exception carries a value. The type of this value is written T_{exn}. For the moment, we leave the precise nature of this type open; below, we discuss several alternatives.

The atomic term `error` is replaced by a term constructor `raise t`, where t is the extra information that we want to pass to the exception handler. The syntax of `try` remains the same, but the handler t_2 in `try` t_1 `with` t_2 is now interpreted as a *function* that takes the extra information as an argument.

The evaluation rule E-TryRaise implements this behavior, taking the extra information carried by a `raise` from the body t_1 and passing it to the handler t_2. E-AppRaise1 and E-AppRaise2 propagate exceptions through applications, just like E-AppErr1 and E-AppErr2 in Figure 14-1. Note, however, that these rules are allowed to propagate only exceptions whose extra information is a value; if we attempt to evaluate a raise with extra information that itself requires some evaluation, these rules will block, forcing us to use E-RAISE to evaluate the extra information first. E-RAISERAISE propagates exceptions that may occur *while* we are evaluating the extra information that is to be sent along in some other exception. E-TRYV tells us that we can throw away a try once its main body has reduced to a value, just as we did in §14.2. E-TRY directs the evaluator to work on the body of a try until it becomes either a value or a raise.

The typing rules reflect these changes in behavior. In T-RAISE we demand that the extra information has type T_{exn}; the whole raise can then be given any type T that may be required by the context. In T-TRY, we check that the handler t_2 is a function that, given the extra information of type T_{exn}, yields a result of the same type as t_1.

Finally, let us consider some alternatives for the type T_{exn}.

1. We can take T_{exn} to be just Nat. This corresponds to the errno convention used, for example, by Unix operating system functions: each system call returns a numeric "error code," with 0 signaling success and other values reporting various exceptional conditions.

2. We can take T_{exn} to be String, which avoids looking up error numbers in tables and allows exception-raising sites to construct more descriptive messages if they wish. The cost of this extra flexibility is that error handlers may now have to *parse* these strings to find out what happened.

3. We can keep the ability to pass more informative exceptions while avoiding string parsing if we define T_{exn} to be a *variant type:*

```
Texn  =  <divideByZero:      Unit,
          overflow:          Unit,
          fileNotFound:      String,
          fileNotReadable:   String,
          ... >
```

This scheme allows a handler to distinguish between kinds of exceptions using a simple case expression. Also, different exceptions can carry different types of additional information: exceptions like divideByZero need no extra baggage, fileNotFound can carry a string indicating which file was being opened when the error occurred, etc.

The problem with this alternative is that it is rather inflexible, demanding that we fix *in advance* the complete set of exceptions that can be raised by any program (i.e., the set of tags of the variant type T_{exn}). This leaves no room for programmers to declare application-specific exceptions.

4. The same idea can be refined to leave room for user-defined exceptions by taking T_{exn} to be an *extensible variant type*. ML adopts this idea, providing a single extensible variant type called exn.[1] The ML declaration exception 1 of T can be understood, in the present setting, as "make sure that 1 is different from any tag already present in the variant type T_{exn},[2] and from now on let T_{exn} be <1_1:T_1...1_n:t_n,1:T>, where 1_1:T_1 through 1_n:t_n were the possible variants before this declaration."

The ML syntax for raising exceptions is raise 1(t), where 1 is an exception tag defined in the current scope. This can be understood as a combination of the tagging operator and our simple raise:

$$\text{raise 1(t)} \quad \overset{\text{def}}{=} \quad \text{raise (<1=t> as } T_{exn})$$

Similarly, the ML try construct can be desugared using our simple try plus a case.

$$\text{try t with 1(x)} \to \text{h} \quad \overset{\text{def}}{=} \quad \begin{array}{l} \text{try t with} \\ \quad \lambda e{:}T_{exn}.\ \text{case e of} \\ \qquad \text{<1=x>} \Rightarrow \text{h} \\ \qquad \mid \_ \Rightarrow \text{raise e} \end{array}$$

The case checks whether the exception that has been raised is tagged with 1. If so, it binds the value carried by the exception to the variable x and evaluates the handler h. If not, it falls through to the else clause, which *re-raises* the exception. The exception will keep propagating (and perhaps being caught and re-raised) until it either reaches a handler that wants to deal with it, or else reaches the top level and aborts the whole program.

5. Java uses classes instead of extensible variants to support user-defined exceptions. The language provides a built-in class Throwable; an instance of Throwable or any of its subclasses can be used in a throw (same as our raise) or try...catch (same as our try...with) statement. New exceptions can be declared simply by defining new subclasses of Throwable.

There is actually a close correspondence between this exception-handling mechanism and that of ML. Roughly speaking, an exception object in Java

---

1. One can go further and provide extensible variant types as a general language feature, but the designers of ML have chosen to simply treat exn as a special case.
2. Since the exception form is a binder, we can always ensure that 1 is different from the tags already used in T_{exn} by alpha-converting it if necessary.

is represented at run time by a tag indicating its class (which corresponds directly to the extensible variant tag in ML) plus a record of instance variables (corresponding to the extra information labeled by this tag).

Java exceptions go a little further than ML in a couple of respects. One is that there is a natural partial order on exception tags, generated by the *subclass* ordering. A handler for the exception 1 will actually trap all exceptions carrying an object of class 1 or any subclass of 1. Another is that Java distinguishes between *exceptions* (subclasses of the built-in class `Exception`—a subclass of `Throwable`), which application programs might want to catch and try to recover from, and *errors* (subclasses of `Error`—also a subclass of `Throwable`), which indicate serious conditions that should normally just terminate execution. The key difference between the two lies in the typechecking rules, which demand that methods explicitly declare which exceptions (but *not* which errors) they might raise.

14.3.1   EXERCISE [★★★]: The explanation of extensible variant types in alternative 4 above is rather informal. Show how to make it precise.   □

14.3.2   EXERCISE [★★★★]: We noted above that Java exceptions (those that are subclasses of `Exception`) are a bit more strictly controlled than exceptions in ML (or the ones we have defined here): every exception that might be raised by a method must be declared in the method's type. Extend your solution to Exercise 14.3.1 so that the type of a function indicates not only its argument and result types, but also the set of exceptions that it may raise. Prove that your system is typesafe.   □

14.3.3   EXERCISE [★★★]: Many other control constructs can be formalized using techniques similar to the ones we have seen in this chapter. Readers familiar with the "call with current continuation" (`call/cc`) operator of Scheme (see Clinger, Friedman, and Wand, 1985; Kelsey, Clinger, and Rees, 1998; Dybvig, 1996; Friedman, Wand, and Haynes, 2001) may enjoy trying to formulate typing rules based on a type `Cont T` of *T-continuations*—i.e., continuations that expect an argument of type T.   □

PART III

Subtyping

15 *Subtyping*

We have spent the last several chapters studying the typing behavior of a variety of language features within the framework of the simply typed lambda-calculus. This chapter addresses a more fundamental extension: *subtyping* (sometimes called *subtype polymorphism*). Unlike the features we have studied up to now, which could be formulated more or less orthogonally to each other, subtyping is a cross-cutting extension, interacting with most other language features in non-trivial ways.

Subtyping is characteristically found in *object-oriented* languages and is often considered an essential feature of the object-oriented style. We will explore this connection in detail in Chapter 18; for now, though, we present subtyping in a more economical setting with just functions and records, where most of the interesting issues already appear. §15.5 discusses the combination of subtyping with some of the other features we have seen in previous chapters. In the final section (15.6) we consider a more refined semantics for subtyping, in which the use of suptyping corresponds to the insertion of run-time *coercions*.

15.1   Subsumption

Without subtyping, the rules of the simply typed lambda-calculus can be annoyingly rigid. The type system's insistence that argument types exactly match the domain types of functions will lead the typechecker to reject many programs that, to the programmer, seem obviously well-behaved. For example, recall the typing rule for function application:

$$\frac{\Gamma \vdash t_1 : T_{11} \rightarrow T_{12} \qquad \Gamma \vdash t_2 : T_{11}}{\Gamma \vdash t_1 \; t_2 : T_{12}} \qquad \text{(T-APP)}$$

The calculus studied in this chapter is $\lambda_{<:}$, the simply typed lambda-calculus with subtyping (Figure 15-1) and records (15-3); the corresponding OCaml implementation is rcdsub. (Some of the examples also use numbers; fullsub is needed to check these.)

According to this rule, the well-behaved term

```
(λr:{x:Nat}. r.x) {x=0,y=1}
```

is not typable, since the type of the argument is {x:Nat,y:Nat}, whereas the function accepts {x:Nat}. But, clearly, the function just requires that its argument is a record with a field x; it doesn't care what other fields the argument may or may not have. Moreover, we can see this from the type of the function—we don't need to look at its body to verify that it doesn't use any fields besides x. It is *always* safe to pass an argument of type {x:Nat,y:Nat} to a function that expects type {x:Nat}.

The goal of subtyping is to refine the typing rules so that they can accept terms like the one above. We accomplish this by formalizing the intuition that some types are more informative than others: we say that S is a *subtype* of T, written S <: T, to mean that any term of type S can safely be used in a context where a term of type T is expected. This view of subtyping is often called the *principle of safe substitution.*

A simpler intuition is to read S <: T as "every value described by S is also described by T," that is, "the elements of S are a subset of the elements of T." We shall see in §15.6 that other, more refined, interpretations of subtyping are sometimes useful, but this *subset semantics* suffices for most purposes.

The bridge between the typing relation and this subtype relation is provided by adding a new typing rule—the so-called rule of *subsumption:*

$$\frac{\Gamma \vdash t : S \qquad S <: T}{\Gamma \vdash t : T} \qquad \text{(T-Sub)}$$

This rule tells us that, if S <: T, then every element t of S is also an element of T. For example, if we define the subtype relation so that {x:Nat,y:Nat} <: {x:Nat}, then we can use rule T-Sub to derive ⊢ {x=0,y=1} : {x:Nat}, which is what we need to make our motivating example typecheck.

15.2   The Subtype Relation

The subtype relation is formalized as a collection of inference rules for deriving statements of the form S <: T, pronounced "S is a subtype of T" (or "T is a supertype of S"). We consider each form of type (function types, record types, etc.) separately; for each one, we introduce one or more rules formalizing situations when it is safe to allow elements of one type of this form to be used where another is expected.

Before we get to the rules for particular type constructors, we make two general stipulations: first, that subtyping should be reflexive,

$$S <: S \qquad \text{(S-Refl)}$$

and second, that it should be transitive:

$$\frac{S <: U \qquad U <: T}{S <: T} \qquad \text{(S-TRANS)}$$

These rules follow directly from the intuition of safe substitution.

Now, for record types, we have already seen that we want to consider the type $S = \{k_1 : S_1 \ldots k_m : S_m\}$ to be a subtype of $T = \{l_1 : T_1 \ldots l_n : T_n\}$ if T has fewer fields than S. In particular, it is safe to "forget" some fields at the end of a record type. The so-called *width subtyping* rule captures this intuition:

$$\{l_i : T_i{}^{i \in 1..n+k}\} <: \{l_i : T_i{}^{i \in 1..n}\} \qquad \text{(S-RCDWIDTH)}$$

It may seem surprising that the "smaller" type—the subtype—is the one with *more* fields. The easiest way to understand this is to adopt a more liberal view of record types than we did in §11.8, regarding a record type $\{x : \text{Nat}\}$ as describing "the set of all records with *at least* a field x of type Nat." Values like $\{x=3\}$ and $\{x=5\}$ are elements of this type, and so are values like $\{x=3, y=100\}$ and $\{x=3, a=\text{true}, b=\text{true}\}$. Similarly, the record type $\{x : \text{Nat}, y : \text{Nat}\}$ describes records with *at least* the fields x and y, both of type Nat. Values like $\{x=3, y=100\}$ and $\{x=3, y=100, z=\text{true}\}$ are members of this type, but $\{x=3\}$ is not, and neither is $\{x=3, a=\text{true}, b=\text{true}\}$. Thus, the set of values belonging to the second type is a proper subset of the set belonging to the first type. A longer record constitutes a more demanding—i.e., more informative—specification, and so describes a smaller set of values.

The width subtyping rule applies only to record types where the common fields are identical. It is also safe to allow the types of individual fields to vary, as long as the types of each corresponding field in the two records are in the subtype relation. The *depth subtyping* rule expresses this intuition:

$$\frac{\text{for each } i \quad S_i <: T_i}{\{l_i : S_i{}^{i \in 1..n}\} <: \{l_i : T_i{}^{i \in 1..n}\}} \qquad \text{(S-RCDDEPTH)}$$

The following subtyping derivation uses S-RCDWIDTH and S-RCDDEPTH together to show that the nested record type $\{x : \{a : \text{Nat}, b : \text{Nat}\}, y : \{m : \text{Nat}\}\}$ is a subtype of $\{x : \{a : \text{Nat}\}, y : \{\}\}$:

$$\frac{\dfrac{}{\{a:\text{Nat},b:\text{Nat}\} <: \{a:\text{Nat}\}}\text{S-RCDWIDTH} \qquad \dfrac{}{\{m:\text{Nat}\} <: \{\}}\text{S-RCDWIDTH}}{\{x:\{a:\text{Nat},b:\text{Nat}\},y:\{m:\text{Nat}\}\} <: \{x:\{a:\text{Nat}\},y:\{\}\}}\text{S-RCDDEPTH}$$

If we want to use S-RCDDEPTH to refine the type of just a single record field (instead of refining every field, as we did in the example above), we can use S-REFL to obtain trivial subtyping derivations for the other fields.

$$\frac{\dfrac{}{\{a:\text{Nat},b:\text{Nat}\} <: \{a:\text{Nat}\}}\text{S-RCDWIDTH} \qquad \dfrac{}{\{m:\text{Nat}\} <: \{m:\text{Nat}\}}\text{S-REFL}}{\{x:\{a:\text{Nat},b:\text{Nat}\},y:\{m:\text{Nat}\}\} <: \{x:\{a:\text{Nat}\},y:\{m:\text{Nat}\}\}}\text{S-RCDDEPTH}$$

We can also use the transitivity rule, S-Trans, to combine width and depth subtyping. For example, we can obtain a supertype by promoting the type of one field while dropping another:

$$\frac{\dfrac{\dfrac{}{\texttt{\{a:Nat,b:Nat\}} \texttt{<: \{a:Nat\}}}\ \text{S-RcdWidth}}{\texttt{\{x:\{a:Nat,b:Nat\}\}} \texttt{<: \{x:\{a:Nat\}\}}}\ \text{S-RcdDepth}}{}$$

```
                                                    ───────────────── S-RcdWidth
                                                     {a:Nat,b:Nat}
                                                      <: {a:Nat}
──────────────────────────── S-RcdWidth        ───────────────────── S-RcdDepth
{x:{a:Nat,b:Nat},y:{m:Nat}}                      {x:{a:Nat,b:Nat}}
   <: {x:{a:Nat,b:Nat}}                            <: {x:{a:Nat}}
──────────────────────────────────────────────────────────────────── S-Trans
        {x:{a:Nat,b:Nat},y:{m:Nat}} <: {x:{a:Nat}}
```

Our final record subtyping rule arises from the observation that the order of fields in a record does not make any difference to how we can safely use it, since the only thing that we can *do* with records once we've built them—i.e., projecting their fields—is insensitive to the order of fields.

$$\frac{\{k_j:S_j{}^{j\in 1..n}\} \text{ is a permutation of } \{l_i:T_i{}^{i\in 1..n}\}}{\{k_j:S_j{}^{j\in 1..n}\} <: \{l_i:T_i{}^{i\in 1..n}\}} \qquad \text{(S-RcdPerm)}$$

For example, S-RcdPerm tells us that $\texttt{\{c:Top,b:Bool,a:Nat\}}$ is a subtype of $\texttt{\{a:Nat,b:Bool,c:Top\}}$, and vice versa. (This implies that the subtype relation will *not* be anti-symmetric.)

S-RcdPerm can be used in combination with S-RcdWidth and S-Trans to drop fields from anywhere in a record type, not just at the end.

15.2.1   EXERCISE [⋆]: Draw a derivation showing that $\texttt{\{x:Nat,y:Nat,z:Nat\}}$ is a subtype of $\texttt{\{y:Nat\}}$. ☐

S-RcdWidth, S-RcdDepth, and S-RcdPerm each embody a different sort of flexibility in the use of records. For purposes of discussion, it is useful to present them as three separate rules. In particular, there are languages that allow some of them but not others; for example, most variants of Abadi and Cardelli's *object calculus* (1996) omit width subtyping. However, for purposes of implementation it is more convenient to combine them into a single macro-rule that does all three things at once. This rule is discussed in the next chapter (cf. page 211).

Since we are working in a higher-order language, where not only numbers and records but also functions can be passed as arguments to other functions, we must also give a subtyping rule for function types—i.e., we must specify under what circumstances it is safe to use a function of one type in a context where a different function type is expected.

$$\frac{T_1 <: S_1 \qquad S_2 <: T_2}{S_1 \rightarrow S_2 <: T_1 \rightarrow T_2} \qquad \text{(S-Arrow)}$$

Notice that the sense of the subtype relation is reversed (*contravariant*) for the argument types in the left-hand premise, while it runs in the same direction (*covariant*) for the result types as for the function types themselves. The intuition is that, if we have a function f of type $S_1 \rightarrow S_2$, then we know that f accepts elements of type S_1; clearly, f will also accept elements of any subtype T_1 of S_1. The type of f also tells us that it returns elements of type S_2; we can also view these results belonging to any supertype T_2 of S_2. That is, any function f of type $S_1 \rightarrow S_2$ can also be viewed as having type $T_1 \rightarrow T_2$.

An alternative view is that it is safe to allow a function of one type $S_1 \rightarrow S_2$ to be used in a context where another type $T_1 \rightarrow T_2$ is expected as long as none of the arguments that may be passed to the function in this context will surprise it ($T_1 <: S_1$) and none of the results that it returns will surprise the context ($S_2 <: T_2$).

Finally, it is convenient to have a type that is a supertype of every type. We introduce a new type constant Top, plus a rule that makes Top a maximum element of the subtype relation.

$$S <: \text{Top} \qquad\qquad (\text{S-Top})$$

§15.4 discusses the Top type further.

Formally, the subtype relation is the least relation closed under the rules we have given. For easy reference, Figures 15-1, 15-2, and 15-3 recapitulate the full definition of the simply typed lambda-calculus with records and subtyping, highlighting the syntactic forms and rules we have added in this chapter. Note that the presence of the reflexivity and transitivity rules means that the subtype relation is clearly a *preorder*; however, because of the record permutation rule, it is not a partial order: there are many pairs of distinct types where each is a subtype of the other.

To finish the discussion of the subtype relation, let us verify that the example at the beginning of the chapter now typechecks. Using the following abbreviations to avoid running off the edge of the page,

$$f \overset{\text{def}}{=} \lambda r{:}\{x{:}Nat\}.\ r.x \qquad Rx \overset{\text{def}}{=} \{x{:}Nat\}$$
$$xy \overset{\text{def}}{=} \{x{=}0,y{=}1\} \qquad Rxy \overset{\text{def}}{=} \{x{:}Nat,y{:}Nat\}$$

and assuming the usual typing rules for numeric constants, we can construct a derivation for the typing statement ⊢ f xy : Nat as follows:

$$\cfrac{\vdots \quad \vdash f : Rx{\rightarrow}Nat \qquad \cfrac{\cfrac{\cfrac{\vdash 0 : Nat \qquad \vdash 1 : Nat}{\vdash xy : Rxy} \text{ T-Rcd} \qquad \cfrac{}{Rxy <: Rx} \text{ S-RcdWidth}}{\vdash xy : Rx} \text{ T-Sub}}{}}{\vdash f\ xy : Nat} \text{ T-App}$$

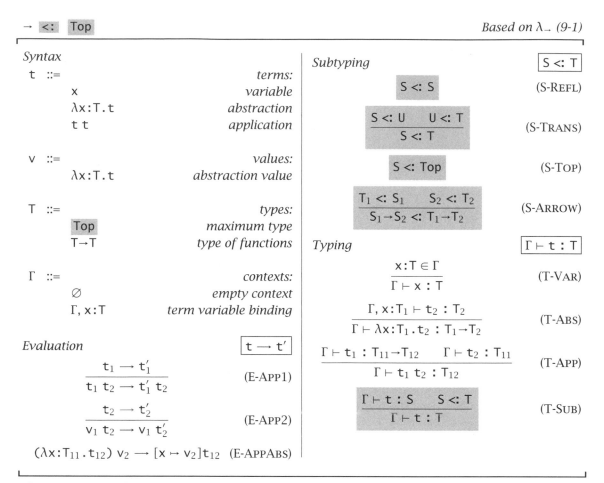

Figure 15-1: Simply typed lambda-calculus with subtyping ($\lambda_{<:}$)

15.2.2   EXERCISE [⋆]: Is this the *only* derivation of the statement ⊢ f xy : Nat?   □

15.2.3   EXERCISE [⋆]: (1) How many different supertypes does {a:Top,b:Top} have?
(2) Can you find an infinite descending chain in the subtype relation—that is,
an infinite sequence of types S_0, S_1, etc. such that each S_{i+1} is a subtype of
S_i? (3) What about an infinite ascending chain?   □

15.2.4   EXERCISE [⋆]: Is there a type that is a subtype of every other type? Is there an
arrow type that is a supertype of every other arrow type?   □

→ {}   *Extends* $\lambda_\to$ *(9-1)*

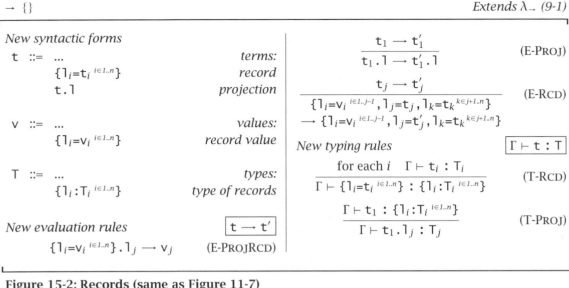

New syntactic forms

$$t ::= \dots \qquad\qquad\qquad\qquad terms:$$
$$\{l_i{=}t_i{}^{i\in 1..n}\} \qquad\qquad record$$
$$t.l \qquad\qquad\qquad projection$$

$$v ::= \dots \qquad\qquad\qquad\qquad values:$$
$$\{l_i{=}v_i{}^{i\in 1..n}\} \qquad\qquad record\ value$$

$$T ::= \dots \qquad\qquad\qquad\qquad types:$$
$$\{l_i{:}T_i{}^{i\in 1..n}\} \qquad\qquad type\ of\ records$$

New evaluation rules $\boxed{t \to t'}$

$$\{l_i{=}v_i{}^{i\in 1..n}\}.l_j \longrightarrow v_j \qquad (\text{E-PROJRCD})$$

$$\frac{t_1 \to t_1'}{t_1.l \to t_1'.l} \qquad (\text{E-PROJ})$$

$$\frac{t_j \to t_j'}{\{l_i{=}v_i{}^{i\in 1..j-1}, l_j{=}t_j, l_k{=}t_k{}^{k\in j+1..n}\} \longrightarrow \{l_i{=}v_i{}^{i\in 1..j-1}, l_j{=}t_j', l_k{=}t_k{}^{k\in j+1..n}\}} \qquad (\text{E-RCD})$$

New typing rules $\boxed{\Gamma \vdash t : T}$

$$\frac{\text{for each } i \quad \Gamma \vdash t_i : T_i}{\Gamma \vdash \{l_i{=}t_i{}^{i\in 1..n}\} : \{l_i{:}T_i{}^{i\in 1..n}\}} \qquad (\text{T-RCD})$$

$$\frac{\Gamma \vdash t_1 : \{l_i{:}T_i{}^{i\in 1..n}\}}{\Gamma \vdash t_1.l_j : T_j} \qquad (\text{T-PROJ})$$

Figure 15-2: Records (same as Figure 11-7)

→ {} <:   *Extends* $\lambda_{<:}$ *(15-1) and simple record rules (15-2)*

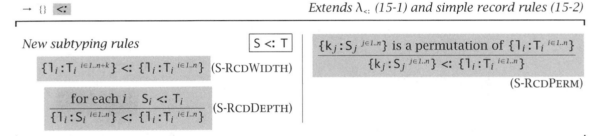

New subtyping rules $\boxed{S <: T}$

$$\{l_i{:}T_i{}^{i\in 1..n+k}\} <: \{l_i{:}T_i{}^{i\in 1..n}\} \qquad (\text{S-RCDWIDTH})$$

$$\frac{\text{for each } i \quad S_i <: T_i}{\{l_i{:}S_i{}^{i\in 1..n}\} <: \{l_i{:}T_i{}^{i\in 1..n}\}} \qquad (\text{S-RCDDEPTH})$$

$$\frac{\{k_j{:}S_j{}^{j\in 1..n}\} \text{ is a permutation of } \{l_i{:}T_i{}^{i\in 1..n}\}}{\{k_j{:}S_j{}^{j\in 1..n}\} <: \{l_i{:}T_i{}^{i\in 1..n}\}} \qquad (\text{S-RCDPERM})$$

Figure 15-3: Records and subtyping

15.2.5   EXERCISE [⋆⋆]: Suppose we extend the calculus with the product type constructor $T_1 \times T_2$ described in §11.6. It is natural to add a subtyping rule

$$\frac{S_1 <: T_1 \qquad S_2 <: T_2}{S_1 \times S_2 <: T_1 \times T_2} \qquad (\text{S-PRODDEPTH})$$

corresponding to S-RCDDEPTH for records. Would it be a good idea to add a width subtyping rule for products

$$T_1 \times T_2 <: T_1 \qquad (\text{S-PRODWIDTH})$$

as well?   □

15.3   Properties of Subtyping and Typing

Having decided on the definition of the lambda-calculus with subtyping, we now have some work to do to verify that it makes sense—in particular, that the preservation and progress theorems of the simply typed lambda-calculus continue to hold in the presence of subtyping.

15.3.1   EXERCISE [RECOMMENDED, ★★]: Before reading on, try to predict where difficulties might arise. In particular, suppose we had made a mistake in defining the subtype relation and included a bogus subtyping rule in addition to those above. Which properties of the system can fail? On the other hand, suppose we *omit* one of the subtyping rules—can any properties then break?   □

We begin by recording one key property of the subtype relation—an analog of the inversion lemma for the typing relation in the simply typed lambda-calculus (Lemma 9.3.1). If we know that some type S is a subtype of an arrow type, then the subtyping inversion lemma tells us that S itself must be an arrow type; moreover, it tells us that the left-hand sides of the arrows must be (contravariantly) related, and so (covariantly) must the right-hand sides. Similar considerations apply when S is known to be a subtype of a record type: we know that S has more fields (S-RCDWIDTH) in some order (S-RCDPERM), and that the types of common fields are in the subtype relation (S-RCDDEPTH).

15.3.2   LEMMA [INVERSION OF THE SUBTYPE RELATION]:

1. If $S <: T_1 \rightarrow T_2$, then S has the form $S_1 \rightarrow S_2$, with $T_1 <: S_1$ and $S_2 <: T_2$.

2. If $S <: \{l_i : T_i{}^{i \in 1..n}\}$, then S has the form $\{k_j : S_j{}^{j \in 1..m}\}$, with at least the labels $\{l_i{}^{i \in 1..n}\}$—i.e., $\{l_i{}^{i \in 1..n}\} \subseteq \{k_j{}^{j \in 1..m}\}$—and with $S_j <: T_i$ for each common label $l_i = k_j$.   □

Proof: EXERCISE [RECOMMENDED, ★★].   □

To prove that types are preserved during evaluation, we begin with an inversion lemma for the typing relation (cf. Lemma 9.3.1 for the simply typed lambda-calculus). Rather than stating the lemma in its most general form, we give here just the cases that are actually needed in the proof of the preservation theorem below. (The general form can be read off from the algorithmic subtype relation in the next chapter, Definition 16.2.2.)

15.3.3   LEMMA:

1. If $\Gamma \vdash \lambda x : S_1.\ s_2 : T_1 \rightarrow T_2$, then $T_1 <: S_1$ and $\Gamma, x : S_1 \vdash s_2 : T_2$.

2. If $\Gamma \vdash \{k_a = s_a{}^{a \in 1..m}\} : \{l_i : T_i{}^{i \in 1..n}\}$, then $\{l_i{}^{i \in 1..n}\} \subseteq \{k_a{}^{a \in 1..m}\}$ and $\Gamma \vdash s_a :$
T_i for each common label $k_a = l_i$.   □

Proof: Straightforward induction on typing derivations, using Lemma 15.3.2
for the T-SUB case.   □

Next, we need a substitution lemma for the typing relation. The statement
of this lemma is unchanged from the simply typed lambda-calculus (Lemma
9.3.8), and its proof is nearly identical.

15.3.4   LEMMA [SUBSTITUTION]: If $\Gamma, x : S \vdash t : T$ and $\Gamma \vdash s : S$, then $\Gamma \vdash [x \mapsto s]t :$
T.   □

Proof: By induction on typing derivations. We need new cases for T-SUB and
for the record typing rules T-RCD and T-PROJ, making straightforward use of
the induction hypothesis. The rest is just like the proof of 9.3.8.   □

Now, the preservation theorem has the same statement as before. Its proof,
though, is somewhat complicated by subtyping at several points.

15.3.5   THEOREM [PRESERVATION]: If $\Gamma \vdash t : T$ and $t \longrightarrow t'$, then $\Gamma \vdash t' : T$.   □

Proof: Straightforward induction on typing derivations. Most of the cases
are similar to the proof of preservation for the simply typed lambda-calculus
(9.3.9). We need new cases for the record typing rules and for subsumption.

Case T-VAR: $t = x$

Can't happen (there are no evaluation rules for variables).

Case T-ABS: $t = \lambda x : T_1 . t_2$

Can't happen (t is already a value).

Case T-APP: $t = t_1\ t_2 \qquad \Gamma \vdash t_1 : T_{11} \rightarrow T_{12} \qquad \Gamma \vdash t_2 : T_{11} \qquad T = T_{12}$

From the evaluation rules in Figures 15-1 and 15-2, we see that there are three
rules by which $t \longrightarrow t'$ can be derived: E-APP1, E-APP2, and E-APPABS. Proceed
by cases.

> *Subcase* E-APP1: $t_1 \longrightarrow t_1' \qquad t' = t_1'\ t_2$
> The result follows from the induction hypothesis and T-APP.

> *Subcase* E-APP2: $t_1 = v_1 \qquad t_2 \longrightarrow t_2' \qquad t' = v_1\ t_2'$
> Similar.

> *Subcase* E-APPABS: $t_1 = \lambda x : S_{11} . t_{12} \qquad t_2 = v_2 \qquad t' = [x \mapsto v_2]t_{12}$
> By Lemma 15.3.3(1), $T_{11} <: S_{11}$ and $\Gamma, x : S_{11} \vdash t_{12} : T_{12}$. By T-SUB, $\Gamma \vdash t_2 :$
> S_{11}. From this and the substitution lemma (15.3.4), we obtain $\Gamma \vdash t' : T_{12}$.

Case T-RCD: $t = \{l_i = t_i \; {}^{i \in 1..n}\}$ $\Gamma \vdash t_i : T_i$ for each i
                  $T = \{l_i : T_i \; {}^{i \in 1..n}\}$

The only evaluation rule whose left-hand side is a record is E-RCD. From the premise of this rule, we see that $t_j \longrightarrow t'_j$ for some field t_j. The result follows from the induction hypothesis (applied to the corresponding assumption $\Gamma \vdash t_j : T_j$) and T-RCD.

Case T-PROJ: $t = t_1 . l_j$ $\Gamma \vdash t_1 : \{l_i : T_i \; {}^{i \in 1..n}\}$ $T = T_j$

From the evaluation rules in Figures 15-1 and 15-2, we see that there are two rules by which $t \longrightarrow t'$ can be derived: E-PROJ, E-PROJRCD.

> *Subcase* E-PROJ: $t_1 \longrightarrow t'_1$ $t' = t'_1 . l_j$
>
> The result follows from the induction hypothesis and T-PROJ.

> *Subcase* E-PROJRCD: $t_1 = \{k_a = v_a \; {}^{a \in 1..m}\}$ $l_j = k_b$ $t' = v_b$
>
> By Lemma 15.3.3(2), we have $\{l_i \; {}^{i \in 1..n}\} \subseteq \{k_a \; {}^{a \in 1..m}\}$ and $\Gamma \vdash v_a : T_i$ for each $k_a = l_i$. In particular, $\Gamma \vdash v_b : T_j$, as desired.

Case T-SUB: $t : S$ $S <: T$

By the induction hypothesis, $\Gamma \vdash t' : S$. By T-SUB, $\Gamma \vdash t : T$. $\square$

To prove that well-typed terms cannot get stuck, we begin (as in Chapter 9) with a canonical forms lemma, which tells us the possible shapes of values belonging to arrow and record types.

15.3.6   LEMMA [CANONICAL FORMS]:

1. If v is a closed value of type $T_1 \rightarrow T_2$, then v has the form $\lambda x : S_1 . t_2$.

2. If v is a closed value of type $\{l_i : T_i \; {}^{i \in 1..n}\}$, then v has the form $\{k_j = v_j \; {}^{a \in 1..m}\}$, with $\{l_i \; {}^{i \in 1..n}\} \subseteq \{k_a \; {}^{a \in 1..m}\}$. $\square$

Proof: EXERCISE [RECOMMENDED, ★★★]. $\square$

The progress theorem and its proof are now quite close to what we saw in the simply typed lambda-calculus. Most of the burden of dealing with subtyping has been pushed into the canonical forms lemma, and only a few small changes are needed here.

15.3.7   THEOREM [PROGRESS]: If t is a closed, well-typed term, then either t is a value or else there is some t' with $t \longrightarrow t'$. $\square$

Proof: By straightforward induction on typing derivations. The variable case cannot occur (because t is closed). The case for lambda-abstractions is immediate, since abstractions are values. The remaining cases are more interesting.

Case T-APP: $t = t_1\ t_2$ $\vdash t_1 : T_{11} \rightarrow T_{12}$ $\vdash t_2 : T_{11}$ $T = T_{12}$

By the induction hypothesis, either t_1 is a value or else it can make a step of evaluation; likewise t_2. If t_1 can take a step, then rule E-APP1 applies to t. If t_1 is a value and t_2 can take a step, then rule E-APP2 applies. Finally, if both t_1 and t_2 are values, then the canonical forms lemma (15.3.6) tells us that t_1 has the form $\lambda x : S_{11}.t_{12}$, so rule E-APPABS applies to t.

Case T-RCD: $t = \{l_i = t_i{}^{i \in 1..n}\}$ for each $i \in 1..n$, $\vdash t_i : T_i$
$\qquad\qquad\quad T = \{l_i : T_i{}^{i \in 1..n}\}$

By the induction hypothesis, each t_i either is already a value or can make a step of evaluation. If all of them are values, then t is a value. On the other hand, if at least one can make a step, then rule E-RCD applies to t.

Case T-PROJ: $t = t_1.l_j$ $\vdash t_1 : \{l_i : T_i{}^{i \in 1..n}\}$ $T = T_j$

By the induction hypothesis, either t_1 is a value or it can make an evaluation step. If t_1 can make a step, then (by E-PROJ) so can t. If t_1 is a value, then by the canonical forms lemma (15.3.6) t_1 has the form $\{k_a = v_j{}^{a \in 1..m}\}$, with $\{l_i{}^{i \in 1..n}\} \subseteq \{k_a{}^{a \in 1..m}\}$ and with $\vdash v_j : T_i$ for each $l_i = k_j$. In particular, l_j is among the labels $\{k_a{}^{a \in 1..m}\}$ of t_1, from which rule E-PROJRCD tells us that t itself can take an evaluation step.

Case T-SUB: $\Gamma \vdash t : S$ $S <: T$

The result follows directly from the induction hypothesis. $\square$

15.4   The Top and Bottom Types

The maximal type Top is not a necessary part of the simply typed lambda-calculus with subtyping; it can be removed without damaging the properties of the system. However, it is included in most presentations, for several reasons. First, it corresponds to the type Object found in most object-oriented languages. Second, Top is a convenient technical device in more sophisticated systems combining subtyping and parametric polymorphism. For example, in System $F_{<:}$ (Chapters 26 and 28), the presence of Top allows us to recover ordinary unbounded quantification from bounded quantification, streamlining the system. Indeed, even records can be encoded in $F_{<:}$, further streamlining the presentation (at least for purposes of formal study); this encoding critically depends on Top. Finally, since Top's behavior is straightforward and it is often useful in examples, there is little reason not to keep it.

It is natural to ask whether we can also complete the subtype relation with a *minimal* element—a type Bot that is a subtype of every type. The answer is that we can: this extension is formalized in Figure 15-4.

The first thing to notice is that Bot is empty—there are no closed values

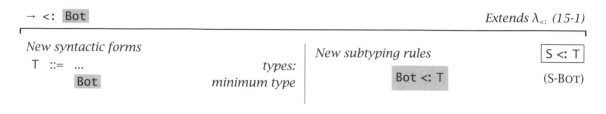

Figure 15-4: Bottom type

of type Bot. If there were one, say v, then the subsumption rule plus S-Bot would allow us to derive ⊢ v : Top→Top, from which the canonical forms lemma (15.3.6, which still holds under the extension) tells us that v must have the form λx:S₁.t₂ for some S₁ and t₂. On the other hand, by subsumption, we also have ⊢ v : {}, from which the canonical forms lemma tells us that v must be a record. The syntax makes it clear that v cannot be both a function and a record, and so assuming that ⊢ v : Bot has led us to a contradiction.

The emptiness of Bot does not make it useless. On the contrary: Bot provides a very convenient way of expressing the fact that some operations (in particular, throwing an exception or invoking a continuation) are not intended to return. Giving such expressions the type Bot has two good effects: first, it signals to the programmer that no result is expected (since if the expression *did* return a result, it would be a value of type Bot); second, it signals to the typechecker that such an expression can safely be used in a context expecting any type of value. For example, if the exception-raising term error from Chapter 14 is given type Bot, then a term like

```
λx:T.
  if <check that x is reasonable> then
    <compute result>
  else
    error
```

will be well typed because, no matter what the type of the normal result is, the term error can always be given the same type by subsumption, so the two branches of the if are compatible, as required by T-If.[1]

Unfortunately, the presence of Bot significantly complicates the problem of building a typechecker for the system. A simple typechecking algorithm for

---

1. In languages with polymorphism, such as ML, we can also use ∀X.X as a result type for error and similar constructs. This achieves the same effect as Bot by different means: instead of giving error a type that can be *promoted* to any type, we give it a type scheme that can be *instantiated* to any type. Though they rest on different foundations, the two solutions are quite similar: in particular, the type ∀X.X is also empty.

a language with subtyping needs to rely on inferences like "if an application t_1 t_2 is well typed, then t_1 must have an arrow type." In the presence of Bot, we must refine this to "if t_1 t_2 is well typed, then t_1 must have either an arrow type or type Bot"; this point is expanded in §16.4. The complications are magnified further in systems with bounded quantification; see §28.8.

These complications show that adding Bot is a more serious step than adding Top. We shall omit it from the systems we consider in the remainder of the book.

15.5 Subtyping and Other Features

As we extend our simple calculus with subtyping toward a full-blown programming language, each new feature must be examined carefully to see how it interacts with subtyping. In this section we consider some of the features we have seen at this point.[2] Later chapters will take up the (significantly more complex) interactions between subtyping and features such as parametric polymorphism (Chapters 26 and 28), recursive types (Chapters 20 and 21), and type operators (Chapter 31).

Ascription and Casting

The *ascription* operator t as T was introduced in §11.4 as a form of checked documentation, allowing the programmer to record in the text of the program the assertion that some subterm of a complex expression has some particular type. In the examples in this book, ascription is also used to control the way in which types are printed, forcing the typechecker to use a more readable abbreviated form instead of the type that it has actually calculated for a term.

In languages with subtyping such as Java and C++, ascription becomes quite a bit more interesting. It is often called *casting* in these languages, and is written (T)t. There are actually two quite different forms of casting—so-called *up-casts* and *down-casts*. The former are straightforward; the latter, which involve *dynamic type-testing*, require a significant extension.

Up-casts, in which a term is ascribed a *supertype* of the type that the typechecker would naturally assign it, are instances of the standard ascription operator. We give a term t and a type T at which we intend to "view" t. The typechecker verifies that T is indeed one of the types of t by attempting to build a derivation

---

2. Most of the extensions discussed in this section are *not* implemented in the fullsub checker.

$$\frac{\quad \vdots \qquad\qquad\quad \vdots \quad}{\cfrac{\Gamma \vdash t : S \qquad S <: T}{\cfrac{\Gamma \vdash t : T}{\Gamma \vdash t \text{ as } T : T} \text{ T-ASCRIBE}} \text{ T-SUB}}$$

using the "natural" typing of t, the subsumption rule T-SUB, and the ascription rule from §11.4:

$$\frac{\Gamma \vdash t_1 : T}{\Gamma \vdash t_1 \text{ as } T : T} \qquad \text{(T-ASCRIBE)}$$

Up-casts can be viewed as a form of *abstraction*—a way of hiding the existence of some parts of a value so that they cannot be used in some surrounding context. For example, if t is a record (or, more generally, an object), then we can use an up-cast to hide some of its fields (methods).

A down-cast, on the other hand, allows us to assign types to terms that the typechecker cannot derive statically. To allow down-casts, we make a somewhat surprising change to the typing rule for as:

$$\frac{\Gamma \vdash t_1 : S}{\Gamma \vdash t_1 \text{ as } T : T} \qquad \text{(T-DOWNCAST)}$$

That is, we check that t_1 is well typed (i.e., that it has some type S) and then assign it type T, without making *any* demand about the relation between S and T. For example, using down-casting we can write a function f that takes any argument whatsoever, casts it down to a record with an a field containing a number, and returns this number:

```
f = λ(x:Top) (x as {a:Nat}).a;
```

In effect, the programmer is saying to the typechecker, "I know (for reasons that are too complex to explain in terms of the typing rules) that f will *always* be applied to record arguments with numeric a fields; I want you to trust me on this one."

Of course, blindly trusting such assertions will have a disastrous effect on the safety of our language: if the programmer somehow makes a mistake and applies f to a record that does not contain an a field, the results might (depending on the details of the compiler) be completely arbitrary! Instead, our motto should be "trust, but verify." At compile time, the typechecker simply accepts the type given in the down-cast. However, it inserts a check that, at run time, will verify that the actual value does indeed have the type claimed. In other words, the evaluation rule for ascriptions should not just discard the annotation, as our original evaluation rule for ascriptions did,

$$v_1 \text{ as } T \longrightarrow v_1 \qquad \text{(E-ASCRIBE)}$$

but should first compare the actual (run-time) type of the value with the declared type:

$$\frac{\vdash v_1 : T}{v_1 \text{ as } T \longrightarrow v_1}$$ (E-Downcast)

For example, if we apply the function f above to the argument {a=5,b=true}, then this rule will check (successfully) that ⊢ {a=5,b=true} : {a:Nat}. On the other hand, if we apply f to {b=true}, then the E-Downcast rule will not apply and evaluation will get stuck at this point. This run-time check recovers the type preservation property.

15.5.1   Exercise [★★ ↛]: Prove this. □

Of course, we lose progress, since a well-typed program can certainly get stuck by attempting to evaluate a bad down-cast. Languages that provide down-casts normally address this in one of two ways: either by making a failed down-cast raise a dynamic exception that can be caught and handled by the program (cf. Chapter 14) or else by replacing the down-cast operator by a form of dynamic type test:

$$\frac{\Gamma \vdash t_1 : S \qquad \Gamma, x{:}T \vdash t_2 : U \qquad \Gamma \vdash t_3 : U}{\Gamma \vdash \text{if } t_1 \text{ in } T \text{ then } x{\rightarrow}t_2 \text{ else } t_3 : U}$$ (T-Typetest)

$$\frac{\vdash v_1 : T}{\text{if } v_1 \text{ in } T \text{ then } x{\rightarrow}t_2 \text{ else } t_3 \longrightarrow [x \mapsto v_1]t_2}$$ (E-Typetest1)

$$\frac{\nvdash v_1 : T}{\text{if } v_1 \text{ in } T \text{ then } x{\rightarrow}t_2 \text{ else } t_3 \longrightarrow t_3}$$ (E-Typetest2)

Uses of down-casts are actually quite common in languages like Java. In particular, down-casts support a kind of "poor-man's polymorphism." For example, "collection classes" such as Set and List are monomorphic in Java: instead of providing a type List T (lists containing elements of type T) for every type T, Java provides just List, the type of lists whose elements belong to the maximal type Object. Since Object is a supertype of every other type of objects in Java, this means that lists may actually contain anything at all: when we want to add an element to a list, we simply use subsumption to promote its type to Object. However, when we take an element *out* of a list, all the typechecker knows about it is that it has type Object. This type does not warrant calling most of the methods of the object, since the type Object mentions only a few very generic methods for printing and such, which are shared by all Java objects. In order to do anything useful with it, we must first downcast it to some expected type T.

It has been argued—for example, by the designers of Pizza (Odersky and Wadler, 1997), GJ (Bracha, Odersky, Stoutamire, and Wadler, 1998), PolyJ (Myers, Bank, and Liskov, 1997), and NextGen (Cartwright and Steele, 1998)—that it is better to extend the Java type system with *real* polymorphism (cf. Chapter 23), which is both safer and more efficient than the down-cast idiom, requiring no run-time tests. On the other hand, such extensions add significant complexity to an already-large language, interacting with many other features of the language and type system (see Igarashi, Pierce, and Wadler, 1999, Igarashi, Pierce, and Wadler, 2001, for example); this fact supports a view that the down-cast idiom offers a reasonable pragmatic compromise between safety and complexity.

Down-casts also play a critical role in Java's facilities for *reflection*. Using reflection, the programmer can tell the Java run-time system to dynamically load a bytecode file and create an instance of some class that it contains. Clearly, there is no way that the typechecker can statically predict the shape of the class that will be loaded at this point (the bytecode file can be obtained on demand from across the net, for example), so the best it can do is to assign the maximal type Object to the newly created instance. Again, in order to do anything useful, we must downcast the new object to some expected type T, handle the run-time exception that may result if the class provided by the bytecode file does not actually match this type, and then go ahead and use it with type T.

To close the discussion of down-casts, a note about implementation is in order. It seems, from the rules we have given, that including down-casts to a language involves adding all the machinery for typechecking to the run-time system. Worse, since values are typically represented differently at run time than inside the compiler (in particular, functions are compiled into bytecodes or native machine instructions), it appears that we will need to write a *different* typechecker for calculating the types needed in dynamic checks. To avoid this, real languages combine down-casts with *type tags*—single-word tags (similar in some ways to ML's datatype constructors and the variant tags in §11.10) that capture a run-time "residue" of compile-time types and that are sufficient to perform dynamic subtype tests. Chapter 19 develops one instance of this mechanism in detail.

Variants

The subtyping rules for variants (cf. §11.10) are nearly identical to the ones for records; the only difference is that the width rule S-VARIANTWIDTH allows new variants to be *added*, not dropped, when moving from a subtype to a supertype. The intuition is that a tagged expression <l=t> belongs to a variant type $<l_i:T_i^{\ i\in 1..n}>$ if its label l is one of the possible labels $\{l_i\}$ listed in the type; adding more labels to this set decreases the information it gives us

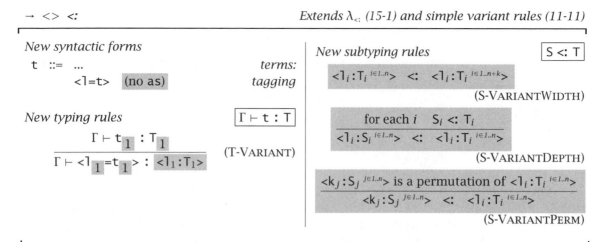

Figure 15-5: Variants and subtyping

about its elements. A singleton variant type $<l_1:T_1>$ tells us precisely what label its elements are tagged with; a two-variant type $<l_1:T_1,l_2:T_2>$ tells us that its elements have either label l_1 or label l_2, etc. Conversely, when we *use* variant values, it is always in the context of a `case` statement, which must have one branch for each variant listed by the type—listing more variants just means forcing `case` statements to include some unnecessary extra branches.

Another consequence of combining subtyping and variants is that we can drop the annotation from the tagging construct, writing just $<l=t>$ instead of $<l=t>$ as $<l_i:T_i^{\ i\in 1..n}>$, as we did in §11.10, and changing the typing rule for tagging so that it assigns $<l_1=t_1>$ the precise type $<l_1:T_1>$. We can then use subsumption plus S-VARIANTWIDTH to obtain any larger variant type.

Lists

We have seen a number of examples of covariant type constructors (records and variants, as well as function types, on their right-hand sides) and one contravariant constructor (arrow, on the left-hand side). The `List` constructor is also covariant: if we have a list whose elements have type S_1, and $S_1 <: T_1$, then we can safely regard our list as having elements of type T_1.

$$\frac{S_1 <: T_1}{\mathsf{List}\ S_1 <: \mathsf{List}\ T_1} \qquad (\text{S-LIST})$$

References

Not all type constructors are covariant or contravariant. The Ref constructor, for example, must be taken to be *invariant* in order to preserve type safety.

$$\frac{S_1 <: T_1 \qquad T_1 <: S_1}{\text{Ref } S_1 <: \text{Ref } T_1} \qquad \text{(S-REF)}$$

For Ref S_1 to be a subtype of Ref T_1, we demand that S_1 and T_1 be *equivalent* under the subtype relation—each a subtype of the other. This gives us the flexibility to reorder the fields of records under a Ref constructor—for example, Ref {a:Bool,b:Nat} <: Ref {b:Nat,a:Bool}—but nothing more.

   The reason for this very restrictive subtyping rule is that a value of type Ref T_1 can be used in a given context in two different ways: for both reading (!) and writing (:=). When it is used for reading, the context expects to obtain a value of type T_1, so if the reference actually yields a value of type S_1 then we need $S_1 <: T_1$ to avoid violating the context's expectations. On the other hand, if the same reference cell is used for writing, then the new value provided by the context will have type T_1. If the actual type of the reference is Ref S_1, then someone else may later read this value and use it as an S_1; this will be safe only if $T_1 <: S_1$.

15.5.2   EXERCISE [★ ⇸]: (1) Write a short program that will fail with a run-time type error (i.e., its evaluation will get stuck) if the first premise of S-REF is dropped. (2) Write another program that will fail if the second premise is dropped.   □

Arrays

Clearly, the motivations behind the invariant subtyping rule for references also apply to arrays, since the operations on arrays include forms of both dereferencing and assignment.

$$\frac{S_1 <: T_1 \qquad T_1 <: S_1}{\text{Array } S_1 <: \text{Array } T_1} \qquad \text{(S-ARRAY)}$$

Interestingly, Java actually permits covariant subtyping of arrays:

$$\frac{S_1 <: T_1}{\text{Array } S_1 <: \text{Array } T_1} \qquad \text{(S-ARRAYJAVA)}$$

(in Java syntax, S_1[] <: T_1[]). This feature was originally introduced to compensate for the lack of parametric polymorphism in the typing of some basic operations such as copying parts of arrays, but is now generally considered a flaw in the language design, since it seriously affects the performance of programs involving arrays. The reason is that the unsound subtyping rule must be compensated with a run-time check on *every* assignment to *any* array, to make sure the value being written belongs to (a subtype of) the actual type of the elements of the array.

15.5.3 EXERCISE [★★★ ↦]: Write a short Java program involving arrays that typechecks but fails (by raising an `ArrayStoreException`) at run time. □

References Again

A more refined analysis of references, first explored by Reynolds in the language Forsythe (1988), can be obtained by introducing two new type constructors, `Source` and `Sink`. Intuitively, `Source T` is thought of as a capability to read values of type T from a cell (but which does not permit assignment), while `Sink T` is a capability to write to a cell. `Ref T` is a combination of these two capabilities, giving permission both to read and to write.

The typing rules for dereferencing and assignment (Figure 13-1) are modified so that they demand only the appropriate capability.

$$\frac{\Gamma \mid \Sigma \vdash t_1 : \text{Source } T_{11}}{\Gamma \mid \Sigma \vdash !t_1 : T_{11}} \quad \text{(T-DEREF)}$$

$$\frac{\Gamma \mid \Sigma \vdash t_1 : \text{Sink } T_{11} \quad \Gamma \mid \Sigma \vdash t_2 : T_{11}}{\Gamma \mid \Sigma \vdash t_1 := t_2 : \text{Unit}} \quad \text{(T-ASSIGN)}$$

Now, if we have only the capability to read values from a cell and if these values are guaranteed to have type S_1, then it is safe to "downgrade" this to a capability to read values of type T_1, as long as S_1 is a subtype of T_1. That is, the `Source` constructor is covariant.

$$\frac{S_1 <: T_1}{\text{Source } S_1 <: \text{Source } T_1} \quad \text{(S-SOURCE)}$$

Conversely, a capability to write values of type S_1 to a given cell can be downgraded to a capability to write values of some *smaller* type T_1: the `Sink` constructor is contravariant.

$$\frac{T_1 <: S_1}{\text{Sink } S_1 <: \text{Sink } T_1} \quad \text{(S-SINK)}$$

Finally, we express the intuition that `Ref` T_1 is a combination of read and write capabilities by two subtyping rules that permit a `Ref` to be downgraded to either a `Source` or a `Sink`.

$$\text{Ref } T_1 <: \text{Source } T_1 \quad \text{(S-REFSOURCE)}$$

$$\text{Ref } T_1 <: \text{Sink } T_1 \quad \text{(S-REFSINK)}$$

Channels

The same intuitions (and identical subtyping rules) form the basis for the treatment of *channel types* in recent concurrent programming languages such as Pict (Pierce and Turner, 2000; Pierce and Sangiorgi, 1993). The key observation is that, from the point of view of typing, a communication channel behaves exactly like a reference cell: it can be used for both reading and writing, and, since it is difficult to determine statically which reads correspond to which writes, the only simple way to ensure type safety is to require that all the values passed along the channel must belong to the same type. Now, if we pass someone only the capability to write to a given channel, then it is safe for them to pass this capability to someone else who promises to write values of a smaller type—the "output channel" type constructor is contravariant. Similarly, if we pass just the capability to read from a channel, then this capability can safely be downgraded to a capability for reading values of any larger type—the "input channel" constructor is covariant.

Base Types

In a full-blown language with a rich set of base types, it is often convenient to introduce primitive subtype relations among these types. For example, in many languages the boolean values `true` and `false` are actually represented by the numbers 1 and 0. We can, if we like, expose this fact to the programmer by introducing a subtyping axiom `Bool <: Nat`. Now we can write compact expressions like 5*b instead of `if b then 5 else 0`.

15.6   Coercion Semantics for Subtyping

Throughout this chapter, our intuition has been that subtyping is "semantically insignificant." The presence of subtyping does not change the way programs are evaluated; rather, subtyping is just a way of obtaining additional flexibility in typing terms. This interpretation is simple and natural, but it carries some performance penalties—particularly for numerical calculations and for accessing record fields—that may not be acceptable in high-performance implementations. We sketch here an alternative *coercion semantics* and discuss some new issues that it, in its turn, raises. This section can be skipped if desired.

Problems with the Subset Semantics

As we saw in §15.5, it can be convenient to allow subtyping between different base types. But some "intuitively reasonable" inclusions between base types may have a detrimental effect on performance. For example, suppose we introduce the axiom Int <: Float, so that integers can be used in floating-point calculations without writing explicit coercions—allowing us to write, for example, 4.5 + 6 instead of 4.5 + intToFloat(6). Under the subset semantics, this implies that the set of integer values must literally be a subset of the set of floats. But, on most real machines, the concrete representations of integers and floats are entirely different: integers are usually represented in twos-complement form, while floats are divided up into mantissa, exponent, and sign, plus some special cases such as NaN (not-a-number).

To reconcile these representational differences with the subset semantics of subtyping, we can adopt a common *tagged* (or *boxed*) representation for numbers: an integer is represented as a machine integer plus a tag (either in a separate header word or in the high-order bits of the same word as the actual integer), and a float is represented as a machine float plus a different tag. The type Float then refers to the entire set of tagged numbers (floats and ints), while Int refers just to the tagged ints.

This scheme is not unreasonable: it corresponds to the representation strategy actually used in many modern language implementations, where the tag bits (or words) are also needed to support garbage collection. The downside is that every primitive operation on numbers must actually be implemented as a tag check on the arguments, a few instructions to unbox the primitive numbers, one instruction for the actual operation, and a couple of instructions for re-boxing the result. Clever compiler optimizations can eliminate some of this overhead, but, even with the best currently available techniques, it significantly degrades performance, especially in heavily numeric code such as graphical and scientific calculations.

A different performance problem arises when records are combined with subtyping—in particular, with the permutation rule. Our simple evaluation rule for field projection

$$\{l_i = v_i \ ^{i \in 1..n}\}.l_j \longrightarrow v_j \qquad \text{(E-ProjRcd)}$$

can be read as "search for l_j among the labels of the record, and yield the associated value v_j." But, in a real implementation, we certainly do not want to perform a linear search at run time through the fields of the record to find the desired label. In a language without subtyping (or with subtyping but without the permutation rule), we can do much better: if the label l_j appears third in the *type* of the record, then we know statically that all run-time values with this type will have l_j as their third field, so at run time we do not need to look at the labels at all (in fact, we can omit them completely from the run-time representation, effectively compiling records into tuples). To obtain the value of the 1_j field, we generate an indirect load through a register pointing to the start of the record, with a constant offset of 3 words. The presence of the permutation rule foils this technique, since knowing that some record value belongs to a type where 1_j appears as the third field tells us nothing at all, now, about where the 1_j field is actually stored in the record. Again, clever optimizations and run-time tricks can palliate this problem, but in general field projection can require some form of search at run time.[3]

Coercion Semantics

We can address both of these problems by adopting a different semantics, in which we "compile away" subtyping by replacing it with run-time coercions. If an Int is promoted to a Float during typechecking, for example, then at run time we physically change this number's representation from a machine integer to a machine float. Similarly, a use of the record permutation sub-typing rule will be compiled into a piece of code that literally rearranges the order of the fields. Primitive numeric operations and field accesses can now proceed without the overhead of unboxing or search.

Intuitively, the coercion semantics for a language with subtyping is expressed as a function that transforms terms from this language into a lower-level language without subtyping. Ultimately, the low-level language might be machine code for some concrete processor. For purposes of illustration, however, we can keep the discussion on a more abstract level. For the source language, we choose the one we have been using for most of the chapter—the simply typed lambda-calculus with subtyping and records. For the low-level target language, we choose the pure simply typed lambda-calculus with records and a Unit type (which we use to interpret Top).

Formally, the compilation consists of three translation functions—one for types, one for subtyping, and one for typing. For types, the translation just replaces Top with Unit. We write this function as $[\![-]\!]$.

$$
\begin{aligned}
[\![\text{Top}]\!] &= \text{Unit} \\
[\![\text{T}_1 \rightarrow \text{T}_2]\!] &= [\![\text{T}_1]\!] \rightarrow [\![\text{T}_2]\!] \\
[\![\{1_i : \text{T}_i\,^{i \in 1..n}\}]\!] &= \{1_i : [\![\text{T}_i]\!]\,^{i \in 1..n}\}
\end{aligned}
$$

---

3. Similar observations apply to accessing fields and methods of objects, in languages where object subtyping allows permutation. This is the reason that Java, for example, restricts subtyping between classes so that new fields can only be added at the end. Subtyping between interfaces (and between classes and interfaces) does allow permutation—if it did not, interfaces would be of hardly any use—and the manual explicitly warns that looking up a method from an interface will in general be slower than from a class.

For example, $[\![\text{Top}\to\{\text{a:Top,b:Top}\}]\!] = \text{Unit}\to\{\text{a:Unit,b:Unit}\}$. (The other translations will also be written $[\![-]\!]$; the context will always make it clear which one we are talking about.)

To translate a term, we need to know where subsumption is used in type-checking it, since these are the places where run-time coercions will be inserted. One convenient way of formalizing this observation is to give the translation as a function on *derivations* of typing statements. Similarly, to generate a coercion function transforming values of type S to type T, we need to know not just *that* S is a subtype of T, but also *why*. We accomplish this by generating coercions from subtyping derivations.

A little notation for naming derivations is needed to formalize the translations. Write $C :: S <: T$ to mean "C is a subtyping derivation tree whose conclusion is $S <: T$." Similarly, write $\mathcal{D} :: \Gamma \vdash t : T$ to mean "$\mathcal{D}$ is a typing derivation whose conclusion is $\Gamma \vdash t : T$."

Let us look first at the function that, given a derivation C for the subtyping statement $S <: T$, generates a coercion $[\![C]\!]$. This coercion is nothing but a function (in the target language of the translation, $\lambda_\to$) from type $[\![S]\!]$ to type $[\![T]\!]$. The definition goes by cases on the final rule used in C.

$$\left[\!\!\left[\dfrac{}{\text{T} <: \text{T}} \text{ (S-Refl)} \right]\!\!\right] \quad = \quad \lambda\text{x:}[\![\text{T}]\!].\ \text{x}$$

$$\left[\!\!\left[\dfrac{}{\text{S} <: \text{Top}} \text{ (S-Top)} \right]\!\!\right] \quad - \quad \lambda\text{x:}[\![\text{S}]\!].\ \text{unit}$$

$$\left[\!\!\left[\dfrac{C_1 :: \text{S} <: \text{U} \qquad C_2 :: \text{U} <: \text{T}}{\text{S} <: \text{T}} \text{ (S-Trans)} \right]\!\!\right] \quad = \quad \lambda\text{x:}[\![\text{S}]\!].\ [\![C_2]\!]([\![C_1]\!]\ \text{x})$$

$$\left[\!\!\left[\dfrac{C_1 :: \text{T}_1 <: \text{S}_1 \qquad C_2 :: \text{S}_2 <: \text{T}_2}{\text{S}_1\to\text{S}_2 <: \text{T}_1\to\text{T}_2} \text{ (S-Arrow)} \right]\!\!\right] \quad = \quad \begin{array}{l}\lambda\text{f:}[\![\text{S}_1\to\text{S}_2]\!].\ \lambda\text{x:}[\![\text{T}_1]\!].\\ \quad [\![C_2]\!](\text{f}([\![C_1]\!]\ \text{x}))\end{array}$$

$$\left[\!\!\left[\dfrac{}{\{\text{l}_i\text{:T}_i{}^{i\in 1..n+k}\} <: \{\text{l}_i\text{:T}_i{}^{i\in 1..n}\}} \text{ (S-RcdWidth)} \right]\!\!\right] \quad = \quad \begin{array}{l}\lambda\text{r:}\{\text{l}_i\text{:}[\![\text{T}_i]\!]{}^{i\in 1..n+k}\}.\\ \quad \{\text{l}_i\text{=r.l}_i{}^{i\in 1..n}\}\end{array}$$

$$\left[\!\!\left[\dfrac{\text{for each } i \quad C_i :: \text{S}_i <: \text{T}_i}{\{\text{l}_i\text{:S}_i{}^{i\in 1..n}\} <: \{\text{l}_i\text{:T}_i{}^{i\in 1..n}\}} \text{ (S-RcdDepth)} \right]\!\!\right] \quad = \quad \begin{array}{l}\lambda\text{r:}\{\text{l}_i\text{:}[\![\text{S}_i]\!]{}^{i\in 1..n}\}.\\ \quad \{\text{l}_i\text{=}[\![C_i]\!](\text{r.l}_i){}^{i\in 1..n}\}\end{array}$$

$$\left[\!\!\left[\dfrac{\{\text{k}_j\text{:S}_j{}^{j\in 1..n}\} \text{ perm. of } \{\text{l}_i\text{:T}_i{}^{i\in 1..n}\}}{\{\text{l}_i\text{:S}_i{}^{i\in 1..n}\} <: \{\text{l}_i\text{:T}_i{}^{i\in 1..n}\}} \text{ (S-RcdPerm)} \right]\!\!\right] \quad = \quad \begin{array}{l}\lambda\text{r:}\{\text{k}_j\text{:}[\![\text{S}_i]\!]{}^{j\in 1..n}\}.\\ \quad \{\text{l}_i\text{=r.l}_i{}^{i\in 1..n}\}\end{array}$$

15.6.1   LEMMA: If $C :: S <: T$, then $\vdash [\![C]\!] : [\![S]\!]\to[\![T]\!]$.   □

Proof: Straightforward induction on C.   □

Typing derivations are translated in a similar way. If $\mathcal{D}$ is a derivation of the statement $\Gamma \vdash t : T$, then its translation $[\![\mathcal{D}]\!]$ is a target-language term of type

$[\![T]\!]$. This translation function is often called the *Penn translation,* after the group at the University of Pennsylvania that first studied it (Breazu-Tannen, Coquand, Gunter, and Scedrov, 1991).

$$\left[\!\!\left[\frac{x:T \in \Gamma}{\Gamma \vdash x : T} \text{(T-Var)} \right]\!\!\right] \qquad\qquad = \quad x$$

$$\left[\!\!\left[\frac{\mathcal{D}_2 :: \Gamma, x:T_1 \vdash t_2 : T_2}{\Gamma \vdash \lambda x:T_1 . T_1 \rightarrow T_2} \text{(T-Abs)} \right]\!\!\right] \qquad = \quad \lambda x:[\![T_1]\!]. \ [\![\mathcal{D}_2]\!]$$

$$\left[\!\!\left[\frac{\mathcal{D}_1 :: \Gamma \vdash t_1 : T_{11} \rightarrow T_{12} \qquad \mathcal{D}_2 :: \Gamma \vdash t_2 : T_{11}}{\Gamma \vdash t_1 \ t_2 : T_{12}} \text{(T-App)} \right]\!\!\right] \quad = \quad [\![\mathcal{D}_1]\!] \ [\![\mathcal{D}_2]\!]$$

$$\left[\!\!\left[\frac{\text{for each } i \quad \mathcal{D}_i :: \Gamma \vdash t_i : T_i}{\Gamma \vdash \{l_i = t_i{}^{i \in 1..n}\} : \{l_i : T_i{}^{i \in 1..n}\}} \text{(T-Rcd)} \right]\!\!\right] \quad = \quad \{l_i = [\![\mathcal{D}_i]\!]^{\ i \in 1..n}\}$$

$$\left[\!\!\left[\frac{\mathcal{D}_1 :: \Gamma \vdash t_1 : \{l_i : T_i{}^{i \in 1..n}\}}{\Gamma \vdash t_1 . l_j : T_j} \text{(T-Proj)} \right]\!\!\right] \qquad = \quad [\![\mathcal{D}_1]\!]. l_j$$

$$\left[\!\!\left[\frac{\mathcal{D} :: \Gamma \vdash t : S \qquad C :: S <: T}{\Gamma \vdash t : T} \text{(T-Sub)} \right]\!\!\right] \qquad = \quad [\![C]\!] \ [\![\mathcal{D}]\!]$$

15.6.2   THEOREM: If $\mathcal{D} :: \Gamma \vdash t : T$, then $[\![\Gamma]\!] \vdash [\![\mathcal{D}]\!] : [\![T]\!]$, where $[\![\Gamma]\!]$ is the point-wise extension of the type translation to contexts: $[\![\varnothing]\!] = \varnothing$ and $[\![\Gamma, x:T]\!] = [\![\Gamma]\!], x:[\![T]\!]$.   □

Proof: Straightforward induction on $\mathcal{D}$, using Lemma 15.6.1 for the T-Sub case.   □

Having defined these translations, we can drop the evaluation rules for the high-level language with subtyping, and instead evaluate terms by typecheck-ing them (using the high-level typing and subtyping rules), translating their typing derivations to the low-level target language, and then using the evalua-tion relation of this language to obtain their operational behavior. This strat-egy is actually used in some high-performance implementations of languages with subtyping, such as the Yale compiler group's experimental Java compiler (League, Shao, and Trifonov, 1999; League, Trifonov, and Shao, 2001).

15.6.3   EXERCISE [★★★ ↛]: Modify the translations above to use simply typed lambda-calculus with *tuples* (instead of records) as a target language. Check that The-orem 15.6.2 still holds.   □

Coherence

When we give a coercion semantics for a language with subtyping, there is a potential pitfall that we need to be careful to avoid. Suppose, for example, that we extend the present language with the base types `Int`, `Bool`, `Float`, and `String`. The following primitive coercions might all be useful:

$$[\![\texttt{Bool} <: \texttt{Int}]\!] \quad = \quad \lambda\texttt{b:Bool. if b then 1 else 0}$$
$$[\![\texttt{Int} <: \texttt{String}]\!] \quad = \quad \texttt{intToString}$$
$$[\![\texttt{Bool} <: \texttt{Float}]\!] \quad = \quad \lambda\texttt{b:Bool. if b then 1.0 else 0.0}$$
$$[\![\texttt{Float} <: \texttt{String}]\!] \quad = \quad \texttt{floatToString}$$

The functions `intToString` and `floatToString` are primitives that construct string representations of numbers. For the sake of the example, suppose that `intToString(1)` = `"1"`, while `floatToString(1.0)` = `"1.000"`.

Now, suppose we are asked to evaluate the term

```
(λx:String.x) true;
```

using the coercion semantics. This term is typable, given the axioms above for the primitive types. In fact, it is typable in two distinct ways: we can either use subsumption to promote `Bool` to `Int` and then to `String`, to show that `true` is an appropriate argument to a function of type `String→String`, or we can promote `Bool` to `Float` and then to `String`. But if we translate these derivations into $\lambda_\rightarrow$, we get different behaviors. If we coerce `true` to type `Int`, we get `1`, from which `intToString` yields the string `"1"`. But if we instead coerce `true` to a float and then, using `floatToString`, to a `String` (following the structure of a typing derivation in which `true : String` is proved by going via `Float`), we obtain `"1.000"`. But `"1"` and `"1.000"` are very different strings: they do not even have the same length. In other words, the choice of how to prove ⊢ `(λx:String. x) true : String` affects the way the translated program behaves! But this choice is completely internal to the compiler—the programmer writes only *terms,* not derivations—so we have designed a language in which programmers cannot control or even predict the behavior of the programs they write.

The appropriate response to such problems is to impose an additional requirement, called *coherence,* on the definition of the translation functions.

15.6.4 DEFINITION: A translation $[\![-]\!]$ from typing derivations in one language to terms in another is *coherent* if, for every pair of derivations $\mathcal{D}_1$ and $\mathcal{D}_2$ with the same conclusion $\Gamma \vdash \texttt{t} : \texttt{T}$, the translations $[\![\mathcal{D}_1]\!]$ and $[\![\mathcal{D}_2]\!]$ are behaviorally equivalent terms of the target language. □

In particular, the translations given above (with no base types) are coherent. To recover coherence when we consider base types (with the axioms above), it suffices to change the definition of the `floatToString` primitive so that `floatToString(0.0)` = `"0"` and `floatToString(1.0)` = `"1"`.

Proving coherence, especially for more complex languages, can be a tricky business. See Reynolds (1980), Breazu-Tannen et al. (1991), Curien and Ghelli (1992), and Reynolds (1991).

15.7   Intersection and Union Types

A powerful refinement of the subtype relation can be obtained by adding an *intersection* operator to the language of types. Intersection types were invented by Coppo, Dezani, Sallé, and Pottinger (Coppo and Dezani-Ciancaglini, 1978; Coppo, Dezani-Ciancaglini, and Sallé, 1979; Pottinger, 1980). Accessible introductions can be found in Reynolds (1988, 1998b), Hindley (1992), and Pierce (1991b).

The inhabitants of the intersection type $T_1 \wedge T_2$ are terms belonging to *both* S and T—that is, $T_1 \wedge T_2$ is an order-theoretic meet (greatest lower bound) of T_1 and T_2. This intuition is captured by three new subtyping rules.

$$T_1 \wedge T_2 <: T_1 \qquad \text{(S-Inter1)}$$

$$T_1 \wedge T_2 <: T_2 \qquad \text{(S-Inter2)}$$

$$\frac{S <: T_1 \qquad S <: T_2}{S <: T_1 \wedge T_2} \qquad \text{(S-Inter3)}$$

One additional rule allows a natural interaction between intersection and arrow types.

$$S{\rightarrow}T_1 \wedge S{\rightarrow}T_2 <: S{\rightarrow}(T_1{\wedge}T_2) \qquad \text{(S-Inter4)}$$

The intuition behind this rule is that, if we know a term has the function types $S{\rightarrow}T_1$ and $S{\rightarrow}T_2$, then we can certainly pass it an S and expect to get back both a T_1 and a T_2.

The power of intersection types is illustrated by the fact that, in a call-by-name variant of the simply typed lambda-calculus with subtyping and intersections, the set of untyped lambda-terms that can be assigned types is exactly the set of *normalizing* terms—i.e., a term is typable iff its evaluation terminates! This immediately implies that the type reconstruction problem (see Chapter 22) for calculi with intersections is undecidable.

More pragmatically, the interest of intersection types is that they support a form of *finitary overloading*. For example, we might assign the type (Nat→Nat→Nat) ∧ (Float→Float→Float) to an addition operator that can be used on both natural numbers and floats (using tag bits in the run-time representation of its arguments, for example, to select the correct instruction).

Unfortunately, the power of intersection types raises some difficult pragmatic issues for language designers. So far, only one full-scale language,

Forsythe (Reynolds, 1988), has included intersections in their most general form. A restricted form known as *refinement types* may prove more manageable (Freeman and Pfenning, 1991; Pfenning, 1993b; Davies, 1997).

The dual notion of *union types,* $T_1 \vee T_2$, also turns out to be quite useful. Unlike sum and variant types (which, confusingly, are sometimes also called "unions"), $T_1 \vee T_2$ denotes the ordinary union of the set of values belonging to T_1 and the set of values belonging to T_2, with no added tag to identify the origin of a given element. Thus, Nat $\vee$ Nat is actually just another name for Nat. Non-disjoint union types have long played an important role in program analysis (Palsberg and Pavlopoulou, 1998), but have featured in few programming languages (notably Algol 68; cf. van Wijngaarden et al., 1975); recently, though, they are increasingly being applied in the context of type systems for processing of "semistructured" database formats such as XML (Buneman and Pierce, 1998; Hosoya, Vouillon, and Pierce, 2001).

The main formal difference between disjoint and non-disjoint union types is that the latter lack any kind of `case` construct: if we know only that a value v has type $T_1 \vee T_2$, then the only operations we can safely perform on v are ones that make sense for *both* T_1 and T_2. (For example, if T_1 and T_2 are records, it makes sense to project v on their common fields.) The untagged `union` type in C is a source of type safety violations precisely because it ignores this restriction, allowing any operation on an element of $T_1 \vee T_2$ that makes sense for *either* T_1 or T_2.

15.8 Notes

The idea of subtyping in programming languages goes back to the 1960s, in Simula (Birtwistle, Dahl, Myhrhaug, and Nygaard, 1979) and its relatives. The first formal treatments are due to Reynolds (1980) and Cardelli (1984).

The typing and—especially—subtyping rules dealing with records are somewhat heavier than most of the other rules we have seen, involving either variable numbers of premises (one for each field) or additional mechanisms like permutations on the indices of fields. There are many other ways of writing these rules, but all either suffer from similar complexity or else avoid it by introducing informal conventions (e.g., ellipsis: "$l_1:T_1 \ldots l_n:T_n$"). Frustration with this state of affairs led Cardelli and Mitchell to develop their calculus of *Operations on Records* (1991), in which the macro operation of creating a multi-field record is broken down into a basic empty record value plus an operation for adding a single field at a time. Additional operations such as in-place field update and record concatenation (Harper and Pierce, 1991) can also be considered in this setting. The typing rules for these operations become rather subtle, especially in the presence of parametric polymorphism, so most language designers prefer to stick with ordinary records. Nevertheless, Cardelli and Mitchell's system remains an important conceptual landmark. An alternative treatment of records based on *row-variable polymorphism* has been developed by Wand (1987, 1988, 1989b), Rémy (1990, 1989, 1992), and others, and forms the basis for the object-oriented features of OCaml (Rémy and Vouillon, 1998; Vouillon, 2000).

The fundamental problem addressed by a type theory is to insure that programs have meaning. The fundamental problem caused by a type theory is that meaningful programs may not have meanings ascribed to them. The quest for richer type systems results from this tension.   —*Mark Manasse*

16 *Metatheory of Subtyping*

The definition in the previous chapter of the simply typed lambda-calculus with subtyping is not immediately suitable for implementation. Unlike the other calculi we have seen, the rules of this system are not *syntax directed*— they cannot just be "read from bottom to top" to yield a typechecking algorithm. The main culprits are the rules of subsumption (T-SUB) in the typing relation and transitivity (S-TRANS) in the subtype relation.

The reason T-SUB is problematic is that the term in its conclusion is specified as a bare metavariable t:

$$\frac{\Gamma \vdash t : S \qquad S <: T}{\Gamma \vdash t : T} \qquad \text{(T-SUB)}$$

Every other typing rule specifies a term of some specific form—T-ABS applies only to lambda-abstractions, T-VAR only to variables, etc.—while T-SUB can be applied to *any* kind of term. This means that, if we are given a term t whose type we are trying to calculate, it will always be possible to apply either T-SUB or the other rule whose conclusion matches the shape of t.

S-TRANS is problematic for the same reason—its conclusion overlaps with the conclusions of all the other rules.

$$\frac{S <: U \qquad U <: T}{S <: T} \qquad \text{(S-TRANS)}$$

Since S and T are bare metavariables, we can potentially use S-TRANS as the final rule in a derivation of any subtyping statement. Thus, a naive "bottom to top" implementation of the subtyping rules would never know whether to try using this rule or whether to try another rule whose more specific conclusion also matches the two types whose membership in the subtype relation we are trying to check.

The calculus studied in this chapter is the simply typed lambda-calculus with subtyping (Figure 15-1) and records (15-3). The corresponding OCaml implementation is rcdsub. §16.3 also deals with booleans and conditionals (8-1); the OCaml implementation for this section is joinsub. §16.4 extends the discussions to Bot; the corresponding implementation is bot.

There is one other problem with S-TRANS. Both of its premises mention the metavariable U, which does not appear in the conclusion. If we read the rule naively from bottom to top, it says that we should *guess* a type U and then attempt to show that S <: U and U <: T. Since there are an infinite number of Us that we could guess, this strategy has little hope of success.

The S-REFL rule also overlaps the conclusions of the other subtyping rules. This is less severe than the problems with T-SUB and S-TRANS: the reflexivity rule has no premises, so if it matches a subtyping statement we are trying to prove, we can succeed immediately. Still, it is another reason why the rules are not syntax directed.

The solution to all of these problems is to replace the ordinary (or *declarative*) subtyping and typing relations by two new relations, called the *algorithmic subtyping* and *algorithmic typing* relations, whose sets of inference rules are syntax directed. We then justify this switch by showing that the original subtyping and typing relations actually coincide with the algorithmic presentations: the statement S <: T is derivable from the algorithmic subtyping rules iff it is derivable from the declarative rules, and a term is typable by the algorithmic typing rules iff it is typable under the declarative rules.

We develop the algorithmic subtype relation in §16.1 and the algorithmic typing relation in §16.2. §16.3 addresses the special typechecking problems of multi-branch constructs like `if...then...else`, which require additional structure (the existence of least upper bounds, or *joins,* in the subtype relation). §16.4 considers the minimal type `Bot`.

16.1   Algorithmic Subtyping

A crucial element of any implementation of a language with subtyping is an algorithm for checking whether one type is a subtype of another. This subtype checker will be called by the typechecker when, for example, it encounters an application $t_1 \; t_2$ where t_1 has type T→U and t_2 has type S. Its function is to decide whether the statement S <: T is derivable from the subtyping rules in Figures 15-1 and 15-3. It accomplishes this by checking whether (S, T) belongs to another relation, written ⊢ S <: T ("S is algorithmically a subtype of T"), which is defined in such a way that membership can be decided simply by following the structure of the types, and which contains the same pairs of types as the ordinary subtype relation. The significant difference between the declarative and algorithmic relations is that the algorithmic relation drops the S-TRANS and S-REFL rules.

To begin with, we need to reorganize the declarative system a little. As we saw on page 184, we need to use transitivity to "paste together" subtyping

$\rightarrow \{\} <:$ *Extends 15-1 and 15-3*

$S <: S$	(S-REFL)	$\dfrac{T_1 <: S_1 \qquad S_2 <: T_2}{S_1 \rightarrow S_2 <: T_1 \rightarrow T_2}$ (S-ARROW)
$\dfrac{S <: U \qquad U <: T}{S <: T}$	(S-TRANS)	
$S <: \text{Top}$	(S-TOP)	$\dfrac{\{l_i^{\;i \in 1..n}\} \subseteq \{k_j^{\;j \in 1..m}\} \quad k_j = l_i \text{ implies } S_j <: T_i}{\{k_j : S_j^{\;j \in 1..m}\} <: \{l_i : T_i^{\;i \in 1..n}\}}$ (S-RCD)

Figure 16-1: Subtype relation with records (compact version)

derivations for records involving combinations of depth, width, and permutation subtyping. Before we can drop S-TRANS, we must first *add* a rule that bundles depth, width, and permutation subtyping into one:

$$\frac{\{l_i^{\;i \in 1..n}\} \subseteq \{k_j^{\;j \in 1..m}\} \qquad k_j = l_i \text{ implies } S_j <: T_i}{\{k_j : S_j^{\;j \in 1..m}\} <: \{l_i : T_i^{\;i \in 1..n}\}} \qquad \text{(S-RCD)}$$

16.1.1   LEMMA: If $S <: T$ is derivable from the subtyping rules including S-RCDDEPTH, S-RCD-WIDTH, and S-RCD-PERM (but not S-RCD), then it can also be derived using S-RCD (and not S-RCDDEPTH, S-RCD-WIDTH, or S-RCD-PERM), and vice versa.   □

Proof: Straightforward induction on derivations.   □

Lemma 16.1.1 justifies eliminating rules S-RCDDEPTH, S-RCD-WIDTH, and S-RCD-PERM in favor of S-RCD. Figure 16-1 summarizes the resulting system.

Next, we show that, in the system of Figure 16-1, the reflexivity and transitivity rules are inessential.

16.1.2   LEMMA:

1. $S <: S$ can be derived for every type S without using S-REFL.

2. If $S <: T$ is derivable, then it can be derived without using S-TRANS.   □

Proof: EXERCISE [RECOMMENDED, ★★★].   □

16.1.3   EXERCISE [★]: If we add the type Bool, how do these properties change?   □

This brings us to the definition of the algorithmic subtype relation.

16.1.4   DEFINITION: The *algorithmic subtyping* relation is the least relation on types closed under the rules in Figure 16-2.   □

$\to$ {} <:

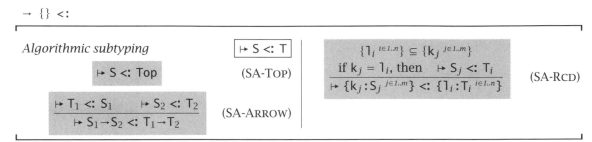

Algorithmic subtyping $\vdash S <: T$

$\vdash S <:$ Top   (SA-Top)

$$\frac{\vdash T_1 <: S_1 \qquad \vdash S_2 <: T_2}{\vdash S_1 \to S_2 <: T_1 \to T_2}$$ (SA-Arrow)

$$\frac{\{l_i{}^{i \in 1..n}\} \subseteq \{k_j{}^{j \in 1..m}\} \quad \text{if } k_j = l_i, \text{ then } \vdash S_j <: T_i}{\vdash \{k_j : S_j{}^{j \in 1..m}\} <: \{l_i : T_i{}^{i \in 1..n}\}}$$ (SA-Rcd)

Figure 16-2: Algorithmic subtyping

We say that the algorithmic rules are *sound* because every statement that can be derived from algorithmic rules can also be derived from the declarative rules (the algorithmic rules do not prove anything new), and *complete* because every statement that can be derived from the declarative rules can also be derived from the algorithmic rules (the algorithmic rules prove everything that could be proved before).

16.1.5   PROPOSITION [SOUNDNESS AND COMPLETENESS]: S <: T iff $\vdash$ S <: T.   □

Proof: Each direction proceeds by induction on derivations, using one of the two previous lemmas.   □

Now the algorithmic rules, being syntax directed, can be read directly as an algorithm for checking the algorithmic subtype relation (and hence also the declarative subtype relation). In a more conventional pseudocode notation, the algorithm looks like this:

$$
\begin{aligned}
\textit{subtype}(S, T) = \ & \text{if } T = \text{Top, then } \textit{true} \\
& \text{else if } S = S_1 \to S_2 \text{ and } T = T_1 \to T_2 \\
& \quad \text{then } \textit{subtype}(T_1, S_1) \ \wedge \ \textit{subtype}(S_2, T_2) \\
& \text{else if } S = \{k_j : S_j{}^{j \in 1..m}\} \text{ and } T = \{l_i : T_i{}^{i \in 1..n}\} \\
& \quad \text{then} \quad \{l_i{}^{i \in 1..n}\} \subseteq \{k_j{}^{j \in 1..m}\} \\
& \qquad\qquad \wedge \text{ for all } i \text{ there is some } j \in 1..m \text{ with } k_j = l_i \\
& \qquad\qquad\qquad \text{and } \textit{subtype}(S_j, T_i) \\
& \text{else } \textit{false}.
\end{aligned}
$$

A concrete realization of this algorithm in ML appears in Chapter 17.

Finally, we need to verify that the algorithmic subtype relation is *total*—i.e., that the recursive function *subtype* derived from the algorithmic rules returns either *true* or *false,* for every pair of inputs, after a finite amount of time.

16.1.6   PROPOSITION [TERMINATION]: If ⊢ S <: T is derivable, then *subtype*(S, T) will
return *true*. If not, then *subtype*(S, T) will return *false*.   □

This theorem, together with the soundness and completeness of the algorithmic rules, essentially asserts that the *subtype* function is a *decision
procedure* for the declarative subtype relation.

Proof: The first claim is easy to check (by a straightforward induction on a
derivation of ⊢ S <: T). Conversely, it is also easy to check that, if *subtype*(S, T)
returns *true,* then ⊢ S <: T. Thus, to establish the second claim, it suffices to
show that *subtype*(S, T) must always return *something*—i.e., that it cannot diverge. This we can do by observing that the sum of the sizes of the input pair
S and T is always strictly larger than the sum of the sizes of the arguments to
any recursive call that that algorithm makes. Since this sum is always positive,
an infinite sequence of recursive calls is not possible.   □

The reader may wonder whether we could have saved ourselves all the work
in this section by simply taking the algorithmic definition of the subtype relation as the official definition and never even mentioning the declarative
version. The answer is a qualified "Yes." We can certainly take the algorithmic definition as the official one when defining the calculus, if we prefer.
However, this does not actually save much work, because, to show that the
typing relation (which depends on the subtype relation) is well-behaved, we
will need to know that subtyping is reflexive and transitive, and these proofs
involve more or less the same work as we have done here. (On the other hand,
language definitions do often adopt an algorithmic presentation of the typing
relation. We will see one example of this in Chapter 19.)

16.2   Algorithmic Typing

Having gotten the subtype relation under control, we need to do the same
with the typing relation. As we saw on page 209, the only non-syntax-directed
typing rule is T-SUB, so this is the one we must deal with. As with S-TRANS
in the previous section, we cannot simply delete the subsumption rule: we
must first examine where it plays a critical role in typing and enrich the other
typing rules to achieve the same effects in a more syntax-directed way.

Clearly, one critical use of subsumption is bridging gaps between the types
expected by functions and the actual types of their arguments. A term like

```
(λr:{x:Nat}. r.x) {x=0,y=1}
```

is not typable without subsumption.

Perhaps surprisingly, this is the *only* situation where subsumption plays a crucial role in typing. In every other case where subsumption is used in a typing proof, the same statement can be proved by a different derivation in which subsumption is "postponed" by moving it down the tree toward the root. To see why this works, it is instructive to experiment a little with typing derivations involving subsumption, taking each typing rule in turn and thinking about how a derivation ending with this rule can be reorganized if one of its immediate subderivations ends with T-SUB.

For example, suppose we are given a typing derivation ending with T-ABS, whose immediate subderivation ends with T-SUB.

$$
\cfrac{
  \cfrac{
    \cfrac{\vdots}{\Gamma, x:S_1 \vdash s_2 : S_2}
    \qquad
    \cfrac{\vdots}{S_2 <: T_2}
  }{\Gamma, x:S_1 \vdash s_2 : T_2} \text{(T-SUB)}
}{\Gamma \vdash \lambda x:S_1.s_2 : S_1 \rightarrow T_2} \text{(T-ABS)}
$$

Such a derivation can be rearranged so that subsumption is used *after* the abstraction rule to achieve the same conclusion:

$$
\cfrac{
  \cfrac{
    \cfrac{\vdots}{\Gamma, x:S_1 \vdash s_2 : S_2}
  }{\Gamma \vdash \lambda x:S_1.s_2 : S_1 \rightarrow S_2} \text{(T-ABS)}
  \qquad
  \cfrac{
    \cfrac{}{S_1 <: S_1} \text{(S-REFL)}
    \qquad
    \cfrac{\vdots}{S_2 <: T_2}
  }{S_1 \rightarrow S_2 <: S_1 \rightarrow T_2} \text{(S-ARROW)}
}{\Gamma \vdash \lambda x:S_1.s_2 : S_1 \rightarrow T_2} \text{(T-SUB)}
$$

A more interesting case is the application rule T-APP. Here there are two subderivations, either of which might end with T-SUB. Consider first the case where subsumption appears at the end of the left-hand subderivation.

$$
\cfrac{
  \cfrac{
    \cfrac{\vdots}{\Gamma \vdash s_1 : S_{11} \rightarrow S_{12}}
    \qquad
    \cfrac{\vdots}{S_{11} \rightarrow S_{12} <: T_{11} \rightarrow T_{12}} \text{(S-ARROW)}
  }{\Gamma \vdash s_1 : T_{11} \rightarrow T_{12}} \text{(T-SUB)}
  \qquad
  \cfrac{\vdots}{\Gamma \vdash s_2 : T_{11}}
}{\Gamma \vdash s_1\, s_2 : T_{12}} \text{(T-APP)}
$$

From the results in the previous section, we may assume that the final rule in the derivation of $S_{11} \rightarrow S_{12} <: T_{11} \rightarrow T_{12}$ is neither S-REFL nor S-TRANS. Given the form of its conclusion, this rule can then only be S-ARROW.

$$
\cfrac{
  \cfrac{\vdots}{\Gamma \vdash s_1 : S_{11} \to S_{12}} \qquad
  \cfrac{
    \cfrac{\vdots}{T_{11} <: S_{11}} \quad \cfrac{\vdots}{S_{12} <: T_{12}}
  }{S_{11} \to S_{12} <: T_{11} \to T_{12}} \text{(S-ARROW)}
}{\Gamma \vdash s_1 : T_{11} \to T_{12}} \text{(T-SUB)} \qquad
\cfrac{\vdots}{\Gamma \vdash s_2 : T_{11}}
$$
$$
\cfrac{}{\Gamma \vdash s_1 \; s_2 : T_{12}} \text{(T-APP)}
$$

Rewriting to eliminate the instance of T-SUB has an interesting effect.

$$
\cfrac{
  \cfrac{
    \cfrac{\vdots}{\Gamma \vdash s_1 : S_{11} \to S_{12}} \qquad
    \cfrac{
      \cfrac{\vdots}{\Gamma \vdash s_2 : T_{11}} \quad \cfrac{\vdots}{T_{11} <: S_{11}}
    }{\Gamma \vdash s_2 : S_{11}} \text{(T-SUB)}
  }{\Gamma \vdash s_1 \; s_2 : S_{12}} \text{(T-APP)} \qquad
  \cfrac{\vdots}{S_{12} <: T_{12}}
}{\Gamma \vdash s_1 \; s_2 : T_{12}} \text{(T-SUB)}
$$

The right-hand subderivation of the original instance of S-ARROW has been pushed down to the bottom of the tree, where a new instance of T-SUB raises the type of the whole application node. On the other hand, the left-hand subderivation has been pushed *up* into the derivation for the argument s_2.

Suppose instead that the instance of T-SUB that we want to relocate occurs at the end of the right-hand subderivation of an instance of T-APP.

$$
\cfrac{
  \cfrac{\vdots}{\Gamma \vdash s_1 : T_{11} \to T_{12}} \qquad
  \cfrac{
    \cfrac{\vdots}{\Gamma \vdash s_2 : T_2} \quad \cfrac{\vdots}{T_2 <: T_{11}}
  }{\Gamma \vdash s_2 : T_{11}} \text{(T-SUB)}
}{\Gamma \vdash s_1 \; s_2 : T_{12}} \text{(T-APP)}
$$

The only thing we can do with this instance of T-SUB is to move it over into the left-hand subderivation—partly reversing the previous transformation.

$$
\cfrac{
  \cfrac{
    \cfrac{\vdots}{\Gamma \vdash s_1 : T_{11} \to T_{12}} \qquad
    \cfrac{
      \cfrac{\vdots}{T_2 <: T_{11}} \quad \cfrac{}{T_{12} <: T_{12}} \text{(S-REFL)}
    }{T_{11} \to T_{12} <: T_2 \to T_{12}} \text{(S-ARROW)}
  }{\Gamma \vdash s_1 : T_2 \to T_{12}} \text{(T-SUB)} \qquad
  \cfrac{\vdots}{\Gamma \vdash s_2 : T_2}
}{\Gamma \vdash s_1 \; s_2 : T_{12}} \text{(T-APP)}
$$

So we see that the use of subsumption for promoting the result type of an application can be moved down past the T-APP rule, but that the use of subsumption for matching the argument type and the domain type of the function cannot be eliminated. It can be moved from one premise to the other—we can promote the type of the argument to match the domain of the function, or we can promote the type of the function (by demoting its argument type) so that it expects an argument of the type we actually plan to give it—but we cannot get rid of the subsumption altogether. This observation corresponds precisely with our intuition that this gap-bridging use of subsumption is essential to the power of the system.

Another case we have to consider is where the last rule in a derivation is subsumption and its immediate subderivation also ends with subsumption. In this case, the two adjacent uses of subsumption can be coalesced into one—i.e., any derivation of the form

$$
\cfrac{\cfrac{\vdots \qquad \vdots}{\cfrac{\Gamma \vdash s : S \qquad S <: U}{\Gamma \vdash s : U} \text{ (T-Sub)} \qquad \cfrac{\vdots}{U <: T}}}{\Gamma \vdash s : T} \text{ (T-Sub)}
$$

can be rewritten:

$$
\cfrac{\cfrac{\vdots}{\Gamma \vdash s : S} \qquad \cfrac{\cfrac{\vdots}{S <: U} \qquad \cfrac{\vdots}{U <: T}}{S <: T} \text{ (S-Trans)}}{\Gamma \vdash s : T} \text{ (T-Sub)}
$$

16.2.1   EXERCISE [⋆ ↠]: To finish the experiment, show how to perform similar rearrangements on derivations in which T-SUB is used before T-RCD or T-PROJ. □

By applying these transformations repeatedly, we can rewrite an arbitrary typing derivation into a special form where T-SUB appears in only two places: at the end of right-hand subderivations of applications, and at the very end of the whole derivation. Moreover, if we simply *delete* the one at the very end, no great harm will result: we will still have a derivation assigning a type to the same term—the only difference is that the type assigned to this term may be a smaller (i.e., better!) one. This leaves just one place, applications, where uses of subsumption can still occur. To deal with this case, we can replace the application rule by a slightly more powerful one

$$
\frac{\Gamma \vdash t_1 : T_{11} {\rightarrow} T_{12} \qquad \Gamma \vdash t_2 : T_2 \qquad T_2 <: T_{11}}{\Gamma \vdash t_1\ t_2 : T_{12}}
$$

incorporating a single instance of subsumption as a premise. Every subderivation of the form application-preceded-by-subsumption can be replaced by a use of this rule, which leaves us with no uses of T-SUB at all. Moreover, the enriched application rule is syntax directed: the shape of the term in the conclusion prevents it from overlapping with the other rules.

→ {} <:

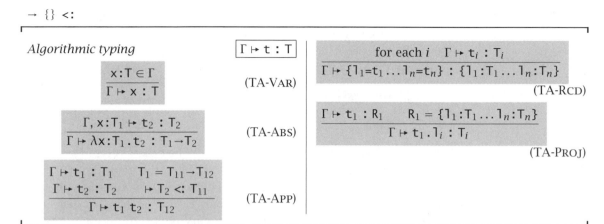

Figure 16-3: Algorithmic typing

This transformation yields a syntax-directed set of typing rules that assigns types to the same terms as the original typing rules. These rules are summarized in the following definition. As we did for the algorithmic subtyping rules, we write the algorithmic relation with a funny turnstile, $\Gamma \Vdash t : T$, to distinguish it from the declarative relation.

16.2.2 DEFINITION: The *algorithmic typing relation* is the least relation closed under the rules in Figure 16-3. The premise $T_1 = T_{11} \rightarrow T_{12}$ in the application rule is simply an explicit reminder of the sequencing of operations during type-checking: first we calculate a type T_1 for t_1; then we check that T_1 has the form $T_{11} \rightarrow T_{12}$, etc. The rule would have exactly the same force if we dropped this premise and instead wrote the first premise as $\Gamma \Vdash t_1 : T_{11} \rightarrow T_{12}$. Similarly for TA-PROJ. Also, the subtyping premise in the application rule is written with a funny turnstile; since we know that the algorithmic and declarative presentations of subtyping are equivalent, this choice is a matter of taste. □

16.2.3 EXERCISE [★ ↦]: Show that the type assigned to a term by the algorithmic rules can *decrease* during evaluation by finding two terms s and t with algorithmic types S and T such that s $\longrightarrow^*$ t and T <: S, but S ≮: T. □

We now need to check formally that the algorithmic typing rules correspond to the original declarative rules. (The transformations on typing derivations that we enumerated above are too informal to be considered a proof. They could be turned into one, but it would be longer and heavier than necessary: it is simpler just to argue by induction on derivations, as usual.) As we did for subtyping, we argue that the algorithmic typing relation is both sound and complete with respect to the original declarative rules.

The soundness property is unchanged: every typing statement that can be derived from the algorithmic rules also follows from the declarative rules.

16.2.4   THEOREM [SOUNDNESS]: If $\Gamma \vdash\!\!\!\!\shortmid\ t : T$, then $\Gamma \vdash t : T$.   □

Proof: Straightforward induction on algorithmic typing derivations.   □

Completeness, though, looks a little different. The ordinary typing relation can be used to assign many types to a term, while the algorithmic typing relation assigns at most one (as can easily be checked). So a straightforward converse of Theorem 16.2.4 is clearly not going to hold. Instead, we can show that if a term t has a type T under the ordinary typing rules, then it has a *better* type S under the algorithmic rules, in the sense that $S <: T$. In other words, the algorithmic rules assign each typable term its smallest possible (*minimal*) type. The completeness theorem is often called the Minimal Typing theorem, since (when combined with Theorem 16.2.4) it amounts to showing that each typable term in the declarative system has a minimal type.

16.2.5   THEOREM [COMPLETENESS, OR MINIMAL TYPING]: If $\Gamma \vdash t : T$, then $\Gamma \vdash\!\!\!\!\shortmid\ t : S$ for some $S <: T$.   □

Proof: EXERCISE [RECOMMENDED, ⋆⋆].   □

16.2.6   EXERCISE [⋆⋆]: If we dropped the arrow subtyping rule S-ARROW but kept the rest of the declarative subtyping and typing rules the same, would the system still have the minimal typing property? If so, prove it. If not, give an example of a typable term with no minimal type.   □

16.3   Joins and Meets

Typechecking expressions with multiple result branches, such as conditionals or `case` expressions, in a language with subtyping requires some additional machinery. For example, recall the declarative typing rule for conditionals.

$$\frac{\Gamma \vdash t_1 : \text{Bool} \qquad \Gamma \vdash t_2 : T \qquad \Gamma \vdash t_3 : T}{\Gamma \vdash \text{if } t_1 \text{ then } t_2 \text{ else } t_3 : T} \tag{T-IF}$$

The rule requires that the types of the two branches be the same, and assigns this type to the whole conditional. But in the presence of subsumption, there may be *many* ways of giving the two branches the same type. For example,

```
if true then {x=true,y=false} else {x=false,z=true};
```

has type {x:Bool}, since the then part has minimal type {x:Bool,y:Bool}, which can be promoted to {x:Bool} using T-SUB, and similarly the else part has minimal type {x:Bool,z:Bool}, which can also be promoted to {x:Bool}. The same term also has types {x:Top} and {}—in fact, *any* type that is a supertype of both {x:Bool,y:Bool} and {x:Bool,z:Bool}. The minimal type for the whole conditional is therefore the least type that is a supertype of both {x:Bool,y:Bool} and {x:Bool,z:Bool}—i.e., {x:Bool}. In general, to calculate the minimal type of an arbitrary conditional expression, we need to calculate the minimal types of its then and else branches and then calculate the least common supertype of these. This type is often called the *join* of the types of the branches, since it corresponds to the usual join of two elements of a partial order.

16.3.1 DEFINITION: A type J is called a *join* of a pair of types S and T, written S ∨ T = J, if S <: J, T <: J, and, for all types U, if S <: U and T <: U, then J <: U. Similarly, we say that a type M is a *meet* of S and T, written S ∧ T = M, if M <: S, M <: T, and, for all types L, if L <: S and L <: T, then L <: M. □

Depending on how the subtype relation in a particular language with subtyping is defined, it may or may not be the case that every pair of types has a join. A given subtype relation is said to *have joins* if, for every S and T, there is some J that is a join of S and T. Similarly, a subtype relation is said to *have meets* if, for every S and T, there is some M that is a meet of S and T.

The subtype relation that we are considering in this section[1] has joins, but not meets. For example, the types {} and Top→Top do not have any common subtypes at all, so they certainly have no greatest one. However, a slightly weaker property does hold. A pair of types S and T is said to be *bounded below* if there is some type L such that L <: S and L <: T. A given subtype relation is said to *have bounded meets* if, for every S and T such that S and T are bounded below, there is some M that is a meet of S and T.

Joins and meets need not be unique. For example, {x:Top,y:Top} and {y:Top,x:Top} are both joins of the pair of types {x:Top,y:Top,z:Top} and {x:Top,y:Top,w:Top}. However, two different joins (or meets) of the same pair of types must each be a subtype of the other.

16.3.2 PROPOSITION [EXISTENCE OF JOINS AND BOUNDED MEETS]:

1. For every pair of types S and T, there is some type J such that S ∨ T = J.

---

1. That is, the relation defined in Figures 15-1 and 15-3, extended with the type Bool. The subtyping behavior of Bool is simple: no rules for it are added to the declarative subtype relation, so its only supertype is Top.

2. For every pair of types S and T with a common subtype, there is some type M such that $S \wedge T = M$.   □

Proof: EXERCISE [RECOMMENDED, ★★★].   □

Using the join operation we can now give an algorithmic rule for the if construct in the presence of subtyping.

$$\frac{\Gamma \vdash t_1 : T_1 \quad T_1 = \text{Bool} \quad \Gamma \vdash t_2 : T_2 \quad \Gamma \vdash t_3 : T_3 \quad T_2 \vee T_3 = T}{\Gamma \vdash \text{if } t_1 \text{ then } t_2 \text{ else } t_3 : T} \quad \text{(TA-IF)}$$

16.3.3   EXERCISE [★★]: What is the minimal type of if true then false else {}? Is this what we want?   □

16.3.4   EXERCISE [★★★]: Is it easy to extend the algorithms for calculating joins and meets to an imperative language with references, as described in §15.5 (on p. 193)? What about the treatment of references in §15.5 (p. 198), where we refine the invariant Ref with covariant Source and contravariant Sink?   □

16.4   Algorithmic Typing and the Bottom Type

If a minimal type Bot (§15.4) is added to the subtype relation, the subtyping and typing algorithms must be extended a little. We add one rule (the obvious one) to the algorithmic subtype relation

$$\Vdash \text{Bot} <: T \quad \text{(SA-BOT)}$$

and two slightly trickier ones to the algorithmic typing relation:

$$\frac{\Gamma \Vdash t_1 : T_1 \quad T_1 = \text{Bot} \quad \Gamma \Vdash t_2 : T_2}{\Gamma \Vdash t_1 \, t_2 : \text{Bot}} \quad \text{(TA-APPBOT)}$$

$$\frac{\Gamma \Vdash t_1 : R_1 \quad R_1 = \text{Bot}}{\Gamma \Vdash t_1.l_i : \text{Bot}} \quad \text{(TA-PROJBOT)}$$

The subtyping rule is clear. The intuition behind the typing rules is that, in the declarative system, we can apply something of type Bot to an argument of absolutely any type (by using subsumption to promote the Bot to whatever function type we like), and assume that the result has any other type, and similarly for projection.

16.4.1   EXERCISE [★]: Suppose we also have conditionals in the language. Do we need to add another algorithmic typing rule for if?   □

The additions needed to support Bot in this language are not overly complicated. We will see in §28.8, though, that more serious complications arise when Bot is combined with bounded quantification.

17 *An ML Implementation of Subtyping*

This chapter extends the OCaml implementation of the simply typed lambda-calculus developed in Chapter 10 with the extra mechanisms needed to support subtyping—in particular, a function for checking the subtype relation.

17.1 Syntax

The datatype definitions for types and terms follow the abstract syntax in Figures 15-1 and 15-3.

```
type ty =
    TyRecord of (string * ty) list
  | TyTop
  | TyArr of ty * ty

type term =
    TmVar of info * int * int
  | TmAbs of info * string * ty * term
  | TmApp of info * term * term
  | TmRecord of info * (string * term) list
  | TmProj of info * term * string
```

The new constructors, compared with the pure simply typed lambda-calculus, are the type TyTop, the type constructor TyRecord, and the term constructors TmRecord and TmProj. We represent records and their types in the simplest possible way, as a list of field names and associated terms or types.

17.2 Subtyping

The pseudocode presentation of the algorithmic subtype relation on page 212 can be translated directly into OCaml as follows.

```
let rec subtype tyS tyT =
  (=) tyS tyT ||
  match (tyS,tyT) with
    (_,TyTop) →
      true
  | (TyArr(tyS1,tyS2),TyArr(tyT1,tyT2)) →
      (subtype tyT1 tyS1) && (subtype tyS2 tyT2)
  | (TyRecord(fS), TyRecord(fT)) →
      List.for_all
        (fun (li,tyTi) →
           try let tySi = List.assoc li fS in
                 subtype tySi tyTi
           with Not_found → false)
        fT
  | (_,_) →
      false
```

We have made one slight change to the algorithm from the pseudocode presentation, adding a reflexivity check at the beginning. (The (=) operator is ordinary equality; it is written in prefix position here because, in some of the other subtyping implementations, it is replaced by a call to a different comparison function. The || operator is a short-circuiting boolean or: if the first branch yields `true`, the second is never evaluated.) Strictly speaking, this check is not needed. However, it is actually an important optimization in real compilers. In the majority of real-world programs, subtyping is used quite rarely—that is, most times when the subtype checker is called, the two types being compared are actually equal. Moreover, if types are represented so that structurally isomorphic types are guaranteed to have physically identical representations—for example, using *hash consing* (Goto, 1974; Appel and Gonçalves, 1993) when constructing types—then this check is just one instruction.

The subtyping rule for records naturally involves a certain amount of fussing around with lists. `List.for_all` applies a predicate (its first argument) to every member of a list and returns `true` iff all these applications return `true`. `List.assoc li fS` looks up the label `li` in the list of fields `fS` and returns the associated field type `tySi`; if `li` is not among the labels in `fS`, it raises `Not_found`, which we catch and convert into a `false` response.

17.3   Typing

The typechecking function is a straightforward extension of the `typeof` function from earlier implementations. The main change is the application clause, where we perform a subtype check between the argument type and the type expected by the function. We also add two new clauses for record construction and projection.

```
let rec typeof ctx t =
  match t with
    TmRecord(fi, fields) →
      let fieldtys =
        List.map (fun (li,ti) → (li, typeof ctx ti)) fields in
      TyRecord(fieldtys)
  | TmProj(fi, t1, l) →
      (match (typeof ctx t1) with
          TyRecord(fieldtys) →
            (try List.assoc l fieldtys
             with Not_found → error fi ("label "^l^" not found"))
        | _ → error fi "Expected record type")
  | TmVar(fi,i,_) → getTypeFromContext fi ctx i
  | TmAbs(fi,x,tyT1,t2) →
      let ctx' = addbinding ctx x (VarBind(tyT1)) in
      let tyT2 = typeof ctx' t2 in
      TyArr(tyT1, tyT2)
  | TmApp(fi,t1,t2) →
      let tyT1 = typeof ctx t1 in
      let tyT2 = typeof ctx t2 in
      (match tyT1 with
          TyArr(tyT11,tyT12) →
            if subtype tyT2 tyT11 then tyT12
            else error fi "parameter type mismatch"
        | _ → error fi "arrow type expected")
```

The record clauses introduce a few features of OCaml that we have not seen before. In the `TmRecord` clause, we calculate the list of field names and types `fieldtys` from the list of names and terms `fields` by using `List.map` to apply the function

```
fun (li,ti) → (li, typeof ctx ti)
```

to each name/term pair in turn. In the `TmProj` clause, we use `List.assoc` again to look up the type of the selected field; if it raises `Not_found`, we raise our own error message (`^` is string concatenation).

17.3.1   EXERCISE [★★★]: §16.3 showed how adding booleans and conditionals to a language with subtyping required extra support functions for calculating the least upper bounds of a given pair of types. The proof of Proposition 16.3.2 (see page 522) gave mathematical descriptions of the necessary algorithms.

The `joinexercise` typechecker is an incomplete implementation of the simply typed lambda-calculus with subtyping, records, and conditionals: basic parsing and printing functions are provided, but the clause for `TmIf` is missing from the `typeof` function, as is the `join` function on which it depends. Add booleans and conditionals (and joins and meets) to this implementation.   □

17.3.2   EXERCISE [★★]: Add a minimal `Bot` type to the `rcdsub` implementation, following the description in §16.4.   □

17.3.3   EXERCISE [★★★ ⇝]: If the subtype check in the application rule fails, the error message that our typechecker prints may not be very helpful to the user. We can improve it by including the expected parameter type and the actual argument type in the error message, but even this may be hard to understand. For example, if the expected type is

  `{x:{},y:{},z:{},a:{},b:{},c:{},d:{},e:{},f:{},g:{}}`

and the actual type is

  `{y:{},z:{},f:{},a:{},x:{},i:{},b:{},e:{},g:{},c:{},h:{}}`

it is not immediately obvious that what's missing from the second type is a `d` field. Error reporting can be greatly improved by changing the `subtype` function so that, instead of returning `true` or `false`, it either returns a trivial value (the unit value `()`) or else raises an exception. Since the exception is raised at the point in the types where something actually failed to match, it can be more precise about what the problem was. Notice that this change doesn't affect the "end-to-end" behavior of the checker: if the subtype checker returns false, the typechecker is always going to raise an exception (by calling `error`) anyway at that point.

Reimplement the `typeof` and `subtype` functions to make *all* of the error messages as informative as possible.   □

17.3.4   EXERCISE [★★★ ⇝]: In §15.6 we defined a *coercion semantics* for a language with records and subtyping using a translation from typing and subtyping derivations into terms of the pure simply typed lambda-calculus. Implement these transformations by modifying the `subtype` function presented above so that it constructs and returns a coercion function (represented as a `term`), and similarly modifying the `typeof` function so that it returns both a type and a translated term. The translated term (rather than the original input term) should then be evaluated, and the result printed as usual.   □

18 *Case Study: Imperative Objects*

In this chapter we come to our first substantial programming example. We will use most of the features we have defined—functions, records, general recursion, mutable references, and subtyping—to build up a collection of programming idioms supporting objects and classes similar to those found in object-oriented languages like Smalltalk and Java. We will not introduce any new concrete syntax for objects or classes in this chapter: what we're after here is to try to *understand* these rather complex language features by showing how to approximate their behavior using lower-level constructs.

For most of the chapter, the approximation is actually quite accurate: we can obtain a satisfactory implementation of most features of objects and classes by regarding them as derived forms that are desugared into simple combinations of features we have already seen. When we get to virtual methods and `self` in §18.9, however, we will encounter some difficulties with evaluation order that make the desugaring a little unrealistic. A more satisfactory account of these features can be obtained by axiomatizing their syntax, operational semantics, and typing rules directly, as we do in Chapter 19.

18.1 What Is Object-Oriented Programming?

Most arguments about "What is the essence of...?" do more to reveal the prejudices of the participants than to uncover any objective truth about the topic of discussion. Attempts to define the term "object-oriented" precisely are no exception. Nonetheless, we can identify a few fundamental features that are found in most object-oriented languages and that, in concert, support a distinctive programming style with well-understood advantages and disadvantages.

The examples in this chapter are terms of the simply typed lambda-calculus with subtyping (Figure 15-1), records (15-3), and references (13-1). The associated OCaml implementation is `fullref`.

1. **Multiple representations.** Perhaps the most basic characteristic of the object-oriented style is that, when an operation is invoked on an object, the object itself determines what code gets executed. Two objects responding to the same set of operations (i.e., with the same *interface*) may use entirely different representations, as long as each carries with it an implementation of the operations that works with its particular representation. These implementations are called the object's *methods*. Invoking an operation on an object—called *method invocation* or, more colorfully, sending it a *message*—involves looking up the operation's name at run time in a method table associated with the object, a process called *dynamic dispatch*.

   By contrast, a conventional *abstract data type* (*ADT*) consists of a set of values plus a *single* implementation of the operations on these values. (This static definition of implementations has both advantages and disadvantages over objects; we explore these further in §24.2.)

2. **Encapsulation.** The internal representation of an object is generally hidden from view outside of the object's definition: only the object's own methods can directly inspect or manipulate its fields.[1] This means that changes to the internal representation of an object can affect only a small, easily identifiable region of the program; this constraint greatly improves the readability and maintainability of large systems.

   Abstract data types offer a similar form of encapsulation, ensuring that the concrete representation of their values is visible only within a certain scope (e.g., a module, or an ADT definition), and that code outside of this

---

1. In some object-oriented languages, such as Smalltalk, this encapsulation is mandatory—the internal fields of an object simply cannot be *named* outside of its definition. Other languages, such as C++ and Java, allow fields to be marked either `public` or `private`. Conversely, all the methods of an object are publicly accessible in Smalltalk, while Java and C++ allow *methods* to be marked `private`, restricting their call sites to other methods in the same object. We will ignore such refinements here, but they have been considered in detail in the research literature (Pierce and Turner, 1993; Fisher and Mitchell, 1998; Fisher, 1996a; Fisher and Mitchell, 1996; Fisher, 1996b; Fisher and Reppy, 1999).

Although most object-oriented languages take encapsulation as an essential notion, there are several that do not. The *multi-methods* found in CLOS (Bobrow, DeMichiel, Gabriel, Keene, Kiczales, and Moon, 1988; Kiczales, des Rivières, and Bobrow, 1991), Cecil (Chambers, 1992, 1993), Dylan (Feinberg, Keene, Mathews, and Withington., 1997; Shalit), and KEA (Mugridge, Hamer, and Hosking, 1991) and in the lambda-& calculus of Castagna, Ghelli, and Longo (1995; Castagna, 1997) keep object states separate from methods, using special type-tags to select appropriate alternatives from overloaded method bodies at method invocation time. The underlying mechanisms for object creation, method invocation, class definition, etc., in these languages are fundamentally different from the ones we describe in this chapter, although the high-level programming idioms that they lead to are quite similar.

scope can manipulate these values only by invoking operations defined within this privileged scope.

3. **Subtyping.** The type of an object—its *interface*—is just the set of names and types of its operations. The object's internal representation does *not* appear in its type, since it does not affect the set of things that we can directly do with the object.

   Object interfaces fit naturally into the subtype relation. If an object satisfies an interface I, then it clearly also satisfies any interface J that lists fewer operations than I, since any context that expects a J-object can invoke only J-operations on it and so providing an I-object should always be safe. (Thus, object subtyping is similar to record subtyping. Indeed, for the model of objects developed in this chapter, they will be the same thing.) The ability to ignore parts of an object's interface allows us to write a single piece of code that manipulates many different sorts of objects in a uniform way, demanding only a certain common set of operations.

4. **Inheritance.** Objects that share parts of their interfaces will also often share some behaviors, and we would like to implement these common behaviors just once. Most object-oriented languages achieve this reuse of behaviors via structures called *classes*—templates from which objects can be instantiated—and a mechanism of *subclassing* that allows new classes to be derived from old ones by adding implementations for new methods and, when necessary, selectively overriding implementations of old methods. (Instead of classes, some object-oriented languages use a mechanism called *delegation,* which combines the features of objects and classes.)

5. **Open recursion.** Another handy feature offered by most languages with objects and classes is the ability for one method body to invoke another method of the same object via a special variable called `self` or, in some languages, `this`. The special behavior of `self` is that it is *late-bound,* allowing a method defined in one class to invoke another method that is defined later, in some subclass of the first.

The remaining sections of this chapter develop these features in succession, beginning with very simple "stand-alone" objects and then considering increasingly powerful forms of classes.

Later chapters examine different accounts of objects and classes. Chapter 19 presents a direct treatment (not an encoding) of objects and classes in the style of Java. Chapter 27 returns to the encoding developed in the present chapter, improving the run-time efficiency of class construction using bounded quantification. Chapter 32 develops a more ambitious version of the encoding that works in a purely functional setting.

18.2   Objects

In its simplest form, an *object* is just a data structure encapsulating some internal *state* and offering access to this state to clients via a collection of *methods*. The internal state is typically organized as a number of mutable *instance variables* (or *fields*) that are shared among the methods and inaccessible to the rest of the program.

Our running example throughout the chapter will be objects representing simple counters. Each counter object holds a single number and provides two methods (i.e., responds to two messages)—get, which causes it to return its current value; and inc, which increments the value.

A straightforward way of obtaining this behavior using the features we have discussed in previous chapters is to use a reference cell for the object's internal state and a record of functions for the methods. A counter object whose current state is 1 looks like this:

```
c = let x = ref 1 in
        {get = λ_:Unit. !x,
         inc = λ_:Unit. x:=succ(!x)};
```
▸ c : {get:Unit→Nat, inc:Unit→Unit}

The method bodies are both written as functions with trivial parameters (written _ because we don't need to refer to them in the bodies). The abstractions block evaluation of the method bodies when the object is created, allowing the bodies to be evaluated repeatedly, later, by applying them over and over to the unit argument. Also, note how the state of this object is shared among the methods and inaccessible to the rest of the program: the encapsulation of the state arises directly from the lexical scope of the variable x.

To invoke a method of the object c, we just extract a field of the record and apply it to an appropriate argument. For example:

```
  c.inc unit;
```
▸ unit : Unit

```
  c.get unit;
```
▸ 2 : Nat

```
  (c.inc unit; c.inc unit; c.get unit);
```
▸ 4 : Nat

The fact that the inc method returns unit allows us to use the ;-notation (§11.3) for sequences of increments. We could equivalently have written the last line above as:

```
let _ = c.inc unit in let _ = c.inc unit in c.get unit;
```

Since we may want to create and manipulate many counters, it is convenient to introduce an abbreviation for their type:

```
Counter = {get:Unit→Nat, inc:Unit→Unit};
```

Our attention in this chapter is focused on how objects are *built,* rather than on how they are *used* in organizing larger programs. However, we do want to see at least one function that uses objects, so that we can verify that it works on objects with different internal representations. Here is a trivial one—a function that takes a counter object and invokes its inc method three times:

```
inc3 = λc:Counter. (c.inc unit; c.inc unit; c.inc unit);
```

▸ inc3 : Counter → Unit

```
(inc3 c; c.get unit);
```

▸ 7 : Nat

18.3   Object Generators

We have seen how to build individual counter objects, one at a time. It is equally easy to write a *counter generator*—a function that creates and returns a new counter every time it is called.

```
newCounter =
  λ_:Unit. let x = ref 1 in
            {get = λ_:Unit. !x,
             inc = λ_:Unit. x:=succ(!x)};
```

▸ newCounter : Unit → Counter

18.4   Subtyping

One of the reasons for the popularity of object-oriented programming styles is that they permit objects of many shapes to be manipulated by the same client code. For example, suppose that, in addition to the Counter objects defined above, we also create some objects with an additional method that allows them to be reset to their initial state (say, 1) at any time.

```
ResetCounter = {get:Unit→Nat, inc:Unit→Unit, reset:Unit→Unit};
```

```
newResetCounter =
  λ_:Unit. let x = ref 1 in
              {get   = λ_:Unit. !x,
               inc   = λ_:Unit. x:=succ(!x),
               reset = λ_:Unit. x:=1};
```

▸ newResetCounter : Unit → ResetCounter

Since ResetCounter has all the fields of Counter (plus one more), the
record subtyping rule tells us that ResetCounter <: Counter. This means
that client functions like inc3 that take counters as arguments can also safely
be used with reset counters:

```
rc = newResetCounter unit;
```

▸ rc : ResetCounter

```
(inc3 rc; rc.reset unit; inc3 rc; rc.get unit);
```

▸ 4 : Nat

18.5   Grouping Instance Variables

So far, the states of our objects have consisted of just a single reference cell.
Obviously, more interesting objects will often have several instance variables.
In the sections that follow, it will be useful to be able to manipulate all of
these instance variables as a single unit. To allow for this, let's change the
internal representation of our counters to be a *record* of reference cells, and
refer to instance variables in method bodies by projecting fields from this
record.

```
c = let r = {x=ref 1} in
      {get = λ_:Unit. !(r.x),
       inc = λ_:Unit. r.x:=succ(!(r.x))};
```

▸ c : Counter

The type of this record of instance variables is called the *representation type*
of the object.

```
CounterRep = {x: Ref Nat};
```

18.6 Simple Classes

The definitions of `newCounter` and `newResetCounter` are identical except for the `reset` method in the latter. Of course, both of these definitions are so short anyway that this makes little difference, but if we imagine them stretching over many pages, as can easily happen in practice, it is clear that we would prefer to have some means for describing the common functionality in one place. The mechanism by which this is achieved in most object-oriented languages is called *classes*.

The class mechanisms in real-world object-oriented languages tend to be complex and loaded with features—`self`, `super`, visibility annotations, static fields and methods, inner classes, friend classes, annotations such as `final` and `Serializable`, etc., etc.[2] We'll ignore most of these here and focus our attention on the most basic aspects of classes: code reuse via inheritance, and the late binding of `self`. For the moment, let's consider just the former.

In its most primitive form, a class is simply a data structure holding a collection of methods that can either be *instantiated* to yield a fresh object or *extended* to yield another class.

Why can't we just reuse the methods from some counter *object* to build a reset counter? Simply because, in any particular counter object, the method bodies contain references to some particular record of instance variables. Clearly, if we want to be able to reuse the same code with a different record of instance variables, what we need to do is to *abstract* the methods with respect to the instance variables. This amounts to breaking our `newCounter` function above into two pieces, one that defines the method bodies with respect to an *arbitrary* record of instance variables,

```
counterClass =
  λr:CounterRep.
    {get = λ_:Unit. !(r.x),
     inc = λ_:Unit. r.x:=succ(!(r.x))};
```
▶ `counterClass : CounterRep → Counter`

and one that allocates a record of instance variables and supplies it to the method bodies to create an object:

```
newCounter =
  λ_:Unit. let r = {x=ref 1} in
              counterClass r;
```

---

2. The main reason for all this complexity is that, in most of these languages, classes are the *only* large-scale structuring mechanism. Indeed, there is just one widely used language—OCaml—that provides both classes and a sophisticated module system. So classes in most languages tend to become the dumping ground for all language features that have anything to do with large-scale program structure.

▸ newCounter : Unit → Counter

The method bodies from `counterClass` can be reused to define new classes, called *subclasses*. For example, we can define a class of reset counters:

```
resetCounterClass =
  λr:CounterRep.
    let super = counterClass r in
      {get   = super.get,
       inc   = super.inc,
       reset = λ_:Unit. r.x:=1};
```

▸ resetCounterClass : CounterRep → ResetCounter

Like `counterClass`, this function takes a record of instance variables and returns an object. Internally, it works by first using `counterClass` to create a counter object with the *same* record of instance variables r; this "parent object" is bound to the variable `super`. It then builds a new object by copying the `get` and `inc` fields from `super` and supplying a new function as the value for the `reset` field. Since `super` was built on r, all three methods share the same instance variables.

To build a reset counter object, we again just allocate memory for its instance variables and call `resetCounterClass`, where the real work happens.

```
newResetCounter =
  λ_:Unit. let r = {x=ref 1} in resetCounterClass r;
```

▸ newResetCounter : Unit → ResetCounter

18.6.1   EXERCISE [RECOMMENDED, ★★]: Write a subclass of `resetCounterClass` with an additional method `dec` that subtracts one from the current value stored in the counter. Use the `fullref` checker to test your new class.   □

18.6.2   EXERCISE [★★ ↛]: The explicit copying of most of the superclass fields into the record of subclass methods is notationally rather clumsy—it avoids explicitly re-entering the code of superclass methods in subclasses, but it still involves a lot of typing. If we were going to develop larger object-oriented programs in this style, we would soon wish for a more compact notation like "`super with {reset = λ_:Unit. r.x:=1}`," meaning "a record just like `super` but with a field `reset` containing the function λ_:Unit. r.x:=1." Write out syntax, operational semantics, and typing rules for this construct. □

We should emphasize that these classes are *values,* not *types.* Also we can, if we like, create many classes that generate objects of exactly the same type. In mainstream object-oriented languages like C++ and , classes have a more complex status—they are used both as compile-time types and as run-time data structures. This point is discussed further in §19.3.

18.7 Adding Instance Variables

It happens that our counter and reset counter objects use exactly the same
internal representation. However, in general a subclass may need to extend
not only the methods but also the instance variables of the superclass from
which it is derived. For example, suppose we want to define a class of "backup
counters" whose reset method resets their state to whatever value it has
when we last called the method backup, instead of resetting it to a constant
value:

```
BackupCounter = {get:Unit→Nat, inc:Unit→Unit,
                 reset:Unit→Unit, backup: Unit→Unit};
```

To implement backup counters, we need an extra instance variable to store
the backed-up value of the state.

```
BackupCounterRep = {x: Ref Nat, b: Ref Nat};
```

Just as we derived resetCounterClass from counterClass by copying
the get and inc methods and adding reset, we derive backupCounterClass
from resetCounterClass by copying get and inc and providing reset and
backup.

```
backupCounterClass =
  λr:BackupCounterRep.
    let super = resetCounterClass r in
       {get     = super.get,
        inc     = super.inc,
        reset   = λ_:Unit. r.x:=!(r.b),
        backup  = λ_:Unit. r.b:=!(r.x)};
```

▸ backupCounterClass : BackupCounterRep → BackupCounter

Two things are interesting about this definition. First, although the parent
object super includes a method reset, we chose to write a fresh implementation because we wanted a different behavior. The new class *overrides* the
reset method of the superclass. Second, subtyping is used in an essential
way here in typing the expression that builds super: resetCounterClass
expects an argument of type CounterRep, which is a supertype of the actual
type, BackupCounterRep, of the argument r. In other words, we are actually
providing the parent object with a larger record of instance variables than its
methods require.

18.7.1   EXERCISE [RECOMMENDED, ★★]: Define a subclass of backupCounterClass
with two new methods, reset2 and backup2, controlling a second "backup

register." This register should be completely separate from the one added by
backupCounterClass: calling reset should restore the counter to its value
at the time of the last call to backup (as it does now) and calling reset2
should restore the counter to its value at the time of the last call to backup2.
Use the fullref checker to test your class.   □

18.8   Calling Superclass Methods

The variable super has been used to copy functionality from superclasses
into new subclasses. We can also use super in the bodies of method definitions to *extend* the superclass's behavior with something extra. Suppose,
for instance, that we want a variant of our backupCounter class in which
every call to the inc method is automatically preceded by a call to backup.
(Goodness knows why such a class would be useful—it's just an example.)

```
funnyBackupCounterClass =
  λr:BackupCounterRep.
    let super = backupCounterClass r in
      {get = super.get,
       inc = λ_:Unit. (super.backup unit; super.inc unit),
       reset = super.reset,
       backup = super.backup};
```

▶ funnyBackupCounterClass : BackupCounterRep → BackupCounter

Note how the calls to super.inc and super.backup in the new definition of
inc avoid repeating the superclass's code for inc or backup here. In larger
examples, the savings of duplicated functionality in such situations can be
substantial.

18.9   Classes with Self

Our final extension is allowing the methods of classes to refer to each other
via self. To motivate this extension, suppose that we want to implement a
class of counters with a set method that can be used from the outside to set
the current count to a particular number.

```
SetCounter = {get:Unit→Nat, set:Nat→Unit, inc:Unit→Unit};
```

Moreover, suppose that we want the inc method in terms of set and get,
rather than directly reading and assigning the instance variable x. (Imagine a
much larger example in which the definitions of set and get each take many

pages.) Since get, set, and inc are all defined in the same class, what we are asking for is essentially to make the methods of this class mutually recursive.

We saw how to build mutually recursive records of functions using the fix operator in §11.11. We simply abstract the record of methods on a parameter that is itself a record of functions (which we call self), and then use the fix operator to "tie the knot," arranging that the very record we are constructing is the one passed as self.

```
setCounterClass =
  λr:CounterRep.
    fix
      (λself: SetCounter.
        {get = λ_:Unit. !(r.x),
         set = λi:Nat.  r.x:=i,
         inc = λ_:Unit. self.set (succ (self.get unit)))});
```

▸ setCounterClass : CounterRep → SetCounter

This class has no parent class, so there is no need for a super variable. Instead, the body of the inc method invokes get and then set from the record of methods passed to it as self. This use of fix is entirely internal to setCounterClass. We then create set-counters in exactly the same way as usual.

```
newSetCounter =
  λ_:Unit. let r = {x=ref 1} in
              setCounterClass r;
```

▸ newSetCounter : Unit → SetCounter

18.10   Open Recursion through Self

Most object-oriented languages actually support a more general form of recursive call between methods, known as *open recursion,* or *late-binding* of self. We can achieve this more general behavior by removing the use of fix from the class definition,

```
setCounterClass =
  λr:CounterRep.
    λself: SetCounter.
      {get = λ_:Unit. !(r.x),
       set = λi:Nat.  r.x:=i,
       inc = λ_:Unit. self.set (succ(self.get unit))};
```

▸ setCounterClass : CounterRep → SetCounter → SetCounter

and instead placing it in the object creation function.

```
newSetCounter =
  λ_:Unit. let r = {x=ref 1} in
             fix (setCounterClass r);
▶ newSetCounter : Unit → SetCounter
```

Notice that moving the use of `fix` changes the type of `setCounterClass`: instead of being abstracted just on a record of instance variables, it is also abstracted on a "`self`-object"; both are supplied at instantiation time.

The reason why open recursion through `self` is interesting is that it allows the methods of a *superclass* to call the methods of a *subclass,* even though the subclass does not exist when the superclass is being defined. In effect, we have changed the interpretation of `self` so that, instead of "the methods of this class," it provides access to "the methods of the class from which the current object was instantiated [which may be a subclass of this one]."

For example, suppose we want to build a subclass of our set-counters that keeps track of how many times the `set` method has been called. The interface of this class includes one extra operation for extracting the access count,

```
InstrCounter = {get:Unit→Nat, set:Nat→Unit,
                inc:Unit→Unit, accesses:Unit→Nat};
```

and the representation includes an instance variable for the access count:

```
InstrCounterRep = {x: Ref Nat, a: Ref Nat};
```

In the definition of the instrumented counter class, the `inc` and `get` methods are copied from the `setCounterClass` that we defined above. The `accesses` method is written out in the ordinary way. In the `set` method, we first increment the access count and then use `super` to invoke the superclass's `set`.

```
instrCounterClass =
  λr:InstrCounterRep.
    λself: InstrCounter.
      let super = setCounterClass r self in
        {get = super.get,
         set = λi:Nat. (r.a:=succ(!(r.a)); super.set i),
         inc = super.inc,
         accesses = λ_:Unit. !(r.a)};
▶ instrCounterClass : InstrCounterRep →
                        InstrCounter → InstrCounter
```

Because of the open recursion through `self`, the call to `set` from the body of `inc` will result in the instance variable `a` being incremented, even though the incrementing behavior of `set` is defined in the subclass and the definition of `inc` appears in the superclass.

18.11   Open Recursion and Evaluation Order

There is one problem with our definition of `instrCounterClass`—we cannot use it to build instances! If we write `newInstrCounter` in the usual way

```
newInstrCounter =
  λ_:Unit. let r = {x=ref 1, a=ref 0} in
              fix (instrCounterClass r);
```

▶ `newInstrCounter : Unit → InstrCounter`

and then attempt to create an instrumented counter by applying it to `unit`,

```
  ic = newInstrCounter unit;
```

the evaluator will diverge. To see how this happens, consider the sequence of evaluation steps that ensue when we start from this term.

1. We first apply `newInstrCounter` to `unit`, yielding

   ```
   let r = {x=ref 1, a=ref 0} in fix (instrCounterClass r)
   ```

2. We next allocate two `ref` cells, package them into a record—let's call it `<ivars>`—and substitute `<ivars>` for `r` in the rest.

   ```
   fix (instrCounterClass <ivars>)
   ```

3. We pass `<ivars>` to `instrCounterClass`. Since `instrCounterClass` begins with two lambda-abstractions, we immediately get back a function that is waiting for `self`,

   ```
   fix (λself:InstrCounter.
           let super = setCounterClass <ivars> self in <imethods>)
   ```

   where `<imethods>` is the record of instrumented-counter methods. Let's call this function `<f>` and write the current state (`fix <f>`).

4. We apply the evaluation rule for `fix` (E-FIX in Figure 11-12, page 144), which "unfolds" `fix <f>` by substituting (`fix <f>`) for `self` in the body of `<f>`, yielding

   ```
   let super = setCounterClass <ivars> (fix <f>) in <imethods>
   ```

5. We now reduce the application of `setCounterClass` to `<ivars>`, yielding:

   ```
   let super = (λself:SetCounter. <smethods>) (fix <f>)
               in <imethods>
   ```

where `<smethods>` is the record of set-counter methods.

6. By the evaluation rules for applications, we cannot reduce the application of (λself:SetCounter. `<smethods>`) to (`fix <f>`) until the latter has been reduced to a value. So the next step of evaluation again unfolds `fix <f>`, yielding:

```
let super = (λself:SetCounter. <smethods>)
                     (let super = setCounterClass <ivars> (fix <f>)
                      in <imethods>)
 in <imethods>
```

7. Since the argument to the outer lambda-abstraction is still not a value, we must continue to work on evaluating the inner one. We perform the application of `setCounterClass` to `<ivars>`, yielding

```
let super = (λself:SetCounter. <smethods>)
                     (let super = (λself:SetCounter. <smethods>)
                                       (fix <f>)
                      in <imethods>)
 in <imethods>
```

8. Now we have created an inner application similar in form to the outer one. Just as before, this inner application cannot be reduced until its argument, `fix <f>`, has been fully evaluated. So our next step is again to unfold `fix <f>`, yielding a yet more deeply nested expression of the same form as in step 6. It should be clear at this point that we are *never* going to get around to evaluating the outer application.

Intuitively, the problem here is that the argument to the `fix` operator is using its own argument, `self`, too early. The operational semantics of `fix` is defined with the expectation that, when we apply `fix` to some function λx.t, the body t should refer to x only in "protected" positions, such as the bodies of inner lambda-abstractions. For example, we defined `iseven` on page 143 by applying `fix` to a function of the form λie. λx. ..., where the recursive reference to `ie` in the body was protected by the abstraction on x. By contrast, the definition of `instrCounterClass` tries to use `self` right away in calculating the value of `super`.

At this point, we can proceed in several ways:

• We can protect the reference to `self` in `instrCounterClass` to prevent it from being evaluated too early, for example by inserting dummy lambda-abstractions. We develop this solution below. We will see that it is not completely satisfactory, but it is straightforward to describe and understand using the mechanisms we have already seen. We will also find it useful later, when we consider purely functional object encodings in Chapter 32.

- We can look for different ways of using low-level language features to model the semantics of classes. For example, instead of using fix to build the method table of a class, we could build it more explicitly using references. We develop this idea in §18.12 and further refine it in Chapter 27.

- We can forget about encoding objects and classes in terms of lambda-abstraction, records, and fix, and instead take them as language primitives, with their own evaluation (and typing) rules. Then we can simply choose evaluation rules that match our intentions about how objects and classes should behave, rather than trying to work around the problems with the given rules for application and fix. This approach will be developed in Chapter 19.

Using dummy lambda-abstractions to control evaluation order is a well-known trick in the functional programming community. The idea is that an arbitrary expression t can be turned into a function λ_:Unit.t, called a *thunk*. This "thunked form" of t is a syntactic value; all the computation involved in evaluating t is postponed until the thunk is applied to unit. This gives us a way to pass t around in unevaluated form and, later, ask for its result.

What we want to do at the moment is to delay the evaluation of self. We can do this by changing its type from an object (e.g. SetCounter) to an object thunk (Unit→SetCounter). This involves (1) changing the type of the self parameter to the class, (2) adding a dummy abstraction before we construct the result object, and (3) changing every occurrence of self in the method bodies to (self unit).

```
setCounterClass =
  λr:CounterRep.
  λself: Unit→SetCounter.
    λ_:Unit.
      {get = λ_:Unit. !(r.x),
       set = λi:Nat.  r.x:=i,
       inc = λ_:Unit. (self unit).set(succ((self unit).get unit))};
▶ setCounterClass : CounterRep →
                (Unit→SetCounter) → Unit → SetCounter
```

Since we do not want the type of newSetCounter to change (it should still return an object), we also need to modify its definition slightly so that it passes a unit argument to the thunk that results when we form the fixed point of setCounterClass.

```
    newSetCounter =
      λ_:Unit. let r = {x=ref 1} in
                  fix (setCounterClass r) unit;
```

▶ newSetCounter : Unit → SetCounter

Similar changes are needed in the definition of instrCounterClass. Note that none of these modifications actually require any thinking: once we have changed the type of self, every other change is dictated by the typing rules.

```
    instrCounterClass =
      λr:InstrCounterRep.
      λself: Unit→InstrCounter.
        λ_:Unit.
          let super = setCounterClass r self unit in
            {get = super.get,
             set = λi:Nat. (r.a:=succ(!(r.a)); super.set i),
             inc = super.inc,
             accesses = λ_:Unit. !(r.a)};
```

▶ instrCounterClass : InstrCounterRep →
                          (Unit→InstrCounter) → Unit → InstrCounter

Finally, we change newInstrCounter so that it supplies a dummy argument to the thunk constructed by fix.

```
    newInstrCounter =
      λ_:Unit. let r = {x=ref 1, a=ref 0} in
                  fix (instrCounterClass r) unit;
```

▶ newInstrCounter : Unit → InstrCounter

We can now use newInstrCounter to actually build an object.

```
    ic = newInstrCounter unit;
```

▶ ic : InstrCounter

Recall that this was the step that diverged before we added thunks.

The following tests demonstrate how the accesses method counts calls to both set and inc, as we intended.

```
    (ic.set 5; ic.accesses unit);
```

▶ 1 : Nat

```
    (ic.inc unit; ic.get unit);
```

▶ 6 : Nat

```
ic.accesses unit;
```

▶ 2 : Nat

18.11.1 EXERCISE [RECOMMENDED, ★★★]: Use the `fullref` checker to implement the following extensions to the classes above:

1. Rewrite `instrCounterClass` so that it also counts calls to `get`.

2. Extend your modified `instrCounterClass` with a subclass that adds a `reset` method, as in §18.4.

3. Add another subclass that also supports backups, as in §18.7.   □

18.12 A More Efficient Implementation

The tests above demonstrate that our implementation of classes matches the "open recursion" behavior of method calls through `self` in languages like Smalltalk, C++, and Java. However, we should note that the implementation is not entirely satisfactory from the point of view of efficiency. All the thunks we have inserted to make the `fix` calculation converge have the effect of postponing the calculation of the method tables of classes. In particular, note that all the calls to `self` inside method bodies have become (`self unit`)— that is, the methods of `self` are being recalculated on the fly every time we make a recursive call to one of them!

We can avoid all this recalculation by using reference cells instead of fixed points to "tie the knot" in the class hierarchy when we build objects.[3] Instead of abstracting classes on a record of methods called `self` that will be constructed later using `fix`, we abstract on a *reference* to a record of methods, and allocate this record *first*. That is, we instantiate a class by first allocating a heap cell for its methods (initialized with a dummy value), then constructing the real methods (passing them a pointer to this heap cell, which they can use to make recursive calls), and finally back-patching the cell to contain the real methods. For example, here is `setCounterClass` again.

```
setCounterClass =
  λr:CounterRep. λself: Ref SetCounter.
    {get = λ_:Unit. !(r.x),
     set = λi:Nat. r.x:=i,
     inc = λ_:Unit. (!self).set (succ ((!self).get unit))};
```

---

3. This is essentially the same idea as we used in the solution to Exercise 13.5.8. I am grateful to James Riely for the insight that it can be applied to class construction by exploiting the covariance of `Source` types.

▸ setCounterClass : CounterRep → (Ref SetCounter) → SetCounter

The self parameter is a pointer to the cell that contains the methods of the current object. When setCounterClass is called, this cell is initialized with a dummy value:

```
dummySetCounter =
  {get = λ_:Unit. 0,
   set = λi:Nat.  unit,
   inc = λ_:Unit. unit};
```

▸ dummySetCounter : SetCounter

```
newSetCounter =
  λ_:Unit.
    let r = {x=ref 1} in
    let cAux = ref dummySetCounter in
    (cAux := (setCounterClass r cAux); !cAux);
```

▸ newSetCounter : Unit → SetCounter

However, since all of the dereference operations (!self) are protected by lambda-abstractions, the cell will not actually be dereferenced until after it has been back-patched by newSetCounter.

To support building subclasses of setCounterClass, we need to make one further refinement in its type. Each class expects its self parameter to have the same type as the record of methods that it constructs. That is, if we define a subclass of instrumented counters, then the self parameter of this class will be a pointer to a record of instrumented counter methods. But, as we saw in §15.5, the types Ref SetCounter and Ref InstrCounter are incompatible—it is unsound to promote the latter to the former. This will lead to trouble (i.e., a parameter type mismatch) when we try to create super in the definition of instrCounterClass.

```
instrCounterClass =
  λr:InstrCounterRep. λself: Ref InstrCounter.
  let super = setCounterClass r self in
  {get = super.get,
   set = λi:Nat. (r.a:=succ(!(r.a)); super.set i),
   inc = super.inc,
   accesses = λ_:Unit. !(r.a)};
```

▸ Error: parameter type mismatch

The way out of this difficulty is to replace the Ref constructor in the type of self by Source—i.e., to pass to the class just the capability to read from the method pointer, not the capability to write to it (which it does not need anyway). As we saw in §15.5, `Source` permits covariant subtyping—i.e., we have `Ref InstrCounter <: Ref SetCounter`—so the creation of `super` in `instrCounterClass` becomes well typed.

```
setCounterClass =
  λr:CounterRep. λself: Source SetCounter.
    {get = λ_:Unit. !(r.x),
     set = λi:Nat. r.x:=i,
     inc = λ_:Unit. (!self).set (succ ((!self).get unit))};
```

▸ `setCounterClass : CounterRep → (Source SetCounter) → SetCounter`

```
instrCounterClass =
  λr:InstrCounterRep. λself: Source InstrCounter.
  let super = setCounterClass r self in
  {get = super.get,
   set = λi:Nat. (r.a:=succ(!(r.a)); super.set i),
   inc = super.inc,
   accesses = λ_:Unit. !(r.a)};
```

▸ `instrCounterClass : InstrCounterRep →`
                       `(Source InstrCounter) → InstrCounter`

To build an instrumented counter object, we first define a dummy collection of instrumented counter methods, as before, to serve as the initial value of the `self` pointer.

```
dummyInstrCounter =
  {get = λ_:Unit. 0,
   set = λi:Nat.  unit,
   inc = λ_:Unit. unit,
   accesses = λ_:Unit. 0};
```

▸ `dummyInstrCounter : InstrCounter`

We then create an object by allocating heap space for the instance variables and methods, calling `instrCounterClass` to construct the actual methods, and back-patching the reference cell.

```
newInstrCounter =
  λ_:Unit.
    let r = {x=ref 1, a=ref 0} in
    let cAux = ref dummyInstrCounter in
    (cAux := (instrCounterClass r cAux); !cAux);
```

▸ `newInstrCounter : Unit → InstrCounter`

The code for constructing the method table (in `instrCounterClass` and `counterClass`) is now called once per object creation, rather than once per method invocation. This achieves what we set out to do, but it is still not quite as efficient as we might wish: after all the method table that we construct for each instrumented counter object is always exactly the same, so it would seem we should be able to compute this method table just *once,* when the class is defined, and never again. We will see in Chapter 27 how this can be accomplished using the *bounded quantification* introduced in Chapter 26.

18.13   Recap

The first section of this chapter listed several characteristic features of the object-oriented programming style. Let us recall these features and briefly discuss how they relate to the examples developed in the chapter.

1. **Multiple representations.** All of the objects that we have seen in this chapter are counters—i.e., they belong to the type `Counter`. But their representations vary widely, from single reference cells in §18.2 to records containing several references in §18.9. Each object is a record of functions, providing implementations of the `Counter` methods (and perhaps others) appropriate to its own internal representation.

2. **Encapsulation.** The fact that the instance variables of an object are accessible only from its methods follows directly from the way we build objects, building the methods by passing the record of instance variables to a constructor function. It is obvious that the instance variables can be *named* only from inside the methods.

3. **Subtyping.** In this setting, subtyping between object types is just ordinary subtyping between types of records of functions.

4. **Inheritance.** We modeled inheritance by copying implementations of methods from an existing superclass to a newly defined subclass. There were a few interesting technicalities here: strictly speaking, both the superclass and the new subclass are *functions* from instance variables to records of methods. The subclass waits for its instance variables, then instantiates the superclass with the instance variables it is given, forming a record of superclass methods operating on the same variables.

5. **Open recursion.** The open recursion provided by `self` (or `this`) in real-world object-oriented languages is modeled here by abstracting classes not only on instance variables but also on a `self` parameter, which can

be used in methods to refer to other methods of the same object. This parameter is resolved at object-creation time by using fix to "tie the knot."

18.13.1   EXERCISE [★★★]: Another feature of objects that is useful for some purposes is a notion of *object identity*—an operation sameObject that yields true if its two arguments evaluate to the very same object, and false if they evaluate to objects that were created at different times (by different calls to new functions). How might the model of objects in this chapter be extended to support object identity?   □

18.14   Notes

Object encodings are a staple source of examples and problems for the programming languages research community. An early encoding was given by Reynolds (1978); general interest in the area was sparked by an article by Cardelli (1984). The understanding of self in terms of fixed points was developed by Cook (1989), Cook and Palsberg (1989), Kamin (1988), and Reddy (1988); relations between these models were explored by Kamin and Reddy (1994) and Bruce (1991).

A number of important early papers in the area are collected in Gunter and Mitchell (1994). Later developments are surveyed by Bruce, Cardelli, and Pierce (1999) and by Abadi and Cardelli (1996). Bruce (2002) gives an up-to-date picture of progress in the area. Alternative foundational approaches to objects and their type systems can be found in Palsberg and Schwartzbach (1994) and Castagna (1997).

Some additional historical notes can be found at the end of Chapter 32.

Inheritance is highly overrated.   —*Grady Booch*

19 *Case Study: Featherweight Java*

We saw in Chapter 18 how a lambda-calculus with subtyping, records, and references can model certain key features of object-oriented programming. The goal in that chapter was to deepen our understanding of these features by *encoding* them in terms of more elementary ones. In this chapter, we take a different approach, showing how to adapt the ideas in previous chapters to a *direct* treatment of a core object-oriented language based on Java. Prior acquaintance with Java is assumed.

19.1 Introduction

Formal modeling can offer a significant boost to the design of complex real-world artifacts such as programming languages. A formal model may be used to describe some aspect of a design precisely, to state and prove its properties, and to direct attention to issues that might otherwise be overlooked. In formulating a model, however, there is a tension between completeness and compactness: the more aspects the model addresses at the same time, the more unwieldy it becomes. Often it is sensible to choose a model that is less complete but more compact, offering maximum insight for minimum investment. This strategy may be seen in a flurry of recent papers on the formal properties of Java, which omit advanced features such as concurrency and reflection and concentrate on fragments of the full language to which well-understood theory can be applied.

Featherweight Java, or FJ, was proposed by Igarashi, Pierce, and Wadler (1999) as a contender for a *minimal* core calculus for modeling Java's type system. The design of FJ favors compactness over completeness almost obsessively, having just five forms of term: object creation, method invocation,

---

The examples in this chapter are terms of FeatherWeight Java (Figures 19-1 through 19-4). There is no associated OCaml implementation; rather, since FJ is designed to be a strict subset of Java, any Java implementation can be used to run the examples.

field access, casting, and variables. Its syntax, typing rules, and operational semantics fit comfortably on a single (letter-sized) page. Indeed, the aim of its design was to omit as many features as possible—even assignment—while retaining the core features of Java typing. There is a direct correspondence between FJ and a purely functional core of Java, in the sense that every FJ program is literally an executable Java program.

FJ is only a little larger than the lambda-calculus or Abadi and Cardelli's object calculus (1996), and is significantly smaller than other formal models of class-based languages like Java, including those of Drossopoulou, Eisenbach, and Khurshid (1999), Syme (1997), Nipkow and Oheimb (1998), and Flatt, Krishnamurthi, and Felleisen (1998a, 1998b). Being smaller, FJ can focus on just a few key issues. For example, we shall see that capturing the behavior of Java's casting construct in a small-step operational semantics is trickier than we might have expected.

FJ's main application is modeling extensions of Java. Because FJ itself is so compact, it focuses attention on essential aspects of an extension. Moreover, because the proof of type safety for pure FJ is very simple, a rigorous safety proof for even a significant extension may remain manageable. The original FJ paper illustrated this utility by enriching FJ with generic classes and methods *à la* GJ (Bracha, Odersky, Stoutamire, and Wadler, 1998). A followup paper (Igarashi, Pierce, and Wadler, 2001) formalized *raw types,* a feature introduced in GJ to ease evolution of Java programs to GJ. Igarashi and Pierce (2000) used FJ as the basis for a study of Java's *inner class* features. FJ has also been used for studies of type-preserving compilation (League, Trifonov, and Shao, 2001) and semantic foundations (Studer, 2001) for Java.

The goal in designing FJ was to make its proof of type safety as concise as possible, while still capturing the essence of the safety argument for the central features of full Java. Any language feature that made the safety proof *longer* without making it significantly *different* was a candidate for omission. Like other studies of its kind, FJ omits advanced features such as concurrency and reflection. Other Java features missing from FJ include assignment, interfaces, overloading, messages to `super`, `null` pointers, base types (`int`, `bool`, etc.), abstract method declarations, inner classes, shadowing of superclass fields by subclass fields, access control (`public`, `private`, etc.), and exceptions. The features of Java that FJ *does* model include mutually recursive class definitions, object creation, field access, method invocation, method override, method recursion through `this`, subtyping, and casting.

A key simplification in FJ is the omission of assignment. We assume that an object's fields are initialized by its constructor and never changed afterwards. This restricts FJ to a "functional" fragment of Java, in which many common Java idioms, such as use of enumerations, cannot be represented.

Nonetheless, this fragment is computationally complete (it is easy to encode the lambda-calculus into it), and is large enough to include useful programs—for example, many of the programs in Felleisen and Friedman's Java text (1998) use a purely functional style.

19.2 Overview

In FJ, a program consists of a collection of class definitions plus a term to be evaluated, corresponding to the body of the `main` method in full Java. Here are some typical class definitions in FJ.

```
class A extends Object { A() { super(); } }

class B extends Object { B() { super(); } }

class Pair extends Object {
  Object fst;
  Object snd;
  // Constructor:
  Pair(Object fst, Object snd) {
    super(); this.fst=fst; this.snd=snd; }
  // Method definition:
  Pair setfst(Object newfst) {
    return new Pair(newfst, this.snd); } }
```

For the sake of syntactic regularity, we always include the superclass (even when it is `Object`), we always write out the constructor (even for the trivial classes A and B), and we always name the receiver in a field access or a method invocation (as in `this.snd`), even when the receiver is `this`. Constructors always take the same stylized form: there is one parameter for each field, with the same name as the field; the `super` constructor is invoked to initialize the fields of the superclass; and then the remaining fields are initialized to the corresponding parameters. In this example, the superclass of all three classes is `Object`, which has no fields, so the invocations of `super` have no arguments. Constructors are the only place where `super` or = appears in an FJ program. Since FJ provides no side-effecting operations, a method body always consists of `return` followed by a term, as in the body of `setfst()`.

There are five forms of term in FJ. In the example, `new A()`, `new B()`, and `new Pair(...,...)` are *object constructors,* and `... .setfst(...)` is a *method invocation.* In the body of `setfst`, the term `this.snd` is a *field access,* and the occurrences of `newfst` and `this` are *variables.*[1] In the context of the above

---

1. The syntax of FJ differs slightly from Java in treating `this` as a variable, not a keyword.

definitions, the term

```
new Pair(new A(), new B()).setfst(new B())
```

evaluates to new Pair(new B(), new B()).

The remaining form of term is a *cast* (see §15.5). The term

```
((Pair)new Pair(new Pair(new A(), new B()),
                new A()).fst).snd
```

evaluates to new B(). The subterm (Pair)t, where t is new Pair(...).fst, is a cast. The cast is required, because t is a field access to fst, which is declared to contain an Object, whereas the next field access, to snd, is valid only on a Pair. At run time, the evaluation rules check whether the Object stored in the fst field is a Pair (in this case the check succeeds).

Dropping side effects has a pleasant side effect: evaluation can easily be formalized entirely within the syntax of FJ, with no additional mechanisms for modeling the heap (see Chapter 13). There are three basic computation rules: one for field access, one for method invocation, and one for casts. Recall that, in the lambda-calculus, the evaluation rule for applications assumes that the function is first simplified to a lambda abstraction. Similarly, in FJ the evaluation rules assume the object operated upon is first simplified to a new term. The slogan in the lambda-calculus is "everything is a function"; here, "everything is an object."

The next example shows the rule for field access (E-PROJNEW) in action:

```
new Pair(new A(), new B()).snd   ⟶   new B()
```

Because of the stylized syntax of object constructors, we know that the constructor has one parameter for each field, in the same order that the fields are declared. Here the fields are fst and snd, and an access to the snd field selects the second parameter.

Here is the rule for method invocation (E-INVKNEW) in action:

```
new Pair(new A(), new B()).setfst(new B())
```

$$
\longrightarrow
\left[
\begin{array}{l}
\text{newfst} \mapsto \text{new B(),} \\
\text{this} \mapsto \text{new Pair(new A(),new B())}
\end{array}
\right]
\text{new Pair(newfst, this.snd)}
$$

```
i.e.,   new Pair(new B(), new Pair(new A(), new B()).snd)
```

The receiver of the invocation is the object new Pair(new A(),new B()), so we look up the setfst method in the Pair class, where we find that it has formal parameter newfst and body new Pair(newfst, this.snd). The invocation reduces to the body with the formal parameter replaced by the actual, and the special variable this replaced by the receiver object. This is similar to the beta-reduction rule (E-APPABS) of the lambda-calculus. The key differences are the fact that the class of the receiver determines where to look for the body (supporting method override), and the substitution of the receiver for this (supporting "open recursion through self").[2] In FJ, as in the lambda-calculus, if the formal parameter appears more than once in the body this may lead to duplication of the argument value, but since there are no side effects this difference from the standard Java semantics cannot be observed.

Here is the rule for casts (E-CASTNEW) in action:

(Pair)new Pair(new A(), new B()) ⟶ new Pair(new A(), new B())

Once the subject of the cast is reduced to an object, it is easy to check that the class of the constructor is a subclass of the target of the cast. If so (as is the case here), the reduction removes the cast. If not, as in the term (A)new B(), then no rule applies and the computation is *stuck*, denoting a run-time error.

There are three ways in which a computation may get stuck: an attempt to access a field not declared for the class, an attempt to invoke a method not declared for the class ("message not understood"), or an attempt to cast to something other than a superclass of an object's run-time class. We will prove that the first two of these never happen in well-typed programs, and that the third never happens in well-typed programs that contain no downcasts (and no "stupid casts"—a technicality explained below).

We adopt a standard call-by-value evaluation strategy. Here are the steps of evaluation for the second example term above, where the next subterm to be reduced is underlined at each step.

$$((\text{Pair})\ \underline{(\text{new Pair}(\text{new Pair}(\text{new A}(),\text{new B}()),\text{ new A}())}$$
$$\underline{.\texttt{fst}}).\texttt{snd}$$
$$\longrightarrow\quad \underline{((\text{Pair})\text{new Pair}(\text{new A}(),\text{new B}()))}.\texttt{snd}$$
$$\longrightarrow\quad \underline{\text{new Pair}(\text{new A}(),\ \text{new B}()).\texttt{snd}}$$
$$\longrightarrow\quad \text{new B}()$$

19.3   Nominal and Structural Type Systems

Before proceeding with the formal definition of FJ, we should pause to examine one fundamental stylistic difference between FJ (and Java) and the typed lambda-calculi that are the main focus in this book. This difference concerns the status of *type names*.

---

2. Readers familiar with Abadi and Cardelli's object calculus (1996) will see a strong similarity to their ς-reduction rule.

In previous chapters, we have often defined short names for long or complex compound types to improve the readability of examples, e.g.:

```
NatPair = {fst:Nat, snd:Nat};
```

Such definitions are purely cosmetic: the name `NatPair` is a simple abbreviation for `{fst:Nat,snd:Nat}`, and the two are interchangeable in every context. Our formal presentations of the calculi have ignored abbreviations.

By contrast, in Java, as in many widely used programming languages, type definitions play a much more significant role. Every compound type used in a Java program has a name, and, when we declare the type of a local variable, a field, or a method parameter, we always do so by giving the name. "Bare" types like `{fst:Nat,snd:Nat}` simply cannot appear in these positions.

These type names play a crucial role in Java's subtype relation. Whenever a new name is introduced (in a class or interface definition), the programmer explicitly declares which classes and interfaces the new one extends (or, in the case of a new class and an existing interface, "implements"). The compiler checks these declarations to make sure that the facilities provided by the new class or interface really extend those of each super-class or super-interface—this check corresponds to record subtyping in a typed lambda-calculus. The subtype relation is now defined between type *names* as the reflexive and transitive closure of the declared immediate-subtype relation. If one name has not been declared to be a subtype of another, then it is not.

Type systems like Java's, in which names are significant and subtyping is explicitly declared, are called *nominal*. Type systems like most of the ones in this book, in which names are inessential and subtyping is defined directly on the structures of types are called *structural*.

Nominal type systems have both advantages and disadvantages over structural presentations. Probably the most important advantage is that the type names in nominal systems are useful not only during typechecking, but at run time as well. Most nominal languages tag each run-time object with a header word containing its type name, represented concretely as a pointer to a run-time data structure describing the type and giving pointers to its immediate supertypes. These type tags are handy for a variety of purposes, including run-time type testing (e.g., Java's `instanceOf` test and downcasting operation), printing, marshaling data structures into binary forms for storage in files or transmission over networks, and reflective facilities that permit a program to dynamically investigate the fields and methods of an object that it has been given. Run-time type tags can also be supported in structural systems (see Glew, 1999; League, Shao, and Trifonov, 1999; League, Trifonov, and Shao, 2001; and the citations given there), but they constitute an additional, separate mechanism; in nominal systems, the run-time tags are identified with the compile-time types.

A less essential, but pleasant, property of nominal systems is that they offer a natural and intuitive account of *recursive types*—types whose definition mentions the type itself. (We will discuss recursive types in detail in Chapter 20.) Such types are ubiquitous in serious programming, being required to describe such common structures as lists and trees, and nominal type systems support them in the most straightforward possible way: referring to List in the body of its own declaration is just as easy as referring to any other type. Indeed, even *mutually* recursive types are straightforward. We view the set of type names as being given from the beginning, so that, if the definition of type A involves the name B and the definition of B refers to A, there is no issue about "which is defined first." Of course, recursive types can also be handled in structural type systems. Indeed, high-level languages with structural typing, such as ML, generally "bundle" recursive types with other features, so that, for the programmer, they are just as natural and easy to use as in nominal languages. But in calculi intended for more foundational purposes, such as type safety proofs, the mechanisms required to deal rigorously with recursive types can become rather heavy, especially if mutually recursive types are allowed. The fact that recursive types come essentially for free in nominal systems is a decided benefit.

Another advantage of nominal systems is that checking whether one type is a subtype of another becomes almost trivial. Of course, the compiler must still do the work of verifying that the declared subtype relations are safe, which essentially duplicates the structural subtype relation, but this work needs to be done only once per type, at the point where it is defined, rather than during every subtype check. This makes it somewhat easier to achieve good performance in typecheckers for nominal type systems. In more serious compilers, though, it is not clear that the difference between nominal and structural styles has much effect on performance, since well-engineered typecheckers for structural systems incorporate representation techniques that reduce most subtype checks to a single comparison—see page 222.

A final advantage often cited for explicit subtype declarations is that they prevent "spurious subsumption," where the typechecker fails to reject a program that uses a value of one type where a completely different, but structurally compatible, type is expected. This point is more contentious than the ones above, since there are other—arguably better—ways of preventing spurious subsumption, for example using single-constructor datatypes (page 138) or abstract data types (Chapter 24).

Given all these advantages—especially the general usefulness of type tags and the simple treatment of recursive types—it is no surprise to find that nominal type systems are the norm in mainstream programming languages. The research literature on programming languages, on the other hand, is almost completely concerned with structural type systems.

One immediate reason for this is that, at least in the absence of recursive types, structural systems are somewhat tidier and more elegant. In a structural setting, a type expression is a closed entity: it carries with it all the information that is needed to understand its meaning. In a nominal system, we are always working with respect to some global collection of type names and associated definitions. This tends to make both definitions and proofs more verbose.

A more interesting reason is that the research literature tends to focus on more advanced features—in particular, on powerful mechanisms for type abstraction (parametric polymorphism, abstract data types, user-defined type operators, functors, etc.)—and on languages such as ML and Haskell that embody these features. Unfortunately, such features do not fit very comfortably into nominal systems. A type like List(T), for example, seems irreducibly compound—there will be just one definition somewhere in the program for the constructor List, and we need to refer to this definition to see how List(T) behaves, so we cannot treat List(T) as an atomic name. A few nominal languages have been extended with such "generic" features (Myers, Bank, and Liskov, 1997; Agesen, Freund, and Mitchell, 1997; Bracha, Odersky, Stoutamire, and Wadler, 1998; Cartwright and Steele, 1998; Stroustrup, 1997), but the results of such extensions are no longer pure nominal systems, but somewhat complex hybrids of the two approaches. Designers of languages with advanced typing features thus tend to favor the structural approach.

A full account of the relation between nominal and structural type systems remains a topic of ongoing research.

19.4   Definitions

We now turn to the formal definition of FJ.

Syntax

The syntax of FJ is given in Figure 19-1. The metavariables A, B, C, D, and E range over class names; f and g range over field names; m ranges over method names; x ranges over parameter names; s and t range over terms; u and v range over values; CL ranges over class declarations; K ranges over constructor declarations; M ranges over method declarations. We assume that the set of variables includes the special variable this, but that this is never used as

Syntax		*Subtyping*	$\boxed{\texttt{C<:D}}$

Syntax

$$\text{CL} ::= \qquad\qquad\qquad \textit{class declarations:}$$
$$\texttt{class C extends C \{}\overline{\texttt{C}}\ \overline{\texttt{f}}\texttt{;}\ \texttt{K}\ \overline{\texttt{M}}\texttt{\}}$$

$$\text{K} ::= \qquad\qquad\qquad \textit{constructor declarations:}$$
$$\texttt{C(}\overline{\texttt{C}}\ \overline{\texttt{f}}\texttt{) \{super(}\overline{\texttt{f}}\texttt{); this.}\overline{\texttt{f}}\texttt{=}\overline{\texttt{f}}\texttt{;\}}$$

$$\text{M} ::= \qquad\qquad\qquad \textit{method declarations:}$$
$$\texttt{C m(}\overline{\texttt{C}}\ \overline{\texttt{x}}\texttt{) \{return t;\}}$$

$$\text{t} ::= \qquad\qquad\qquad\qquad\qquad \textit{terms:}$$

$\texttt{x}$	*variable*
$\texttt{t.f}$	*field access*
$\texttt{t.m(}\overline{\texttt{t}}\texttt{)}$	*method invocation*
$\texttt{new C(}\overline{\texttt{t}}\texttt{)}$	*object creation*
$\texttt{(C) t}$	*cast*

$$\text{v} ::= \qquad\qquad\qquad\qquad\qquad \textit{values:}$$

$\texttt{new C(}\overline{\texttt{v}}\texttt{)}$	*object creation*

Subtyping

$$\texttt{C <: C}$$

$$\frac{\texttt{C <: D} \qquad \texttt{D <: E}}{\texttt{C <: E}}$$

$$\frac{CT(\texttt{C}) = \texttt{class C extends D \{...\}}}{\texttt{C <: D}}$$

Figure 19-1: Featherweight Java (syntax and subtyping)

the name of an argument to a method. Instead, it is considered to be implicitly bound in every method declaration. The evaluation rule for method invocation (rule E-INVKNEW in Figure 19-3) will substitute an appropriate object for $\texttt{this}$ in addition to substituting argument values for parameters.

We write $\overline{\texttt{f}}$ as shorthand for $\texttt{f}_1, \ldots, \texttt{f}_n$ (similarly $\overline{\texttt{C}}$, $\overline{\texttt{x}}$, $\overline{\texttt{t}}$, etc.) and write $\overline{\texttt{M}}$ for $\texttt{M}_1 \ldots \texttt{M}_n$ (with no commas). We abbreviate operations on pairs of sequences similarly, writing "$\overline{\texttt{C}}\ \overline{\texttt{f}}$" for "$\texttt{C}_1\ \texttt{f}_1, \ldots, \texttt{C}_n\ \texttt{f}_n$", where n is the length of $\overline{\texttt{C}}$ and $\overline{\texttt{f}}$, "$\overline{\texttt{C}}\ \overline{\texttt{f}}\texttt{;}$" for the declarations "$\texttt{C}_1\ \texttt{f}_1\texttt{;} \ldots \texttt{C}_n\ \texttt{f}_n\texttt{;}$" and "$\texttt{this.}\overline{\texttt{f}}\texttt{=}\overline{\texttt{f}}\texttt{;}$" for "$\texttt{this.f}_1\texttt{=f}_1\texttt{;} \ldots \texttt{;this.f}_n\texttt{=f}_n\texttt{;}$". Sequences of field declarations, parameter names, and method declarations are assumed to contain no duplicate names.

The declaration $\texttt{class C extends D \{}\overline{\texttt{C}}\ \overline{\texttt{f}}\texttt{;}\ \texttt{K}\ \overline{\texttt{M}}\texttt{\}}$ introduces a class named $\texttt{C}$ with superclass $\texttt{D}$. The new class has fields $\overline{\texttt{f}}$ with types $\overline{\texttt{C}}$, a single constructor $\texttt{K}$, and a suite of methods $\overline{\texttt{M}}$. The instance variables declared by $\texttt{C}$ are added to the ones declared by $\texttt{D}$ and its superclasses, and should have names distinct from these.[3] The methods of $\texttt{C}$, on the other hand, may either over-

---

3. In Java, instance variables of superclasses may be redeclared—the redeclaration shadows

ride methods with the same names that are already present in D or add new functionality special to C.

The constructor declaration $C(\overline{D}\ \overline{g},\ \overline{C}\ \overline{f})$ {super($\overline{g}$); this.$\overline{f}$=$\overline{f}$;} shows how to initialize the fields of an instance of C. Its form is completely determined by the instance variable declarations of C and its superclasses: it *must* take exactly as many parameters as there are instance variables, and its body *must* consist of a call to the superclass constructor to initialize its fields from the parameters $\overline{g}$, followed by an assignment of the parameters $\overline{f}$ to the new fields of the same names declared by C. (These constraints are enforced by the typing rule for classes in Figure 19-4.) In full Java, a subclass constructor must contain a call to its superclass constructor (when the superclass constructor takes arguments); this is the reason that the constructor body here calls super to initialize the superclass's instance variables. If we did not care about making FJ a literal subset of Java, we could drop the call to super and make each constructor initialize all the instance variables directly.

The method declaration $D\ m(\overline{C}\ \overline{x})$ {return t;} introduces a method named m with result type D and parameters $\overline{x}$ of types $\overline{C}$. The body of the method is the single statement return t. The variables $\overline{x}$ are bound in t. The special variable this is also considered bound in t.

A class table *CT* is a mapping from class names C to class declarations CL. A program is a pair (CT, t) of a class table and a term. To lighten the notation in what follows, we always assume a *fixed* class table *CT*.

Every class has a superclass, declared with extends. This raises a question: what is the superclass of the Object class? There are various ways to deal with this issue; the simplest one (which we adopt here) is to take Object as a distinguished class name whose definition does *not* appear in the class table. The auxiliary function that looks up fields in the class table is equipped with a special case for Object that returns the empty sequence of fields, denoted •; Object is also assumed to have no methods.[4]

By looking at the class table, we can read off the subtype relation between classes. We write C <: D when C is a subtype of D—i.e., subtyping is the reflexive and transitive closure of the immediate subclass relation given by the extends clauses in *CT*. It is defined formally in Figure 19-1.

The given class table is assumed to satisfy some sanity conditions: (1) $CT(C)$ = class C... for every $C \in dom(CT)$; (2) Object $\notin dom(CT)$; (3) for every class name C (except Object) appearing anywhere in *CT*, we have $C \in dom(CT)$; and (4) there are no cycles in the subtype relation induced by *CT*—that is, the <: relation is antisymmetric.

---

the original in the current class and its subclasses. We omit this feature in FJ.

4. In full Java, the class Object actually has several methods. We ignore these in FJ.

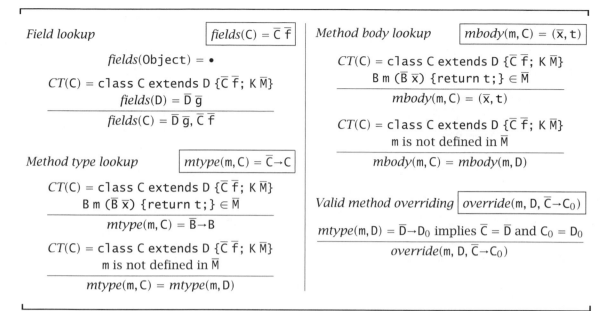

Figure 19-2: Featherweight Java (auxiliary definitions)

Note that the types defined by the class table *are* allowed to be recursive, in the sense that the definition of a class A may use the name A in the types of its methods and instance variables. Mutual recursion between class definitions is also allowed.

19.4.1 EXERCISE [⋆]: By analogy with the S-TOP rule in our lambda-calculus with subtyping, one might expect to see a rule stating that Object is a supertype of every class. Why don't we need it here? □

Auxiliary Definitions

For the typing and evaluation rules, we will need a few auxiliary definitions; these are given in Figure 19-2. The fields of a class C, written *fields*(C), is a sequence $\overline{C}\,\overline{f}$ pairing the class of each field with its name, for all the fields declared in class C and all of its superclasses. The type of the method m in class C, written *mtype*(m, C), is a pair, written $\overline{B}{\rightarrow}B$, of a sequence of argument types $\overline{B}$ and a single result type B. Similarly, the body of the method m in class C, written *mbody*(m, C), is a pair, written $(\overline{x}, t)$, of a sequence of parameters $\overline{x}$ and a term t. The predicate *override*(m, D, $\overline{C}{\rightarrow}C_0$) judges whether a method m with argument types $\overline{C}$ and a result type C_0 may be defined in a subclass of

Evaluation $\boxed{t \longrightarrow t'}$

$$\frac{\textit{fields}(C) = \overline{C}\,\overline{f}}{(\text{new } C(\overline{v})).f_i \longrightarrow v_i} \quad \text{(E-ProjNew)}$$

$$\frac{\textit{mbody}(m, C) = (\overline{x}, t_0)}{(\text{new } C(\overline{v})).m(\overline{u})} \quad \text{(E-InvkNew)}$$
$$\longrightarrow [\overline{x} \mapsto \overline{u}, \text{this} \mapsto \text{new } C(\overline{v})]t_0$$

$$\frac{C <: D}{(D)(\text{new } C(\overline{v})) \longrightarrow \text{new } C(\overline{v})} \quad \text{(E-CastNew)}$$

$$\frac{t_0 \longrightarrow t'_0}{t_0.f \longrightarrow t'_0.f} \quad \text{(E-Field)}$$

$$\frac{t_0 \longrightarrow t'_0}{t_0.m(\overline{t}) \longrightarrow t'_0.m(\overline{t})} \quad \text{(E-Invk-Recv)}$$

$$\frac{t_i \longrightarrow t'_i}{\substack{v_0.m(\overline{v}, t_i, \overline{t}) \\ \longrightarrow v_0.m(\overline{v}, t'_i, \overline{t})}} \quad \text{(E-Invk-Arg)}$$

$$\frac{t_i \longrightarrow t'_i}{\substack{\text{new } C(\overline{v}, t_i, \overline{t}) \\ \longrightarrow \text{new } C(\overline{v}, t'_i, \overline{t})}} \quad \text{(E-New-Arg)}$$

$$\frac{t_0 \longrightarrow t'_0}{(C)t_0 \longrightarrow (C)t'_0} \quad \text{(E-Cast)}$$

Figure 19-3: Featherweight Java (evaluation)

D. In case of overriding, if a method with the same name is declared in the superclass then it must have the same type.

Evaluation

We use a standard call-by-value operational semantics (Figure 19-3). The three computation rules—for field access, method invocation, and casting—were explained in §19.2. The rest of the rules formalize the call-by-value strategy. The values that can result from normal termination of the evaluator are fully evaluated object creation terms of the form new $C(\overline{v})$.

Note that the run-time behavior of the cast operation is to test whether the actual type of the object being cast is a subtype of the type declared in the cast. If it is, then the cast operation is thrown away and the result is the object itself. This corresponds exactly to the semantics of Java: a run-time cast does not change an object in any way—it simply either succeeds or else fails and raises an exception. In FJ, instead of raising an exception a failing cast will just get stuck, since there will be no evaluation rule that applies.

Typing

The typing rules for terms, method declarations, and class declarations are given in Figure 19-4. An environment Γ is a finite mapping from variables to types, written $\overline{x}{:}\overline{C}$. Typing statements for terms have the form $\Gamma \vdash t : C$,

Term typing

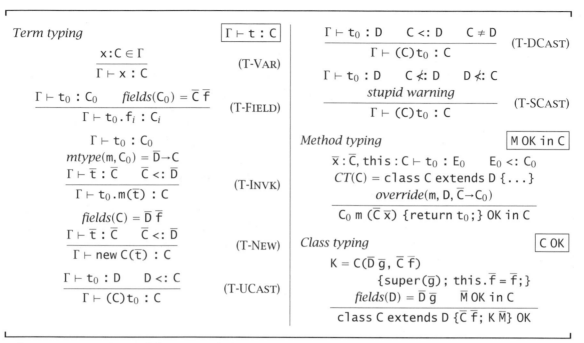

$$\frac{x : C \in \Gamma}{\Gamma \vdash x : C} \quad \text{(T-VAR)}$$

$$\frac{\Gamma \vdash t_0 : C_0 \qquad \mathit{fields}(C_0) = \overline{C}\ \overline{f}}{\Gamma \vdash t_0 . f_i : C_i} \quad \text{(T-FIELD)}$$

$$\frac{\begin{array}{c} \Gamma \vdash t_0 : C_0 \\ \mathit{mtype}(m, C_0) = \overline{D} \to C \\ \Gamma \vdash \overline{t} : \overline{C} \qquad \overline{C} <: \overline{D} \end{array}}{\Gamma \vdash t_0 . m(\overline{t}) : C} \quad \text{(T-INVK)}$$

$$\frac{\begin{array}{c} \mathit{fields}(C) = \overline{D}\ \overline{f} \\ \Gamma \vdash \overline{t} : \overline{C} \qquad \overline{C} <: \overline{D} \end{array}}{\Gamma \vdash \mathtt{new}\ C(\overline{t}) : C} \quad \text{(T-NEW)}$$

$$\frac{\Gamma \vdash t_0 : D \qquad D <: C}{\Gamma \vdash (C)t_0 : C} \quad \text{(T-UCAST)}$$

$$\frac{\Gamma \vdash t_0 : D \qquad C <: D \qquad C \ne D}{\Gamma \vdash (C)t_0 : C} \quad \text{(T-DCAST)}$$

$$\frac{\Gamma \vdash t_0 : D \qquad C \not<: D \qquad D \not<: C}{\mathit{stupid\ warning}} \quad \text{(T-SCAST)}$$
$$\overline{\Gamma \vdash (C)t_0 : C}$$

Method typing $\boxed{\text{M OK in C}}$

$$\frac{\begin{array}{c} \overline{x} : \overline{C}, \mathtt{this} : C \vdash t_0 : E_0 \qquad E_0 <: C_0 \\ CT(C) = \mathtt{class}\ C\ \mathtt{extends}\ D\ \{\ldots\} \\ \mathit{override}(m, D, \overline{C} \to C_0) \end{array}}{C_0\ m\ (\overline{C}\ \overline{x})\ \{\mathtt{return}\ t_0;\}\ \text{OK in C}}$$

Class typing $\boxed{\text{C OK}}$

$$\frac{\begin{array}{c} K = C(\overline{D}\ \overline{g}, \overline{C}\ \overline{f}) \\ \{\mathtt{super}(\overline{g}); \mathtt{this}.\overline{f} = \overline{f};\} \\ \mathit{fields}(D) = \overline{D}\ \overline{g} \qquad \overline{M}\ \text{OK in C} \end{array}}{\mathtt{class}\ C\ \mathtt{extends}\ D\ \{\overline{C}\ \overline{f}; K\ \overline{M}\}\ \text{OK}}$$

Figure 19-4: Featherweight Java (typing)

read "in the environment Γ, term t has type C." The typing rules are syntax directed,[5] with one rule for each form of term, save that there are three rules for casts (discussed below). The typing rules for constructors and method invocations check that each argument has a type that is a subtype of the one declared for the corresponding formal parameter. We abbreviate typing statements on sequences in the obvious way, writing $\Gamma \vdash \overline{t} : \overline{C}$ as shorthand for $\Gamma \vdash t_1 : C_1, \ldots, \Gamma \vdash t_n : C_n$ and $\overline{C} <: \overline{D}$ as shorthand for $C_1 <: D_1, \ldots, C_n <: D_n$.

One minor technical innovation in FJ is the introduction of "stupid" casts. There are three rules for type casts: in an *upcast* the subject is a subclass of the target, in a *downcast* the target is a subclass of the subject, and in a *stupid* cast the target is unrelated to the subject. The Java compiler rejects as ill typed a term containing a stupid cast, but we must allow stupid casts in FJ if we are to formulate type safety as a type preservation theorem for a small-step semantics. This is because a sensible term may be reduced to

---

5. We follow full Java in choosing an algorithmic formulation of the typing relation. Interestingly, in full Java this choice is actually forced. See Exercise 19.4.6.

one containing a stupid cast. For example, consider the following, which uses classes A and B as defined in §19.2:

(A)(Object)new B() $\longrightarrow$ (A)new B()

We indicate the special nature of stupid casts by including the hypothesis *stupid warning* in the type rule for stupid casts (T-SCAST); an FJ typing corresponds to a legal Java typing only if it does not contain this rule.

Typing statements for method declarations have the form M OK in C, read "method declaration M is well formed if it occurs in class C." It uses the term typing relation on the body of the method, where the free variables are the parameters of the method with their declared types, plus the special variable this with type C.

Typing statements for class declarations have the form CL OK, read "class declaration CL is well formed." It checks that the constructor applies super to the fields of the superclass and initializes the fields declared in this class, and that each method declaration in the class is ok.

The type of a term may depend on the type of any methods it invokes, and the type of a method depends on the type of a term (its body), so it behooves us to check that there is no ill-defined circularity here. Indeed there is none: the circle is broken because the type of each method is explicitly declared. It is possible to load the class table and use it for typechecking before all the classes in it have been checked, so long as each class is eventually checked.

19.4.2   EXERCISE [★★]: A number of design decisions in FJ are dictated by the desire to make it a subset of Java, in the sense that every well- or ill-typed FJ program is well- or ill-typed as a Java program, and the well-typed programs behave the same. Suppose this requirement were dropped—i.e., suppose all we wanted was a Java-*like* core calculus. How would you change the design of FJ to make it simpler or more elegant?   □

19.4.3   EXERCISE [RECOMMENDED, ★★★ ↦]: The operation of assigning a new value to the field of an object is omitted from FJ to simplify its presentation, but it can be added without changing the basic character of the calculus very much. Do this, using the treatment of references in Chapter 13 as a model.   □

19.4.4   EXERCISE [★★★ ↦]: Extend FJ with analogs of Java's raise and try forms, using the treatment of exceptions in Chapter 14 as a model.   □

19.4.5   EXERCISE [★★ ↦]: FJ, like full Java, presents the typing relation in algorithmic form. There is no subsumption rule; instead, several of the other rules include subtyping checks among their premises. Can the system be reformulated in a more declarative style, dropping most or all of these premises in favor of a single subsumption rule?   □

19.4.6 EXERCISE [★★★]: Full Java provides both classes and *interfaces,* which specify the types of methods, but not their implementations. Interfaces are useful because they permit a richer, non-tree-structured, subtype relation: each class has a single superclass (from which it inherits instance variables and method bodies), but may additionally implement any number of interfaces.

The presence of interfaces in Java actually forces the choice of an algorithmic presentation of the typing relation, which gives each typable term a unique (minimal) type. The reason is an interaction between conditional expressions (written $t_1 \ ? \ t_2 \ : \ t_3$ in Java) and interfaces.

1. Show how to extend FJ with interfaces in the style of Java.

2. Show that, in the presence of interfaces, the subtype relation is not necessarily closed under joins. (Recall from §16.3 that the existence of joins played a critical role in the minimal typing property for conditionals.)

3. What is Java's typing rule for conditional expressions? Is it reasonable? □

19.4.7 EXERCISE [★★★]: FJ includes Java's `this` keyword, but omits `super`. Show how to add it. □

19.5 Properties

We can prove a standard type-preservation theorem for FJ.

19.5.1 THEOREM [PRESERVATION]: If $\Gamma \vdash t : C$ and $t \longrightarrow t'$, then $\Gamma \vdash t' : C'$ for some $C' <: C$. □

Proof: Exercise [★★★]. □

We can also show a variant of the standard progress theorem: if a program is well typed, then the only way it can get stuck is if it reaches a point where it cannot perform a downcast. We use the mechanism of *evaluation contexts* to identify the failing downcast in the latter case.

19.5.2 LEMMA: Suppose t is a well-typed term.

1. If $t = \text{new } C_0(\overline{t}).f$, then $fields(C_0) = \overline{C} \ \overline{f}$ and $f \in \overline{f}$.

2. If $t = \text{new } C_0(\overline{t}).m(\overline{s})$, then $mbody(m, C_0) = (\overline{x}, t_0)$ and $|\overline{x}| = |\overline{s}|$. □

Proof: Straightforward. □

19.5.3   DEFINITION: The set of *evaluation contexts* for FJ is defined as follows:

$$
\begin{array}{lll}
E & ::= & \textit{evaluation contexts:} \\
  & [\,] & \textit{hole} \\
  & E.\mathsf{f} & \textit{field access} \\
  & E.\mathsf{m}(\overline{\mathsf{t}}) & \textit{method invocation (receiver)} \\
  & \mathsf{v}.\mathsf{m}(\overline{\mathsf{v}},E,\overline{\mathsf{t}}) & \textit{method invocation (arg)} \\
  & \mathsf{new}\ \mathsf{C}(\overline{\mathsf{v}},E,\overline{\mathsf{t}}) & \textit{object creation (arg)} \\
  & (\mathsf{C})E & \textit{cast}
\end{array}
$$

Each evaluation context is a term with a hole (written $[\,]$) somewhere inside it. We write $E[\mathsf{t}]$ for the ordinary term obtained by replacing the hole in E with t.   □

Evaluation contexts capture the notion of the "next subterm to be reduced," in the sense that, if $\mathsf{t} \longrightarrow \mathsf{t}'$, then we can express t and t' as $\mathsf{t} = E[\mathsf{r}]$ and $\mathsf{t}' = E[\mathsf{r}']$ for a unique E, r, and r', with $\mathsf{r} \longrightarrow \mathsf{r}'$ by one of the computation rules E-PROJNEW, E-INVKNEW, or E-CASTNEW.

19.5.4   THEOREM [PROGRESS]: Suppose t is a closed, well-typed normal form. Then either (1) t is a value, or (2) for some evaluation context E, we can express t as $\mathsf{t} = E[(\mathsf{C})(\mathsf{new}\ \mathsf{D}(\overline{\mathsf{v}}))]$, with $\mathsf{D} \not<: \mathsf{C}$.   □

Proof: Straightforward induction on typing derivations.   □

The progress property can be sharpened a little: if t contains only upcasts, then it cannot get stuck (and, if the original program contains only upcasts, then evaluation will never produce any casts that are not upcasts). But, in general, we want to use casting to *lower* the static types of objects, and so we must live with the possibility that casts can fail at run time. In full Java, of course, a cast failure does not stop the whole program: it generates an exception that can be caught by a surrounding exception handler.

19.5.5   EXERCISE [★★★ ↛]: Starting from one of the lambda-calculus typecheckers, build a typechecker and interpreter for Featherweight Java.   □

19.5.6   EXERCISE [★★★★ ↛]: The original FJ paper (Igarashi, Pierce, and Wadler, 1999) also formalizes polymorphic types in the style of GJ. Extend the typechecker and interpreter from Exercise 19.5.5 to include these features. (You will need to read Chapters 23, 25, 26, and 28 before attempting this exercise.)   □

19.6   Encodings vs. Primitive Objects

We have seen two contrasting approaches to the semantics and typing of simple object-oriented languages. In Chapter 18, we used combinations of features from the simply typed lambda-calculus with records, references, and subtyping to encode objects, classes, and inheritance. In the present chapter, we gave a direct account of a simple language in which objects and classes are primitive mechanisms.

Each of these approaches has its uses. Studying object encodings lays bare the fundamental mechanisms of encapsulation and reuse and allows us to compare them to other mechanisms with related aims. These encodings also help in understanding the way objects are translated into yet lower-level languages by compilers, and in understanding the interactions between objects and other language features. Treating objects as primitive, on the other hand, allows us to talk about their operational semantics and typing behavior directly; this kind of presentation is a better tool for high-level language design and documentation.

Ultimately, of course, we would like to have both views—a high-level language including primitive features for objects, classes, etc., with its own typing rules and operational semantics, plus a translation from this language to some lower-level language with just records and functions (or, indeed, an even lower-level language with nothing but registers, pointers, and instruction sequences), and finally a proof that this translation is a correct implementation of the high-level language, in the sense that the translation preserves the evaluation and typing properties of the high-level language. Many variants of this exercise have been carried out—for FJ itself by League, Trifonov, and Shao (2001), and for other object-oriented core calculi by Hofmann and Pierce (1995b), Bruce (1994, 2002), Abadi, Cardelli, and Viswanathan (1996), and others.

19.7 Notes

This chapter is adapted from the original FJ article by Igarashi, Pierce, and Wadler (1999). The main difference in presentation is that we have used a call-by-value operational semantics, for consistency with the rest of the book, while the original used a nondeterministic beta-reduction relation.

There have been several proofs of type safety for subsets of Java. In the earliest, Drossopoulou, Eisenbach, and Khurshid (1999), using a technique later mechanically checked by Syme (1997), prove safety for a substantial subset of sequential Java. Like FJ, they use a small-step operational semantics, but they avoid the subtleties of "stupid casts" by omitting casting entirely. Nipkow and Oheimb (1998) give a mechanically checked proof of safety for a somewhat larger core language. Their language does include casts, but it is formulated using a "big-step" operational semantics, which sidesteps the stupid cast problem. Flatt, Krishnamurthi, and Felleisen (1998a, 1998b) use a small-step semantics and formalize a language with both assignment and casting, treating stupid casts as in FJ. Their system is somewhat larger than FJ (the syntax, typing, and operational semantics rules take perhaps three times the space), and its safety proof, though correspondingly longer, is of similar complexity.

Of these three studies, Flatt, Krishnamurthi, and Felleisen's is closest to FJ in an important sense: the goal there, as here, is to choose a core calculus that is as *small* as possible, capturing just the features of Java that are relevant to some particular task. In their case, the task is analyzing an extension of Java with Common Lisp style mixins. The goal of the other two systems mentioned above, on the other hand, is to include as *large* a subset of Java as possible, since their primary interest is proving the safety of Java itself.

The literature on foundations of object-oriented languages contains many papers on formalizing class-based object-oriented languages, either taking classes as primitive (e.g., Wand, 1989a, Bruce, 1994, Bono, Patel, Shmatikov, and Mitchell, 1999b, Bono, Patel, and Shmatikov, 1999a) or translating classes into lower-level mechanisms (e.g., Fisher and Mitchell, 1998, Bono and Fisher, 1998, Abadi and Cardelli, 1996, Pierce and Turner, 1994).

A related thread of work considers models of object-oriented languages in which classes are replaced by some form of *method override* or *delegation* (Ungar and Smith, 1987), where individual objects may inherit behaviors from other *objects*. The resulting calculi tend to be somewhat simpler than those for class-based languages, since they deal with a smaller set of concepts. The most highly developed and best known of these is Abadi and Cardelli's *object calculus* (1996). Another popular one was developed by Fisher, Honsell, and Mitchell (1994).

A rather different approach to objects, classes, and inheritance, known as *multi-methods,* has been formalized by Castagna, Ghelli, and Longo (1995). The footnote on page 226 gives additional citations.

> *Inside every large language is a small language struggling to get out....*
> —*Igarashi, Pierce, and Wadler (1999)*

> *Inside every large program is a small program struggling to get out....*
> —*Tony Hoare,* Efficient Production of Large Programs *(1970)*

> *I'm fat, but I'm thin inside.*
> *Has it ever struck you that there's a thin man inside every fat man?*
> —*George Orwell,* Coming Up For Air *(1939)*

PART IV

Recursive Types

20 *Recursive Types*

We saw in §11.12 how to extend a simple type system to include a type constructor List(T) whose elements are lists with elements of type T. Lists are just one example of a large class of common structures—also including queues, binary trees, labeled trees, abstract syntax trees, etc.—that may grow to arbitrary size, but that have a simple, regular structure. An element of List(Nat), for example, is always either nil or else a pair (a "cons cell") of a number and another List(Nat). Clearly, it does not make sense to provide every one of these structures as a separate, primitive language feature. Instead, we need a general mechanism with which they can be defined from simpler elements, as needed. This mechanism is called *recursive types*.

Consider again the type of lists of numbers.[1] We can represent the fact that a list is either nil or a pair using the variant and tuple types defined in §11.10 and §11.7:

    NatList = <nil:Unit, cons:{...,...}>;

The data value carried by nil is trivial, since the nil tag itself already tells us everything that we need to know about an empty list. The value carried by the cons tag, on the other hand, is a pair consisting of a number and another list. The first component of this pair has type Nat,

    NatList = <nil:Unit, cons: {Nat, ...}>;

while the second component is a list of numbers—i.e., an element of the very type NatList that we are defining:

    NatList = <nil:Unit, cons:{Nat,NatList}>;

The system studied in this chapter is the simply typed calculus with recursive types. The examples use a variety of features from earlier chapters; the associated checker for these is fullequirec. For §20.2, the associated checker is fullisorec.

1. We ignore, in the rest of this chapter, the question of how to give a single, generic definition of lists with elements of an arbitrary type T. To deal with this, we also need the mechanism of *type operators*, which will be introduced in Chapter 29.

This equation is not just a simple definition—that is, we are not giving a new name to a phrase whose meaning we already understand—since the right-hand side mentions the very name that we are in the process of defining. Instead, we can think of it as a specification of an infinite tree:

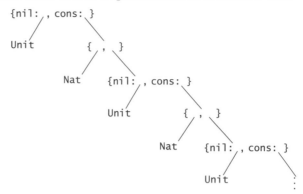

The recursive equation specifying this infinite tree type is similar to the equation specifying the recursive `factorial` function on page 52. Here, as there, it is convenient to make this equation into a proper definition by moving the "loop" over to the right-hand side of the =.[2] We do this by introducing an explicit recursion operator μ for types:

    NatList = μX. <nil:Unit, cons:{Nat,X}>;

Intuitively, this definition is read, "Let NatList be the infinite type satisfying the equation X = <nil:Unit, cons:{Nat,X}>."

We will see in §20.2 that there are actually two somewhat different ways of formalizing recursive types—the so-called *equi-recursive* and *iso-recursive* presentations—differing in the amount of help that the programmer is expected to give to the typechecker in the form of type annotations. In the programming examples in the following section, we use the lighter equi-recursive presentation.

20.1   Examples

Lists

First, let's finish off the example of lists of numbers that we started above. To program with lists, we need a constant `nil`, a constructor `cons` for adding

---

2. The reason this move is convenient is that it allows us to talk about recursive types without giving them names. However, there are also some advantages to working with explicitly named recursive types—see the discussion of *nominal* vs. *structural* type systems in §19.3.

an element to the front of an existing list, an `isnil` operation that takes a list and returns a boolean, and destructors `hd` and `tl` for extracting the head and tail of a non-empty list. We defined all these as built-in operations in Figure 11-13; our job here is to build them from simpler parts.

The definitions of `nil` and `cons` follow directly from the definition of `NatList` as a two-field variant type.

```
nil = <nil=unit> as NatList;
```

▸ `nil : NatList`

```
cons = λn:Nat. λl:NatList. <cons={n,l}> as NatList;
```

▸ `cons : Nat → NatList → NatList`

(Recall from §11.10 that expressions of the form `<l=t> as T` are used to introduce values of variant types: the value `t` is tagged with the label `l` and "injected" into the variant type `T`. Also, note that the typechecker here automatically "unfolds" the recursive type `NatList` to the variant type `<nil:Unit, cons:{Nat,NatList}>`.)

The rest of the basic operations on lists involve testing their structure and extracting appropriate parts. They are all implemented in terms of `case`.

```
isnil = λl:NatList. case l of
                      <nil=u> ⇒ true
                    | <cons=p> ⇒ false;
```

▸ `isnil : NatList → Bool`

```
hd = λl:NatList. case l of <nil=u> ⇒ 0 | <cons=p> ⇒ p.1;
```

▸ `hd : NatList → Nat`

```
tl = λl:NatList. case l of <nil=u> ⇒ l | <cons=p> ⇒ p.2;
```

▸ `tl : NatList → NatList`

We've arbitrarily decided to define `hd` of an empty list to be 0 and `tl` of the empty list to be the empty list. We might alternatively have raised exceptions in these cases.

We can use all these definitions together to write a recursive function that sums the elements of a list:

```
sumlist = fix (λs:NatList→Nat. λl:NatList.
                  if isnil l then 0 else plus (hd l) (s (tl l)));
```

▸ `sumlist : NatList → Nat`

```
mylist = cons 2 (cons 3 (cons 5 nil));
sumlist mylist;
```

▸ 10 : Nat

Note that, although `NatList` itself is an infinitely long type expression, all its elements are *finite* lists (because there is no way to use the pairing and tagging primitives or the call-by-value `fix` to build infinitely large structures).

20.1.1 EXERCISE [★★]: One presentation of labeled binary trees defines a tree to be either a leaf (with no label) or else an interior node with a numeric label and two child trees. Define a type `NatTree` and suitable operations for constructing, destructing, and testing trees. Write a function that performs a depth-first traversal of a tree and returns a list of the labels it finds. Use the `fullequirec` checker to test your code.   □

Hungry Functions

Another example illustrating a somewhat trickier use of recursive types is a type of "hungry functions" that can accept any number of numeric arguments and always return a new function that is hungry for more:

```
Hungry = μA. Nat→A;
```

An element of this type can be defined using the `fix` operator:

```
f = fix (λf: Nat→Hungry. λn:Nat. f);
```

▸ f : Hungry

```
f 0 1 2 3 4 5;
```

▸ <fun> : Hungry

Streams

A more useful variant of the `Hungry` type above is the type `Stream` of functions that can consume an arbitrary number of `unit` values, each time returning a pair of a number and a new stream.

```
Stream = μA. Unit→{Nat,A};
```

We can define two "destructors" for streams; if `s` is a stream, then `hd s` is the first number it returns when we pass it `unit`.

```
hd = λs:Stream. (s unit).1;
```
▶ hd : Stream → Nat

Similarly, tl s is the new stream that we obtain when we pass unit to s.

```
tl = λs:Stream. (s unit).2;
```
▶ tl : Stream → Stream

To construct a stream, we use fix as above:

```
upfrom0 = fix (λf: Nat→Stream. λn:Nat. λ_:Unit. {n,f (succ n)}) 0;
```
▶ upfrom0 : Stream

```
hd upfrom0;
```
▶ 0 : Nat

```
hd (tl (tl (tl upfrom0)));
```
▶ 3 : Nat

20.1.2   EXERCISE [RECOMMENDED, ★★]: Define a stream that yields successive elements of the Fibonacci sequence (1, 1, 2, 3, 5, 8, 13, . . .).   □

Streams can be further generalized to a simple form of *processes*—functions that accept a number and return a number and a new process.

```
Process = μA. Nat→{Nat,A};
```

For example, here is a process that, at each step, returns the sum of all the numbers it has been given so far:

```
p = fix (λf: Nat→Process. λacc:Nat. λn:Nat.
            let newacc = plus acc n in
            {newacc, f newacc}) 0;
```
▶ p : Process

As we did for streams, we can define auxiliary functions for interacting with processes:

```
curr = λs:Process. (s 0).1;
```
▶ curr : Process → Nat

```
send = λn:Nat. λs:Process. (s n).2;
```
▶ send : Nat → Process → Process

If we send the process p the numbers 5, 3, and 20, the number it returns in response to the last interaction is 28.

```
curr (send 20 (send 3 (send 5 p)));
```
▶ 28 : Nat

Objects

A slight rearrangement of the last example gives us another familiar idiom of interacting with data: objects. For instance, here is the type of counter objects that keep track of a number and allow us to either query or increment it:

```
Counter = μC. {get:Nat, inc:Unit→C};
```

Note that our treatment of objects here is *purely functional* (like the one in Chapter 19 and unlike Chapter 18): sending a counter object the `inc` message does not cause this object to mutate its state internally; instead, the operation returns a *new* counter object with incremented internal state. The use of recursive types here allows us to specify that the returned object has exactly the same type as the original.

The only difference between these objects and the processes discussed above is that an object is a recursively defined *record* (containing a function), whereas a process was a recursively defined *function* (returning a tuple). The reason this change in point of view is useful is that we can extend our record to include more than one function—for example, a decrement operation:

```
Counter = μC. {get:Nat, inc:Unit→C, dec:Unit→C};
```

To create a counter object, we use the fixed-point combinator, as we did above.

```
c = let create = fix (λf: {x:Nat}→Counter. λs: {x:Nat}.
                          {get = s.x,
                           inc = λ_:Unit. f {x=succ(s.x)},
                           dec = λ_:Unit. f {x=pred(s.x)} })
        in create {x=0};
```

▸ c : Counter

To invoke one of c's operations, we simply project out the appropriate field:

```
c1 = c.inc unit;
c2 = c1.inc unit;
c2.get;
```

▸ 2 : Nat

20.1.3   EXERCISE [★★]: Extend the `Counter` type and the counter c above to include `backup` and `reset` operations (as we did in §18.7): invoking `backup` causes the counter to store its current value in a separate internal register; calling `reset` causes the counter's value to be reset to the value in this register.   □

Recursive Values from Recursive Types

A more surprising use of recursive types—and one that clearly reveals their expressive power—is a well-typed implementation of the fixed-point combinator. For any type T, we can define a fixed-point constructor for functions on T as follows.

```
fix_T = λf:T→T. (λx:(μA.A→T). f (x x)) (λx:(μA.A→T). f (x x));
```

▸ fix$_T$: (T→T) → T

Note that, if we erase types, this term is precisely the untyped fixed point combinator that we saw on page 65.

The key trick here is using a recursive type to type the two occurrences of the subexpression x x. As we observed in Exercise 9.3.2, typing this term requires that x have an arrow type whose domain is the type of x itself. Clearly, there is no finite type with this property, but the *infinite* type μA.A→T does the job perfectly.

A corollary of this example is that the presence of recursive types breaks the strong normalization property: we can use the fix$_T$ combinator to write a well-typed term whose evaluation (when applied to unit) will diverge.

```
diverge_T = λ_:Unit. fix_T (λx:T. x);
```

▸ diverge$_T$: Unit → T

Moreover, since we can can obtain such terms for every type, it follows that every type in this system is inhabited, unlike λ$_→$.[3]

Untyped Lambda-Calculus, Redux

Perhaps the best illustration of the power of recursive types is the fact that we can embed the whole untyped lambda-calculus—in a well-typed way—into a statically typed language with recursive types. Let D be the following type:[4]

```
D = μX.X→X;
```

Define an "injection function" lam mapping functions from D to D into elements of D as follows:

---

3. This fact makes systems with recursive types useless as logics: if we interpret types as logical propositions following the Curry-Howard correspondence (see §9.4) and read "type T is inhabited" as "proposition T is provable," then the fact that every type is inhabited means that every proposition in the logic is provable—that is, the logic is inconsistent.

4. Readers familiar with denotational semantics will observe that D's definition is precisely the defining property of the *universal domains* used in semantic models of the pure lambda-calculus.

```
lam = λf:D→D. f as D;
```

▸ lam : D

To apply one element of D to another, we simply unfold the type of the first, yielding a function, and apply this to the second:

```
ap = λf:D. λa:D. f a;
```

▸ ap : D

Now, suppose M is a closed lambda-term involving just variables, abstractions, and applications. Then we can construct an element of D representing M, written M*, in a uniform way as follows:

```
x*          =   x
(λx.M)*     =   lam (λx:D. M*)
(M N)*      =   ap M* N*
```

For example, here is the untyped fixed point combinator expressed as an element of D:

```
fixD = lam (λf:D.
            ap (lam (λx:D. ap f (ap x x)))
               (lam (λx:D. ap f (ap x x))));
```

▸ fixD : D

This embedding of the pure lambda-calculus can be extended to include features such as numbers. We change the definition of D to a variant type with one tag for numbers and one for functions:

```
D = μX. <nat:Nat, fn:X→X>;
```

That is, an element of D is either a number or a function from D to D, tagged nat or fn, respectively. The implementation of the lam constructor is essentially the same as before:

```
lam = λf:D→D. <fn=f> as D;
```

▸ lam : (D→D) → D

The implementation of ap, though, is different in an interesting way:

```
ap = λf:D. λa:D.
        case f of
          <nat=n> ⇒ divergeD unit
        | <fn=f> ⇒ f a;
```

▸ ap : D → D → D

Before we can apply f to a, we need to extract a function from f with a case. This forces us to specify how application behaves when f is *not* a function. (In this example, we just diverge; we could also raise an exception.) Note how closely the tag-checking here resembles the run-time tag checking in an implementation of a dynamically typed language such as Scheme. In this sense, typed computation may be said to "include" untyped or dynamically typed computation.

Similar tag checking is needed in order to define the successor function on elements of D:

```
suc = λf:D. case f of
                <nat=n> ⇒ (<nat=succ n> as D)
            | <fn=f> ⇒ diverge_D unit;
```

▸ suc : D → D

The injection of 0 into D is trivial:

```
zro = <nat=0> as D;
```

▸ zro : D

20.1.4   EXERCISE [⋆]: Extend this encoding with booleans and conditionals, and encode the terms if false then 1 else 0 and if false then 1 else false as elements of D. What happens when we evaluate these terms?   □

20.1.5   EXERCISE [RECOMMENDED, ⋆⋆]: Extend the datatype D to include records

```
D = μX. <nat:Nat, fn:X→X, rcd:Nat→X>;
```

and implement record construction and field projection. For simplicity, use natural numbers as field labels—i.e., records are represented as functions from natural numbers to elements of D. Use the fullequirec checker to test your extension.   □

20.2   Formalities

In the literature on type systems, there are two basic approaches to recursive types. The essential difference between them is captured in their response to a simple question: What is the relation between the type μX.T and its one-step unfolding? For example, what is the relation between NatList and <nil:Unit,cons:{Nat,NatList}>?

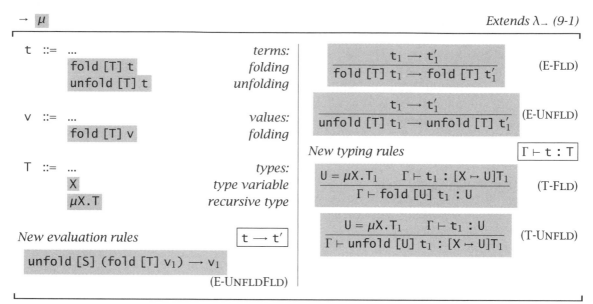

Figure 20-1: Iso-recursive types (λμ)

1. The *equi-recursive* approach takes these two type expressions as *definitionally equal*—interchangeable in all contexts—since they stand for the same infinite tree.[5] It is the typechecker's responsibility to make sure that a term of one type will be allowed as an argument to a function expecting the other, etc.

   The pleasant thing about the equi-recursive treatment is that allowing type expressions to be infinite[6] is the only alteration to the declarative presentations of the systems we already understand. Existing definitions, safety theorems, and proofs remain unchanged, as long as they do not depend on induction on type expressions (which naturally no longer works).

   Of course, the *implementation* of equi-recursive types requires some work, since typechecking algorithms cannot work directly with infinite structures. Exactly how this can be achieved is the topic of Chapter 21.

2. The *iso-recursive* approach, on the other hand, takes a recursive type and its unfolding as different, but *isomorphic*.

   Formally, the unfolding of a recursive type $\mu X.T$ is the type obtained by taking the body T and replacing all occurrences of X by the whole recur-

---

5. The mapping from μ-types to their infinite tree expansions is defined precisely in §21.8.
6. Strictly speaking, we should say *regular*—see §21.7.

sive type—i.e., using the standard notation for substitution, it is $[X \mapsto (\mu X.T)]T$. For example, the type NatList, i.e.,

μX.<nil:Unit,cons:{Nat,X}>,

unfolds to

<nil:Unit, cons:{Nat, μX.<nil:Unit,cons:{Nat,X}>}>.

In a system with iso-recursive types, we introduce, for each recursive type $\mu X.T$, a pair of functions

unfold[μX.T]   : $\mu X.T \rightarrow [X \mapsto \mu X.T]T$
fold[μX.T]   : $[X \mapsto \mu X.T]T \rightarrow \mu X.T$

that "witness the isomorphism" by mapping values back and forth between the two types:

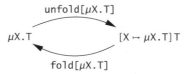

The fold and unfold maps are provided as primitives by the language, as described in Figure 20-1. The fact that they form an isomorphism is captured by the evaluation rule E-UNFLDFLD, which annihilates a fold when it meets a corresponding unfold. (The evaluation rule does not require the type annotations on the fold and the unfold to be the same, since we would have to invoke the typechecker at run time to verify such a constraint. However, in the evaluation of a well-typed program, these two type annotations *will* be equal whenever E-UNFLDFLD is applied.)

Both approaches are widely used in both theoretical studies and programming language designs. The equi-recursive style is arguably more intuitive, but places stronger demands on the typechecker, which must effectively infer the points where fold and unfold annotations should occur. Moreover, the interactions between equi-recursive types and other advanced typing features such as bounded quantification and type operators can be quite complex, leading to significant theoretical difficulties (e.g. Ghelli, 1993; Colazzo and Ghelli, 1999) or even undecidable typechecking problems (Solomon, 1978).

The iso-recursive style is notationally somewhat heavier, requiring programs to be decorated with fold and unfold instructions wherever recursive types are used. In practice, however, these annotations can often be "hidden" by coalescing them with other annotations. In languages in the ML family, for example, every `datatype` definition implicitly introduces a recursive type. Each use of one of the constructors to build a value of the datatype implicitly includes a `fold`, and each constructor appearing in a pattern match implicitly forces an `unfold`. Similarly, in Java each class definition implicitly introduces a recursive type, and invoking a method on an object involves an implicit `unfold`. This felicitous overlap of mechanisms makes the iso-recursive style quite palatable in practice.

For example, here is the `NatList` example in iso-recursive form. First, it is convenient to define an abbreviation for the unfolded form of `NatList`:

```
NLBody = <nil:Unit, cons:{Nat,NatList}>;
```

Now, `nil` is defined by building a variant, of type `NLBody`, and then folding it up as a `NatList`; `cons` is similar.

```
nil = fold [NatList] (<nil=unit> as NLBody);
cons = λn:Nat. λl:NatList. fold [NatList] <cons={n,l}> as NLBody;
```

Conversely, the definitions of the `isnil`, `hd`, and `tl` operations need to take a `NatList` and consider it as a variant so that they can perform a case analysis on its tag. This is achieved by unfolding the argument `l`:

```
isnil = λl:NatList.
          case unfold [NatList] l of
            <nil=u> ⇒ true
          | <cons=p> ⇒ false;
hd = λl:NatList.
        case unfold [NatList] l of
          <nil=u> ⇒ 0
        | <cons=p> ⇒ p.1;
tl = λl:NatList.
        case unfold [NatList] l of
          <nil=u> ⇒ l
        | <cons=p> ⇒ p.2;
```

20.2.1   EXERCISE [RECOMMENDED, ★★]: Reformulate some of the other examples in §20.1 (in particular, the fix_T example on page 273) with explicit `fold` and `unfold` annotations. Check them using the `fullisorec` checker.   □

20.2.2   EXERCISE [★★ ↛]: Sketch proofs of the progress and preservation theorems for the iso-recursive system.   □

20.3   Subtyping

The final question that we need to address in this chapter concerns the combination of recursive types with the other major refinement of the simply typed lambda-calculus that we have seen so far—subtyping. For example, supposing that the type Even is a subtype of Nat, what should be the relation between the types $\mu X.\text{Nat}\rightarrow(\text{Even}\times X)$ and $\mu X.\text{Even}\rightarrow(\text{Nat}\times X)$?

The simplest way to think through such questions is to view them "in the limit"—i.e., using an equi-recursive treatment of recursive types. In the present example, the elements inhabiting both types can be thought of as simple reactive processes (cf. page 271): given a number, they return another number plus a new process that is ready to receive a number, and so on. Processes belonging to the first type always yield even numbers and are capable of accepting arbitrary numbers. Those belonging to the second type yield arbitrary numbers, but expect always to be given even numbers. The constraints both on what arguments the function must accept and on what results it may return are more demanding for the first type, so intuitively we expect the first to be a subtype of the second. We can draw a picture summarizing these calculations as follows:

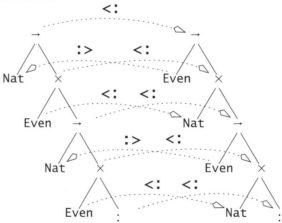

Can this intuitive argument be made precise? Indeed it can, as we shall see in Chapter 21.

20.4   Notes

Recursive types in computer science go back at least to Morris (1968). Basic syntactic and semantic properties (without subtyping) are collected in Cardone and Coppo (1991). Properties of infinite and regular trees are surveyed by Courcelle (1983). Basic syntactic and semantic properties of recursive types without subtyping were established in early papers by Huet (1976) and MacQueen, Plotkin, and Sethi (1986). The relation between iso- and equirecursive systems was explored by Abadi and Fiore (1996). Additional citations on recursive types with subtyping can be found in §21.12.

Morris (1968, pp. 122–124) first observed that recursive types can be used to construct a well-typed `fix` operator for terms (§20.1).

The two formulations of recursive types have been around since the earliest work in the area, but the pleasantly mnemonic terms *iso-recursive* and *equirecursive* are a recent coinage by Crary, Harper, and Puri (1999).

21 *Metatheory of Recursive Types*

In Chapter 20 we saw two alternative presentations of recursive types: equi-recursive types, which are definitionally equivalent to their unfoldings, and iso-recursive types, where this equivalence is explicitly witnessed by `fold` and `unfold` terms. In this chapter, we develop the theoretical foundations of typecheckers for equi-recursive types. (Implementing iso-recursive types is comparatively straightforward.) We will deal with a system including both recursive types and subtyping, since these are often combined in practice. A system with equi-recursive types but not subtyping would be only a little simpler, since we would still need to check equivalence of recursive types.

We saw in Chapter 20 that subtyping for equi-recursive types can be understood intuitively in terms of infinite subtyping derivations over infinite types. Our job here is to make these intuitions precise using the mathematical framework of *coinduction,* and to draw a precise connection between infinite trees and derivations and the finite representations manipulated by an actual subtyping algorithm.

We begin in §21.1 by reviewing the basic theory of inductive and coinductive definitions and their associated proof principles. §21.2 and §21.3 instantiate this general theory for the case of subtyping, defining both the familiar inductive subtype relation on finite types and its coinductive extension to infinite types. §21.4 makes a brief detour to consider some issues connected with the rule of transitivity (a notorious troublemaker in subtyping systems, as we have seen). §21.5 derives simple algorithms for checking membership in inductively and co-inductively defined sets; §21.6 considers more refined algorithms. These algorithms are applied to subtyping for the important special case of "regular" infinite types in §21.7. §21.8 introduces μ-types as a finite notation for representing infinite types and proves that the more complex (but finitely implementable) subtype relation on μ-types corresponds to

---

The system studied in this chapter is the simply typed calculus with subtyping (Figure 15-1), products (11-5), and equi-recursive types. The corresponding checker is `equirec`.

the ordinary coinductive definition of subtyping between infinite types. §21.9 proves termination of the subtyping algorithm for μ-types. §21.10 compares this algorithm with another algorithm due to Amadio and Cardelli. §21.11 briefly discusses iso-recursive types.

21.1   Induction and Coinduction

Assume we have fixed some *universal set* $\mathcal{U}$ as the domain of discourse for our inductive and coinductive definitions. $\mathcal{U}$ represents the set of "everything in the world," and the role of an inductive or coinductive definition will be to pick out some subset of $\mathcal{U}$. (Later on, we are going to choose $\mathcal{U}$ to be the set of all pairs of types, so that subsets of $\mathcal{U}$ are relations on types. For the present discussion, an arbitrary set $\mathcal{U}$ will do.)

21.1.1   DEFINITION: A function $F \in \mathcal{P}(\mathcal{U}) \rightarrow \mathcal{P}(\mathcal{U})$ is *monotone* if $X \subseteq Y$ implies $F(X) \subseteq F(Y)$. (Recall that $\mathcal{P}(\mathcal{U})$ is the set of all subsets of $\mathcal{U}$.)   □

In the following, we assume that F is some monotone function on $\mathcal{P}(\mathcal{U})$. We often refer to F as a *generating function*.

21.1.2   DEFINITION: Let X be a subset of $\mathcal{U}$.

1. X is *F-closed* if $F(X) \subseteq X$.

2. X is *F-consistent* if $X \subseteq F(X)$.

3. X is a *fixed point* of F if $F(X) = X$.   □

A useful intuition for these definitions is to think of the elements of $\mathcal{U}$ as some sort of statements or assertions, and of F as representing a "justification" relation that, given some set of statements (premises), tells us what new statements (conclusions) follow from them. An F-closed set, then, is one that cannot be made any bigger by adding elements justified by F—it already contains all the conclusions that are justified by its members. An F-consistent set, on the other hand, is one that is "self-justifying": every assertion in it is justified by other assertions that are also in it. A fixed point of F is a set that is both closed and consistent: it includes all the justifications required by its members, all the conclusions that follow from its members, and nothing else.

21.1.3   EXAMPLE: Consider the following generating function on the three-element universe $\mathcal{U} = \{a, b, c\}$:

$$
\begin{array}{llll}
E_1(\varnothing) & = & \{c\} & \qquad E_1(\{a,b\}) & = & \{c\} \\
E_1(\{a\}) & = & \{c\} & \qquad E_1(\{a,c\}) & = & \{b,c\} \\
E_1(\{b\}) & = & \{c\} & \qquad E_1(\{b,c\}) & = & \{a,b,c\} \\
E_1(\{c\}) & = & \{b,c\} & \qquad E_1(\{a,b,c\}) & = & \{a,b,c\}
\end{array}
$$

There is just one E_1-closed set—$\{a,b,c\}$—and four E_1-consistent sets—$\varnothing$, $\{c\}$, $\{b,c\}$, $\{a,b,c\}$.

E_1 can be represented compactly by a collection of *inference rules:*

$$\frac{}{c} \qquad \frac{c}{b} \qquad \frac{b \quad c}{a}$$

Each rule states that if all of the elements above the bar are in the input set, then the element below is in the output set. □

21.1.4   THEOREM [KNASTER-TARSKI (TARSKI, 1955)]:

1. The intersection of all F-closed sets is the least fixed point of F.

2. The union of all F-consistent sets is the greatest fixed point of F. □

Proof: We consider only part (2); the proof of part (1) is symmetric. Let $C = \{X \mid X \subseteq F(X)\}$ be the collection of all F-consistent sets, and let P be the union of all these sets. Taking into account the fact that F is monotone and that, for any $X \in C$, we know both that X is F-consistent and that $X \subseteq P$, we obtain $X \subseteq F(X) \subseteq F(P)$. Consequently, $P = \bigcup_{X \in C} X \subseteq F(P)$, i.e. P is F-consistent. Moreover, by its definition, P is the largest F-consistent set. Using the monotonicity of F again, we obtain $F(P) \subseteq F(F(P))$. This means, by the definition of C, that $F(P) \in C$. Hence, as for any member of C, we have $F(P) \subseteq P$, i.e. P is F-closed. Now we have established both that P is the largest F-consistent set and that P is a fixed point of F, so P is the largest fixed point. □

21.1.5   DEFINITION: The least fixed point of F is written μF. The greatest fixed point of F is written νF. □

21.1.6   EXAMPLE: For the sample generating function E_1 shown above, we have $\mu E_1 = \nu E_1 = \{a,b,c\}$. □

21.1.7   EXERCISE [⋆]: Suppose a generating function E_2 on the universe $\{a,b,c\}$ is defined by the following inference rules:

$$\frac{}{a} \qquad \frac{c}{b} \qquad \frac{a \quad b}{c}$$

Write out the set of pairs in the relation E_2 explicitly, as we did for E_1 above. List all the E_2-closed and E_2-consistent sets. What are μE_2 and νE_2? □

Note that μF itself is F-closed (hence, it is the smallest F-closed set) and that νF is F-consistent (hence, it is the largest F-consistent set). This observation gives us a pair of fundamental reasoning tools:

21.1.8   COROLLARY [OF 21.1.4]:

1. *Principle of induction:* If X is F-closed, then $\mu F \subseteq X$.

2. *Principle of coinduction:* If X is F-consistent, then $X \subseteq \nu F$.   □

The intuition behind these principles comes from thinking of the set X as a predicate, represented as its characteristic set—the subset of $\mathcal{U}$ for which the predicate is true; showing that property X holds of an element x is the same as showing that x is in the set X. Now, the induction principle says that any property whose characteristic set is closed under F (i.e., the property is preserved by F) is true of all the elements of the inductively defined set μF.

The coinduction principle, on the other hand, gives us a method for establishing that an element x is *in* the coinductively defined set νF. To show $x \in \nu F$, it suffices to find a set X such that $x \in X$ and X is F-consistent. Although it is a little less familiar than induction, the principle of coinduction is central to many areas of computer science; for example, it is the main proof technique in theories of concurrency based on *bisimulation*, and it lies at the heart of many *model checking* algorithms.

The principles of induction and coinduction are used heavily throughout the chapter. We do not write out every inductive argument in terms of generating functions and predicates; instead, in the interest of brevity, we often rely on familiar abbreviations such as structural induction. Coinductive arguments are presented more explicitly.

21.1.9   EXERCISE [RECOMMENDED, ★★★]: Show that the principles of ordinary induction on natural numbers (2.4.1) and lexicographic induction on pairs of numbers (2.4.4) follow from the principle of induction in 21.1.8.   □

21.2   Finite and Infinite Types

We are going to instantiate the general definitions of greatest fixed points and the coinductive proof method with the specifics of subtyping. Before we can do this, though, we need to show precisely how to view types as (finite or infinite) trees.

For brevity, we deal in this chapter with just three type constructors: $\rightarrow$, $\times$, and Top. We represent types as (possibly infinite) trees with nodes labeled by one of the symbols $\to$, $\times$, or Top. The definition is specialized to our present needs; for a general treatment of infinite labeled trees see Courcelle (1983).

We write $\{1,2\}^*$ for the set of sequences of 1s and 2s. Recall that the empty sequence is written $\bullet$, and i^k stands for k copies of i. If π and σ are sequences, then π,σ denotes the concatenation of π and σ.

21.2.1   DEFINITION: A *tree type*[1] (or, simply, a *tree*) is a partial function $T \in \{1,2\}^* \to \{\to, \times, \text{Top}\}$ satisfying the following constraints:

- $T(\bullet)$ is defined;

- if $T(\pi,\sigma)$ is defined then $T(\pi)$ is defined;

- if $T(\pi) = \to$ or $T(\pi) = \times$ then $T(\pi,1)$ and $T(\pi,2)$ are defined;

- if $T(\pi) = \text{Top}$ then $T(\pi,1)$ and $T(\pi,2)$ are undefined.

A tree type T is *finite* if $dom(T)$ is finite. The set of all tree types is written $\mathcal{T}$; the subset of all finite tree types is written $\mathcal{T}_f$.   □

For notational convenience, we write Top for the tree T with $T(\bullet) = \text{Top}$. When T_1 and T_2 are trees, we write $T_1 \times T_2$ for the tree with $(T_1 \times T_2)(\bullet) = \times$ and $(T_1 \times T_2)(i,\pi) = T_i(\pi)$ and $T_1 \to T_2$ for the tree with $(T_1 \to T_2)(\bullet) = \to$ and $(T_1 \to T_2)(i,\pi) = T_i(\pi)$, for $i = 1, 2$. For example, $(\text{Top} \times \text{Top}) \to \text{Top}$ denotes the finite tree type T defined by the function with $T(\bullet) = \to$ and $T(1) = \times$ and $T(2) = T(1,1) = T(1,2) = \text{Top}$. We use ellipses informally for describing non-finite tree types. For example, $\text{Top} \to (\text{Top} \to (\text{Top} \to \ldots))$ corresponds to the type T defined by $T(2^k) = \to$, for all $k \geq 0$, and $T(2^k,1) = \text{Top}$, for all $k \geq 0$. Figure 21-1 illustrates these conventions.

The set of finite tree types can be defined more compactly by a grammar:

$$
\begin{array}{rcl}
T & ::= & \text{Top} \\
  &   & T \times T \\
  &   & T \to T
\end{array}
$$

Formally, $\mathcal{T}_f$ is the least fixed point of the generating function described by the grammar. The universe of this generating function is the set of all finite and infinite trees labeled with Top, $\to$, and $\times$ (i.e., the set formed by generalizing Definition 21.2.1 by dropping its two last conditions). The whole set $\mathcal{T}$ can be derived from the same generating function by taking the greatest fixed point instead of the least.

---

1. The locution "tree type" is slightly awkward, but it will help to keep things straight when we discuss the alternative presentation of recursive types as finite expressions involving μ ("μ-types") in §21.8.

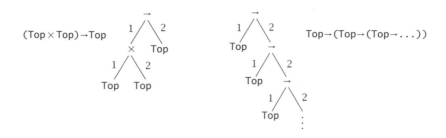

Figure 21-1: Sample tree types.

21.2.2   EXERCISE [RECOMMENDED, ★★]: Following the ideas in the previous paragraph, suggest a universe $\mathcal{U}$ and a generating function $F \in \mathcal{P}(\mathcal{U}) \to \mathcal{P}(\mathcal{U})$ such that the set of finite tree types $\mathcal{T}_f$ is the least fixed point of F and the set of all tree types $\mathcal{T}$ is its greatest fixed point.   □

21.3   Subtyping

We define subtype relations on finite tree types and on tree types in general as least and greatest fixed points, respectively, of monotone functions on certain universes. For subtyping on finite tree types the universe is the set $\mathcal{T}_f \times \mathcal{T}_f$ of pairs of finite tree types; our generating function will map subsets of this universe—that is, relations on $\mathcal{T}_f$—to other subsets, and their fixed points will also be relations on $\mathcal{T}_f$. For subtyping on arbitrary (finite or infinite) trees, the universe is $\mathcal{T} \times \mathcal{T}$.

21.3.1   DEFINITION [FINITE SUBTYPING]: Two finite tree types S and T are in the subtype relation ("S is a subtype of T") if $(S, T) \in \mu S_f$, where the monotone function $S_f \in \mathcal{P}(\mathcal{T}_f \times \mathcal{T}_f) \to \mathcal{P}(\mathcal{T}_f \times \mathcal{T}_f)$ is defined by

$$
\begin{aligned}
S_f(R) \quad = \quad & \{(\mathsf{T}, \mathsf{Top}) \mid \mathsf{T} \in \mathcal{T}_f\} \\
\cup \quad & \{(\mathsf{S}_1 \times \mathsf{S}_2, \mathsf{T}_1 \times \mathsf{T}_2) \mid (\mathsf{S}_1, \mathsf{T}_1), (\mathsf{S}_2, \mathsf{T}_2) \in R\} \\
\cup \quad & \{(\mathsf{S}_1 \to \mathsf{S}_2, \mathsf{T}_1 \to \mathsf{T}_2) \mid (\mathsf{T}_1, \mathsf{S}_1), (\mathsf{S}_2, \mathsf{T}_2) \in R\}.
\end{aligned}
$$

This generating function precisely captures the effect of the standard definition of the subtype relation by a collection of inference rules:

$$\frac{}{\mathsf{T} <: \mathsf{Top}}$$

$$\frac{\mathsf{S}_1 <: \mathsf{T}_1 \qquad \mathsf{S}_2 <: \mathsf{T}_2}{\mathsf{S}_1 \times \mathsf{S}_2 <: \mathsf{T}_1 \times \mathsf{T}_2}$$

$$\frac{T_1 <: S_1 \quad S_2 <: T_2}{S_1 \to S_2 <: T_1 \to T_2}$$

The statement S <: T above the line in the second and third rules should be read as "if the pair (S, T) is in the argument to S_f" and below the line as "then (S, T) is in the result." □

21.3.2 DEFINITION [INFINITE SUBTYPING]: Two (finite or infinite) tree types S and T are in the subtype relation if $(S, T) \in \nu S$, where $S \in \mathcal{P}(\mathcal{T} \times \mathcal{T}) \to \mathcal{P}(\mathcal{T} \times \mathcal{T})$ is defined by:

$$
\begin{aligned}
S(R) \quad = \quad & \{(T, \mathsf{Top}) \mid T \in \mathcal{T}\} \\
\cup \quad & \{(S_1 \times S_2, T_1 \times T_2) \mid (S_1, T_1), (S_2, T_2) \in R\} \\
\cup \quad & \{(S_1 \to S_2, T_1 \to T_2) \mid (T_1, S_1), (S_2, T_2) \in R\}.
\end{aligned}
$$

Note that the inference rule presentation of this relation is precisely the same as for the inductive relation above: all that changes is that we consider a larger universe of types and take a greatest instead of a least fixed point. □

21.3.3 EXERCISE [⋆]: Check that νS is not the whole of $\mathcal{T} \times \mathcal{T}$ by exhibiting a pair (S, T) that is not in νS. □

21.3.4 EXERCISE [⋆]: Is there a pair of types (S, T) that is related by νS, but not by μS? What about a pair of types (S, T) that is related by νS_f, but not by μS_f? □

One fundamental property of the subtype relation on infinite tree types—the fact that it is transitive—should be verified right away. (We have already seen in §16.1 that subtyping on finite types is transitive.) If the subtype relation were *not* transitive, the critical property of preservation of types under evaluation would immediately fail. To see this, suppose that there were types S, T, and U with S<:T and T<:U but not S<:U. Let s be a value of type S and f a function of type U→Top. Then the term (λx:T. f x) s could be typed, using the rule of subsumption once for each application, but this term reduces in one step to the ill-typed term f s.

21.3.5 DEFINITION: A relation $R \subseteq \mathcal{U} \times \mathcal{U}$ is *transitive* if R is closed under the monotone function $TR(R) = \{(x, y) \mid \exists z \in \mathcal{U}. (x, z), (z, y) \in R\}$—i.e., if $TR(R) \subseteq R$. □

21.3.6 LEMMA: Let $F \in \mathcal{P}(\mathcal{U} \times \mathcal{U}) \to \mathcal{P}(\mathcal{U} \times \mathcal{U})$ be a monotone function. If $TR(F(R)) \subseteq F(TR(R))$ for any $R \subseteq \mathcal{U} \times \mathcal{U}$, then νF is transitive. □

Proof: Since νF is a fixed point, $\nu F = F(\nu F)$, implying $TR(\nu F) = TR(F(\nu F))$. Therefore, by the lemma's assumption, $TR(\nu F) \subseteq F(TR(\nu F))$. In other words, $TR(\nu F)$ is F-consistent, so, by the principle of coinduction, $TR(\nu F) \subseteq \nu F$. Equivalently, νF is transitive by Definition 21.3.5. □

This lemma is reminiscent of the traditional technique for establishing redundancy of the transitivity rule in inference systems, often called "cut-elimination proofs" (see §16.1). The condition $TR(F(R)) \subseteq F(TR(R))$ corresponds to the crucial step in this technique: given that a certain statement can be obtained by taking some statements from R, applying rules from F, and then applying the rule of transitivity TR, we argue that the statement can instead be obtained by reversing the steps—first applying the rule of transitivity, and then rules from F. We use the lemma to establish transitivity of the subtype relation.

21.3.7   THEOREM: νS is transitive.   □

Proof: By Lemma 21.3.6, it suffices to show that $TR(S(R)) \subseteq S(TR(R))$ for any $R \subseteq \mathcal{T} \times \mathcal{T}$. Let $(\mathsf{S}, \mathsf{T}) \in TR(S(R))$. By the definition of TR, there exists some $\mathsf{U} \in \mathcal{T}$ such that $(\mathsf{S}, \mathsf{U}), (\mathsf{U}, \mathsf{T}) \in S(R)$. Our goal is to show that $(\mathsf{S}, \mathsf{T}) \in S(TR(R))$. Consider the possible shapes of U.

Case: $\mathsf{U} = \mathsf{Top}$

Since $(\mathsf{U}, \mathsf{T}) \in S(R)$, the definition of S implies that T must be Top. But $(\mathsf{A}, \mathsf{Top}) \in S(Q)$ for any A and Q; in particular, $(\mathsf{S}, \mathsf{T}) = (\mathsf{S}, \mathsf{Top}) \in S(TR(R))$.

Case: $\mathsf{U} = \mathsf{U}_1 \times \mathsf{U}_2$

If $\mathsf{T} = \mathsf{Top}$, then $(\mathsf{S}, \mathsf{T}) \in S(TR(R))$ as in the previous case. Otherwise, $(\mathsf{U}, \mathsf{T}) \in S(R)$ implies $\mathsf{T} = \mathsf{T}_1 \times \mathsf{T}_2$, with $(\mathsf{U}_1, \mathsf{T}_1), (\mathsf{U}_2, \mathsf{T}_2) \in R$. Similarly, $(\mathsf{S}, \mathsf{U}) \in S(R)$ implies $\mathsf{S} = \mathsf{S}_1 \times \mathsf{S}_2$, with $(\mathsf{S}_1, \mathsf{U}_1), (\mathsf{S}_2, \mathsf{U}_2) \in R$. By the definition of TR, we have $(\mathsf{S}_1, \mathsf{T}_1), (\mathsf{S}_2, \mathsf{T}_2) \in TR(R)$, from which $(\mathsf{S}_1 \times \mathsf{S}_2, \mathsf{T}_1 \times \mathsf{T}_2) \in S(TR(R))$ follows from the definition of S.

Case: $\mathsf{U} = \mathsf{U}_1 \rightarrow \mathsf{U}_2$

Similar.   □

21.3.8   EXERCISE [RECOMMENDED, ★★]: Show that the subtype relation on infinite tree types is also reflexive.   □

The following section continues the discussion of transitivity by comparing its treatment in standard accounts of subtyping for finite types and in the present account of subtyping for infinite tree types. It can be skipped or skimmed on a first reading.

21.4   A Digression on Transitivity

We saw in Chapter 16 that standard formulations of inductively defined subtype relations generally come in two forms: a *declarative* presentation that is optimized for readability and an *algorithmic* presentation that corresponds more or less directly to an implementation. In simple systems, the two presentations are fairly similar; in more complex systems, they can be quite different, and proving that they define the same relation on types can pose a significant challenge. (We will see an example of this in Chapter 28; many others have been studied.)

One of the most distinctive differences between declarative and algorithmic presentations is that declarative presentations include an explicit rule of transitivity—if S<:U and U<:T then S<:T—while algorithmic systems do not. This rule is useless in an algorithm, since applying it in a goal-directed manner would involve guessing U.

The rule of transitivity plays two useful roles in declarative systems. First, it makes it obvious to the reader that the subtype relation is, indeed, transitive. Second, transitivity often allows other rules to be stated in simpler, more primitive forms; in algorithmic presentations, these simple rules need to be combined into heavier mega-rules that take into account all possible combinations of the simpler ones. For example, in the presence of transitivity, the rules for "depth subtyping" within record fields, "width subtyping" by adding new fields, and "permutation" of fields can be stated separately, making them all easier to understand, as we did in §15.2. Without transitivity, the three rules must be merged into a single one that takes width, depth, and permutation into account all at once, as we did in §16.1.

Somewhat surprisingly, the possibility of giving a declarative presentation with the rule of transitivity turns out to be a consequence of a "trick" that can be played with inductive, but not coinductive, definitions. To see why, observe that the property of transitivity is a *closure property*—it demands that the subtype relation be closed under the transitivity rule. Since the subtype relation for finite types is itself defined as the closure of a set of rules, we can achieve closure under transitivity simply by adding it to the other rules. This is a general property of inductive definitions and closure properties: the union of two sets of rules, when applied inductively, generates the least relation that is closed under both sets of rules separately. This fact can be formulated more abstractly in terms of generating functions:

21.4.1 PROPOSITION: Suppose F and G are monotone functions, and let $H(X) = F(X) \cup G(X)$. Then μH is the smallest set that is both F-closed and G-closed. □

Proof: First, we show that μH is closed under both F and G. By definition, $\mu H = H(\mu H) = F(\mu H) \cup G(\mu H)$, so $F(\mu H) \subseteq \mu H$ and $G(\mu H) \subseteq \mu H$. Second, we show that μH is the *least* set closed under both F and G. Suppose there is some set X such that $F(X) \subseteq X$ and $G(X) \subseteq X$. Then $H(X) = F(X) \cup G(X) \subseteq X$, that is, X is H-closed. Since μH is the least H-closed set (by the Knaster-Tarski theorem), we have $\mu H \subseteq X$.   □

Unfortunately, this trick for achieving transitive closure does not work when we are dealing with coinductive definitions. As the following exercise shows, adding transitivity to the rules generating a coinductively defined relation always gives us a degenerate relation.

21.4.2   EXERCISE [⋆]: Suppose F is a generating function on the universe $\mathcal{U}$. Show that the greatest fixed point νF^{TR} of the generating function

$$F^{TR}(R) = F(R) \cup TR(R)$$

is the *total* relation on $\mathcal{U} \times \mathcal{U}$.   □

In the coinductive setting, then, we drop declarative presentations and work just with algorithmic ones.

21.5   Membership Checking

We now turn our attention to the central question of the chapter: how to decide, given a generating function F on some universe $\mathcal{U}$ and an element $x \in \mathcal{U}$, whether or not x falls in the greatest fixed point of F. Membership checking for least fixed points is addressed more briefly (in Exercise 21.5.13).

A given element $x \in \mathcal{U}$ can, in general, be generated by F in many ways. That is, there can be more than one set $X \subseteq \mathcal{U}$ such that $x \in F(X)$. Call any such set X a *generating set* for x. Because of the monotonicity of F, any superset of a generating set for x is also a generating set for x, so it makes sense to restrict our attention to minimal generating sets. Going one step further, we can focus on the class of "invertible" generating functions, where each x has at most one minimal generating set.

21.5.1   DEFINITION: A generating function F is said to be *invertible* if, for all $x \in \mathcal{U}$, the collection of sets

$$G_x = \{X \subseteq \mathcal{U} \mid x \in F(X)\}$$

either is empty or contains a unique member that is a subset of all the others. When F is invertible, the partial function $support_F \in \mathcal{U} \rightharpoonup \mathcal{P}(\mathcal{U})$ is defined as follows[2]:

$$support_F(x) = \begin{cases} X & \text{if } X \in G_x \text{ and } \forall X' \in G_x.\ X \subseteq X' \\ \uparrow & \text{if } G_x = \varnothing \end{cases}$$

---

2. We assume that functions f similar to *support* have a special value for "failure" in their range domain. The notation $f(x){\downarrow}$ indicates that f results in a value when applied to x, while $f(x) \uparrow$ says that f fails on x. We also write $f(x) = {\uparrow}$ in the latter case.

The *support* function is lifted to sets as follows:

$$support_F(X) = \begin{cases} \bigcup_{x \in X} support_F(x) & \text{if } \forall x \in X.\ support_F(x){\downarrow} \\ \uparrow & \text{otherwise} \end{cases}$$

When F is clear from context, we will often omit the subscript in $support_F$ (and similar functions based on F that we define later). □

21.5.2 EXERCISE [⋆⋆]: Verify that S_f and S, the generating functions for the subtyping relations from Definitions 21.3.1 and 21.3.2, are invertible, and give their support functions. □

Our goal is to develop algorithms for checking membership in the least and greatest fixed points of a generating function F. The basic steps in these algorithms will involve "running F backwards": to check membership for an element x, we need to ask how x could have been generated by F. The advantage of an invertible F is that there is at most one way to generate a given x. For a non-invertible F, elements can be generated in multiple ways, leading to a combinatorial explosion in the number of paths that the algorithm must explore. From now on, we restrict our attention to invertible generating functions.

21.5.3 DEFINITION: An element x is *F-supported* if $support_F(x){\downarrow}$; otherwise, x is *F-unsupported*. An *F*-supported element is called *F-ground* if $support_F(x) = \varnothing$. □

Note that an unsupported element x does not appear in $F(X)$ for any X, while a ground x is in $F(X)$ for every X.

An invertible function can be visualized as a *support graph*. For example, Figure 21-2 defines a function E on the universe $\{a, b, c, d, e, f, g, h, i\}$ by showing which elements are needed to support a given element of the universe: for a given x, the set $support_E(x)$ contains every y for which there is an arrow from x to y. An unsupported element is denoted by a slashed circle. In this example, i is the only unsupported element and g is the only ground element. (Note that, according to our definition, h *is* supported, even though its support set includes an unsupported element.)

21.5.4 EXERCISE [⋆]: Give inference rules corresponding to this function, as we did in Example 21.1.3. Check that $E(\{b,c\}) = \{g, a, d\}$, that $E(\{a, i\}) = \{g, h\}$, and that the sets of elements marked in the figure as μE and νE are indeed the least and the greatest fixed points of E. □

Thinking about the graph in Figure 21-2 suggests the idea that an element x is in the greatest fixed point iff no unsupported element is reachable from

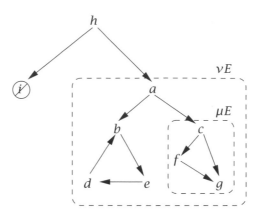

Figure 21-2: A sample *support* function

x in the support graph. This suggests an algorithmic strategy for checking
whether x is in νF: enumerate all elements reachable from x via the *support*
function; return failure if an unsupported element occurs in the enumeration;
otherwise, succeed. Observe, however, that there can be cycles of reachability
between the elements, and the enumeration procedure must take some pre-
cautions against falling into an infinite loop. We will pursue this idea for the
remainder of this section.

21.5.5   DEFINITION: Suppose F is an invertible generating function. Define the boolean-
valued function gfp_F (or just gfp) as follows:[3]

$$gfp(X) \quad = \quad \text{if } support(X) \uparrow, \text{ then } false$$
$$\text{else if } support(X) \subseteq X, \text{ then } true$$
$$\text{else } gfp(support(X) \cup X).$$

Intuitively, *gfp* starts from X and keeps enriching it using *support* until either
it becomes consistent or else an unsupported element is found. We extend
gfp to individual elements by taking $gfp(x) = gfp(\{x\})$.   □

21.5.6   EXERCISE [★]: Another observation that can be made from Figure 21-2 is that
an element x of νF is not a member of μF if x participates in a cycle in the
support graph (or if there is a path from x to an element that participates in

---

3. We use here the standard notation for defining recursive functions, i.e., we intend that *gfp* is
the *smallest* partial function satisfying the stated equation. Such definitions can themselves be
viewed more formally as least fixed points of appropriate generating functions. Details can be
found in any standard treatment of denotational semantics, e.g. the in texts of Gunter (1992),
Winskel (1993), or Mitchell (1996).

a cycle). Is the converse also true—that is, if x is a member of νF but not μF, is it necessarily the case that x leads to a cycle?   □

The remainder of the section is devoted to proving the correctness and termination of *gfp*. (First-time readers may want to skip this material and jump to the next section.) We start by observing a couple of properties of the *support* function.

21.5.7   LEMMA: $X \subseteq F(Y)$ iff *support*$_F(X)\downarrow$ and *support*$_F(X) \subseteq Y$.   □

Proof: It suffices to show that $x \in F(Y)$ iff *support*$(x)\downarrow$ and *support*$(x) \subseteq Y$. Suppose first that $x \in F(Y)$. Then $Y \in G_x = \{X \subseteq \mathcal{U} \mid x \in F(X)\}$—that is, $G_x \neq \varnothing$. Therefore, since F is invertible, *support*(x), the smallest set in G_x, exists and *support*$(x) \subseteq Y$. Conversely, if *support*$(x) \subseteq Y$, then $F(support(x)) \subseteq F(Y)$ by monotonicity. But $x \in F(support(x))$ by the definition of *support*, so $x \in F(Y)$.   □

21.5.8   LEMMA: Suppose P is a fixed point of F. Then $X \subseteq P$ iff *support*$_F(X)\downarrow$ and *support*$_F(X) \subseteq P$.   □

Proof: Recall that $P = F(P)$ and apply Lemma 21.5.7.   □

Now we can prove partial correctness of *gfp*. (We are not concerned with total correctness yet, because some generating functions will make *gfp* diverge. We prove termination for a restricted class of generating functions later in the section.)

21.5.9   THEOREM: (1) If *gfp*$_F(X)$ = *true*, then $X \subseteq \nu F$. (2) If *gfp*$_F(X)$ = *false*, then $X \not\subseteq \nu F$.   □

Proof: The proof of each clause proceeds by induction on the recursive structure of a run of the algorithm.

1. From the definition of *gfp*, it is easy to see that there are two cases where *gfp*(X) can return *true*. If *gfp*(X) = *true* because *support*$(X) \subseteq X$, then, by Lemma 21.5.7, we have $X \subseteq F(X)$, i.e., X is F-consistent; thus, $X \subseteq \nu F$ by the coinduction principle. On the other hand, if *gfp*(X) = *true* because *gfp*$(support(X) \cup X)$ = *true*, then, by the induction hypothesis, *support*$(X) \cup X \subseteq \nu F$, and so $X \subseteq \nu F$.

2. Again, there are two ways to get *gfp*(X) = *false*. Suppose first that *gfp*(X) = *false* because *support*$(X)\uparrow$. Then $X \not\subseteq \nu F$ by Lemma 21.5.8. On the other hand, suppose *gfp*(X) = *false* because *gfp*$(support(X) \cup X)$ = *false*. By the induction hypothesis, *support*$(X) \cup X \not\subseteq \nu F$. Equivalently, $X \not\subseteq \nu F$ or *support*$(X) \not\subseteq \nu F$. Either way, $X \not\subseteq \nu F$ (using Lemma 21.5.8 in the second case).   □

Next, we identify a sufficient termination condition for *gfp*, giving a class of generating functions for which the algorithm is guaranteed to terminate. To describe the class, we need some additional terminology.

21.5.10   DEFINITION: Given an invertible generating function F and an element $x \in \mathcal{U}$, the set $pred_F(x)$ (or just $pred(x)$) of immediate predecessors of x is

$$pred(x) = \begin{cases} \varnothing & \text{if } support(x) \uparrow \\ support(x) & \text{if } support(x) \downarrow \end{cases}$$

and its extension to sets $X \subseteq \mathcal{U}$ is

$$pred(X) = \bigcup_{x \in X} pred(x).$$

The set $reachable_F(X)$ (or just $reachable(X)$) of all elements reachable from a set X via *support* is defined as

$$reachable(X) = \bigcup_{n \geq 0} pred^n(X).$$

and its extension to single elements $x \in \mathcal{U}$ is

$$reachable(x) = reachable(\{x\}).$$

An element $y \in \mathcal{U}$ is *reachable* from an element x if $y \in reachable(x)$.   □

21.5.11   DEFINITION: An invertible generating function F is said to be *finite state* if $reachable(x)$ is finite for each $x \in \mathcal{U}$.   □

For a finite-state generating function, the search space explored by *gfp* is finite and *gfp* always terminates:

21.5.12   THEOREM: If $reachable_F(X)$ is finite, then $gfp_F(X)$ is defined. Consequently, if F is finite state, then $gfp_F(X)$ terminates for any finite $X \subseteq \mathcal{U}$.   □

Proof: For each recursive call $gfp(Y)$ in the call graph generated by the original invocation $gfp(X)$, we have $Y \subseteq reachable(X)$. Moreover, Y strictly increases on each call. Since $reachable(X)$ is finite, $m(Y) = |reachable(X)| - |Y|$ serves as a termination measure for *gfp*.   □

21.5.13   EXERCISE [★★★]: Suppose F is an invertible generating function. Define the function lfp_F (or just lfp) as follows:

$$lfp(X) \quad = \quad \begin{aligned} &\text{if } support(X) \uparrow, \text{ then } \textit{false} \\ &\text{else if } X = \varnothing, \text{ then } \textit{true} \\ &\text{else } lfp(support(X)). \end{aligned}$$

Intuitively, *lfp* works by starting with a set X and using the *support* relation to reduce it until it becomes empty. Prove that this algorithm is partially correct, in the sense that

1. If $lfp_F(X) = true$, then $X \subseteq \mu F$.

2. If $lfp_F(X) = false$, then $X \nsubseteq \mu F$.

Can you find a class of generating functions for which lfp_F is guaranteed to terminate on all finite inputs? □

21.6 More Efficient Algorithms

Although the *gfp* algorithm is correct, it is not very efficient, since it has to recompute the *support* of the whole set X every time it makes a recursive call. For example, in the following trace of *gfp* on the function E from Figure 21-2,

$$gfp(\{a\})$$
$$= \quad gfp(\{a, b, c\})$$
$$= \quad gfp(\{a, b, c, e, f, g\})$$
$$= \quad gfp(\{a, b, c, e, f, g, d\})$$
$$= \quad true.$$

Note that *support*(a) is recomputed four times. We can refine the algorithm to eliminate this redundant recomputation by maintaining a set A of *assumptions* whose *support* sets have already been considered and a set X of *goals* whose *support* has not yet been considered.

21.6.1 DEFINITION: Suppose F is an invertible generating function. Define the function gfp_F^a (or just gfp^a) as follows (the superscript "a" is for "assumptions"):

$$gfp^a(A, X) \quad = \quad \text{if } support(X) \uparrow, \text{ then } false$$
$$\text{else if } X = \varnothing, \text{ then } true$$
$$\text{else } gfp^a(A \cup X, support(X) \setminus (A \cup X)).$$

In order to check $x \in \nu F$, compute $gfp^a(\varnothing, \{x\})$. □

This algorithm (like the two following algorithms in this section) computes the support of each element at most once. A trace for the above example looks like this:

$$gfp^a(\varnothing, \{a\})$$
$$= \quad gfp^a(\{a\}, \{b, c\})$$
$$= \quad gfp^a(\{a, b, c\}, \{e, f, g\})$$
$$= \quad gfp^a(\{a, b, c, e, f, g\}, \{d\})$$
$$= \quad gfp^a(\{a, b, c, e, f, g, d\}, \varnothing)$$
$$= \quad true.$$

Naturally, the correctness statement for this algorithm is slightly more elaborate than the one we saw in the previous section.

21.6.2   THEOREM:

1. If $support_F(A) \subseteq A \cup X$ and $gfp_F^a(A, X) = true$, then $A \cup X \subseteq \nu F$.

2. If $gfp_F^a(A, X) = false$, then $X \nsubseteq \nu F$. $\square$

Proof: Similar to 21.5.9. $\square$

The remainder of this section examines two more variations on the *gfp* algorithm that correspond more closely to well-known subtyping algorithms for recursive types. First-time readers may want to skip to the beginning of the next section.

21.6.3   DEFINITION: A small variation on gfp^a has the algorithm pick just one element at a time from X and expand its *support*. The new algorithm is called gfp_F^s (or just gfp^s, "s" being for "single").

$$gfp^s(A, X) \quad = \quad \text{if } X = \varnothing, \text{ then } true$$
$$\text{else let } x \text{ be some element of } X \text{ in}$$
$$\text{if } x \in A \text{ then } gfp^s(A, X \setminus \{x\})$$
$$\text{else if } support(x) \uparrow \text{ then } false$$
$$\text{else } gfp^s(A \cup \{x\}, (X \cup support(x)) \setminus (A \cup \{x\})).$$

The correctness statement (i.e., the invariant of the recursive "loop") for this algorithm is exactly the same as Theorem 21.6.2.

Unlike the above algorithm, many existing algorithms for recursive subtyping take just one candidate element, rather than a set, as an argument. Another small modification to our algorithm makes it more similar to these. The modified algorithm is no longer tail recursive,[4] since it uses the call stack to remember subgoals that have not yet been checked. Another change is that the algorithm both takes a set of assumptions A as an argument and returns a new set of assumptions as a result. This allows it to record the subtyping assumptions that have been generated during completed recursive calls and reuse them in later calls. In effect, the set of assumptions is "threaded" through the recursive call graph—whence the name of the algorithm, gfp^t.

---

4. A *tail-recursive* call (or *tail call*) is a recursive call that is the last action of the calling function—i.e., such that the result returned from the recursive call will also be caller's result. Tail calls are interesting because most compilers for functional languages will implement a tail call as a simple branch, re-using the stack space of the caller instead of allocating a new stack frame for the recursive call. This means that a loop implemented as a tail-recursive function compiles into the same machine code as an equivalent `while` loop.

21.6.4   DEFINITION: Given an invertible generating function F, define the function gfp_F^t (or just gfp^t) as follows:

$$gfp^t(A, x) \ = \ \text{if } x \in A, \text{ then } A$$

else if $support(x) \uparrow$, then *fail*

else

    let $\{x_1, \ldots, x_n\} = support(x)$ in

    let $A_0 = A \cup \{x\}$ in

    let $A_1 = gfp^t(A_0, x_1)$ in

    $\ldots$

    let $A_n = gfp^t(A_{n-1}, x_n)$ in

    A_n.

To check $x \in \nu F$, compute $gfp^t(\varnothing, x)$. If this call succeeds, then $x \in \nu F$; if it fails, then $x \notin \nu F$. We use the following convention for failure: if an expression B fails, then "let $A = B$ in C" also fails. This avoids writing explicit "exception handling" clauses for every recursive invocation of gfp^t. $\square$

The correctness statement for this algorithm must again be refined from what we had above, taking into account the non-tail-recursive nature of this formulation by positing an extra "stack" X of elements whose supports remain to be checked.

21.6.5   LEMMA:

1. If $gfp_F^t(A, x) = A'$, then $A \cup \{x\} \subseteq A'$.

2. For all X, if $support_F(A) \subseteq A \cup X \cup \{x\}$ and $gfp_F^t(A, x) = A'$, then $support_F(A') \subseteq A' \cup X$. $\square$

Proof: Part (1) is a routine induction on the recursive structure of a run of the algorithm.

Part (2) also goes by induction on the recursive structure of a run of the algorithm. If $x \in A$, then $A' = A$ and the desired conclusion follows immediately from the assumption. On the other hand, suppose $A' \neq A$, and consider the special case where $support(x)$ contains two elements x_1 and x_2—the general case (not shown here) is proved similarly, using an inner induction on the size of $support(x)$. The algorithm calculates A_0, A_1, and A_2 and returns A_2. We want to show, for an arbitrary X_0, that if $support(A) \subseteq A \cup \{x\} \cup X_0$, then $support(A_2) \subseteq A_2 \cup X_0$. Let $X_1 = X_0 \cup \{x_2\}$. Since

$$
\begin{aligned}
support(A_0) \ &= \ support(A) \cup support(x) \\
&= \ support(A) \cup \{x_1, x_2\} \\
&\subseteq \ A \cup \{x\} \cup X_0 \cup \{x_1, x_2\} \\
&= \ A_0 \cup X_0 \cup \{x_1, x_2\} \\
&= \ A_0 \cup X_1 \cup \{x_1\},
\end{aligned}
$$

we can apply the induction hypothesis to the first recursive call by instantiating the universally quantified X with X_1. This yields $support(A_1) \subseteq A_1 \cup X_1 = A_1 \cup \{x_2\} \cup X_0$. Now, we can apply the induction hypothesis to the second recursive call by instantiating the universally quantified X with X_0 to obtain the desired result: $support(A_2) \subseteq A_2 \cup X_0$. $\qquad\square$

21.6.6   THEOREM:

1. If $gfp_F^t(\varnothing, x) = A'$, then $x \in \nu F$.

2. If $gfp_F^t(\varnothing, x) = fail$, then $x \notin \nu F$. $\qquad\square$

Proof: For part (1), observe that, by Lemma 21.6.5(1), $x \in A'$. Instantiating part (2) of the lemma with $X = \varnothing$, we obtain $support(A') \subseteq A'$—that is, A' is F-consistent by Lemma 21.5.7, and so $A' \subseteq \nu F$ by coinduction. For part (2), we argue (by an easy induction on the depth of a run of the gfp_F^t algorithm, using Lemma 21.5.8) that if, for some A, we have $gfp_F^t(A, x) = fail$, then $x \notin \nu F$. $\quad\square$

Since all of the algorithms in this section examine the reachable set, a sufficient termination condition for all of them is the same as that of the original *gfp* algorithm: they terminate on all inputs when F is finite state.

21.7   Regular Trees

At this point, we have developed generic algorithms for checking membership in a set defined as the greatest fixed point of a generating function F, assuming that F is invertible and finite state; separately, we have shown how to define subtyping between infinite trees as the greatest fixed point of a particular generating function S. The obvious next step is to instantiate one of our algorithms with S. Of course, this concrete algorithm will not terminate on all inputs, since in general the set of states reachable from a given pair of infinite types can be infinite. But, as we shall see in this section, if we restrict ourselves to infinite types of a certain well-behaved form, so-called *regular types,* then the sets of reachable states will be guaranteed to remain finite and the subtype checking algorithm will always terminate.

21.7.1   DEFINITION: A tree type S is a *subtree* of a tree type T if $S = \lambda\sigma.\, T(\pi,\sigma)$ for some π—that is, if the function S from paths to symbols can be obtained from the function T by adding some constant prefix π to the argument paths we give to T; the prefix π corresponds to the path from the root of T to the root of S. We write *subtrees*(T) for the set of all subtrees of T. $\quad\square$

21.7.2   DEFINITION: A tree type $T \in \mathcal{T}$ is *regular* if *subtrees*(T) is finite—i.e., if T has finitely many distinct subtrees. The set of regular tree types is written $\mathcal{T}_r$. $\quad\square$

21.7.3   EXAMPLES:

1. Every finite tree type is regular; the number of distinct subtrees is at most the number of nodes. The number of distinct subtrees of a tree type can be strictly less than the number of nodes. For example, T = Top→(Top × Top) has five nodes but only three distinct subtrees (T itself, Top × Top, and Top).

2. Some infinite tree types are regular. For example, the tree

   T = Top × (Top × (Top × ...))

   has just two distinct subtrees (T itself and Top).

3. The tree type

   T = B × (A × (B × (A × (A × (B × (A × (A × (A × (B × ...)

   where pairs of consecutive Bs are separated by increasingly many As, is not regular. Because T is irregular, the set $reachable_S(\mathsf{T},\mathsf{T})$ containing all the subtyping pairs needed to justify the statement T<:T is infinite.   □

21.7.4   PROPOSITION: The restriction S_r of the generating function S to regular tree types is finite state.   □

Proof: We need to show that for any pair (S,T) of regular tree types, the set $reachable_{S_r}(\mathsf{S},\mathsf{T})$ is finite. Observe that $reachable_{S_r}(\mathsf{S},\mathsf{T}) \subseteq subtrees(\mathsf{S}) \times subtrees(\mathsf{T})$; the latter is finite, since both $subtrees(\mathsf{S})$ and $subtrees(\mathsf{T})$ are.   □

This means that we can obtain a decision procedure for the subtype relation on regular tree types by instantiating one of the membership algorithms with S. Naturally, for this to work in a practical implementation, regular trees must be represented by some finite structures. One such representation, μ-notation, is discussed in the next section.

21.8 μ-Types

This section develops the finite μ-notation, defines subtyping on μ-expressions, and establishes the correspondence between this notion of subtyping and the subtyping on tree types.

21.8.1   DEFINITION: Let X range over a fixed countable set $\{X_1, X_2, \ldots\}$ of type variables. The set $\mathcal{T}_m^{raw}$ of *raw μ-types* is the set of expressions defined by the following grammar:

$$
\begin{array}{lll}
\mathsf{T} & ::= & \mathsf{X} \\
           &   & \mathsf{Top} \\
           &   & \mathsf{T \times T} \\
           &   & \mathsf{T \to T} \\
           &   & \mu\mathsf{X.T}
\end{array}
$$

The syntactic operator μ is a binder, and gives rise, in the standard way, to notions of bound and free variables, closed raw μ-types, and equivalence of raw μ-types up to renaming of bound variables. *FV*(T) denotes the set of free variables of a raw μ-type T. The capture-avoiding substitution $[\mathsf{X} \mapsto \mathsf{S}]\mathsf{T}$ of a raw μ-type S for free occurrences of X in a raw μ-type T is defined as usual. □

Raw μ-types have to be restricted a little to achieve a tight correspondence with regular trees: we want to be able to "read off" a tree type as the infinite unfolding of a given μ-type, but there are raw μ-types that cannot be reasonably interpreted as representations of tree types. These types have subexpressions of the form $\mu\mathsf{X}.\mu\mathsf{X}_1\ldots\mu\mathsf{X}_n.\mathsf{X}$, where the variables X_1 through X_n are distinct from X. For example, consider $\mathsf{T} = \mu\mathsf{X}.\mathsf{X}$. Unfolding of T gives T again, so we cannot read off any tree by unfolding T. This leads us to the following restriction.

21.8.2   DEFINITION: A raw μ-type T is *contractive* if, for any subexpression of T of the form $\mu\mathsf{X}.\mu\mathsf{X}_1\ldots\mu\mathsf{X}_n.\mathsf{S}$, the body S is not X. Equivalently, a raw μ-type is contractive if every occurrence of a μ-bound variable in the body is separated from its binder by at least one $\to$ or $\times$.

A raw μ-type is called simply a μ-*type* if it is contractive. The set of μ-types is written $\mathcal{T}_m$.

When T is a μ-type, we write μ-*height*(*T*) for the number of μ-bindings at the front of T.   □

The common understanding of μ-types as finite notation for infinite regular tree types is formalized by the following function.

21.8.3   DEFINITION: The function *treeof*, mapping closed μ-types to tree types, is defined inductively as follows:

$$
\begin{array}{lll}
\textit{treeof}(\mathsf{Top})(\bullet) & = & \mathsf{Top} \\[4pt]
\textit{treeof}(\mathsf{T}_1 \to \mathsf{T}_2)(\bullet) & = & \to \\
\textit{treeof}(\mathsf{T}_1 \to \mathsf{T}_2)(i,\pi) & = & \textit{treeof}(\mathsf{T}_i)(\pi) \\[4pt]
\textit{treeof}(\mathsf{T}_1 \times \mathsf{T}_2)(\bullet) & = & \times \\
\textit{treeof}(\mathsf{T}_1 \times \mathsf{T}_2)(i,\pi) & = & \textit{treeof}(\mathsf{T}_i)(\pi) \\[4pt]
\textit{treeof}(\mu\mathsf{X}.\mathsf{T})(\pi) & = & \textit{treeof}([\mathsf{X} \mapsto \mu\mathsf{X}.\mathsf{T}]\mathsf{T})(\pi)
\end{array}
$$

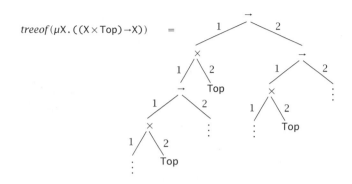

Figure 21-3: Sample *treeof* application

To verify that this definition is proper (i.e., exhaustive and terminating), note the following:

1. Every recursive use of *treeof* on the right-hand side reduces the lexicographic size of the pair $(|\pi|, \mu\text{-}height(\mathsf{T}))$: the cases for $\mathsf{S} \rightarrow \mathsf{T}$ and $\mathsf{S} \times \mathsf{T}$ reduce $|\pi|$ and the case for $\mu\mathsf{X}.\mathsf{T}$ preserves $|\pi|$ but reduces $\mu\text{-}height(\mathsf{T})$.

2. All recursive calls preserve contractiveness and closure of the argument types. In particular, the type $\mu\mathsf{X}.\mathsf{T}$ is contractive and closed iff its unfolding $[\mathsf{X} \mapsto \mu\mathsf{X}.\mathsf{T}]\mathsf{T}$ is. This justifies the unfolding step in the definition of $treeof(\mu\mathsf{X}.\mathsf{T})$.

The *treeof* function is lifted to pairs of types by defining $treeof(\mathsf{S},\mathsf{T}) = (treeof(\mathsf{S}), treeof(\mathsf{T}))$.   □

A sample application of *treeof* to a μ-type is shown in Figure 21-3.

The subtype relation for tree types was defined in §21.3 as the greatest fixed point of the generating function S. In the present section, we extended the syntax of types with μ-types, whose behavior is intuitively described by the rules of (right and left, correspondingly) *μ-folding*:

$$\frac{\mathsf{S} <: [\mathsf{X} \mapsto \mu\mathsf{X}.\mathsf{T}]\mathsf{T}}{\mathsf{S} <: \mu\mathsf{X}.\mathsf{T}} \quad \text{and} \quad \frac{[\mathsf{X} \mapsto \mu\mathsf{X}.\mathsf{S}]\mathsf{S} <: \mathsf{T}}{\mu\mathsf{X}.\mathsf{S} <: \mathsf{T}}$$

Formally, we define subtyping for μ-types by giving a generating function S_m, with three clauses identical to the definition of S and two additional clauses corresponding to the μ-folding rules.

21.8.4   DEFINITION: Two μ-types S and T are said to be in the subtype relation if
$(S, T) \in \nu S_m$, where the monotone function $S_m \in \mathcal{P}(\mathcal{T}_m \times \mathcal{T}_m) \to \mathcal{P}(\mathcal{T}_m \times \mathcal{T}_m)$
is defined by:

$$
\begin{aligned}
S_m(R) \;=\; & \{(S, \mathsf{Top}) \mid S \in \mathcal{T}_m\} \\
\cup\; & \{(S_1 \times S_2, T_1 \times T_2) \mid (S_1, T_1), (S_2, T_2) \in R\} \\
\cup\; & \{(S_1 {\to} S_2, T_1 {\to} T_2) \mid (T_1, S_1), (S_2, T_2) \in R\} \\
\cup\; & \{(S, \mu X.T) \mid (S, [X \mapsto \mu X.T]T) \in R\} \\
\cup\; & \{(\mu X.S, T) \mid ([X \mapsto \mu X.S]S, T) \in R, \; T \ne \mathsf{Top}, \text{ and } T \ne \mu Y.T_1\}.
\end{aligned}
$$

Note that this definition does not embody precisely the μ-folding rules above:
we have introduced an asymmetry between its final and penultimate clauses
to make it invertible (otherwise, the clauses would overlap). However, as the
next exercise shows, S_m generates the same subtype relation as the more
natural generating function[5] S_d whose clauses exactly correspond to the inference rules.   □

21.8.5   EXERCISE [★★★]: Write down the function S_d mentioned above, and demonstrate that it is not invertible. Prove that $\nu S_d = \nu S_m$.   □

The generating function S_m is invertible because the corresponding support function is well-defined:

$$
\mathit{support}_{S_m}(S, T) = \begin{cases}
\varnothing & \text{if } T = \mathsf{Top} \\
\{(S_1, T_1), (S_2, T_2)\} & \text{if } S = S_1 \times S_2 \text{ and} \\
& \quad T = T_1 \times T_2 \\
\{(T_1, S_1), (S_2, T_2)\} & \text{if } S = S_1 {\to} S_2 \text{ and} \\
& \quad T = T_1 {\to} T_2 \\
\{(S, [X \mapsto \mu X.T_1]T_1)\} & \text{if } T = \mu X.T_1 \\
\{([X \mapsto \mu X.S_1]S_1, T)\} & \text{if } S = \mu X.S_1 \text{ and} \\
& \quad T \ne \mu X.T_1, \; T \ne \mathsf{Top} \\
\uparrow & \text{otherwise.}
\end{cases}
$$

The subtype relation on μ-types so far has been introduced independently
of the previously defined subtyping on tree types. Since we think of μ-types
as just a way of representing regular types in a finite form, it is necessary
to ensure that the two notions of subtyping correspond to each other. The
next theorem (21.8.7) establishes this correspondence. But first, we need a
technical lemma.

21.8.6   LEMMA: Suppose that $R \subseteq \mathcal{T}_m \times \mathcal{T}_m$ is S_m-consistent. For any $(S, T) \in R$, there
is some $(S', T') \in R$ such that $\mathit{treeof}(S', T') = \mathit{treeof}(S, T)$ and neither S' nor
T' starts with μ.   □

---

5. The "d" in S_d is a reminder that the function is based on the "declarative" inference rules
for μ-folding, in contrast to the "algorithmic" versions used in S_m.

Proof: By induction on the total number of μs at the front of S and T. If neither S nor T starts with μ, then we can take $(S', T') = (S, T)$. On the other hand, if $(S, T) = (S, \mu X. T_1)$, then by the S_m-consistency of R, we have $(S, T) \in S_m(R)$, so $(S'', T'') = (S, [X \mapsto \mu X. T_1]T_1) \in R$. Since T is contractive, the result T″ of unfolding T has one fewer μ at the front than T does. By the induction hypothesis, there is some $(S', T') \in R$ such that neither S′ nor T′ starts with μ and such that $treeof(S'', T'') = (S', T')$. Since, by the definition of *treeof*, $treeof(S, T) = treeof(S'', T'')$, the pair (S', T') is the one we need. The case where $(S, T) = (\mu X. S_1, T)$ is similar. □

21.8.7   THEOREM: Let $(S, T) \in \mathcal{T}_m \times \mathcal{T}_m$. Then $(S, T) \in \nu S_m$ iff $treeof(S, T) \in \nu S$.   □

Proof: First, let us consider the "only if" direction—that $(S, T) \in \nu S_m$ implies $treeof(S, T) \in \nu S$. Let $(A, B) = treeof(S, T) \in \mathcal{T} \times \mathcal{T}$. By the coinduction principle, the result will follow if we can exhibit an S-consistent set $Q \in \mathcal{T} \times \mathcal{T}$ such that $(A, B) \in Q$. Our claim is that $Q = treeof(\nu S_m)$ is such a set. To verify this, we must show that $(A', B') \in S(Q)$ for every $(A', B') \in Q$.

Let $(S', T') \in \nu S_m$ be a pair of μ-types such that $treeof(S', T') = (A', B')$. By Lemma 21.8.6, we may assume that neither S′ nor T′ starts with μ. Since νS_m is S_m-consistent, (S', T') must be supported by one of the clauses in the definition of S_m—i.e., it must have one of the following shapes.

Case: $(S', T') = (S', \mathsf{Top})$

Then $B' = \mathsf{Top}$, and $(A', B') \in S(Q)$ by the definition of S.

Case: $(S', T') = (S_1 \times S_2, T_1 \times T_2)$ with $(S_1, T_1), (S_2, T_2) \in \nu S_m$

By the definition of *treeof*, we have $B' = treeof(T') = B_1 \times B_2$, where each $B_i = treeof(T_i)$. Similarly, $A' = A_1 \times A_2$, where $A_i = treeof(S_i)$. Applying *treeof* to these pairs gives $(A_1, B_1), (A_2, B_2) \in Q$. But then, by the definition of S, we have $(A, B) = (A_1 \times A_2, B_1 \times B_2) \in S(Q)$.

Case: $(S', T') = (S_1 \rightarrow S_2, T_1 \rightarrow T_2)$ with $(T_1, S_1), (S_2, T_2) \in \nu S_m$

Similar.

Next, let us check the "if" direction of the theorem—that $treeof(S, T) \in \nu S$ implies $(S, T) \in \nu S_m$. By the coinduction principle, it suffices to exhibit an S_m-consistent set $R \in \mathcal{T}_m \times \mathcal{T}_m$ with $(S, T) \in R$. We claim that $R = \{(S', T') \in \mathcal{T}_m \times \mathcal{T}_m \mid treeof(S', T') \in \nu S\}$ is such a set. Clearly, $(S, T) \in R$. To finish the proof, we must now show that $(S', T') \in R$ implies $(S', T') \in S_m(R)$.

Note that, since νS is S-consistent, any pair $(A', B') \in \nu S$ must have one of the forms (A', Top), $(A_1 \times A_2, B_1 \times B_2)$, or $(A_1 \rightarrow A_2, B_1 \rightarrow B_2)$. From this and the definition of *treeof*, we see that any pair $(S', T') \in R$ must have one of the forms (S', Top), $(S_1 \times S_2, T_1 \times T_2)$, $(S_1 \rightarrow S_2, T_1 \rightarrow T_2)$, $(S', \mu X. T_1)$, or $(\mu X. S_1, T')$. We consider each of these cases in turn.

Case: $(S', T') = (S', \text{Top})$

Then $(S', T') \in S_m(R)$ immediately, by the definition of S_m.

Case: $(S', T') = (S_1 \times S_2, T_1 \times T_2)$

Let $(A', B') = \textit{treeof}(S', T')$. Then $(A', B') = (A_1 \times A_2, B_1 \times B_2)$, with $A_i = \textit{treeof}(S_i)$ and $B_i = \textit{treeof}(T_i)$. Since $(A', B') \in \nu S$, the S-consistency of νS implies that $(A_i, B_i) \in \nu S$, which in turn yields $(S_i, T_i) \in R$, by the definition of R. The definition of S_m yields $(S', T') = (S_1 \times S_2, T_1 \times T_2) \in S_m(R)$.

Case: $(S', T') = (S_1 \rightarrow S_2, T_1 \rightarrow T_2)$

Similar.

Case: $(S', T') = (S', \mu X.T_1)$

Let $T'' = [X \mapsto \mu X.T_1]T_1$. By definition, $\textit{treeof}(T'') = \textit{treeof}(T')$. Therefore, by the definition of R, we have $(S', T'') \in R$, and so $(S', T') \in S_m(R)$, by the definition of S_m.

Case: $(S', T') = (\mu X.S_1, T')$

If $T' = \text{Top}$ or T' starts with μ, then one of the cases above applies; otherwise, the argument is similar to the previous one. $\square$

The correspondence established by the theorem is a statement of soundness and completeness of subtyping between μ-types, as defined in this section, with respect to the ordinary subtype relation between infinite tree types, restricted to those tree types that can be represented by finite μ-expressions.

21.9   Counting Subexpressions

Instantiating the generic algorithm $\textit{gfp}^t$ (21.6.4) with the specific support function $\textit{support}_{S_m}$ for the subtype relation on μ-types (21.8.4) yields the subtyping algorithm shown in Figure 21-4. The argument in Section 21.6 shows that the termination of this algorithm can be guaranteed if $\textit{reachable}_{S_m}(S, T)$ is finite for any pair of μ-types (S, T). The present section is devoted to proving that this is the case (Proposition 21.9.11).

At first glance, the property seems almost obvious, but proving it rigorously requires a surprising amount of work. The difficulty is that there are two possible ways of defining the set of "closed subexpressions" of a μ-type. One, which we call *top-down* subexpressions, directly corresponds to the subexpressions generated by $\textit{support}_{S_m}$. The other, called *bottom-up* subexpressions, supports a straightforward proof that the set of closed subexpressions of every closed μ-type is finite. The termination proof proceeds by defining both of these sets and showing that the former is a subset of the

$$
\begin{aligned}
subtype(A, \mathsf{S}, \mathsf{T}) \quad = \quad & \text{if } (\mathsf{S}, \mathsf{T}) \in A, \text{ then} \\
& \quad A \\
& \text{else let } A_0 = A \cup \{(\mathsf{S}, \mathsf{T})\} \text{ in} \\
& \quad \text{if } \mathsf{T} = \mathsf{Top}, \text{ then} \\
& \qquad A_0 \\
& \quad \text{else if } \mathsf{S} = \mathsf{S}_1 \times \mathsf{S}_2 \text{ and } \mathsf{T} = \mathsf{T}_1 \times \mathsf{T}_2, \text{ then} \\
& \qquad \text{let } A_1 = subtype(A_0, \mathsf{S}_1, \mathsf{T}_1) \text{ in} \\
& \qquad subtype(A_1, \mathsf{S}_2, \mathsf{T}_2) \\
& \quad \text{else if } \mathsf{S} = \mathsf{S}_1 {\rightarrow} \mathsf{S}_2 \text{ and } \mathsf{T} = \mathsf{T}_1 {\rightarrow} \mathsf{T}_2, \text{ then} \\
& \qquad \text{let } A_1 = subtype(A_0, \mathsf{T}_1, \mathsf{S}_1) \text{ in} \\
& \qquad subtype(A_1, \mathsf{S}_2, \mathsf{T}_2) \\
& \quad \text{else if } \mathsf{T} = \mu \mathsf{X}.\mathsf{T}_1, \text{ then} \\
& \qquad subtype(A_0, \mathsf{S}, [\mathsf{X} \mapsto \mu \mathsf{X}.\mathsf{T}_1]\mathsf{T}_1) \\
& \quad \text{else if } \mathsf{S} = \mu \mathsf{X}.\mathsf{S}_1, \text{ then} \\
& \qquad subtype(A_0, [\mathsf{X} \mapsto \mu \mathsf{X}.\mathsf{S}_1]\mathsf{S}_1, \mathsf{T}) \\
& \quad \text{else} \\
& \qquad \text{*fail*}
\end{aligned}
$$

Figure 21-4: Concrete subtyping algorithm for μ-types

latter (Proposition 21.9.10). The development here is based on Brandt and Henglein's (1997).

21.9.1   DEFINITION: A μ-type S is a *top-down subexpression* of a μ-type T, written $\mathsf{S} \sqsubseteq \mathsf{T}$, if the pair (S, T) is in the least fixed point of the following generating function:

$$
\begin{aligned}
TD(R) \quad = \quad & \{(\mathsf{T}, \mathsf{T}) \mid \mathsf{T} \in \mathcal{T}_m\} \\
\cup \quad & \{(\mathsf{S}, \mathsf{T}_1 \times \mathsf{T}_2) \mid (\mathsf{S}, \mathsf{T}_1) \in R\} \\
\cup \quad & \{(\mathsf{S}, \mathsf{T}_1 \times \mathsf{T}_2) \mid (\mathsf{S}, \mathsf{T}_2) \in R\} \\
\cup \quad & \{(\mathsf{S}, \mathsf{T}_1 {\rightarrow} \mathsf{T}_2) \mid (\mathsf{S}, \mathsf{T}_1) \in R\} \\
\cup \quad & \{(\mathsf{S}, \mathsf{T}_1 {\rightarrow} \mathsf{T}_2) \mid (\mathsf{S}, \mathsf{T}_2) \in R\} \\
\cup \quad & \{(\mathsf{S}, \mu \mathsf{X}.\mathsf{T}) \mid (\mathsf{S}, [\mathsf{X} \mapsto \mu \mathsf{X}.\mathsf{T}]\mathsf{T}) \in R\}
\end{aligned}
$$

21.9.2   EXERCISE [$\star$]: Give an equivalent definition of the relation $\mathsf{S} \sqsubseteq \mathsf{T}$ as a set of inference rules.   □

From the definition of $support_{S_m}$ it is easy to see that, for any μ-types S and T, all the pairs contained in $support_{S_m}(\mathsf{S}, \mathsf{T})$ are formed from top-down subexpressions of S and T:

21.9.3   LEMMA: If $(\mathsf{S}', \mathsf{T}') \in support_{S_m}(\mathsf{S}, \mathsf{T})$, then either $\mathsf{S}' \sqsubseteq \mathsf{S}$ or $\mathsf{S}' \sqsubseteq \mathsf{T}$, and either $\mathsf{T}' \sqsubseteq \mathsf{S}$ or $\mathsf{T}' \sqsubseteq \mathsf{T}$.   □

Proof: Straightforward inspection of the definition of *support*$_{S_m}$.   □

Also, the top-down subexpression relation is transitive:

21.9.4   LEMMA: If $S \sqsubseteq U$ and $U \sqsubseteq T$, then $S \sqsubseteq T$.   □

Proof: The statement of the lemma is equivalent to $\forall U,T. \ U \sqsubseteq T \Rightarrow (\forall S. \ S \sqsubseteq U \Rightarrow S \sqsubseteq T)$. In other words, we must show that $\mu(TD) \subseteq R$, where $R = \{(U,T) \mid \forall S. \ S \sqsubseteq U \Rightarrow S \sqsubseteq T\}$. By the induction principle, it suffices to show that R is TD-closed—that is, that $TD(R) \subseteq R$. So suppose $(U,T) \in TD(R)$. Proceed by cases on the clauses in the definition of TD.

Case: $(U,T) = (T,T)$

Clearly, $(T,T) \in R$.

Case: $(U,T) = (U,T_1 \times T_2)$ and $(U,T_1) \in R$

Since $(U,T_1) \in R$, it must be the case that $S \sqsubseteq U \Rightarrow S \sqsubseteq T_1$ for all S. By the definition of $\sqsubseteq$, it must also be the case that $S \sqsubseteq U \Rightarrow S \sqsubseteq T_1 \times T_2$ for all S. Thus, $(U,T) = (U,T_1 \times T_2) \in R$, by the definition of R.

Other cases:

Similar.   □

Combining the two previous lemmas gives us the proposition that motivates the introduction of top-down subexpressions:

21.9.5   PROPOSITION: If $(S',T') \in reachable_{S_m}(S,T)$, then $S' \sqsubseteq S$ or $S' \sqsubseteq T$, and $T' \sqsubseteq S$ or $T' \sqsubseteq T$.   □

Proof: By induction on the definition of $reachable_{S_m}$, using transitivity of $\sqsubseteq$.   □

The finiteness of $reachable_{S_m}(S,T)$ will follow (in Proposition 21.9.11) from the above proposition and the fact that any μ-type U has only a finite number of top-down subexpressions. Unfortunately, the latter fact is not obvious from the definition of $\sqsubseteq$. Attempting to prove it by structural induction on U using the definition of TD does not work because the last clause of TD breaks the induction: to construct the subexpressions of $U = \mu X.T$, it refers to a potentially *larger* expression $[X \mapsto \mu X.T]T$.

The alternative notion of bottom-up subexpressions avoids this problem by performing the substitution of μ-types for recursion variables *after* calculating the subexpressions instead of before. This change will lead to a simple proof of finiteness.

21.9.6   DEFINITION: A μ-type S is a *bottom-up subexpression* of a μ-type T, written
S $\preceq$ T, if the pair (S, T) is in the least fixed point of the following generating
function:

$$
\begin{aligned}
BU(R) \;=\; & \{(T, T) \mid T \in \mathcal{T}_m\} \\
\cup\; & \{(S, T_1 \times T_2) \mid (S, T_1) \in R\} \\
\cup\; & \{(S, T_1 \times T_2) \mid (S, T_2) \in R\} \\
\cup\; & \{(S, T_1 \rightarrow T_2) \mid (S, T_1) \in R\} \\
\cup\; & \{(S, T_1 \rightarrow T_2) \mid (S, T_2) \in R\} \\
\cup\; & \{([X \mapsto \mu X.T]S, \mu X.T) \mid (S, T) \in R\}
\end{aligned}
$$

This new definition of subexpressions differs from the old one only in the
clause for a type starting with a μ binder. To obtain the top-down subexpressions of such a type, we unfolded it first and then collected the subexpressions of the unfolding. To obtain the bottom-up subexpressions, we first
collect the (not necessarily closed) subexpressions of the body, and then close
them by applying the unfolding substitution.

21.9.7   EXERCISE [$\star\star$]: Give an equivalent definition of the relation S $\preceq$ T as a set of
inference rules.   □

The fact that an expression has only finitely many bottom-up subexpressions is easily proved.

21.9.8   LEMMA: $\{S \mid S \preceq T\}$ is finite for each T.   □

Proof: Straightforward structural induction on T, using the following observations, which follow from the definition of *BU* and $\preceq$:

- if T = Top or T = X then $\{S \mid S \preceq T\} = \{T\}$;

- if T = $T_1 \times T_2$ or T = $T_1 \rightarrow T_2$ then $\{S \mid S \preceq T\} = \{T\} \cup \{S \mid S \preceq T_1\} \cup \{S \mid S \preceq T_2\}$;

- if T = $\mu X.T'$ then $\{S \mid S \preceq T\} = \{T\} \cup \{[X \mapsto T]S \mid S \preceq T'\}$.   □

To prove that the bottom-up subexpressions of a type include its top-down
subexpressions, we will need the following lemma relating bottom-up subexpressions and substitution.

21.9.9   LEMMA: If S $\preceq$ [X $\mapsto$ Q]T, then either S $\preceq$ Q or else S = [X $\mapsto$ Q]S' for some S'
with S' $\preceq$ T.   □

Proof: By structural induction on T.

Case: T = Top

Only the reflexivity clause of *BU* allows Top as the right-hand element of the pair, so we must have S = Top. Taking S′ = Top yields the desired result.

Case: T = Y

If Y = X, we have S ⪯ [X ↦ Q]T = Q, and the desired result holds by assumption. If Y ≠ X, we have S = [X ↦ Q]T = Y. Only the reflexivity clause of *BU* can justify this pair, so we must have S = Y. Take S′ = Y to get the desired result.

Case: $T = T_1 \times T_2$

We have $S \preceq [X \mapsto Q]T = [X \mapsto Q]T_1 \times [X \mapsto Q]T_2$. According to the definition of *BU*, there are three ways in which S can be a bottom-up subexpression of this product type. We consider each in turn.

Subcase: S = [X ↦ Q]T

Then take S′ = T.

Subcase: $S \preceq [X \mapsto Q]T_1$

By the induction hypothesis, either S ⪯ Q (in which case we are done) or else S = [X ↦ Q]S′ for some $S' \preceq T_1$. The latter alternative implies the desired result $S' \preceq T_1 \times T_2$ by the definition of *BU*.

Subcase: $S \preceq [X \mapsto Q]T_2$

Similar.

Case: $T = T_1 \rightarrow T_2$

Similar to the product case.

Case: $T = \mu Y . T'$

We have $S \preceq [X \mapsto Q]T = \mu Y.[X \mapsto Q]T'$. There are two ways in which S can be a bottom-up subexpression of this μ-type.

Subcase: S = [X ↦ Q]T

Take S′ = T

Subcase: $S = [Y \mapsto \mu Y.[X \mapsto Q]T']S_1$ with $S_1 \preceq [X \mapsto Q]T'$

Applying the induction hypothesis gives us two possible alternatives:

- $S_1 \preceq Q$. By our conventions on bound variable names, we know that $Y \notin FV(Q)$, so it must be that $Y \notin FV(S_1)$. But then $S = [Y \mapsto \mu Y.[X \mapsto Q]T']S_1 = S_1$, so $S \preceq Q$.

- $S_1 = [X \mapsto Q]S_2$ for some S_2 such that $S_2 \preceq T'$. In this case, $S = [Y \mapsto \mu Y.[X \mapsto Q]T']S_1 = [Y \mapsto \mu Y.[X \mapsto Q]T'][X \mapsto Q]S_2 = [X \mapsto Q][Y \mapsto \mu Y.T']S_2$. Take $S' = [Y \mapsto \mu Y.S']S_2$ to obtain the desired result.   □

The final piece of the proof establishes that every top-down subexpression of a μ-type can be found among its bottom-up subexpressions.

21.9.10   PROPOSITION: If $S \subseteq T$, then $S \preceq T$.   □

Proof: We want to show that $\mu TD \subseteq \mu BU$. By the principle of induction, this will follow if we can show that μBU is *TD*-closed—that is, $TD(\mu BU) \subseteq \mu BU$. In other words, we want to show that $(A, B) \in TD(\mu BU)$ implies $(A, B) \in \mu BU = BU(\mu BU)$. The latter will be true if every clause of *TD* that could have generated (A, B) from μBU is matched by a clause of *BU* that also generates (A, B) from μBU. This is trivially true for all the clauses of *TD* except the last, since they are exactly the same as the corresponding clauses of *BU*. In the last clause, $(A, B) = (S, \mu X.T) \in TD(\mu BU)$ and $(S, [X \mapsto \mu X.T]T) \in \mu BU$ or, equivalently, $S \preceq [X \mapsto \mu X.T]T$. By Lemma 21.9.9, either $S \preceq \mu X.T$, which is $(S, \mu X.T) \in \mu BU$, what is needed, or $S = [X \mapsto \mu X.T]S'$ for some S' with $(S', T) \in \mu BU$. The latter implies $(S, \mu X.T) \in BU(\mu BU) = \mu BU$, by the last clause of *BU*.   □

Combining the facts established in this section gives us the final result.

21.9.11   PROPOSITION: For any μ-types S and T, the set $reachable_{S_m}(S, T)$ is finite.   □

Proof: For S and T, let *Td* be the set of all their top-down subexpressions, and *Bu* be the set of all their bottom-up subexpressions. According to Proposition 21.9.5, $reachable_{S_m}(S, T) \subseteq Td \times Td$. By Proposition 21.9.10, $Td \times Td \subseteq Bu \times Bu$. By Lemma 21.9.8, the latter set is finite, so $reachable_{S_m}(S, T)$ is finite.   □

21.10   Digression: An Exponential Algorithm

The algorithm *subtype* presented at the beginning of §21.9 (Figure 21-4) can be simplified a bit more by making it return just a boolean value rather than a new set of assumptions (see Figure 21-5). The resulting procedure, *subtype*^{ac}, corresponds to Amadio and Cardelli's algorithm for checking subtyping (1993). It computes the same relation as the one computed by *subtype*, but much less efficiently because it does not remember pairs of types in the subtype relation across the recursive calls in the $\rightarrow$ and $\times$ cases. This seemingly innocent change results in a blowup of the number of recursive calls the algorithm makes. Whereas the number of recursive calls made by *subtype* is proportional to the square of the total number of subexpressions in the two argument types (as can be seen by inspecting the proofs of Lemma 21.9.8 and Proposition 21.9.11), in the case of *subtype*^{ac} it is exponential.

$$\begin{aligned}
subtype^{ac}\,(A, \mathsf{S}, \mathsf{T}) \quad = \quad &\text{if } (\mathsf{S}, \mathsf{T}) \in A, \text{ then } true \\
&\text{else let } A_0 = A \cup (\mathsf{S}, \mathsf{T}) \text{ in} \\
&\quad \text{if } \mathsf{T} = \mathsf{Top}, \text{ then } true \\
&\quad \text{else if } \mathsf{S} = \mathsf{S}_1 \times \mathsf{S}_2 \text{ and } \mathsf{T} = \mathsf{T}_1 \times \mathsf{T}_2, \text{ then} \\
&\quad\quad subtype^{ac}\,(A_0, \mathsf{S}_1, \mathsf{T}_1) \text{ and} \\
&\quad\quad subtype^{ac}\,(A_0, \mathsf{S}_2, \mathsf{T}_2) \\
&\quad \text{else if } \mathsf{S} = \mathsf{S}_1 {\rightarrow} \mathsf{S}_2 \text{ and } \mathsf{T} = \mathsf{T}_1 {\rightarrow} \mathsf{T}_2, \text{ then} \\
&\quad\quad subtype^{ac}\,(A_0, \mathsf{T}_1, \mathsf{S}_1) \text{ and} \\
&\quad\quad subtype^{ac}\,(A_0, \mathsf{S}_2, \mathsf{T}_2) \\
&\quad \text{else if } \mathsf{S} = \mu \mathsf{X}.\,\mathsf{S}_1, \text{ then} \\
&\quad\quad subtype^{ac}\,(A_0, [\mathsf{X} \mapsto \mu \mathsf{X}.\,\mathsf{S}_1]\mathsf{S}_1, \mathsf{T}) \\
&\quad \text{else if } \mathsf{T} = \mu \mathsf{X}.\,\mathsf{T}_1, \text{ then} \\
&\quad\quad subtype^{ac}\,(A_0, \mathsf{S}, [\mathsf{X} \mapsto \mu \mathsf{X}.\,\mathsf{T}_1]\mathsf{T}_1) \\
&\quad \text{else } false.
\end{aligned}$$

Figure 21-5: Amadio and Cardelli's subtyping algorithm

The exponential behavior of $subtype^{ac}$ can be seen clearly in the following example. Define families of types S_n and T_n inductively as follows:

$$\begin{aligned}
\mathsf{S}_0 &= \mu \mathsf{X}.\,\mathsf{Top} \times \mathsf{X} & \mathsf{S}_{n+1} &= \mu \mathsf{X}.\,\mathsf{X}{\rightarrow}\mathsf{S}_n \\
\mathsf{T}_0 &= \mu \mathsf{X}.\,\mathsf{Top} \times (\mathsf{Top} \times \mathsf{X}) & \mathsf{T}_{n+1} &= \mu \mathsf{X}.\,\mathsf{X}{\rightarrow}\mathsf{T}_n.
\end{aligned}$$

Since S_n and T_n each contain just one occurrence of S_{n-1} and T_{n-1}, respectively, their size (after expanding abbreviations) will be linear in n. Checking $\mathsf{S}_n <: \mathsf{T}_n$ generates an exponential derivation, however, as can be seen by the following sequence of recursive calls

$$\begin{aligned}
&\quad subtype^{ac}\,(\varnothing, \mathsf{S}_n, \mathsf{T}_n) \\
=\ &\quad subtype^{ac}\,(A_1, \mathsf{S}_n{\rightarrow}\mathsf{S}_{n-1}, \mathsf{T}_n) \\
=\ &\quad subtype^{ac}\,(A_2, \mathsf{S}_n{\rightarrow}\mathsf{S}_{n-1}, \mathsf{T}_n{\rightarrow}\mathsf{T}_{n-1}) \\
=\ &\quad subtype^{ac}\,(A_3, \mathsf{T}_n, \mathsf{S}_n) \text{ and } \underline{subtype^{ac}\,(A_3, \mathsf{S}_{n-1}, \mathsf{T}_{n-1})} \\
=\ &\quad subtype^{ac}\,(A_4, \mathsf{T}_n{\rightarrow}\mathsf{T}_{n-1}, \mathsf{S}_n) \text{ and } \dots \\
=\ &\quad subtype^{ac}\,(A_5, \mathsf{T}_n{\rightarrow}\mathsf{T}_{n-1}, \mathsf{S}_n{\rightarrow}\mathsf{S}_{n-1}) \text{ and } \dots \\
=\ &\quad subtype^{ac}\,(A_6, \mathsf{S}_n, \mathsf{T}_n) \text{ and } \underline{subtype^{ac}\,(A_6, \mathsf{T}_{n-1}, \mathsf{S}_{n-1})} \text{ and } \dots \\
=\ &\quad \text{etc.,}
\end{aligned}$$

where

$$\begin{aligned}
A_1 &= \{(\mathsf{S}_n, \mathsf{T}_n)\} \\
A_2 &= A_1 \cup \{(\mathsf{S}_n{\rightarrow}\mathsf{S}_{n-1}, \mathsf{T}_n)\} \\
A_3 &= A_2 \cup \{(\mathsf{S}_n{\rightarrow}\mathsf{S}_{n-1}, \mathsf{T}_n{\rightarrow}\mathsf{T}_{n-1})\} \\
A_4 &= A_3 \cup \{(\mathsf{T}_n, \mathsf{S}_n)\} \\
A_5 &= A_4 \cup \{(\mathsf{T}_n{\rightarrow}\mathsf{T}_{n-1}, \mathsf{S}_n)\} \\
A_6 &= A_5 \cup \{(\mathsf{T}_n{\rightarrow}\mathsf{T}_{n-1}, \mathsf{S}_n{\rightarrow}\mathsf{S}_{n-1})\}.
\end{aligned}$$

Notice that the initial call $subtype^{ac}(\emptyset, S_n, T_n)$ results in the two underlined recursive calls of the same form involving S_{n-1} and T_{n-1}. These, in turn, will each give rise to two recursive calls involving S_{n-2} and T_{n-2}, and so on. The total number of recursive calls is thus proportional to 2^n.

21.11 Subtyping Iso-Recursive Types

We remarked in §20.2 that some treatments of recursive types adopt an *iso-recursive* presentation, where the folding and unfolding of recursive types is witnessed explicitly by the term constructors fold and unfold. In such languages, the μ type constructor is "rigid," in the sense that its position in a type affects how terms belonging to this type can be used.

If we add subtyping to a language with iso-recursive types, the rigidity of the μ constructor also affects the subtype relation. Instead of intuitively "unrolling to the limit, then subtyping," as we have done in most of this chapter, we must define subtyping rules involving recursive types directly.

The most common definition of iso-recursive subtyping is the *Amber rule*—so-called because it was popularized by Cardelli's Amber language (1986):

$$\frac{\Sigma, X{<}{:}Y \vdash S <: T}{\Sigma \vdash \mu X.S <: \mu Y.T} \quad \text{(S-AMBER)}$$

Intuitively, this rule can be read, "To show that $\mu X.S$ is a subtype of $\mu Y.T$ under some set of assumptions Σ, it suffices to show S <: T under the additional assumption that X <: Y."[6] Σ here is just a set of pairs of recursion variables, recording the pairs of recursive types that have already been considered. These assumptions are used by another subtyping rule

$$\frac{(X <: Y) \in \Sigma}{\Sigma \vdash X <: Y} \quad \text{(S-ASSUMPTION)}$$

that allows us to conclude X <: Y if we are currently assuming it.

In effect, adding these two rules to the usual subtyping algorithm from Chapter 16 (and extending the other rules so that they pass Σ through from premises to conclusion) yields an algorithm that behaves somewhat like the $subtype^{ac}$ algorithm in Figure 21-5, with Σ playing the role of A. The differences are that (1) we "unfold" recursive types only when they appear on *both* sides of the <: at once, and (2) we do not substitute the recursive types into their bodies (we just leave them as variables), which makes it easy to see that the algorithm terminates.

---

6. Note that this rule, unlike most rules involving binding constructs on both sides, such as S-ALL in Figure 26-1, demands that the bound variables X and Y be renamed to be *distinct* before the rule is applied.

The subtyping rules found in *nominal* type systems (such as Featherweight Java, Chapter 19) are closely related to the Amber rule.

21.11.1   EXERCISE [RECOMMENDED, ⋆⋆]: Find recursive types S and T such that S <: T using the equi-recursive definition, but not using the Amber rule.   □

21.12   Notes

This chapter is based on a tutorial article by Gapeyev, Levin, and Pierce (2000).

Background on coinduction can be found in Barwise and Moss's *Vicious Circles* (1996), Gordon's tutorial on coinduction and functional programming (1995), and Milner and Tofte's expository article on coinduction in programming language semantics (1991a). For basic information on monotone functions and fixed points see Aczel (1977) and Davey and Priestley (1990).

The use of coinductive proof methods in computer science dates from the 1970s, for example in the work of Milner (1980) and Park (1981) on concurrency; also see Arbib and Manes's categorical discussion of duality in automata theory (1975). But the use of induction in its dual "co-" form was familiar to mathematicians considerably earlier and is developed explicitly in, for example, universal algebra and category theory. Aczel's seminal book (1988) on non-well-founded sets includes a brief historical survey.

Amadio and Cardelli (1993) gave the first subtyping algorithm for recursive types. Their paper defines three relations: an inclusion relation between infinite trees, an algorithm that checks subtyping between μ-types, and a reference subtype relation between μ-types defined as the least fixed point of a set of declarative inference rules; these relations are proved to be equivalent, and connected to a model construction based on partial equivalence relations. Coinduction is not used; instead, to reason about infinite trees, a notion of finite approximations of an infinite tree is introduced. This notion plays a key role in many of the proofs.

Brandt and Henglein (1997) laid bare the underlying coinductive nature of Amadio and Cardelli's system, giving a new inductive axiomatization of the subtype relation that is sound and complete with respect to that of Amadio and Cardelli. The so-called ARROW/FIX rule of the axiomatization embodies the coinductiveness of the system. The paper describes a general method for deriving an inductive axiomatization for relations that are naturally defined by coinduction and presents a detailed proof of termination for a subtyping algorithm. §21.9 of the present chapter closely follows the latter proof. Brandt and Henglein establish that the complexity of their algorithm is $O(n^2)$.

Kozen, Palsberg, and Schwartzbach (1993) obtain an elegant quadratic subtyping algorithm by observing that a regular recursive type corresponds to

an automaton with labeled states. They define a product of two automata
that yields a conventional word automaton accepting a word iff the types
corresponding to the original automata are not in the subtype relation. A
linear-time emptiness test now solves the subtyping problem. This fact, plus
the quadratic complexity of product construction and linear-time conversion
from types to automata, gives an overall quadratic complexity.

Hosoya, Vouillon, and Pierce (2001) use a related automata-theoretic approach, associating recursive types (with unions) to tree automata in a subtyping algorithm tuned to XML processing applications.

Jim and Palsberg (1999) address type *reconstruction* (see Chapter 22) for
languages with subtyping and recursive types. As we have done in this chapter, they adopt a coinductive view of the subtype relation over infinite trees
and motivate a subtype checking algorithm as a procedure building the minimal simulation (i.e., consistent set, in our terminology) from a given pair of
types. They define the notions of consistency and $P1$-closure of a relation
over types, which correspond to our consistency and reachable sets.

If you think about it long enough, you'll see that it's obvious.   —*Saul Gorn*

PART V

Polymorphism

22 *Type Reconstruction*

The typechecking algorithms for the calculi we have seen so far all depend on explicit type annotations—in particular, they require that lambda-abstractions be annotated with their argument types. In this chapter, we develop a more powerful *type reconstruction* algorithm, capable of calculating a *principal type* for a term in which some or all of these annotations are left unspecified. Related algorithms lie at the heart of languages like ML and Haskell.

Combining type reconstruction with other language features is often a somewhat delicate matter. In particular, both records and subtyping pose significant challenges. To keep things simple, we consider type reconstruction here only for simple types; §22.8 gives some starting points for further reading on other combinations.

22.1 Type Variables and Substitutions

In some of the calculi in previous chapters, we have assumed that the set of types includes an infinite collection of *uninterpreted* base types (§11.1). Unlike interpreted base types such as Bool and Nat, these types come with no operations for introducing or eliminating terms; intuitively, they are just placeholders for some particular types whose exact identities we do not care about. In this chapter, we will be asking questions like "if we instantiate the placeholder X in the term t with the concrete type Bool, do we obtain a typable term?" In other words, we will treat our uninterpreted base types as *type variables,* which can be *substituted* or *instantiated* with other types.

For the technical development in this chapter, it is convenient to separate the operation of substituting types for type variables into two parts: *describing* a mapping σ from type variables to types, called a *type substitution,* and

---

The system studied in this chapter is the simply typed lambda-calculus (Figure 9-1) with booleans (8-1), numbers (8-2), and an infinite collection of base types (11-1). The corresponding OCaml implementations are recon and fullrecon.

applying this mapping to a particular type T to obtain an instance σT. For example, we might define $\sigma = [X \mapsto \text{Bool}]$ and then apply σ to the type X→X to obtain $\sigma(X→X) = \text{Bool}→\text{Bool}$.

22.1.1   DEFINITION: Formally, a *type substitution* (or just *substitution,* when it's clear that we're talking about types) is a finite mapping from type variables to types. For example, we write $[X \mapsto T, Y \mapsto U]$ for the substitution that associates X with T and Y with U. We write $dom(\sigma)$ for the set of type variables appearing on the left-hand sides of pairs in σ, and $range(\sigma)$ for the set of types appearing on the right-hand sides. Note that the same variable may occur in both the domain and the range of a substitution. Like term substitutions, the intention in such cases is that all the clauses of the substitution are applied simultaneously; for example, $[X \mapsto \text{Bool}, Y \mapsto X→X]$ maps X to Bool and Y to X→X, not Bool→Bool.

Application of a substitution to a type is defined in the obvious way:

$$\sigma(X) = \begin{cases} T & \text{if } (X \mapsto T) \in \sigma \\ X & \text{if } X \text{ is not in the domain of } \sigma \end{cases}$$

$$\sigma(\text{Nat}) = \text{Nat}$$
$$\sigma(\text{Bool}) = \text{Bool}$$
$$\sigma(T_1→T_2) = \sigma T_1 → \sigma T_2$$

Note that we do not need to make any special provisions to avoid variable capture during type substitution, because there are no constructs in the language of type expressions that *bind* type variables. (We'll get to these in Chapter 23.)

Type substitution is extended pointwise to contexts by defining

$$\sigma(x_1 : T_1, \ldots, x_n : T_n) = (x_1 : \sigma T_1, \ldots, x_n : \sigma T_n).$$

Similarly, a substitution is applied to a term t by applying it to all types appearing in annotations in t.

If σ and γ are substitutions, we write $\sigma \circ \gamma$ for the substitution formed by composing them as follows:

$$\sigma \circ \gamma = \begin{bmatrix} X \mapsto \sigma(T) & \text{for each } (X \mapsto T) \in \gamma \\ X \mapsto T & \text{for each } (X \mapsto T) \in \sigma \text{ with } X \notin dom(\gamma) \end{bmatrix}$$

Note that $(\sigma \circ \gamma)S = \sigma(\gamma S)$.   □

A crucial property of type substitutions is that they preserve the validity of typing statements: if a term involving variables is well typed, then so are all of its substitution instances.

22.1.2   THEOREM [PRESERVATION OF TYPING UNDER TYPE SUBSTITUTION]: If σ is any type substitution and $\Gamma \vdash t : T$, then $\sigma\Gamma \vdash \sigma t : \sigma T$.   □

Proof: Straightforward induction on typing derivations.   □

22.2   Two Views of Type Variables

Suppose that t is a term containing type variables and Γ is an associated context (possibly also containing type variables). There are two quite different questions that we can ask about t:

1. "Are *all* substitution instances of t well typed?" That is, for every σ, do we have $\sigma\Gamma \vdash \sigma t : T$ for some T?

2. "Is *some* substitution instance of t well typed?" That is, can we find a σ such that $\sigma\Gamma \vdash \sigma t : T$ for some T?

According to the first view, type variables should be *held abstract* during typechecking, thus ensuring that a well-typed term will behave properly no matter what concrete types are later substituted for its type variables. For example, the term

```
λf:X→X. λa:X. f (f a);
```

has type $(X{\to}X){\to}X{\to}X$, and, whenever we replace X by a concrete type T, the instance

```
λf:T→T. λa:T. f (f a);
```

is well typed. Holding type variables abstract in this way leads us to *parametric polymorphism,* where type variables are used to encode the fact that a term can be used in many concrete contexts with different concrete types. We will return to parametric polymorphism later in this chapter (in §22.7) and, in more depth, in Chapter 23.

On the second view, the original term t may not even be well typed; what we want to know is whether it can be *instantiated* to a well typed term by choosing appropriate values for some of its type variables. For example, the term

```
λf:Y. λa:X. f (f a);
```

is not typable as it stands, but if we replace Y by $\mathtt{Nat}{\to}\mathtt{Nat}$ and X by $\mathtt{Nat}$, we obtain

```
λf:Nat→Nat. λa:Nat. f (f a);
```

of type $(\mathtt{Nat}{\to}\mathtt{Nat}){\to}\mathtt{Nat}{\to}\mathtt{Nat}$. Or, if we simply replace Y by $X{\to}X$, we obtain the term

```
λf:X→X. λa:X. f (f a);
```

which is well typed even though it contains variables. Indeed, this term is a *most general* instance of λf:Y. λa:X. f (f a), in the sense that it makes the smallest commitment about the values of type variables that yields a well-typed term.

Looking for valid instantiations of type variables leads to the idea of *type reconstruction* (sometimes called *type inference*), in which the compiler helps fill in type information that has been left out by the programmer. In the limit, we may, as in ML, allow the programmer to leave out *all* type annotations and write in the syntax of the bare, untyped lambda-calculus. During parsing, we annotate each bare lambda-abstraction λx.t with a type variable, λx:X.t, choosing X to be different from the type variables on all the other abstractions in the program. We then perform type reconstruction to find the most general values for all these variables that make the term typecheck. (This story becomes a little more complicated in the presence of ML's let-polymorphism; we return to this in §22.6 and §22.7.)

To formalize type reconstruction, we will need a concise way of talking about the possible ways that type variables can be substituted by types, in a term and its associated context, to obtain a valid typing statement.[1]

22.2.1   DEFINITION: Let Γ be a context and t a term. A *solution* for (Γ, t) is a pair (σ, T) such that $\sigma\Gamma \vdash \sigma t : T$.   □

22.2.2   EXAMPLE: Let Γ = f:X, a:Y and t = f a. Then

$$([X \mapsto Y{\to}Nat],\ Nat) \qquad\qquad ([X \mapsto Y{\to}Z],\ Z)$$
$$([X \mapsto Y{\to}Z,\ Z \mapsto Nat],\ Z) \qquad ([X \mapsto Y{\to}Nat{\to}Nat],\ Nat{\to}Nat)$$
$$([X \mapsto Nat{\to}Nat,\ Y \mapsto Nat],\ Nat)$$

are all solutions for (Γ, t).   □

22.2.3   EXERCISE [★ ↦]: Find three different solutions for the term

   λx:X. λy:Y. λz:Z. (x z) (y z).

in the empty context.   □

---

1. There are other ways of setting up these basic definitions. One is to use a general mechanism called *existential unificands,* due to Kirchner and Jouannaud (1990), instead of all the individual freshness conditions in the constraint generation rules in Figure 22-1. Another possible improvement, employed by Rémy (1992a, 1992b, long version, 1998, Chapter 5), is to treat typing statements themselves as unificands; we begin with a triple (Γ, t, T), where all three components may contain type variables, and look for substitutions σ such that $\sigma\Gamma \vdash \sigma(t) : \sigma(T)$, i.e., substitutions that *unify* the schematic typing statement $\Gamma \vdash t : T$.

22.3   Constraint-Based Typing

We now present an algorithm that, given a term t and a context Γ, calculates a set of constraints—equations between type expressions (possibly involving type variables)—that must be satisfied by any solution for (Γ, t). The intuition behind this algorithm is essentially the same as the ordinary typechecking algorithm; the only difference is that, instead of *checking* constraints, it simply *records* them for later consideration. For example, when presented with an application $t_1\ t_2$ with $Γ ⊢ t_1 : T_1$ and $Γ ⊢ t_2 : T_2$, rather than checking that T_1 has the form $T_2 {\rightarrow} T_{12}$ and returning T_{12} as the type of the application, it instead chooses a fresh type variable X, records the constraint $T_1 = T_2 {\rightarrow} X$, and returns X as the type of the application.

22.3.1   DEFINITION: A *constraint set* C is a set of equations $\{S_i = T_i\ ^{i \in 1..n}\}$. A substitution σ is said to *unify* an equation S = T if the substitution instances σS and σT are identical. We say that σ *unifies* (or *satisfies*) C if it unifies every equation in C.   □

22.3.2   DEFINITION: The *constraint typing relation* $Γ ⊢ t : T \mid_X C$ is defined by the rules in Figure 22-1. Informally, $Γ ⊢ t : T \mid_X C$ can be read "term t has type T under assumptions Γ whenever constraints C are satisfied." In rule T-APP, we write *FV*(T) for the set of all type variables mentioned in T.

The *X* subscripts are used to track the type variables introduced in each subderivation and make sure that the fresh variables created in different subderivations are actually distinct. On a first reading of the rules, it may be helpful to ignore these subscripts and all the premises involving them. On the next reading, observe that these annotations and premises ensure two things. First, whenever a type variable is chosen by the final rule in some derivation, it must be different from any variables chosen in subderivations. Second, whenever a rule involves two or more subderivations, the sets of variables chosen by these subderivations must be disjoint. Also, note that these conditions never prevent us from building *some* derivation for a given term; they merely prevent us from building a derivation in which the same variable is used "fresh" in two different places. Since there is an infinite supply of type variable names, we can always find a way of satisfying the freshness requirements.

When read from bottom to top, the constraint typing rules determine a straightforward procedure that, given Γ and t, calculates T and C (and *X*) such that $Γ ⊢ t : T \mid_X C$. However, unlike the ordinary typing algorithm for the simply typed lambda-calculus, this one never fails, in the sense that for every Γ and t there are always some T and C such that $Γ ⊢ t : T \mid_X C$, and moreover that T and C are uniquely determined by Γ and t. (Strictly

$$\frac{x{:}T \in \Gamma}{\Gamma \vdash x : T \;\mid_\varnothing \{\}} \quad \text{(CT-VAR)}$$

$$\frac{\Gamma, x{:}T_1 \vdash t_2 : T_2 \;\mid_{\mathcal{X}} C}{\Gamma \vdash \lambda x{:}T_1.t_2 : T_1{\to}T_2 \;\mid_{\mathcal{X}} C} \quad \text{(CT-ABS)}$$

$$\frac{\begin{array}{c}\Gamma \vdash t_1 : T_1 \;\mid_{\mathcal{X}_1} C_1 \quad \Gamma \vdash t_2 : T_2 \;\mid_{\mathcal{X}_2} C_2 \\ \mathcal{X}_1 \cap \mathcal{X}_2 = \mathcal{X}_1 \cap FV(T_2) = \mathcal{X}_2 \cap FV(T_1) = \varnothing \\ X \notin \mathcal{X}_1, \mathcal{X}_2, T_1, T_2, C_1, C_2, \Gamma, t_1, \text{ or } t_2 \\ C' = C_1 \cup C_2 \cup \{T_1 = T_2{\to}X\}\end{array}}{\Gamma \vdash t_1\, t_2 : X \;\mid_{\mathcal{X}_1 \cup \mathcal{X}_2 \cup \{X\}} C'} \quad \text{(CT-APP)}$$

$$\Gamma \vdash 0 : \mathsf{Nat} \;\mid_\varnothing \{\} \quad \text{(CT-ZERO)}$$

$$\frac{\begin{array}{c}\Gamma \vdash t_1 : T \;\mid_{\mathcal{X}} C \\ C' = C \cup \{T = \mathsf{Nat}\}\end{array}}{\Gamma \vdash \mathsf{succ}\; t_1 : \mathsf{Nat} \;\mid_{\mathcal{X}} C'} \quad \text{(CT-SUCC)}$$

$$\frac{\begin{array}{c}\Gamma \vdash t_1 : T \;\mid_{\mathcal{X}} C \\ C' = C \cup \{T = \mathsf{Nat}\}\end{array}}{\Gamma \vdash \mathsf{pred}\; t_1 : \mathsf{Nat} \;\mid_{\mathcal{X}} C'} \quad \text{(CT-PRED)}$$

$$\frac{\begin{array}{c}\Gamma \vdash t_1 : T \;\mid_{\mathcal{X}} C \\ C' = C \cup \{T = \mathsf{Nat}\}\end{array}}{\Gamma \vdash \mathsf{iszero}\; t_1 : \mathsf{Bool} \;\mid_{\mathcal{X}} C'} \quad \text{(CT-ISZERO)}$$

$$\Gamma \vdash \mathsf{true} : \mathsf{Bool} \;\mid_\varnothing \{\} \quad \text{(CT-TRUE)}$$

$$\Gamma \vdash \mathsf{false} : \mathsf{Bool} \;\mid_\varnothing \{\} \quad \text{(CT-FALSE)}$$

$$\frac{\begin{array}{c}\Gamma \vdash t_1 : T_1 \;\mid_{\mathcal{X}_1} C_1 \\ \Gamma \vdash t_2 : T_2 \;\mid_{\mathcal{X}_2} C_2 \quad \Gamma \vdash t_3 : T_3 \;\mid_{\mathcal{X}_3} C_3 \\ \mathcal{X}_1, \mathcal{X}_2, \mathcal{X}_3 \text{ nonoverlapping} \\ C' = C_1 \cup C_2 \cup C_3 \cup \{T_1 = \mathsf{Bool}, T_2 = T_3\}\end{array}}{\Gamma \vdash \mathsf{if}\; t_1 \;\mathsf{then}\; t_2 \;\mathsf{else}\; t_3 : T_2 \;\mid_{\mathcal{X}_1 \cup \mathcal{X}_2 \cup \mathcal{X}_3} C'} \quad \text{(CT-IF)}$$

Figure 22-1: Constraint typing rules

speaking, the algorithm is deterministic only if we consider it "modulo the choice of fresh names." We return to this point in Exercise 22.3.9.)

To lighten the notation in the following discussion, we sometimes elide the $\mathcal{X}$ and write just $\Gamma \vdash t : T \mid C$. □

22.3.3   EXERCISE [⋆ ↦]: Construct a constraint typing derivation whose conclusion is

$$\vdash \lambda x{:}X.\; \lambda y{:}Y.\; \lambda z{:}Z.\; (x\; z)\; (y\; z) : S \;\mid_{\mathcal{X}} C$$

for some S, $\mathcal{X}$, and C. □

The idea of the constraint typing relation is that, given a term t and a context Γ, we can check whether t is typable under Γ by first collecting the constraints C that must be satisfied in order for t to have a type, together with a result type S, sharing variables with C, that characterizes the possible types of t in terms of these variables. Then, to find solutions for t, we just look for substitutions σ that satisfy C (i.e., that make all the equations in C into identities); for each such σ, the type σS is a possible type of t. If we find that there are *no* substitutions that satisfy C, then we know that t cannot be instantiated in such a way as to make it typable.

For example, the constraint set generated by the algorithm for the term $t = \lambda x : X \rightarrow Y.\ x\ 0$ is $\{Nat \rightarrow Z = X \rightarrow Y\}$, and the associated result type is $(X \rightarrow Y) \rightarrow Z$. The substitution $\sigma = [X \mapsto Nat,\ Z \mapsto Bool,\ Y \mapsto Bool]$ makes the equation $Nat \rightarrow Z = X \rightarrow Y$ into an identity, so we know that $\sigma((X \rightarrow Y) \rightarrow Z)$, i.e., $(Nat \rightarrow Bool) \rightarrow Bool$, is a possible type for t.

This idea is captured formally by the following definition.

22.3.4   DEFINITION: Suppose that $\Gamma \vdash t : S\ |\ C$. A *solution* for (Γ, t, S, C) is a pair (σ, T) such that σ satisfies C and $\sigma S = T$.   □

The algorithmic problem of finding substitutions unifying a given constraint set C will be taken up in the next section. First, though, we should check that our constraint typing algorithm corresponds in a suitable sense to the original, declarative typing relation.

Given a context Γ and a term t, we have two different ways of characterizing the possible ways of instantiating type variables in Γ and t to produce a valid typing:

1. [DECLARATIVE] as the set of all solutions for (Γ, t) in the sense of Definition 22.2.1; or

2. [ALGORITHMIC] via the constraint typing relation, by finding S and C such that $\Gamma \vdash t : S\ |\ C$ and then taking the set of solutions for (Γ, t, S, C).

We show the equivalence of these two characterizations in two steps. First we show that every solution for (Γ, t, S, C) is also a solution for (Γ, t) (Theorem 22.3.5). Then we show that every solution for (Γ, t) can be *extended* to a solution for (Γ, t, S, C) (Theorem 22.3.7) by giving values for the type variables introduced by constraint generation.

22.3.5   THEOREM [SOUNDNESS OF CONSTRAINT TYPING]: Suppose that $\Gamma \vdash t : S\ |\ C$. If (σ, T) is a solution for (Γ, t, S, C), then it is also a solution for (Γ, t).   □

For this direction of the argument, the fresh variable sets X are secondary and can be elided.

Proof: By induction on the given constraint typing derivation for $\Gamma \vdash t : S\ |\ C$, reasoning by cases on the last rule used.

Case CT-VAR: $t = x$ $x : S \in \Gamma$ $C = \{\}$

We are given that (σ, T) is a solution for (Γ, t, S, C); since C is empty, this means just that $\sigma S = T$. But then by T-VAR we immediately obtain $\sigma \Gamma \vdash x : T$, as required.

Case CT-ABS: $t = \lambda x{:}T_1.t_2$ $S = T_1{\rightarrow}S_2$ $\Gamma, x{:}T_1 \vdash t_2 : S_2 \mid C$

We are given that (σ, T) is a solution for (Γ, t, S, C), that is, σ unifies C and $T = \sigma S = \sigma T_1 \rightarrow \sigma S_2$. So $(\sigma, \sigma S_2)$ is a solution for $((\Gamma, x{:}T_1), t_2, S_2, C)$. By the induction hypothesis, $(\sigma, \sigma S_2)$ is a solution for $((\Gamma, x{:}T_1), t_2)$, i.e., $\sigma\Gamma, x{:}\sigma T_1 \vdash \sigma t_2 : \sigma S_2$. By T-ABS, $\sigma\Gamma \vdash \lambda x{:}\sigma T_1.\sigma t_2 : \sigma T_1{\rightarrow}\sigma S_2 = \sigma(T_1{\rightarrow}S_2) = T$, as required.

Case CT-APP: $t = t_1\ t_2$ $S = X$
$\qquad\qquad\qquad \Gamma \vdash t_1 : S_1 \mid C_1 \qquad \Gamma \vdash t_2 : S_2 \mid C_2$
$\qquad\qquad\qquad C = C_1 \cup C_2 \cup \{S_1 = S_2{\rightarrow}X\}$

By definition, σ unifies C_1 and C_2 and $\sigma S_1 = \sigma(S_2{\rightarrow}X)$. So $(\sigma, \sigma S_1)$ and $(\sigma, \sigma S_2)$ are solutions for (Γ, t_1, S_1, C_1) and (Γ, t_2, S_2, C_2), from which the induction hypothesis gives us $\sigma\Gamma \vdash \sigma t_1 : \sigma S_1$ and $\sigma\Gamma \vdash \sigma t_2 : \sigma S_2$. But since $\sigma S_1 = \sigma S_2{\rightarrow}\sigma X$, we have $\sigma\Gamma \vdash \sigma t_1 : \sigma S_2{\rightarrow}\sigma X$, and, by T-APP, $\sigma\Gamma \vdash \sigma(t_1\ t_2) : \sigma X = T$.

Other cases:

Similar. $\square$

The argument for the *completeness* of constraint typing with respect to the ordinary typing relation is a bit more delicate, because we must deal carefully with fresh names.

22.3.6   DEFINITION: Write $\sigma \backslash X$ for the substitution that is undefined for all the variables in X and otherwise behaves like σ. $\square$

22.3.7   THEOREM [COMPLETENESS OF CONSTRAINT TYPING]: Suppose $\Gamma \vdash t : S \mid_X C$. If (σ, T) is a solution for (Γ, t) and $dom(\sigma) \cap X = \varnothing$, then there is some solution (σ', T) for (Γ, t, S, C) such that $\sigma' \backslash X = \sigma$. $\square$

Proof: By induction on the given constraint typing derivation.

Case CT-VAR: $t = x$ $x{:}S \in \Gamma$

From the assumption that (σ, T) is a solution for (Γ, x), the inversion lemma for the typing relation (9.3.1) tells us that $T = \sigma S$. But then (σ, T) is also a $(\Gamma, x, S, \{\})$-solution.

Case CT-ABS: $t = \lambda x{:}T_1.t_2$ $\Gamma, x{:}T_1 \vdash t_2 : S_2 \mid_X C$ $S = T_1{\rightarrow}S_2$

From the assumption that (σ, T) is a solution for $(\Gamma, \lambda x{:}T_1.t_2)$, the inversion lemma for the typing relation yields $\sigma\Gamma, x{:}\sigma T_1 \vdash \sigma t_2 : T_2$ and $T = \sigma T_1{\rightarrow}T_2$ for some T_2. By the induction hypothesis, there is a solution (σ', T_2) for $((\Gamma, x{:}T_1), t_2, S_2, C)$ such that $\sigma' \backslash X$ agrees with σ. Now, X cannot include any of the type variables in T_1. So $\sigma' T_1 = \sigma T_1$, and $\sigma'(S) = \sigma'(T_1{\rightarrow}S_2) = \sigma T_1{\rightarrow}\sigma' S_2 = \sigma T_1{\rightarrow}T_2 = T$. Thus, we see that (σ', T) is a solution for $(\Gamma, (\lambda x{:}T_1.t_2), T_1{\rightarrow}S_2, C)$.

Case CT-APP: $t = t_1 \; t_2$ $\Gamma \vdash t_1 : S_1 \mid_{X_1} C_1$ $\Gamma \vdash t_2 : S_2 \mid_{X_2} C_2$
$X_1 \cap X_2 = \varnothing$
$X_1 \cap FV(S_2) = \varnothing$
$X_2 \cap FV(S_1) = \varnothing$
X not mentioned in $X_1, X_2, S_1, S_2, C_1, C_2$
$S = X$ $X = X_1 \cup X_2 \cup \{X\}$ $C = C_1 \cup C_2 \cup \{S_1 = S_2 \rightarrow X\}$

From the assumption that (σ, T) is a solution for $(\Gamma, t_1 \; t_2)$, the inversion
lemma for the typing relation yields $\sigma\Gamma \vdash \sigma t_1 : T_1 \rightarrow T$ and $\sigma\Gamma \vdash \sigma t_2 : T_1$.
By the induction hypothesis, there are solutions $(\sigma_1, T_1 \rightarrow T)$ for (Γ, t_1, S_1, C_1)
and (σ_2, T_1) for (Γ, t_2, S_2, C_2), and $\sigma_1 \backslash X_1 = \sigma = \sigma_2 \backslash X_2$. We must exhibit a
substitution σ' such that: (1) $\sigma' \backslash X$ agrees with σ; (2) $\sigma' X = T$; (3) σ' unifies
C_1 and C_2; and (4) σ' unifies $\{S_1 = S_2 \rightarrow X\}$, i.e., $\sigma' S_1 = \sigma' S_2 \rightarrow \sigma' X$. Define σ'
as follows:

$$
\sigma' = \left[\begin{array}{ll}
Y \mapsto U & \text{if } Y \notin X \text{ and } (Y \mapsto U) \in \sigma, \\
Y_1 \mapsto U_1 & \text{if } Y_1 \in X_1 \text{ and } (Y_1 \mapsto U_1) \in \sigma_1, \\
Y_2 \mapsto U_2 & \text{if } Y_2 \in X_2 \text{ and } (Y_2 \mapsto U_2) \in \sigma_2, \\
X \mapsto T
\end{array} \right]
$$

Conditions (1) and (2) are obviously satisfied. (3) is satisfied because X_1 and
X_2 do not overlap. To check (4), first note that the side-conditions about
freshness guarantee that $FV(S_1) \cap (X_2 \cup \{X\}) = \varnothing$, so that $\sigma' S_1 = \sigma_1 S_1$.
Now calculate as follows: $\sigma' S_1 = \sigma_1 S_1 = T_1 \rightarrow T = \sigma_2 S_2 \rightarrow T = \sigma' S_2 \rightarrow \sigma' X = \sigma'(S_2 \rightarrow X)$.

Other cases:

Similar.   □

22.3.8   COROLLARY: Suppose $\Gamma \vdash t : S \mid C$. There is some solution for (Γ, t) iff there
is some solution for (Γ, t, S, C).   □

Proof: By Theorems 22.3.5 and 22.3.7.   □

22.3.9   EXERCISE [RECOMMENDED, ★★★]: In a production compiler, the nondeterministic choice of a fresh type variable name in the rule CT-APP would typically be
replaced by a call to a *function* that generates a new type variable—different
from all others that it ever generates, and from all type variables mentioned
explicitly in the context or term being checked—each time it is called. Because
such global "gensym" operations work by side effects on a hidden global
variable, they are difficult to reason about formally. However, we can mimic
their behavior in a fairly accurate and mathematically more tractable way
by "threading" a sequence of unused variable names through the constraint
generation rules.

Let F denote a sequence of distinct type variable names. Then, instead of writing $\Gamma \vdash t : T \mid_X C$ for the constraint generation relation, we write $\Gamma \vdash_F t : T \mid_{F'} C$, where Γ, F, and t are inputs to the algorithm and T, F', and C are outputs. Whenever it needs a fresh type variable, the algorithm takes the front element of F and returns the rest of F as F'.

Write out the rules for this algorithm. Prove that they are equivalent, in an appropriate sense, to the original constraint generation rules.   □

22.3.10   EXERCISE [RECOMMENDED, ★★]: Implement the algorithm from Exercise 22.3.9 in ML. Use the datatype

```
type ty =
    TyBool
  | TyNat
  | TyArr of ty * ty
  | TyId of string
```

for types, and

```
type constr = (ty * ty) list
```

for constraint sets. You will also need a representation for infinite sequences of fresh variable names. There are lots of ways of doing this; here is a fairly direct one using a recursive datatype:

```
type nextuvar = NextUVar of string * uvargenerator
and uvargenerator = unit → nextuvar

let uvargen =
  let rec f n () = NextUVar("?X_" ∧ string_of_int n, f (n+1))
  in f 0
```

That is, `uvargen` is a function that, when called with argument (), returns a value of the form `NextUVar(x,f)`, where `x` is a fresh type variable name and `f` is another function of the same form.   □

22.3.11   EXERCISE [★★]: Show how to extend the constraint generation algorithm to deal with general recursive function definitions (§11.11).   □

22.4   Unification

To calculate solutions to constraint sets, we use the idea, due to Hindley (1969) and Milner (1978), of using *unification* (Robinson, 1971) to check that the set of solutions is nonempty and, if so, to find a "best" element, in the sense that all solutions can be generated straightforwardly from this one.

$$
\begin{aligned}
unify(C) \quad = \quad & \text{if } C = \emptyset, \text{ then } [\,] \\
& \text{else let } \{S = T\} \cup C' = C \text{ in} \\
& \quad \text{if } S = T \\
& \quad \quad \text{then } unify(C') \\
& \quad \text{else if } S = X \text{ and } X \notin FV(T) \\
& \quad \quad \text{then } unify([X \mapsto T]C') \circ [X \mapsto T] \\
& \quad \text{else if } T = X \text{ and } X \notin FV(S) \\
& \quad \quad \text{then } unify([X \mapsto S]C') \circ [X \mapsto S] \\
& \quad \text{else if } S = S_1 {\rightarrow} S_2 \text{ and } T = T_1 {\rightarrow} T_2 \\
& \quad \quad \text{then } unify(C' \cup \{S_1 = T_1, S_2 = T_2\}) \\
& \quad \text{else} \\
& \quad \quad fail
\end{aligned}
$$

Figure 22-2: Unification algorithm

22.4.1   DEFINITION: A substitution σ is *less specific* (or *more general*) *than* a substitution σ', written $\sigma \sqsubseteq \sigma'$, if $\sigma' = \gamma \circ \sigma$ for some substitution γ.   □

22.4.2   DEFINITION: A *principal unifier* (or sometimes *most general unifier*) for a constraint set C is a substitution σ that satisfies C and such that $\sigma \sqsubseteq \sigma'$ for every substitution σ' satisfying C.   □

22.4.3   EXERCISE [⋆]: Write down principal unifiers (when they exist) for the following sets of constraints:

$\{X = Nat, Y = X{\rightarrow}X\}$	$\{Nat{\rightarrow}Nat = X{\rightarrow}Y\}$
$\{X{\rightarrow}Y = Y{\rightarrow}Z, Z = U{\rightarrow}W\}$	$\{Nat = Nat{\rightarrow}Y\}$
$\{Y = Nat{\rightarrow}Y\}$	$\{\}$ (the empty set of constraints)

   □

22.4.4   DEFINITION: The *unification algorithm* for types is defined in Figure 22-2.[2] The phrase "let $\{S = T\} \cup C' = C$" in the second line should be read as "choose a constraint S=T from the set C and let C' denote the remaining constraints from C."   □

The side conditions $X \notin FV(T)$ in the fifth line and $X \notin FV(S)$ in the seventh are known as the *occur check*. Their effect is to prevent the algorithm from generating a solution involving a cyclic substitution like $X \mapsto X{\rightarrow}X$, which

---

2. Note that nothing in this algorithm depends on the fact that we are unifying type expressions as opposed to some other sort of expressions; the same algorithm can be used to solve equality constraints between any kind of (first-order) expressions.

makes no sense if we are talking about finite type expressions. (If we expand our language to include *infinite* type expressions—i.e. recursive types in the sense of Chapters 20 and 21—then the occur check can be omitted.)

22.4.5   THEOREM: The algorithm *unify* always terminates, failing when given a non-unifiable constraint set as input and otherwise returning a principal unifier. More formally:

1. *unify*(C) halts, either by failing or by returning a substitution, for all C;

2. if *unify*(C) = σ, then σ is a unifier for C;

3. if δ is a unifier for C, then *unify*(C) = σ with σ ⊑ δ.   □

Proof: For part (1), define the *degree* of a constraint set C to be the pair (m, n), where m is the number of distinct type variables in C and n is the total size of the types in C. It is easy to check that each clause of the *unify* algorithm either terminates immediately (with success in the first case or failure in the last) or else makes a recursive call to *unify* with a constraint set of lexicographically smaller degree.

Part (2) is a straightforward induction on the number of recursive calls in the computation of *unify*(C). All the cases are trivial except for the two involving variables, which depend on the observation that, if σ unifies [X ↦ T]D, then σ ∘ [X ↦ T] unifies {X = T} ∪ D for any constraint set D.

Part (3) again proceeds by induction on the number of recursive calls in the computation of *unify*(C). If C is empty, then *unify*(C) immediately returns the trivial substitution [ ]; since δ = δ ∘ [ ], we have [ ] ⊑ δ as required. If C is non-empty, then *unify*(C) chooses some pair (S, T) from C and continues by cases on the shapes of S and T.

Case: S = T

Since δ is a unifier for C, it also unifies C′. By the induction hypothesis, *unify*(C) = σ with σ ⊑ δ, as required.

Case: S = X and X ∉ *FV*(T)

Since δ unifies S and T, we have δ(X) = δ(T). So, for any type U, we have δ(U) = δ([X ↦ T]U); in particular, since δ unifies C′, it must also unify [X ↦ T]C′. The induction hypothesis then tells us that *unify*([X ↦ T]C′) = σ′, with δ = γ ∘ σ′ for some γ. Since *unify*(C) = σ′ ∘ [X ↦ T], showing that δ = γ ∘ (σ′ ∘ [X ↦ T]) will complete the argument. So consider any type variable Y. If Y ≠ X, then clearly (γ ∘ (σ′ ∘ [X ↦ T]))Y = (γ ∘ σ′)Y = δY. On the other hand, (γ ∘ (σ′ ∘ [X ↦ T]))X = (γ ∘ σ′)T = δX, as we saw above. Combining these observations, we see that δY = (γ ∘ (σ′ ∘ [X ↦ T]))Y for all variables Y, that is, δ = (γ ∘ (σ′ ∘ [X ↦ T])).

Case: T = X and X ∉ *FV*(S)

Similar.

Case: S = $S_1 \rightarrow S_2$ and T = $T_1 \rightarrow T_2$

Straightforward. Just note that δ is a unifier of $\{S_1 \rightarrow S_2 = T_1 \rightarrow T_2\} \cup C'$ iff it is a unifier of $C' \cup \{S_1 = T_1, S_2 = T_2\}$.

If none of the above cases apply to S and T, then *unify*(C) fails. But this can happen in only two ways: either S is Nat and T is an arrow type (or vice versa), or else S = X and X ∈ T (or vice versa). The first case obviously contradicts the assumption that C is unifiable. To see that the second does too, recall that, by assumption, δS = δT; if X occurred in T, then δT would always be strictly larger than δS. Thus, if *unify*(C) fails, then C is not unifiable, contradicting our assumption that δ is a unifier for C; so this case cannot occur.   □

22.4.6   EXERCISE [RECOMMENDED, ★★★]: Implement the unification algorithm.   □

22.5   Principal Types

We remarked above that if there is *some* way to instantiate the type variables in a term so that it becomes typable, then there is a *most general* or *principal* way of doing so. We now formalize this observation.

22.5.1   DEFINITION: A *principal solution* for (Γ, t, S, C) is a solution (σ, T) such that, whenever (σ', T') is also a solution for (Γ, t, S, C), we have $\sigma \sqsubseteq \sigma'$. When (σ, T) is a principal solution, we call T a *principal type* of t under Γ.[3]   □

22.5.2   EXERCISE [★ ↛]: Find a principal type for λx:X. λy:Y. λz:Z. (x z) (y z). □

22.5.3   THEOREM [PRINCIPAL TYPES]: If (Γ, t, S, C) has any solution, then it has a principal one. The unification algorithm in Figure 22-2 can be used to determine whether (Γ, t, S, C) has a solution and, if so, to calculate a principal one.   □

Proof: By the definition of a solution for (Γ, t, S, C) and the properties of unification.   □

22.5.4   COROLLARY: It is decidable whether (Γ, t) has a solution.   □

Proof: By Corollary 22.3.8 and Theorem 22.5.3.   □

---

3. Principal types should not be confused with *principal typings*. See page 337.

22.5.5   EXERCISE [RECOMMENDED, ★★★ ↠]: Combine the constraint generation and
unification algorithms from Exercises 22.3.10 and 22.4.6 to build a typechecker that calculates principal types, taking the `reconbase` checker as a
starting point. A typical interaction with your typechecker might look like:

λx:X. x;

▸ <fun> : X → X

λz:ZZ. λy:YY. z (y true);

▸ <fun> : $(?X_0{\to}?X_1)$ → $(Bool{\to}?X_0)$ → $?X_1$

λw:W. if true then false else w false;

▸ <fun> : $(Bool{\to}Bool)$ → Bool

Type variables with names like $?X_0$ are automatically generated.   □

22.5.6   EXERCISE [★★★]: What difficulties arise in extending the definitions above
(22.3.2, etc.) to deal with records? How might they be addressed?   □

The idea of principal types can be used to build a type reconstruction algorithm that works more incrementally than the one we have developed here.
Instead of generating all the constraints first and then trying to solve them,
we can interleave generation and solving, so that the type reconstruction algorithm actually returns a principal type at each step. The fact that the types
are always principal ensures that the algorithm never needs to re-analyze a
subterm: it makes only the minimum commitments needed to achieve typability at each step. One major advantage of such an algorithm is that it can
pinpoint errors in the user's program much more precisely.

22.5.7   EXERCISE [★★★ ↠]: Modify your solution to Exercise 22.5.5 so that it performs unification incrementally and returns principal types.   □

22.6   Implicit Type Annotations

Languages supporting type reconstruction typically allow programmers to
completely omit type annotations on lambda-abstractions. One way to achieve
this (as we remarked in §22.2) is simply to make the parser fill in omitted annotations with freshly generated type variables. A better alternative is to add
un-annotated abstractions to the syntax of terms and a corresponding rule to
the constraint typing relation.

$$\frac{X \notin \mathcal{X} \qquad \Gamma, x{:}X \vdash t_1 : T \mid_{\mathcal{X}} C}{\Gamma \vdash \lambda x.t_1 : X {\to} T \mid_{\mathcal{X} \cup \{X\}} C} \qquad \text{(CT-ABSINF)}$$

This account of un-annotated abstractions is a bit more direct than regarding them as syntactic sugar. It is also more expressive, in a small but useful way: if we make several *copies* of an un-annotated abstraction, the CT-ABSINF rule will allow us to choose a *different* variable as the argument type of each copy. By contrast, if we regard a bare abstraction as being annotated with an invisible type variable, then making copies will yield several expressions sharing the *same* argument type. This difference is important for the discussion of let-polymorphism in the following section.

22.7 Let-Polymorphism

The term *polymorphism* refers to a range of language mechanisms that allow a single part of a program to be used with different types in different contexts (§23.2 discusses several varieties of polymorphism in more detail). The type reconstruction algorithm shown above can be generalized to provide a simple form of polymorphism known as *let-polymorphism* (also *ML-style* or *Damas-Milner* polymorphism). This feature was introduced in the original dialect of ML (Milner, 1978) and has been incorporated in a number of successful language designs, where it forms the basis of powerful *generic libraries* of commonly used structures (lists, arrays, trees, hash tables, streams, user-interface widgets, etc.).

The motivation for let-polymorphism arises from examples like the following. Suppose we define and use a simple function `double`, which applies its first argument twice in succession to its second:

```
let double = λf:Nat→Nat. λa:Nat. f(f(a)) in
double (λx:Nat. succ (succ x)) 2;
```

Because we want to apply `double` to a function of type `Nat→Nat`, we choose type annotations that give it type `(Nat→Nat)→(Nat→Nat)`. We can alternatively define `double` so that it can be used to double a boolean function:

```
let double = λf:Bool→Bool. λa:Bool. f(f(a)) in
double (λx:Bool. x) false;
```

What we *cannot* do is use the same `double` function with both booleans and numbers: if we need both in the same program, we must define two versions that are identical except for type annotations.

```
let doubleNat = λf:Nat→Nat. λa:Nat. f(f(a)) in
let doubleBool = λf:Bool→Bool. λa:Bool. f(f(a)) in
```

```
let a = doubleNat (λx:Nat. succ (succ x)) 1 in
let b = doubleBool (λx:Bool. x) false in ...
```

Even annotating the abstractions in double with a *type variable*

```
let double = λf:X→X. λa:X. f(f(a)) in ...
```

does not help. For example, if we write

```
let double = λf:X→X. λa:X. f(f(a)) in
let a = double (λx:Nat. succ (succ x)) 1 in
let b = double (λx:Bool. x) false in ...
```

then the use of double in the definition of a generates the constraint $X→X =$ $Nat→Nat$, while the use of double in the definition of b generates the constraint $X→X = Bool→Bool$. These constraints place unsatisfiable demands on X, making the whole program untypable.

What went wrong here? The variable X plays two distinct roles in the example. First, it captures the constraint that the first argument to double in the calculation of a must be a function whose domain and range types are the same as the type (Nat) of the other argument to double. Second, it captures the constraint that the arguments to double in the calculation of b must be similarly related. Unfortunately, because the same variable X is used in both cases, we also end up with the spurious constraint that the second arguments to the two uses of double must have the same type.

What we'd like is to break this last connection—i.e., to associate a *different* variable X with each use of double. Fortunately, this is easily accomplished. The first step is to change the ordinary typing rule for let so that, instead of calculating a type for the right-hand side t_1 and then using this as the type of the bound variable x while calculating a type for the body t_2,

$$\frac{\Gamma \vdash t_1 : T_1 \qquad \Gamma, x{:}T_1 \vdash t_2 : T_2}{\Gamma \vdash \texttt{let } x{=}t_1 \texttt{ in } t_2 : T_2} \qquad\qquad \text{(T-LET)}$$

it instead *substitutes* t_1 for x in the body, and then typechecks this expanded expression:

$$\frac{\Gamma \vdash [x \mapsto t_1]t_2 : T_2}{\Gamma \vdash \texttt{let } x{=}t_1 \texttt{ in } t_2 : T_2} \qquad\qquad \text{(T-LETPOLY)}$$

We write a constraint-typing rule for let in a similar way:

$$\frac{\Gamma \vdash [x \mapsto t_1]t_2 : T_2 \ |_X\ C}{\Gamma \vdash \texttt{let } x{=}t_1 \texttt{ in } t_2 : T_2 \ |_X\ C} \qquad\qquad \text{(CT-LETPOLY)}$$

In essence, what we've done is to change the typing rules for let so that they perform a step of evaluation

$$\texttt{let } x{=}v_1 \texttt{ in } t_2 \ \longrightarrow\ [x \mapsto v_1]t_2 \qquad\qquad \text{(E-LETV)}$$

before calculating types.

The second step is to rewrite the definition of `double` using the *implicitly annotated* lambda-abstractions from §22.6.

```
let double = λf. λa. f(f(a)) in
let a = double (λx:Nat. succ (succ x)) 1 in
let b = double (λx:Bool. x) false in ...
```

The combination of the constraint typing rules for `let` (CT-LETPOLY) and the implicitly annotated lambda-abstraction (CT-ABSINF) gives us exactly what we need: CT-LETPOLY makes two copies of the definition of `double`, and CT-ABSINF assigns each of the abstractions a different type variable. The ordinary process of constraint solving does the rest.

However, this scheme has some flaws that need to be addressed before we can use it in practice. One obvious one is that, if we don't happen to actually use the `let`-bound variable in the body of the `let`, then the definition will never actually be typechecked. For example, a program like

```
let x = <utter garbage> in 5
```

will pass the typechecker. This can be repaired by adding a premise to the typing rule

$$\frac{\Gamma \vdash [x \mapsto t_1]t_2 : T_2 \quad \Gamma \vdash t_1 : T_1}{\Gamma \vdash \text{let } x=t_1 \text{ in } t_2 : T_2} \qquad \text{(T-LETPOLY)}$$

and a corresponding premise to CT-LETPOLY, ensuring that t_1 is well typed.

A related problem is that, if the body of the `let` contains *many* occurrences of the `let`-bound variable, then the whole right-hand side of the `let`-definition will be checked once per occurrence, whether or not it contains any implicitly annotated lambda-abstractions. Since the right-hand side itself can contain `let`-bindings, this typing rule can cause the typechecker to perform an amount of work that is exponential in the size of the original term!

To avoid this re-typechecking, practical implementations of languages with let-polymorphism actually use a more clever (though formally equivalent) re-formulation of the typing rules. In outline, the typechecking of a term `let x=t₁ in t₂` in a context Γ proceeds as follows:

1. We use the constraint typing rules to calculate a type S_1 and a set C_1 of associated constraints for the right-hand side t_1.

2. We use unification to find a most general solution σ to the constraints C_1 and apply σ to S_1 (and Γ) to obtain t_1's *principal type* T_1.

3. We *generalize* any variables remaining in T_1. If $X_1 \ldots X_n$ are the remaining variables, we write $\forall X_1 \ldots X_n . T_1$ for the principal *type scheme* of t_1.

One caveat here is that we need to be careful *not* to generalize variables T_1 that are also mentioned in Γ, since these correspond to real constraints between t_1 and its environment. For example, in

```
λf:X→X. λx:X. let g=f in g(x);
```

we should not generalize the variable X in the type X→X of g, since doing so would allow us to type wrong programs like this one:

```
(λf:X→X. λx:X. let g=f in g(0))
  (λx:Bool. if x then true else false)
  true;
```

4. We extend the context to record the type scheme $\forall X_1 \ldots X_n . T_1$ for the bound variable x, and start typechecking the body t_2. In general, the context now associates each free variable with a type scheme, not just a type.

5. Each time we encounter an occurrence of x in t_2, we look up its type scheme $\forall X_1 \ldots X_n . T_1$. We now generate fresh type variables $Y_1 \ldots Y_n$ and use them to *instantiate* the type scheme, yielding $[X_1 \mapsto Y_1, \ldots, X_n \mapsto Y_n]T_1$, which we use as the type of x.[4]

This algorithm is much more efficient than the simplistic approach of substituting away `let` expressions before typechecking. Indeed, decades of experience have shown that in practice it appears "essentially linear" in the size of the input program. It therefore came as a significant surprise when Kfoury, Tiuryn, and Urzyczyn (1990) and independently Mairson (1990) showed that its worst-case complexity is still exponential! The example they constructed involves using deeply nested sequences of `let`s in the right-hand sides of other `let`s—rather than in their bodies, where nesting of `let`s is common—to build expressions whose types grow exponentially larger than the expressions themselves. For example, the following OCaml program, due to Mairson (1990), is well typed but takes a very long time to typecheck.

```
let f₀ = fun x → (x,x) in
  let f₁ = fun y → f₀(f₀ y) in
    let f₂ = fun y → f₁(f₁ y) in
      let f₃ = fun y → f₂(f₂ y) in
        let f₄ = fun y → f₃(f₃ y) in
          let f₅ = fun y → f₄(f₄ y) in
            f₅ (fun z → z)
```

---

4. The difference between a lambda-abstraction that is explicitly annotated with a type variable and an un-annotated abstraction for which the constraint generation algorithm creates a variable becomes moot once we introduce generalization and instantiation. Either way, the right-hand side of a `let` is assigned a type involving a variable, which is generalized before being added to the context and replaced by a fresh variable every time it is instantiated.

To see why, try entering f_0, f_1, etc., one at a time, into the OCaml top-level. See Kfoury, Tiuryn, and Urzyczyn (1994) for further discussion.

A final point worth mentioning is that, in designing full-blown programming languages with let-polymorphism, we need to be a bit careful of the interaction of polymorphism and side-effecting features such as mutable storage cells. A simple example illustrates the danger:

```
let r = ref (λx. x) in
(r:=(λx:Nat. succ x); (!r)true);
```

Using the algorithm sketched above, we calculate $Ref(X{\rightarrow}X)$ as the principal type of the right-hand side of the `let`; since X appears nowhere else, this type can be generalized to $\forall X.Ref(X{\rightarrow}X)$, and we assign this type scheme to r when we add it to the context. When typechecking the assignment in the second line, we instantiate this type to $Ref(Nat{\rightarrow}Nat)$. When typechecking the third line, we instantiate it to $Ref(Bool{\rightarrow}Bool)$. But this is unsound, since when the term is evaluated it will end up applying `succ` to `true`.

The problem here is that the typing rules have gotten out of sync with the evaluation rules. The typing rules introduced in this section tell us that, when we see a `let` expression, we should *immediately* substitute the right-hand side into the body. But the evaluation rules tell us that we may perform this substitution only *after* the right-hand side has been reduced to a value. The typing rules see two uses of the `ref` constructor, and analyze them under different assumptions, but at run time only one `ref` is actually allocated.

We can correct this mismatch in two ways—by adjusting evaluation or typing. In the former case, the evaluation rule for `let` would become[5]

$$\text{let } x{=}t_1 \text{ in } t_2 \longrightarrow [x \mapsto t_1]t_2 \qquad \text{(E-LET)}$$

Under this strategy, the first step in evaluating our dangerous example from above would replace r by its definition, yielding

```
(ref (λx. x)) := (λx:Nat. succ x) in
(!(ref (λx. x))) true;
```

which is perfectly safe! The first line creates a reference cell initially containing the identity function, and stores (λx:Nat. succ x) into it. The second creates *another* reference containing the identity, extracts its contents, and applies it to `true`. However, this calculation also demonstrates that changing the evaluation rule to fit the typing rule gives us a language with a rather

---

5. Strictly speaking, we should annotate this rule with a *store,* as we did in Chapter 13, since we are talking about a language with references:

$$\text{let } x{=}t_1 \text{ in } t_2 \mid \mu \longrightarrow [x \mapsto t_1]t_2 \mid \mu \qquad \text{(E-LET)}$$

strange semantics that no longer matches standard intuitions about call-by-value evaluation order. (Imperative languages with non-CBV evaluation strategies are not unheard-of [Augustsson, 1984], but they have never become popular because of the difficulty of understanding and controlling the ordering of side effects at run time.)

It is better to change the typing rule to match the evaluation rule. Fortunately, this is easy: we just impose the restriction (often called the *value restriction*) that a let-binding can be treated polymorphically—i.e., its free type variables can be generalized—only if its right-hand side is a syntactic value. This means that, in the dangerous example, the type assigned to r when we add it to the context will be X→X, not ∀X.X→X. The constraints imposed by the second line will force X to be Nat, and this will cause the typechecking of the third line to fail, since Nat cannot be unified with Bool.

The value restriction solves our problem with type safety, at some cost in expressiveness: we can no longer write programs in which the right-hand sides of let expressions can both perform some interesting computation and be assigned a polymorphic type scheme. What is surprising is that this restriction makes hardly any difference in practice. Wright (1995) settled this point by analyzing a huge corpus of code written in an ML dialect—the 1990 definition of Standard ML (Milner, Tofte, and Harper, 1990)—that provided a more flexible let-typing rule based on *weak type variables* and observing that all but a tiny handful of right-hand sides were syntactic values anyway. This observation more or less closed the argument, and all major languages with ML-style let-polymorphism now adopt the value restriction.

22.7.1   EXERCISE [★★★ ↛]: Implement the algorithm sketched in this section.   □

22.8   Notes

Notions of principal types for the lambda-calculus go back at least to the work of Curry in the 1950s (Curry and Feys, 1958). An algorithm for calculating principal types based on Curry's ideas was given by Hindley (1969); similar algorithms were discovered independently by Morris (1968) and Milner (1978). In the world of propositional logic, the ideas go back still further, perhaps to Tarski in the 1920s and certainly to the Meredith cousins in the 1950s (Lemmon, Meredith, Meredith, Prior, and Thomas, 1957); their first implementation on a computer was by David Meredith in 1957. Additional historical remarks on principal types can be found in Hindley (1997).

Unification (Robinson, 1971) is fundamental to many areas of computer science. Thorough introductions can be found, for example, in Baader and Nipkow (1998), Baader and Siekmann (1994), and Lassez and Plotkin (1991).

ML-style let-polymorphism was first described by Milner (1978). A number of type reconstruction algorithms have been proposed, notably the classic *Algorithm W (Damas and Milner)* of Damas and Milner (1982; also see Lee and Yi, 1998). The main difference between Algorithm W and the presentation in this chapter is that the former is specialized for "pure type reconstruction"—assigning principal types to completely *untyped* lambda-terms—while we have mixed type checking and type reconstruction, permitting terms to include explicit type annotations that may, but need not, contain variables. This makes our technical presentation a bit more involved (especially the proof of completeness, Theorem 22.3.7, where we must be careful to keep the programmer's type variables separate from the ones introduced by the constraint generation rules), but it meshes better with the style of the other chapters.

A classic paper by Cardelli (1987) lays out a number of implementation issues. Other expositions of type reconstruction algorithms can be found in Appel (1998), Aho et al. (1986), and Reade (1989). A particularly elegant presentation of the core system called *mini-ML* (Clement, Despeyroux, Despeyroux, and Kahn, 1986) often forms the basis for theoretical discussions. Tiuryn (1990) surveys a range of type reconstruction problems.

Principal types should not be confused with the similar notion of *principal typings*. The difference is that, when we calculate principal types, the context Γ and term t are considered as inputs to the algorithm, while the principal type T is the output. An algorithm for calculating principal typings takes just t as input and yields both Γ and T as outputs—i.e., it calculates the *minimal assumptions* about the types of the free variables in t. Principal typings are useful in supporting separate compilation and "smartest recompilation," performing incremental type inference, and pinpointing type errors. Unfortunately, many languages, in particular ML, have principal types but not principal typings. See Jim (1996).

ML-style polymorphism, with its striking combination of power and simplicity, hits a "sweet spot" in the language design space; mixing it with other sophisticated typing features has often proved quite delicate. The biggest success story in this arena is the elegant account of type reconstruction for record types proposed by Wand (1987) and further developed by Wand (1988, 1989b), Remy (1989, 1990; 1992a, 1992b, 1998), and many others. The idea is to introduce a new kind of variable, called a *row variable*, that ranges not over types but over entire "rows" of field labels and associated types. A simple form of *equational unification* is used solve constraint sets involving row variables. See Exercise 22.5.6. Garrigue (1994) and others have developed related methods for variant types. These techniques have been extended to general notions of *type classes* (Kaes, 1988; Wadler and Blott, 1989), *constraint types*

(Odersky, Sulzmann, and Wehr, 1999), and *qualified types* (Jones, 1994b,a), which form the basis of Haskell's system of *type classes* (Hall et al., 1996; Hudak et al., 1992; Thompson, 1999); similar ideas appear in Mercury (Somogyi, Henderson, and Conway, 1996) and Clean (Plasmeijer, 1998).

Type reconstruction for the more powerful form of *impredicative polymorphism* discussed in Chapter 23 was shown to be undecidable by Wells (1994). Indeed, several forms of *partial type reconstruction* for this system also turn out to be undecidable. §23.6 and §23.8 give more information on these results and on methods for combining ML-style type reconstruction with stronger forms of polymorphism such as *rank-2 polymorphism*.

For the combination of subtyping with ML-style type reconstruction, some promising initial results have been reported (Aiken and Wimmers, 1993; Eifrig, Smith, and Trifonov, 1995; Jagannathan and Wright, 1995; Trifonov and Smith, 1996; Odersky, Sulzmann, and Wehr, 1999; Flanagan and Felleisen, 1997; Pottier, 1997), but practical checkers have yet to see widespread use.

Extending ML-style type reconstruction to handle recursive types (Chapter 20) has been shown *not* to pose significant difficulties (Huet, 1975, 1976). The only significant difference from the algorithms presented in this chapter appears in the definition of unification, where we omit the *occur check* (which ordinarily ensures that the substitution returned by the unification algorithm is acyclic). Having done this, to ensure termination we also need to modify the representation used by the unification algorithm so that it maintains sharing, e.g., by using destructive operations on (potentially cyclic) pointer structures. Such representations are common in high-performance implementations.

The mixture of type reconstruction with recursively defined *terms,* on the other hand, raises one tricky problem, known as *polymorphic recursion*. A simple (and unproblematic) typing rule for recursive function definitions in ML specifies that a recursive function can be used within the body of its definition only monomorphically (i.e., all recursive calls must have identically typed arguments and results), while occurrences in the rest of the program may be used polymorphically (with arguments and results of different types). Mycroft (1984) and Meertens (1983) proposed a polymorphic typing rule for recursive definitions that allows recursive calls to a recursive function from its own body to be instantiated with different types. This extension, often called the *Milner-Mycroft Calculus,* was shown to have an undecidable reconstruction problem by Henglein (1993) and independently by Kfoury, Tiuryn, and Urzyczyn (1993a); both of these proofs depend on the undecidability of the (unrestricted) semi-unification problem, shown by Kfoury, Tiuryn, and Urzyczyn (1993b).

23 *Universal Types*

In the previous chapter, we studied the simple form of *let-polymorphism* found in ML. In this chapter, we consider a more general form of polymorphism in the setting of a powerful calculus known as *System F*.

23.1 Motivation

As we remarked in §22.7, we can write an infinite number of "doubling" functions in the simply typed lambda-calculus...

```
doubleNat = λf:Nat→Nat. λx:Nat. f (f x);
doubleRcd = λf:{l:Bool}→{l:Bool}. λx:{l:Bool}. f (f x);
doubleFun = λf:(Nat→Nat)→(Nat→Nat). λx:Nat→Nat. f (f x);
```

Each of these functions is applicable to a different type of argument, but all share precisely the same behavior (indeed, they share precisely the same program text, aside from the typing annotations). If we want apply the doubling operation to different types of arguments within the same program, we will need to write out separate definitions of doubleT for each T. This kind of cut-and-paste programming violates a basic dictum of software engineering:

> ABSTRACTION PRINCIPLE: Each significant piece of functionality in a program should be implemented in just one place in the source code. Where similar functions are carried out by distinct pieces of code, it is generally beneficial to combine them into one by *abstracting out* the varying parts.

The system studied in most of this chapter is pure System F (Figure 23-1); the examples in §23.4 use various extensions with previously studied features. The associated OCaml implementation is fullpoly. (The examples involving pairs and lists require the fullomega checker.)

Here, the varying parts are the types! What we need, then, are facilities for abstracting out a type from a term and later instantiating this abstract term with concrete type annotations.

23.2   Varieties of Polymorphism

Type systems that allow a single piece of code to be used with multiple types are collectively known as *polymorphic* systems (*poly* = many, *morph* = form). Several varieties of polymorphism can be found in modern languages (this classification comes from Strachey, 1967, and Cardelli and Wegner, 1985).

Parametric polymorphism, the topic of this chapter, allows a single piece of code to be typed "generically," using variables in place of actual types, and then instantiated with particular types as needed. Parametric definitions are *uniform:* all of their instances behave the same.

The most powerful form of parametric polymorphism is the *impredicative* or *first-class polymorphism* developed in this chapter. More common in practice is the form known as *ML-style* or *let-polymorphism,* which restricts polymorphism to top-level let-bindings, disallowing functions that take polymorphic values as arguments, and obtains in return a convenient and natural form of automatic *type reconstruction* (Chapter 22). First-class parametric polymorphism is also becoming popular in programming languages, and forms the technical foundation for the powerful module systems of languages like ML (see Harper and Stone, 2000).

Ad-hoc polymorphism, by contrast, allows a polymorphic value to exhibit different behaviors when "viewed" at different types. The most common example of ad-hoc polymorphism is *overloading,* which associates a single function symbol with many implementations; the compiler (or the runtime system, depending on whether overloading resolution is *static* or *dynamic*) chooses an appropriate implementation for each application of the function, based on the types of the arguments.

A generalization of function overloading forms the basis for *multi-method dispatch* in languages such as CLOS (Bobrow et al., 1988; Kiczales et al., 1991) and Cecil (Chambers, 1992; Chambers and Leavens, 1994). This mechanism has been formalized in the λ-& calculus of Castagna, Ghelli, and Longo (1995; cf. Castagna, 1997).

A more powerful form of ad-hoc polymorphism known as *intensional polymorphism* (Harper and Morrisett, 1995; Crary, Weirich, and Morrisett, 1998) permits restricted computation over types at run time. Intensional polymorphism is an enabling technology for a variety of advanced implementation techniques for polymorphic languages, including tag-free garbage collection, "unboxed" function arguments, polymorphic marshaling, and space-efficient "flattened" data structures.

Yet more powerful forms of ad-hoc polymorphism can be built from a `typecase` primitive, which permits arbitrary pattern-matching on type information at run time (Abadi, Cardelli, Pierce, and Rémy, 1995; Abadi, Cardelli, Pierce, and Plotkin, 1991b; Henglein, 1994; Leroy and Mauny, 1991; Thatte, 1990). Language features such as Java's `instanceof` test can be viewed as restricted forms of `typecase`.

The *subtype polymorphism* of Chapter 15 gives a single term many types using the rule of subsumption, allowing us to selectively "forget" information about the term's behavior.

These categories are not exclusive: different forms of polymorphism can be mixed in the same language. For example, Standard ML offers both parametric polymorphism and simple overloading of built-in arithmetic operations, but not subtyping, while Java includes subtyping, overloading, and simple ad-hoc polymorphism (`instanceof`), but not (at the time of this writing) parametric polymorphism. There are several proposals for adding parametric polymorphism to Java; the best known of these is GJ (Bracha, Odersky, Stoutamire, and Wadler, 1998).

The unqualified term "polymorphism" causes a certain amount of confusion between programming language communities. Among functional programers (i.e., those who use or design languages like ML, Haskell, etc.), it almost always refers to parametric polymorphism. Among object-oriented programmers, on the other hand, it almost always means subtype polymorphism, while the term *genericity* (or *generics*) is used for parametric polymorphism.

23.3   System F

The system we will be studying in this chapter, commonly called *System F*, was first discovered by Jean-Yves Girard (1972), in the context of proof theory in logic. A little later, a type system with essentially the same power was developed, independently, by a computer scientist, John Reynolds (1974), who called it the *polymorphic lambda-calculus*. This system has been used extensively as a research vehicle for foundational work on polymorphism and as the basis for numerous programming language designs. It is also sometimes called the *second-order lambda-calculus,* because it corresponds, via the *Curry-Howard correspondence,* to second-order intuitionistic logic, which allows quantification not only over individuals [terms], but also over predicates [types].

The definition of System F is a straightforward extension of $\lambda_\rightarrow$, the simply typed lambda-calculus. In $\lambda_\rightarrow$, lambda-abstraction is used to abstract terms out of terms, and application is used to supply values for the abstracted parts. Since we want here a mechanism for abstracting *types* out of terms and filling them in later, we introduce a new form of abstraction, written $\lambda X.t$, whose parameter is a type, and a new form of application, $t\ [T]$, in which the argument is a type expression. We call our new abstractions *type abstractions* and the new application construct *type application* or *instantiation*.

When, during evaluation, a type abstraction meets a type application, the pair forms a redex, just as in $\lambda_\rightarrow$. We add a reduction rule

$$(\lambda X.t_{12})\ [T_2] \longrightarrow [X \mapsto T_2]t_{12} \qquad\qquad \text{(E-TappTabs)}$$

analogous to the ordinary reduction rule for abstractions and applications.

$$(\lambda x{:}T_{11}.t_{12})\ v_2 \longrightarrow [x \mapsto v_2]t_{12} \qquad\qquad \text{(E-AppAbs)}$$

For example, when the *polymorphic identity function*

```
id = λX. λx:X. x;
```

is applied to Nat by writing id [Nat], the result is $[X \mapsto \text{Nat}](\lambda x{:}X.x)$, i.e., $\lambda x{:}\text{Nat}.x$, the identity function on natural numbers.

Finally, we need to specify the *type* of a polymorphic abstraction. We use types like Nat→Nat for classifying ordinary functions like λx:Nat.x; we now need a different form of "arrow type" whose domain is a type, for classifying polymorphic functions like id. Notice that, for each argument T to which it is applied, id yields a function of type T→T; that is, the type of the result of id depends on the actual type that we pass it as argument. To capture this dependency, we write the type of id as ∀X.X→X. The typing rules for polymorphic abstraction and application are analogous to the rules for term-level abstraction and application.

$$\frac{\Gamma, X \vdash t_2 : T_2}{\Gamma \vdash \lambda X.t_2 : \forall X.T_2} \qquad\qquad \text{(T-TAbs)}$$

$$\frac{\Gamma \vdash t_1 : \forall X.T_{12}}{\Gamma \vdash t_1\ [T_2] : [X \mapsto T_2]T_{12}} \qquad\qquad \text{(T-TApp)}$$

Note that we include the type variable X in the context used by the subderivation for t. We continue the convention (5.3.4) that the names of (term or type) variables should be chosen so as to be different from all the names already bound by Γ, and that lambda-bound type variables may be renamed at will in order to satisfy this condition. (In some presentations of System F, this freshness condition is given as an explicit side condition on the T-TAbs rule, instead of being built into the rules about how contexts are constructed, as we are doing here.) For the moment, the only role of type variables in contexts

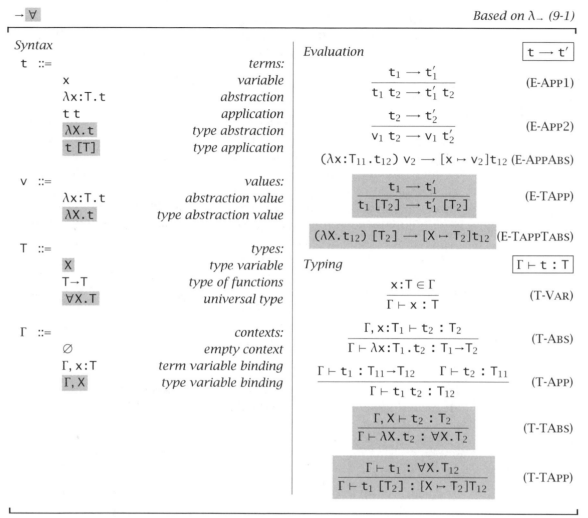

Figure 23-1: Polymorphic lambda-calculus (System F)

is to keep track of scopes and make sure that the same type variable is not added twice to a context. In later chapters, we will annotate type variables with information of various kinds, such as *bounds* (Chapter 26) and *kinds* (Chapter 29).

Figure 23-1 shows the complete definition of the polymorphic lambda-calculus, with differences from λ₋ highlighted. As usual, this summary defines just the pure calculus, omitting other type constructors such as records, base types such as `Nat` and `Bool`, and term-language extensions such as `let` and `fix`. These extra constructs can be added straightforwardly to the pure system, and we will use them freely in the examples that follow.

23.4   Examples

We now develop several examples of programming with polymorphism. To warm up, we start with a few small but increasingly tricky examples, showing sóme of the expressive power of System F. We then review the basic ideas of "ordinary" polymorphic programming with lists, trees, etc. The last two subsections introduce typed versions of the Church encodings of simple algebraic datatypes like booleans, numbers, and lists that we saw in Chapter 5 for the untyped lambda-calculus. Although these encodings are of small practical importance—it is easier to compile good code for these important features if they are built into high-level programming languages as primitives— they make excellent exercises for understanding both the intricacies and the power of System F. In Chapter 24, we will see some additional applications of polymorphism in the domain of *modular programming* and *abstract data types.*

Warm-ups

We have seen already how type abstraction and application can be used to define a single polymorphic identity function

```
id = λX. λx:X. x;
```

▶ id : ∀X. X → X

and instantiate it to yield any concrete identity function that may be required:

```
id [Nat];
```

▶ <fun> : Nat → Nat

```
id [Nat] 0;
```

▶ 0 : Nat

A more useful example is the polymorphic doubling function:

```
double = λX. λf:X→X. λa:X. f (f a);
```

▶ double : ∀X. (X→X) → X → X

The abstraction on the type X allows us to obtain doubling functions for specific types by instantiating double with different type arguments:

```
doubleNat = double [Nat];
```

▸ doubleNat : (Nat→Nat) → Nat → Nat

```
doubleNatArrowNat = double [Nat→Nat];
```

▸ doubleNatArrowNat : ((Nat→Nat)→Nat→Nat) →
                      (Nat→Nat) → Nat → Nat

Once instantiated with a type argument, double can be further applied to an actual function and argument of appropriate types:

```
double [Nat] (λx:Nat. succ(succ(x))) 3;
```

▸ 7 : Nat

Here is a slightly trickier example: polymorphic self-application. Recall that, in the simply typed lambda-calculus, there is no way to type the untyped term λx. x x (Exercise 9.3.2). In System F, on the other hand, this term becomes typable if we give x a polymorphic type and instantiate it appropriately:

```
selfApp = λx:∀X.X→X.  x [∀X.X→X] x;
```

▸ selfApp : (∀X. X→X) → (∀X. X → X)

As a (slightly) more useful example of self application, we can apply the polymorphic double function to itself, yielding a polymorphic quadrupling function:

```
quadruple = λX. double [X→X] (double [X]);
```

▸ quadruple : ∀X. (X→X) → X → X

23.4.1 EXERCISE [★ ↠]: Using the typing rules in Figure 23-1, convince yourself that the terms above have the types given.   □

Polymorphic Lists

Most real-world programming with polymorphism is much more pedestrian than the tricky examples above. As an example of straightforward polymorphic programming, suppose our programming language is equipped with a type constructor List and term constructors for the usual list manipulation primitives, with the following types.

```
▸ nil : ∀X. List X
  cons : ∀X. X → List X → List X
  isnil : ∀X. List X → Bool
  head : ∀X. List X → X
  tail : ∀X. List X → List X
```

When we first introduced lists in §11.12, we used "custom" inference rules to allow the operations to be applied to lists with elements of any type. Here, we can give the operations polymorphic types expressing exactly the same constraints—that is, lists no longer need to be "baked into" the core language, but can simply be considered as a library providing several constants with particular polymorphic types. The same holds for the Ref type and the primitive operations on reference cells in Chapter 13, and many other common data and control structures.

We can use these primitives to define our own polymorphic operations on lists. For example, here is a polymorphic map function that takes a function from X to Y and a list of Xs and returns a list of Ys.

```
map = λX. λY.
        λf: X→Y.
          (fix (λm: (List X) → (List Y).
                 λl: List X.
                   if isnil [X] l
                     then nil [Y]
                     else cons [Y] (f (head [X] l))
                                   (m (tail [X] l))));
▸ map : ∀X. ∀Y. (X→Y) → List X → List Y

  l = cons [Nat] 4 (cons [Nat] 3 (cons [Nat] 2 (nil [Nat])));
▸ l : List Nat

  head [Nat] (map [Nat] [Nat] (λx:Nat. succ x) l);
▸ 5 : Nat
```

23.4.2   EXERCISE [★ ⇀]: Convince yourself that map really has the type shown.   □

23.4.3   EXERCISE [RECOMMENDED, ★★]: Using map as a model, write a polymorphic list-reversing function:

    reverse : ∀X. List X → List X.

This exercise is best done on-line. Use the fullomega checker and copy the contents of the file test.f from the fullomega directory to the top of your own input file. (The file contains definitions of the List constructor and associated operations that require the powerful abstraction facilities of System F_ω, discussed in Chapter 29. You do not need to understand exactly how they work to proceed with the present exercise.)   □

23.4.4   EXERCISE [★★ ↦]: Write a simple polymorphic sorting function

$$\text{sort} : \forall X.\ (X{\to}X{\to}\text{Bool}) \to (\text{List}\ X) \to \text{List}\ X$$

where the first argument is a comparison function for elements of type X.   □

Church Encodings

We saw in §5.2 that a variety of primitive data values such as booleans, numbers, and lists can be encoded as functions in the pure untyped lambda-calculus. In this section, we show how these *Church encodings* can also be carried out in System F. Readers may want to refer to §5.2 to refresh their intuitions about Church encodings.

These encodings are interesting for two reasons. First, they give our understanding of type abstraction and application a good workout. Second, they demonstrate that System F, like the pure untyped lambda-calculus, is computationally a very rich language, in the sense that the pure system can express a large range of data and control structures. This means that, if we later design a full-scale programming language with System F as its core, we can add these features as primitives (for efficiency, and so that we can equip them with more convenient concrete syntax) without disturbing the fundamental properties of the core language. This will not be true of all interesting high-level language features, of course. For example, adding *references* to System F, as we did for λ₋ in Chapter 13, represents a real change in the fundamental computational nature of the system.

Let us begin with the Church booleans. Recall that, in the untyped lambda-calculus, we represented the boolean constants true and false by lambda-terms tru and fls defined like this:

```
tru = λt. λf. t;
fls = λt. λf. f;
```

Each of these terms takes two arguments and returns one of them. If we want to assign a common type to tru and fls, we had better assume that the two arguments have the same type (since the caller will not know whether it is interacting with tru or fls), but this type may be arbitrary (since tru and fls do not need to do anything with their arguments except return one of them). This leads us to the following type for tru and fls.

```
CBool = ∀X.X→X→X;
```

The System-F terms tru and fls are obtained by adding appropriate type annotations to the untyped versions above.

```
tru = λX. λt:X. λf:X. t;
```

▸ tru : CBool

```
fls = λX. λt:X. λf:X. f;
```

▸ fls : CBool

We can write common boolean operations like not by constructing a new boolean that uses an existing one to decide which of its arguments to return:

```
not = λb:CBool. λX. λt:X. λf:X. b [X] f t;
```

▸ not : CBool → CBool

23.4.5   EXERCISE [RECOMMENDED, ★]: Write a term and that takes two arguments of type CBool and computes their conjunction.   □

We can play a similar game with numbers. The *Church numerals* introduced in §5.2 encode each natural number n as a function that take two arguments s and z and applies s to z, n times:

```
c₀ = λs. λz. z;
c₁ = λs. λz. s z;
c₂ = λs. λz. s (s z);
c₃ = λs. λz. s (s (s z));
```

Clearly, the z argument should have the same type as the domain of s, and the result returned by s should again have the same type. This leads us to the following type for Church numerals in System F:

```
CNat = ∀X. (X→X) → X → X;
```

The elements of this type are obtained by adding appropriate annotations to the untyped Church numerals:

```
c₀   =   λX. λs:X→X. λz:X. z;
```

▸ c₀ : CNat

```
c₁   =   λX. λs:X→X. λz:X. s z;
```

▸ c₁ : CNat

```
c₂   =   λX. λs:X→X. λz:X. s (s z);
```

▸ c₂ : CNat

A typed successor function on Church numerals can be defined as follows.

```
csucc = λn:CNat. λX. λs:X→X. λz:X. s (n [X] s z);
```

▸ csucc : CNat → CNat

That is, csucc n returns an element of CNat that, given s and z, applies s to z, n times (by applying n to s and z), and then once more. Other arithmetic operations can be defined similarly. For example, addition can be defined either in terms of successor,

```
cplus = λm:CNat. λn:CNat. m [CNat] csucc n;
```

▸ cplus : CNat → CNat → CNat

or more directly:

```
cplus = λm:CNat. λn:CNat.  λX. λs:X→X. λz:X. m [X] s (n [X] s z);
```

▸ cplus : CNat → CNat → CNat

If our language also includes primitive numbers (Figure 8-2), then we can convert from Church numerals to ordinary ones using the following function:

```
cnat2nat = λm:CNat. m [Nat] (λx:Nat. succ(x)) 0;
```

▸ cnat2nat : CNat → Nat

This allows us to verify that our operations on Church numerals actually compute the desired arithmetic functions:

```
cnat2nat (cplus (csucc c₀) (csucc (csucc c₀)));
```

▸ 3 : Nat

23.4.6 EXERCISE [RECOMMENDED, ⋆⋆]: Write a function iszero that will return tru when applied to the Church numeral c_0 and fls otherwise. □

23.4.7 EXERCISE [⋆⋆ ↛]: Verify that the terms

```
ctimes = λm:CNat. λn:CNat.  λX. λs:X→X. n [X] (m [X] s);
```

▸ ctimes : CNat → CNat → CNat

```
cexp = λm:CNat. λn:CNat.  λX. n [X→X] (m [X]);
```

▸ cexp : CNat → CNat → CNat

have the indicated types. Give an informal argument that they implement the arithmetic multiplication and exponentiation operators. □

23.4.8 EXERCISE [RECOMMENDED, ⋆⋆]: Show that the type

PairNat = ∀X. (CNat→CNat→X) → X;

can be used to represent pairs of numbers, by writing functions

```
pairNat : CNat→CNat→PairNat;
fstNat  : PairNat→CNat;
sndNat  : PairNat→CNat;
```

for constructing elements of this type from pairs of numbers and for accessing their first and second components.   □

23.4.9   EXERCISE [RECOMMENDED, ★★★]: Use the functions defined in Exercise 23.4.8
to write a function `pred` that computes the predecessor of a Church numeral
(returning 0 if its input is 0). Hint: the key idea is developed in the example
in §5.2. Define a function f : PairNat→PairNat that maps the pair (i, j)
into $(i + 1, i)$—that is, it throws away the second component of its argument,
copies the first component to the second, and increments the first. Then n
applications of f to the starting pair $(0, 0)$ yields the pair $(n, n - 1)$, from
which we extract the predecessor of n by projecting the second component. □

23.4.10 EXERCISE [★★★]: There is another way of computing the predecessor function
on Church numerals. Let k stand for the untyped lambda-term $\lambda x. \lambda y. x$ and
i for $\lambda x. x$. The untyped lambda-term

vpred = $\lambda n. \lambda s. \lambda z. n\ (\lambda p. \lambda q.\ q\ (p\ s))\ (k\ z)\ i$

(from Barendregt, 1992, who attributes it to J. Velmans) computes the predecessor of an untyped Church numeral. Show that this term can be typed
in System F by adding type abstractions and applications as necessary and
annotating the bound variables in the untyped term with appropriate types.
For extra credit, explain why it works!   □

Encoding Lists

As a final example, let us extend the Church encodings of numbers to lists.
This is a nice demonstration of the expressive power of pure System F, since it
shows that all of the programming examples in the subsection above on polymorphic list manipulation can actually be expressed in the pure language.
(For convenience, we do use the `fix` construct for defining general recursive
functions, but essentially the same constructions can be carried out without
it. See Exercises 23.4.11 and 23.4.12.)

We saw in Exercise 5.2.8 that lists can be encoded in the untyped lambda-
calculus in a fashion quite similar to the encoding of natural numbers. In
effect, a number in unary notation is like a list of dummy elements. Generalizing this idea to elements of any type, we arrive at a Church encoding

for lists, where a list with elements x, y, and z is represented as a function that, given any function f and starting value v, calculates f x (f y (f z v)). In OCaml terminology, a list is represented as its own fold_right function.

The type List X of lists with elements of type X is defined as follows:

List X = ∀R. (X→R→R) → R → R;

The nil value for this representation of lists easy to write.[1]

nil = λX. (λR. λc:X→R→R. λn:R. n) as List X;

▸ nil : ∀X. List X

The cons and isnil operations are also easy:

cons = λX. λhd:X. λtl:List X.
            (λR. λc:X→R→R. λn:R. c hd (tl [R] c n)) as List X;

▸ cons : ∀X. X → List X → List X

isnil = λX. λl:List X. l [Bool] (λhd:X. λtl:Bool. false) true;

▸ isnil : ∀X. List X → Bool

For the head operation, we need to work a little harder. The first difficulty is what to do about head of the empty list. We can address this by recalling that, if we have a general fixed point operator in the language, we can use it to construct an expression of any type. In fact, using type abstraction, we can go further and write a single, uniform function that, given a type X, yields a function from Unit to X that diverges when applied to unit.

diverge = λX. λ_:Unit. fix (λx:X. x);

▸ diverge : ∀X. Unit → X

Now we can use diverge [X] unit as the "result" of head [X] nil.

head = λX. λl:List X. l [X] (λhd:X. λtl:X. hd) (diverge [X] unit);

▸ head : ∀X. List X → X

Unfortunately, this definition is not yet quite what we want: it will *always* diverge, even when applied to non-empty lists. To get the right behavior, we need to reorganize it a little so that diverge[X] is not actually passed its Unit argument when it is supplied as an argument to l. This is accomplished by removing the unit argument and changing the type of the first argument to l correspondingly:

---

1. The as annotation here helps the typechecker print the type of nil in a readable form. As we saw in §11.4, all the typecheckers used in this book perform a simple abbreviation-collapsing step before printing types, but the collapsing function is not smart enough to deal automatically with "parametric abbreviations" like List.

```
head =
  λX. λl:List X.
    (l [Unit→X] (λhd:X. λtl:Unit→X. λ_:Unit. hd) (diverge [X]))
    unit;
```

▸ head : ∀X. List X → X

That is, l is applied to a function of type X→(Unit→X)→(Unit→X) and a
base value of type Unit→X, and it constructs a function of type Unit→X. In
the case where l represents the empty list, this result will be diverge[X];
but in the case where l represents a non-empty list, the result will be a function that takes unit and returns the head element of l. The result from l
is applied to unit at the end to get the actual head element (or, if we are
unlucky, diverge), so that head has the type we expect.

For the tail function, we use the abbreviation Pair X Y (generalizing the
PairNat type from Exercise 23.4.8) for the Church encoding of pairs with
first component of type X and second component of type Y:

```
Pair X Y = ∀R. (X→Y→R) → R;
```

The operations on pairs are simple generalizations of the operations on the
type PairNat above:

▸ pair : ∀X. ∀Y. X → Y → Pair X Y
  fst : ∀X. ∀Y. Pair X Y → X
  snd : ∀X. ∀Y. Pair X Y → Y

Now the tail function can be written like this:

```
tail =
  λX. λl: List X.
    (fst [List X] [List X] (
        l [Pair (List X) (List X)]
          (λhd: X. λtl: Pair (List X) (List X).
            pair [List X] [List X]
              (snd [List X] [List X] tl)
              (cons [X] hd (snd [List X] [List X] tl)))
          (pair [List X] [List X] (nil [X]) (nil [X])))));
```

▸ tail : ∀X. List X → List X

23.4.11   EXERCISE [★★]: Strictly speaking, the examples in this subsection have not
          been expressed in pure System F, since we used the fix operator to con-
          struct a value to be "returned" when head is applied to an empty list. Write
          an alternative version of head that takes an extra parameter to be returned
          (instead of diverging) when the list is empty.   □

23.4.12 EXERCISE [RECOMMENDED, ★★★]: In pure System F (without `fix`), write a function `insert` of type

$$\forall X.\ (X \rightarrow X \rightarrow Bool) \rightarrow List\ X \rightarrow X \rightarrow List\ X$$

that takes a comparison function, a sorted list, and a new element, and inserts the element into the list at the appropriate point (i.e., after all the elements smaller than it). Next, use `insert` to build a sorting function for lists in pure System F. □

23.5 Basic Properties

The fundamental properties of System F are very similar to those of the simply typed lambda-calculus. In particular, the proofs of type preservation and progress are straightforward extensions of the ones we saw in Chapter 9.

23.5.1 THEOREM [PRESERVATION]: If $\Gamma \vdash t : T$ and $t \longrightarrow t'$, then $\Gamma \vdash t' : T$. □

Proof: EXERCISE [RECOMMENDED, ★★★]. □

23.5.2 THEOREM [PROGRESS]: If t is a closed, well-typed term, then either t is a value or else there is some t' with $t \longrightarrow t'$. □

Proof: EXERCISE [RECOMMENDED, ★★★]. □

System F also shares with $\lambda_\rightarrow$ the property of *normalization*—the fact that the evaluation of every well-typed program terminates.[2] Unlike the type safety theorems above, normalization is quite difficult to prove (indeed, it is somewhat astonishing that it holds at all, considering that we can code things like sorting functions in the pure language, as we did in Exercise 23.4.12, without resorting to `fix`). This proof, based on a generalization of the method presented in Chapter 12, was a major achievement of Girard's doctoral thesis (1972; also see Girard, Lafont, and Taylor, 1989). Since then, his proof technique has been analyzed and reworked by many others; see Gallier (1990).

23.5.3 THEOREM [NORMALIZATION]: Well-typed System F terms are normalizing. □

---

2. Indeed, presentations of System F with more permissive operational semantics based on full beta-reduction have the *strong normalization* property: every reduction path starting from a well-typed term is guaranteed to terminate.

23.6   Erasure, Typability, and Type Reconstruction

As we did for $\lambda_\rightarrow$ in §9.5, we can define a *type erasure* function mapping System F terms to untyped lambda-terms by stripping out all their type annotations (including all type abstractions and applications):

$$
\begin{array}{lcl}
erase(\mathsf{x}) & = & \mathsf{x} \\
erase(\lambda\mathsf{x}{:}\mathsf{T}_1.\ \mathsf{t}_2) & = & \lambda\mathsf{x}.\ erase(\mathsf{t}_2) \\
erase(\mathsf{t}_1\ \mathsf{t}_2) & = & erase(\mathsf{t}_1)\ erase(\mathsf{t}_2) \\
erase(\lambda\mathsf{X}.\ \mathsf{t}_2) & = & erase(\mathsf{t}_2) \\
erase(\mathsf{t}_1\ [\mathsf{T}_2]) & = & erase(\mathsf{t}_1)
\end{array}
$$

A term M in the untyped lambda-calculus is said to be *typable* in System F if there is some well-typed term t such that $erase(\mathsf{t}) = \mathsf{m}$. The *type reconstruction* problem then asks, given an untyped term m, whether we can find some well-typed term that erases to m.

Type reconstruction for System F was one of the longest-standing problems in the programming languages literature, remaining open from the early 1970s until it was finally settled (negatively) by Wells in the early 1990s.

23.6.1   THEOREM [WELLS, 1994]: It is undecidable whether, given a closed term m of the untyped lambda-calculus, there is some well-typed term t in System F such that $erase(\mathsf{t}) = \mathsf{m}$.   □

Not only full type reconstruction but also various forms of partial type reconstruction are known to be undecidable for System F. For example, consider the following "partial erasure" function, which leaves intact all typing annotations except the arguments to type applications:

$$
\begin{array}{lcl}
erase_p(\mathsf{x}) & = & \mathsf{x} \\
erase_p(\lambda\mathsf{x}{:}\mathsf{T}_1.\ \mathsf{t}_2) & = & \lambda\mathsf{x}{:}\mathsf{T}_1.\ erase_p(\mathsf{t}_2) \\
erase_p(\mathsf{t}_1\ \mathsf{t}_2) & = & erase_p(\mathsf{t}_1)\ erase_p(\mathsf{t}_2) \\
erase_p(\lambda\mathsf{X}.\ \mathsf{t}_2) & = & \lambda\mathsf{X}.\ erase_p(\mathsf{t}_2) \\
erase_p(\mathsf{t}_1\ [\mathsf{T}_2]) & = & erase_p(\mathsf{t}_1)\ [\,]
\end{array}
$$

Note that type applications are still marked (with empty square brackets) in the erased terms; we can see where they must occur, but not what type must be supplied.

23.6.2   THEOREM [BOEHM 1985, 1989]: It is undecidable whether, given a closed term s in which type applications are marked but the arguments are omitted, there is some well-typed System F term t such that $erase_p(\mathsf{t}) = \mathsf{s}$.   □

Boehm showed that this form of type reconstruction was just as hard as higher-order unification, hence undecidable. Interestingly, this negative result led directly to a useful partial type reconstruction technique (Pfenning,

1988, 1993a) based on Huet's earlier work on efficient semi-algorithms for higher-order unification (Huet, 1975). Later improvements in this line of development have included using a more refined algorithm for higher-order constraint solving (Dowek, Hardin, Kirchner, and Pfenning, 1996), eliminating the troublesome possibilities of nontermination or generation of non-unique solutions. Experience with related algorithms in languages such as LEAP (Pfenning and Lee, 1991), Elf (Pfenning, 1989), and FX (O'Toole and Gifford, 1989) has shown them to be quite well behaved in practice.

A different approach to partial type reconstruction was sparked by Perry's observation that first-class existential types (see Chapter 24) can be integrated with ML's `datatype` mechanism (Perry, 1990); the idea was further developed by Läufer and Odersky (Läufer, 1992; Läufer and Odersky, 1994). In essence, `datatype` constructors and destructors can be regarded as explicit type annotations, marking where values must be injected into and projected from disjoint union types, where recursive types must be folded and unfolded, and (when existentials are added) where packing and unpacking must occur. This idea was extended to include first-class (impredicative) universal quantifiers by Rémy (1994). A more recent proposal by Odersky and Läufer (1996), further developed by Garrigue and Rémy (1997), conservatively extends ML-style type reconstruction by allowing programmers to explicitly annotate function arguments with types, which may (unlike the annotations that can be inferred automatically) contain embedded universal quantifiers, thus partly bridging the gap between ML and more powerful impredicative systems. This family of approaches to type reconstruction has the advantage of relative simplicity and clean integration with the polymorphism of ML.

A pragmatic approach to partial type reconstruction for systems involving both *subtyping* and impredicative polymorphism, called *local type inference* (or *local type reconstruction*), was proposed by Pierce and Turner (1998; also see Pierce and Turner, 1997; Hosoya and Pierce, 1999). Local type inference has appeared in several recent language designs, including GJ (Bracha, Odersky, Stoutamire, and Wadler, 1998) and Funnel (Odersky and Zenger, 2001), the latter introducing a more powerful form called *colored local type inference* (Odersky, Zenger, and Zenger, 2001).

A simpler but less predictable *greedy type inference* algorithm was proposed by Cardelli (1993); similar algorithms have also been used in proof-checkers for dependent type theories, such as NuPrl (Howe, 1988) and Lego (Pollack, 1990). The idea here is that any type annotation may be omitted by the programmer: a fresh unification variable X will be generated for each one by the parser. During typechecking, the subtype-checking algorithm may be asked to check whether some type S is a subtype T, where both S and T may contain unification variables. Subtype-checking proceeds as usual until a subgoal of the form X <: T or T <: X is encountered, at which point X is instantiated to T, thus satisfying the immediate constraint in the simplest possible way. However, setting X to T may not be the best possible choice, and this may cause later subtype-checks for types involving X to fail when a different choice would have allowed them to succeed; but, again, practical experience with this algorithm in Cardelli's implementation and in an early version of the Pict language (Pierce and Turner, 2000) shows that the algorithm's greedy choice is correct in nearly all cases. However, when it goes wrong, the greedy algorithm's behavior can be quite puzzling to the programmer, yielding mysterious errors far from the point where a suboptimal instantiation is made.

23.6.3   EXERCISE [★★★★]: The normalization property implies that the untyped term omega = (λx. x x) (λy. y y) cannot be typed in System F, since reduction of omega never reaches a normal form. However, it is possible to give a more direct, "combinatorial" proof of this fact, using just the rules defining the typing relation.

1. Let us call a System F term *exposed* if it is a variable, an abstraction λx:T.t, or an application t s (i.e., if it is *not* a type abstraction λX.t or type application t [S]).

   Show that if t is well typed (in some context) and $erase(t) = m$, then there is some exposed term s such that $erase(s) = m$ and s is well typed (possibly in a different context).

2. Write $\lambda \overline{X}.t$ as shorthand for a nested sequence of type abstractions of the form $\lambda X_1 \ldots \lambda X_n.t$. Similarly, write $t\ [\overline{A}]$ for a nested sequence of type applications $((t\ [A_1]) \ldots [A_{n-1}])\ [A_n]$ and $\forall \overline{X}.T$ for a nested sequence of polymorphic types $\forall X_1 \ldots \forall X_n.T$. Note that these sequences are allowed to be empty. For example, if $\overline{X}$ is the empty sequence of type variables, then $\forall \overline{X}.T$ is just T.

   Show that if $erase(t) = m$ and $\Gamma \vdash t : T$, then there exists some s of the form $\lambda \overline{X}.\ (u\ [\overline{A}])$, for some sequence of type variables $\overline{X}$, some sequence of types $\overline{A}$, and some exposed term u, with $erase(s) = m$ and $\Gamma \vdash s : T$.

3. Show that if t is an exposed term of type T (under Γ) and $erase(t) = m\ n$, then t has the form s u for some terms s and u such that $erase(s) = m$ and $erase(u) = n$, with $\Gamma \vdash s : U {\rightarrow} T$ and $\Gamma \vdash u : U$.

4. Suppose $x{:}T \in \Gamma$. Show that if $\Gamma \vdash u : U$ and $erase(u) = x\ x$, then either

   (a) $T = \forall \overline{X}.X_i$, where $X_i \in \overline{X}$, or else

   (b) $T = \forall \overline{X}_1 \overline{X}_2.T_1 {\rightarrow} T_2$, where $[\overline{X}_1 \overline{X}_2 \mapsto \overline{A}]T_1 = [\overline{X}_1 \mapsto \overline{B}](\forall \overline{Z}.T_1 {\rightarrow} T_2)$ for some sequences of types $\overline{A}$ and $\overline{B}$ with $|\overline{A}| = |\overline{X}_1 \overline{X}_2|$ and $|\overline{B}| = |\overline{X}_1|$.

5. Show that if *erase*(s) = λx.m and $\Gamma \vdash$ s : S, then S has the form $\forall \overline{X}.S_1 \rightarrow S_2$, for some $\overline{X}$, S_1, and S_2.

6. Define the *leftmost leaf* of a type T as follows:

leftmost-leaf(X)	=	X
leftmost-leaf(S$\rightarrow$T)	=	*leftmost-leaf*(S)
leftmost-leaf($\forall$X.S)	=	*leftmost-leaf*(S).

   Show that if $[\overline{X}_1\overline{X}_2 \mapsto \overline{A}](\forall\overline{Y}.T_1) = [\overline{X}_1 \mapsto \overline{B}](\forall\overline{Z}.(\forall\overline{Y}.T_1)\rightarrow T_2)$, then it must be the case that *leftmost-leaf*(T$_1$) = X$_i$ for some $X_i \in \overline{X}_1\overline{X}_2$.

7. Show that omega is not typable in System F. □

23.7 Erasure and Evaluation Order

The operational semantics given to System F in Figure 23-1 is a *type-passing semantics:* when a polymorphic function meets a type argument, the type is actually substituted into the body of the function. The ML implementation of System F in Chapter 25 does exactly this.

In a more realistic interpreter or compiler for a programming language based on System F, this manipulation of types at run time could impose a significant cost. Moreover, it is easy to see that type annotations play no significant role at run time, in the sense that no run-time decisions are made on the basis of types: we can take a well-typed program, rewrite its type annotations in an arbitrary way, and obtain a program that behaves just the same. For these reasons, many polymorphic languages instead adopt a *type-erasure semantics,* where, after the typechecking phase, all the types are erased and the resulting *un*typed terms are interpreted or compiled to machine code.[3]

However, in a full-blown programming language, which may include side-effecting features such as mutable reference cells or exceptions, the type-erasure function needs to be defined a little more delicately than the full erasure function in §23.6. For example, if we extend System F with an exception-raising primitive error (§14.1), then the term

```
let f = (λX.error) in 0;
```

─────────

3. In some languages, the presence of features like *casts* (§15.5) forces a type-passing implementation. High-performance implementations of these languages typically attempt to maintain only a vestigial form of type information at run time, e.g., passing types only to polymorphic functions where they may actually be used.

evaluates to 0 because λX.error is a syntactic value and the error in its body is never evaluated, while its erasure

```
let f = error in 0;
```

raises an exception when evaluated.[4] What this shows is that type abstractions *do* play a significant semantic role, since they stop evaluation under a call-by-value evaluation strategy and hence can postpone or prevent the evaluation of side-effecting primitives.

We can repair this discrepancy by introducing a new form of erasure appropriate for call-by-value evaluation, in which we erase a type abstraction to a *term*-abstraction

$$
\begin{array}{lcl}
erase_v(\text{x}) & = & \text{x} \\
erase_v(\lambda \text{x} : \text{T}_1.\ \text{t}_2) & = & \lambda \text{x}.\ erase_v(\text{t}_2) \\
erase_v(\text{t}_1\ \text{t}_2) & = & erase_v(\text{t}_1)\ erase_v(\text{t}_2) \\
erase_v(\lambda \text{X}.\ \text{t}_2) & = & \lambda\_.\ erase_v(\text{t}_2) \\
erase_v(\text{t}_1\ [\text{T}_2]) & = & erase_v(\text{t}_1)\ \text{dummyv}
\end{array}
$$

where dummyv is some arbitrary untyped value, such as unit.[5] The appropriateness of this new erasure function is expressed by the observation that it "commutes" with untyped evaluation, in the sense that erasure and evaluation can be performed in either order:

23.7.2   THEOREM: If $erase_v(\text{t}) = \text{u}$, then either (1) both t and u are normal forms according to their respective evaluation relations, or (2) $\text{t} \longrightarrow \text{t}'$ and $\text{u} \longrightarrow \text{u}'$, with $erase_v(\text{t}') = \text{u}'$.   □

23.8   Fragments of System F

The elegance and power of System F have earned it a central role in theoretical studies of polymorphism. For language design, however, the loss of type

---

4. This is related to the problem we saw with the unsound combination of references and ML-style let-polymorphism in §22.7. The *generalization* of the let-body in that example corresponds to the explicit type abstraction here.

23.7.1   EXERCISE [★★]: Translate the unsound example on page 335 into System F extended with references (Figure 13-1).   □

5. In contrast, the *value restriction* that we imposed in order to recover soundness of ML-style type reconstruction in the presence of side effects in §22.7 does erase type-abstractions—generalizing a type variable is essentially the opposite of erasing a type abstraction—but ensures soundness by permitting such generalizations only when the inferred type abstraction would occur immediately adjacent to a term abstraction or other syntactic value-constructor, since these also stop evaluation.

reconstruction is sometimes considered to be too heavy a price to pay for a feature whose full power is seldom used. This has led to various proposals for restricted fragments of System F with more tractable reconstruction problems.

The most popular of these is the let-polymorphism of ML (§22.7), which is sometimes called *prenex polymorphism* because it can be viewed as a fragment of System F in which type variables range only over quantifier-free types (*monotypes*) and in which quantified types (*polytypes,* or *type schemes*) are not allowed to appear on the left-hand sides of arrows. The special role of let in ML makes the correspondence slightly tricky to state precisely; see Jim (1995) for details.

Another well-studied restriction of System F is *rank-2 polymorphism,* introduced by Leivant (1983) and further investigated by many others (see Jim, 1995, 1996). A type is said to be of rank 2 if no path from its root to a ∀ quantifier passes to the left of 2 or more arrows, when the type is drawn as a tree. For example, (∀X.X→X)→Nat is of rank 2, as are Nat→Nat and Nat→(∀X.X→X)→Nat→Nat, but ((∀X.X→X)→Nat)→Nat is not. In the rank-2 system, all types are restricted to be of rank 2. This system is slightly more powerful than the prenex (ML) fragment, in the sense that it can assign types to more untyped lambda-terms.

Kfoury and Tiuryn (1990) proved that the complexity of type reconstruction for the rank-2 fragment of System F is identical to that of ML (i.e., DExptime-complete). Kfoury and Wells (1999) gave the first correct type reconstruction algorithm for the rank 2 system and showed that type reconstruction for ranks 3 and higher of System F is undecidable.

The rank-2 restriction can be applied to other powerful type constructors besides quantifiers. For example, *intersection types* (see §15.7) can be restricted to rank 2 by excluding types in which an intersection appears to the left of 2 or more arrows (Kfoury, Mairson, Turbak, and Wells, 1999). The rank-2 fragments of System F and of the first-order intersection type system are closely related. Indeed, Jim (1995) showed that they can type exactly the same untyped terms.

23.9 Parametricity

Recall from §23.4 how we defined the type CBool of Church booleans

    CBool = ∀X.X→X→X;

and the constants tru and fls:

    tru = λX. λt:X. λf:X. t;

▸ `tru : CBool`

   `fls = λX. λt:X. λf:X. f;`

▸ `fls : CBool`

Given the type `CBool`, we can actually write the definitions of `tru` and `fls` rather mechanically, simply by looking at the structure of the type. Since `CBool` begins with a ∀, any value of type `CBool` must be a type abstraction, so `tru` and `fls` must both begin with a λX. Then, since the body of `CBool` is an arrow type X→X→X, every value of this type must take two arguments of type X—i.e., the bodies of `tru` and `fls` must each begin λt:X.λf:X. Finally, since the result type of `CBool` is X, any value of type `CBool` must return an element of type X. But since X is a parameter, the only values of this type that we can possibly return are the bound variables t and f—we have no other way of obtaining or constructing values of this type ourselves. In other words, `tru` and `fls` are essentially the *only* inhabitants of the type `CBool`. Strictly speaking, `CBool` contains some other terms like (λb:CBool.b) `tru`, but it is intuitively clear that every one of them must behave like either `tru` or `fls`.

This observation is a simple consequence of a powerful principle known as *parametricity,* which formalizes the uniform behavior of polymorphic programs. Parametricity was introduced by Reynolds (1974, 1983) and has been further explored, along with related notions, by Reynolds (1984, Reynolds and Plotkin, 1993), Bainbridge et al. (1990), Ma (1992), Mitchell (1986), Mitchell and Meyer (1985), Hasegawa (1991), Pitts (1987, 1989, 2000), Abadi, Cardelli, Curien, and Plotkin (Abadi, Cardelli, and Curien, 1993; Plotkin and Abadi, 1993; Plotkin, Abadi, and Cardelli, 1994), Wadler (1989, 2001), and others. See Wadler (1989) for an expository introduction.

23.10   Impredicativity

The polymorphism of System F is often called *impredicative.* In general, a definition (of a set, a type, etc.) is called "impredicative" if it involves a quantifier whose domain includes the very thing being defined. For example, in System F, the type variable X in the type T = ∀X.X→X ranges over all types, including T itself (so that, for example, we can instantiate a term of type T at type T, yielding a function from T to T). The polymorphism found in ML, on the other hand, is often called *predicative* (or *stratified*), because the range of type variables is restricted to monotypes, which do not contain quantifiers.

The terms "predicative" and "impredicative" originate in logic. Quine (1987) offers a lucid summary of their history:

In exchanges with Henri Poincaré... Russell attributed [Russell's] paradox tentatively to what he called a vicious-circle fallacy. The "fallacy" consisted in specifying a class by a membership condition that makes reference directly or indirectly to a range of classes one of which is the very class that is being specified. For instance the membership condition behind Russell's Paradox is non-self-membership: x not a member of x. The paradox comes of letting the x of the membership condition be, among other things, the very class that is being defined by the membership condition. Russell and Poincaré came to call such a membership condition *impredicative,* and disqualified it as a means of specifying a class. The paradoxes of set theory, Russell's and others, were thus dismantled...

Speaking of terminology, whence "predicative" and "impredicative"? Our tattered platitude about classes and membership conditions was, in Russell's phrase, that every predicate determines a class; and then he accommodates the tattering of the platitude by withdrawing the title of predicate from such membership conditions as were no longer to be seen as determining classes. "Predicative" thus did not connote the hierarchical approach in particular, or the metaphor of progressive construction; that was just Russell and Poincaré's particular proposal of what membership conditions to accept as class-productive, or "predicative." But the tail soon came to wag the dog. Today predicative set theory is constructive set theory, and impredicative definition is strictly as explained in the foregoing paragraph, regardless of what membership conditions one may choose to regard as determining classes.

23.11 Notes

Further reading on System F can be found in Reynolds's introductory article (1990) and his *Theories of Programming Languages* (1998b).

24 *Existential Types*

Having examined the role of universal quantifiers in type systems (Chapter 23), it is natural to wonder whether *existential* quantifiers might also be useful in programming. Indeed they are, offering an elegant foundation for data abstraction and information hiding.

24.1 Motivation

Existential types are fundamentally no more complicated than universal types (in fact, we will see in §24.3 that existentials can straightforwardly be encoded in terms of universals). However, the introduction and elimination forms for existential types are syntactically a bit heavier than the simple type abstraction and application associated with universals, and some people find them slightly puzzling initially. The following intuitions may be helpful in getting through this phase.

The universal types in Chapter 23 can be viewed in two different ways. A *logical intuition* is that an element of the type $\forall X.T$ is a value that has type $[X \mapsto S]T$ for all choices of S. This intuition corresponds to a type-erasure view of behavior: for example, the polymorphic identity function $\lambda X.\lambda x:X.x$ erases to the untyped identity function $\lambda x.x$, which maps an argument from any type S to a result of the same type. By contrast, a more *operational intuition* is that an element of $\forall X.T$ is a function mapping a type S to a specialized term with type $[X \mapsto S]T$. This intuition corresponds to our definition of System F in Chapter 23, where the reduction of a type application is considered an actual step of computation.

Similarly, there are two different ways of looking at an existential type, written $\{\exists X,T\}$. The *logical intuition* is that an element of $\{\exists X,T\}$ is a value

---

The system studied in most of this chapter is System F (Figure 23-1) with existentials (24-1). The examples also use records (11-7) and numbers (8-2). The associated OCaml implementation is `fullpoly`.

of type $[X \mapsto S]T$, for *some* type S. The *operational intuition,* on the other hand, is that an element of $\{\exists X,T\}$ is a *pair,* written $\{*S,t\}$, of a type S and a term t of type $[X \mapsto S]T$.

We will emphasize the operational view of existential types in this chapter, because it provides a closer analogy between existentials and the modules and abstract data types found in programming languages. Our concrete syntax for existential types reflects this analogy: we write $\{\exists X,T\}$—the curly braces emphasizing that an existential value is a form of tuple—instead of the more standard notation $\exists X.T$.

To understand existential types, we need to know two things: how to *build* (or *introduce,* in the jargon of §9.4) elements that inhabit them, and how to *use* (or *eliminate*) these values in computations.

An existentially typed value is introduced by pairing a type with a term, written $\{*S,t\}$.[1] A useful concrete intuition is to think of a value $\{*S,t\}$ of type $\{\exists X,T\}$ as a simple form of *package* or *module* with one (hidden) type component and one term component.[2] The type S is often called the *hidden representation type,* or sometimes (to emphasize a connection with logic, cf. §9.4) the *witness type* of the package. For example, the package p = $\{*Nat, \{a=5, f=\lambda x:Nat. succ(x)\}\}$ has the existential type $\{\exists X, \{a:X, f:X\rightarrow X\}\}$. The type component of p is Nat, and the value component is a record containing a field a of type X and a field f of type $X\rightarrow X$, for some X (namely Nat).

The same package p *also* has the type $\{\exists X, \{a:X, f:X\rightarrow Nat\}\}$, since its right-hand component is a record with fields a and f of type X and $X\rightarrow Nat$, for some X (namely Nat). This example shows that, in general, the typechecker cannot make an automatic decision about which existential type a given package belongs to: the programmer must specify which one is intended. The simplest way to do this is just to add an annotation to every package that explicitly gives its intended type. So the full introduction form for existentials will look like this,

> p = $\{*Nat, \{a=5, f=\lambda x:Nat. succ(x)\}\}$ as $\{\exists X, \{a:X, f:X\rightarrow X\}\}$;

> ▸ p : $\{\exists X, \{a:X,f:X\rightarrow X\}\}$

---

1. We mark the type component of the pair with a * to avoid confusion with ordinary term-tuples (§11.7). Another common notation for existential introduction is pack X=S with t.
2. Obviously, one could imagine generalizing these modules to many type and/or term components, but let's stick with just one of each to keep the notation tractable. The effect of multiple type components can be achieved by nesting single-type existentials, while the effect of multiple term components can be achieved by using a tuple or record as the right-hand component:

$$\{*S_1, *S_2, t_1, t_2\} \overset{\text{def}}{=} \{*S_1, \{*S_2, \{t_1, t_2\}\}\}$$

or (the same package with a different type):

```
p1 = {*Nat, {a=5, f=λx:Nat. succ(x)}} as {∃X, {a:X, f:X→Nat}};
```

▸ `p1 : {∃X, {a:X,f:X→Nat}}`

The type annotation introduced by `as` is similar to the ascription construct introduced in §11.4, which allows *any* term to be annotated with its intended type. We are essentially incorporating a single ascription as part of the concrete syntax of the package construct. The typing rule for existential introduction is as follows:

$$\frac{\Gamma \vdash t_2 : [X \mapsto U]T_2}{\Gamma \vdash \{*U,t_2\} \text{ as } \{\exists X,T_2\} : \{\exists X,T_2\}} \qquad \text{(T-PACK)}$$

One thing to notice about this rule is that packages with *different* hidden representation types can inhabit the *same* existential type. For example:

```
p2 = {*Nat, 0} as {∃X,X};
```

▸ `p2 : {∃X, X}`

```
p3 = {*Bool, true} as {∃X,X};
```

▸ `p3 : {∃X, X}`

Or, more usefully:

```
p4 = {*Nat, {a=0, f=λx:Nat. succ(x)}} as {∃X, {a:X, f:X→Nat}};
```

▸ `p4 : {∃X, {a:X,f:X→Nat}}`

```
p5 = {*Bool, {a=true, f=λx:Bool. 0}} as {∃X, {a:X, f:X→Nat}};
```

▸ `p5 : {∃X, {a:X,f:X→Nat}}`

24.1.1 EXERCISE [⋆]: Here are three more variations on the same theme:

```
p6 = {*Nat, {a=0, f=λx:Nat. succ(x)}} as {∃X, {a:X, f:X→X}};
```

▸ `p6 : {∃X, {a:X,f:X→X}}`

```
p7 = {*Nat, {a=0, f=λx:Nat. succ(x)}} as {∃X, {a:X, f:Nat→X}};
```

▸ `p7 : {∃X, {a:X,f:Nat→X}}`

```
p8 = {*Nat, {a=0, f=λx:Nat. succ(x)}} as {∃X, {a:Nat, f:Nat→Nat}};
```

▸ `p8 : {∃X, {a:Nat,f:Nat→Nat}}`

In what ways are these less useful than p4 and p5? □

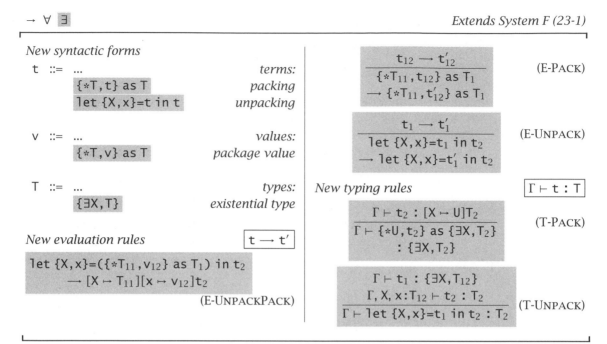

Figure 24-1: Existential types

The analogy with modules also offers a helpful intuition for the existential elimination construct. If an existential package corresponds to a module, then package elimination is like an open or import directive: it allows the components of the module to be used in some other part of the program, but holds abstract the identity of the module's type component. This can be achieved with a kind of pattern-matching binding:

$$\frac{\Gamma \vdash t_1 : \{\exists X, T_{12}\} \qquad \Gamma, X, x{:}T_{12} \vdash t_2 : T_2}{\Gamma \vdash \text{let } \{X, x\} = t_1 \text{ in } t_2 : T_2} \qquad \text{(T-Unpack)}$$

That is, if t_1 is an expression that yields an existential package, then we can bind its type and term components to the pattern variables X and x and use them in computing t_2. (Another common concrete syntax for existential elimination is open t_1 as $\{X, x\}$ in t_2.)

For example, take the package p4, of type $\{\exists X, \{a{:}X, f{:}X{\to}Nat\}\}$, defined above. The elimination expression

```
let {X,x}=p4 in (x.f x.a);
```

▸ 1 : Nat

opens p4 and uses the fields of its body (x.f and x.a) to compute a numeric result. The body of the elimination form can also involve the type variable X:

```
let {X,x}=p4 in (λy:X. x.f y) x.a;
```
▶ 1 : Nat

The fact that the package's representation type is held abstract during the typechecking of the body means that the only operations allowed on x are those warranted by its "abstract type" {a:X,f:X→Nat}. In particular, we are not allowed to use x.a concretely as a number:

```
let {X,x}=p4 in succ(x.a);
```
▶ Error: argument of succ is not a number

This restriction makes good sense, since we saw above that a package with the same existential type as p4 might use either Nat or Bool (or anything else) as its representation type.

There is another, more subtle, way in which typechecking of the existential elimination construct may fail. In the rule T-UNPACK, the type variable X appears in the context in which t_2's type is calculated, but does *not* appear in the context of the rule's conclusion. This means that the result type T_2 cannot contain X free, since any free occurrences of X will be out of scope in the conclusion.

```
let {X,x}=p in x.a;
```
▶ Error: Scoping error!

This point is discussed in more detail in §25.5.

The computation rule for existentials is straightforward:

$$\text{let } \{X,x\}=(\{*T_{11},v_{12}\} \text{ as } T_1) \text{ in } t_2 \qquad \text{(E-UNPACKPACK)}$$
$$\longrightarrow [X \mapsto T_{11}][x \mapsto v_{12}]t_2$$

If the first subexpression of the let has already been reduced to a concrete package, then we may substitute the components of this package for the variables X and x in the body t_2. In terms of the analogy with modules, this rule can be viewed as a *linking* step, in which symbolic names (X and x) referring to the components of a separately compiled module are replaced by the actual contents of the module.

Since the type variable X is substituted away by this rule, the resulting program actually has concrete access to the package's internals. This is just another example of a phenomenon we have seen several times: expressions can become "more typed" as computation proceeds—in particular an ill-typed expression can reduce to a well-typed one.

The rules defining the extension of System F with existential types are summarized in Figure 24-1.

24.2   Data Abstraction with Existentials

The introductory chapter (§1.2) argued that the uses of type systems go far beyond their role in detecting small-scale programming errors like 2+true: they also offer crucial support for programming in the large. In particular, types can be used to enforce not only the abstractions built into the language, but also *programmer-defined abstractions*—i.e., not only protecting the machine from the program, but protecting parts of the program from each other.[3]   This section considers two different styles of abstraction—classical *abstract data types,* and *objects*—using existential types as a common framework for discussion.

Unlike the object encodings that we have already encountered in Chapter 18, all the examples in this section are *purely functional* programs. This is purely an expository choice: mechanisms for modularity and abstraction are almost completely orthogonal to the statefulness or statelessness of the abstractions being defined. (Exercises 24.2.2 and 24.2.4 illustrate this point by developing stateful versions of some of the purely functional examples in the text.) The reasons for preferring purely functional examples here are that (1) this choice implies that our examples live in a simpler and more economical formal framework, and (2) working with purely functional programs sometimes makes the typing problems more interesting (and their solutions correspondingly more revealing). The reason for this is that, in imperative programming, mutable variables provide a "side-channel" allowing direct communication between distant parts of a program. In purely functional programs, all information that passes between different parts of the program must go via the arguments and results of functions, where it is "visible" to the type system. This is particularly true in the case of objects, and it will force us to postpone treatment of some important features (subtyping and inheritance) until Chapter 32, where we will have some more powerful type-theoretic machinery at our disposal.

Abstract Data Types

A conventional *abstract data type* (or *ADT*) consists of (1) a type name A, (2) a concrete representation type T, (3) implementations of some operations for creating, querying, and manipulating values of type T, and (4) an *abstraction boundary* enclosing the representation and operations. Inside this bound-

---

3. For the sake of fairness, we should note that types are not the only way of protecting programmer-defined abstractions. In untyped languages, similar effects can be achieved using function closures, objects, or special-purpose constructs such as MzScheme's *units* (Flatt and Felleisen, 1998).

ary, elements of the type are viewed concretely (with type T). Outside, they
are viewed abstractly, with type A. Values of type A may be passed around,
stored in data structures, etc., but not directly examined or changed—the
only operations allowed on A are those provided by the ADT.

For example, here is a declaration of an abstract data type of purely functional counters, in a pseudocode notation similar to Ada (U.S. Dept. of Defense, 1980) or Clu (Liskov et al., 1981).

```
ADT counter =
  type Counter
  representation Nat
  signature
      new : Counter,
      get : Counter→Nat,
      inc : Counter→Counter;
  operations
      new = 1,
      get = λi:Nat. i,
      inc = λi:Nat. succ(i);

  counter.get (counter.inc counter.new);
```

The abstract type name is Counter; its concrete representation is Nat. The
implementations of the operations deal with Counter objects concretely, as
Nats: new is just the constant 1; the inc operation is the successor function;
get is the identity. The signature section specifies how these operations are
to be used externally, replacing some instances of Nat in their concrete types
by Counter. The abstraction boundary extends from the ADT keyword to the
terminating semicolon; in the remainder of the program (i.e., the last line),
the association between Counter and Nat is broken, so that the only thing
that can be done with the constant counter.new is to use it as an argument
to counter.get or counter.inc.

We can translate this pseudocode almost symbol for symbol into our calculus with existentials. We first create an existential package containing the
internals of the ADT:

```
counterADT =
    {*Nat,
     {new = 1,
      get = λi:Nat. i,
      inc = λi:Nat. succ(i)}}
  as {∃Counter,
      {new: Counter,
       get: Counter→Nat,
       inc: Counter→Counter}};
```

```
▶ counterADT : {∃Counter,
                {new:Counter,get:Counter→Nat,inc:Counter→Counter}}
```

We then open the package, introducing the type variable `Counter` as a place-holder for the hidden representation type of the package and a term variable `counter` providing access to the operations:

```
let {Counter,counter} = counterADT in
counter.get (counter.inc counter.new);
```

```
▶ 2 : Nat
```

The version using existential types is slightly harder on the eye, compared to the syntactically sugared pseudocode, but the two are identical in structure.

In general, the body of the `let` that opens the existential package contains the whole remainder of the program:

```
let {Counter,counter} = <counter package> in
<rest of program>
```

In the remainder, the type name `Counter` can be used just like the base types built into the language. We can define functions that operate on counters:

```
let {Counter,counter}=counterADT in
let add3 = λc:Counter. counter.inc (counter.inc (counter.inc c)) in
counter.get (add3 counter.new);
```

```
▶ 4 : Nat
```

We can even define new abstract data types whose representation involves counters. For example, the following program defines an ADT of flip-flops, using a counter as its (not particularly efficient) representation type:

```
let {Counter,counter} = counterADT in

let {FlipFlop,flipflop} =
    {*Counter,
     {new    = counter.new,
      read   = λc:Counter. iseven (counter.get c),
      toggle = λc:Counter. counter.inc c,
      reset  = λc:Counter. counter.new}}
   as {∃FlipFlop,
       {new:    FlipFlop, read: FlipFlop→Bool,
        toggle: FlipFlop→FlipFlop, reset: FlipFlop→FlipFlop}} in

flipflop.read (flipflop.toggle (flipflop.toggle flipflop.new));
```

```
▶ false : Bool
```

In this way, a large program can be broken up into a long sequence of ATD declarations, each using the types and operations provided by its predecessors to implement its own, and packaging these up for its successors as a clean, well-defined abstraction.

A key property of the kind of information hiding we are doing here is *representation independence*. We can substitute an alternative implementation of the Counter ADT—for example, one where the internal representation is a record containing a Nat rather than just a single Nat,

```
counterADT =
  {*{x:Nat},
    {new = {x=1},
     get = λi:{x:Nat}. i.x,
     inc = λi:{x:Nat}. {x=succ(i.x)}}}
  as {∃Counter,
      {new: Counter, get: Counter→Nat, inc: Counter→Counter}};

▸ counterADT : {∃Counter,
                {new:Counter,get:Counter→Nat,inc:Counter→Counter}}
```

in complete confidence that the whole program will remain typesafe, since we are guaranteed that the rest of the program cannot access instances of Counter except using get and inc.

Experience has shown that a programming style based on abstract data types can yield huge improvements in robustness and maintainability of large systems. There are several reasons for this. First, this style limits the scope of changes to the program. As we saw just above, we can replace one implementation of an ADT by another, possibly changing both its concrete representation type and the implementations of its operations, without affecting the rest of the program, because the typing rules for existential packages ensure that the rest of the program cannot depend on the ADT's internal representation. Second, it encourages programmers to limit the dependencies between the parts of a program by making the signatures of ADTs as small as possible. Finally, and perhaps most importantly, by making the signatures of the operations explicit, it forces programmers to think about *designing abstractions*.

24.2.1 EXERCISE [RECOMMENDED, ★★★]: Follow the model of the above example to define an abstract data type of *stacks* of numbers, with operations new, push, top (returning the current top element), pop (returning a new stack without the top element), and isempty. Use the List type introduced in Exercise 23.4.3 as the underlying representation. Write a simple main program that creates a stack, pushes a couple of numbers onto it, and gets its top element. This exercise is best done on-line. Use the `fullomega` checker and copy the contents of the file `test.f` (which contains definitions of the `List` constructor and associated operations) to the top of your own input file.   □

24.2.2   EXERCISE [RECOMMENDED, ⋆⋆]: Build an ADT of *mutable* counters, using the reference cells defined in Chapter 13. Change `new` from a constant to a function taking a `Unit` argument and returning a `Counter`, and change the result type of the `inc` operation to `Unit` instead of `Counter`. (The `fullomega` checker provides references in addition to existentials.)   □

Existential Objects

The "pack and then open" idiom that we saw in the last subsection is the hallmark of ADT-style programming using existential packages. A package defines an abstract type and its associated operations, and we open each package immediately after it is built, binding a type variable for the abstract type and exposing the ADT's operations abstractly. In this section, we show how a simple form of *object*-style data abstraction can also be viewed as a different programming idiom based on existentials. This object model is developed further in Chapter 32.

We will again use simple counters as our running example, as we did both in the existential ADTs above and in our earlier encounters with objects in Chapters 18 and 19. We again choose a purely functional style, where sending the message `inc` to a counter does not change its internal state in-place, but rather returns a *fresh* counter object with incremented internal state.

A counter object comprises two basic components: a number (its internal state), and a pair of methods, `get` and `inc`, that can be used to manipulate the state. We also need to ensure that the only way that the state can be queried or updated is by using one of these two methods. This can be accomplished by wrapping the state and methods in an existential package, abstracting the type of the state. For example, a counter object holding the value 5 might be written

```
c = {*Nat,
    {state = 5,
     methods = {get = λx:Nat. x,
                inc = λx:Nat. succ(x)}}}
    as Counter;
```

where:

```
Counter = {∃X, {state:X, methods: {get:X→Nat, inc:X→X}}};
```

To use a method of a counter object, we open the existential and apply the appropriate element of its `methods` to its `state` field. For example, to get the current value of `c` we can write:

```
let {X,body} = c in body.methods.get(body.state);
```

▸ 5 : Nat

More generally, we can define a little function that "sends the `get` message" to any counter:

```
sendget = λc:Counter.
            let {X,body} = c in
            body.methods.get(body.state);
```

▸ sendget : Counter → Nat

Invoking the `inc` method of a counter object is a little more complicated. If we simply do the same as for `get`, the typechecker complains

```
let {X,body} = c in  body.methods.inc(body.state);
```

▸ Error: Scoping error!

because the type variable X appears free in the type of the body of the `let`. Indeed, what we've written doesn't make intuitive sense either, since the result of the `inc` method is a bare internal state, not an object. To satisfy both the typechecker and our informal understanding of what invoking `inc` should do, we must take this fresh internal state and repackage it as a counter object, using the same record of methods and the same internal state type as in the original object:

```
c1 = let {X,body} = c in
        {*X,
         {state = body.methods.inc(body.state),
          methods = body.methods}}
      as Counter;
```

More generally, to "send the `inc` message" to a counter, we can write:

```
sendinc = λc:Counter.
            let {X,body} = c in
              {*X,
               {state = body.methods.inc(body.state),
                methods = body.methods}}
              as Counter;
```

▸ sendinc : Counter → Counter

More complex operations on counters can be implemented in terms of these
two basic operations:

```
add3 = λc:Counter. sendinc (sendinc (sendinc c));
▸ add3 : Counter → Counter
```

24.2.3   EXERCISE [RECOMMENDED, ★★★]: Implement FlipFlop objects with Counter
objects as their internal representation type, using the FlipFlop ADT above
as a model.   □

24.2.4   EXERCISE [RECOMMENDED, ★★]: Use the fullomega checker to implement a
stateful variant of Counter objects, following Exercise 24.2.2.   □

Objects vs. ADTs

The examples in the previous section do not constitute a full-blown model
of object-oriented programming. Many of the features that we saw in Chapters 18 and 19, including subtyping, classes, inheritance, and recursion via
self and super, are missing here. We will come back to modeling these features in Chapter 32, when we have added some necessary refinements to our
type system. But there are already several interesting comparisons to be made
between these simple objects and the ADTs discussed previously.

At the coarsest level, the two programming idioms fall at opposite ends of a
spectrum: when programming with ADTs, packages are opened immediately
after they are built; on the other hand, when packages are used to model
objects they are kept closed as long as possible—until the moment when they
must be opened so that one of the methods can be applied to the internal
state.

A consequence of this difference is that "the abstract type of counters"
refers to different things in the two styles. In an ADT-style program, the
counter values manipulated by client code such as the add3 function are elements of the underlying representation type (e.g., simple numbers). In an
object-style program, each counter is a whole package—including not only
a number, but also the implementations of the get and inc methods. This
stylistic difference is reflected in the fact that, in the ADT style, the type
Counter is a bound type variable introduced by the let construct, while in
the object style Counter stands for the whole existential type

$$\{\exists X, \{state:X, methods: \{get:X \rightarrow Nat, inc:X \rightarrow X\}\}\}.$$

Thus, at run time, all the counter values generated from the counter ADT are
just bare elements of the same internal representation type, and there is a single implementation of the counter operations that works on this internal representation. By contrast, each counter object carries its own representation

type together with its own set of methods that work for this representation type.

These differences between objects and ADTs lead to contrasting pragmatic advantages. One obvious one is that, since each object chooses its own representation and carries its own operations, a single program can freely intermix many different implementations of the same object type. This is particularly convenient in the presence of subtyping and inheritance: we can define a single, general class of objects and then produce many different refinements, each with its own slightly (or completely) different representation. Since instances of these refined classes all share the same general type, they can be manipulated by the same generic code, stored together in lists, etc.

For example, a user-interface library may define a generic `Window` class, with subclasses like `TextWindow`, `ContainerWindow`, `ScrollableWindow`, `TitledWindow`, `DialogBox`, etc. Each of these subclasses will include its own particular instance variables (e.g., a `TextWindow` may use a `String` instance variable to represent its current contents, whereas a `ContainerWindow` might use a list of `Window` objects), and provide specialized implementations of operations like `repaint` and `handleMouseEvent`. Defining `Window` as an ADT, on the other hand, leads to a less flexible structure. The concrete representation type of `Window` will need to include a variant type (§11.10) with one case for each specific sort of window, carrying the specialized data relevant to that type of window. Operations like `repaint` will perform a `case` on the variant and execute the appropriate specialized code. If there are many special forms of windows, this monolithic declaration of the `Window` ADT can easily grow to be quite large and unwieldy.

A second major pragmatic difference between objects and ADTs concerns the status of *binary operations*—operations that accept two or more arguments of the same abstract type. To discuss this point coherently, we need to distinguish between two kinds of binary operations:

- Some binary operations can be implemented entirely in terms of the publicly available operations on two abstract values. For example, to implement an equality operation for counters, all we need to do is ask each for its current value (using `get`) and compare the two numbers that we get back—i.e., the `equal` operation can just as well live outside the abstraction boundary that protects the concrete representation of counters. We call such operations *weak binary operations*.

- Other binary operations cannot be implemented without concrete, privileged access to the representations of both abstract values. For example, suppose we are implementing an abstraction representing sets of numbers. After scouring several algorithms textbooks, we choose a concrete representation of sets as labeled trees obeying some particular complex invariant. An efficient implementation of the union operation on two sets will need to view both of them concretely, as trees. However, we do *not* want to expose this concrete representation anywhere in the public interface to our set abstraction. So we will need to arrange for union to have privileged access to both of its arguments that is not available to ordinary client code—i.e., the union operation must live inside the abstraction boundary. We call such operations *strong binary operations.*

Weak binary operations are an easy case for both of the styles of abstraction we are considering, since it does not make much difference whether we place them inside or outside of the abstraction boundary. If we choose to place them outside, then they may simply be defined as free-standing functions (taking either objects or values of an ADT, as appropriate). Placing them inside an ADT is exactly the same (they will then have concrete access to the representations of their arguments, even though they don't really need it). Placing a weak binary operation inside of an object is only slightly more demanding, since the type of the object now becomes recursive:[4]

$$\texttt{EqCounter} = \{\exists \texttt{X, \{state:X, methods: \{get:X}\rightarrow\texttt{Nat, inc:X}\rightarrow\texttt{X,}}$$
$$\texttt{eq:X}\rightarrow\texttt{EqCounter}\rightarrow\texttt{Bool}\}\}\}$$

Strong binary operations, on the other hand, cannot be expressed as methods of objects in our model. We can express their *types* just as we did for weak binary methods above:

$$\texttt{NatSet} = \{\exists \texttt{X, \{state:X, methods: \{empty:X, singleton:Nat}\rightarrow\texttt{X,}}$$
$$\texttt{member:X}\rightarrow\texttt{Nat}\rightarrow\texttt{Bool,}$$
$$\texttt{union:X}\rightarrow\texttt{NatSet}\rightarrow\texttt{X}\}\}\}$$

But there is no satisfactory way to *implement* an object of this type: all we know about the second argument of the union operation is that it provides the operations of NatSet, but these do not give us any way to find out what its elements are so that we can compute the union.

24.2.5   EXERCISE [⋆]: Why can't we use the type

$$\texttt{NatSet} = \{\exists \texttt{X, \{state:X, methods: \{empty:X, singleton:Nat}\rightarrow\texttt{X,}}$$
$$\texttt{member:X}\rightarrow\texttt{Nat}\rightarrow\texttt{Bool,}$$
$$\texttt{union:X}\rightarrow\texttt{X}\rightarrow\texttt{X}\}\}\}$$

instead?   □

----

4. This sort of recursion in object types interacts with inheritance in some tricky ways. See Bruce et al. (1996).

In summary, the single representations of ADTs directly support binary operations, while the multiple representations of objects give up binary methods in return for useful flexibility. These advantages are complementary; neither style dominates the other.

One caveat should be added to this discussion. These comparisons apply to the simple, "purist" model of objects presented earlier in the chapter. The classes in mainstream object-oriented languages like C++ and Java *are* designed to allow some forms of strong binary methods, and are actually best described as a kind of compromise between the pure objects and pure ADTs that we have seen in this chapter. In these languages, the type of an object is exactly the name of the class from which it was instantiated, and this type is considered distinct from the names of other classes, even if they provide exactly the same operations (cf. §19.3). That is, a given object type in these languages has a *single* implementation given by the corresponding class declaration. Moreover, subclasses in these languages can add instance variables only to those inherited from superclasses. These constraints mean that every object belonging to type C is guaranteed to have all the instance variables defined by the (unique) declaration of class C (and possibly some more). It now makes sense for a method of such an object to take another C as an argument and concretely access its instance variables, as long as it uses only instance variables defined by C. This permits strong binary operations such as set union to be defined as methods. "Hybrid" object models of this sort have been formalized by Pierce and Turner (1993) and Katiyar et al. (1994), and elaborated in more detail by Fisher and Mitchell (Fisher and Mitchell, 1996, 1998; Fisher, 1996b,a).

24.3   Encoding Existentials

The encoding of pairs as a polymorphic type in §23.4 suggests a similar encoding for existential types in terms of universal types, using the intuition that an element of an existential type is a pair of a type and a value:

$$\{\exists X, T\} \overset{\text{def}}{=} \forall Y. \ (\forall X. \ T \rightarrow Y) \rightarrow Y.$$

That is, an existential package is thought of as a data value that, given a result type and a *continuation,* calls the continuation to yield a final result. The continuation takes two arguments—a type X and a value of type T—and uses them in computing the final result.

Given this encoding of existential types, the encoding of the packaging and unpackaging constructs is essentially forced. To encode a package

$$\{*S, t\} \text{ as } \{\exists X, T\}$$

we must use S and t to build a value of type $\forall Y. (\forall X. T \rightarrow Y) \rightarrow Y$. This type begins with a universal quantifier, the body of which is an arrow type. An element of this type should therefore begin with two abstractions:

$$\{*S,t\} \text{ as } \{\exists X,T\} \quad \overset{\text{def}}{=} \quad \lambda Y. \lambda f:(\forall X.T \rightarrow Y). \ldots$$

To complete the job, we need to return a result of type Y; clearly, the only way to do this is to apply f to some appropriate arguments. First, we supply the type S (this is a natural choice, being the only type we have lying around at the moment):

$$\{*S,t\} \text{ as } \{\exists X,T\} \quad \overset{\text{def}}{=} \quad \lambda Y. \lambda f:(\forall X.T \rightarrow Y). f [S] \ldots$$

Now, the type application f [S] has type $[X \mapsto S](T \rightarrow Y)$, i.e., $([X \mapsto S]T) \rightarrow Y$. We can thus supply t (which, by rule T-PACK, has type $[X \mapsto S]T$) as the next argument:

$$\{*S,t\} \text{ as } \{\exists X,T\} \quad \overset{\text{def}}{=} \quad \lambda Y. \lambda f:(\forall X.T \rightarrow Y). f [S] t$$

The type of the whole application f [S] t is now Y, as required.

To encode the unpacking construct let $\{X,x\}=t_1$ in t_2, we proceed similarly. First, the typing rule T-UNPACK tells us that t_1 should have some type $\{\exists X,T_{11}\}$, that t_2 should have type T_2 (under an extended context binding X and $x:T_{11}$), and that T_2 is the type we expect for the whole let...in... expression.[5] As in the Church encodings in §23.4, the intuition here is that the introduction form ($\{*S,t\}$) is encoded as an active value that "performs its own elimination." So the encoding of the elimination form here should simply take the existential package t_1 and apply it to enough arguments to yield a result of the desired type T_2:

$$\text{let } \{X,x\}=t_1 \text{ in } t_2 \quad \overset{\text{def}}{=} \quad t_1 \ldots$$

The first argument to t_1 should be the desired result type of the whole expression, i.e., T_2:

$$\text{let } \{X,x\}=t_1 \text{ in } t_2 \quad \overset{\text{def}}{=} \quad t_1 [T_2] \ldots$$

Now, the application $t_1 [T_2]$ has type $(\forall X. T_{11} \rightarrow T_2) \rightarrow T_2$. That is, if we can now supply another argument of type $(\forall X.T_{11} \rightarrow T_2)$, we will be finished. Such

---

5. Strictly speaking, the fact that the translation requires these extra bits of type information not present in the syntax of terms means that what we are translating is actually *typing derivations,* not terms. We have seen a similar situation in the definition of the *coercion semantics* for subtyping in §15.6.

an argument can be obtained by *abstracting* the body t_2 on the variables X and x:

$$\texttt{let } \{X,x\}=t_1 \texttt{ in } t_2 \quad \overset{\mathrm{def}}{=} \quad t_1 \ [T_2] \ (\lambda X. \ \lambda x{:}T_{11}. \ t_2).$$

This finishes the encoding.

24.3.1 EXERCISE [RECOMMENDED, ★★ ⇸]: Take a blank piece of paper and, without looking at the above encoding, regenerate it from scratch. □

24.3.2 EXERCISE [★★★]: What must we prove to be confident that this encoding of existentials is correct? □

24.3.3 EXERCISE [★★★★]: Can we go the other direction, encoding universal types in terms of existential types? □

24.4 Notes

The correspondence between ADTs and existential types was first developed by Mitchell and Plotkin (1988), who also noticed the connection with objects. Pierce and Turner (1994) elaborated this connection in detail—see Chapter 32 for details and further citations. The tradeoffs between objects and ADTs have been discussed by Reynolds (1975), Cook (1991), Bruce et al. (1996) and many others. In particular, Bruce et al. (1996) is an extended discussion of binary methods.

We have seen how existential types offer natural type-theoretic foundations for a simple form of abstract data types. To account for the (related, but much more powerful) *module systems* found in languages like ML, a variety of more sophisticated mechanisms have been studied. Good starting points for reading in this area are Cardelli and Leroy (1990), Leroy (1994), Harper and Lillibridge (1994), Lillibridge (1997), Harper and Stone (2000), and Crary et al. (2002).

> *Type structure is a syntactic discipline for enforcing levels of abstraction.*
> *—John Reynolds (1983)*

25 *An ML Implementation of System F*

We now extend our implementation of λ₋ from Chapter 10 to include the universal and existential types from Chapters 23 and 24. Since the rules defining this system are syntax directed (like λ₋ itself, but unlike calculi with subtyping or equi-recursive types), its OCaml realization is quite straightforward. The most interesting extension to the implementation of λ₋ is a representation for types that may include variable bindings (in quantifiers). For these, we use the technique of *de Bruijn indices* introduced in Chapter 6.

25.1 Nameless Representation of Types

We begin by extending the syntax of types with type variables and universal and existential quantifiers.

```
type ty =
    TyVar of int * int
  | TyArr of ty * ty
  | TyAll of string * ty
  | TySome of string * ty
```

The conventions here are exactly the same as for the representation of terms in §7.1. Type variables consist of two integers: the first specifies the distance to the variable's binder, while the second, as a consistency check, specifies the expected total size of the context. Quantifiers are annotated with a string name for the variable they bind, as a hint for the printing functions.

We next extend contexts to carry bindings for type variables in addition to term variables, by adding a new constructor to the `binding` type:

```
type binding =
    NameBind
  | VarBind of ty
  | TyVarBind
```

As in our earlier implementations, the NameBind binder is used only by the parsing and printing functions. The VarBind constructor carries a type, as before. The new TyVarBind constructor carries no additional data value, since (unlike term variables) type variables in this system are not annotated with any additional assumptions. In a system with bounded quantification (Chapter 26) or higher kinds (Chapter 29), we would add an appropriate annotation to each TyVarBind.

25.2   Type Shifting and Substitution

Since types now contain variables, we need to define functions for shifting and substitution of types.

25.2.1   EXERCISE [⋆]: Using the term-shifting function in Definition 6.2.1 (page 79) as a model, write down a mathematical definition of an analogous function that shifts the variables in types.   □

In §7.2, we showed shifting and substitution for terms as two separate functions, but remarked that the implementation available from the book's web site actually uses a generic "mapping" function to perform both tasks. A similar mapping function can be used to define shifting and substitution for types. Let us look, now, at these mapping functions.

The basic observation is that shifting and substitution have exactly the same behavior on all constructors except variables. If we abstract out their behavior on variables, then they become identical. For example, here is the specialized shifting function for types that we get by mechanically transcribing the solution to Exercise 25.2.1 into OCaml:

```
let typeShiftAbove d c tyT =
  let rec walk c tyT = match tyT with
      TyVar(x,n) → if x>=c then TyVar(x+d,n+d) else TyVar(x,n+d)
    | TyArr(tyT1,tyT2) → TyArr(walk c tyT1,walk c tyT2)
    | TyAll(tyX,tyT2) → TyAll(tyX,walk (c+1) tyT2)
    | TySome(tyX,tyT2) → TySome(tyX,walk (c+1) tyT2)
  in walk c tyT
```

The arguments to this function include an amount d by which free variables should be shifted, a cutoff c below which we should *not* shift (to avoid shifting variables bound by quantifiers within the type), and a type tyT to be shifted.

Now, if we abstract out the TyVar clause from typeShiftAbove into a new argument onvar and drop the argument d, which was only mentioned in the TyVar clause, we obtain a generic mapping function

```
let tymap onvar c tyT =
  let rec walk c tyT = match tyT with
    TyArr(tyT1,tyT2) → TyArr(walk c tyT1,walk c tyT2)
  | TyVar(x,n) → onvar c x n
  | TyAll(tyX,tyT2) → TyAll(tyX,walk (c+1) tyT2)
  | TySome(tyX,tyT2) → TySome(tyX,walk (c+1) tyT2)
  in walk c tyT
```

from which we can recover the shifting function by supplying the TyVar clause (as a function abstracted on c, x, and n) as a parameter:

```
let typeShiftAbove d c tyT =
  tymap
    (fun c x n → if x>=c then TyVar(x+d,n+d) else TyVar(x,n+d))
    c tyT
```

It is also convenient to define a specialized version of typeShiftAbove, to be used when the initial cut-off is 0:

```
let typeShift d tyT = typeShiftAbove d 0 tyT
```

We can also instantiate tymap to implement the operation of substituting a type tyS for the type variable numbered j in a type tyT:

```
let typeSubst tyS j tyT =
  tymap
    (fun j x n → if x=j then (typeShift j tyS) else (TyVar(x,n)))
    j tyT
```

When we use type substitution during typechecking and evaluation, we will always be substituting for the 0th (outermost) variable, and we will want to shift the result so that that variable disappears. The helper function typeSubstTop does this for us.

```
let typeSubstTop tyS tyT =
  typeShift (-1) (typeSubst (typeShift 1 tyS) 0 tyT)
```

25.3   Terms

At the level of terms, the work to be done is similar. We begin by extending the term datatype from Chapter 10 with the introduction and elimination forms for universal and existential types.

```
type term =
    TmVar of info * int * int
  | TmAbs of info * string * ty * term
```

```
| TmApp of info * term * term
| TmTAbs of info * string * term
| TmTApp of info * term * ty
| TmPack of info * ty * term * ty
| TmUnpack of info * string * string * term * term
```

The definitions of shifting and substitution for terms are similar to those in Chapter 10. However, let us write them here in terms of a common generic mapping function, as we did for types in the previous section. The mapping function looks like this:

```
let tmmap onvar ontype c t =
  let rec walk c t = match t with
    TmVar(fi,x,n) → onvar fi c x n
  | TmAbs(fi,x,tyT1,t2) → TmAbs(fi,x,ontype c tyT1,walk (c+1) t2)
  | TmApp(fi,t1,t2) → TmApp(fi,walk c t1,walk c t2)
  | TmTAbs(fi,tyX,t2) → TmTAbs(fi,tyX,walk (c+1) t2)
  | TmTApp(fi,t1,tyT2) → TmTApp(fi,walk c t1,ontype c tyT2)
  | TmPack(fi,tyT1,t2,tyT3) →
      TmPack(fi,ontype c tyT1,walk c t2,ontype c tyT3)
  | TmUnpack(fi,tyX,x,t1,t2) →
      TmUnpack(fi,tyX,x,walk c t1,walk (c+2) t2)
  in walk c t
```

Note that `tmmap` takes *four* arguments—one more than `tymap`. To see why, notice that terms may contain two different types of variables: term variables as well as type variables embedded in type annotations in terms. So during shifting, for example, there are two kinds of "leaves" where we may need to do some real work: term variables and types. The `ontype` parameter tells the term mapper what to do when processing a term constructor containing a type annotation, as in the `TmAbs` case. If we were dealing with a larger language, there would be several more such cases.

Term shifting can be defined by giving `tmmap` appropriate arguments.

```
let termShiftAbove d c t =
  tmmap
    (fun fi c x n → if x>=c then TmVar(fi,x+d,n+d)
                           else TmVar(fi,x,n+d))
    (typeShiftAbove d)
    c t

let termShift d t = termShiftAbove d 0 t
```

On term variables, we check the cutoff and construct a new variable, just as we did in `typeShiftAbove`. For types, we call the type shifting function defined in the previous section.

The function for substituting one term into another is similar.

```
let termSubst j s t =
  tmmap
    (fun fi j x n → if x=j then termShift j s else TmVar(fi,x,n))
    (fun j tyT → tyT)
    j t
```

Note that type annotations are not changed by `termSubst` (types cannot contain term variables, so a term substitution will never affect them).

We also need a function for substituting a *type* into a *term*—used, for example, in the evaluation rule for type applications:

$$(\lambda X.t_{12})\ [T_2] \longrightarrow [X \mapsto T_2]t_{12} \qquad \text{(E-TAPPTABS)}$$

This one can also be defined using the term mapper:

```
let rec tytermSubst tyS j t =
  tmmap (fun fi c x n → TmVar(fi,x,n))
        (fun j tyT → typeSubst tyS j tyT) j t
```

This time, the function that we pass to `tmmap` for dealing with term variables is the identity (it just reconstructs the original term variable); when we reach a type annotation, we perform a type-level substitution on it.

Finally, as we did for types, we define convenience functions packaging the basic substitution functions for use by `eval` and `typeof`.

```
let termSubstTop s t =
  termShift (-1) (termSubst 0 (termShift 1 s) t)
let tytermSubstTop tyS t =
  termShift (-1) (tytermSubst (typeShift 1 tyS) 0 t)
```

25.4   Evaluation

The extensions to the `eval` function are straightforward transcriptions of the evaluation rules introduced in Figures 23-1 and 24-1. The hard work is done by the substitution functions defined in the previous section.

```
let rec eval1 ctx t = match t with
    ...
  | TmTApp(fi,TmTAbs(_,x,t11),tyT2) →
      tytermSubstTop tyT2 t11
  | TmTApp(fi,t1,tyT2) →
      let t1' = eval1 ctx t1 in
      TmTApp(fi, t1', tyT2)
```

```
        | TmUnpack(fi,_,_,TmPack(_,tyT11,v12,_),t2) when isval ctx v12 →
             tytermSubstTop tyT11 (termSubstTop (termShift 1 v12) t2)
        | TmUnpack(fi,tyX,x,t1,t2) →
             let t1' = eval1 ctx t1 in
             TmUnpack(fi,tyX,x,t1',t2)
        | TmPack(fi,tyT1,t2,tyT3) →
             let t2' = eval1 ctx t2 in
             TmPack(fi,tyT1,t2',tyT3)
        ...
```

25.4.1   EXERCISE [⋆]: Why is the `termShift` needed in the first `TmUnpack` case?   □

25.5   Typing

The new clauses of the `typeof` function also follow directly from the typing
rules for type abstraction and application and for packing and opening existentials. We show the full definition of `typeof`, so that the new `TmTAbs` and
`TmTApp` clauses may be compared with the old clauses for ordinary abstraction and application.

```
        let rec typeof ctx t =
          match t with
            TmVar(fi,i,_) → getTypeFromContext fi ctx i
          | TmAbs(fi,x,tyT1,t2) →
              let ctx' = addbinding ctx x (VarBind(tyT1)) in
              let tyT2 = typeof ctx' t2 in
              TyArr(tyT1, typeShift (-1) tyT2)
          | TmApp(fi,t1,t2) →
              let tyT1 = typeof ctx t1 in
              let tyT2 = typeof ctx t2 in
              (match tyT1 with
                  TyArr(tyT11,tyT12) →
                    if (=) tyT2 tyT11 then tyT12
                    else error fi "parameter type mismatch"
                | _ → error fi "arrow type expected")
          | TmTAbs(fi,tyX,t2) →
              let ctx = addbinding ctx tyX TyVarBind in
              let tyT2 = typeof ctx t2 in
              TyAll(tyX,tyT2)
          | TmTApp(fi,t1,tyT2) →
              let tyT1 = typeof ctx t1 in
              (match tyT1 with
                  TyAll(_,tyT12) → typeSubstTop tyT2 tyT12
                | _ → error fi "universal type expected")
```

```
| TmPack(fi,tyT1,t2,tyT) →
    (match tyT with
        TySome(tyY,tyT2) →
          let tyU = typeof ctx t2 in
          let tyU' = typeSubstTop tyT1 tyT2 in
          if (=) tyU tyU' then tyT
          else error fi "doesn't match declared type"
      | _ → error fi "existential type expected")
| TmUnpack(fi,tyX,x,t1,t2) →
    let tyT1 = typeof ctx t1 in
    (match tyT1 with
        TySome(tyY,tyT11) →
          let ctx' = addbinding ctx tyX TyVarBind in
          let ctx" = addbinding ctx' x (VarBind tyT11) in
          let tyT2 = typeof ctx" t2 in
          typeShift (-2) tyT2
      | _ → error fi "existential type expected")
```

The most interesting new clause is the one for TmUnpack. It involves the following steps. (1) We check the subexpression t_1 and ensure that it has an existential type $\{\exists X.T_{11}\}$. (2) We extend the context Γ with a type-variable binding X and a term-variable binding $x:T_{11}$, and check that t_2 has some type T_2. (3) We shift the indices of free variables in T_2 *down* by two, so that it makes sense with respect to the original Γ. (4) We return the resulting type as the type of the whole let...in... expression.

Clearly, if X occurs free in T_2, then the shift in step (3) will yield a nonsensical type containing free variables with negative indices; typechecking must fail at this point. We can ensure this by redefining typeShiftAbove so that it notices when it is about to construct a type variable with a negative index and signals an error instead of returning nonsense.

```
let typeShiftAbove d c tyT =
  tymap
    (fun c x n → if x>=c then
                    if x+d<0 then err "Scoping error!"
                    else TyVar(x+d,n+d)
                  else TyVar(x,n+d))
    c tyT
```

This check will report a scoping error whenever the type that we calculate for the body t_2 of an existential elimination expression let $\{X,x\}=t_1$ in t_2 contains the bound type variable X.

```
let {X,x}=({*Nat,0} as {∃X,X}) in x;
▶ Error: Scoping error!
```

26 *Bounded Quantification*

Many of the interesting issues in programming languages arise from interactions between features that are relatively straightforward when considered individually. This chapter introduces *bounded quantification,* which arises when polymorphism and subtyping are combined, substantially increasing both the expressive power of the system and its metatheoretic complexity. The calculus we will be studying, called $F_{<:}$ ("F sub"), has played a central role in programming language research since it was developed in the mid '80s, in particular in studies on the foundations of object-oriented programming.

26.1 Motivation

The simplest way of combining subtyping and polymorphism is to take them as completely orthogonal features—i.e., to consider a system that is essentially the union of the systems from Chapters 15 and 23. This system is theoretically unproblematic, and is useful for all of the reasons that subtyping and polymorphism are individually. However, once we have both features in the same language, it is tempting to mix them in more interesting ways. To illustrate, let us consider a very simple example—we will see others in §26.3 and some larger and more pragmatic case studies in Chapters 27 and 32.

Suppose f is the identity function on records with a numeric field a:

```
f = λx:{a:Nat}. x;
```

▶ `f : {a:Nat} → {a:Nat}`

If ra is a record with an a field,

The system studied in most of this chapter is pure $F_{<:}$ (Figure 26-1). The examples also use records (11-7) and numbers (8-2). The associated OCaml implementations are fullfsub and fullfomsub. (The fullfsub checker suffices for most of the examples; fullfomsub is needed for the ones involving type abbreviations with parameters, such as Pair.)

```
ra = {a=0};
```

then we can apply f to ra—in any of the type systems that we have seen in previous chapters—yielding a record of the same type.

```
f ra;
```

▸ {a=0} : {a:Nat}

Similarly, if we define a larger record rab with two fields, a and b,

```
rab = {a=0, b=true};
```

we can also apply f to rab by using the rule of subsumption (T-SUB, Figure 15-1) to promote the type of rab to {a:Nat} to match the type expected by f.

```
f rab;
```

▸ {a=0, b=true} : {a:Nat}

However, the result type of this application has only the field a, which means that a term like (f rab).b will be judged ill typed. In other words, by passing rab through the identity function, we have lost the ability to access its b field!

Using the polymorphism of System F, we can write f in a different way:

```
fpoly = λX. λx:X. x;
```

▸ fpoly : ∀X. X → X

The application of fpoly to rab (and an appropriate type argument) yields the desired result:

```
fpoly [{a:Nat, b:Bool}] rab;
```

▸ {a=0, b=true} : {a:Nat, b:Bool}

But in making the type of x into a variable, we have given up some information that we might have wanted to use. For example, suppose we want to write a different version of f that returns a pair of its original argument and the numeric successor of its a field.

```
f2 = λx:{a:Nat}. {orig=x, asucc=succ(x.a)};
```

▸ f2 : {a:Nat} → {orig:{a:Nat}, asucc:Nat}

Again, using subtyping, we can apply f2 to both ra and rab, losing the b field in the second case.

```
f2 ra;
```

▸ {orig={a=0}, asucc=1} : {orig:{a:Nat}, asucc:Nat}

  f2 rab;

▸ {orig={a=0,b=true}, asucc=1} : {orig:{a:Nat}, asucc:Nat}

But this time polymorphism offers us no solution. If we replace the type of x by a variable X as before, we lose the constraint that x must be a record with an a field, which is required to compute the asucc field of the result.

    f2poly = λX. λx:X. {orig=x, asucc=succ(x.a)};

▸ Error: Expected record type

The fact about the operational behavior of f2 that we want to express in its type is that it takes an argument of any record type R that includes a numeric a field and returns as its result a record containing a field of type R and a field of type Nat. We can use the subtype relation to express this concisely: f2 takes an argument of any subtype R of the type {a:Nat} and returns a record containing a field of type R and a field of type Nat. This intuition can be formalized by introducing a *subtyping constraint* on the bound variable X of f2poly.

    f2poly = λX<:{a:Nat}. λx:X. {orig=x, asucc=succ(x.a)};

▸ f2poly : ∀X<:{a:Nat}. X → {orig:X, asucc:Nat}

This so-called *bounded quantification* is the characteristic feature of System $F_{<:}$.

26.2   Definitions

Formally, $F_{<:}$ is obtained by combining the types and terms of System F from Chapter 23 with the subtype relation from Chapter 15 and refining universal quantifiers to carry subtyping constraints. Bounded existential quantifiers can be defined similarly, as we shall see in §26.5.

There are actually two reasonable ways of defining the subtyping relation of $F_{<:}$, differing in their formulation of the rule for comparing bounded quantifiers (S-ALL): a more tractable but less flexible version called the *kernel* rule, and a more expressive but technically somewhat problematic *full* subtyping rule. We discuss both versions in detail in the following subsections, introducing the kernel variant in the first several subsections and then the full variant in §26-1. When we need to be precise about which variant we are talking about, we call the versions of the whole system with these rules *kernel* $F_{<:}$ and *full* $F_{<:}$, respectively. The unqualified name $F_{<:}$ refers to both systems.

Figure 26-1 presents the full definition of kernel $F_{<:}$, with differences from previous systems highlighted.

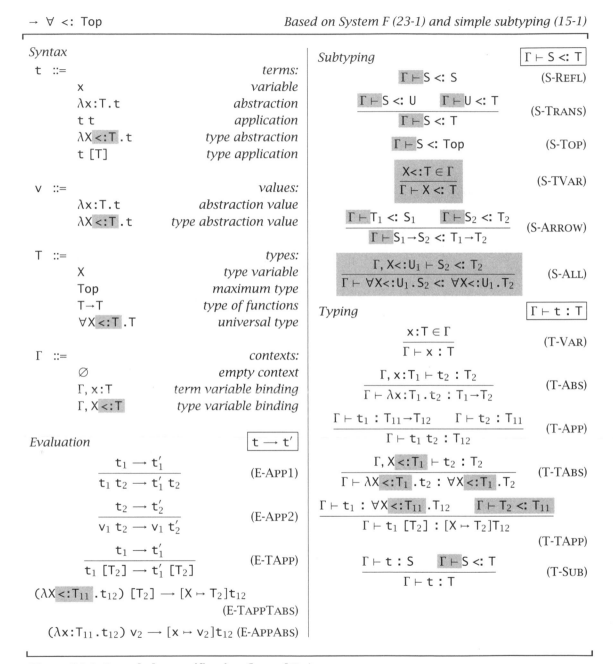

→ ∀ <: Top   *Based on System F (23-1) and simple subtyping (15-1)*

Syntax

t ::=   *terms:*
  x   *variable*
  λx:T.t   *abstraction*
  t t   *application*
  λX<:T.t   *type abstraction*
  t [T]   *type application*

v ::=   *values:*
  λx:T.t   *abstraction value*
  λX<:T.t   *type abstraction value*

T ::=   *types:*
  X   *type variable*
  Top   *maximum type*
  T→T   *type of functions*
  ∀X<:T.T   *universal type*

Γ ::=   *contexts:*
  ∅   *empty context*
  Γ, x:T   *term variable binding*
  Γ, X<:T   *type variable binding*

Evaluation $\boxed{t \longrightarrow t'}$

$$\frac{t_1 \longrightarrow t_1'}{t_1\ t_2 \longrightarrow t_1'\ t_2} \quad \text{(E-App1)}$$

$$\frac{t_2 \longrightarrow t_2'}{v_1\ t_2 \longrightarrow v_1\ t_2'} \quad \text{(E-App2)}$$

$$\frac{t_1 \longrightarrow t_1'}{t_1\ [T_2] \longrightarrow t_1'\ [T_2]} \quad \text{(E-TApp)}$$

$$(\lambda X{<:}T_{11}.t_{12})\ [T_2] \longrightarrow [X \mapsto T_2]t_{12}$$
$$\text{(E-TappTabs)}$$

$$(\lambda x{:}T_{11}.t_{12})\ v_2 \longrightarrow [x \mapsto v_2]t_{12} \quad \text{(E-AppAbs)}$$

Subtyping $\boxed{\Gamma \vdash S <: T}$

$$\Gamma \vdash S <: S \quad \text{(S-Refl)}$$

$$\frac{\Gamma \vdash S <: U \qquad \Gamma \vdash U <: T}{\Gamma \vdash S <: T} \quad \text{(S-Trans)}$$

$$\Gamma \vdash S <: \text{Top} \quad \text{(S-Top)}$$

$$\frac{X{<:}T \in \Gamma}{\Gamma \vdash X <: T} \quad \text{(S-TVar)}$$

$$\frac{\Gamma \vdash T_1 <: S_1 \qquad \Gamma \vdash S_2 <: T_2}{\Gamma \vdash S_1{\to}S_2 <: T_1{\to}T_2} \quad \text{(S-Arrow)}$$

$$\frac{\Gamma, X{<:}U_1 \vdash S_2 <: T_2}{\Gamma \vdash \forall X{<:}U_1.S_2 <: \forall X{<:}U_1.T_2} \quad \text{(S-All)}$$

Typing $\boxed{\Gamma \vdash t : T}$

$$\frac{x{:}T \in \Gamma}{\Gamma \vdash x : T} \quad \text{(T-Var)}$$

$$\frac{\Gamma, x{:}T_1 \vdash t_2 : T_2}{\Gamma \vdash \lambda x{:}T_1.t_2 : T_1{\to}T_2} \quad \text{(T-Abs)}$$

$$\frac{\Gamma \vdash t_1 : T_{11}{\to}T_{12} \qquad \Gamma \vdash t_2 : T_{11}}{\Gamma \vdash t_1\ t_2 : T_{12}} \quad \text{(T-App)}$$

$$\frac{\Gamma, X{<:}T_1 \vdash t_2 : T_2}{\Gamma \vdash \lambda X{<:}T_1.t_2 : \forall X{<:}T_1.T_2} \quad \text{(T-TAbs)}$$

$$\frac{\Gamma \vdash t_1 : \forall X{<:}T_{11}.T_{12} \qquad \Gamma \vdash T_2 <: T_{11}}{\Gamma \vdash t_1\ [T_2] : [X \mapsto T_2]T_{12}} \quad \text{(T-TApp)}$$

$$\frac{\Gamma \vdash t : S \qquad \Gamma \vdash S <: T}{\Gamma \vdash t : T} \quad \text{(T-Sub)}$$

Figure 26-1: Bounded quantification (kernel $F_{<:}$)

Bounded and Unbounded Quantification

One point that is immediately obvious from this figure is that the syntax of $F_{<:}$ provides *only* bounded quantification: the ordinary, unbounded quantification of pure System F has disappeared. The reason for this is that we do not need it: a bounded quantifier whose bound is Top ranges over all subtypes of Top—that is, over all types. So we recover unbounded quantification as an abbreviation:

$$\forall X.T \quad \overset{\text{def}}{=} \quad \forall X{<}{:}Top.T$$

We use this abbreviation frequently below.

Scoping

An important technical detail that is not obvious in Figure 26-1 concerns the scoping of type variables. Obviously, whenever we talk about a typing statement of the form $\Gamma \vdash t : T$, we intend that the free type variables in t and T should be in the domain of Γ. But what about free type variables appearing in the types *inside* Γ? In particular, which of the following contexts should be considered to be well-scoped?

$$
\begin{array}{rcl}
\Gamma_1 &=& X{<}{:}Top, y{:}X{\rightarrow}Nat \\
\Gamma_2 &=& y{:}X{\rightarrow}Nat, X{<}{:}Top \\
\Gamma_3 &=& X{<}{:}\{a{:}Nat,b{:}X\} \\
\Gamma_4 &=& X{<}{:}\{a{:}Nat,b{:}Y\}, Y{<}{:}\{c{:}Bool,d{:}X\}
\end{array}
$$

Γ_1 is certainly well-scoped: it introduces a type variable X and then a term variable y whose type involves X. A term that might give rise to this context during typechecking would have the form $\lambda X{<}{:}Top. \lambda y{:}X{\rightarrow}Nat. t$, and it is clear that the X in the type of y is bound by the enclosing λ. On the other hand, by the same reasoning Γ_2 looks wrong, since in the sort of term that would give rise to it—e.g., $\lambda y{:}X{\rightarrow}Nat. \lambda X{<}{:}Top. t$—is it not clear what the intended scope of X is.

Γ_3 is a more interesting case. We could argue that it *is* clear, in a term like $\lambda X{<}{:}\{a{:}Nat,b{:}X\}. t$, where the second X is bound. All we need to do is to regard the scope of the binding for X as including its own upper bound (and everything to the right of the binding, as usual). The variety of bounded quantification incorporating this refinement is called *F-bounded quantification* (Canning, Cook, Hill, Olthoff, and Mitchell, 1989b). F-bounded quantification often appears in discussions of types for object-oriented programming, and has been used in the GJ language design (Bracha, Odersky, Stoutamire, and Wadler, 1998). However, its theory is somewhat more complex than that of ordinary $F_{<:}$ (Ghelli, 1997; Baldan, Ghelli, and Raffaetà, 1999), and it only becomes really interesting when recursive types are also included in the system (no non-recursive type X could satisfy a constraint like X<:{a:Nat,b:X}).

Yet more general contexts like Γ_4, permitting mutual recursion between type variables via their upper bounds, are not unheard of. In such calculi, each new variable binding is generally allowed to introduce an arbitrary set of inequations involving the new variable and all the existing ones.

We will not consider F-bounded quantification further in this book, and will take all of Γ_2, Γ_3, and Γ_4 to be ill-scoped. More formally, we will require that, whenever we mention a type T in a context, the free variables of T should be bound in the portion of the context to the left of where T appears.

Subtyping

Type variables in $F_{<:}$ have associated bounds (just as ordinary term variables have associated types), and we must keep track of these bounds during both subtyping and typechecking. We do this by changing the type bindings in contexts to include an upper bound for each type variable. These bounds are used during subtyping to justify steps of the form "the type variable X is a subtype of the type T because we assumed it was."

$$\frac{X<:T \in \Gamma}{\Gamma \vdash X <: T} \tag{S-TVAR}$$

Adding this rule implies that subtyping now becomes a *three*-place relation— that is, every subtyping statement will now have the form $\Gamma \vdash S <: T$, pronounced "S is a subtype of T under assumptions Γ." We complete this refinement by adding contexts to all the other subtyping rules (see Figure 26-1).

Besides the new rule for variables, we must also add a subtyping rule for comparing quantified types (S-ALL). Figure 26-1 gives the simpler variant, called the *kernel* rule, in which the bounds of the two quantifiers being compared must be identical.

$$\frac{\Gamma, X<:U_1 \vdash S_2 <: T_2}{\Gamma \vdash \forall X<:U_1.S_2 <: \forall X<:U_1.T_2} \tag{S-ALL}$$

The term "kernel" comes from Cardelli and Wegner's original paper (1985), where this variant of $F_{<:}$ was called *Kernel Fun.*

26.2.1   EXERCISE [⋆ ↛]: Draw a subtyping derivation tree showing that B→Y <: X→B under the context Γ = B<:Top, X<:B, Y<:X.   □

Typing

We must also refine the typing rules for ordinary universal types. These extensions are straightforward: in the introduction rule for bounded quanti-

→ ∀ <: Top *full*   *Extends* F$_{<:}$ *(26-1)*

New subtyping rules $\boxed{\Gamma \vdash S <: T}$

$$\frac{\Gamma \vdash T_1 <: S_1 \qquad \Gamma, X<:T_1 \vdash S_2 <: T_2}{\Gamma \vdash \forall X<:S_1.S_2 <: \forall X<:T_1.T_2} \quad \text{(S-ALL)}$$

Figure 26-2: "Full" bounded quantification

fiers, we carry the bound from the abstraction into the context during the typechecking of the body,

$$\frac{\Gamma, X<:T \vdash t_2 : T_2}{\Gamma \vdash \lambda X<:T.t_2 : \forall X<:T.T_2} \quad \text{(T-TABS)}$$

and in the elimination rule we check that the supplied type argument actually satisfies the bound:

$$\frac{\Gamma \vdash t_1 : \forall X<:T_{11}.T_{12} \qquad \Gamma \vdash T_2 <: T_{11}}{\Gamma \vdash t_1 [T_2] : [X \mapsto T_2]T_{12}} \quad \text{(T-TAPP)}$$

Full F$_{<:}$

In kernel F$_{<:}$, two quantified types can be compared only if their upper bounds are identical. If we think of a quantifier as a sort of arrow type (whose elements are functions from types to terms), then the kernel rule corresponds to a "covariant" restriction of the standard subtyping rule for arrows, in which the domain of an arrow type is not allowed to vary in subtypes:

$$\frac{S_2 <: T_2}{U{\rightarrow}S_2 <: U{\rightarrow}T_2}$$

This restriction looks rather unnatural, both for arrows and for quantifiers. This analogy suggests that we should refine the kernel S-ALL rule to allow contravariant subtyping in the "left-hand side" of bounded quantifiers, as shown in Figure 26-2.

Intuitively, the full version of S-ALL can be understood as follows. A type $T = \forall X<:T_1.T_2$ describes a collection of functions from types to values, each mapping subtypes of T_1 to instances of T_2. If T_1 is a subtype of S_1, then the domain of T is smaller than that of $S = \forall X<:S_1.S_2$, so S is a stronger constraint and describes a smaller collection of polymorphic values. Moreover, if, for each type U that is an acceptable argument to the functions in both collections (i.e., one that satisfies the more stringent requirement $U <: T_1$), the

U-instance of S_2 is a subtype of the U-instance of T_2, then S is a "pointwise stronger" constraint and again describes a smaller collection of values.

The system with just the kernel subtyping rule for quantified types is called Kernel $F_{<:}$. The same system with the full quantifier subtyping rule is called Full $F_{<:}$. The bare name $F_{<:}$ refers ambiguously to both systems.

26.2.2   EXERCISE [★ ↛]: Give a couple of examples of pairs of types that are related by the subtype relation of full $F_{<:}$ but are not subtypes in kernel $F_{<:}$.   □

26.2.3   EXERCISE [★★★★]: Can you find any *useful* examples with this property?   □

26.3   Examples

This section presents some small examples of programming in $F_{<:}$. These examples are intended to illustrate the properties of the system, rather than to demonstrate its practical application; larger and more sophisticated examples will be found in later chapters (27 and 32). All the examples in this chapter work in both kernel and full $F_{<:}$.

Encoding Products

In §23.4, we gave an encoding of pairs of numbers in System F. This encoding can easily be generalized to pairs of arbitrary types: the elements of the type

```
Pair T₁ T₂ = ∀X. (T₁→T₂→X) → X;
```

represent pairs of T_1 and T_2. The constructor pair and the destructors fst and snd are defined as follows. (The ascription in the definition of pair helps the typechecker print its type in a readable form.)

```
pair = λX. λY. λx:X. λy:Y. (λR. λp:X→Y→R. p x y) as Pair X Y;
```

▸ pair : ∀X. ∀Y. X → Y → Pair X Y

```
fst = λX. λY. λp: Pair X Y. p [X] (λx:X. λy:Y. x);
```

▸ fst : ∀X. ∀Y. Pair X Y → X

```
snd = λX. λY. λp: Pair X Y. p [Y] (λx:X. λy:Y. y);
```

▸ snd : ∀X. ∀Y. Pair X Y → Y

Clearly, the same encoding can be used in $F_{<:}$, since $F_{<:}$ contains all the features of System F. What is more interesting, though, is that this encoding also has some natural subtyping properties. In fact, the expected subtyping rule for pairs

$$\frac{\Gamma \vdash S_1 <: T_1 \qquad \Gamma \vdash S_2 <: T_2}{\Gamma \vdash \mathtt{Pair}\ S_1\ S_2 <: \mathtt{Pair}\ T_1\ T_2}$$

follows directly from the encoding.

26.3.1 EXERCISE [⋆ ↛]: Show this. □

Encoding Records

It is interesting to observe that records and record types—including their subtyping laws—can actually be encoded in pure $F_{<:}$. The encoding presented here was discovered by Cardelli (1992).

We begin by defining *flexible tuples* as follows. They are "flexible" because they can be expanded on the right during subtyping, unlike ordinary tuples.

26.3.2 DEFINITION: For each $n \geq 0$ and types T_1 through T_n, let

$$\{T_i^{\ i \in 1..n}\} \stackrel{\text{def}}{=} \mathtt{Pair}\ T_1\ (\mathtt{Pair}\ T_2\ \ldots\ (\mathtt{Pair}\ T_n\ \mathtt{Top})\ldots).$$

In particular, $\{\} \stackrel{\text{def}}{=} \mathtt{Top}$. Similarly, for terms t_1 through t_n, let

$$\{t_i^{\ i \in 1..n}\} \stackrel{\text{def}}{=} \mathtt{pair}\ t_1\ (\mathtt{pair}\ t_2\ \ldots\ (\mathtt{pair}\ t_n\ \mathtt{top})\ldots),$$

where we elide the type arguments to `pair`, for the sake of brevity. (The term `top` here is just some arbitrary element of Top—i.e., an arbitrary closed, well-typed term.) The projection `t.n` (again eliding type arguments) is:

$$\mathtt{fst}\ (\underbrace{\mathtt{snd}\ (\mathtt{snd}\ldots\ (\mathtt{snd}}_{n-1\ \text{times}}\ \mathtt{t})\ldots)$$ □

From this abbreviation, we immediately obtain the following rules for subtyping and typing of flexible tuples.

$$\frac{\Gamma \vdash^{\ i \in 1..n} S_i <: T_i}{\Gamma \vdash \{S_i^{\ i \in 1..n+k}\} <: \{T_i^{\ i \in 1..n}\}}$$

$$\frac{\Gamma \vdash^{\ i \in 1..n} t_i : T_i}{\Gamma \vdash \{t_i^{\ i \in 1..n}\} : \{T_i^{\ i \in 1..n}\}}$$

$$\frac{\Gamma \vdash t : \{T_i^{\ i \in 1..n}\}}{\Gamma \vdash t.i : T_i}$$

Now, let $\mathcal{L}$ be a countable set of labels, with a fixed total ordering given by the bijective function *label-with-index* : $\mathbb{N} \rightarrow \mathcal{L}$. We define records as follows.

26.3.3   DEFINITION: Let L be a finite subset of $\mathcal{L}$ and let S_l be a type for each $l \in L$. Let m be the maximal index of any element of L, and

$$\hat{S}_i = \begin{cases} S_l & \text{if } label\text{-}with\text{-}index(i) = l \in L \\ \text{Top} & \text{if } label\text{-}with\text{-}index(i) \notin L. \end{cases}$$

The record type $\{l\!:\!S_l{}^{l \in L}\}$ is defined as the flexible tuple $\{\hat{S}_i{}^{i \in 1..m}\}$. Similarly, if t_l is a term for each $l : L$, then

$$\hat{t}_i = \begin{cases} t_l & \text{if } label\text{-}with\text{-}index(i) = l \in L \\ \text{top} & \text{if } label\text{-}with\text{-}index(i) \notin L. \end{cases}$$

The record value $\{l\!=\!t_l{}^{l \in L}\}$ is $\{\hat{t}_i{}^{i \in 1..m}\}$. The projection t.l is just the tuple projection t.i, where $label\text{-}with\text{-}index(i) = l$.   □

This encoding validates the expected rules for typing and subtyping of records (rules S-RCDWIDTH, S-RCDDEPTH, S-RCDPERM, T-RCD, and T-PROJ from Figures 15-2 and 15-3). However, its interest is mainly theoretical—from a practical standpoint, the reliance on a global ordering of all field labels is a serious drawback: it means that, in a language with separate compilation, numbers cannot be assigned to labels on a module-by-module basis, but must instead be assigned all at once, i.e., at link time.

Church Encodings with Subtyping

As a final illustration of the expressiveness of $F_{<:}$, let's look at what happens when we add bounded quantification to the encoding of Church numerals in System F (§23.4). There, the type of Church numerals was:

```
CNat = ∀X. (X→X) → X → X;
```

An intuitive anthropomorphic reading of this type is: "Tell me a result type T; now give me a function on T and a 'base element' of T, and I'll give you back another element of T formed by iterating the function you gave me n times over the base element you gave."

We can generalize this by adding two bounded quantifiers and refining the types of the parameters s and z.

```
SNat = ∀X<:Top. ∀S<:X. ∀Z<:X. (X→S) → Z → X;
```

Intuitively, this type reads: "Give me a generic result type X and two subtypes S and Z. Now give me a function that maps from the whole set X into the subset S and an element of the special set Z, and I'll return you an element of X formed by iterating the function n times over the base element."

To see why this is interesting, consider this slightly different type:

```
SZero = ∀X<:Top. ∀S<:X. ∀Z<:X. (X→S) → Z → Z;
```

Although SZero has almost the same form as SNat, it says something much
stronger about the behavior of its elements, since it promises that its final
result will be an element of Z, not just of X. In fact, there is just one way that
this can happen—namely by yielding the argument z itself. In other words,
the value

```
szero = λX. λS<:X. λZ<:X. λs:X→S. λz:Z. z;
```

▶ szero : SZero

is the *only* inhabitant of the type SZero (in the sense that every other element
of SZero behaves the same as szero). Since SZero is a subtype of SNat, we
also have szero : SNat.

On the other hand, the similar type

```
SPos = ∀X<:Top. ∀S<:X. ∀Z<:X. (X→S) → Z → S;
```

has more inhabitants; for example,

```
sone   = λX. λS<:X. λZ<:X. λs:X→S. λz:Z. s z;
stwo   = λX. λS<:X. λZ<:X. λs:X→S. λz:Z. s (s z);
sthree = λX. λS<:X. λZ<:X. λs:X→S. λz:Z. s (s (s z));
```

and so on. Indeed, SPos is inhabited by all the elements of SNat *except* zsero.

We can similarly refine the typings of operations defined on Church numerals. For example, the type system can be used to check that the successor
function always returns a positive number:

```
ssucc = λn:SNat.
          λX. λS<:X. λZ<:X. λs:X→S. λz:Z.
            s (n [X] [S] [Z] s z);
```

▶ ssucc : SNat → SPos

Similarly, by refining the types of its parameters, we can write the function
plus in such a way that the typechecker gives it the type SPos→SPos→SPos.

```
spluspp = λn:SPos. λm:SPos.
            λX. λS<:X. λZ<:X. λs:X→S. λz:Z.
              n [X] [S] [S] s (m [X] [S] [Z] s z);
```

▶ spluspp : SPos → SPos → SPos

26.3.4   EXERCISE [★★]: Write another variant of plus, identical to the one above except for type annotations, that has type SZero→SZero→SZero. Write one
with type SPos→SNat→SPos.   □

The previous example and exercise raise an interesting point. Clearly, we don't want to write several different versions of plus with different names and then have to decide which to apply based on the expected types of its arguments: we want to have a *single* version of plus whose type contains all these possibilities—something like

plus :   SZero→SZero→SZero
       ∧ SNat→SPos→SPos
       ∧ SPos→SNat→SPos
       ∧ SNat→SNat→SNat

where t : S∧T means "t has *both* type S *and* type T." The desire to support this kind of overloading has led to the study of systems combining *intersection types* (§15.7) with bounded quantification. See Pierce (1997b).

26.3.5   EXERCISE [RECOMMENDED, ★★]: Following the model of SNat and friends, generalize the type CBool of Church booleans (§23.4) to a type SBool and two subtypes STrue and SFalse. Write a function notft with type SFalse→STrue and a similar one nottf with type STrue→SFalse.   □

26.3.6   EXERCISE [★ ↛]: We observed in the introduction to this chapter that subtyping and polymorphism can be combined in a more straightforward and orthogonal way than is done in $F_{<:}$. We start with System F (perhaps enriched with records, etc.) and add a subtype relation (as in the simply typed lambda-calculus with subtyping) but leave quantification *un*bounded. The only extension to the subtype relation is a covariant subtyping rule for the bodies of ordinary quantifiers:

$$\frac{S <: T}{\forall X.S <: \forall X.T}$$

Which examples in this chapter can be formulated in this simpler system?   □

26.4   Safety

The type preservation property can be established quite directly for both the kernel and full variants of $F_{<:}$. We give proofs in detail here for kernel $F_{<:}$; the argument for full $F_{<:}$ is very similar. When we consider subtyping and type-checking algorithms in Chapter 28, however, the two variants will turn out to be more different than the basic arguments in this chapter might suggest. We will find many points where the full system is much more complex to analyze than the kernel system, or indeed where the full system lacks useful properties (including decidable typechecking!) enjoyed by the kernel system.

We begin with some preliminary technical facts about the typing and subtype relations. Their proofs proceed by routine induction on derivations.

26.4.1   LEMMA [PERMUTATION]: Suppose that Γ is a well-formed context and that Δ is a permutation of Γ—that is, Δ has the same bindings as Γ, and their ordering in Δ preserves the scopes of type variables from Γ, in the sense that, if one binding in Γ introduces a type variable that is mentioned in another binding further to the right, then these bindings appear in the same order in Δ.

1. If $\Gamma \vdash t : T$, then $\Delta \vdash t : T$.

2. If $\Gamma \vdash S <: T$, then $\Delta \vdash S <: T$. □

26.4.2   LEMMA [WEAKENING]:

1. If $\Gamma \vdash t : T$ and $\Gamma, x:U$ is well formed, then $\Gamma, x:U \vdash t : T$.

2. If $\Gamma \vdash t : T$ and $\Gamma, X<:U$ is well formed, then $\Gamma, X<:U \vdash t : T$.

3. If $\Gamma \vdash S <: T$ and $\Gamma, x:U$ is well formed, then $\Gamma, x:U \vdash S <: T$.

4. If $\Gamma \vdash S <: T$ and $\Gamma, X<:U$ is well formed, then $\Gamma, X<:U \vdash S <: T$. □

26.4.3   EXERCISE [⋆]: Where does the proof of weakening rely on permutation? □

26.4.4   LEMMA [STRENGTHENING FOR TERM VARIABLES IN SUBTYPING DERIVATIONS]: If $\Gamma, x:T, \Delta \vdash S <: T$, then $\Gamma, \Delta \vdash S <: T$. □

Proof: Obvious: typing assumptions play no role in subtype derivations. □

As usual, the proof of type preservation relies on several lemmas relating substitution with the typing and subtype relations.

26.4.5   LEMMA [NARROWING]:

1. If $\Gamma, X<:Q, \Delta \vdash S <: T$ and $\Gamma \vdash P <: Q$, then $\Gamma, X<:P, \Delta \vdash S <: T$.

2. If $\Gamma, X<:Q, \Delta \vdash t : T$ and $\Gamma \vdash P <: Q$, then $\Gamma, X<:P, \Delta \vdash t : T$.

These properties are often called *narrowing* because they involve restricting (narrowing) the range of the variable X. □

Proof: EXERCISE [⋆]. □

Next, we have the usual lemma relating substitution and the typing relation.

26.4.6   LEMMA [SUBSTITUTION PRESERVES TYPING]: If $\Gamma, x:Q, \Delta \vdash t : T$ and $\Gamma \vdash q : Q$, then $\Gamma, \Delta \vdash [x \mapsto q]t : T$. □

Proof: Induction on a derivation of $\Gamma, x:Q, \Delta \vdash t : T$, using the properties above.   □

Since we may substitute types for type variables during reduction, we also need a lemma relating type substitution and typing. The proof of this lemma (specifically, the T-SUB case) depends on a new lemma relating substitution and subtyping.

26.4.7   DEFINITION: We write $[X \mapsto S]\Gamma$ for the context obtained by substituting S for X in the right-hand sides of all of the bindings in Γ.   □

26.4.8   LEMMA [TYPE SUBSTITUTION PRESERVES SUBTYPING]: If $\Gamma, X<:Q, \Delta \vdash S <: T$ and $\Gamma \vdash P <: Q$, then $\Gamma, [X \mapsto P]\Delta \vdash [X \mapsto P]S <: [X \mapsto P]T$.   □

Note that we need to substitute for X only in the part of the environment that *follows* the binding of X, since our conventions about scoping require that the types to the left of the binding of X do not contain X.

Proof: By induction on a derivation of $\Gamma, X<:Q, \Delta \vdash S <: T$. The only interesting cases are the last two:

Case S-TVAR: $S = Y$ $Y<:T \in (\Gamma, X<:Q, \Delta)$

There are two subcases to consider. If $Y \neq X$, then the result is immediate from S-TVAR. On the other hand, if $Y = X$, then we have $T = Q$ and $[X \mapsto P]S = Q$, so the result follows by S-REFL.

Case S-ALL: $S = \forall Z<:U_1.S_2$ $T = \forall Z<:U_1.T_2$
                                    $\Gamma, X<:Q, \Delta, Z<:U_1 \vdash S_2 <: T_2$

By the induction hypothesis, $\Gamma, [X \mapsto P]\Delta, Z<:[X \mapsto P]U_1 \vdash [X \mapsto P]S_2 <: [X \mapsto P]T_2$. By S-ALL, $\Gamma, [X \mapsto P]\Delta \vdash \forall Z<:[X \mapsto P]U_1.[X \mapsto P]S_2 <: \forall Z<:[X \mapsto P]U_1.[X \mapsto P]T_2$, that is, $\Gamma, [X \mapsto P]\Delta \vdash [X \mapsto P](\forall Z<:U_1.S_2) <: [X \mapsto P](\forall Z<:U_1.T_2)$, as required.   □

A similar lemma relates type substitution and typing.

26.4.9   LEMMA [TYPE SUBSTITUTION PRESERVES TYPING]: If $\Gamma, X<:Q, \Delta \vdash t : T$ and $\Gamma \vdash P <: Q$, then $\Gamma, [X \mapsto P]\Delta \vdash [X \mapsto P]t : [X \mapsto P]T$.   □

Proof: By induction on a derivation of $\Gamma, X<:Q, \Delta \vdash t : T$. We give just the interesting cases.

Case T-TAPP: $t = t_1 [T_2]$ $\Gamma, X<:Q, \Delta \vdash t_1 : \forall Z<:T_{11}.T_{12}$
                                    $T = [Z \mapsto T_2]T_{12}$

By the induction hypothesis, $\Gamma, [X \mapsto P]\Delta \vdash [X \mapsto P]t_1 : [X \mapsto P](\forall Z<:T_{11}.T_{12})$, i.e, $\Gamma, [X \mapsto P]\Delta \vdash [X \mapsto P]t_1 : \forall Z<:T_{11}.[X \mapsto P]T_{12}$. By T-TAPP, $\Gamma, [X \mapsto P]\Delta \vdash [X \mapsto P]t_1 [[X \mapsto P]T_2] : [Z \mapsto [X \mapsto P]T_2]([X \mapsto P]T_{12})$, i.e., $\Gamma, [X \mapsto P]\Delta \vdash [X \mapsto P](t_1 [T_2]) : [X \mapsto P]([Z \mapsto T_2]T_{12})$.

Case T-SUB: $\Gamma, X<:Q, \Delta \vdash t : S\Gamma, X<:Q, \Delta \vdash S <: T$

By the induction hypothesis, $\Gamma, [X \mapsto P]\Delta \vdash [X \mapsto P]t : [X \mapsto P]T$. By the preservation of subtyping under substitution (Lemma 26.4.8), we have $\Gamma, [X \mapsto P]\Delta \vdash [X \mapsto P]S <: [X \mapsto P]T$, and the result follows by T-SUB. □

Next, we establish some simple structural properties of subtyping.

26.4.10   LEMMA [INVERSION OF THE SUBTYPE RELATION, FROM RIGHT TO LEFT]:

1. If $\Gamma \vdash S <: X$, then S is a type variable.

2. If $\Gamma \vdash S <: T_1 \rightarrow T_2$, then either S is a type variable or else S has the form $S_1 \rightarrow S_2$, with $\Gamma \vdash T_1 <: S_1$ and $\Gamma \vdash S_2 <: T_2$.

3. If $\Gamma \vdash S <: \forall X<:U_1.T_2$, then either S is a type variable or else S has the form $\forall X<:U_1.S_2$ with $\Gamma, X<:U_1 \vdash S_2 <: T_2$. □

Proof: Part (1) is an easy induction on subtyping derivations. The only interesting case is the rule S-TRANS, which proceeds by two uses of the induction hypothesis, first on the right premise and then on the left premise. The arguments for the other parts are similar, using part (1) in the transitivity cases. □

26.4.11   EXERCISE [RECOMMENDED, ⋆⋆]: Show the following "left to right inversion" properties:

1. If $\Gamma \vdash S_1 \rightarrow S_2 <: T$, then either $T = Top$ or else $T = T_1 \rightarrow T_2$ with $\Gamma \vdash T_1 <: S_1$ and $\Gamma \vdash S_2 <: T_2$.

2. If $\Gamma \vdash \forall X<:U.S_2 <: T$, then either $T = Top$ or else $T = \forall X<:U.T_2$ with $\Gamma, X<:U \vdash S_2 <: T_2$.

3. If $\Gamma \vdash X <: T$, then either $T = Top$ or $T = X$ or $\Gamma \vdash S <: T$ with $X<:S \in \Gamma$.

4. If $\Gamma \vdash Top <: T$, then $T = Top$. □

Lemma 26.4.10 is used, in turn, to establish one straightforward structural property of the typing relation that is needed in the critical cases of the type preservation proof.

26.4.12   LEMMA:

1. If $\Gamma \vdash \lambda x:S_1.s_2 : T$ and $\Gamma \vdash T <: U_1 \rightarrow U_2$, then $\Gamma \vdash U_1 <: S_1$ and there is some S_2 such that $\Gamma, x:S_1 \vdash s_2 : S_2$ and $\Gamma \vdash S_2 <: U_2$.

2. If $\Gamma \vdash \lambda X<:S_1.s_2 : T$ and $\Gamma \vdash T <: \forall X<:U_1.U_2$, then $U_1 = S_1$ and there is some S_2 such that $\Gamma, X<:S_1 \vdash s_2 : S_2$ and $\Gamma, X<:S_1 \vdash S_2 <: U_2$. □

Proof: Straightforward induction on typing derivations, using Lemma 26.4.10 for the induction case (rule T-SUB). $\qquad\square$

With these facts in hand, the proof of type preservation is straightforward.

26.4.13   THEOREM [PRESERVATION]: If $\Gamma \vdash t : T$ and $t \longrightarrow t'$, then $\Gamma \vdash t' : T$. $\qquad\square$

Proof: By induction on a derivation of $\Gamma \vdash t : T$. All of the cases are straightforward, using the facts established above.

Case T-VAR, T-ABS, T-TABS: $t = x$, $t = \lambda x : T_1 . t_2$,   or $t = \lambda X <: U . t$

These case cannot actually arise, since we assumed $t \longrightarrow t'$ and there are no evaluation rules for variables, abstractions, or type abstractions.

Case T-APP: $t = t_1\ t_2$ $\Gamma \vdash t_1 : T_{11} \rightarrow T_{12}$ $T = T_{12}$ $\Gamma \vdash t_2 : T_{11}$

By the definition of the evaluation relation, there are three subcases:

> *Subcase:* $t_1 \longrightarrow t_1'$ $t' = t_1'\ t_2$
>
> Then the result follows from the induction hypothesis and T-APP.

> *Subcase:* t_1 is a value $t_2 \longrightarrow t_2'$ $t' = t_1\ t_2'$
> Ditto.

> *Subcase:* $t_1 = \lambda x : U_{11} . u_{12}$ $t' = [x \mapsto t_2]u_{12}$
>
> By Lemma 26.4.12, $\Gamma, x : U_{11} \vdash u_{12} : U_{12}$ for some U_{12} with $\Gamma \vdash T_{11} <: U_{11}$ and $\Gamma \vdash U_{12} <: T_{12}$. By the preservation of typing under substitution (Lemma 26.4.6), $\Gamma \vdash [x \mapsto t_2]u_{12} : U_{12}$, from which we obtain $\Gamma \vdash [x \mapsto t_2]u_{12} : T_{12}$ by T-SUB.

Case T-TAPP: $t = t_1\ [T_2]$ $\Gamma \vdash t : \forall X <: T_{11} . T_{12}$
 $T = [X \mapsto T_2]T_{12}$ $\Gamma \vdash T_2 <: T_{11}$

By the definition of the evaluation relation, there are two subcases:

> *Subcase:* $t_1 \longrightarrow t_1'$ $t' = t_1'\ [T_2]$
>
> The result follows from the induction hypothesis and T-TAPP.

> *Subcase:* $t_1 = \lambda X <: U_{11} . u_{12}$ $t' = [X \mapsto T_2]u_{12}$
>
> By Lemma 26.4.12, $U_{11} = T_{11}$ and $\Gamma, X <: U_{11} \vdash u_{12} : U_{12}$ with $\Gamma, X <: U_{11} \vdash U_{12} <: T_{12}$. By the preservation of typing under substitution (Lemma 26.4.6), $\Gamma \vdash [X \mapsto T_2]u_{12} : [X \mapsto T_2]U_{12}$, from which $\Gamma \vdash [X \mapsto T_2]u_{12} : [X \mapsto T_2]T_{12}$ follows by Lemma 26.4.8 and T-SUB.

Case T-Sub: $\Gamma \vdash t : S \qquad \Gamma \vdash S <: T$

By the induction hypothesis, $\Gamma \vdash t' : S$, and the result follows by T-Sub.   □

The progress theorem for $F_{<:}$ is a straightforward extension of the one for the simply typed lambda-calculus with subtyping. As always, we begin by recording a canonical forms property telling us the possible shapes of closed values of arrow and quantifier types.

26.4.14   LEMMA [CANONICAL FORMS]:

1. If v is a closed value of type $T_1 \rightarrow T_2$, then v has the form $\lambda x : S_1 . t_2$.

2. If v is a closed value of type $\forall X <: T_1 . T_2$, then v has the form $\lambda X <: T_1 . t_2$. □

Proof: Both parts proceed by induction on typing derivations; we give the argument just for the second part. By inspection of the typing rules, it is clear that the final rule in a derivation of $\vdash v : \forall X <: T_1 . T_2$ must be either T-TAbs or T-Sub. If it is T-TAbs, then the desired result is immediate from the premise of the rule. So suppose the last rule is T-Sub. From the premises of this rule, we have $\vdash v : S$ and $S <: \forall X <: T_1 . T_2$. From the inversion lemma (26.4.10), we know that S has the form $\forall X <: T_1 \rightarrow S_2$. The result now follows from the induction hypothesis.   □

With this in hand, the proof of progress is straightforward.

26.4.15   THEOREM [PROGRESS]: If t is a closed, well-typed $F_{<:}$ term, then either t is a value or else there is some t' with $t \longrightarrow t'$.   □

Proof: By induction on typing derivations. The variable case cannot occur because t is closed. The two cases for lambda-abstractions are immediate, since both term and type abstractions are values. The cases for application, type application, and subsumption are more interesting; we show just the latter two (term application is similar to type application).

Case T-TApp: $t = t_1 \ [T_2] \qquad \vdash t_1 : \forall X <: T_{11} . T_{12}$
$$\Gamma \vdash T_2 <: T_{11} \quad T = [X \mapsto T_2]T_{12}$$

By the induction hypothesis, either t_1 is a value or else it can make a step of evaluation. If t_1 can take a step, then rule E-TApp1 applies to t. Otherwise, if t_1 is a value, then part (2) of the canonical forms lemma (26.4.14) tells us that t_1 has the form $\lambda X <: T_{11} . t_{12}$, so rule E-TAppTAbs applies to t.

Case T-Sub: $\Gamma \vdash t : S \qquad \Gamma \vdash S <: T$

The result follows directly from the induction hypothesis.   □

26.4.16   EXERCISE [★★★ ↝]: Extend the argument in this section to full $F_{<:}$.   □

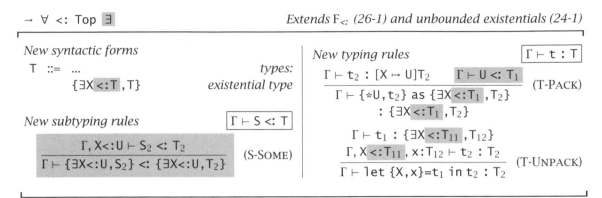

Figure 26-3: Bounded existential quantification (kernel variant)

26.5 Bounded Existential Types

We can add bounds to existential types (Chapter 24) just as we have done for universal types, obtaining *bounded existentials* as shown in Figure 26-3. As with bounded universals, the subtyping rule S-SOME comes in two flavors, one where the bounds of the two quantifiers being compared must be identical, and one where they may be different.

26.5.1   EXERCISE [⋆]: What is the *full* variant of S-SOME?   □

26.5.2   EXERCISE [⋆]: In pure System F with records and existential types (but no subtyping), how many different ways can you find of choosing T to make

```
{*Nat, {a=5,b=7}} as T;
```

well typed? If we add subtyping and bounded existentials, do we get more? □

We saw in §24.2 how ordinary existentials can be used to implement abstract data types. When we add bounds to existential quantifiers, we obtain a corresponding refinement at the level of ADTs, dubbed *partially abstract types* by Cardelli and Wegner (1985). The key intuition is that a bounded existential reveals *some* of the structure of its representation type to the outside world, while keeping the exact identity of the representation type hidden.

For example, suppose we implement an ADT of counters as in §24.2, but add the bound Counter<:Nat to the type annotation.

```
counterADT =
    {*Nat, {new = 1, get = λi:Nat. i, inc = λi:Nat. succ(i)}}
    as {∃Counter<:Nat,
        {new: Counter, get: Counter→Nat, inc: Counter→Counter}};
```

▶ counterADT : {∃Counter<:Nat,
                 {new:Counter,get:Counter→Nat,inc:Counter→Counter}}

We can use this counter ADT exactly as we did before, binding its type and term components to the variables Counter and counter and then using the fields of counter to perform operations on counters

```
let {Counter,counter} = counterADT in
counter.get (counter.inc (counter.inc counter.new));
```

▶ 3 : Nat

Moreover, we are now permitted to use Counter values directly as numbers:

```
let {Counter,counter} = counterADT in
succ (succ (counter.inc counter.new));
```

▶ 4 : Nat

On the other hand, we are still not able to use numbers as Counters:

```
let {Counter,counter} = counterADT in
counter.inc 3;
```

▶ Error: parameter type mismatch

In effect, in this version of the counter abstraction, we have chosen to make it easier for the outside world to use counters by revealing their representation, while retaining control over how counters can be created.

26.5.3   EXERCISE [★★★]: Suppose we want to define two abstract data types, Counter and ResetCounter, such that (1) both ADTs provide operations new, get, and inc, (2) ResetCounter additionally provides a reset operation that takes a counter and returns a new counter set to some fixed value, say 1, (3) clients of the two ADTs are allowed to use a ResetCounter in place of a Counter (i.e., we have ResetCounter <: Counter), and (4) nothing more is revealed to clients about how counters and reset counters are represented. Can this be accomplished using bounded existential packages?   □

We can make a similar refinement of our encodings of objects in terms of existentials from §24.2. There, the witness types of existential packages were used to represent the types of the internal states of objects, which were records of instance variables. By using a bounded existential in place of an unbounded one, we can reveal the names and types of some, but not all, of an object's instance variables to the outside world. For example, here is a counter object with a partially visible internal state that shows just its x field while restricting the visibility of its (not very interesting) private field:

```
c = {*{x:Nat, private:Bool},
      {state = {x=5, private=false},
       methods = {get = λs:{x:Nat}. s.x,
                  inc = λs:{x:Nat,private:Bool}.
                             {x=succ(s.x), private=s.private}}}}
     as {∃X<:{x:Nat}, {state:X, methods: {get:X→Nat, inc:X→X}}};
▶ c : {∃X<:{x:Nat}, {state:X,methods:{get:X→Nat,inc:X→X}}}
```

As with our partially abstract counter ADT above, such a counter object gives us the choice of accessing its value either by invoking its `get` method or by directly reaching inside and looking at the x field of its state.

26.5.4   EXERCISE [★★]: Show how to extend the encoding of existentials in terms of universals from §24.3 to an encoding of bounded existentials in terms of bounded universals. Check that the subtyping rule S-SOME follows from the encoding and the subtyping rules for bounded universals.   □

26.6   Notes

CLU (Liskov et al., 1977, 1981; Schaffert, 1978; Scheifler, 1978) appears to have been the earliest language with typesafe bounded quantification. CLU's notion of parameter bounds is essentially quantification-bounded quantification (§26.2) generalized to multiple type parameters.

The idea of bounded quantification in the form presented here was introduced by Cardelli and Wegner (1985) in the language Fun. Their "Kernel Fun" calculus corresponds to our kernel $F_{<:}$. Based on earlier informal ideas by Cardelli and formalized using techniques developed by Mitchell (1984b), Fun integrated Girard-Reynolds polymorphism (Girard, 1972; Reynolds, 1974) with Cardelli's first-order calculus of subtyping (1984). The original Fun was simplified and slightly generalized by Bruce and Longo (1990), and again by Curien and Ghelli (1992), yielding the calculus we call full $F_{<:}$. The most comprehensive paper on bounded quantification is the survey by Cardelli, Martini, Mitchell, and Scedrov (1994).

$F_{<:}$ and its relatives have been studied extensively by programming language theorists and designers. Cardelli and Wegner's survey paper gives the first programming examples using bounded quantification; more are developed in Cardelli's study of power kinds (1988a). Curien and Ghelli (1992, Ghelli, 1990) address a number of syntactic properties of $F_{<:}$. Semantic aspects of closely related systems have been studied by Bruce and Longo (1990), Martini (1988), Breazu-Tannen, Coquand, Gunter, and Scedrov (1991), Cardone (1989), Cardelli and Longo (1991), Cardelli, Martini, Mitchell, and Scedrov (1994), Curien and Ghelli (1992, 1991), and Bruce and Mitchell (1992).

$F_{<:}$ has been extended to include record types and richer notions of inheritance by Cardelli and Mitchell (1991), Bruce (Bruce, 1991), Cardelli (1992), and Canning, Cook, Hill, Olthoff, and Mitchell (1989b). Bounded quantification also plays a key role in Cardelli's programming language Quest (1991, Cardelli and Longo, 1991), in the Abel language developed at HP Labs (Canning, Cook, Hill, and Olthoff, 1989a; Canning, Cook, Hill, Olthoff, and Mitchell, 1989b; Canning, Hill, and Olthoff, 1988; Cook, Hill, and Canning, 1990), and in more recent designs such as GJ (Bracha, Odersky, Stoutamire, and Wadler, 1998), Pict (Pierce and Turner, 2000), and Funnel (Odersky, 2000).

The effect of bounded quantification on Church encodings of algebraic datatypes (§26.3) was considered by Ghelli (1990) and by Cardelli, Martini, Mitchell, and Scedrov (1994).

An extension of $F_{<:}$ with intersection types (§15.7) was studied by Pierce (1991b, 1997b). A variant of the system with higher kinds was applied to the modeling of object-oriented languages with multiple inheritance by Compagnoni and Pierce (1996); its metatheoretic properties were analyzed by Compagnoni (1994).

27 *Case Study: Imperative Objects, Redux*

Chapter 18 developed a collection of idioms in a simply typed calculus with records, references, and subtyping, modeling the core of an imperative object-oriented programming style. At the end of that chapter (in §18.12) we spent some effort in improving the run-time efficiency of our objects by moving the work of building an object's method table from method invocation time to object creation time. In this chapter, we use bounded quantification to further improve the efficiency of the model.

The key idea in §18.12 was to pass a *reference* to the "self method table" to a class when we call it. The class uses this reference in defining its own methods, and we later back-patch the reference to point to the completed method table returned by the class. For example, if SetCounter and SetCounterRep are the public interface and the internal representation type of a class of counter objects with get, set, and inc methods,

```
SetCounter = {get:Unit→Nat, set:Nat→Unit, inc:Unit→Unit};

CounterRep = {x: Ref Nat};
```

then we can implement a class of set counters like this:

```
setCounterClass =
  λr:CounterRep. λself: Source SetCounter.
    {get = λ_:Unit. !(r.x),
     set = λi:Nat. r.x:=i,
     inc = λ_:Unit. (!self).set
                         (succ ((!self).get unit))};
```
▸ setCounterClass : CounterRep → (Source SetCounter) → SetCounter

We use the type Source SetCounter instead of Ref SetCounter for the self parameter because, when we define a subclass of setCounterClass, this new

---

The examples in this chapter are terms of $F_{<:}$ with records (Figure 15-3), and references (13-1). The associated OCaml implementation is fullfsubref.

class's `self` will have a different type. For example, if `InstrCounter` and `InstrCounterRep` are the interface and representation types for a class of instrumented counter objects,

```
InstrCounter = {get:Unit→Nat, set:Nat→Unit,
                inc:Unit→Unit, accesses:Unit→Nat};

InstrCounterRep = {x: Ref Nat, a: Ref Nat};
```

then we can define the class itself as follows:

```
instrCounterClass =
  λr:InstrCounterRep. λself: Source InstrCounter.
  let super = setCounterClass r self in
  {get = super.get,
   set = λi:Nat. (r.a:=succ(!(r.a)); super.set i),
   inc = super.inc,
   accesses = λ_:Unit.
                 !(r.a)};
```

```
▶ instrCounterClass : InstrCounterRep →
                      (Source InstrCounter) → InstrCounter
```

The type of the `self` parameter here is `Source InstrCounter`, and we need to be able coerce from `Source InstrCounter` to `Source SetCounter` in order to pass this `self` as the `self` argument of `setCounterClass` when we build `super`. The covariant `Source` constructor permits this coercion, whereas the invariant `Ref` constructor would not.

However, as we observed at the end of §18.12, the efficiency of this model of classes is still not optimal. Since the same method table is associated with every object instantiated from a given class, we ought to be able to build this table just once, at *class* creation time, and re-use it every time an object is created. This would more accurately reflect the implementation conventions of real-world object-oriented languages, where an object does not carry any methods but just a pointer to a data structure representing its class, which is where the methods are actually stored.[1]

Another way of saying the same thing is to observe that the order of parameters to the classes above (first instance variables, then `self`) is backwards:

---

1. In fact, real-world object oriented-languages go one step further. Rather than calculating and storing a complete method table, each class stores just the methods that it adds or overrides with respect to its superclass. So the method table in our sense never gets built at all—at method invocation time, we simply walk up the class hierarchy, starting from the actual class of the receiver object, until we find a definition of the method we want. This kind of run-time search poses tricky problems for a static type analysis, and we will not deal with it here.

the `self` parameter is needed to build the class table, but the record of instance variables r is not used until a method is actually called. If `self` were the first argument, then we could compute the method table before being passed the r argument; we could partially apply the class, once, to its `self` argument, perform this computation once and for all, and make multiple copies of the resulting method table by applying it to multiple records of instance variables. Concretely, we would like to rewrite the `setCounterClass` like this:

```
setCounterClass =
  λself: Source (CounterRep→SetCounter).
  λr:CounterRep.
    {get = λ_:Unit. !(r.x),
     set = λi:Nat. r.x:=i,
     inc = λ_:Unit. (!self r).set
                           (succ ((!self r).get unit))};
```

▸ setCounterClass : (Source (CounterRep→SetCounter)) →
                             CounterRep → SetCounter

There are three significant differences between this version and the previous one. First, the new version takes `self` before r. Second, the type of `self` has changed from `SetCounter` to `CounterRep→SetCounter`. This change is forced by the first, since the type of `self` must be the same as the type of the method table returned by the class. And third, every use of `!self` in the body of the class becomes (`!self r`). This change is forced by the second one.

The instantiation function for our new counters is defined like this:

```
newSetCounter =
  let m = ref (λr:CounterRep. error as SetCounter) in
  let m' = setCounterClass m in
  (m := m';
   λ_:Unit. let r = {x=ref 1} in m' r);
```

▸ newSetCounter : Unit → SetCounter

Notice that the first three lines of this definition are evaluated just once, when `newSetCounter` is defined. Evaluation stops at the trivial abstraction on the last line, which can then be applied over and over to create objects; each time, it will allocate storage for a fresh record r of instance variables and instantiate the method table m′ with r to yield a fresh object.

Unfortunately, by rearranging `setCounterClass` in this way, we have introduced a *contravariant* occurrence of the state type `CounterRep`, and this comes back to haunt us when we try to define a subclass of `setCounterClass`.

```
instrCounterClass =
  λself: Source (InstrCounterRep→InstrCounter).
  let super = setCounterClass self in
  λr:InstrCounterRep.
  {get = (super r).get,
   set = λi:Nat. (r.a:=succ(!(r.a)); (super r).set i),
   inc = (super r).inc,
   accesses = λ_:Unit. !(r.a)};
```

▶ Error: parameter type mismatch

The mismatch arises in the definition of super, where we instantiate the superclass setCounterClass with the same self that was passed to the subclass. Unfortunately, the present self is (a reference to) a function of type InstrCounterRep→InstrCounter, which is not a subtype of CounterRep→ SetCounter because the left-hand sides of the arrows are the wrong way around.

We can address this difficulty by rewriting setCounterClass once more, this time using bounded quantification.

```
setCounterClass =
  λR<:CounterRep.
  λself: Source(R→SetCounter).
    λr: R.
      {get = λ_:Unit. !(r.x),
       set = λi:Nat.  r.x:=i,
       inc = λ_:Unit. (!self r).set (succ((!self r).get unit))};
```

▶ setCounterClass : ∀R<:CounterRep.
                        (Source (R→SetCounter)) → R → SetCounter

What this change accomplishes is that it makes setCounterClass a bit less demanding about the self parameter it is passed. Anthropomorphizing a little, we could characterize the previous version of setCounterClass as saying to its environment, "Please pass me a self parameter that accepts a CounterRep as a parameter, and I will use it to build a method table that also expects a CounterRep parameter." The new version, says, instead, "Please tell me the representation type R for an object that we are building; this type must have at least an x field, because I need to use it. Then give me a (reference to a) self that accepts R as a parameter and returns a method table with at least the methods of the SetCounter interface, and I will build and return another of the same kind."

We can see the effect of this change most clearly when we define the subclass instrCounterClass.

```
instrCounterClass =
  λR<:InstrCounterRep.
  λself: Source(R→InstrCounter).
    λr: R.
      let super = setCounterClass [R] self in
        {get = (super r).get,
         set = λi:Nat. (r.a:=succ(!(r.a)); (super r).set i),
         inc = (super r).inc,
         accesses = λ_:Unit. !(r.a)};
```

▸ instrCounterClass : ∀R<:InstrCounterRep.
                     (Source (R→InstrCounter)) →
                     R → InstrCounter

The reason this definition works where the previous one failed lies in the different uses of subsumption in the expression bound to super, where we promote the type of self to make it acceptable to the superclass. Previously, we were trying to show

$$\text{Source(InstrCounterRep→InstrCounter)}$$
$$<:\quad \text{Source(CounterRep→SetCounter)},$$

which was false. Now all we have to show is

$$\text{Source(R→InstrCounter)} <: \text{Source(R→SetCounter)},$$

which is true.

The object creation functions for our new encoding of classes are very similar to the old ones. For example, here is the creator for the instrumented counter subclass.

```
newInstrCounter =
  let m = ref (λr:InstrCounterRep. error as InstrCounter) in
  let m' = instrCounterClass [InstrCounterRep] m in
  (m := m';
   λ_:Unit. let r = {x=ref 1, a=ref 0} in m' r);
```

▸ newInstrCounter : Unit → InstrCounter

The only difference is that we need to instantiate instrCounterClass with the actual type InstrCounterRep of the instance variable record. As before, the first three lines are executed just once, at the point when the binding of newInstrCounter is made.

Finally, here are a few tests to demonstrate that our counters are behaving the way we expect.

```
ic = newInstrCounter unit;
ic.inc unit;
ic.get unit;
```

▸ 2 : Nat

```
ic.accesses unit;
```

▸ 1 : Nat

27.1   EXERCISE [RECOMMENDED, ★★★]: Our new encoding of classes relies on the
covariance of the Source type constructor. Is it possible to achieve the same
efficiency (i.e., to give a well-typed encoding of classes with the same operational behavior) in a language with just bounded quantification and the
invariant Ref constructor?   □

28 *Metatheory of Bounded Quantification*

In this chapter we develop subtyping and typechecking algorithms for $F_{<:}$. We study both the kernel and the full variants of the system, which behave somewhat differently. Some properties are enjoyed by both but harder to prove for the full variant, while others are lost outright in full $F_{<:}$ — the price we pay for the extra expressiveness of this system.

We first present a typechecking algorithm that works for both systems in §28.1 and §28.2. Then we consider subtype checking, taking first the kernel system in §28.3 and then the full system in §28.4. §28.5 continues the discussion of subtyping in full $F_{<:}$, focusing on the surprising fact that the subtype relation is undecidable. §28.6 shows that the kernel system has joins and meets, while the full system does not. §28.7 touches on some issues raised by bounded existentials, and §28.8 considers the effects of adding a minimal Bot type.

28.1 Exposure

In the typechecking algorithm in §16.2 for the simply typed lambda-calculus with subtyping, the key idea was to calculate a *minimal type* for each term from the minimal types of its subterms. We can use the same basic idea for $F_{<:}$, but we need to take into account one small complication arising from the presence of type variables in the system. Consider the term

```
f = λX<:Nat→Nat. λy:X. y 5;
```

▸ f : ∀X<:Nat→Nat. X → Nat

This term is clearly well typed, since the type of the variable y in the application y 5 can be promoted to Nat→Nat by T-SUB. But the *minimal* type of y is

---

The system studied in this chapter is pure $F_{<:}$ (Figure 26-1). The corresponding implementation is purefsub; the fullfsub implementation also includes existentials (24-1) and several extensions from Chapter 11.

Figure 28-1: Exposure Algorithm for $F_{<:}$

X, which is not an arrow type. In order to find the minimal type of the whole application, we need to find the smallest arrow type that y possesses—i.e., the minimal arrow type that is a supertype of the type variable X. Not too surprisingly, we can find this type by *promoting* the minimal type of y until it becomes something other than a type variable.

Formally, we write $\Gamma \vdash S \Uparrow T$ (pronounced "S exposes to T under Γ") to mean "T is the least nonvariable supertype of S." Exposure is defined by repeated promotion of variables, as shown in Figure 28-1.

It is easy to see that these rules define a total function. Moreover, the result of exposing a type is always the least supertype that has some shape other than a variable. For example, if Γ = X<:Top, Y<:Nat→Nat, Z<:Y, W<:Z, then:

$$\Gamma \vdash \mathsf{Top} \Uparrow \mathsf{Top} \qquad \Gamma \vdash \mathsf{Y} \Uparrow \mathsf{Nat{\to}Nat} \qquad \Gamma \vdash \mathsf{W} \Uparrow \mathsf{Nat{\to}Nat}$$
$$\Gamma \vdash \mathsf{X} \Uparrow \mathsf{Top} \qquad \Gamma \vdash \mathsf{Z} \Uparrow \mathsf{Nat{\to}Nat}$$

The essential properties of exposure can be summarized as follows.

28.1.1   LEMMA [EXPOSURE]: Suppose $\Gamma \vdash S \Uparrow T$. Then:

1. $\Gamma \vdash S <: T$.

2. If $\Gamma \vdash S <: U$ and U is not a variable, then $\Gamma \vdash T <: U$.   □

Proof: Part (1) goes by induction on a derivation of $\Gamma \vdash S \Uparrow T$, part (2) by induction on a derivation of $\Gamma \vdash S <: U$.   □

28.2   Minimal Typing

The algorithm for calculating minimal types is now built along the same lines as the one for the simply typed lambda-calculus with subtyping, with one additional twist: when we typecheck an application, we calculate the minimal type of the left-hand side and then *expose* this type to obtain an arrow type, as

$$\rightarrow \forall <: \text{Top} \qquad\qquad\qquad\qquad \textit{Extends } \lambda_{<:} \textit{ (16-3)}$$

Algorithmic typing $\boxed{\Gamma \vdash t : T}$

$$\frac{x{:}T \in \Gamma}{\Gamma \vdash x : T} \qquad \text{(TA-VAR)}$$

$$\frac{\Gamma, x{:}T_1 \vdash t_2 : T_2}{\Gamma \vdash \lambda x{:}T_1.t_2 : T_1 {\rightarrow} T_2} \qquad \text{(TA-ABS)}$$

$$\frac{\Gamma \vdash t_1 : T_1 \qquad \Gamma \vdash T_1 \Uparrow (T_{11} {\rightarrow} T_{12})}{\Gamma \vdash t_2 : T_2 \qquad \Gamma \vdash T_2 <: T_{11}}{\Gamma \vdash t_1\ t_2 : T_{12}} \qquad \text{(TA-APP)}$$

$$\frac{\Gamma, X <: T_1 \vdash t_2 : T_2}{\Gamma \vdash \lambda X <: T_1.t_2 : \forall X <: T_1.T_2} \qquad \text{(TA-TABS)}$$

$$\frac{\Gamma \vdash t_1 : T_1 \qquad \Gamma \vdash T_1 \Uparrow \forall X <: T_{11}.T_{12}}{\Gamma \vdash T_2 <: T_{11}}{\Gamma \vdash t_1\ [T_2] : [X \mapsto T_2]T_{12}} \qquad \text{(TA-TAPP)}$$

Figure 28-2: Algorithmic typing for $F_{<:}$

shown in Figure 28-2. If the exposure of the left-hand side does not yield an arrow type, then rule TA-APP does not apply and the application is ill-typed. Similarly, we typecheck a type application by exposing its left-hand side to obtain a quantified type.

The soundness and completeness of this algorithm with respect to the original typing rules are easy to show. We give the proof for kernel $F_{<:}$ (the argument for full $F_{<:}$ is similar; cf. Exercise 28.2.3).

28.2.1   THEOREM [MINIMAL TYPING]:

1. If $\Gamma \vdash t : T$, then $\Gamma \vdash t : T$.

2. If $\Gamma \vdash t : T$, then $\Gamma \vdash t : M$ with $\Gamma \vdash M <: T$.   □

Proof: Part (1) is a straightforward induction on algorithmic derivations, using part (1) of Lemma 28.1.1 for the application cases. Part (2) goes by induction on a derivation of $\Gamma \vdash t : T$, with a case analysis on the final rule used in the derivation. The most interesting cases are those for T-APP and T-TAPP.

Case T-VAR: $t = x$ $x{:}T \in \Gamma$

By TA-VAR, $\Gamma \vdash x : T$. By S-REFL, $\Gamma \vdash T <: T$.

Case T-ABS: $t = \lambda x{:}T_1.t_2$ $\Gamma, x{:}T_1 \vdash t_2 : T_2$ $T = T_1 {\rightarrow} T_2$

By the induction hypothesis, $\Gamma, x{:}T_1 \vdash t_2 : M_2$ for some M_2 with $\Gamma, x{:}T_1 \vdash M_2 <: T_2$—i.e., with $\Gamma \vdash M_2 <: T_2$, since subtyping does not depend on term variable bindings in the context (Lemma 26.4.4). By TA-ABS, $\Gamma \vdash t : T_1 {\rightarrow} M_2$. By S-REFL and S-ARROW, $\Gamma \vdash T_1 {\rightarrow} M_2 <: T_1 {\rightarrow} T_2$.

Case T-App: $t = t_1\ t_2$ $\Gamma \vdash t_1 : T_{11} \rightarrow T_{12}$ $T = T_{12}$ $\Gamma \vdash t_2 : T_{11}$

From the induction hypothesis, we obtain $\Gamma \Vdash t_1 : M_1$ and $\Gamma \Vdash t_2 : M_2$, with $\Gamma \vdash M_1 <: T_{11} \rightarrow T_{12}$ and $\Gamma \vdash M_2 <: T_{11}$. Let N_1 be the least nonvariable supertype of M_1—i.e., $\Gamma \vdash M_1 \Uparrow N_1$. By part (2) of Lemma 28.1.1, $\Gamma \vdash N_1 <: T_{11} \rightarrow T_{12}$. Since we know that N_1 is not a variable, the inversion lemma for the subtype relation (26.4.10) tells us that $N_1 = N_{11} \rightarrow N_{12}$, with $\Gamma \vdash T_{11} <: N_{11}$ and $\Gamma \vdash N_{12} <: T_{12}$. By transitivity, $\Gamma \vdash M_2 <: N_{11}$, so rule TA-App applies to give us $\Gamma \Vdash t_1\ t_2 : N_{12}$, which satisfies the requirements.

Case T-TABS: $t = \lambda X{<:}T_1.t_2$ $\Gamma, X{<:}T_1 \vdash t_2 : T_2$ $T = \forall X{<:}T_1.T_2$

By the induction hypothesis, $\Gamma, X{<:}T_1 \Vdash t_2 : M_2$ for some M_2 with $\Gamma, X{<:}T_1 \vdash M_2 <: T_2$. By TA-TABS, $\Gamma \Vdash t : \forall X{<:}T_1.M_2$. By S-ALL, $\Gamma \vdash \forall X{<:}T_1.M_2 <: \forall X{<:}T_1.T_2$.

Case T-TApp: $t = t_1\ [T_2]$ $\Gamma \vdash t_1 : \forall X{<:}T_{11}.T_{12}$
                 $T = [X \mapsto T_2]T_{12}$ $\Gamma \vdash T_2 <: T_{11}$

By the induction hypothesis, we have $\Gamma \Vdash t_1 : M_1$, with $\Gamma \vdash M_1 <: \forall X{<:}T_{11}.T_{12}$. Let N_1 be the least nonvariable supertype of M_1—i.e., $\Gamma \vdash M_1 \Uparrow N_1$. By the exposure lemma (28.1.1), $\Gamma \vdash N_1 <: \forall X{<:}T_{11}.T_{12}$. But we know that N_1 is not a variable, so the inversion lemma for the subtype relation (26.4.10) tells us that $N_1 = \forall X{<:}T_{11}.N_{12}$, with $\Gamma, X{<:}T_{11} \vdash N_{12} <: T_{12}$. Rule TA-TApp gives us $\Gamma \Vdash t_1\ [T_2] : [X \mapsto T_2]N_{12}$, and the preservation of subtyping under substitution (Lemma 26.4.8) yields $\Gamma \vdash [X \mapsto T_2]N_{12} <: [X \mapsto T_2]T_{12} = T$.

Case T-Sub: $\Gamma \vdash t : S$ $\Gamma \vdash S <: T$

By the induction hypothesis, $\Gamma \Vdash t : M$ with $\Gamma \vdash M <: S$. By transitivity, $\Gamma \vdash M <: T$.   □

28.2.2   COROLLARY [DECIDABILITY OF TYPING]: The kernel $F_{<:}$ typing relation is decidable, given a decision procedure for the subtype relation.   □

Proof: For any Γ and t, we can check whether there is some T such that $\Gamma \vdash t : T$ by using the algorithmic typing rules to generate a proof of $\Gamma \Vdash t : T$. If we succeed, then this T is also a type for t in the original typing relation, by part (1) of 28.2.1. If not, then part (2) of 28.2.1 implies that t has no type in the original typing relation. Finally, note that the algorithmic typing rules correspond to a terminating algorithm, since they are syntax directed (at most one applies to a given term t) and they always reduce the size of t when read from bottom to top.   □

28.2.3   EXERCISE [★★]: Where do the proofs above need to be changed for full $F_{<:}$?   □

28.3 Subtyping in Kernel F<:

In §16.1, we remarked that the declarative subtype relation for the simply typed lambda-calculus with subtyping is not syntax directed—i.e., it cannot be read directly as a subtyping algorithm—for two reasons: (1) the conclusions of S-Refl and S-Trans overlap with the other rules (so, reading the rules from bottom to top, we would not know which one to try to apply), and (2) the premises of S-Trans mention a metavariable that does not appear in the conclusion (which a naive algorithm would have to somehow "guess"). We saw that these problems can be fixed by simply dropping the two offending rules from the system, but that, before doing so, we must fix up the system a little by combining the three separate record subtyping rules into one.

For kernel F<:, the story is similar. Again, the offending rules are S-Refl and S-Trans, and we obtain an algorithm by dropping these rules and fixing up the remaining rules a little to account for the essential uses of the dropped rules.

In the simply typed lambda-calculus with subtyping, there were no essential uses of the reflexivity rule—we could just drop it without changing the set of derivable subtyping statements (Lemma 16.1.2, part 1). In F<:, on the other hand, subtyping statements of the form $\Gamma \vdash X <: X$ can be proved only by reflexivity. So, when we remove the full reflexivity rule, we should add in its place a restricted reflexivity axiom that applies only to variables.

$$\Gamma \vdash X <: X$$

Similarly, to eliminate S-Trans, we must first understand which of its uses are essential. Here, the interesting interaction is with the S-TVar rule, which allows assumptions about type variables to be used in deriving subtyping statements. For example, if $\Gamma = W<:Top, X<:W, Y<:X, Z<:Y$, then the statement $\Gamma \vdash Z <: W$ cannot be proved if S-Trans is removed from the system. An instance of S-Trans whose left-hand subderivation is an instance of the axiom S-TVar, as in

$$\frac{\dfrac{Z <: Y \in \Gamma}{\Gamma \vdash Z <: Y} \text{(S-TVar)} \qquad \dfrac{\vdots}{\Gamma \vdash Y <: W}}{\Gamma \vdash Z <: W} \text{(S-Trans)}$$

cannot, in general, be eliminated.

Fortunately, derivations of this form are the *only* essential uses of transitivity in subtyping. This observation can be made precise by introducing a new subtyping rule

$$\frac{X<:U \in \Gamma \qquad \Gamma \vdash U <: T}{\Gamma \vdash X <: T}$$

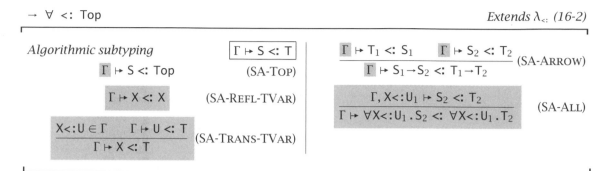

Figure 28-3: Algorithmic subtyping for kernel F$_{<:}$

that captures exactly this pattern of variable lookup followed by transitivity, and showing that replacing the transitivity and variable rules by this one does not change the set of derivable subtyping statements.

These changes lead us to the algorithmic subtype relation for kernel F$_{<:}$, shown in Figure 28-3. We add an arrowhead to the turnstile symbol in algorithmic typing statements so that we can distinguish them from original typing statements in discussions involving both.

The fact that the new SA-REFL-TVAR and SA-TRANS-TVAR rules are sufficient replacements for the old reflexivity and transitivity rules is captured by the next two lemmas.

28.3.1   LEMMA [REFLEXIVITY OF THE ALGORITHMIC SUBTYPE RELATION]: $\Gamma \vdash T <: T$ is provable for every Γ and T.   □

Proof: By induction on T.   □

28.3.2   LEMMA [TRANSITIVITY OF THE ALGORITHMIC SUBTYPE RELATION]: If $\Gamma \vdash S <: Q$ and $\Gamma \vdash Q <: T$, then $\Gamma \vdash S <: T$.   □

Proof: By induction on the sum of the sizes of the two derivations. Given two derivations, we proceed by a case analysis of the final rules in both.

If the right-hand derivation is an instance of SA-TOP, then we are done, since $\Gamma \vdash S <: \text{Top}$ by SA-TOP. If the left-hand derivation is an instance of SA-TOP, then $Q = \text{Top}$ and by looking at the algorithmic rules we see that the right-hand derivation must also be an instance of SA-TOP.

If either derivation is an instance of SA-REFL-TVAR, then we are again done since the other derivation is exactly the desired result.

If the left-hand derivation ends with an instance of SA-TRANS-TVAR, then $S = Y$ with $Y<:U \in \Gamma$ and we have a subderivation with conclusion $\Gamma \vdash U <: Q$.

By the induction hypothesis, $\Gamma \vdash U <: T$, and, by SA-TRANS-TVAR again, $\Gamma \vdash Y <: T$, as required.

If the left-hand derivation ends with an instance of SA-ARROW, then we have $S = S_1 \rightarrow S_2$ and $Q = Q_1 \rightarrow Q_2$, with subderivations $\Gamma \vdash Q_1 <: S_1$ and $\Gamma \vdash S_2 <: Q_2$. But since we have already considered the case where the right-hand derivation is SA-TOP, the only remaining possibility is that this derivation also ends with SA-ARROW; we therefore have $T = T_1 \rightarrow T_2$ and two more subderivations $\Gamma \vdash T_1 <: Q_1$ and $\Gamma \vdash Q_2 <: T_2$. We now apply the induction hypothesis twice, obtaining $\Gamma \vdash T_1 <: S_1$ and $\Gamma \vdash S_2 <: T_2$. SA-ARROW now yields $\Gamma \vdash S_1 \rightarrow S_2 <: T_1 \rightarrow T_2$, as required.

If the case where the left-hand derivation ends with an instance of SA-ALL, the argument is similar. We have $S = \forall X <: U_1 . S_2$ and $Q = \forall X <: U_1 . Q_2$, with a subderivation $\Gamma, X <: U_1 \vdash S_2 <: Q_2$. But again, since we have already considered the case where the right-hand derivation is SA-TOP, it must end with SA-ALL; so $T = \forall X <: U_1 . T_2$ with a subderivation $\Gamma, X <: U_1 \vdash Q_2 <: T_2$. We apply the induction hypothesis to obtain $\Gamma, X <: U_1 \vdash S_2 <: T_2$, and SA-ALL to obtain $\Gamma \vdash \forall X <: U_1 . S_2 <: \forall X <: U_1 . T_2$. $\square$

28.3.3   THEOREM [SOUNDNESS AND COMPLETENESS OF ALGORITHMIC SUBTYPING]: $\Gamma \vdash S <: T$ iff $\Gamma \vdash S <: T$. $\square$

Proof: Both directions proceed by induction on derivations. Soundness ($\Leftarrow$) is routine. Completeness ($\Rightarrow$) relies on Lemmas 28.3.1 and 28.3.2. $\square$

Finally, we need to check that the subtyping rules define an algorithm that is *total*—i.e., that terminates on all inputs. We do this by assigning a weight to each subtyping statement and checking that the algorithmic rules all have conclusions with strictly greater weight than their premises.

28.3.4   DEFINITION: The *weight* of a type T in a context Γ, written $weight_\Gamma(T)$, is defined as follows:

$$
\begin{aligned}
weight_\Gamma(X) &= weight_{\Gamma_1}(U) + 1 && \text{if } \Gamma = \Gamma_1, X <: U, \Gamma_2 \\
weight_\Gamma(\text{Top}) &= 1 \\
weight_\Gamma(T_1 \rightarrow T_2) &= weight_\Gamma(T_1) + weight_\Gamma(T_2) + 1 \\
weight_\Gamma(\forall X <: T_1 . T_2) &= weight_{\Gamma, X <: T_1}(T_2) + 1
\end{aligned}
$$

The *weight* of a subtyping statement $\Gamma \vdash S <: T$ is the maximum weight of S and T in Γ. $\square$

28.3.5   THEOREM: The subtyping algorithm terminates on all inputs. $\square$

Proof: The weight of the conclusion in an instance of any of the algorithmic subtyping rules is strictly greater than the weight of any of the premises. $\square$

28.3.6   COROLLARY: Subtyping in kernel F<: is decidable. $\square$

$\rightarrow \forall <:$ Top *full*   *Extends 28-3*

Algorithmic subtyping $\boxed{\Gamma \vdash S <: T}$

$\qquad \Gamma \vdash S <:$ Top   (SA-TOP)

$\qquad \Gamma \vdash X <: X$ (SA-REFL-TVAR)

$$\frac{X{<:}U \in \Gamma \qquad \Gamma \vdash U <: T}{\Gamma \vdash X <: T} \quad \text{(SA-TRANS-TVAR)}$$

$$\frac{\Gamma \vdash T_1 <: S_1 \qquad \Gamma \vdash S_2 <: T_2}{\Gamma \vdash S_1 {\rightarrow} S_2 <: T_1 {\rightarrow} T_2} \quad \text{(SA-ARROW)}$$

$$\frac{\Gamma \vdash T_1 <: S_1 \qquad \Gamma, X{<:}T_1 \vdash S_2 <: T_2}{\Gamma \vdash \forall X{<:}S_1.S_2 <: \forall X{<:}T_1.T_2} \quad \text{(SA-ALL)}$$

Figure 28-4: Algorithmic subtyping for full $F_{<:}$

28.4 Subtyping in Full $F_{<:}$

The subtype checking algorithm for full $F_{<:}$, summarized in Figure 28-4, is nearly the same as for kernel $F_{<:}$: the only change is replacing SA-ALL with its more flexible variant. As with kernel $F_{<:}$, the soundness and completeness of this algorithmic relation with respect to the original subtype relation follow directly from the fact that the algorithmic relation is reflexive and transitive.

For reflexivity, the argument is exactly the same as before, but transitivity is a bit more delicate. To see why, recall the proof of transitivity for kernel $F_{<:}$ from the previous section (Lemma 28.3.2). The idea there was to take two subtyping derivations ending with the statements $\Gamma \vdash S <: Q$ and $\Gamma \vdash Q <: T$, and to show how to rearrange and reassemble their subderivations to construct a derivation of $\Gamma \vdash S <: T$ without using the transitivity rule, given (as an induction hypothesis) that it is possible to do the same with pairs of smaller derivations. Now, suppose we have two derivations ending with the new SA-ALL rule:

$$\frac{\vdots \qquad\qquad \vdots}{\dfrac{\Gamma \vdash Q_1 <: S_1 \qquad \Gamma, X{<:}Q_1 \vdash S_2 <: Q_2}{\Gamma \vdash \forall X{<:}S_1.S_2 <: \forall X{<:}Q_1.Q_2}} \qquad \frac{\vdots \qquad\qquad \vdots}{\dfrac{\Gamma \vdash T_1 <: Q_1 \qquad \Gamma, X{<:}T_1 \vdash Q_2 <: T_2}{\Gamma \vdash \forall X{<:}Q_1.Q_2 <: \forall X{<:}T_1.T_2}}$$

Following the pattern of the earlier proof, we would like to use the induction hypothesis to combine the left- and right-hand subderivations and finish with a single use of SA-ALL with the conclusion $\Gamma \vdash \forall X{<:}S_1.S_2 <: \forall X{<:}T_1.T_2$. For the left-hand subderivations, there is no problem; the induction hypothesis gives us a transitivity-free derivation of $\Gamma \vdash T_1 <: S_1$. For the right-hand subderivations, however, the induction hypothesis does not apply because the contexts in the subderivations are different—the upper bound for X is Q_1 in one and T_1 in the other.

Fortunately, we know a way to *make* the contexts the same: the *narrowing* property from Chapter 26 (Lemma 26.4.5) tells us that a valid subtyping statement remains valid if we replace a bound in the context by one of its subtypes. So it would seem we can just narrow the subderivation of $\Gamma, X{<:}Q_1 \vdash S_2 <: Q_2$ to $\Gamma, X{<:}T_1 \vdash S_2 <: Q_2$, thereby enabling the induction hypothesis.

However, we need to be a little careful. Lemma 26.4.5 shows that we can take any derivation and construct a derivation with a narrowed conclusion, but it does *not* guarantee that the new derivation will be the same size as the old one. Indeed, if we examine the lemma's proof, it is clear that narrowing generally yields a bigger derivation, since it involves splicing in a copy of an arbitrarily large derivation at each place where the S-TVAR axiom is used to look up the variable being narrowed. Moreover, this splicing operation involves creating new instances of transitivity, which is precisely the rule that we are trying to show is admissible in the present system.

The solution to these difficulties is to prove transitivity and narrowing *together,* using an induction hypothesis based on the size of the intermediate type Q in the transitivity property and the original bound Q in the narrowing property.

We preface this argument with an easy lemma recording the fact that permuting the order or adding fresh type variable bindings to the context does not invalidate any derivable subtyping statements.

28.4.1   LEMMA [PERMUTATION AND WEAKENING]:

1. Suppose that Δ is a well-formed permutation of Γ (cf. 26.4.1). If $\Gamma \vdash S <: T$, then $\Delta \vdash S <: T$.

2. If $\Gamma \vdash S <: T$ and $dom(\Delta) \cap dom(\Gamma) = \emptyset$, then $\Gamma, \Delta \vdash S <: T$.   □

Proof: Routine inductions. Part (1) is used in the SA-ALL case of part (2).   □

28.4.2   LEMMA [TRANSITIVITY AND NARROWING FOR FULL F$_{<:}$]:

1. If $\Gamma \vdash S <: Q$ and $\Gamma \vdash Q <: T$, then $\Gamma \vdash S <: T$.

2. If $\Gamma, X{<:}Q, \Delta \vdash M <: N$ and $\Gamma \vdash P <: Q$ then $\Gamma, X{<:}P, \Delta \vdash M <: N$.   □

Proof: The two parts are proved simultaneously, by induction on the size of Q. At each stage of the induction, the argument for part (2) assumes that part (1) has been established already for the Q in question; part (1) uses part (2) only for strictly smaller Qs.

1. We proceed by an inner induction on the size of the first given derivation, with a case analysis on the final rules in both derivations. All but one of the

cases are like the proof of Lemma 28.3.2; the difference is in the SA-ALL case.

If the right-hand derivation is an instance of SA-TOP, then we are done, since $\Gamma \vdash S <: \text{Top}$ by SA-TOP. If the left-hand derivation is an instance of SA-TOP, then $Q = \text{Top}$, and, inspecting the algorithmic rules, we see that the right-hand derivation must also be an instance of SA-TOP. If either derivation is an instance of SA-REFL-TVAR, then we are again done, since the other derivation is exactly the desired result.

If the left-hand derivation ends with an instance of SA-TRANS-TVAR, then we have $S = Y$ with $Y{<}{:}U \in \Gamma$ and a subderivation of $\Gamma \vdash U <: Q$. By the inner induction hypothesis, $\Gamma \Vdash U <: T$, and, by SA-TRANS-TVAR again, $\Gamma \Vdash Y <: T$, as required.

If the left-hand derivation ends with an instance of SA-ARROW or SA-ALL, then, since we have already considered the case where the right-hand derivation ends with SA-TOP, it must end with the same rule as the left. If this rule is SA-ARROW, then we have $S = S_1 \rightarrow S_2$, $Q = Q_1 \rightarrow Q_2$, and $T = T_1 \rightarrow T_2$, with subderivations $\Gamma \Vdash Q_1 <: S_1$, $\Gamma \Vdash S_2 <: Q_2$, $\Gamma \Vdash T_1 <: Q_1$, and $\Gamma \Vdash Q_2 <: T_2$. We apply part (1) of the outer induction hypothesis twice (noting that Q_1 and Q_2 are both smaller than Q) to obtain $\Gamma \Vdash T_1 <: S_1$ and $\Gamma \Vdash S_2 <: T_2$, and then use SA-ARROW to obtain $\Gamma \Vdash S_1 \rightarrow S_2 <: T_1 \rightarrow T_2$.

In the case where the two derivations end with SA-ALL, we have $S = \forall X{<}{:}S_1.S_2$, $Q = \forall X{<}{:}Q_1.Q_2$, and $T = \forall X{<}{:}T_1.T_2$, with

$$\begin{array}{ll} \Gamma \Vdash Q_1 <: S_1 & \Gamma, X{<}{:}Q_1 \Vdash S_2 <: Q_2 \\ \Gamma \Vdash T_1 <: Q_1 & \Gamma, X{<}{:}T_1 \Vdash Q_2 <: T_2 \end{array}$$

as subderivations. By part (1) of the outer induction hypothesis (Q_1 being smaller than Q), we can combine the two subderivations for the bounds to obtain $\Gamma \Vdash T_1 <: S_1$. For the bodies, we need to work a little harder, since the two contexts do not quite agree. We first use part (2) of the outer induction hypothesis (noting again that Q_1 is smaller than Q) to narrow the bound of X in the derivation of $\Gamma, X{<}{:}Q_1 \Vdash S_2 <: Q_2$, obtaining $\Gamma, X{<}{:}T_1 \Vdash S_2 <: Q_2$. Now part (1) of the outer induction hypothesis applies (Q_2 being smaller than Q), yielding $\Gamma, X{<}{:}T_1 \Vdash S_2 <: T_2$. Finally, by SA-ALL, $\Gamma \Vdash \forall X{<}{:}S_1.S_2 <: \forall X{<}{:}T_1.T_2$.

2. We again proceed by an inner induction on the size of the first given derivation, with a case analysis on the final rule of this derivation. Most of the cases proceed by straightforward use of the inner induction hypothesis. The interesting case is SA-TRANS-TVAR with $M = X$ and we have

Γ, X<:Q, Δ $\vdash$ Q <: N as a subderivation. Applying the inner induction hypothesis to this subderivation yields Γ, X<:P, Δ $\vdash$ Q <: N. Also, applying weakening (Lemma 28.4.1, part 2) to the second given derivation yields Γ, X<:P, Δ $\vdash$ P <: Q. Now, by part (1) of the outer induction hypothesis (with the same Q), we have Γ, X<:P, Δ $\vdash$ P <: N. Rule SA-TRANS-TVAR yields Γ, X<:P, Δ $\vdash$ X <: N, as required. $\square$

28.4.3   EXERCISE [$\star\star\star\star$ $\rightarrowtail$]: There is another reasonable variant of the quantifier subtyping rule that is a bit more flexible than the kernel F$_{<:}$ rule but substantially less so than the full F$_{<:}$ rule:

$$\frac{\Gamma \vdash S_1 <: T_1 \qquad \Gamma \vdash T_1 <: S_1 \qquad \Gamma, X{<:}T_1 \vdash S_2 <: T_2}{\Gamma \vdash \forall X{<:}S_1.S_2 <: \forall X{<:}T_1.T_2} \qquad \text{(S-ALL)}$$

This rule is close to the kernel F$_{<:}$ variant, but instead of requiring that the bounds of the two quantifiers be syntactically identical, it demands only that they be equivalent—each a subtype of the other. The difference between the kernel rule and this one actually appears only when we enrich the language with some construct whose subtyping rules generate non-trivial equivalence classes, such as records. For example, in pure kernel F$_{<:}$ with records, the type $\forall X{<:}\{a{:}Top,b{:}Top\}.X$ would not be a subtype of $\forall X{<:}\{b{:}Top,a{:}Top\}.X$, whereas with the above rule it would be. Is subtyping decidable for the system with this rule? $\square$

28.5   Undecidability of Full F$_{<:}$

We established in the previous section that the algorithmic subtyping rules for full F$_{<:}$ are sound and complete—that is, that the smallest relation closed under these rules contains the same statements as the smallest relation closed under the original declarative rules. This leaves the question of whether an algorithm implementing these rules terminates on all inputs. Unfortunately—and, to many people at the time this was discovered, quite surprisingly—it does not.

28.5.1   EXERCISE [$\star$]: If the algorithmic rules for full F$_{<:}$ do not define an algorithm that always terminates, then clearly the proof of termination for the kernel F$_{<:}$ algorithm cannot be carried over to the rules for the full system. Precisely where does it break down? $\square$

Here is an example, due to Ghelli (1995), that makes the subtyping algorithm diverge. We first define the following abbreviation:

$$\neg S \quad \overset{\text{def}}{=} \quad \forall X{<:}S.X.$$

The crucial property of the $\neg$ operator is that it allows the left- and right-hand sides of subtyping statements to be swapped.

28.5.2   FACT: $\Gamma \vdash \neg S <: \neg T$ iff $\Gamma \vdash T <: S$.   □

Proof: EXERCISE [★★ ↛].   □

Now, define a type T as follows:

$$T \quad = \quad \forall X<:\texttt{Top}.\ \neg(\forall Y<:X.\ \neg Y).$$

If we use the algorithmic subtyping rules bottom-to-top to attempt to construct a subtyping derivation for the statement

$$X_0<:T \quad \mapsto \quad X_0 \quad <: \quad \forall X_1<:X_0.\ \neg X_1$$

we end up in an infinite regress of larger and larger subgoals:

$$
\begin{array}{lllll}
X_0<:T & \mapsto & X_0 & <: & \forall X_1<:X_0.\ \neg X_1 \\
X_0<:T & \mapsto & \forall X_1<:\texttt{Top}.\ \neg(\forall X_2<:X_1.\ \neg X_2) & <: & \forall X_1<:X_0.\ \neg X_1 \\
X_0<:T, X_1<:X_0 & \mapsto & \neg(\forall X_2<:X_1.\ \neg X_2) & <: & \neg X_1 \\
X_0<:T, X_1<:X_0 & \mapsto & X_1 & <: & \forall X_2<:X_1.\ \neg X_2 \\
X_0<:T, X_1<:X_0 & \mapsto & X_0 & <: & \forall X_2<:X_1.\ \neg X_2 \\
\end{array}
$$

etc.

The renaming steps necessary to maintain the well-formedness of the context when new variables are added are performed tacitly here, choosing new names so as to clarify the pattern of regress. The crucial trick is the "re-bounding" that occurs, for instance, between the second and third lines, where the bound of X_1 on the left-hand side changes from $\texttt{Top}$ in line 2 to X_0 in line 3. Since the whole left-hand side in line 2 is itself the upper-bound of X_0, this re-bounding creates a cyclic pattern where longer and longer chains of variables in the context must be traversed on each loop. (The reader is cautioned not to look for *semantic* intuitions behind this example; in particular, $\neg T$ is a negation only in a syntactic sense.)

Worse yet, not only does this particular algorithm fail to terminate on some inputs, it can be shown (Pierce, 1994) that there is *no* algorithm that is sound and complete for the original full $F_{<:}$ subtype relation and that terminates on all inputs. The proof of this fact is too large for this book. However, to get a sense of its flavor, let's look at one more example.

28.5.3   DEFINITION: The *positive* and *negative* occurrences in a type T are defined as follows. T itself is a positive occurrence in T. If $T_1 \rightarrow T_2$ is a positive (respectively, negative) occurrence, then T_1 is a negative (resp. positive) occurrence and T$_2$ is a positive (negative) occurrence. If ∀X<:T$_1$.T$_2$ is a positive (respectively, negative) occurrence, then T$_1$ is a negative (resp. positive) occurrence and T$_2$ is a positive (negative) occurrence. The positive and negative occurrences in a subtyping statement Γ ⊢ S <: T are defined as follows: the type S and the bounds of type variables in Γ are negative occurrences. The type T is a positive occurrence.   □

The words "positive" and "negative" come from logic. According to the well-known *Curry-Howard correspondence* between propositions and types (§9.4), the type S→T corresponds to the logical proposition S ⇒ T, which, by the definition of logical implication, is equivalent to ¬S ∨ T. The subproposition S here is obviously in a "negative" position—that is, inside of an odd number of negations—if and only if the whole implication appears inside an even number of negations. Note that a positive occurrence in T corresponds to a negative occurrence in ¬T.

28.5.4   FACT: If X occurs only positively in S and negatively in T, then X<:U ⊢ S <: T iff ⊢ [X ↦ U]S <: [X ↦ U]T.   □

Proof: EXERCISE [★★ ↛].   □

Now, let T be the following type

$$T \quad = \quad ∀X_0{<:}Top.\,∀X_1{<:}Top.\,∀X_2{<:}Top.$$
$$¬(∀Y_0{<:}X_0.\,∀Y_1{<:}X_1.\,∀Y_2{<:}X_2.\,¬X_0)$$

and consider the subtyping statement

$$⊢ \quad T \quad <: \quad ∀X_0{<:}T.\,∀X_1{<:}P.\,∀X_2{<:}Q.$$
$$¬(∀Y_0{<:}Top.\,∀Y_1{<:}Top.\,∀Y_2{<:}Top.$$
$$¬(∀Z_0{<:}Y_0.\,∀Z_1{<:}Y_2.\,∀Z_2{<:}Y_1.\,U)).$$

We can think of this statement as a description of the state of a simple computer. The variables X$_1$ and X$_2$ are the "registers" of this machine. Their current contents are the types P and Q. The "instruction stream" of the machine is the third line: the first instruction is encoded in the bounds (Y$_2$ and Y$_1$— note their order) of the variables Z$_1$ and Z$_2$, and the unspecified type U is the remaining instructions in the program. The type T, the nested negations, and the bound variables X$_0$ and Y$_0$ here play much the same role as their counterparts in the simpler example above: they allow us to "turn the crank" and get back to a subgoal of the same shape as the original goal. One turn of the crank will correspond to one cycle of our machine.

In this example, the instruction at the front of the instruction stream encodes the command "switch the contents of registers 1 and 2." To see this, we use the two facts stated above to calculate as follows. (The values P and Q in the two registers are highlighted, to make them easier to follow.)

$$
\begin{array}{rll}
\vdash & \mathsf{T} & \\
<: & \forall X_0 <:\mathsf{T}.\, \forall X_1 <:\boxed{\mathsf{P}}.\, \forall X_2 <:\boxed{\mathsf{Q}}. & \\
& \quad \neg(\forall Y_0 <:\mathsf{Top}.\, \forall Y_1 <:\mathsf{Top}.\, \forall Y_2 <:\mathsf{Top}. & \\
& \quad\quad \neg(\forall Z_0 <:Y_0.\, \forall Z_1 <:Y_2.\, \forall Z_2 <:Y_1.\, \mathsf{U})) & \\
\text{iff}\quad \vdash & \neg(\forall Y_0 <:\mathsf{T}.\, \forall Y_1 <:\boxed{\mathsf{P}}.\, \forall Y_2 <:\boxed{\mathsf{Q}}.\, \neg\mathsf{T}) & \\
<: & \neg(\forall Y_0 <:\mathsf{Top}.\, \forall Y_1 <:\mathsf{Top}.\, \forall Y_2 <:\mathsf{Top}. & \text{by Fact 28.5.4} \\
& \quad \neg(\forall Z_0 <:Y_0.\, \forall Z_1 <:Y_2.\, \forall Z_2 <:Y_1.\, \mathsf{U})) & \\
\text{iff}\quad \vdash & (\forall Y_0 <:\mathsf{Top}.\, \forall Y_1 <:\mathsf{Top}.\, \forall Y_2 <:\mathsf{Top}. & \\
& \quad \neg(\forall Z_0 <:Y_0.\, \forall Z_1 <:Y_2.\, \forall Z_2 <:Y_1.\, \mathsf{U})) & \\
<: & (\forall Y_0 <:\mathsf{T}.\, \forall Y_1 <:\boxed{\mathsf{P}}.\, \forall Y_2 <:\boxed{\mathsf{Q}}.\, \neg\mathsf{T}) & \text{by Fact 28.5.2} \\
\text{iff}\quad \vdash & \neg(\forall Z_0 <:\mathsf{T}.\, \forall Z_1 <:\boxed{\mathsf{Q}}.\, \forall Z_2 <:\boxed{\mathsf{P}}.\, \mathsf{U})) & \\
<: & \neg\mathsf{T} & \text{by Fact 28.5.4} \\
\text{iff}\quad \vdash & \mathsf{T} & \\
<: & (\forall Z_0 <:\mathsf{T}.\, \forall Z_1 <:\boxed{\mathsf{Q}}.\, \forall Z_2 <:\boxed{\mathsf{P}}.\, \mathsf{U})) & \text{by Fact 28.5.2}
\end{array}
$$

Note that, at the end of the derivation, not only have the values P and Q switched places, but the instruction that caused this to happen has been used up in the process, leaving U at the front of the instruction stream to be "executed" next. By choosing a value of U that begins in the same way as the instruction we just executed

$$
\begin{aligned}
\mathsf{U} \;=\; & \neg(\forall Y_0 <:\mathsf{Top}.\, \forall Y_1 <:\mathsf{Top}.\, \forall Y_2 <:\mathsf{Top}. \\
& \quad \neg(\forall Z_0 <:Y_0.\, \forall Z_1 <:Y_2.\, \forall Z_2 <:Y_1.\, \mathsf{U}'))
\end{aligned}
$$

we can perform another swap and return the registers to their original state before continuing with U'. Alternatively, we can choose other values for U that cause different sorts of behavior. For example, if

$$
\begin{aligned}
\mathsf{U} \;=\; & \neg(\forall Y_0 <:\mathsf{Top}.\, \forall Y_1 <:\mathsf{Top}.\, \forall Y_2 <:\mathsf{Top}. \\
& \quad \neg(\forall Z_0 <:Y_0.\, \forall Z_1 <:Y_1.\, \forall Z_2 <:Y_2.\, Y_1))
\end{aligned}
$$

then, on the next cycle of the machine, the current value of register 1, i.e., Q, will appear in the position of U—in effect, performing an "indirect branch" through register 1 to the stream of instructions represented by Q. Conditional constructs and arithmetic (successor, predecessor, and zero-test) can be encoded using a generalization of this trick.

Putting all of this together, we arrive at a proof of undecidability via a reduction from two-counter machines—a simple variant on ordinary Turing machines, consisting of a finite control and two counters, each holding a natural number—to subtyping statements.

28.5.5   THEOREM [PIERCE, 1994]:   For each two-counter machine M, there exists a subtyping statement $S(M)$ such that $S(M)$ is derivable in full F<: iff the execution
of M halts.   □

Thus, if we could decide whether any subtype statement is provable, then
we could also decide whether any given two-counter machine will eventually
halt. Since the halting problem for two-counter machines is undecidable (cf.
Hopcroft and Ullman, 1979), so is the subtyping problem for full F<: .

We should emphasize, again, that the undecidability of the subtype relation
does not imply that the semi-algorithm for subtyping developed in §28.4 is either unsound or incomplete. If the statement $\Gamma \vdash S <: T$ is provable according
to the declarative subtyping rules, then the algorithm will definitely terminate
and yield *true*. If $\Gamma \vdash S <: T$ is *not* provable according to the declarative subtyping rules, then the algorithm will either diverge or yield *false*. The point is
that a given subtyping statement may fail to be provable from the algorithmic rules in two different ways: either by generating an infinite sequence of
subgoals (meaning that there is no finite derivation with this conclusion) or
else by leading to an obvious inconsistency like Top <: S→T. The subtyping
algorithm can detect one of these cases, but not the other.

Does the undecidability of full F<: mean that the system is useless in practice? Actually, it is generally held that the undecidability of F<: is not, *per se,*
a terribly serious deficiency. For one thing, it has been shown (Ghelli, 1995)
that, in order to cause the subtype checker to diverge, we must present it
with a goal with three quite special properties, each one of which is difficult to imagine programmers creating by accident. Also, there are a number
of popular languages whose typechecking or type reconstruction problems
are, in principle, either extremely expensive—like ML and Haskell, as we saw
in §22.7—or even undecidable, like C++ and λProlog (Felty, Gunter, Hannan,
Miller, Nadathur, and Scedrov, 1988). In fact, experience has shown the lack of
joins and meets mentioned in the following section (cf. Exercise 28.6.3) to be a
significantly more problematic shortcoming of full F<: than its undecidability.

28.5.6   EXERCISE [★★★★]:   (1) Define a variant of full F<: with no Top type but with
both X<:T and X bindings for variables (i.e., with both bounded and unbounded quantification); this variant is called *completely bounded quantification.* (2) Show that the subtype relation for this system is decidable. (3) Does
this restriction offer a satisfactory solution to the basic problems raised in
this section? In particular, does it work for languages with additional features
such as numbers, records, variants, etc.?   □

→ ∀ <: Top

$\Gamma \vdash S \vee T =$

$$
\begin{cases}
T & \text{if } \Gamma \vdash S <: T \\
S & \text{if } \Gamma \vdash T <: S \\
J & \text{if } S = X \\
& \quad X<:U \in \Gamma \\
& \quad \Gamma \vdash U \vee T = J \\
J & \text{if } T = X \\
& \quad X<:U \in \Gamma \\
& \quad \Gamma \vdash S \vee U = J \\
M_1 \rightarrow J_2 & \text{if } S = S_1 \rightarrow S_2 \\
& \quad T = T_1 \rightarrow T_2 \\
& \quad \Gamma \vdash S_1 \wedge T_1 = M_1 \\
& \quad \Gamma \vdash S_2 \vee T_2 = J_2 \\
\forall X<:U_1.J_2 & \text{if } S = \forall X<:U_1.S_2 \\
& \quad T = \forall X<:U_1.T_2 \\
& \quad \Gamma, X<:U_1 \vdash S_2 \vee T_2 = J_2 \\
Top & \text{otherwise}
\end{cases}
$$

$\Gamma \vdash S \wedge T =$

$$
\begin{cases}
S & \text{if } \Gamma \vdash S <: T \\
T & \text{if } \Gamma \vdash T <: S \\
J_1 \rightarrow M_2 & \text{if } S = S_1 \rightarrow S_2 \\
& \quad T = T_1 \rightarrow T_2 \\
& \quad \Gamma \vdash S_1 \vee T_1 = J_1 \\
& \quad \Gamma \vdash S_2 \wedge T_2 = M_2 \\
\forall X<:U_1.M_2 & \text{if } S = \forall X<:U_1.S_2 \\
& \quad T = \forall X<:U_1.T_2 \\
& \quad \Gamma, X<:U_1 \vdash S_2 \wedge T_2 = M_2 \\
fail & \text{otherwise}
\end{cases}
$$

Figure 28-5: Join and meet algorithms for kernel $F_{<:}$

28.6   Joins and Meets

We saw in §16.3 that a desirable property of languages with subtyping is the existence of a *join* for every pair of types S and T—that is, a type J that is minimal among all the common supertypes of S and T. We show in this section that the subtype relation of kernel $F_{<:}$ does indeed have a join for every S and T, as well as a meet for every S and T with at least one subtype in common, by giving algorithms for calculating them. (On the other hand, both of these properties fail for full $F_{<:}$; see Exercise 28.6.3.)

We write $\Gamma \vdash S \vee T = J$ for "J is the join of S and T in context Γ" and $\Gamma \vdash S \wedge T = M$ for "M is the meet of S and T in Γ." The algorithms for calculating these relations are defined simultaneously, in Figure 28-5. Note that some of the cases in each definition overlap; to read the definitions as deterministic algorithms, we stipulate that the first clause that applies is always chosen.

It is easy to check that ∨ and ∧ are total functions, in the sense that ∨ always returns a type and ∧ either returns a type or fails. We just observe that the total weight (cf. Definition 28.3.4) of S and T with respect to Γ is always reduced in recursive calls.

Now let us verify that these definitions actually calculate joins and meets. The argument is divided into two parts: Proposition 28.6.1 shows that the calculated join is an upper bound of S and T and the meet (when it exists) is a lower bound; Proposition 28.6.2 then shows that the calculated join is less than every common upper bound of S and T and that the meet is greater than every common lower bound (and exists whenever S and T have a common lower bound).

28.6.1   PROPOSITION:

1. If $\Gamma \vdash S \vee T = J$, then $\Gamma \vdash S <: J$ and $\Gamma \vdash T <: J$.

2. If $\Gamma \vdash S \wedge T = M$, then $\Gamma \vdash M <: S$ and $\Gamma \vdash M <: T$.   □

Proof: By a straightforward induction on the size of a derivation of $\Gamma \vdash S \vee T = J$ or $\Gamma \vdash S \wedge T = M$ (i.e., the number of recursive calls needed to calculate J or M).   □

28.6.2   PROPOSITION:

1. If $\Gamma \vdash S <: V$ and $\Gamma \vdash T <: V$, then $\Gamma \vdash S \vee T = J$ for some J with $\Gamma \vdash J <: V$.

2. If $\Gamma \vdash L <: S$ and $\Gamma \vdash L <: T$, then $\Gamma \vdash S \wedge T = M$ for some M with $\Gamma \vdash L <: M$.   □

Proof: It is easiest to prove the two parts by simultaneous induction on the total sizes of *algorithmic* derivations of $\Gamma \vdash S <: V$ and $\Gamma \vdash T <: V$ for part 1 and of $\Gamma \vdash L <: S$ and $\Gamma \vdash L <: T$ for part 2. (Theorem 28.3.3 assures us that these algorithmic counterparts of the given derivations always exist.)

1. If either of the two derivations is an instance of SA-TOP, then $V = \mathsf{Top}$ and the desired result, $\Gamma \vdash J <: V$, is immediate.

   If the derivation of $\Gamma \vdash T <: V$ is an instance of SA-REFL-TVAR, then $T = V$. But then the first given derivation tells us that $\Gamma \vdash S <: V = T$, so the first clause in the definition of the join applies, giving us $\Gamma \vdash S \vee T = T$ and satisfying the requirements. Similarly, if the derivation of $\Gamma \vdash S <: V$ is an instance of SA-REFL-TVAR, then $S = V$. But then the second given derivation tells us that $\Gamma \vdash T <: V = S$, so the second clause in the definition of the join applies, giving us $\Gamma \vdash S \vee T = S$ and again satisfying the requirements.

   If the derivation of $\Gamma \vdash S <: V$ ends with an instance of SA-TRANS-TVAR, then we have $S = X$ with $X{<:}U \in \Gamma$ and a subderivation of $\Gamma \vdash U \vee T = J$. The third clause in the definition of the join gives us $\Gamma \vdash S \vee T = J$, and the induction hypothesis yields $\Gamma \vdash J <: V$. Similarly if the derivation of $\Gamma \vdash T <: V$ ends with SA-TRANS-TVAR.

It is now easy to check, from the form of the algorithmic subtyping rules, that the only remaining possibilities are that both of the given derivations end with either SA-ARROW or SA-ALL.

If both end with SA-ARROW, then we have $S = S_1 \rightarrow S_2$, $T = T_1 \rightarrow T_2$, and $V = V_1 \rightarrow V_2$, with $\Gamma \vdash V_1 <: S_1$, $\Gamma \vdash S_2 <: V_2$, $\Gamma \vdash V_1 <: T_1$, and $\Gamma \vdash T_2 <: V_2$. By part (2) of the induction hypothesis, $\Gamma \vdash S_1 \wedge T_1 = M_1$ for some M_1 with $\Gamma \vdash V_1 <: M_1$, and by part (1), $\Gamma \vdash S_2 \vee T_2 = J_2$ for some J_2 with $\Gamma \vdash J_2 <: V_2$. The fifth clause in the definition of joins gives us $\Gamma \vdash S_1 \rightarrow S_2 \vee T_1 \rightarrow T_2 = M_1 \rightarrow J_2$, and we obtain $\Gamma \vdash M_1 \rightarrow J_2 <: V_1 \rightarrow V_2$ by S-ARROW.

Finally, if both of the given derivations end with SA-ALL, then we have $S = \forall X <: U_1 . S_2$, $T = \forall X <: U_1 \rightarrow T_2$, and $V = \forall X <: U_1 . V_2$, with $\Gamma, X <: U_1 \vdash S_2 <: V_2$ and $\Gamma, X <: U_1 \vdash T_2 <: V_2$. By part (1) of the induction hypothesis, $\Gamma, X <: U_1 \vdash S_2 \vee T_2 = J_2$ with $\Gamma, X <: U_1 \vdash J_2 <: V_2$. The sixth clause in the definition of joins gives us $J = \forall X <: U_1 . J_2$, and we obtain $\Gamma \vdash \forall X <: U_1 . J_2 <: \forall X <: U_1 . V_2$ by S-ALL.

2. If the derivation of $\Gamma \vdash L <: T$ ends in SA-TOP, then T is Top, so $\Gamma \vdash S <: T$ and, from the first clause of the definition of the meet, $\Gamma \vdash S \wedge T = S$. But, from the other given derivation, we know that $\Gamma \vdash L <: S$, so we are finished. Similarly if the derivation of $\Gamma \vdash L <: S$ ends in SA-TOP.

    If the derivation of $\Gamma \vdash L <: S$ ends in SA-REFL-TVAR, then $L = S$ and the other given derivation tells us $\Gamma \vdash L = S <: T$, from which the definition of the meet yields $\Gamma \vdash S \wedge T = S$ and we are done. Similarly if the derivation of $\Gamma \vdash L <: T$ ends in SA-REFL-TVAR.

    The only remaining possibilities are that both of the given derivations end with SA-TRANS-TVAR, SA-ARROW, or SA-ALL.

    If both derivations end with SA-TRANS-TVAR, then we have $L = X$ with $X <: U \in \Gamma$ and two subderivations $\Gamma \vdash U <: S$ and $\Gamma \vdash U <: T$. By part (2) of the induction hypothesis, $\Gamma \vdash U <: M$, from which we obtain $\Gamma \vdash L <: M$ from S-TVAR and transitivity.

    If both derivations end with SA-ARROW, then we have $S = S_1 \rightarrow S_2$, $T = T_1 \rightarrow T_2$, and $L = L_1 \rightarrow L_2$, with $\Gamma \vdash S_1 <: L_1$, $\Gamma \vdash L_2 <: S_2$, $\Gamma \vdash T_1 <: L_1$, and $\Gamma \vdash L_2 <: T_2$. By part (1) of the induction hypothesis, $\Gamma \vdash S_1 \vee T_1 = J_1$ for some J_1 with $\Gamma \vdash J_1 <: L_1$, and by part (2), $\Gamma \vdash S_2 \wedge T_2 = M_2$ for some M_2 with $\Gamma \vdash L_2 <: M_2$. The definition of meets tells us that $\Gamma \vdash S_1 \rightarrow S_2 \wedge T_1 \rightarrow T_2 = J_1 \rightarrow M_2$, and we obtain $\Gamma \vdash L_1 \rightarrow L_2 <: J_1 \rightarrow M_2$ by S-ARROW.

    The case where both derivations end with SA-ALL is similar.   □

28.6.3 EXERCISE [RECOMMENDED, ★★★]: Consider the pair of types (due to Ghelli, 1990) S = ∀X<:Y→Z.Y→Z and T = ∀X<:Y′→Z′.Y′→Z′ and the context Γ = Y<:Top, Z<:Top, Y′<:Y, Z′<:Z. (1) In full F$_{<:}$, how many types are there that are subtypes of both S and T under Γ? (2) Show that, in full F$_{<:}$, the types S and T have no meet under Γ. (3) Find a pair of types that has no join under Γ in full F$_{<:}$. □

28.7 Bounded Existentials

To extend the kernel F$_{<:}$ typechecking algorithm to a language with existential types, we must deal with one additional subtlety. Recall the declarative elimination rule for existentials:

$$\frac{\Gamma \vdash t_1 : \{\exists X <: T_{11}, T_{12}\} \qquad \Gamma, X <: T_{11}, x : T_{12} \vdash t_2 : T_2}{\Gamma \vdash \texttt{let } \{X, x\} = t_1 \texttt{ in } t_2 : T_2} \quad \text{(T-UNPACK)}$$

In §24-1 we remarked that the type variable X appears in the context in which t$_2$'s type is calculated in the second premise but *not* in the context of the rule's conclusion. This means that the type T$_2$ must not contain X free, since any free occurrences of X will be out of scope in the conclusion. This point was discussed in more detail in §25.5, where we observed that the change in the context from premise to conclusion corresponds to a *negative* shift of variable indices in T$_2$, when we represent types in the nameless deBruijn format; this shift will fail if T$_2$ happens to contain X free.

What are the implications of this observation for a minimal typing algorithm for a language with existentials? In particular, what should we do with an expression like t = let {X,x} = p in x, where p has type {∃X,Nat→X}? The most natural type of the body x is Nat→X, which mentions the bound variable X. However, according to the declarative typing relation (with the subsumption rule), x also has the types Nat→Top and Top. Since neither of these mentions X, the whole term t can legally be assigned the types Nat→Top and Top in the declarative system. More generally, we are always free to promote the body of an unpacking expression to any type that does not involve the bound type variable X and then apply T-UNPACK. So, if we want our minimal typing algorithm to be complete, it should not simply fail when it encounters an unpacking expression where the minimal type T$_2$ of the body contains a free occurrence of the bound variable X. Instead, it should try to promote T$_2$ to some supertype that does not mention X. The key observation that we need to make this work is that the set of X-free supertypes of a given type always has a minimal element, as the following exercise (whose solution is due to Ghelli and Pierce, 1998) shows.

28.7.1   EXERCISE [★★★]: Give an algorithm for calculating, in kernel $F_{<:}$ with bounded existentials, the minimal X-free supertype of a given type T with respect to a context Γ, written $R_{X,\Gamma}(T)$.   □

The algorithmic typing rule for existential elimination can now be written like this:

$$\frac{\Gamma \vdash t_1 : T_1 \qquad \Gamma \vdash T_1 \Uparrow \{\exists X{<:}T_{11}, T_{12}\}}{\Gamma, X{<:}T_{11}, x{:}T_{12} \vdash t_2 : T_2 \qquad R_{X,(\Gamma, X{<:}T_{11}, x{:}T_{12})}(T_2) = T_2'}{\Gamma \vdash \mathtt{let}\ \{X,x\}{=}t_1\ \mathtt{in}\ t_2 : T_2'} \quad \text{(TA-UNPACK)}$$

For *full* $F_{<:}$ with bounded existentials, the situation is more problematic, as might be expected. Ghelli and Pierce (1998) give an example of a type T, a context Γ, and a variable X such that the set of X-free supertypes T under Γ has no minimal element. It immediately follows that the typing relation for this system lacks minimal types.

28.7.2   EXERCISE [★★★]: Show that the subtyping relation for a variant of full $F_{<:}$ with just bounded existential types (no universal types) is also undecidable.   □

28.8   Bounded Quantification and the Bottom Type

The addition of a minimal Bot type (§15.4) somewhat complicates the metatheoretic properties of $F_{<:}$. The reason for this is that, in a type of the form $\forall X{<:}\mathtt{Bot}.T$, the variable X is actually a *synonym* for Bot inside T, since X is a subtype of Bot by assumption and Bot is a subtype of X by the rule S-BOT. This, in turn, means that pairs of types such as $\forall X{<:}\mathtt{Bot}.X{\rightarrow}X$ and $\forall X{<:}\mathtt{Bot}.\mathtt{Bot}{\rightarrow}\mathtt{Bot}$ are equivalent in the subtype relation, even though they are not syntactically identical. Moreover, if the ambient context contains the assumptions $X{<:}\mathtt{Bot}$ and $Y{<:}\mathtt{Bot}$, then the types $X{\rightarrow}Y$ and $Y{\rightarrow}X$ are equivalent even though neither of them mentions Bot explicitly. Despite these difficulties, the essential properties of kernel $F_{<:}$ can still be established in the presence of Bot. Details can be found in Pierce (1997a).

PART VI

Higher-Order Systems

29 *Type Operators and Kinding*

In previous chapters, we have often made use of abbreviations like

    CBool = ∀X. X → X → X;

and

    Pair Y Z = ∀X. (Y→Z→X) → X;

to make examples easier to read, writing λx:Pair Nat Bool. x, for instance, instead of the more cumbersome λx:∀X.(Nat→Bool→X)→X. x.

CBool is a simple abbreviation; when we see it in an example, we should just replace it by the right-hand side of its definition. Pair, on the other hand, is a *parametric abbreviation;* when we encounter Pair S T, we must substitute the actual types S and T for the parameters Y and Z in its definition. In other words, abbreviations like Pair give us an informal notation for defining functions at the level of type expressions.

We have also used type-level expressions like Array T and Ref T involving the *type constructors* Array and Ref. Although these type constructors are built into the language, rather than being defined by the programmer, they are also a form of functions at the level of types. We can view Ref, for example, as a function that, for each type T, yields the type of reference cells containing an element of T.

Our task in this and the next two chapters is to treat these type-level functions, collectively called *type operators,* more formally. In this chapter, we introduce basic mechanisms of abstraction and application at the level of types, along with a precise definition of when two type expressions should be regarded as equivalent and a well-formedness relation, called *kinding,* that prevents us from writing nonsensical type expressions. Chapter 30 goes a

---

The system introduced in this chapter is the pure simply typed lambda-calculus with type operators, λ_ω (Figure 29-1). The examples also use numbers and booleans (8-2) and universal types (23-1). The associated OCaml implementation is fullomega.

step further and treats type operators as *first-class citizens*—i.e., as entities that can be passed as arguments to functions; that chapter introduces the well-known System F_ω, generalizing the quantification over types in System F (Chapter 23) to *higher-order quantification* over type operators. Chapter 31 considers the combination of type operators, higher-order quantification, and subtyping.

29.1   Intuitions

To study functions at the level of types, the first thing we need is some notation for abstraction and application. It is standard practice to use the *same* notations for these as for abstraction and application at the level of terms, indicating abstraction by λ and application by juxtaposition.[1] For example, we write $\lambda X.\{a:X,b:X\}$ for the function that, given a type T, yields the record type $\{a:T,b:T\}$. The application of this function to the argument Bool is written $(\lambda X.\{a:X,b:X\})$ Bool.

Like ordinary functions, type functions with multiple arguments can be built from one-argument functions by *currying*. For example, the type expression $\lambda Y.\ \lambda Z.\ \forall X.\ (Y{\to}Z{\to}X)\ \to\ X$ represents a two-argument function— or, strictly speaking, a one-argument function that, when applied to a type S, yields another one-argument function that, when applied to a type T, yields the type $\forall X.\ (S{\to}T{\to}X){\to}X$.

We will continue to use informal abbreviations for long type expressions, including type operators. For example, in the remainder of this chapter we will assume we have the abbreviation

    Pair = λY. λZ. ∀X. (Y→Z→X) → X;

When we write Pair S T in examples, what we really mean is

    (λY. λZ. ∀X. (Y→Z→X) → X) S T.

In other words, we are replacing the informal convention of parametric abbreviation that we have used up to this point with the more elementary informal convention of expanding simple abbreviations to their right-hand sides whenever we see them, plus formal mechanisms for definition and instantiation of type operators. The operations of defining and expanding abbreviations can

---

1. The one drawback of this notational parsimony is that the terminology for different sorts of expressions can become a little contorted. In particular, the phrase "type abstraction" might now mean an abstraction that expects a type as its argument (i.e., a term like $\lambda X.t$), or it might equally mean an abstraction at the level of types (i.e., a type expression like $\lambda X.\{a:X\}$). In contexts where both are possible, people tend to use "polymorphic function" for the first sense and "type-level abstraction" or "operator abstraction" for the second.

also be treated formally—i.e., we can make them operations in the object language, instead of conventions in the meta-language—but we will not do so here. Interested readers are referred to the literature on type systems with *definitions* or *singleton kinds;* see Severi and Poll (1994), Stone and Harper (2000), Crary (2000), and other works cited there.

Introducing abstraction and application at the level of types gives us the possibility of writing the same type in different ways. For example, if `Id` is an abbreviation for the type operator λX.X, then the expressions

$$\begin{array}{lll}
\texttt{Nat} \rightarrow \texttt{Bool} & \texttt{Nat} \rightarrow \texttt{Id Bool} & \texttt{Id Nat} \rightarrow \texttt{Id Bool} \\
\texttt{Id Nat} \rightarrow \texttt{Bool} & \texttt{Id (Nat} \rightarrow \texttt{Bool)} & \texttt{Id (Id (Id Nat} \rightarrow \texttt{Bool))}
\end{array}$$

are all names for the same arrow type. To make this intuition precise, we introduce a *definitional equivalence* relation on types, written $S \equiv T$. The most important clause in the definition of this relation

$$(\lambda X :: K_{11} . T_{12}) \ T_2 \equiv [X \mapsto T_2] T_{12} \qquad \text{(Q-ApAbs)}$$

tells us that a type-level abstraction applied to an argument is equivalent to the body of the abstraction with the argument substituted for the formal parameter. We exploit definitional equivalence in typechecking by a new rule

$$\frac{\Gamma \vdash t : S \qquad S \equiv T}{\Gamma \vdash t : T} \qquad \text{(T-Eq)}$$

precisely capturing the intuition that, if two types are equivalent, then the members of one are all members of the other.

Another new possibility that abstraction and application mechanisms give us is the ability to write meaningless type expressions. For example, applying one proper type to another, as in the type expression (`Bool Nat`), makes no more sense than applying `true` to `6` at the term level. To prevent this sort of nonsense, we introduce a system of *kinds* that classify type expressions according to their arity, just as arrow types tell us about the arities of terms.

Kinds are built from a single atomic kind, written ∗ and pronounced "type," and a single constructor ⇒. They include, for example:

∗	the kind of proper types (like `Bool` and `Bool→Bool`)
∗⇒∗	the kind of type operators (i.e., functions from proper types to proper types)
∗⇒∗⇒∗	the kind of functions from proper types to type operators (i.e., two-argument operators)
(∗⇒∗)⇒∗	the kind of functions from type operators to proper types

Kinds, then, are "the types of types." In essence, the system of kinds is a copy of the simply typed lambda-calculus, "one level up."

In what follows, we use the word *type* for any type-level expression—i.e., both for ordinary types like Nat→Nat and ∀X.X→X and for type operators like λX.X. When we want to focus on ordinary types (i.e., the sorts of type expressions that are actually used to classify terms), we call them *proper types*.

Type expressions with kinds like (∗⇒∗)⇒∗ are called *higher-order type operators*. Unlike higher-order functions at the term level, which are often extremely useful, higher-order type operators are somewhat esoteric. We will see one class of examples that use them in Chapter 32.

To simplify the problem of checking the well-kindedness of type expressions, we annotate each type-level abstraction with a kind for its bound variable. For example, the official form of the Pair operator is:

```
Pair = λA::∗. λB::∗. ∀X.  (A→B→X) → X;
```

(Note the doubled colon.) However, since almost all of these annotations will be ∗, we will continue to write λX.T as an abbreviation for λX::∗.T.

A few pictures may help clarify. The expressions of our language are now divided into three separate classes: terms, types, and kinds. The level of terms contains basic data values (integers, floats), compound data values (records, etc.), value-level abstractions, applications, type abstractions, and type applications.

Terms

```
  5                λx:Nat.x
                                          (λx:Nat.x) true
                      λX.λx:X.x
     (λx:Nat.x) 5                pair [Nat] [Bool] 5 false
```

The level of types contains two sorts of expressions. First, there are proper types like Nat, Nat→Nat, Pair Nat Bool, and ∀X.X→X, which are inhabited by terms. (Of course, not all terms have a type; for example (λx:Nat.x) true does not.)

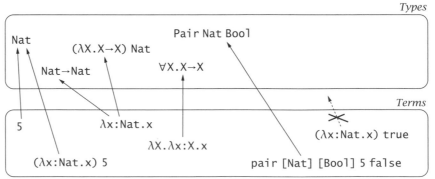

Then there are type operators like Pair and λX.X→X, which do *not* themselves classify terms (it does not make sense to ask "What terms have type λX.X→X?"), but which can be applied to type arguments to form proper types like (λX.X→X)Nat that do classify terms.

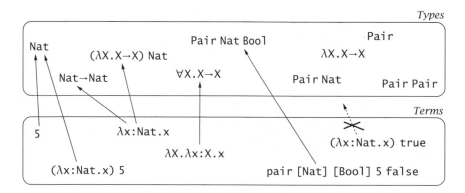

Note that proper types—i.e., type expressions of kind ∗—may include type operators of higher kinds as subphrases, as in (λX.X→X) Nat or Pair Nat Bool, just as term expressions belonging to base types like Nat may include lambda-abstractions as subexpressions, as in (λx:Nat.x) 5.

Finally, we have the level of kinds. The simplest kind is ∗, which has all proper types as members.

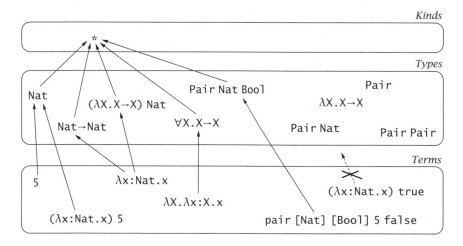

Type operators like λX.X→X and Pair belong to arrow kinds like ∗⇒∗ and ∗⇒∗⇒∗. Ill-formed type-level expressions, like Pair Pair, do not belong to any kind.

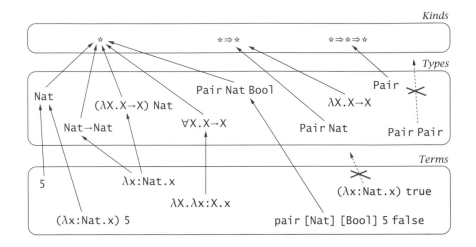

29.1.1   EXERCISE [★]: What is the difference in meaning between the type-level expressions ∀X.X→X and λX.X→X?   □

29.1.2   EXERCISE [★]: Why doesn't an arrow type like Nat→Nat have an arrow kind like ∗⇒∗?   □

A natural question at this point is "Why stop at three levels of expressions?" Couldn't we go on to introduce functions from kinds to kinds, application at the level of kinds, etc., add a fourth level to classify kind expressions according to their functionality, and continue on in this way *ad infinitum*? Such systems have been investigated by the *pure type systems* community (Terlouw, 1989; Berardi, 1988; Barendregt, 1991, 1992; Jutting, McKinna, and Pollack, 1994; McKinna and Pollack, 1993; Pollack, 1994). For programming languages, however, three levels have proved sufficient.

Indeed, while type operators can be found, in some form, in essentially all statically typed programming languages, it is relatively rare for language designers to offer programmers even the full power of the present formulation. Some languages (e.g., Java) offer only a few built-in type operators like Array, with no facilities for defining new ones. Others bundle type operators together with other language features; in ML, for example, type operators are provided as part of the datatype mechanism; we can define *parametric datatypes* like[2]

_____

2. We're ignoring ML's conventions for capitalization of identifiers for the sake of the example. In OCaml, this definition would really be written

```
type 'a tyop = Tyoptag of ('a → 'a);
```

```
type 'a Tyop = tyoptag of ('a → 'a);
```

which we would write as

```
Tyop = λX. <tyoptag:X→X>;
```

In other words, in ML we can define parametric variants, but not arbitrary parametric types. The benefit of this restriction is that, wherever the type operator Tyop appears in a program at the level of types, the corresponding tag tyoptag will appear at the level of terms—that is, every place where the typechecker needs to use the definitional equivalence relation to replace a type like Tyop Nat by its reduced form Nat→Nat will be marked in the program by an explicit occurrence of tyoptag. This substantially simplifies the typechecking algorithm.[3]

The ⇒ constructor on kinds is the only one that we have space to discuss here, but a great many others have been studied; indeed, the range of kinding systems for checking and tracking various properties of type expressions rivals the range of type systems for analyzing properties of terms. There are *record kinds* (whose elements are records of types—not to be confused with the types of records; they offer a natural way of defining systems of mutually recursive types), *row kinds* (which describe "rows of fields" that can be used to assemble record types in systems with row variable polymorphism—see page 337), *power kinds* or *power types* (which offer an alternate presentation of subtyping—see Cardelli, 1988a), *singleton kinds* (related to *definitions*—see page 441—and to module systems with *sharing*—see page 465), *dependent kinds* (an analog "one level up" of the dependent types discussed in §30.5), and many more.

29.2 Definitions

Figure 29-1 presents the complete definition of a core lambda-calculus with type operators. At the term level, this calculus includes just the variables, abstraction, and application of the simply typed lambda-calculus (for this reason, it is called the *simply typed lambda-calculus with type operators*). The type level includes the usual arrow types and type variables, plus operator abstraction and application. Quantified types like ∀X.T are omitted from this system; we return to them in detail in Chapter 30.

---

3. This restriction is similar to ML's treatment of recursive types, discussed in §20-1. The bundling of recursive types into datatype definitions gives the programmer the convenience of equi-recursive types and the typechecker the simplicity of iso-recursive types by hiding the fold/unfold annotations in the tagging and case analysis operations associated with variant types.

→ $\boxed{\Rightarrow}$ *Extends* $\lambda_\rightarrow$ *(9-1)*

Syntax

t ::=		*terms:*
	x	*variable*
	λx:T.t	*abstraction*
	t t	*application*
v ::=		*values:*
	λx:T.t	*abstraction value*
T ::=		*types:*
	X	*type variable*
	λX::K.T	*operator abstraction*
	T T	*operator application*
	T→T	*type of functions*
Γ ::=		*contexts:*
	$\varnothing$	*empty context*
	Γ, x:T	*term variable binding*
	Γ, X::K	*type variable binding*
K ::=		*kinds:*
	*	*kind of proper types*
	K$\Rightarrow$K	*kind of operators*

Evaluation $\boxed{t \longrightarrow t'}$

$$\frac{t_1 \longrightarrow t_1'}{t_1\ t_2 \longrightarrow t_1'\ t_2} \quad \text{(E-App1)}$$

$$\frac{t_2 \longrightarrow t_2'}{v_1\ t_2 \longrightarrow v_1\ t_2'} \quad \text{(E-App2)}$$

$$(\lambda x{:}T_{11}.t_{12})\ v_2 \longrightarrow [x \mapsto v_2]t_{12} \quad \text{(E-AppAbs)}$$

Kinding $\boxed{\Gamma \vdash T :: K}$

$$\frac{X{::}K \in \Gamma}{\Gamma \vdash X :: K} \quad \text{(K-TVar)}$$

$$\frac{\Gamma, X{::}K_1 \vdash T_2 :: K_2}{\Gamma \vdash \lambda X{::}K_1.T_2 :: K_1 \Rightarrow K_2} \quad \text{(K-Abs)}$$

$$\frac{\Gamma \vdash T_1 :: K_{11} \Rightarrow K_{12} \qquad \Gamma \vdash T_2 :: K_{11}}{\Gamma \vdash T_1\ T_2 :: K_{12}} \quad \text{(K-App)}$$

$$\frac{\Gamma \vdash T_1 :: * \qquad \Gamma \vdash T_2 :: *}{\Gamma \vdash T_1 {\rightarrow} T_2 :: *} \quad \text{(K-Arrow)}$$

Type equivalence $\boxed{S \equiv T}$

$$T \equiv T \quad \text{(Q-Refl)}$$

$$\frac{T \equiv S}{S \equiv T} \quad \text{(Q-Symm)}$$

$$\frac{S \equiv U \qquad U \equiv T}{S \equiv T} \quad \text{(Q-Trans)}$$

$$\frac{S_1 \equiv T_1 \qquad S_2 \equiv T_2}{S_1 {\rightarrow} S_2 \equiv T_1 {\rightarrow} T_2} \quad \text{(Q-Arrow)}$$

$$\frac{S_2 \equiv T_2}{\lambda X{::}K_1.S_2 \equiv \lambda X{::}K_1.T_2} \quad \text{(Q-Abs)}$$

$$\frac{S_1 \equiv T_1 \qquad S_2 \equiv T_2}{S_1\ S_2 \equiv T_1\ T_2} \quad \text{(Q-App)}$$

$$(\lambda X{::}K_{11}.T_{12})\ T_2 \equiv [X \mapsto T_2]T_{12} \quad \text{(Q-AppAbs)}$$

continued...

Figure 29-1: Type operators and kinding (λ_ω)

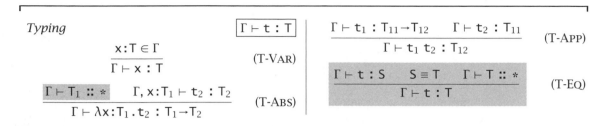

Typing

$$\frac{x{:}T \in \Gamma}{\Gamma \vdash x : T} \quad \text{(T-VAR)}$$

$$\frac{\Gamma \vdash T_1 :: * \quad \Gamma, x{:}T_1 \vdash t_2 : T_2}{\Gamma \vdash \lambda x{:}T_1 . t_2 : T_1 {\to} T_2} \quad \text{(T-ABS)}$$

$\Gamma \vdash t : T$

$$\frac{\Gamma \vdash t_1 : T_{11}{\to}T_{12} \quad \Gamma \vdash t_2 : T_{11}}{\Gamma \vdash t_1 \, t_2 : T_{12}} \quad \text{(T-APP)}$$

$$\frac{\Gamma \vdash t : S \quad S \equiv T \quad \Gamma \vdash T :: *}{\Gamma \vdash t : T} \quad \text{(T-EQ)}$$

Figure 29-1: Type operators and kinding (continued)

The presentation of the system extends the framework of the simply typed lambda-calculus in three ways. First, we add a collection of rules of *kinding*, which specify how type expressions can be combined to yield new type expressions. We write $\Gamma \vdash T :: K$ for "type T has kind K in context Γ." Note the similarity between these kinding rules and the typing rules of the original simply typed lambda-calculus (Figure 9-1).

Second, whenever a type T appears in a term (as in $\lambda x{:}T . t$), we must check that T is well formed. This involves adding a new premise to the old T-ABS rule that checks $\Gamma \vdash T :: *$. Note that T must have exactly kind $*$—i.e., it must be a proper type—since it is being used to describe the values that the term-variable x may range over. The typing rules maintain the invariant that, whenever we can derive a statement $\Gamma \vdash t : T$, the statement $\Gamma \vdash T :: *$ is also derivable (as long as all the types appearing in the context are well kinded). This point is discussed in more detail in §30-3.

Third, we add a collection of rules for the *definitional equivalence* relation between types. We write $S \equiv T$ for "types S and T are definitionally equivalent." This relation is quite similar to the reduction relation at the level of terms. The effect of definitional equivalence on typing is captured by the new T-EQ rule. The kinding premise (which was elided when we discussed the rule in the previous section) maintains the invariant mentioned above, that "typable terms always have kindable types." Note the similarity of this rule to the rule of subsumption (T-SUB) in systems with subtyping.

The basic metatheoretic properties of this system require a little work to develop, since the type equivalence relation introduces significant flexibility in the "shapes" of the types assigned to terms. We postpone the development of this theory to Chapter 30.

30 *Higher-Order Polymorphism*

Having seen in Chapter 29 how to add type operators to $\lambda_\rightarrow$, the natural next step is to mix them with the other typing features we have studied throughout the book. In this chapter, we combine type operators with the polymorphism of System F, yielding a well-known system called F_ω (Girard, 1972). Chapter 31 enriches this system with subtyping to form System $F_{<:}^\omega$, which is the setting for our final case study of purely functional objects in Chapter 32.

The definition of F_ω is a straightforward combination of features from λ_ω and System F. However, proving the basic properties of this system (in particular, preservation and progress) requires somewhat harder work than most of the systems we have seen, because we must deal with the fact that type-checking now requires evaluation at the level of types. These proofs will be the main job of this chapter.

30.1 Definitions

System F_ω is formed by combining System F from Chapter 23 and λ_ω from Chapter 29, adding kinding annotations (X::K) in places where type variables are bound (i.e., in type abstractions and quantifiers). The formal definition for the system with just universal quantifiers (not existentials) is given in Figure 30-1. We list the rules in full, even though the differences from earlier systems are minor, for easy reference in the proofs in §30.3.

We abbreviate $\forall X::*.T$ as $\forall X.T$ and $\{\exists X::*,T\}$ as $\{\exists X,T\}$, so that terms of System F can be read directly as terms of F_ω.

Similarly, we obtain the higher-order variant of existential types by generalizing bindings from X to X::K in the original presentation of existentials in Chapter 24. Figure 30-2 summarizes this extension.

The examples in this chapter are terms of F_ω (Figure 30-1) with records, booleans, and existentials (30-2). The associated OCaml implementation is `fullomega`. No implementation is provided for the dependent types mentioned in §30.5.

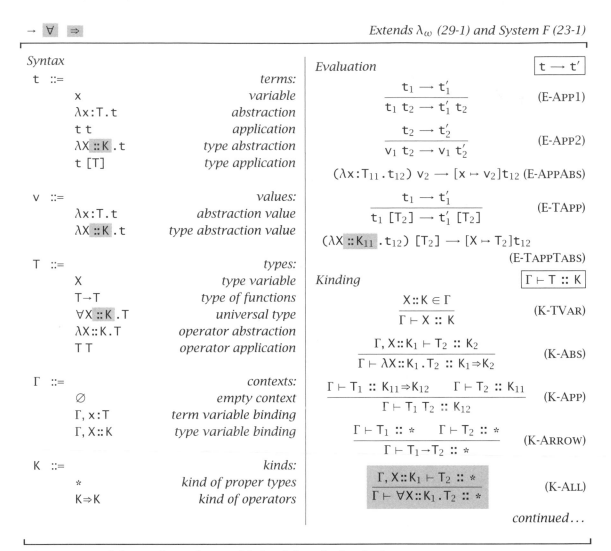

$\rightarrow$ $\forall$ $\Rightarrow$ *Extends* λ_ω *(29-1) and System F (23-1)*

Syntax

t	::=		*terms:*
		x	*variable*
		λx:T.t	*abstraction*
		t t	*application*
		λX::K.t	*type abstraction*
		t [T]	*type application*

v	::=		*values:*
		λx:T.t	*abstraction value*
		λX::K.t	*type abstraction value*

T	::=		*types:*
		X	*type variable*
		T→T	*type of functions*
		∀X::K.T	*universal type*
		λX::K.T	*operator abstraction*
		T T	*operator application*

Γ	::=		*contexts:*
		∅	*empty context*
		Γ,x:T	*term variable binding*
		Γ,X::K	*type variable binding*

K	::=		*kinds:*
		*	*kind of proper types*
		K⇒K	*kind of operators*

Evaluation $\boxed{\mathsf{t} \longrightarrow \mathsf{t}'}$

$$\frac{\mathsf{t}_1 \longrightarrow \mathsf{t}_1'}{\mathsf{t}_1\ \mathsf{t}_2 \longrightarrow \mathsf{t}_1'\ \mathsf{t}_2} \quad (\text{E-App1})$$

$$\frac{\mathsf{t}_2 \longrightarrow \mathsf{t}_2'}{\mathsf{v}_1\ \mathsf{t}_2 \longrightarrow \mathsf{v}_1\ \mathsf{t}_2'} \quad (\text{E-App2})$$

$$(\lambda\mathsf{x}{:}\mathsf{T}_{11}.\mathsf{t}_{12})\ \mathsf{v}_2 \longrightarrow [\mathsf{x} \mapsto \mathsf{v}_2]\mathsf{t}_{12} \quad (\text{E-AppAbs})$$

$$\frac{\mathsf{t}_1 \longrightarrow \mathsf{t}_1'}{\mathsf{t}_1\ [\mathsf{T}_2] \longrightarrow \mathsf{t}_1'\ [\mathsf{T}_2]} \quad (\text{E-TApp})$$

$$(\lambda\mathsf{X}{::}\mathsf{K}_{11}.\mathsf{t}_{12})\ [\mathsf{T}_2] \longrightarrow [\mathsf{X} \mapsto \mathsf{T}_2]\mathsf{t}_{12}$$
$$(\text{E-TappTabs})$$

Kinding $\boxed{\Gamma \vdash \mathsf{T} :: \mathsf{K}}$

$$\frac{\mathsf{X}{::}\mathsf{K} \in \Gamma}{\Gamma \vdash \mathsf{X} :: \mathsf{K}} \quad (\text{K-TVar})$$

$$\frac{\Gamma, \mathsf{X}{::}\mathsf{K}_1 \vdash \mathsf{T}_2 :: \mathsf{K}_2}{\Gamma \vdash \lambda\mathsf{X}{::}\mathsf{K}_1.\mathsf{T}_2 :: \mathsf{K}_1{\Rightarrow}\mathsf{K}_2} \quad (\text{K-Abs})$$

$$\frac{\Gamma \vdash \mathsf{T}_1 :: \mathsf{K}_{11}{\Rightarrow}\mathsf{K}_{12} \qquad \Gamma \vdash \mathsf{T}_2 :: \mathsf{K}_{11}}{\Gamma \vdash \mathsf{T}_1\ \mathsf{T}_2 :: \mathsf{K}_{12}} \quad (\text{K-App})$$

$$\frac{\Gamma \vdash \mathsf{T}_1 :: * \qquad \Gamma \vdash \mathsf{T}_2 :: *}{\Gamma \vdash \mathsf{T}_1{\rightarrow}\mathsf{T}_2 :: *} \quad (\text{K-Arrow})$$

$$\frac{\Gamma, \mathsf{X}{::}\mathsf{K}_1 \vdash \mathsf{T}_2 :: *}{\Gamma \vdash \forall\mathsf{X}{::}\mathsf{K}_1.\mathsf{T}_2 :: *} \quad (\text{K-All})$$

continued...

Figure 30-1: Higher-order polymorphic lambda-calculus ($\mathbf{F}_\omega$)

30.2   Example

We will see an extended example of programming using abstractions ranging over type operators in Chapter 32. Here is a much smaller one.

Recall the encoding of abstract data types in terms of existentials from §24.2. Suppose now that we want to implement an ADT of pairs, in the same way as we earlier implemented ADTs of types like counters. This ADT should

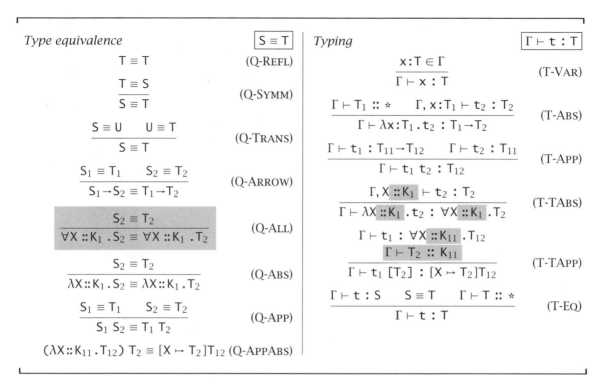

Type equivalence $\boxed{S \equiv T}$

$$T \equiv T \qquad \text{(Q-Refl)}$$

$$\frac{T \equiv S}{S \equiv T} \qquad \text{(Q-Symm)}$$

$$\frac{S \equiv U \qquad U \equiv T}{S \equiv T} \qquad \text{(Q-Trans)}$$

$$\frac{S_1 \equiv T_1 \qquad S_2 \equiv T_2}{S_1 {\rightarrow} S_2 \equiv T_1 {\rightarrow} T_2} \qquad \text{(Q-Arrow)}$$

$$\frac{S_2 \equiv T_2}{\forall X :: K_1 . S_2 \equiv \forall X :: K_1 . T_2} \qquad \text{(Q-All)}$$

$$\frac{S_2 \equiv T_2}{\lambda X :: K_1 . S_2 \equiv \lambda X :: K_1 . T_2} \qquad \text{(Q-Abs)}$$

$$\frac{S_1 \equiv T_1 \qquad S_2 \equiv T_2}{S_1 \ S_2 \equiv T_1 \ T_2} \qquad \text{(Q-App)}$$

$$(\lambda X :: K_{11} . T_{12}) \ T_2 \equiv [X \mapsto T_2] T_{12} \quad \text{(Q-AppAbs)}$$

Typing $\boxed{\Gamma \vdash t : T}$

$$\frac{x : T \in \Gamma}{\Gamma \vdash x : T} \qquad \text{(T-Var)}$$

$$\frac{\Gamma \vdash T_1 :: * \qquad \Gamma, x : T_1 \vdash t_2 : T_2}{\Gamma \vdash \lambda x : T_1 . t_2 : T_1 {\rightarrow} T_2} \qquad \text{(T-Abs)}$$

$$\frac{\Gamma \vdash t_1 : T_{11} {\rightarrow} T_{12} \qquad \Gamma \vdash t_2 : T_{11}}{\Gamma \vdash t_1 \ t_2 : T_{12}} \qquad \text{(T-App)}$$

$$\frac{\Gamma, X :: K_1 \vdash t_2 : T_2}{\Gamma \vdash \lambda X :: K_1 . t_2 : \forall X :: K_1 . T_2} \qquad \text{(T-TAbs)}$$

$$\frac{\Gamma \vdash t_1 : \forall X :: K_{11} . T_{12} \qquad \Gamma \vdash T_2 :: K_{11}}{\Gamma \vdash t_1 \ [T_2] : [X \mapsto T_2] T_{12}} \qquad \text{(T-TApp)}$$

$$\frac{\Gamma \vdash t : S \qquad S \equiv T \qquad \Gamma \vdash T :: *}{\Gamma \vdash t : T} \qquad \text{(T-Eq)}$$

Figure 30-1: Higher-order polymorphic lambda-calculus (F_ω), continued

provide operations for building pairs and taking them apart. Moreover, we would like these operations to be *polymorphic,* so that we can use them to build and use pairs of elements from any types S and T. That is, the abstract type that we provide should not be a proper type, but rather an abstract type *constructor* (or *operator*). It should be abstract in the same sense as the earlier ADTs: for each S and T, the `pair` operation should take an element of S and one of T and return an element of `Pair S T`, while `fst` and `snd` should take a `Pair S T` and return, respectively, an S or a T, and these facts should be all that a client of our abstraction knows about it.

From these requirements, we can read off the signature that we want our pair ADT to present to the world:

```
PairSig = {∃Pair::*⇒*⇒*,
          {pair: ∀X. ∀Y. X→Y→(Pair X Y),
           fst: ∀X. ∀Y. (Pair X Y)→X,
           snd: ∀X. ∀Y. (Pair X Y)→Y}};
```

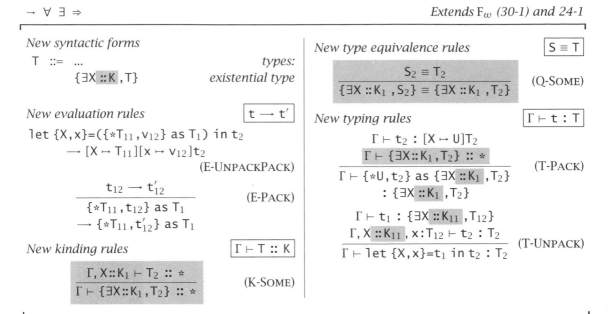

Figure 30-2: Higher-order existential types

That is, an implementation of pairs should provide a type operator `Pair` plus polymorphic functions `pair`, `fst`, and `snd` of the given types.

Here is one way of building a package with this type:

```
pairADT =
    {*λX. λY. ∀R. (X→Y→R) → R,
     {pair = λX. λY. λx:X. λy:Y.
                λR. λp:X→Y→R. p x y,
      fst = λX. λY. λp: ∀R. (X→Y→R) → R.
                p [X] (λx:X. λy:Y. x),
      snd = λX. λY. λp: ∀R. (X→Y→R) → R.
                p [Y] (λx:X. λy:Y. y)}}  as PairSig;
```

▶ pairADT : PairSig

The hidden representation type is the operator λX. λY. ∀R. (X→Y→R) → R that we have used before (§23.4) to represent pairs. The components `pair`, `fst`, and `snd` of the body are appropriate polymorphic functions.

Having defined `pairADT`, we can unpack it in the usual way.

```
let {Pair,pair}=pairADT
in pair.fst [Nat] [Bool] (pair.pair [Nat] [Bool] 5 true);
```

▶ 5 : Nat

30.3   Properties

We now turn to establishing the basic properties of F_ω—in particular the usual preservation and progress theorems. The ideas behind these proofs are similar to what we've seen before, but we need to proceed carefully because we are now dealing with a somewhat larger and more complicated system. In particular, it will require some work to analyze the structure of the type equivalence relation. To shorten the proofs, we treat only the universal part of F_ω, the system defined in Figure 30-1. Extending the arguments to cover existential types is straightforward.

Basic Properties

We begin with some simple properties that will be needed later.

30.3.1   LEMMA [STRENGTHENING]:

If $\Gamma, x:S, \Delta \vdash T :: K$, then $\Gamma, \Delta \vdash T :: K$.   □

Proof: The kinding relation does not refer to term variable bindings.   □

For the sake of variety, let us prove permutation and weakening for F_ω together, rather than one after the other as we have done previously.

30.3.2   LEMMA [PERMUTATION AND WEAKENING]: Suppose we have contexts Γ and Δ such that Δ is a well-formed permutation of Γ, Σ for some context Σ—that is, Δ is a permutation of an extension of Γ.

1. If $\Gamma \vdash T :: K$, then $\Delta \vdash T :: K$.

2. If $\Gamma \vdash t : T$, then $\Delta \vdash t : T$.   □

Proof: Straightforward induction on derivations.   □

30.3.3   LEMMA [TERM SUBSTITUTION]: If $\Gamma, x:S, \Delta \vdash t : T$ and $\Gamma \vdash s : S$, then $\Gamma, \Delta \vdash [x \mapsto s]t : T$.   □

Proof: By induction on derivations. (EXERCISE [$\star$]: Where is Lemma 30.3.1 used? What about Lemma 30.3.2?)   □

30.3.4   LEMMA [TYPE SUBSTITUTION]:

1. If $\Gamma, Y::J, \Delta \vdash T :: K$ and $\Gamma \vdash S :: J$, then $\Gamma, [Y \mapsto S]\Delta \vdash [Y \mapsto S]T :: K$.

2. If $T \equiv U$, then $[Y \mapsto S]T \equiv [Y \mapsto S]U$.

Parallel reduction $\boxed{S \Rrightarrow T}$

$$T \Rrightarrow T \qquad \text{(QR-REFL)}$$

$$\frac{S_2 \Rrightarrow T_2}{\lambda X :: K_1 . S_2 \Rrightarrow \lambda X :: K_1 . T_2} \quad \text{(QR-ABS)}$$

$$\frac{S_1 \Rrightarrow T_1 \qquad S_2 \Rrightarrow T_2}{S_1 {\rightarrow} S_2 \Rrightarrow T_1 {\rightarrow} T_2} \quad \text{(QR-ARROW)}$$

$$\frac{S_1 \Rrightarrow T_1 \qquad S_2 \Rrightarrow T_2}{S_1 \ S_2 \Rrightarrow T_1 \ T_2} \quad \text{(QR-APP)}$$

$$\frac{S_2 \Rrightarrow T_2}{\forall X :: K_1 . S_2 \Rrightarrow \forall X :: K_1 . T_2} \quad \text{(QR-ALL)}$$

$$\frac{S_{12} \Rrightarrow T_{12} \qquad S_2 \Rrightarrow T_2}{(\lambda X :: K_{11} . S_{12}) \ S_2 \Rrightarrow [X \mapsto T_2] T_{12}} \ \text{(QR-APPABS)}$$

Figure 30-3: Parallel reduction on types

3. If $\Gamma, Y :: J, \Delta \vdash t : T$ and $\Gamma \vdash S :: J$, then $\Gamma, [Y \mapsto S]\Delta \vdash [Y \mapsto S]t : [Y \mapsto S]T$. □

Proof: Straightforward induction on derivations, using weakening (Lemma 30.3.2) for the K-TVAR, and T-VAR cases. For the Q-APPABS case, we also need the observation that $[X \mapsto [Y \mapsto S]T_2]([Y \mapsto S]T_{12})$ is the same thing as $[Y \mapsto S]([X \mapsto T_2]T_{12})$. □

Type Equivalence and Reduction

For establishing the properties of typing in F_ω, it is convenient to use a directed variant of the type equivalence relation, called *parallel reduction* (see Figure 30-3). The differences from type equivalence are that the rules of symmetry and transitivity are dropped, and that the QR-APPABS rule allows reductions in the subphrases of the redex. Dropping symmetry gives the reduction relation a more "computational" feel, with $(\lambda X :: K_{11} . T_{12}) \ T_2$ reducing to $[X \mapsto T_2]T_{12}$, but not the other way around; this directedness makes the relation easier to analyze, e.g., in the proof of Lemma 30.3.12 below. Dropping transitivity and allowing reduction of the components at the same time as reducing a lambda-redex are technicalities: we make these changes to obtain a relation with the single-step diamond property stated in Lemma 30.3.8 below.

A key property of the parallel reduction relation is that its transitive and symmetric closure, written $\Leftrightarrow^*$, coincides with type equivalence.

30.3.5   LEMMA: $S \equiv T$ iff $S \Leftrightarrow^* T$. □

Proof: The ($\Leftarrow$) direction is obvious. For the ($\Rightarrow$) direction, the only difficulty is the fact that a type equivalence derivation may use instances of Q-SYMM and Q-TRANS at arbitrary points, while the definition of the $\Leftrightarrow^*$ relation permits uses of symmetry and transitivity only at the outermost level. This can be dealt with by observing that any derivation of $S \equiv T$ can be transformed into a chain of transitivity-free derivations $S = S_0 \equiv S_1 \equiv S_2 \equiv \cdots \equiv S_n = T$ glued together with transitivity at the top, where, in each subderivation $S_i \equiv S_{i+1}$, Q-SYMM is used only as the final rule (or not at all). □

Moreover, parallel reduction is easily seen to be *confluent,* as the next few lemmas show. (Confluence is often called the *Church-Rosser property.*)

30.3.6 LEMMA: If $S \Rightarrow S'$, then $[Y \mapsto S]T \Rightarrow [Y \mapsto S']T$ for any type T. □

Proof: By induction on the structure of T. □

30.3.7 LEMMA: If $S \Rightarrow S'$ and $T \Rightarrow T'$, then $[Y \mapsto S]T \Rightarrow [Y \mapsto S']T'$. □

Proof: By induction on the second given derivation. The QR-REFL case uses Lemma 30.3.6. The cases for QR-ABS, QR-APP, QR-ARROW, and QR-ALL proceed by straightforward use of the induction hypothesis. In QR-APPABS case, we have $T = (\lambda X :: K_{11}. T_{12})\, T_2$ and $T' = [X \mapsto T'_2]T'_{12}$, with $T_{12} \Rightarrow T'_{12}$ and $T_2 \Rightarrow T'_2$. By the induction hypothesis, $[Y \mapsto S]T_{12} \Rightarrow [Y \mapsto S']T'_{12}$ and $[Y \mapsto S]T_2 \Rightarrow [Y \mapsto S']T'_2$. Applying QR-APPABS, we obtain $(\lambda X :: K_{11}. [Y \mapsto S]T_{12})\, [Y \mapsto S]T_2 \Rightarrow [X \mapsto [Y \mapsto S']T'_2]([Y \mapsto S']T'_{12})$, i.e., $[Y \mapsto S]((\lambda X :: K_{11}. T_{12})\, T_2) \Rightarrow [Y \mapsto S']([X \mapsto T'_2]T'_{12})$. □

30.3.8 LEMMA [SINGLE-STEP DIAMOND PROPERTY OF REDUCTION]: If $S \Rightarrow T$ and $S \Rightarrow U$, then there is some type V such that $T \Rightarrow V$ and $U \Rightarrow V$. □

Proof: EXERCISE [RECOMMENDED, ★★★]. □

30.3.9 LEMMA [CONFLUENCE]: If $S \Rightarrow^* T$ and $S \Rightarrow^* U$, then there is some type V such that $T \Rightarrow^* V$ and $U \Rightarrow^* V$. □

Proof: If we visualize the individual steps of reduction from S to T and from S to U like this,

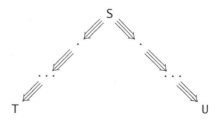

then we can repeatedly use Lemma 30.3.8 to tile the interior of the diagram

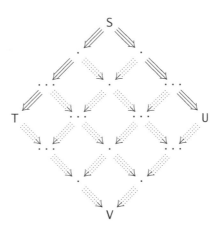

to obtain a large diamond. The lower edges of this diamond are the required reductions.   □

30.3.10   PROPOSITION: If $S \Leftrightarrow^* T$, then there is some U such that $S \Rightarrow^* U$ and $T \Rightarrow^* U$. □

Proof: EXERCISE [★★].   □

This brings us to the crucial observation relating equivalence and reduction: if two types are equivalent, then they share a common reduct. This gives us the structure we need to prove the inversion properties that follow.

30.3.11   COROLLARY: If $S \equiv T$, then there is some U such that $S \Rightarrow^* U$ and $T \Rightarrow^* U$.   □

Preservation

We are now almost ready for the main proof that types are preserved during reduction. The only other thing we need is, as usual, an *inversion lemma* that, given a typing derivation whose conclusion has a certain shape, tells us about the shape of its subderivations. This lemma, in turn, depends on a simple observation about parallel reduction.

30.3.12   LEMMA [PRESERVATION OF SHAPES UNDER REDUCTION]:

1. If $S_1 \rightarrow S_2 \Rightarrow^* T$, then $T = T_1 \rightarrow T_2$ with $S_1 \Rightarrow^* T_1$ and $S_2 \Rightarrow^* T_2$.

2. If $\forall X :: K_1 . S_2 \Rightarrow^* T$, then $T = \forall X :: K_1 . T_2$ with $S_2 \Rightarrow^* T_2$.   □

Proof: Straightforward induction.   □

30.3.13   L EMMA [I NVERSION]:

1. If $\Gamma \vdash \lambda x : S_1 . s_2 : T_1 \to T_2$, then $T_1 \equiv S_1$ and $\Gamma, x : S_1 \vdash s_2 : T_2$. Also, $\Gamma \vdash S_1 :: *$.

2. If $\Gamma \vdash \lambda X :: J_1 . s_2 : \forall X :: K_1 . T_2$, then $J_1 = K_1$ and $\Gamma, X :: J_1 \vdash s_2 : T_2$.   □

Proof: For part 1, we prove, by induction, the following slightly more general statement: If $\Gamma \vdash \lambda x : S_1 . s_2 : S$ and $S \equiv T_1 \to T_2$, then $T_1 \equiv S_1$ and $\Gamma, x : S_1 \vdash s_2 : T_2$. The induction step, rule T-E Q is straightforward. The interesting case is the base of the induction, rule T-A BS. In this case, S has the form $S_1 \to S_2$, where $\Gamma, x : S_1 \vdash s_2 : S_2$. Lemma 30.3.12(1) gives us $T_1 \equiv S_1$ and $T_2 \equiv S_2$, from which T-E Q gives $\Gamma, x : S_1 \vdash s_2 : T_2$. Moreover, the other premise of T-A BS gives us $\Gamma \vdash S_1 :: *$. Part 2 is similar.   □

30.3.14   T HEOREM [P RESERVATION]: If $\Gamma \vdash t : T$ and $t \longrightarrow t'$, then $\Gamma \vdash t' : T$.   □

Proof: Straightforward induction on typing derivations. The argument is similar to the proof of preservation for the simply typed lambda-calculus with subtyping (15.3.5).

Case T-V AR *:* $t = x$

Can't happen (there are no evaluation rules for variables).

Case T-A BS *:* $t = \lambda x : T_1 . t_2$

Can't happen (t is already a value).

Case T-A PP *:* $t = t_1\ t_2$ $\Gamma \vdash t_1 : T_{11} \to T_{12}$ $\Gamma \vdash t_2 : T_{11}$ $T = T_{12}$

From Figure 30-1, we see that there are three rules by which $t \longrightarrow t'$ can be derived: E-A PP1, E-A PP2, and E-A PPA BS. For the first two, the result follows by straightforward use of the induction hypothesis. The third is more interesting:

Subcase E-A PPA BS *:* $t_1 = \lambda x : S_{11} . t_{12}$ $t_2 = v_2$ $t' = [x \mapsto v_2] t_{12}$

By Lemma 30.3.13(1), $T_{11} \equiv S_{11}$ and $\Gamma, x : S_{11} \vdash t_{12} : T_{12}$. By T-E Q, $\Gamma \vdash t_2 : S_{11}$. From this and the substitution lemma (30.3.3), we obtain $\Gamma \vdash t' : T_{12}$.

Case T-TA BS *:* $t = \lambda X :: K_1 . t_2$

Can't happen (t is already a value).

Case T-TA PP *:* $t = t_1\ [T_2]$ $\Gamma \vdash t_1 : \forall X :: K_{11} . T_{12}$ $\Gamma \vdash T_2 :: K_{11}$
$\qquad\qquad\qquad\quad T = [X \mapsto T_2] T_{12}$

Similar to the T-A PP case, using the type substitution lemma (30.3.4) in place of the term substitution lemma (30.3.3).

Case T-Eq: $\Gamma \vdash t : S$ $S \equiv T$ $\Gamma \vdash T :: *$

By the induction hypothesis, $\Gamma \vdash t' : S$. By T-Eq, $\Gamma \vdash t' : T$.   □

Progress

Our next task is the progress theorem. Again, we already have most of what we need for the proof—all that remains is a standard canonical forms lemma that tells us about the shapes of closed values.

30.3.15   LEMMA [CANONICAL FORMS]:

1. If t is a closed value with $\vdash t : T_1 \rightarrow T_2$, then t is an abstraction.

2. If t is a closed value with $\vdash t : \forall X :: K_1 . T_2$, then t is a type abstraction.   □

Proof: The arguments for the two parts are similar; we show just (1). Since there are only two forms of values, if t is a value and not an abstraction, then it must be a type abstraction. So suppose (for a contradiction) that it is a type abstraction. Then the given typing derivation for $\vdash t : T_1 \rightarrow T_2$ must end with a use of T-TABS followed by a nonempty sequence of uses of T-Eq. That is, it must have the following form (eliding kinding premises):

$$\cfrac{\cfrac{\vdots}{\vdash t : \forall X :: K_{11} . S_{12}}\text{(T-Tabs)} \qquad \forall X :: K_{11} . S_{12} \equiv U_1}{\vdash t : U_1}\text{(T-Eq)}$$

$$\vdots$$

$$\cfrac{\cfrac{\vdash t : U_{n-1} \qquad U_{n-1} \equiv U_n}{\vdash t : U_n}\text{(T-Eq)} \qquad U_n \equiv T_1 \rightarrow T_2}{\vdash t : T_1 \rightarrow T_2}\text{(T-Eq)}$$

Since type equivalence is transitive, we can collapse all of these uses of equivalence into one and conclude that $\forall X :: K_{11} . S_{12} \equiv T_1 \rightarrow T_2$. Now, by Proposition 30.3.11, there must be some type U such that $\forall X :: K_{11} . S_{12} \Rightarrow^* U$ and $T_1 \rightarrow T_2 \Rightarrow^* U$. By Lemma 30.3.12, such a U must have both a quantifier and an arrow as its outermost constructor, a contradiction.   □

30.3.16   THEOREM [PROGRESS]: Suppose t is a closed, well-typed term (that is, $\vdash t : T$ for some T). Then either t is a value or else there is some t' with $t \longrightarrow t'$.   □

Proof: By induction on typing derivations. The T-VAR case cannot occur, because t is closed. The T-ABS and T-TABS cases are immediate, since abstractions are values. The T-Eq case follows directly from the induction hypothesis. The remaining cases, for application and type application, are more interesting. We give just the case for type application; the other is similar.

Case T-TAPP: $t = t_1 [T_2]$ $\vdash t_1 : \forall X{::}K_{11}.T_{12}$ $\vdash T_2 :: K_{11}$

By the induction hypothesis, either t_1 is a value or else it can make a step of evaluation. If t_1 can take a step, then rule E-TAPP applies to t. If t_1 is a value, then the canonical forms lemma (30.3.15) tells us that t_1 is a type abstraction, so rule E-TAPPTABS applies to t.   □

30.3.17   EXERCISE [RECOMMENDED, ★★]: Suppose we add to the type equivalence relation the following peculiar rule:

$$T{\to}T \equiv \forall X{::}{*}.T$$

Which, if any, of the basic properties of the system would fail? On the other hand, suppose that we add this rule:

$$S{\to}T \equiv T{\to}S$$

Now which properties fail, if any?   □

Kinding

In the definition of F_ω in Figure 30-1 we took some pains to ensure the well-kindedness of the types we can derive for terms using the rules. In particular, T-ABS checks that the type annotation on a lambda-abstraction is well formed before adding it to the context, and T-EQ checks that the type T being attributed to t has kind $*$. The precise sense in which these checks ensure well-formedness is given by the following proposition.

30.3.18   DEFINITION: A context Γ is said to be *well formed* if (1) Γ is empty, or (2) $\Gamma = \Gamma_1, x{:}T$ with Γ_1 well formed and $\Gamma \vdash T :: *$, or (3) $\Gamma = \Gamma_1, X{::}K$ with Γ_1 well formed.   □

30.3.19   PROPOSITION: If $\Gamma \vdash t : T$ and Γ is well formed, then $\Gamma \vdash T :: *$.   □

Proof: Routine induction, using Lemma 30.3.4(1) for the T-TAPP case.   □

Decidability

Space constraints preclude the inclusion in this book of a full proof of decidability for F_ω—i.e., a typechecking algorithm and proofs of its soundness, completeness, and termination—but almost all the required ideas are already familiar from the minimal typing algorithm for System $F_{<:}$ in Chapter 28.

We begin by observing that the kinding relation is decidable (since its rules are syntax directed). This is no surprise, since we have seen that kinding is essentially a copy of the simply typed lambda-calculus "one level up." This assures us that the well-kindedness checks in the typing rules can be implemented effectively.

Next, we remove the one non-syntax-directed rule, T-Eq, from the typing relation, just as we removed T-Sub from $F_{<:}$. We then examine the other rules to see which premises must be generalized in order to account for essential uses of the now-missing T-Eq rule. It turns out there are two critical points.

1. In the first premise of rules T-App and T-TApp, we may need to use T-Eq to rewrite the type of the left-hand subexpression t_1 to bring an arrow or a quantifier to the outside. (For example, if the context associates variable x with type $(\lambda X.X \rightarrow X)$Nat, then the application x 5 has type Nat only because we can rewrite x's type as Nat$\rightarrow$Nat.)

   We accomplish this by introducing an analog of the exposure relation from §28.1. Here, rather than *promoting* t_1's minimal type until it becomes an arrow or quantifier, as appropriate, we *reduce* it—for example, by repeatedly applying the rules in Figure 30-3 until no more nontrivial reductions are possible.[1]

   To be sure that this process will terminate, we need to show that our reduction rules are normalizing. Of course, on ill-kinded terms, reduction will *not* be normalizing, since the syntax of types in F_ω includes all the primitives we need to encode divergent terms such as omega (page 65). Fortunately, it follows from Proposition 30.3.19 that, as long as we start with a well-formed context (and perform appropriate kind-checks as we go along to ensure that any annotation we put into the context is well kinded), we need to deal only with well-kinded terms, and for these it is possible to show (by adapting the technique of Chapter 12, for example) that reduction always leads to a unique normal form.

2. In the second premise of T-App, we may need to use equivalence to match the type T_2 calculated for t_2 with the left-hand side T_{11} of the arrow type of t_1. An algorithmic variant of this rule will therefore include an equivalence *check* between T_2 and T_{11}. This check can be implemented, for example, by reducing both T_2 and T_{11} to their respective normal forms and then testing whether these are identical (modulo the names of bound variables).

30.3.20   EXERCISE [★★★★]: Implement a typechecker for F_ω based on these ideas, using the purefsub checker as a starting point.   □

---

1. Actually, most typecheckers for F_ω use a less aggressive form of reduction known as *weak head reduction,* in which only leftmost, outermost redexes are reduced and we stop when some concrete constructor—i.e., anything other than an application—comes to the front of the type.

30.4   Fragments of F$_\omega$

Intuitively, it is clear that both $\lambda_\to$ and System F are contained in F$_\omega$. We can make this intuition precise by defining a hierarchy of systems, F$_1$, F$_2$, F$_3$, etc., whose limit is F$_\omega$.

30.4.1   DEFINITION: In System F$_1$, the only kind is $*$ and no quantification ($\forall$) or abstraction (λ) over types is permitted. The remaining systems are defined with reference to a hierarchy of *kinds at level i*, defined as follows:

$$
\begin{aligned}
\mathcal{K}_1 &= \varnothing \\
\mathcal{K}_{i+1} &= \{*\} \cup \{\mathsf{J} \Rightarrow \mathsf{K} \mid \mathsf{J} \in \mathcal{K}_i \text{ and } \mathsf{K} \in \mathcal{K}_{i+1}\} \\
\mathcal{K}_\omega &= \bigcup_{1 \le i} \mathcal{K}_i
\end{aligned}
$$

In System F$_2$, we still have only kind $*$ and no lambda-abstraction at the level of types, but we allow quantification over proper types (of kind $*$). In F$_3$, we allow quantification over type operators (i.e., we can write type expressions of the form $\forall \mathsf{X}{::}\mathsf{K}.\mathsf{T}$, where $\mathsf{K} \in \mathcal{K}_3$) and introduce abstraction over proper types (i.e., we consider type expressions of the form $\lambda \mathsf{X}{::}{*}.\mathsf{T}$, giving them kinds like $* \Rightarrow *$). In general, F$_{i+1}$ permits quantification over types with kinds in $\mathcal{K}_{i+1}$ and abstraction over types with kinds in $\mathcal{K}_i$.   □

F$_1$ is just our simply typed lambda-calculus, $\lambda_\to$. Its definition is superficially more complicated than Figure 9-1 because it includes kinding and type equivalence relations, but these are both trivial: every syntactically well formed type is also well kinded, with kind $*$, and the only type equivalent to a type T is T itself. F$_2$ is our System F; its position in this hierarchy is the reason why it is often called the *second-order lambda-calculus*. F$_3$ is the first system where the kinding and type equivalence relations become non-degenerate.

Interestingly, all the programs in this book live in F$_3$. (Strictly speaking, the type operators `Object` and `Class` in Chapter 32 are in F$_4$, since their argument is a type operator of kind $(* \Rightarrow *) \Rightarrow *$, but we could just as well treat these two as abbreviation mechanisms of the metalanguage rather than full-fledged expressions of the calculus, as we did with `Pair` before Chapter 29, since in the examples using `Object` and `Class` we do not need to *quantify* over types of this kind.) On the other hand, restricting our programming language to F$_3$ instead of using full F$_\omega$ does not actually simplify things very much, in terms of either implementation difficulty or metatheoretic intricacy, since the key mechanisms of type operator abstraction and type equivalence are already present at this level.

30.4.2   EXERCISE [★★★★ ↛]: Are there any useful programs that can be written in F$_4$ but not F$_3$?   □

30.5   Going Further: Dependent Types

Much of this book has been concerned with formalizing abstraction mechanisms of various sorts. In the simply typed lambda-calculus, we formalized the operation of taking a term and abstracting out a subterm, yielding a function that can later be instantiated by applying it to different terms. In System F, we considered the operation of taking a term and abstracting out a *type,* yielding a term that can be instantiated by applying it to various types. In λ_ω, we recapitulated the mechanisms of the simply typed lambda-calculus "one level up," taking a type and abstracting out a subexpression to obtain a type operator that can later be instantiated by applying it to different types.

A convenient way of thinking of all these forms of abstraction is in terms of *families* of expressions, *indexed by* other expressions. An ordinary lambda-abstraction $\lambda x{:}T_1.t_2$ is a family of terms $[x \mapsto s]t_1$ indexed by terms s. Similarly, a type abstraction $\lambda X{::}K_1.t_2$ is a family of terms indexed by types, and a type operator is a family of types indexed by types.

$$\begin{array}{ll} \lambda x{:}T_1.t_2 & \text{family of terms indexed by terms} \\ \lambda X{::}K_1.t_2 & \text{family of terms indexed by types} \\ \lambda X{::}K_1.T_2 & \text{family of types indexed by types.} \end{array}$$

Looking at this list, it is clear that there is one possibility that we have not considered yet: families of *types* indexed by *terms*. This form of abstraction has also been studied extensively, under the rubric of *dependent types.*

Dependent types offer a degree of precision in describing program behaviors that goes far beyond the other typing features we have seen. As a simple example of this, suppose we have a built-in type `FloatList` with the usual associated operations:

```
nil   :  FloatList
cons  :  Float → FloatList → FloatList
hd    :  FloatList → Float
tl    :  FloatList → FloatList
isnil :  FloatList → Bool
```

In a language with dependent types, we can refine the simple type `FloatList` to a family of types `FloatList n`—the types of lists with n elements.

To take advantage of this refinement, we sharpen the types of the basic list operations. To begin with, we give the constant `nil` type `FloatList 0`. To give more accurate types to the rest of the operations, we need to refine the notation for function types to express the *dependency* between their arguments and the types of their results. For example, the type of `cons` should be roughly "a function that takes a `Float` and a list of length *n* and returns a list of length $n+1$." If we make the binding of n explicit by providing it as an initial argument, this description becomes "a function that takes a number n, a Float, and a list of length n, and returns a list of length succ n." That is, what we need to capture in the type is the dependency between the *value* of the first argument (n) and the *types* of the third argument (FloatList n) and the result (FloatList (succ n)). We accomplish this by binding a name to the first argument, writing Πn:Nat. ... instead of Nat→.... The types of cons and the other list operations then become

```
nil   :  FloatList 0
cons  :  Πn:Nat. Float → FloatList n → FloatList (succ n)
hd    :  Πn:Nat. FloatList (succ n) → Float
tl    :  Πn:Nat. FloatList (succ n) → FloatList n.
```

The types of nil, cons, and tl tell us exactly how many elements are in their results, while hd and tl demand non-empty lists as arguments. Also, note that we don't need isnil any more, since we can tell whether an element of FloatList n is nil just by testing whether n is 0.

Dependent function types of the form Πx:T_1.T_2 are a more precise form of arrow types $T_1 \rightarrow T_2$, where we bind a variable x representing the function's argument so that we can mention it in the result type T_2. In the degenerate case, when T_2 does not mention x, we write Πx:T_1.T_2 as $T_1 \rightarrow T_2$.

Of course, we can also define new terms with dependent function types. For example, the function

```
consthree = λn:Nat. λf:Float. λl:FloatList n.
              cons (succ(succ n)) f
                (cons (succ n) f
                   (cons n f l));
```

which prepends three copies of its second argument (f) at the front of its third argument (l), has type

```
Πn:Nat. Float → FloatList n → FloatList (succ(succ(succ n))).
```

Note that the first argument to each of the three calls to cons is different, reflecting the different lengths of their list arguments.

There is an extensive literature on dependent types in computer science and logic. Some good starting points are Smith, Nordström, and Petersson (1990), Thompson (1991), Luo (1994), and Hofmann (1997).

30.5.1   EXERCISE [★★]: Fixing the type of the elements of lists to be Float keeps the example simple, but we can generalize it to lists of an arbitrary type T using ordinary type operators. Show how to do this.   □

Continuing along the same lines, we can build higher-level list-manipulating functions with similarly refined types. For example, we can write a sorting function whose type,

sort : Πn:Nat. FloatList n → FloatList n,

tells us that it returns a list of the same length as its input. Indeed, by further refining the type families involved, we can even write a sort function whose type tells us that the list it returns is always sorted. Checking that this sort function actually belongs to this type will then amount to *proving* that it meets its specification!

Such examples conjure up an alluring picture of a world in which programs are *correct by construction,* where a program's type tells us everything we want to know about its behavior and an "ok" from the typechecker gives us complete confidence that the program behaves as we expect. This vision is related to the idea of programming by "extracting the computational content" from a proof that a specification is satisfiable. The key observation is that a constructive proof of a theorem of the form "For every x there exists a y such that P" can be viewed as a function mapping x to y, together with some evidence (which is computationally inessential—i.e., of interest only to the typechecker) that this function has the property P. These ideas have been pursued by researchers in the Nuprl (Constable et al., 1986), LEGO (Luo and Pollack, 1992; Pollack, 1994) and Coq (Paulin-Mohring, 1989) projects, among others.

Unfortunately, the power of dependent types is a two-edged sword. Blurring the distinction between checking types and carrying out proofs of arbitrary theorems does not magically make theorem proving simple—on the contrary, it makes typechecking computationally intractable! Mathematicians working with mechanical proof assistants do not just type in a theorem, press a button, and sit back to wait for a Yes or No: they spend significant effort writing *proof scripts* and *tactics* to guide the tool in constructing and verifying a proof. If we carry the idea of correctness by construction to its limit, programmers should expect to expend similar amounts of effort annotating programs with hints and explanations to guide the typechecker. For certain critical programming tasks, this degree of effort may be justified, but for day-to-day programming it is almost certainly too costly.

Nonetheless, there have been several attempts to use dependent types in the design of practical programming languges, including Russell (Donahue and Demers, 1985; Hook, 1984), Cayenne (Augustsson, 1998), Dependent ML (Xi and Pfenning, 1998, 1999), Dependently Typed Assembly Language (Xi and Harper, 2001), and the *shape types* of Jay and Sekanina (1997). The trend in these languages is toward restricting the power of dependent types in various ways, obtaining more tractable systems, for which typechecking can be better automated. For example, in the languages of Xi et al., dependent types are used only for static elimination of run-time bounds checking on array accesses; the "theorem proving" problems generated during typechecking in these languages are just systems of linear constraints, for which good automatic procedures exist.

One area where dependent types have a long history of influence on programming languages is in the design of *module systems* that incorporate mechanisms for tracking *sharing* between inter-module dependencies. Landmarks in this area include Pebble (Burstall and Lampson, 1984), MacQueen (1986), Mitchell and Harper (1988), Harper et al. (1990), and Harper and Stone (2000). Recent papers in this area have adopted the technical device of *singleton kinds,* in which module dependency is tracked at the level of kinds instead of types (e.g., Stone and Harper, 2000; Crary, 2000; also see Hayashi, 1991; Aspinall, 1994).

The combination of dependent types with subtyping was first considered by Cardelli (1988b), and has been further developed and generalized by Aspinall (1994), Pfenning (1993b), Aspinall and Compagnoni (2001), Chen and Longo (1996), and Zwanenburg (1999).

Another important application of dependent types in computer science is in building proof assistants and automated theorem provers. In particular, simple type systems with dependent types are often called *logical frameworks*. The most famous of these is the pure simply typed calculus with dependent types, *LF* (Harper, Honsell, and Plotkin, 1992). LF and its relatives, in particular the *calculus of constructions* (Coquand and Huet, 1988; Luo, 1994), have formed the basis for a long line of theorem proving environments, including AutoMath (de Bruijn, 1980), NuPRL (Constable et al., 1986), LEGO (Luo and Pollack, 1992; Pollack, 1994), Coq (Barras et al., 1997), ALF (Magnusson and Nordström, 1994), and ELF (Pfenning, 1994). Pfenning (1996) surveys this area in more depth.

The four forms of abstraction discussed earlier in this section are neatly summarized by the following diagram, known as the *Barendregt cube:*[2]

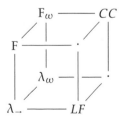

2. Barendregt (1991) called it the *lambda cube*.

All the systems of the cube include ordinary term abstraction. The top face represents systems with polymorphism (families of terms indexed by types), the back face systems with type operators, and the right face systems with dependent types. In the far right corner is the calculus of constructions, containing all four forms of abstraction. The other corner that we have mentioned above is LF, the simply typed lambda-calculus with dependent types. All the systems of the Barendregt cube, and many others, can be presented as instances of the general framework of *pure type systems* (Terlouw, 1989; Berardi, 1988; Barendregt, 1991, 1992; Jutting, McKinna, and Pollack, 1994; McKinna and Pollack, 1993; Pollack, 1994).

31 *Higher-Order Subtyping*

The last system we will consider, called $F^\omega_{<:}$ ("F-omega-sub"), is again a combination of features we have previously studied in isolation—this time, of type operators and subtyping. It can be viewed as the extension of System $F_{<:}$, the second-order polymorphic lambda-calculus with bounded quantification, with type operators. The most interesting new feature is the extension of the subtyping relation from kind $*$ to types of higher kinds.

Several different versions of $F^\omega_{<:}$ have been proposed, varying in expressiveness and metatheoretic complexity. The one used here is very close to that of Pierce and Steffen (1994), one of the simplest. We will not prove any properties of the system; interested readers are referred to Pierce and Steffen (1994), or to Compagnoni (1994) or Abadi and Cardelli (1996), which treat similar systems. (Multiplying the complexity of Chapter 28 by that of §30.3 gives an indication of how much space these proofs consume.)

The main reason for discussing $F^\omega_{<:}$ is that it forms the setting for the last case study in object-oriented programming (Chapter 32). The examples do not exercise any esoteric aspects of $F^\omega_{<:}$'s definition—all that is needed is the ability to write a bounded quantifier ranging over the subtypes of a given type operator. Readers may therefore wish to skim this chapter on a first reading and come back to it later if questions arise.

31.1 Intuitions

The interaction of subtyping and bounded quantification with type operators raises several design issues in the formulation of the combined system. We discuss these briefly before proceeding to the definition of the system.

The first question is whether, in the presence of subtyping, type operators like $\lambda X :: K_1 . T_2$ should be generalized to *bounded type operators* of the form

---

The system studied in this chapter is pure $F^\omega_{<:}$ (Figure 31-1). The associated implementation is fomsub (the fullfomsub implementation includes various extensions such as existentials).

$\lambda X <: T_1 . T_2$. We choose simplicity over regularity in this chapter, defining a system with bounded quantification and *un*bounded type operators.

The next issue is how to extend the subtype relation to include type operators. There are several alternatives. The simplest one, which we choose here, is to lift the subtype relation on proper types *pointwise* to type operators. For abstractions, we say that $\lambda X.S$ is a subtype of $\lambda X.T$ whenever applying both to any argument U yields types that are in the subtype relation. For example, $\lambda X.\mathsf{Top} \to X$ is a subtype of $\lambda X.X \to \mathsf{Top}$ because $\mathsf{Top} \to U$ is a subtype of $U \to \mathsf{Top}$ for every U. Equivalently, we can say that $\lambda X.S$ is a subtype of $\lambda X.T$ if S is a subtype of T when we hold X *abstract,* making no assumptions about its subtypes and supertypes. The latter view leads directly to the following rule:

$$\frac{\Gamma, X \vdash S <: T}{\Gamma \vdash \lambda X.S <: \lambda X.T} \qquad \text{(S-ABS)}$$

Conversely, if F and G are type operators with $F <: G$, then $F\,U <: G\,U$.

$$\frac{\Gamma \vdash F <: G}{\Gamma \vdash F\,U <: G\,U} \qquad \text{(S-APP)}$$

Note that this rule applies only when F and G are applied to the *same* argument U—knowing that F is pointwise a subtype of G tells us nothing about their behavior when applied to different arguments. (Some more complex variants of $F^\omega_{<:}$ that do consider this case are mentioned in §31.4.)

One additional rule arises from the intended meaning of the type equivalence relation. If $S \equiv T$, then S and T have the same members. But types that have the same members are surely subtypes of one another. This leads to another subtyping rule, which includes definitional equivalence as a base case.

$$\frac{\Gamma \vdash S :: K \qquad \Gamma \vdash T :: K \qquad S \equiv T}{\Gamma \vdash S <: T} \qquad \text{(S-EQ)}$$

Having lifted subtyping from kind $*$ to kind $* \Rightarrow *$, we can repeat the process for more complex kinds. For example, if P and Q are type operators of kind $* \Rightarrow * \Rightarrow *$, then we say $P <: Q$ if, for each U, the application $P\,U$ is a subtype of $Q\,U$ in kind $* \Rightarrow *$.

A useful side effect of this definition is that the subtype relations for higher kinds all have maximal elements. If we let $\mathsf{Top}[*] = \mathsf{Top}$ and define(maximal elements of higher kinds)

$$\mathsf{Top}[K_1 \Rightarrow K_2] \stackrel{\mathrm{def}}{=} \lambda X :: K_1 . \mathsf{Top}[K_2],$$

then a simple induction shows that $\Gamma \vdash S <: \mathsf{Top}[K]$ (whenever S has kind K). We exploit this effect in the rules in the following section.

The step from ordinary bounded quantifiers to *higher-order bounded quantifiers* is a straightforward one. $F^\omega_{<:}$ inherits from $F_{<:}$ bounded quantifiers of the form $\forall X<:T_1.T_2$. Generalizing to higher-order (i.e., to quantification over type operators) requires no change to this syntax: we just observe that T_1 here may be any type expression, including a type operator. The unbounded higher-order quantifiers that we inherit from F_ω can be treated as abbreviations for bounded quantifiers with maximal bounds—i.e., we regard $\forall X::K_1.T_2$ as an abbreviation for $\forall X<:\text{Top}[K_1].T_2$.

Lastly, $F^\omega_{<:}$ inherits from $F_{<:}$ the issue of whether to use the more tractable kernel variant or the more powerful full variant of the rule S-ALL. We choose the kernel variant here; the full variant also makes semantic sense, but its metatheoretic properties (even those that one would expect should hold, by analogy with full $F_{<:}$) have not yet been established.

31.2 Definitions

The rules defining $F^\omega_{<:}$ are listed in Figure 31-1. One technicality in the definition is that, although the system provides two different sorts of binding for type variables ($X::K$ in type operators and $X<:T$ in quantifiers), we allow only the latter form of binding in contexts. When we move an $X::K$ binder from the right-hand side of the turnstile to the left, in rules K-ABS and S-ABS, we change it to $X<:\text{Top}[K]$.

Another fine point is that the rules S-REFL from $F_{<:}$ and T-EQ from F_ω are dropped in $F^\omega_{<:}$. Instances of the old S-REFL are immediate consequences of S-EQ and Q-REFL, while T-EQ is derivable from T-SUB and S-EQ.

31.2.1 EXERCISE [⋆]: If we define $\text{Id} = \lambda X.X$ and

$$\Gamma = B<:\text{Top}, A<:B, F <: \text{Id}$$

then which of the following subtype statements are derivable?

Γ	$\vdash$	A	$<:$ $\text{Id } B$
Γ	$\vdash$	$\text{Id } A$	$<:$ B
Γ	$\vdash$	$\lambda X.X$	$<:$ $\lambda X.\text{Top}$
Γ	$\vdash$	$\lambda X.\ \forall Y<:X.\ Y$	$<:$ $\lambda X.\ \forall Y<:\text{Top}.\ Y$
Γ	$\vdash$	$\lambda X.\ \forall Y<:X.\ Y$	$<:$ $\lambda X.\ \forall Y<:X.\ X$
Γ	$\vdash$	$F\ B$	$<:$ B
Γ	$\vdash$	B	$<:$ $F\ B$
Γ	$\vdash$	$F\ B$	$<:$ $F\ B$
Γ	$\vdash$	$\forall F<:(\lambda Y.\text{Top}{\to}Y).\ F\ A$	$<:$ $\forall F<:(\lambda Y.\text{Top}{\to}Y).\ \text{Top}{\to}B$
Γ	$\vdash$	$\forall F<:(\lambda Y.\text{Top}{\to}Y).\ F\ A$	$<:$ $\forall F<:(\lambda Y.\text{Top}{\to}Y).\ F\ B$
Γ	$\vdash$	$\text{Top}[{\ast}{\Rightarrow}{\ast}]$	$<:$ $\text{Top}[{\ast}{\Rightarrow}{\ast}{\Rightarrow}{\ast}]$

□

→ ∀ ⇒ <: Top   *Based on* F$_\omega$ *(30-1) and kernel* F$_{<:}$ *(26-1)*

Syntax

t ::=		*terms:*
	x	*variable*
	λx:T.t	*abstraction*
	t t	*application*
	λX<:T.t	*type abstraction*
	t [T]	*type application*

v ::=		*values:*
	λx:T.t	*abstraction value*
	λX<:T.t	*type abstraction value*

T ::=		*types:*
	Top	*maximum type*
	X	*type variable*
	T→T	*type of functions*
	∀X<:T.T	*universal type*
	λX::K.T	*operator abstraction*
	T T	*operator application*

Γ ::=		*contexts:*
	∅	*empty context*
	Γ, x:T	*term variable binding*
	Γ, X<:T	*type variable binding*

K ::=		*kinds:*
	*	*kind of proper types*
	K⇒K	*kind of operators*

Evaluation $\boxed{\text{t} \longrightarrow \text{t}'}$

$$\frac{\text{t}_1 \longrightarrow \text{t}'_1}{\text{t}_1 \; \text{t}_2 \longrightarrow \text{t}'_1 \; \text{t}_2} \tag{E-App1}$$

$$\frac{\text{t}_2 \longrightarrow \text{t}'_2}{\text{v}_1 \; \text{t}_2 \longrightarrow \text{v}_1 \; \text{t}'_2} \tag{E-App2}$$

$$(\lambda\text{x}:\text{T}_{11}.\text{t}_{12}) \; \text{v}_2 \longrightarrow [\text{x} \mapsto \text{v}_2]\text{t}_{12} \tag{E-AppAbs}$$

$$\frac{\text{t}_1 \longrightarrow \text{t}'_1}{\text{t}_1 \; [\text{T}_2] \longrightarrow \text{t}'_1 \; [\text{T}_2]} \tag{E-TApp}$$

$$(\lambda\text{X}{<:}\text{T}_{11}.\text{t}_{12}) \; [\text{T}_2] \longrightarrow [\text{X} \mapsto \text{T}_2]\text{t}_{12}$$
$$\tag{E-TAppTAbs}$$

Kinding $\boxed{\Gamma \vdash \text{T} :: \text{K}}$

$$\Gamma \vdash \text{Top} :: * \tag{K-Top}$$

$$\frac{\text{X}{<:}\text{T} \in \Gamma \qquad \Gamma \vdash \text{T} :: \text{K}}{\Gamma \vdash \text{X} :: \text{K}} \tag{K-TVar}$$

$$\frac{\Gamma, \text{X}{<:}\text{Top}[\text{K}_1] \vdash \text{T}_2 :: \text{K}_2}{\Gamma \vdash \lambda\text{X}::\text{K}_1.\text{T}_2 :: \text{K}_1{\Rightarrow}\text{K}_2} \tag{K-Abs}$$

$$\frac{\Gamma \vdash \text{T}_1 :: \text{K}_{11}{\Rightarrow}\text{K}_{12} \qquad \Gamma \vdash \text{T}_2 :: \text{K}_{11}}{\Gamma \vdash \text{T}_1 \; \text{T}_2 :: \text{K}_{12}} \tag{K-App}$$

$$\frac{\Gamma \vdash \text{T}_1 :: * \qquad \Gamma \vdash \text{T}_2 :: *}{\Gamma \vdash \text{T}_1{\rightarrow}\text{T}_2 :: *} \tag{K-Arrow}$$

$$\frac{\Gamma, \text{X}{<:}\text{T}_1 \vdash \text{T}_2 :: *}{\Gamma \vdash \forall\text{X}{<:}\text{T}_1.\text{T}_2 :: *} \tag{K-All}$$

continued...

Figure 31-1: Higher-order bounded quantification (F$_{<:}^\omega$)

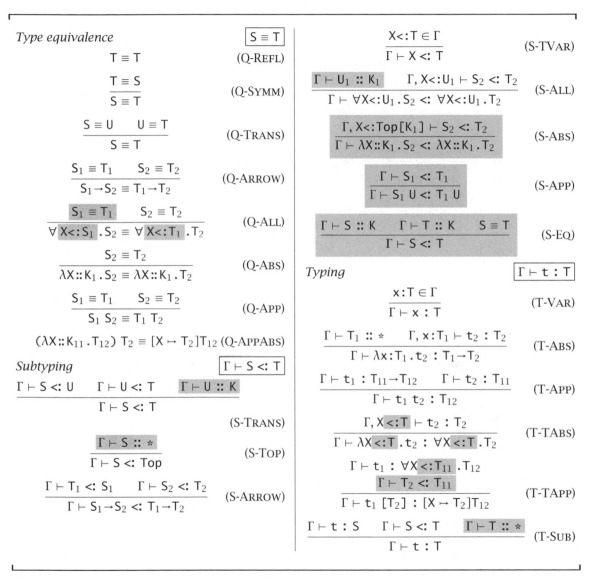

Figure 31-1: Higher-order bounded quantification (continued)

31.3   Properties

Proofs of fundamental properties of $F^{\omega}_{<:}$, including preservation of types during reduction, progress, and minimal typing, for (a near relative of) this system can be found in the papers cited at the beginning of the chapter. These proofs must, of course, address all the issues raised by subtyping, bounded quantification, and type operators in isolation. In addition, one significant new complication arises when we try to define an alternative, syntax-directed presentation of the subtyping rules: not only can the type variable rule be used in combination with transitivity in an essential way in subtyping derivations (as we saw in §28.3), but so can type equivalence (rule S-EQ) together with transitivity.

For example, in the context $\Gamma = X<:\text{Top}, F<:\lambda Y.Y$, the statement $\Gamma \vdash F\,X <: X$ is provable as follows (ignoring kinding):

$$
\cfrac{
\cfrac{
\cfrac{}{\Gamma \vdash F <: \lambda Y.Y}\ \text{S-TVAR}
}{\Gamma \vdash F\,X <: (\lambda Y.Y)\,X}\ \text{S-APP}
\qquad
\cfrac{}{\Gamma \vdash (\lambda Y.Y)\,X <: X}\ \text{S-EQ}
}{\Gamma \vdash F\,X <: X}\ \text{S-TRANS}
$$

Moreover, note that we cannot get around this interaction simply by reducing all type expressions to their normal forms, since the expression $F\,A$ is not a redex—it only becomes one when, during subtype checking, the variable F is *promoted* to its upper bound $\lambda Y.Y$. The solution is to normalize type expressions once at the beginning of the subtype check and then re-normalize as necessary during the promotion operation.

31.4   Notes

Many of the ideas behind $F^{\omega}_{<:}$ are due to Cardelli, particularly to his paper, "Structural Subtyping and the Notion of Power Type" (1988a); the extension of the subtype relation to type operators was developed by Cardelli (1990) and Mitchell (1990a). An early semantic model was given by Cardelli and Longo (1991) using partial equivalence relations. Compagnoni and Pierce (1996) gave a model for an extension of $F^{\omega}_{<:}$ with intersection types. A more powerful model including recursive types was given by Bruce and Mitchell (1992); a related model can be found in Abadi and Cardelli (1996).

Basic metatheoretic properties of the variant of $F^{\omega}_{<:}$ given here were proved by Pierce and Steffen (1994), and independently (using a cleverer proof technique that simplifies one of the main arguments) by Compagnoni (1994). Compagnoni's technique was also used by Abadi and Cardelli (1996) for a variant of $F^\omega_{<:}$ with their object calculus, rather than the lambda-calculus, as its core term language.

The pointwise definition of subtyping between type operators can be generalized to allow subtyping between applications of different type operators to different arguments (F S <: G T) if we refine the kind system so that it tracks the *polarity* of type operators. We says that an operator F is *covariant* if F S <: F T whenever S <: T and *contravariant* if F T <: F S whenever S <: T. If we introduce two new subtyping rules reflecting these properties

$$\frac{\Gamma \vdash S <: T \qquad \text{F is covariant}}{\Gamma \vdash F S <: F T}$$

$$\frac{\Gamma \vdash S <: T \qquad \text{F is contravariant}}{\Gamma \vdash F T <: F S}$$

then it follows (by transitivity) that F S <: G T if F <: G, S <: T, and G is covariant. To make all this work, we also need to mark type variables with their polarities, and to restrict higher-order quantifiers to range only over operators with certain polarities. Versions of $F^\omega_{<:}$ with polarities have been considered by Cardelli (1990), Steffen (1998), and Duggan and Compagnoni (1999).

Another possible generalization of the presentation of $F^\omega_{<:}$ used here is generalizing unbounded type operators $\lambda X{::}K_1.T_2$ to *bounded type operators* $\lambda X{<:}T_1.T_2$. This is an appealing step, because it matches the way we generalized quantifiers to bounded quantifiers when we formed $F_{<:}$ by adding subtyping to System F. On the other hand, it substantially complicates the system, since we must also generalize the kind system to include kinds like $\forall X{<:}T_1.K_2$; this, in turn, introduces a mutual dependency between the kinding and subtyping rules that requires significant work to untangle. See Compagnoni and Goguen (1997a; 1997b).

Extensions of $F^\omega_{<:}$ with dependent types have been studied by Chen and Longo (1996) and Zwanenburg (1999).

32 *Case Study: Purely Functional Objects*

Our final case study continues the development of the *existential object model*. This model was introduced briefly in §24.2, which showed how existential packages could be regarded as simple objects, and compared the properties of this style of abstraction with the use of existentials to implement more conventional abstract data types. In this chapter, we use the tools developed in the past few chapters (type operators and higher-order subtyping, plus one new feature, *polymorphic update,* that we introduce in §32.7) to extend these simple existential objects to a set of idioms offering the flexibility of full-blown object-oriented programming, including classes and inheritance.

32.1 Simple Objects

Let us begin by recalling, from §24.2, the type of purely functional `Counter` objects:

```
Counter = {∃X, {state:X, methods:{get:X→Nat,inc:X→X}}};
```

The elements of this type are packages with a hidden *state type* X, a *state* of type X, and a record of *methods* of type `{get:X→Nat,inc:X→X}`.

For the first few sections of this chapter, we will use the type `{x:Nat}` as the representation type of all our objects. (In §32.8 we will see how to define objects with multiple instance variables, as well as classes that add new instance variables.) We will consistently use the abbreviation `CounterR` when we are talking about the internal state type.

```
CounterR = {x:Nat};
```

A counter object is an element of the type `Counter`, defined according to the rule for existential introduction (T-PACK in Figure 24-1).

The examples in this chapter are terms of $F^{\omega}_{<:}$ (Figure 31-1) with records (11-7), numbers (8-2) and polymorphic update (32-1). The associated OCaml implementation is `fullupdate`.

```
c = {*CounterR,
      {state = {x=5},
       methods = {get = λr:CounterR. r.x,
                  inc = λr:CounterR. {x=succ(r.x)}}}}} as Counter;
```
▸ c : Counter

Invoking the methods of a Counter involves unpacking it, selecting the appropriate field from its methods, and applying it to the state,

```
sendget = λc:Counter.
             let {X,body} = c in
             body.methods.get(body.state);
```
▸ sendget : Counter → Nat

and finally (in the case of inc, which must return a new object, not just a bare number) repackaging the result into a new object with the same representation type and methods as the original.

```
sendinc = λc:Counter.
             let {X,body} = c in
               {*X,
                {state = body.methods.inc(body.state),
                 methods = body.methods}} as Counter;
```
▸ sendinc : Counter → Counter

These basic functions can be used to build up more complex terms that manipulate Counter objects.

```
addthree = λc:Counter. sendinc (sendinc (sendinc c));
```
▸ addthree : Counter → Counter

32.2 Subtyping

A pleasant feature of this existential encoding of objects is that the subtype inclusions that we expect between object types follow directly from the subtyping rules for existentials and records. To check this, recall (from 26-3) the subtyping rule for existential types.[1]

$$\frac{\Gamma, X{<}{:}U \vdash S_2 <: T_2}{\Gamma \vdash \{\exists X{<}{:}U, S_2\} <: \{\exists X{<}{:}U, T_2\}} \quad \text{(S-Some)}$$

This rule tells us immediately that if we define an object type with more methods than Counter, e.g.,

---

1. We use only the kernel variant of the rule here; the power of the full version is not needed. In fact, we do not need *bounded* existentials at all in this chapter—the bounds of all our existentials are Top.

```
ResetCounter =
  {∃X, {state:X, methods:{get: X→Nat, inc:X→X, reset:X→X}}};
```

then it will be a subtype of Counter, i.e., ResetCounter <: Counter. This means that, if we define a reset counter object,

```
rc = {*CounterR,
      {state = {x=0},
       methods = {get = λr:CounterR. r.x,
                  inc = λr:CounterR. {x=succ(r.x)},
                  reset = λr:CounterR. {x=0}}}} as ResetCounter;
```

▸ rc : ResetCounter

we can use subsumption to pass this object to functions defined on Counter, such sendget, sendinc, and addthree:

```
rc3 = addthree rc;
```

▸ rc3 : Counter

Notice, though, that we lose type information when we do this: the type of rc3 here is just Counter, not ResetCounter.

32.3 Bounded Quantification

Of course, it was precisely this sort of information loss due to subsumption that motivated the introduction of bounded quantification in Chapter 26. However, bounded quantification by itself is not quite enough—to be useful in addressing the problem at hand, it needs to be enriched with some additional mechanism.

To see why, observe that the obvious refinement of the type of sendinc using bounded quantification is ∀C<:Counter. C→C. If we had a sendinc of this type, then we could write addthree as

```
addthree = λC<:Counter. λc:C.
             sendinc [C] (sendinc [C] (sendinc [C] c));
```

▸ addthree : ∀C<:Counter. C → C

and apply it to rc to obtain a result of type ResetCounter.

```
rc3 = addthree [ResetCounter] rc;
```

▸ rc3 : ResetCounter

Unfortunately, there is no way to write such a function—or rather, no way to write a function that behaves the way we want and give it this type. We can, of course, write an *identity* function that belongs to this type,

```
wrongsendinc = λC<:Counter. λc:C. c;
```

▸ wrongsendinc : ∀C<:Counter. C → C

but if we try to refine the real implementation of sendinc from above by adding a bounded type abstraction at the front, we get something that fails to typecheck.

```
sendinc =
  λC<:Counter. λc:C.
    let {X,body} = c in
      {*X,
        {state = body.methods.inc(body.state),
         methods = body.methods}}
      as C;
```

▸ Error: existential type expected

The problem here is in the last line. The annotation as C tells the typechecker "use the existential type C for the package being created here." But C is *not* an existential type—it is a type variable. This is not just a silly restriction of the typing rules that we have defined—e.g., a consequence of the fact that the rules do not "know" that every subtype of an existential type is an existential type. On the contrary, it would actually be *wrong* to give the package

```
{*X,
  {state = body.methods.inc(body.state),
   methods = body.methods}}
```

the type C. Observe, for example, that the type

```
{∃X, {state:X, methods:{get:X→Nat,inc:X→X}, junk:Bool}}
```

is a subtype of Counter. But the package above certainly does not have this type: it lacks the field junk. So it is not the case that, for any subtype C of Counter, the body of sendinc above "really" has type C, if only the typing rules could see it. Indeed, it can be shown (e.g., by appealing to a denotational model for $F_{<:}$—see Robinson and Tennent, 1988) that, in pure $F_{<:}$, types of the form ∀C<:T.C→C contain *only* identity functions.

Several ways of addressing this shortcoming of $F_{<:}$ have been proposed. One possibility is to move from $F_{<:}$ to $F_{<:}^\omega$ and use higher-order bounded quantification to give yet more refined types to functions like sendinc. Another possibility is to keep the type ∀C<:Counter.C→C, but to add features to the language that can be used to build interesting inhabitants of this type. A final possibility is simply to add references to the language. However, we have already gone down that path in Chapter 27; the aim in the present chapter is to experiment with what can be achieved—and how to achieve it—in a purely functional setting.

The development that follows combines two of these methods—$F^{\omega}_{<:}$ to address the problem with quantification over object types that we noticed in the previous section, and a new primitive for *polymorphic record update* (defined in §32.7) to address a related problem that arises in the treatment of instance variables (§32.8).

32.4 Interface Types

Using type operators, we can express Counter as the combination of two pieces

    Counter = Object CounterM;

where

    CounterM = λR. {get: R→Nat, inc:R→R};

is a type operator of kind $* \Rightarrow *$ representing the specific method interface of counter objects and

    Object = λM::*⇒*. {∃X, {state:X, methods:M X}};

is a type operator of kind $(* \Rightarrow *) \Rightarrow *$ that captures the common structure of all object types. What we achieve by this reformulation is a separation of the varying part (the method interface), where we want to allow subtyping, from the fixed skeleton of objects (the existential packaging, and the pair of state and methods), where we do not because it gets in the way of the repackaging.

We need bounded quantification over a type *operator* to achieve this splitting because it allows us to pull out the method interface from an object type, even though the interface mentions the existentially bound state type X, by abstracting the method interface itself on X. The interface thus becomes a "parametric parameter." The iterated character of the parameterization here is reflected both in the kind of Object and in the steps by which the application Object CounterM is simplified: first, CounterM is substituted into the body of Object, yielding

    {∃X, {state:X, methods:(λR. {get: R→Nat, inc:R→R}) X}}

and then X is substituted into the body of CounterM, yielding

   {∃X, {state:X, methods:{get:X→Nat,inc:X→X}}}.

If we split ResetCounter in the same way,

   ResetCounterM = λR. {get: R→Nat, inc:R→R, reset:R→R};
   ResetCounter = Object ResetCounterM;

then we have not only

   ResetCounter <: Counter

as before but also

   ResetCounterM <: CounterM

by the rules above for subtyping between type operators. That is, our separation of object types into generic boilerplate plus a specific interface gives us a meaningful sense of *interface subtyping* that is separate from the subtype relations between complete object types.

Interface subtyping is closely related—both conceptually and technically—to the idea of *matching* introduced by Bruce et al. (1997) and further studied by Abadi and Cardelli (1995; 1996).

32.5   Sending Messages to Objects

We can now repair the broken version of sendinc from §32.3 by abstracting over sub-*interfaces* of CounterM rather than sub-*types* of Counter.

```
sendinc =
  λM<:CounterM. λc:Object M.
    let {X, b} = c in
      {*X,
       {state = b.methods.inc(b.state),
        methods = b.methods}}
       as Object M;
```

▸ sendinc : ∀M<:CounterM. Object M → Object M

Intuitively, the type of sendinc can be read "give me an object interface refining the interface of counters, then give me an object with that interface, and I'll return you another object with the same interface."

32.5.1   EXERCISE [⋆]: Why is this sendinc well typed whereas the previous one was not?   □

To invoke the methods of counter and reset counter objects, we instantiate
the polymorphic method invocation functions with the appropriate interface
signature, CounterM or ResetCounterM (assuming sendget and sendreset
have been defined analogously).

```
sendget [CounterM] (sendinc [CounterM] c);
```

▸ 6 : Nat

```
sendget [ResetCounterM]
          (sendreset [ResetCounterM]
              (sendinc [ResetCounterM] rc));
```

▸ 0 : Nat

32.5.2   EXERCISE [RECOMMENDED, ★★]: Define sendget and sendreset.   □

32.6   Simple Classes

Now let us consider classes, beginning (as we did in Chapter 18) with *simple
classes* without self.

In §18.6, we defined a simple class (for the imperative object encoding,
where objects were records of methods) to be a function from states to
objects—a way of manufacturing multiple objects with the same methods
but each with a freshly allocated set of instance variables. In this chapter,
an object is more than just a record of methods: it includes a representation
type and a state as well. On the other hand, since this is a purely functional
model, each of the methods takes the state as a parameter (and, if necessary,
returns an object with an updated state), so we don't need to pass the state to
the class at object-creation time. In fact, a class here—given that we are still
assuming that all objects use the same representation type—can be viewed
as simply a record of methods,

```
counterClass =
    {get = λr:CounterR. r.x,
     inc = λr:CounterR. {x=succ(r.x)}}
  as {get: CounterR→Nat, inc:CounterR→CounterR};
```

▸ counterClass : {get:CounterR→Nat, inc:CounterR→CounterR}

or, using the CounterM operator to write the annotation more tersely:

```
counterClass =
    {get = λr:CounterR. r.x,
     inc = λr:CounterR. {x=succ(r.x)}}
    as CounterM CounterR;
```

▶ counterClass : CounterM CounterR

We build instances of such classes by supplying an initial value for the state and packaging this state with the methods (i.e., the class) into an object.

```
c = {*CounterR,
     {state = {x=0},
      methods = counterClass}}
   as Counter;
```

▶ c : Counter

Defining a subclass is simply a matter of building a new record of methods, copying some of its fields from a previously defined one.

```
resetCounterClass =
   let super = counterClass in
   {get = super.get,
    inc = super.inc,
    reset = λr:CounterR. {x=0}}
   as ResetCounterM CounterR;
```

▶ resetCounterClass : ResetCounterM CounterR

To generalize these simple classes to handle the same sorts of examples that we closed with in Chapter 18, two more things are needed: the ability to add new instance variables in subclasses, and a treatment of `self`. The next two sections address the first of these; §32.9 closes the chapter with a treatment of `self`.

32.7   Polymorphic Update

To add instance variables to classes, we need to add one new mechanism—a primitive for in-place *polymorphic update* of record fields and an associated refinement to record types. The need for these features arises from the fact that allowing variation in instance variables between classes means making superclasses polymorphic in the instance variables of their subclasses. Let us look at how this happens.

Suppose that we want to define a subclass of `resetCounterClass`, adding a `backup` method that saves the current value of the counter and changing the behavior of `reset` to revert to this saved value instead of to a constant initial value. To hold this saved value, we will need to extend our state type from {x:Nat} to {x:Nat, old:Nat}. This difference in representations immediately creates a technical difficulty. Our ability to reuse the `inc` method from `resetCounterClass` when defining `backupCounterClass` depends on this method behaving the same in both classes. However, if the sets of instance variables are different, then it does *not* behave quite the same: the `inc` of a `ResetCounter` expects a state of type `{x:Nat}` and returns a new state of the same type, while the `inc` of `BackupCounter` expects and produces states of type `{x:Nat,old:Nat}`.

To resolve this difficulty, it suffices to observe that the `inc` method does not really need to know that the state type *is* `{x:Nat}` or `{x:Nat,old:Nat}`, but only that the state *contains* an instance variable x. In other words, we can unify these two methods by giving them both type `∀S<:{x:Nat}.S→S`.

Now the same difficulty arises with states as with whole objects in §32.3: the type `∀S<:{x:Nat}.S→S` in our present language is inhabited only by the identity function. Again, to address this difficulty, we need some mechanism that permits a more precise form of bounded quantification; here, the most direct mechanism is to add a primitive for *polymorphic update* of record fields.[2] If r is a record with a field x of type T and t is a term of type T, then we write `r←x=t` to mean "a record that is just like r except that its x field has the value t." Note that this is a purely functional form of update operation—it does not change r, but instead makes a clone with a different x field.

Using this record update primitive, a function that captures the intended behavior of the `inc` method body can be written roughly as follows:

```
f = λX<:{a:Nat}. λr:X. r←a = succ(r.a);
```

However, we have to be a little careful. A naive typing rule for the update operator would be:

$$\frac{\Gamma \vdash r : R \qquad \Gamma \vdash R <: \{l_j:T_j\} \qquad \Gamma \vdash t : T_j}{\Gamma \vdash r{\leftarrow}l_j{=}t : R}$$

But this rule is unsound. For example, suppose we have:

```
s = {x={a=5,b=6},y=true};
```

Since s : `{x:{a:Nat,b:Nat},y:Bool}`, and `{x:{a:Nat,b:Nat},y:Bool}` <: `{x:{a:Nat}}`, the above rule would allow us to derive

```
s←x={a=8} : {x:{a:Nat,b:Nat},y:Bool},
```

which would be wrong, since `s←x={a=8}` reduces to `{x={a=8},y=true}`.

This problem was caused by the use of depth subtyping on the field x to derive `{x:{a:Nat,b:Nat},y:Bool}` <: `{x:{a:Nat}}`. Depth subtyping should

---

2. As before, there are actually several ways of achieving similar effects—by introducing different primitives (some are listed in §32.10), or by using polymorphism, as in Pierce and Turner (1994)—a notationally heavier but theoretically more elementary alternative. The one used here is chosen for its simplicity, and because it fits naturally with the examples that follow.

→ ∀ <: Top {} ←

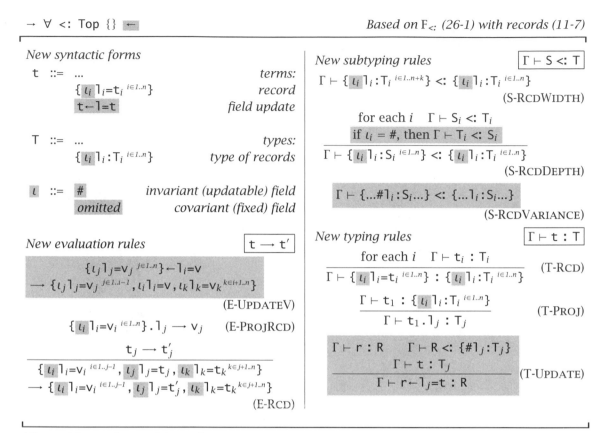

Figure 32-1: Polymorphic update

not be allowed in fields that might be updated. We can achieve this by the simple expedient of annotating such fields with a special mark, written #.

The rules for these "updatable records" and for the update operation itself are given in Figure 32-1. We refine the syntax of record types so that every field is annotated with a *variance* tag that indicates whether depth subtyping is allowed—# to forbid subtyping in this field and the empty string to permit it (choosing the empty string here means that unmarked records will behave as they always have). The depth subtyping rule S-RCDDEPTH is refined to allow subtyping only in unmarked fields. Finally, we add a subtyping rule S-RCDVARIANCE that permits marks on fields to be changed from # to the empty string—in other words, to "forget" that a given field is updatable. The typing rule for the update primitive demands that the field being replaced is marked #. The E-UPDATE rule implements the update operation.

The function f above is now written like this,

```
f = λX<:{#a:Nat}. λr:X. r←a = succ(r.a);
```

▶ f : ∀X<:{#a:Nat}. X → X

and used like this:

```
r = {#a=0, b=true};
f [{#a:Nat,b:Bool}] r;
```

▶ {#a=1, b=true} : {#a:Nat, b:Bool}

The soundness of the update operation rests on the following observation about the refined subtype relation:

32.7.1   FACT: If ⊢ R <: {#1:T_1}, then R = {...#1:R_1...} with ⊢ R_1 <: T_1 and ⊢ T_1 <: R_1.   □

32.7.2   EXERCISE [RECOMMENDED, ★★★]: Does the minimal typing property hold for this calculus? If so, prove it. If not, find a way to repair it.   □

32.8   Adding Instance Variables

Using the features from the previous section, we can write a `counterClass` that is polymorphic in the type of the internal state.

```
CounterR = {#x:Nat};

counterClass =
    λR<:CounterR.
       {get = λs:R. s.x,
        inc = λs:R. s←x=succ(s.x)}
       as CounterM R;
```

▶ counterClass : ∀R<:CounterR. CounterM R

To build an object from the new `counterClass`, we simply supply CounterR as the representation type:

```
c = {*CounterR,
      {state = {#x=0},
       methods = counterClass [CounterR]}}
      as Object CounterM;
```

▶ c : Counter

Note that objects built from the new class have the same type `Counter` = `Object CounterM` as the ones above: the changes to the treatment of instance variables are entirely internal to the classes. The method invocation functions above can also be used with objects instantiated from the new classes.

We can write `resetCounterClass` in the same style.

```
resetCounterClass =
  λR<:CounterR.
    let super = counterClass [R] in
      {get = super.get,
       inc = super.inc,
       reset = λs:R. s←x=0}
      as ResetCounterM R;
▶ resetCounterClass : ∀R<:CounterR. ResetCounterM R
```

Finally, we can write a `backupCounterClass`, this time abstracting over a subtype of `BackupCounterR` (which was the point of the whole exercise).

```
BackupCounterM = λR. {get:R→Nat,inc:R→R,reset:R→R,backup:R→R};
BackupCounterR = {#x:Nat,#old:Nat};
backupCounterClass =
  λR<:BackupCounterR.
    let super = resetCounterClass [R] in
     {get = super.get,
      inc = super.inc,
      reset = λs:R. s←x=s.old,
      backup = λs:R. s←old=s.x}
     as BackupCounterM R;
▶ backupCounterClass : ∀R<:BackupCounterR. BackupCounterM R
```

32.9   Classes with "Self"

In §18.9, we saw how to extend imperative classes with a mechanism allowing the methods of a class to refer to each other recursively. This extension also makes sense in the purely functional setting.

We begin by abstracting `counterClass` on a collection of methods `self` appropriate for the same representation type R.

```
counterClass =
  λR<:CounterR.
  λself: Unit→CounterM R.
  λ_:Unit.
    {get = λs:R. s.x,
     inc = λs:R. s←x=succ(s.x)}
    as CounterM R;
```

As in §18.9, the Unit argument to the class is used to postpone evaluation during the fix operation that creates the methods of an object. The type of self includes a matching Unit abstraction.

To build an object from this class, we take the fixed point of the function counterClass and apply it to unit.

```
c = {*CounterR,
     {state = {#x=0},
      methods = fix (counterClass [CounterR]) unit}}
   as Object CounterM;
```

▶ c : Counter

We next define a subclass offering a set operation, with the following interface:

```
SetCounterM = λR. {get: R→Nat, set:R→Nat→R, inc:R→R};
```

The implementation of setCounterClass defines a set method and uses the set and get methods from self in the implementation of its inc method:

```
setCounterClass =
   λR<:CounterR.
   λself: Unit→SetCounterM R.
   λ_:Unit.
      let super = counterClass [R] self unit in
      {get = super.get,
       set = λs:R. λn:Nat. s←x=n,
       inc = λs:R. (self unit).set s (succ((self unit).get s))}
   as SetCounterM R;
```

Finally, bringing together all the mechanisms from the chapter, we can build a subclass of instrumented counters whose set operation counts the number of times that it has been called.

```
InstrCounterM =
   λR. {get: R→Nat, set:R→Nat→R, inc:R→R, accesses:R→Nat};

InstrCounterR = {#x:Nat,#count:Nat};

instrCounterClass =
   λR<:InstrCounterR.
   λself: Unit→InstrCounterM R.
   λ_:Unit.
      let super = setCounterClass [R] self unit in
      {get = super.get,
```

```
      set = λs:R. λn:Nat.
              let r = super.set s n in
              r←count=succ(r.count),
      inc = super.inc,
      accesses = λs:R. s.count}
  as InstrCounterM R;
```

Note that calls to `inc` are included in the access count, since `inc` is implemented in terms of the `set` method from `self`.

To wrap up, let's build an instrumented counter object and send it some
messages.

```
ic = {*InstrCounterR,
        {state = {#x=0,#count=0},
         methods = fix (instrCounterClass [InstrCounterR]) unit}}
        as Object InstrCounterM;
```

▸ ic : Object InstrCounterM

```
sendaccesses [InstrCounterM] (sendinc [InstrCounterM] ic);
```

▸ 1 : Nat

32.9.1   EXERCISE [RECOMMENDED, ★★★]: Define a subclass of `instrCounterClass`
that adds `backup` and `reset` methods.   □

32.10   Notes

The first "purely functional" interpretation of objects in a typed lambda-
calculus was based on recursively-defined records; it was introduced by Cardelli
(1984) and studied in many variations by Kamin and Reddy (Reddy, 1988;
Kamin and Reddy, 1994), Cook and Palsberg (1989), and Mitchell (1990a). In
its untyped form, this model was used rather effectively for the denotational
semantics of untyped object-oriented languages. In its typed form, it was
used to encode individual object-oriented examples, but it caused difficulties
with uniform interpretations of typed object-oriented languages. The most
successful effort in this direction was carried out by Cook and his co-workers
(Cook, Hill, and Canning, 1990; Canning, Cook, Hill, and Olthoff, 1989a; Canning, Cook, Hill, Olthoff, and Mitchell, 1989b).

Pierce and Turner (1994) introduced an encoding that relied only on a type
system with existential types, but no recursive types. This led Hofmann and
Pierce (1995b) to the first uniform, type-driven interpretation of objects in a
functional calculus. At the same conference, Bruce presented a paper (1994)

on the semantics of a functional object-oriented language. This semantics was originally presented as a direct mapping into a denotational model of $F_{<:}^\omega$, but has recently been reformulated as an object encoding that depends on both existential and recursive types. Meanwhile, frustrated by the difficulties of encoding objects in lambda calculi, Abadi and Cardelli introduced a calculus of primitive objects (1996). Later, however, Abadi, Cardelli, and Viswanathan (1996) discovered a faithful encoding of that object calculus in terms of bounded existentials and recursive types. These developments are surveyed by Bruce et al. (1999) and Abadi and Cardelli (1996).

The object encoding in this chapter has been extended to include *multiple inheritance*—classes with more than one superclass—by Compagnoni and Pierce (1996). The key technical idea is the extension of $F_{<:}^\omega$ with *intersection types* (§15.7).

There have been numerous proposals for addressing the shortcomings of pure second-order bounded quantification that we observed in §32.3. Besides the two that we saw in this chapter—higher-order bounded quantification and a polymorphic record update primitive—there are several other styles of polymorphic record update (Cardelli and Mitchell, 1991; Cardelli, 1992; Fisher and Mitchell, 1996; Poll, 1996), as well as *structural unfolding* for recursive types (Abadi and Cardelli, 1996), *positive subtyping* (Hofmann and Pierce, 1995a), *polymorphic repacking* for existential types (Pierce, 1996), and *type destructors* (Hofmann and Pierce, 1998).

A different line of attack based on *row-variable polymorphism* has been developed by Wand (1987, 1988, 1989b), Rémy (1990, 1989, 1992), Vouillon (2000, 2001) and others, and forms the basis for the object-oriented features of OCaml (Rémy and Vouillon, 1998).

"Begin at the beginning," the King said, very gravely, "and go on till you come to the end: then stop."
—Lewis Carroll

Appendices

A Solutions to Selected Exercises

3.2.4 SOLUTION: $|S_{i+1}| = |S_i|^3 + |S_i| \times 3 + 3$, and $|S_0| = 0$. So $|S_3| = 59439$.

3.2.5 SOLUTION: A straightforward inductive proof does the trick. When $i = 0$, there is nothing to prove. Next, supposing that $i = j + 1$, for some $j > 0$, and that $S_j \subseteq S_i$, we must show that $S_i \subseteq S_{i+1}$—that is, for any term $t \in S_i$, we must show $t \in S_{i+1}$. So suppose we have $t \in S_i$. By the definition of S_i as the union of three sets, we know that t must have one of three forms:

1. $t \in \{\texttt{true}, \texttt{false}, \texttt{0}\}$. In this case, we obviously have $t \in S_{i+1}$, by the definition of S_{i+1}.

2. $t = \texttt{succ } t_1$, $\texttt{pred } t_1$, or $\texttt{iszero } t_1$, where $t_1 \in S_j$. Since $S_j \subseteq S_i$ by the induction hypothesis, we have $t_1 \in S_i$, so $t \in S_{i+1}$ by definition of S_{i+1}.

3. $t = \texttt{if } t_1 \texttt{ then } t_2 \texttt{ else } t_3$, where $t_1, t_2, t_3 \in S_j$. Again, since $S_j \subseteq S_i$ by the induction hypothesis, we have $t \in S_{i+1}$, by the definition of S_{i+1}.

3.3.4 SOLUTION: (We give the argument just for the depth-induction principle; the others are similar.) We are told that, for each term s, if $P(r)$ for all r with smaller depth than s, then $P(s)$; we must now prove that $P(s)$ holds for all s. Define a new predicate Q on natural numbers as follows:

$$Q(n) \quad = \quad \forall s \text{ with } depth(s) = n. \ P(s)$$

Now use natural number induction (2.4.2) to prove that $Q(n)$ holds for all n.

3.5.5 SOLUTION: Suppose P is a predicate on derivations of evaluation statements.

> If, for each derivation $\mathcal{D}$,
>> given $P(C)$ for all immediate subderivations C
>> we can show $P(\mathcal{D})$,
> then $P(\mathcal{D})$ holds for all $\mathcal{D}$.

3.5.10   SOLUTION:

$$\frac{t \longrightarrow t'}{t \longrightarrow^* t'}$$

$$t \longrightarrow^* t$$

$$\frac{t \longrightarrow^* t' \qquad t' \longrightarrow^* t''}{t \longrightarrow^* t''}$$

3.5.13   SOLUTION: (1) 3.5.4 and 3.5.11 fail. 3.5.7, 3.5.8, and 3.5.12 remain valid. (2) Now just 3.5.4 fails; the rest remain valid. The interesting fact in the second part is that, even though single-step evaluation becomes nondeterministic in the presence of this rule, the final results of multi-step evaluation are still deterministic: all roads lead to Rome. Indeed, a rigorous proof of this fact is not very hard, though it is not as trivial as before. The main observation is that the single-step evaluation relation has the so-called *diamond property*:

A.1   LEMMA [DIAMOND PROPERTY]: If $r \longrightarrow s$ and $r \longrightarrow t$, with $s \neq t$, then there is some term u such that $s \longrightarrow u$ and $t \longrightarrow u$.   □

Proof: From the evaluation rules, it is clear that this situation can arise only when r has the form if r_1 then r_2 else r_3. We proceed by induction on the *pair* of derivations used to derive $r \longrightarrow s$ and $r \longrightarrow t$, with a case analysis on the final rules in both derivations.

Case i:

Suppose $r \longrightarrow s$ by E-IFTRUE and $r \longrightarrow t$ by E-FUNNY2. Then, from the forms of these rules, we know that $s = r_2$ and that $t = $ if true then r_2' else r_3, where $r_2 \longrightarrow r_2'$. But then choosing $u = r_2'$ gives us what we need, since we know that $s \longrightarrow r_2'$ and we can see that $t \longrightarrow r_2'$ by E-IFTRUE.

Case ii:

Suppose the final rule in the derivations of both $r \longrightarrow s$ and $r \longrightarrow t$ is E-IF. By the form of E-IF, we know s must have the form if r_1' then r_2 else r_3 and t must have the form if r_1'' then r_2 else r_3, where $r_1 \longrightarrow r_1'$ and $r_1 \longrightarrow r_1''$. But then, by the induction hypothesis, there is some term r_1''' with $r_1' \longrightarrow r_1'''$ and $r_1'' \longrightarrow r_1'''$. We can complete the argument for this case by taking $u = $ if r_1''' then r_2 else r_3 and observing that $s \longrightarrow u$ and $t \longrightarrow u$ by E-IF.

The arguments for the other cases are similar.   □

The proof of uniqueness of results now follows by a straightforward "diagram chase." Suppose that $r \longrightarrow^* s$ and $r \longrightarrow^* t$.

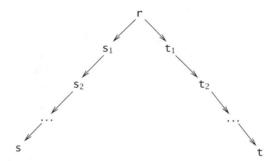

Then we can use Lemma A.1 to "pull together" s_1 and t_1

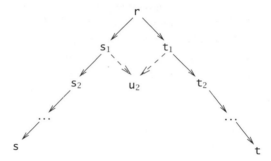

then use it to pull together s_2 and u_2 and again to pull together u_2 and t_2

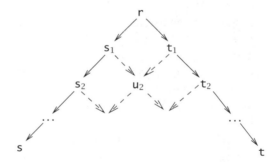

and so on until we have pulled together s and t, building a complete large diamond out of individual single-step diamonds.

It follows that, if r can be evaluated to v and to w, then they must *be* the same (they are both normal forms, so the only way they can evaluate to the same thing is to start out the same).

3.5.14   SOLUTION: By induction on the structure of t.

Case: t is a value

Since every value is in normal form, this case cannot occur.

Case: t = succ t_1

Looking at the evaluation rules, we find that only the rule E-SUCC could possibly be used to derive $t \longrightarrow t'$ and $t \longrightarrow t''$ (all the other rules have left-hand sides whose outermost constructor is something other than succ). So there must be two subderivations with conclusions of the form $t_1 \longrightarrow t_1'$ and $t_1 \longrightarrow t_1''$. By the induction hypothesis (which applies because t_1 is a subterm of t), we obtain $t_1' = t_1''$. But then succ t_1' = succ t_1'', as required.

Case: t = pred t_1

Here there are three evaluation rules (E-PRED, E-PREDZERO, and E-PREDSUCC) that might have been used to reduce t to t' and t''. Notice, however, that these rules do not overlap: if t matches the left-hand side of one rule, then it definitely does *not* match the left-hand side of the others. (For example, if t matches E-PRED, then t_1 is definitely not a value, in particular not 0 or succ v.) This tells us that the *same* rule must have been used to derive $t \longrightarrow t'$ and $t \longrightarrow t''$. If that rule was E-PRED, then we use the induction hypothesis as in the previous case. If it was E-PREDZERO or E-PREDSUCC, then the result is immediate.

Case: Other cases

Similar.

3.5.16   SOLUTION: Let us use the metavariable t to range over the new set of terms extended with wrong (including all terms with wrong as a subphrase), and g to range over the original set of "good" terms that do not involve wrong. Write $t \overset{w}{\longrightarrow} t'$ for the new evaluation relation augmented with wrong transitions, and $g \overset{o}{\longrightarrow} g'$ for the original form of evaluation. Now, the claim that the two treatments agree can be formulated precisely as follows: any (original) term whose evaluation gets stuck in the original semantics will evaluate to wrong in the new semantics, and vice versa. Formally:

A.2   PROPOSITION: For all original terms g, $(g \overset{o}{\longrightarrow}{}^* g'$, where g' is stuck) iff $(g \overset{w}{\longrightarrow}{}^*$ wrong).   ☐

To prove this, we proceed in several steps. First, we remark that the new transitions we have added do not invalidate Theorem 3.5.14.

A.3   LEMMA: The augmented evaluation relation is deterministic.   ☐

This means that whenever g can take a single step to g' in the original semantics, it can also step to g' in the augmented semantics, and furthermore that g' is the *only* term g can step to in the new semantics.

Next, we show that a term that is (already) stuck in the original semantics will always evaluate to wrong in the augmented semantics.

A.4   LEMMA: If g is stuck then g $\xrightarrow{w}{}^*$ wrong.   □

Proof: By induction on the structure of g.

Case: g = true, false, or 0

Can't happen (we assumed that g is stuck).

Case: g = if g$_1$ then g$_2$ else g$_3$

Since g is stuck, g$_1$ must be in normal form (or else E-IF would apply). Clearly, g$_1$ cannot be true or false (otherwise one of E-IFTRUE or E-IFFALSE would apply and g would not be stuck). Consider the remaining cases:

> *Subcase:*   g$_1$ = if g$_{11}$ then g$_{12}$ else g$_{13}$
>
> Since g$_1$ is in normal form and obviously not a value, it is stuck. The induction hypothesis tells us that g$_1$ $\xrightarrow{w}{}^*$ wrong. From this, we can construct a derivation of g $\xrightarrow{w}{}^*$ if wrong then g$_2$ else g$_3$. Adding a final instance of rule E-IF-WRONG yields g $\xrightarrow{w}{}^*$ wrong, as required.
>
> *Subcase:*   g$_1$ = succ g$_{11}$
>
> If g$_{11}$ is a numeric value, then g$_1$ is a badbool and rule E-IF-WRONG immediately yields g $\xrightarrow{w}$ wrong. Otherwise, by definition g$_1$ is stuck, and the induction hypothesis tells us that g$_1$ $\xrightarrow{w}{}^*$ wrong. From this derivation, we construct a derivation of g $\xrightarrow{w}{}^*$ if wrong then g$_2$ else g$_3$. Adding a final instance of rule E-IF-WRONG yields g $\xrightarrow{w}{}^*$ wrong.
>
> *Other subcases:*
>
> Similar.

Case: g = succ g$_1$

Since g is stuck, we know (from the definition of values) that g$_1$ must be in normal form and not a numeric value. There are two possibilities: either g$_1$ is true or false, or else g$_1$ itself is not a value, hence stuck. In the first case, rule E-SUCC-WRONG immediately yields g $\xrightarrow{w}$ wrong; in the second case, the induction hypothesis gives us g$_1$ $\xrightarrow{w}{}^*$ wrong and we proceed as before.

Other cases:

Similar.   □

Lemmas A.3 and A.4 together give us the "only if" ($\Longrightarrow$) half of Proposition A.2. For the other half, we need to show that a term that is "about to go wrong" in the augmented semantics is stuck in the original semantics.

A.5   LEMMA: If $g \xrightarrow{w} t$ in the augmented semantics and t contains wrong as a subterm, then g is stuck in the original semantics.   □

Proof: Straightforward induction on (augmented) evaluation derivations.   □

   Combining this with Lemma A.3 yields the "if" ($\Leftarrow$) half of Proposition A.2, and we are finished.

3.5.17   SOLUTION: We prove the two directions of the "iff" separately, in Propositions A.7 and A.9. In each case, we begin with a technical lemma establishing some useful properties of multi-(small-)step evaluation.

A.6   LEMMA: If $t_1 \longrightarrow^* t_1'$ then if t_1 then t_2 else $t_3 \longrightarrow^*$ if t_1' then t_2 else t_3 (and similarly for the other term constructors).   □

Proof: Easy induction.   □

A.7   PROPOSITION: If $t \Downarrow v$ then $t \longrightarrow^* v$.   □

Proof: By induction on the derivation of $t \Downarrow v$, with a case analysis on the final rule used.

Case B-VALUE*:* $t = v$

Immediate.

Case B-IFTRUE*:* $t =$ if t_1 then t_2 else t_3
                      $t_1 \Downarrow$ true
                      $t_2 \Downarrow v$

By the induction hypothesis, $t_1 \longrightarrow^*$ true. By Lemma A.6,

   if t_1 then t_2 else $t_3 \longrightarrow^*$ if true then t_2 else t_3.

By E-IFTRUE, if true then t_2 else $t_3 \longrightarrow t_2$. By the induction hypothesis, $t_2 \longrightarrow^* v$. The result then follows by the transitivity of $\longrightarrow^*$.
   The other cases are similar.   □

A.8   LEMMA: If

   if t_1 then t_2 else $t_3 \longrightarrow^* v$,

then either $t_1 \longrightarrow^*$ true and $t_2 \longrightarrow^* v$ or $t_1 \longrightarrow^*$ false and $t_3 \longrightarrow^* v$. Moreover, the evaluation sequences for t_1 and t_2 or t_3 are strictly shorter than the given evaluation sequence. (And similarly for the other term constructors.)   □

Proof: By induction on the length of the given evaluation sequence. Since a condition is not a value, there must be at least one step of evaluation. Proceed by case analysis on the final rule used in this step (note that it must be one of the IF rules).

Case E-IF: if t_1 then t_2 else $t_3 \longrightarrow$ if t_1' then t_2 else $t_3 \longrightarrow^*$ v
$\qquad\qquad$ $t_1 \longrightarrow t_1'$

By the induction hypothesis, either $t_1' \longrightarrow^*$ true and $t_2 \longrightarrow^*$ v or $t_1' \longrightarrow^*$ false
and $t_3 \longrightarrow^*$ v. Adding the initial step $t_1 \longrightarrow t_1'$ to the derivation of $t_1' \longrightarrow^*$ true
or $t_1' \longrightarrow^*$ false yields the desired result. It is easy to check that the resulting
evaluation sequences are shorter than the original.

Case E-IFTRUE: if true then t_2 else $t_2 \longrightarrow t_2 \longrightarrow^*$ v

Immediate.

Case E-IFFALSE: if false then t_2 else $t_2 \longrightarrow t_3 \longrightarrow^*$ v

Immediate.   □

A.9   PROPOSITION: If $t \longrightarrow^*$ v then $t \Downarrow$ v.   □

Proof: By induction on the number of steps of small-step evaluation in the
given derivation of $t \longrightarrow^*$ v.

If $t \longrightarrow^*$ v in 0 steps, then $t = v$ and the result follows by B-VALUE. Otherwise, we proceed by case analysis on the form of t.

Case: $t =$ if t_1 then t_2 else t_3

By Lemma A.8, either (1) $t_1 \longrightarrow^*$ true and $t_2 \longrightarrow^*$ v or (2) $t_1 \longrightarrow^*$ false and
$t_3 \longrightarrow^*$ v. The arguments in both cases are similar, so suppose we have case
(1). Lemma A.8 also tells us that the evaluation sequences for $t_1 \longrightarrow^*$ true
and $t_2 \longrightarrow^*$ v are shorter than the given one for t, so the induction hypothesis
applies, giving us $t_1 \Downarrow$ true and $t_2 \Downarrow$ v. From these, we can use rule B-IFTRUE
to derive $t \Downarrow$ v.

The cases for the other term constructors are similar.   □

4.2.1   SOLUTION: Each time eval calls itself, it adds a try handler to the call stack.
Since there is one recursive call for each step of evaluation, the stack will
eventually overflow. In essence, wrapping the recursive call to eval in a try
means that it is not a tail call, although it looks like one. A better (but less
readable) version of eval is:

```
let rec eval t =
  let t'opt = try ∃(eval1 t) with NoRuleApplies → None in
  match t'opt with
    ∃(t') → eval t'
  | None → t
```

5.2.1   SOLUTION:

```
or = λb. λc. b tru c;
not = λb. b fls tru;
```

5.2.2   SOLUTION:

```
scc2 = λn. λs. λz. n s (s z);
```

5.2.3   SOLUTION:

```
times2 = λm. λn. λs. λz. m (n s) z;
```

Or, more compactly:

```
times3 = λm. λn. λs. m (n s);
```

5.2.4   SOLUTION: Again, there is more than one way to do it:

```
power1 = λm. λn. m (times n) c₁;
power2 = λm. λn. m n;
```

5.2.5   SOLUTION:

```
subtract1 = λm. λn. n prd m;
```

5.2.6   SOLUTION: Evaluating prd c_n takes $O(n)$ steps, since prd uses n to construct a sequence of n pairs of numbers and then selects the first component of the last pair of the sequence.

5.2.7   SOLUTION: Here's a simple one:

```
equal = λm. λn.
            and (iszro (m prd n))
                (iszro (n prd m));
```

5.2.8   SOLUTION: This is the solution I had in mind:

```
nil = λc. λn. n;
cons = λh. λt. λc. λn. c h (t c n);
head = λl. l (λh.λt.h) fls;
tail = λl.
          fst (l (λx. λp. pair (snd p) (cons x (snd p)))
                  (pair nil nil));
isnil = λl. l (λh.λt.fls) tru;
```

Here is a rather different approach:

```
nil = pair tru tru;
cons = λh. λt. pair fls (pair h t);
head = λz. fst (snd z);
tail = λz. snd (snd z);
isnil = fst;
```

5.2.9 SOLUTION: We used if rather than test to prevent both branches of the conditional always being evaluated, which would make factorial diverge. To prevent this divergence when using test, we need to protect both branches by wrapping them in dummy lambda-abstractions. Since abstractions are values, our call-by-value evaluation strategy does not look underneath them, but instead passes them verbatim to test, which chooses one and passes it back. We then apply the whole test expression to a dummy argument, say c_0, to force evaluation of the chosen branch.

```
ff = λf. λn.
      test
        (iszro n) (λx. c₁) (λx. (times n (f (prd n)))) c₀;
factorial = fix ff;
equal c₆ (factorial c₃);
```

▸ (λx. λy. x)

5.2.10 SOLUTION: Here's a recursive function that does the job:

```
cn = λf. λm. if iszero m then c₀ else scc (f (pred m));
churchnat = fix cn;
```

A quick test that it works:

```
equal (churchnat 4) c₄;
```

▸ (λx. λy. x)

5.2.11 SOLUTION:

```
ff = λf. λl.
      test (isnil l)
        (λx. c₀) (λx. (plus (head l) (f (tail l)))) c₀;
sumlist = fix ff;

l = cons c₂ (cons c₃ (cons c₄ nil));
equal (sumlist l) c₉;
```

▸ (λx. λy. x)

A list-summing function can also, of course, be written without using fix:

```
sumlist' = λl. l plus c₀;
equal (sumlist l) c₉;
```

▸ (λx. λy. x)

5.3.3 SOLUTION: By induction on the size of t. Assuming the desired property for terms smaller than t, we must prove it for t itself; if we succeed, we may conclude that the property holds for all t. There are three cases to consider:

Case: $t = x$

Immediate: $|FV(t)| = |\{x\}| = 1 = size(t)$.

Case: $t = \lambda x.t_1$

By the induction hypothesis, $|FV(t_1)| \leq size(t_1)$. We now calculate as follows: $|FV(t)| = |FV(t_1) \setminus \{x\}| \leq |FV(t_1)| \leq size(t_1) < size(t)$.

Case: $t = t_1\ t_2$

By the induction hypothesis, $|FV(t_1)| \leq size(t_1)$ and $|FV(t_2)| \leq size(t_2)$. We now calculate as follows: $|FV(t)| = |FV(t_1) \cup FV(t_2)| \leq |FV(t_1)| + |FV(t_2)| \leq size(t_1) + size(t_2) < size(t)$.

5.3.6   SOLUTION: For full (non-deterministic) beta-reduction, the rules are:

$$\frac{t_1 \longrightarrow t_1'}{t_1\ t_2 \longrightarrow t_1'\ t_2} \qquad \text{(E-APP1)}$$

$$\frac{t_2 \longrightarrow t_2'}{t_1\ t_2 \longrightarrow t_1\ t_2'} \qquad \text{(E-APP2)}$$

$$(\lambda x.t_{12})\ t_2 \longrightarrow [x \mapsto t_2]t_{12} \qquad \text{(E-APPABS)}$$

(Note that the syntactic category of values is not used.)

For the normal-order strategy, one way of writing the rules is

$$\frac{na_1 \longrightarrow na_1'}{na_1\ t_2 \longrightarrow na_1'\ t_2} \qquad \text{(E-APP1)}$$

$$\frac{t_2 \longrightarrow t_2'}{nanf_1\ t_2 \longrightarrow nanf_1\ t_2'} \qquad \text{(E-APP2)}$$

$$\frac{t_1 \longrightarrow t_1'}{\lambda x.t_1 \longrightarrow \lambda x.t_1'} \qquad \text{(E-ABS)}$$

$$(\lambda x.t_{12})\ t_2 \longrightarrow [x \mapsto t_2]t_{12} \qquad \text{(E-APPABS)}$$

where the syntactic categories of normal forms, non-abstraction normal forms, and non-abstractions are defined as follows:

```
nf  ::=                                                    normal forms:
        λx.nf
        nanf
nanf ::=                                      non-abstraction normal forms:
        x
        nanf nf
```

na ::=   *non-abstractions:*
>   x
>   t₁ t₂

(This definition is a bit awkward compared to the others. Normal-order reduction is usually defined by just saying "it's like full beta-reduction, except that the left-most, outermost redex is always chosen first.")

The lazy strategy defines values as arbitrary abstractions—the same as call by value. The evaluation rules are:

$$\frac{t_1 \longrightarrow t_1'}{t_1\ t_2 \longrightarrow t_1'\ t_2} \qquad\qquad \text{(E-App1)}$$

$$(\lambda x.t_{12})\ t_2 \longrightarrow [x \mapsto t_2]t_{12} \qquad\qquad \text{(E-AppAbs)}$$

5.3.8   SOLUTION:

$$\lambda x.t \Downarrow \lambda x.t$$

$$\frac{t_1 \Downarrow \lambda x.t_{12} \qquad t_2 \Downarrow v_2 \qquad [x \mapsto v_2]t_{12} \Downarrow v}{t_1\ t_2 \Downarrow v}$$

6.1.1   SOLUTION:

```
c₀ = λ. λ. 0;
c₂ = λ. λ. 1 (1 0);
plus = λ. λ. λ. λ. 3 1 (2 0 1);
fix = λ. (λ. 1 (λ. (1 1) 0)) (λ. 1 (λ. (1 1) 0));
foo = (λ. (λ. 0)) (λ. 0);
```

6.1.5   SOLUTION: The two functions can be defined as follows:

removenames$_\Gamma$(x)	=	the index of the rightmost x in Γ
removenames$_\Gamma$(λx.t₁)	=	λ. *removenames*$_{\Gamma,x}$(t₁)
removenames$_\Gamma$(t₁ t₂)	=	*removenames*$_{\Gamma,x}$(t₁) *removenames*$_{\Gamma,x}$(t₂)
restorenames$_\Gamma$(k)	=	the kth name in Γ
restorenames$_\Gamma$(λ.t₁)	=	λx. *restorenames*$_{\Gamma,x}$(t₁)
		where x is the first name not in *dom*(Γ)
restorenames$_\Gamma$(t₁ t₂)	=	*restorenames*$_{\Gamma,x}$(t₁) *restorenames*$_{\Gamma,x}$(t₂)

The required properties of *removenames* and *restorenames* are proved by straightforward structural induction on terms.

6.2.2   SOLUTION:

1. $\lambda. \lambda.$ 1 (0 4)

2. $\lambda.$ 0 3 ($\lambda.$ 0 1 4)

6.2.5   SOLUTION:

$$
\begin{aligned}
[0 \mapsto 1]\,(0\ (\lambda.\lambda.2)) &= 1\ (\lambda.\ \lambda.\ 3) \\
&\text{i.e.,}\quad a\ (\lambda x.\ \lambda y.\ a) \\[4pt]
[0 \mapsto 1\ (\lambda.2)]\,(0\ (\lambda.1)) &= (1\ (\lambda.2))\ (\lambda.(2\ (\lambda.3))) \\
&\text{i.e.,}\quad (a\ (\lambda z.a))\ (\lambda x.(a\ (\lambda z.a))) \\[4pt]
[0 \mapsto 1]\,(\lambda.\ 0\ 2) &= \lambda.\ 0\ 2 \\
&\text{i.e.,}\quad \lambda b.\ b\ a \\[4pt]
[0 \mapsto 1]\,(\lambda.\ 1\ 0) &= \lambda.\ 2\ 0 \\
&\text{i.e.,}\quad \lambda a'.\ a\ a'
\end{aligned}
$$

6.2.8   SOLUTION: If Γ is a naming context, write $\Gamma(x)$ for the index of x in Γ, counting from the right. Now, the property that we want is that

$$removenames_\Gamma([x \mapsto s]t) \;=\; [\Gamma(x) \mapsto removenames_\Gamma(s)](removenames_\Gamma(t)).$$

The proof proceeds by induction on t, using Definitions 5.3.5 and 6.2.4, some simple calculations, and some easy lemmas about *removenames* and the other basic operations on terms. Convention 5.3.4 plays a crucial role in the abstraction case.

6.3.1   SOLUTION: The only way an index could become negative would be if the variable numbered 0 actually occurred anywhere in the term we shift. But this cannot happen, since we've just performed a substitution for variable 0 (and since the term that we substituted for variable 0 was already shifted *up*, so it obviously cannot contain any instances of variable number 0).

6.3.2   SOLUTION: The proof of equivalence of the presentations using indices and levels can be found in Lescanne and Rouyer-Degli (1995). De Bruijn levels are also discussed by de Bruijn (1972) and Filinski (1999, Section 5.2).

8.3.5   SOLUTION: No: removing this rule breaks the progress property. If we really object to defining the predecessor of 0, we need to handle it in another way— e.g., by raising an exception (Chapter 14) if a program attempts it, or re-fining the type of pred to make clear that it can legally be applied only to strictly positive numbers, perhaps using intersection types (§15.7) or dependent types (§30.5).

8.3.6   SOLUTION: Here's a counterexample: the term (if false then true else 0) is ill-typed, but evaluates to the well-typed term 0.

8.3.7   SOLUTION: The type preservation property for the big-step semantics is similar to the one we gave for the small-step semantics: if a well-typed term evaluates to some final value, then this value has the same type as the original term. The proof is similar to the one we gave. The progress property, on the other hand, now makes a much stronger claim: it says that every well-typed term can be evaluated to some final value—that is, that evaluation always terminates on well-typed terms. For arithmetic expressions, this happens to be the case, but for more interesting languages (languages involving general recursion, for example—cf. §11.11) it will often not be true. For such languages, we simply *have* no progress property: in effect, there is no way to tell the difference between reaching an error state and failing to terminate. This is one reason that language theorists generally prefer the small-step style.

A different alternative is to give a big-step semantics with explicit wrong transitions, in the style of Exercise 8.3.8. This style is used, for example, by Abadi and Cardelli for the operational semantics of their object calculus (Abadi and Cardelli, 1996, p. 87).

8.3.8   SOLUTION: In the augmented semantics there are no stuck states at all—every non-value term either evaluates to another term in the ordinary way or else goes explicitly to wrong (this must be *proved,* of course)—so the progress property is trivial. The subject-reduction theorem, on the other hand, now tells us a little more. Since wrong has no type, saying that a well-typed term can evaluate only to another well-typed term tells us, in particular, that a well-typed term cannot take a step to wrong. In effect, the proof of the old progress theorem becomes part of the new proof of preservation.

9.2.1   SOLUTION: Because the set of type expressions is empty (there is no base case in the syntax of types).

9.2.3   SOLUTION: One such context is

$$\Gamma = \text{f:Bool} \rightarrow \text{Bool} \rightarrow \text{Bool, x:Bool, y:Bool}.$$

In general, any context of the form

$$\Gamma = \text{f:S} \rightarrow \text{T} \rightarrow \text{Bool, x:S, y:T}$$

where S and T are arbitrary types, will do the job. This sort of reasoning is central to the *type reconstruction* algorithm developed in Chapter 22.

9.3.2   SOLUTION: Suppose, for a contradiction, that the term x x does have a type T. Then, by the inversion lemma, the left-hand subterm (x) must have a type $T_1 \rightarrow T_2$ and the right-hand subterm (also x) must have type T_1. Using the variable case of the inversion lemma, we find that $x:T_1 \rightarrow T_2$ and $x:T_1$ must both come from assumptions in Γ. Since there can only be *one* binding for x in Γ, this means that $T_1 \rightarrow T_2 = T_1$. But this means that $size(T_1)$ is strictly greater than $size(T_1 \rightarrow T_2)$, an impossibility, and we have our contradiction.

Notice that if types were allowed to be infinitely large, then we *could* construct a solution to the equation $T_1 \rightarrow T_2 = T_1$. We will return to this point in detail in Chapter 20.

9.3.3   SOLUTION: Suppose that $\Gamma \vdash t : S$ and $\Gamma \vdash t : T$. We show, by induction on a derivation of $\Gamma \vdash t : T$, that $S = T$.

Case T-VAR: $t = x$
                 with $x : T \in \Gamma$

By case (1) of the inversion lemma (9.3.1), the final rule in any derivation of $\Gamma \vdash t : S$ must also be T-VAR, and $S = T$.

Case T-ABS: $t = \lambda y : T_2 . t_1$
                 $T = T_2 \rightarrow T_1$
                 $\Gamma, y : T_2 \vdash t_1 : T_1$

By case (2) of the inversion lemma, the final rule in any derivation of $\Gamma \vdash t : S$ must also be T-ABS, and this derivation must have a subderivation with conclusion $\Gamma, y : T_2 \vdash t_1 : S_1$, with $S = T_2 \rightarrow S_1$. By the induction hypothesis (on the subderivation with conclusion $(\Gamma, y : T_2 \vdash t_1 : T_1)$, we obtain $S_1 = T_1$, from which $S = T$ is immediate.

Case T-APP, T-TRUE, T-FALSE, T-IF:

Similar.

9.3.9   SOLUTION: By induction on a derivation of $\Gamma \vdash t : T$. At each step of the induction, we assume that the desired property holds for all subderivations (i.e., that if $\Gamma \vdash s : S$ and $s \longrightarrow s'$, then $\Gamma \vdash s' : S$, whenever $\Gamma \vdash s : S$ is proved by a subderivation of the present one) and proceed by case analysis on the last rule used in the derivation.

Case T-VAR: $t = x$ $x : T \in \Gamma$

Can't happen (there are no evaluation rules with a variable as the left-hand side).

Case T-ABS: $t = \lambda x : T_1 . t_2$

Can't happen.

Case T-APP: $t = t_1 \, t_2$ $\Gamma \vdash t_1 : T_{11} \rightarrow T_{12}$ $\Gamma \vdash t_2 : T_{11}$
                 $T = T_{12}$

Looking at the evaluation rules in Figure 9-1 with applications on the left-hand side, we find that there are three rules by which $t \longrightarrow t'$ can be derived: E-APP1, E-APP2, and E-APPABS. We consider each case separately.

Subcase E-APP1: $t_1 \longrightarrow t_1'$ $t' = t_1' \, t_2$

From the assumptions of the T-APP case, we have a subderivation of the original typing derivation whose conclusion is $\Gamma \vdash t_1 : T_{11} \rightarrow T_{12}$. We can apply the induction hypothesis to this subderivation, obtaining $\Gamma \vdash t_1' : T_{11} \rightarrow T_{12}$. Combining this with the fact (also from the assumptions of the T-APP case) that $\Gamma \vdash t_2 : T_{11}$, we can apply rule T-APP to conclude that $\Gamma \vdash t' : T$.

Subcase E-APP2: $t_1 = v_1$ (i.e., t_1 is a value)

$t_2 \longrightarrow t_2'$

$t' = v_1 \ t_2'$

Similar.

Subcase E-APPABS: $t_1 = \lambda x{:}T_{11}.\ t_{12}$

$t_2 = v_2$

$t' = [x \mapsto v_2]t_{12}$

Using the inversion lemma, we can deconstruct the typing derivation for $\lambda x{:}T_{11}.\ t_{12}$, yielding $\Gamma, x{:}T_{11} \vdash t_{12} : T_{12}$. From this and the substitution lemma (9.3.8), we obtain $\Gamma \vdash t' : T_{12}$.

The cases for boolean constants and conditional expressions are the same as in 8.3.3.

9.3.10 SOLUTION: The term $(\lambda x{:}Bool.\ \lambda y{:}Bool.\ y)\ (true\ true)$ is ill typed, but reduces to $(\lambda y{:}Bool.y)$, which is well typed.

9.4.1 SOLUTION: T-TRUE and T-FALSE are introduction rules. T-IF is an elimination rule. T-ZERO and T-SUCC are introduction rules. T-PRED and T-ISZERO are elimination rules. Deciding whether succ and pred are introduction or elimination forms requires a little thought, since they can be viewed as both creating *and* using numbers. The key observation is that, when pred and succ meet, they make a redex. Similarly for iszero.

11.2.1 SOLUTION: t_1 = $(\lambda x{:}Unit.x)\ unit$

t_{i+1} = $(\lambda f{:}Unit \rightarrow Unit.\ f(f(unit)))\ (\lambda x{:}Unit.t_i)$

11.3.2 SOLUTION:

$$\frac{\Gamma \vdash t_2 : T_2}{\Gamma \vdash \lambda\_{:}T_1.t_2 : T_1 \rightarrow T_2} \qquad \text{(T-WILDCARD)}$$

$$(\lambda\_{:}T_{11}.t_{12})\ v_2 \longrightarrow t_{12} \qquad \text{(E-WILDCARD)}$$

The proof that these rules are derived from the abbreviation goes exactly like Theorem 11.3.1.

11.4.1 SOLUTION: The first part is easy: if we desugar ascription using the rule t as T = $(\lambda x{:}T.\ x)$ t,x then it is straightforward to check that both the typing and the evaluation rules for ascription can be derived directly from the rules for abstraction and application.

If we change the evaluation rule for ascription to an eager version, then we need a more refined desugaring that delays evaluation of t until after the ascription has been thrown away. For example, we can use this one:

$$\texttt{t as T} \quad \stackrel{\text{def}}{=} \quad (\lambda\texttt{x:Unit→T. x unit}) \ (\lambda\texttt{y:Unit. t}) \quad \text{where y is fresh.}$$

Of course, the choice of Unit here is inessential: any type would do.

The subtlety here is that this desugaring, though intuitively correct, does *not* give us exactly the properties of Theorem 11.3.1. The reason is that a desugared ascription takes *two* steps of evaluation to disappear, while the high-level rule E-ASCRIBE works in a single step. However, this should not surprise us: we can think of this desugaring as a simple form of compilation, and observe that the compiled forms of nearly *every* high-level construct require multiple steps of evaluation in the target language for each atomic reduction in the source language. What we should do, then, is weaken the requirements of 11.3.1 to demand only that each high-level evaluation step should be matched by some *sequence* of low-level steps:

$$\text{if } \texttt{t} \longrightarrow_E \texttt{t}', \text{ then } e(\texttt{t}) \longrightarrow^*_I e(\texttt{t}').$$

A final subtlety is that the other direction—i.e., the fact that reductions of a desugared term can always be "mapped back" to reductions of the original term—requires a little care to state precisely, since the elimination of a desugared ascription takes two steps, and after the first step the low-level term does *not* correspond to the desugaring of either the original term with a high-level ascription or the term in which it has been eliminated. What *is* true, though, is that the first reduction of a desugared term can always be "completed" by taking it one more step to reach the desugaring of another high-level term. Formally, if $e(\texttt{t}) \longrightarrow_I s$, then $s \longrightarrow^* e(\texttt{t}')$, with $\texttt{t} \longrightarrow_E \texttt{t}'$.

11.5.1   SOLUTION: Here is what you need to add:

```
let rec eval1 ctx t = match t with
    ...
  | TmLet(fi,x,v1,t2) when isval ctx v1 →
      termSubstTop v1 t2
  | TmLet(fi,x,t1,t2) →
      let t1' = eval1 ctx t1 in
      TmLet(fi, x, t1', t2)
    ...

let rec typeof ctx t =
```

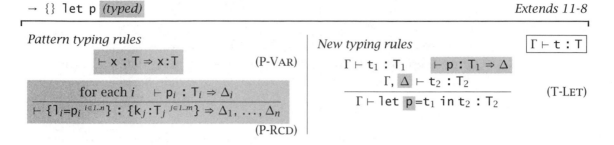

Figure A-1: Typed record patterns

```
match t with
  ...
| TmLet(fi,x,t1,t2) →
    let tyT1 = typeof ctx t1 in
    let ctx' = addbinding ctx x (VarBind(tyT1)) in
    (typeof ctx' t2)
```

11.5.2   SOLUTION: This definition doesn't work very well. For one thing, it changes the order of evaluation: the rules E-LETV and E-LET specify a call-by-value order, where t_1 in let x=t_1 in t_2 must be reduced to a value before we are allowed to substitute it for x and begin working on t_2. For another thing, although the validity of the typing rule T-LET is preserved by this translation—this follows directly from the substitution lemma (9.3.8)—the property of *ill*-typedness of terms is *not* preserved. For example, the ill-typed term

```
let x = unit(unit) in unit
```

is translated to the well-typed term unit: since x does not appear in the body unit, the ill-typed subterm unit(unit) simply disappears.

11.8.2   SOLUTION: One proposal for adding types to record patterns is summarized in Figure A-1. The typing rule for the generalized let construct, T-LET, refers to a separate "pattern typing" relation that (viewed algorithmically) takes a pattern and a type as input and, if it succeeds, returns a context giving appropriate bindings for the variables in the pattern. T-LET adds this context to the current context Γ during the typechecking of the body t_2. (We assume throughout that the sets of variables bound by different fields of a record pattern are disjoint.)

Note that we can, if we like, refine the record pattern typing rule a little, allowing the pattern to mention fewer fields than will actually be provided by the value it will match:

$$\frac{\{\mathsf{l}_i \;^{i \in 1..n}\} \subseteq \{\mathsf{k}_j \;^{j \in 1..m}\} \\ \forall \;^{i \in 1..n}. \; \exists \;^{j \in 1..m}. \; \mathsf{l}_i = \mathsf{k}_j \text{ and } \vdash \mathsf{p}_i : \mathsf{T}_j \Rightarrow \Delta_i}{\vdash \{\mathsf{l}_i = \mathsf{p}_i \;^{i \in 1..n}\} \in \{\mathsf{k}_j : \mathsf{T}_j \;^{j \in 1..m}\} \Rightarrow \Delta_1, \dots, \Delta_n} \qquad \text{(P-RCD')}$$

If we adopt this rule, we can eliminate the record projection form as a primitive construct, since it can now be treated as syntactic sugar:

$$\mathsf{t.l} \quad \overset{\mathrm{def}}{=} \quad \mathsf{let}\; \{\mathsf{l=x}\}\mathsf{=t}\; \mathsf{in}\; \mathsf{x}$$

Proving preservation for the extended system is almost the same as for the simply typed lambda-calculus. The only extension that we need is a lemma connecting the pattern typing relation with the run-time matching operation. If σ is a substitution and Δ is a context with the same domain as σ, then $\Gamma \vdash \sigma \vDash \Delta$ means that, for each $\mathsf{x} \in dom(\Delta)$, we have $\Gamma \vdash \sigma(\mathsf{x}) : \Delta(\mathsf{x})$.

LEMMA: If $\Gamma \vdash \mathsf{t} : \mathsf{T}$ and $\vdash \mathsf{p} : \mathsf{T} \Rightarrow \Delta$, then $match(\mathsf{p}, \mathsf{t}) = \sigma$, with $\Gamma \vdash \sigma \vDash \Delta$.

The extra notations we've introduced require a slight generalization of the standard substitution lemma (9.3.8):

LEMMA: $\Gamma, \Delta \vdash \mathsf{t} : \mathsf{T}$ and $\Gamma \vdash \sigma \vDash \Delta$, then $\Gamma \vdash \sigma \mathsf{t} : \mathsf{T}$.

The preservation argument for the C-LET rule now follows the same pattern as before, using these lemmas for the C-LET case.

11.9.1   SOLUTION:

Bool	$\overset{\mathrm{def}}{=}$	Unit+Unit
true	$\overset{\mathrm{def}}{=}$	inl unit
false	$\overset{\mathrm{def}}{=}$	inr unit
if t_0 then t_1 else t_2	$\overset{\mathrm{def}}{=}$	case t_0 of inl $\mathsf{x}_1 \Rightarrow \mathsf{t}_1$ | inr $\mathsf{x}_2 \Rightarrow \mathsf{t}_2$ where x_1 and x_2 are fresh.

11.11.1   SOLUTION:

```
equal =
  fix
    (λeq:Nat→Nat→Bool.
      λm:Nat. λn:Nat.
        if iszero m then iszero n
        else if iszero n then false
        else eq (pred m) (pred n));

▶ equal : Nat → Nat → Bool
```

```
        plus = fix (λp:Nat→Nat→Nat.
                    λm:Nat. λn:Nat.
                      if iszero m then n else succ (p (pred m) n));
```

▸ plus : Nat → Nat → Nat

```
        times = fix (λt:Nat→Nat→Nat.
                     λm:Nat. λn:Nat.
                       if iszero m then 0 else plus n (t (pred m) n));
```

▸ times : Nat → Nat → Nat

```
        factorial = fix (λf:Nat→Nat.
                         λm:Nat.
                           if iszero m then 1 else times m (f (pred m)));
```

▸ factorial : Nat → Nat

```
        factorial 5;
```

▸ 120 : Nat

11.11.2 SOLUTION:

```
        letrec plus : Nat→Nat→Nat =
          λm:Nat. λn:Nat.
            if iszero m then n else succ (plus (pred m) n) in
        letrec times : Nat→Nat→Nat =
          λm:Nat. λn:Nat.
            if iszero m then 0 else plus n (times (pred m) n) in
        letrec factorial : Nat→Nat =
          λm:Nat.
            if iszero m then 1 else times m (factorial (pred m)) in
        factorial 5;
```

▸ 120 : Nat

11.12.1   SOLUTION: Surprise! Actually, the progress theorem does *not* hold. For example, the expression head[T] nil[T] is stuck—no evaluation rule applies to it, but it is not a value. In a full-blown programming language, this situation would be handled by making head[T] nil[T] raise an exception rather than getting stuck: we consider exceptions in Chapter 14.

11.12.2   SOLUTION: Not quite all: if we erase the annotation on nil, then we lose the Uniqueness of Types theorem. Operationally, when the typechecker sees a nil it knows it has to assign it the type List T for some T, but it does not know how to choose T without some form of guessing. Of course, more sophisticated typing algorithms such as the one used by the OCaml compiler do precisely this sort of guessing. We will return to this point in Chapter 22.

12.1.1   SOLUTION: In the case for applications. Suppose we are trying to show that $t_1\ t_2$ is normalizing. We know by the induction hypothesis that both t_1 and t_2 are normalizing; let v_1 and v_2 be their normal forms. By the inversion lemma for the typing relation (9.3.1), we know that v_1 has type $T_{11}\rightarrow T_{12}$ for some T_{11} and T_{12}. So, by the canonical forms lemma (9.3.4), v_1 must have the form $\lambda x{:}T_{11}.t_{12}$. But reducing $t_1\ t_2$ to $(\lambda x{:}T_{11}.t_{12})\ v_2$ does not give us a normal form, since the E-APPABS rule now applies, yielding $[x \mapsto v_2]t_{12}$, so to finish the proof we must argue that this term is normalizable. But here we get stuck, since this term may, in general, be bigger than the original term $t_1\ t_2$ (because the substitution can make as many copies of v_2 as there are occurrences of x in t_{12}).

12.1.7   SOLUTION: Definition 12.1.2 is extended with two additional clauses:

- $R_{\mathsf{Bool}}(t)$ iff t halts.

- $R_{T_1 \times T_2}(t)$ iff t halts, $R_{T_1}(t.1)$, and $R_{T_2}(t.2)$.

The proof of Lemma 12.1.4 is extended with one additional case:

- Suppose that $T = T_1 \times T_2$ for some T_1 and T_2. For the "only if" direction ($\Longrightarrow$) we suppose that $R_T(t)$ and we must show $R_T(t')$, where $t \longrightarrow t'$. We know that $R_{T_1}t.1$ and $R_{T_2}(t.2)$ from the definition of $R_{T_1 \times T_2}$. But the evaluation rules E-PROJ1 and E-PROJ2 tell us that $t.1 \longrightarrow t'.1$ and $t.2 \longrightarrow t'.2$, so, by the induction hypothesis, $R_{T_1}(t'.1)$ and $R_{T_2}(t'.2)$. From these, the definition of $R_{T_1 \times T_2}$ yields $R_{T_1 \times T_2}(t')$. The "if" direction is similar.

Finally, we need to add some cases (one for each new typing rule) to the proof of Lemma 12.1.5:

Case T-IF: $t = \mathsf{if}\ t_1\ \mathsf{then}\ t_2\ \mathsf{else}\ t_3$ $\Gamma \vdash t_1 : \mathsf{Bool}$
$\Gamma \vdash t_2 : T$ $\Gamma \vdash t_3 : T$
where $\Gamma = x_1{:}T_1, \ldots, x_n{:}T_n$

Let $\sigma = [x_1 \mapsto v_1] \cdots [x_n \mapsto v_n]$. By the induction hypothesis, we have $R_{\mathsf{Bool}}(\sigma t_1)$, $R_T(\sigma t_2)$, and $R_T(\sigma t_3)$. By Lemma 12.1.3, σt_1, σt_2, and σt_3 are all normalizing; let us write v_1, v_2, and v_3 for their values. Lemma 12.1.4 gives us $R_{\mathsf{Bool}}(v_1)$, $R_T(v_2)$, and $R_T(v_3)$. Also, σt itself is clearly normalizing.

We now continue by induction on T.

- If $T = A$ or $T = \mathsf{Bool}$, then $R_T(\sigma t)$ follows immediately from the fact that σt is normalizing.

- If $T = T_1 \rightarrow T_2$, then we must show $R_{T_2} \sigma t\ s$ for an arbitrary $s \in R_{T_1}$. So suppose $s \in R_{T_1}$. Then, by the evaluation rules for if expressions, we see that either $\sigma t\ s \longrightarrow^* v_2\ s$ or else $\sigma t\ s \longrightarrow^* v_3\ s$, depending on whether v_1 is true or false. But we know that $R_{T_2}(v_2\ s)$ and $R_{T_2}(v_3\ s)$ by the definition of $R_{T_1 \rightarrow T_2}$ and the fact that both $R_{T_1 \rightarrow T_2} v_2$ and $R_{T_1 \rightarrow T_2} v_3$. By Lemma 12.1.4, $R_{T_1 \rightarrow T_2}(\sigma t\ s)$, as required.

Case T-TRUE: $t = \text{true}$ $T = \text{Bool}$

Immediate.

Case T-FALSE: $t = \text{false}$ $T = \text{Bool}$

Immediate.

Case T-PAIR: $t = \{t_1, t_2\}$ $\Gamma \vdash t_1 : T_1$ $\Gamma \vdash t_2 : T_2$ $T = T_1 \times T_2$

By the induction hypothesis, $R_{T_i}(\sigma t_i)$ for $i = 1, 2$. Let v_i be the normal form of each σt_i. Note, by Lemma 12.1.4, that $R_{T_i}(v_i)$.

The evaluation rules for the first and second projections tell us that $\{\sigma t_1, \sigma t_2\}.i \longrightarrow^* v_i$, from which we obtain, by Lemma 12.1.4, that $R_{T_i}(\{\sigma t_1, \sigma t_2\}.i)$. The definition of $R_{T_1 \times T_2}$ yields $R_{T_1 \times T_2}(\{\sigma t_1, \sigma t_2\})$, that is, $R_{T_1 \times T_2}(\sigma\{t_1, t_2\})$.

Case T-PROJ1: $t = t_0.1$ $\Gamma \vdash t_0 : T_1 \times T_2$ $T = T_1$

Immediate from the definition of $R_{T_1 \times T_2}$.

13.1.1 SOLUTION:

13.1.2 SOLUTION: No—calls to lookup with any index other than the one given to update will now diverge. The point is that we need to make sure we look up the value stored in a *before* we overwrite it with the new function. Otherwise, when we get around to doing the lookup, we will find the new function, not the original one.

13.1.3 SOLUTION: Suppose the language provides a primitive free that takes a reference cell as argument and releases its storage so that (say) the very next allocation of a reference cell will obtain the same piece of memory. Then the program

```
let r = ref 0 in
let s = r in
free r;
let t = ref true in
t := false;
succ (!s)
```

will evaluate to the stuck term `succ false`. Note that aliasing plays a crucial role here in setting up the problem, since it prevents us from detecting invalid deallocations by simply making `free r` illegal if the variable r appears free in the remainder of the expression.

This sort of example is easy to mimic in a language like C with manual memory management (our `ref` constructor corresponds to C's `malloc`, our `free` to a simplified version of C's `free`).

13.3.1   SOLUTION: A simple account of garbage collection might go like this.

1. Model the finiteness of memory by taking the set $\mathcal{L}$ of locations to be finite.

2. Define *reachability* of locations in the store as follows. Write *locations*(t) for the set of locations mentioned in t. Say that a location l' is *reachable in one step* from a location l in a store μ if $l' \in locations(\mu(l))$. Say that l' is *reachable* from l if there is a finite sequence of locations beginning with l and ending with l', with each reachable in one step from the previous one. Finally, define the set of locations reachable from a term t in a store μ, written *reachable*(t, μ) as the locations reachable in μ from *locations*(t).

3. Model the action of garbage collection as a relation t | $\mu \longrightarrow_{gc}$ t | μ' defined by the following rule:

$$\frac{\mu' = \mu \text{ restricted to } reachable(t, \mu)}{t \mid \mu \longrightarrow_{gc} t \mid \mu'} \qquad \text{(E-GC)}$$

(That is, the domain of μ' is just *reachable*(t, μ), and its value on every location in this domain is the same as that of μ.)

4. Define evaluation sequences to be sequences of ordinary evaluation steps interleaved with garbage collection: $\xrightarrow{gc}_* \stackrel{\text{def}}{=} (\longrightarrow \cup \longrightarrow_{gc})^*$. Note that we do *not* want to just add the rule GC to the ordinary single-step evaluation relation: it is important that we perform garbage collection only "at the outermost level," where we can see the whole term being evaluated. If we allowed garbage collection "inside" of the evaluation of the left-hand side of an application, for example, we might incorrectly re-use locations that are actually mentioned in the right-hand side of the application, since by

looking at the left-hand side we would not be able to see that they were still accessible.

5. Justify these refinements to the definition of evaluation by showing that they do not affect final results, except for introducing the possibility of memory exhaustion:

(a) If $t \mid \mu \xrightarrow{gc} {}^* t' \mid \mu''$, then $t \mid \mu \longrightarrow^* t' \mid \mu'$, for some μ' such that μ' has a larger domain than μ'' and the two coincide where both are defined.

(b) If $t \mid \mu \longrightarrow^* t' \mid \mu'$, then either

    i. $t \mid \mu \xrightarrow{gc} {}^* t' \mid \mu''$, for some μ'' such that μ'' has a smaller domain than μ' and coincides with μ' where μ' is defined, or else

    ii. evaluation of $t \mid \mu$ runs out of memory—i.e., reaches a state $t''' \mid \mu'''$, where the next step of evaluating t''' needs to allocate a fresh location, but none is available because $reachable(t''', \mu''') = \mathcal{L}$.

This simple treatment of garbage collection ignores several aspects of real stores, such as the fact that storing different kinds of values typically requires different amounts of memory, as well as some more advanced language features, such as *finalizers* (pieces of code that will be executed when the run-time system is just about to garbage collect a data structure to which they are attached) and *weak pointers* (pointers that are not counted as "real references" to a data structure, so that the structure may be garbage collected even though weak pointers to it still exist). A more sophisticated treatment of garbage collection in operational semantics can be found in Morrisett et al. (1995).

13.4.1   SOLUTION:

```
let r₁ = ref (λx:Nat.0) in
let r₂ = ref (λx:Nat.(!r₁)x) in
(r₁ := (λx:Nat.(!r₂)x);
 r₂);
```

13.5.2   SOLUTION: Let μ be a store with a single location 1

$$\mu \quad = \quad (1 \mapsto \lambda x{:}\mathsf{Unit}.\ (!1)(x)),$$

and Γ the empty context. Then μ is well typed with respect to both of the following store typings:

$$\Sigma_1 \quad = \quad 1{:}\mathsf{Unit}{\to}\mathsf{Unit}$$
$$\Sigma_2 \quad = \quad 1{:}\mathsf{Unit}{\to}(\mathsf{Unit}{\to}\mathsf{Unit}).$$

13.5.8   SOLUTION: There are well-typed terms in this system that are not strongly normalizing. Exercise 13.1.2 gave one. Here is another:

```
t1 = λr:Ref (Unit→Unit).
        (r := (λx:Unit. (!r)x);
        (!r) unit);
t2 = ref (λx:Unit. x);
```

Applying t1 to t2 yields a (well-typed) divergent term.

More generally, we can use the following steps to define arbitrary recursive functions using references. (This technique is actually used in some implementations of functional languages.)

1. Allocate a ref cell and initialize it with a dummy function of the appropriate type:

    $fact_{ref}$ = ref (λn:Nat.0);

    ▸ $fact_{ref}$: Ref (Nat→Nat)

2. Define the body of the function we are interested in, using the contents of the reference cell for making recursive calls:

    ```
    factbody =
        λn:Nat.
            if iszero n then 1 else times n ((!factref)(pred n));
    ```

    ▸ $fact_{body}$: Nat → Nat

3. "Backpatch" by storing the real body into the reference cell:

    $fact_{ref}$:= $fact_{body}$;

4. Extract the contents of the reference cell and use it as desired:

    ```
    fact = !factref;
    fact 5;
    ```

    ▸ 120 : Nat

14.1.1   SOLUTION: Annotating error with its intended type would break the type preservation property. For example, the well-typed term

(λx:Nat.x) ((λy:Bool.5) (error as Bool));

(where error as T is the type-annotated syntax for exceptions) would evaluate in one step to an ill-typed term:

```
(λx:Nat.x) (error as Bool);
```

As the evaluation rules propagate an `error` from the point where it occurs up to the top-level of a program, we may view it as having different types. The flexibility in the T-ERROR rule permits us to do this.

14.3.1 SOLUTION: The Definition of Standard ML (Milner, Tofte, Harper, and Mac-Queen, 1997; Milner and Tofte, 1991b) formalizes the `exn` type. A related treatment can be found in Harper and Stone (2000).

14.3.2 SOLUTION: See Leroy and Pessaux (2000).

14.3.3 SOLUTION: See Harper et al. (1993).

15.2.1 SOLUTION:

$$
\cfrac{
\cfrac{}{\begin{array}{l}\{x{:}Nat,y{:}Nat,z{:}Nat\} \\ <: \{y{:}Nat,x{:}Nat,z{:}Nat\}\end{array}}\text{ S-RcdPerm} \quad
\cfrac{}{\begin{array}{l}\{y{:}Nat,x{:}Nat,z{:}Nat\} \\ <: \{y{:}Nat\}\end{array}}\text{ S-RcdWidth}
}{\{x{:}Nat,y{:}Nat,z{:}Nat\} <: \{y{:}Nat\}}\text{ S-Trans}
$$

15.2.2 SOLUTION: There are lots of other derivations with the same conclusion. Here is one:

$$
\cfrac{
\cfrac{\vdots}{\vdash f : Rx{\rightarrow}Nat} \quad
\cfrac{\cfrac{}{Rxy <: Rx}\text{ S-Rcd-Width} \quad \cfrac{}{Nat <: Nat}\text{ S-Refl}}{Rx{\rightarrow}Nat <: Rxy{\rightarrow}Nat}\text{ S-Arrow}
}{\cfrac{\vdash f : Rxy{\rightarrow}Nat}{} \text{ T-Sub} \qquad \cfrac{\vdots}{\vdash xy : Rxy}}
$$
$$
\cfrac{}{\vdash f\,xy : Nat}\text{ T-App}
$$

Here is another:

$$
\cfrac{
\cfrac{\vdots}{\vdash f : Rx{\rightarrow}Nat} \qquad
\cfrac{\cfrac{\vdots}{\vdash xy : Rxy}\text{ T-Rcd} \quad \cfrac{\cfrac{}{Rxy <: Rx}\text{ S-RcdWidth} \quad \cfrac{}{Rx <: Rx}\text{ S-Refl}}{Rxy <: Rx}\text{ S-Trans}}{\vdash xy : Rx}\text{ T-Sub}
}{\vdash f\,xy : Nat}\text{ T-App}
$$

In fact, as the second example suggests, there are actually *infinitely many* typing derivations for *any* derivable statement in this calculus.

15.2.3 SOLUTION:

1. I count six: {a:Top,b:Top}, {b:Top,a:Top}, {a:Top}, {b:Top}, {}, and Top.

2. For example, let

$$
\begin{aligned}
S_0 &= \{\} \\
S_1 &= \{\texttt{a:Top}\} \\
S_2 &= \{\texttt{a:Top,b:Top}\} \\
S_2 &= \{\texttt{a:Top,b:Top,c:Top}\} \\
\textit{etc.}
\end{aligned}
$$

3. For example, let $T_0 = S_0 \rightarrow \mathsf{Top}$, $T_1 = S_1 \rightarrow \mathsf{Top}$ $T_2 = S_2 \rightarrow \mathsf{Top}$, etc.

15.2.4   SOLUTION: (1) No. If there were, it would have to be either an arrow or a record (it obviously can't be Top). But a record type would not be a subtype of any of the arrow types, and vice versa. (2) No again. If there *were* such an arrow type $T_1 \rightarrow T_2$, its domain type T_1 would have to be a subtype of every other type S_1; but we have just seen that this is not possible.

15.2.5   SOLUTION: Adding this rule would not be a good idea if we want to keep the existing evaluation semantics. The new rule would allow us to derive, for example, that $\mathsf{Nat} \times \mathsf{Bool} <: \mathsf{Nat}$, which would mean that the stuck term (succ (5,true)) would be well typed, violating the progress theorem. The rule is safe in a "coercion semantics" (see §15.6), though even there it raises some algorithmic difficulties for subtype checking.

15.3.1   SOLUTION: By adding bogus pairs to the subtype relation, we can break both preservation and progress. For example, adding the axiom

$$\{\texttt{x:}\{\}\} <: \{\texttt{x:Top}\rightarrow\texttt{Top}\}$$

allows us to derive $\Gamma \vdash \texttt{t : Top}$, where $\texttt{t} = (\{\texttt{x=}\{\}\}.\texttt{x})\{\}$. But $\texttt{t} \longrightarrow \{\}\{\}$, which is not typable—a violation of preservation. Alternatively, if we add the axiom

$$\{\} <: \mathsf{Top}\rightarrow\mathsf{Top}$$

then the term $\{\}\{\}$ *is* typable, but this term is stuck and not a value—a violation of progress.
    On the other hand, taking away pairs from the subtype relation is actually harmless. The only place where the typing relation is mentioned in the statement of the progress property is in the premises, so restricting the subtype relation, and hence the typing relation, can only make it easier for progress to hold. In the case of the preservation property, we might worry that taking away the transitivity rule, in particular, would cause trouble. The reason it does not is, intuitively, that its role in the system is actually inessential, in the sense that the subsumption rule T-SUB can be used to recover transitivity.

For example, instead of

$$
\cfrac{
  \cfrac{\vdots}{\Gamma \vdash t \in S}
  \qquad
  \cfrac{
    \cfrac{\vdots}{S <: U} \quad \cfrac{\vdots}{U <: T}
  }{S <: T}\ \text{S-Trans}
}{\Gamma \vdash t : T}\ \text{T-Sub}
$$

we can always write:

$$
\cfrac{
  \cfrac{
    \cfrac{\vdots}{\Gamma \vdash t : S} \quad \cfrac{\vdots}{S <: U}
  }{\Gamma \vdash t \in U}\ \text{T-Sub}
  \qquad
  \cfrac{\vdots}{U <: T}
}{\Gamma \vdash t : T}\ \text{T-Sub}
$$

15.3.2   SOLUTION:

1. By induction on subtyping derivations. By inspection of the subtyping rules in Figures 15-1 and 15-3, it is clear that the final rule in the derivation of $S <: T_1 \rightarrow T_2$ must be S-REFL, S-TRANS, or S-ARROW.

   If the final rule is S-REFL, then the result is immediate (since in this case $S = T_1 \rightarrow T_2$, and we can derive both $T_1 <: T_1$ and $T_2 <: T_2$ by reflexivity).

   If the final rule is S-TRANS, then we have subderivations with conclusions $S <: U$ and $U <: T_1 \rightarrow T_2$ for some type U. Applying the induction hypothesis to the second subderivation, we see that U has the form $U_1 \rightarrow U_2$, with $T_1 <: U_1$ and $U_2 <: T_2$. Now, since we know that U is an arrow type, we can apply the induction hypothesis to the first subderivation to obtain $S = S_1 \rightarrow S_2$ with $U_1 <: S_1$ and $S_2 <: U_2$. Finally, we can use S-TRANS twice to reassemble the facts we have established, obtaining $T_1 <: S_1$ (from $T_1 <: U_1$ and $U_1 <: S_1$) and $S_2 <: T_2$ (from $S_2 <: U_2$ and $U_2 <: T_2$).

   If the final rule is S-ARROW, then S has the desired form and the immediate subderivations are exactly the facts we need about the parts of S.

2. By induction on subtyping derivations. Again, inspecting the subtyping rules reveals that the final rule in the derivation of $S <: \{l_i : T_i{}^{i \in 1..n}\}$ must be S-REFL, S-TRANS, S-RCDWIDTH, S-RCDDEPTH, or S-RCDPERM. The case for S-REFL is trivial. The cases for S-RCDWIDTH, S-RCDDEPTH, and S-RCDPERM are all immediate.

   If the final rule is S-TRANS, then we have subderivations with conclusions $S <: U$ and $U <: \{l_i : T_i{}^{i \in 1..n}\}$ for some type U. Applying the induction hypothesis to the second subderivation, we see that U has the form

$\{u_a : U_a{}^{a \in 1..o}\}$, with $\{l_i{}^{i \in 1..n}\} \subseteq \{u_a{}^{a \in 1..o}\}$ and with $U_a <: T_i$ for each $l_i = u_a$. Now, since we know that U is a record type, we can apply the induction hypothesis to the first subderivation to obtain $S = \{k_j : S_j{}^{j \in 1..m}\}$, with $\{u_a{}^{a \in 1..o}\} \subseteq \{k_j{}^{j \in 1..m}\}$ and with $S_j <: U_a$ for each $u_a = k_j$. Reassembling these facts, we obtain $\{l_i{}^{i \in 1..n}\} \subseteq \{k_j{}^{j \in 1..m}\}$ by the transitivity of set inclusion, and $S_j <: T_i$ by S-TRANS for each $l_i = k_j$, since each label in T must also be in U (i.e., l_i must be equal to u_a for some a), and then we know $S_j <: U_a$ and $U_a <: T_i$. (The awkward choice of metavariable names here is unavoidable: there just aren't enough roman letters to go around.)

15.3.6   SOLUTION: Both parts proceed by induction on typing derivations. We show the argument just for the first part.

By inspection of the typing rules, it is clear that the final rule in a derivation of $\vdash v : T_1 \rightarrow T_2$ must be either T-ABS or T-SUB. If it is T-ABS, then the desired result is immediate from the premise of the rule. So suppose the last rule is T-SUB.

From the premises of T-SUB, we have $\vdash v : S$ and $S <: T_1 \rightarrow T_2$. From the inversion lemma (15.3.2), we know that S has the form $S_1 \rightarrow S_2$. The result now follows from the induction hypothesis.

16.1.2   SOLUTION: Part (1) is a straightforward induction on the structure of S.

For part (2), we first note that, by part (1), if there is any derivation of $S <: T$, then there is a reflexivity-free one. We now proceed by induction on the size of a reflexivity-free derivation of $S <: T$. Note that we are arguing by induction on the *size* of the derivation, rather than on its structure, as we have done in the past. This is necessary because, in the arrow and record cases, we apply the induction hypothesis to *newly constructed* derivations that do not appear as subderivations of the original.

If the final rule in the derivation is anything other than S-TRANS, then the result follows directly by the induction hypothesis (i.e., by the induction hypothesis, all of the subderivations of this final rule can be replaced by derivations not involving transitivity; since the final rule itself is not transitivity either, the whole derivation is now transitivity-free). So suppose the final rule is S-TRANS—i.e., that we are given subderivations with conclusions $S <: U$ and $U <: T$, for some type U. We proceed by cases on the pair of final rules in both of these subderivations.

Case ANY/S-TOP: $T = \mathsf{Top}$

If the right-hand derivation ends with S-TOP, then the result is immediate, since $S <: \mathsf{Top}$ can be derived from S-TOP no matter what S is.

Case S-TOP/ANY: $U = \mathsf{Top}$

If the left-hand subderivation ends with S-TOP, we first note that, by the induction hypothesis, we may suppose that the right-hand subderivation is transitivity-free. Now, inspecting the subtyping rules, we see that the final rule in this subderivation must be S-Top (we have already eliminated reflexivity, and all the other rules demand that U be either an arrow or a record). The result then follows by S-Top.

Case S-ARROW/S-ARROW: $S = S_1 \rightarrow S_2$ $U = U_1 \rightarrow U_2$ $T = T_1 \rightarrow T_2$

$$U_1 <: S_1 \qquad S_2 <: U_2$$
$$T_1 <: U_1 \qquad U_2 <: T_2$$

Using S-TRANS, we can construct derivations of $T_1 <: S_1$ and $S_2 <: T_2$ from the given subderivations. Moreover, these new derivations are strictly smaller than the original derivation, so the induction hypothesis can be applied to obtain transitivity-free derivations of $T_1 <: S_1$ and $S_2 <: T_2$. Combining these with S-ARROW, we obtain a transitivity-free derivation of $S_1 \rightarrow S_2 <: T_1 \rightarrow T_2$.

Case S-RCD/S-RCD:

Similar.

Other cases:

The other combinations (S-ARROW/S-RCD and S-RCD/S-ARROW) are not possible, since they place incompatible constraints on the form of U.

16.1.3   SOLUTION: If we add Bool, then the first part of Lemma 16.1.2 needs to be modified a little. It should now read, "S <: S can be derived for every type S without using S-REFL *except at type Bool*." Alternatively, we can add a rule

$$Bool <: Bool$$

to the definition of subtyping and then show that S-REFL can be dropped from the enriched system.

16.2.5   SOLUTION: By induction on declarative typing derivations. Proceed by cases on the final rule in the derivation.

Case T-VAR: $t = x$ $\Gamma(x) = T$

Immediate, by TA-VAR.

Case T-ABS: $t = \lambda x:T_1.t_2$ $\Gamma, x:T_1 \vdash t_2 : T_2$ $T = T_1 \rightarrow T_2$

By the induction hypothesis, $\Gamma, x:T_1 \Vdash t_2 : S_2$, for some $S_2 <: T_2$. By TA-ABS, $\Gamma \Vdash t : T_1 \rightarrow S_2$. By S-ARROW, $T_1 \rightarrow S_2 <: T_1 \rightarrow T_2$, as required.

Case T-APP: $t = t_1\ t_2$ $\Gamma \vdash t_1 : T_{11} \rightarrow T_{12}$ $\Gamma \vdash t_2 : T_{11}$ $T = T_{12}$

By the induction hypothesis, $\Gamma \Vdash t_1 : S_1$ for some $S_1 <: T_{11} \rightarrow T_{12}$ and $\Gamma \Vdash t_2 : S_2$ for some $S_2 <: T_{11}$. By the inversion lemma for the subtype relation (15.3.2), S_1 must have the form $S_{11} \rightarrow S_{12}$, for some S_{11} and S_{12} with $T_{11} <: S_{11}$ and $S_{12} <: T_{12}$. By transitivity, $S_2 <: S_{11}$. By the completeness of algorithmic subtyping, $\vdash S_2 <: S_{11}$. Now, by TA-APP, $\Gamma \vdash t_1\ t_2 : S_{12}$, which finishes this case (since we already have $S_{12} <: T_{12}$).

Case T-RCD: $t = \{l_i{=}t_i{}^{i\in 1..n}\}$ $\Gamma \vdash t_i : T_i$ for each i
                  $T = \{l_i{:}T_i{}^{i\in 1..n}\}$

Straightforward.

Case T-PROJ: $t = t_1.l_j$ $\Gamma \vdash t_1 : \{l_i{:}T_i{}^{i\in 1..n}\}$ $T = T_j$

Similar to the application case.

Case T-SUB: $t : S$ $S <: T$

By the induction hypothesis and transitivity of subtyping.

16.2.6   SOLUTION: The term $\lambda x{:}\{a{:}Nat\}.x$ has both the types $\{a{:}Nat\}{\rightarrow}\{a{:}Nat\}$ and $\{a{:}Nat\}{\rightarrow}Top$ under the declarative rules. But without S-ARROW, these types are incomparable (and there is no type that lies beneath both of them).

16.3.2   SOLUTION: We begin by giving a mutually recursive pair of algorithms that, we claim (and will show, below), calculate the join J and meet M, respectively, of a pair of types S and T. The second algorithm may also fail, signaling that S and T have no meet.

$$S \vee T \;=\; \begin{cases} \text{Bool} & \text{if } S = T = \text{Bool} \\ M_1 \rightarrow J_2 & \text{if } S = S_1 \rightarrow S_2 \qquad T = T_1 \rightarrow T_2 \\ & \qquad S_1 \wedge T_1 = M_1 \quad S_2 \vee T_2 = J_2 \\ \{j_l{:}J_l{}^{l\in 1..q}\} & \text{if } S = \{k_j{:}S_j{}^{j\in 1..m}\} \\ & \qquad T = \{l_i{:}T_i{}^{i\in 1..n}\} \\ & \qquad \{j_l{}^{l\in 1..q}\} = \{k_j{}^{j\in 1..m}\} \cap \{l_i{}^{i\in 1..n}\} \\ & \qquad S_j \vee T_i = J_l \quad \text{for each } j_l = k_j = l_i \\ \text{Top} & \text{otherwise} \end{cases}$$

$$S \wedge T \;=\; \begin{cases} S & \text{if } T = \text{Top} \\ T & \text{if } S = \text{Top} \\ \text{Bool} & \text{if } S = T = \text{Bool} \\ J_1 \rightarrow M_2 & \text{if } S = S_1 \rightarrow S_2 \qquad T = T_1 \rightarrow T_2 \\ & \qquad S_1 \vee T_1 = J_1 \quad S_2 \wedge T_2 = M_2 \\ \{m_l{:}M_l{}^{l\in 1..q}\} & \text{if } S = \{k_j{:}S_j{}^{j\in 1..m}\} \\ & \qquad T = \{l_i{:}T_i{}^{i\in 1..n}\} \\ & \qquad \{m_l{}^{l\in 1..q}\} = \{k_j{}^{j\in 1..m}\} \cup \{l_i{}^{i\in 1..n}\} \\ & \qquad S_j \wedge T_i = M_l \quad \text{for each } m_l = k_j = l_i \\ & \qquad M_l = S_j \qquad \text{if } m_l = k_j \text{ occurs only in S} \\ & \qquad M_l = T_i \qquad \text{if } m_l = l_i \text{ occurs only in T} \\ \textit{fail} & \text{otherwise} \end{cases}$$

In the arrow case of the first algorithm, the call to the second algorithm may result in failure; in this case the first algorithm falls through to the last case and the result is Top. For example $\text{Bool} \rightarrow \text{Top} \vee \{\} \rightarrow \text{Top} = \text{Top}$.

It is easy to check that $\vee$ and $\wedge$ are total functions (i.e., never diverge): just note that the total size of S and T is always reduced in recursive calls. Also, the $\wedge$ algorithm never fails when its inputs are bounded below:

A.10   LEMMA: If $L <: S$ and $L <: T$, then $S \wedge T = M$ for some M.   □

Proof: By induction on the size of S (or, equivalently, T), with a case analysis on the shapes of S and T. If either S or T is Top, then one of the first two cases in the definition applies, and the result is either T or S, respectively. The cases where S and T have different shapes cannot occur, since the inversion lemma for the subtype relation (15.3.2) would make inconsistent demands on the shape of L; for example, if S is an arrow, then so must L be, but if T is a record, then so is L.[1] So we have three cases left.

If both S and T are Bool, then the third case in the definition applies and we are finished.

Suppose instead that $S = S_1 \rightarrow S_2$ and $T = T_1 \rightarrow T_2$. The totality of the $\vee$ algorithm tells us that the first recursive call returns some type J_1. Also, by the inversion lemma, L must have the form $L_1 \rightarrow L_2$ with $L_2 <: S_2$ and $L_2 <: T_2$. That is, L_2 is a common lower bound of S_2 and T_2, so the induction hypothesis applies and tells us that $S_2 \wedge L_2$ does not fail, but rather returns a type M_2. So $S \wedge T = J_1 \rightarrow M_2$.

Finally, suppose that $S = \{k_j : S_j{}^{j \in 1..m}\}$ and $T = \{l_i : T_i{}^{i \in 1..n}\}$. By the inversion lemma, L must be a record type whose labels include all the labels that occur in either of S and T. Moreover, for each label in *both* S and T, the inversion lemma tells us that the corresponding field in L is a common subtype of the fields in S and T. This assures us that the recursive calls to the $\wedge$ algorithm for the common labels all succeed.   □

Now let us verify that these definitions calculate joins and meets. The argument is divided into two parts: Proposition A.11 shows that the calculated meet is a lower bound of S and T and the join is an upper bound; Proposition A.12 shows that the calculated meet is greater than every common lower bound of S and T and the join less than every common upper bound.

A.11   PROPOSITION:

1. If $S \vee T = J$, then $S <: J$ and $T <: J$.

---

[1]. Strictly speaking, Lemma 15.3.2 did not deal with Bool. The additional case for Bool just says that the only subtype of Bool is Bool itself.

2. If $S \wedge T = M$, then $M <: S$ and $M <: T$.   □

Proof: By a straightforward induction on the size of a "derivation" of $S \wedge T = M$ or $S \vee T = J$ (i.e., the number of recursive calls to the definitions of $\wedge$ and $\vee$ needed to calculate M or J).   □

A.12   PROPOSITION:

1. Suppose that $S \vee T = J$ and, for some U, that $S <: U$ and $T <: U$. Then $J <: U$.

2. Suppose that $S \wedge T = M$ and, for some L, that $L <: S$ and $L <: T$. Then $L <: M$.   □

Proof: The two parts are proved together, by induction on the sizes of S and T (actually, induction on almost anything will do). Given S and T, we consider the two parts in turn.

For part (1), proceed by cases on the form of U. If U is Top, then we are done, since $J <: $ Top no matter what J is. If $U = $ Bool, then the inversion lemma (15.3.2) tells us that S and T must also be Bool, so $J = $ Bool and we are finished. The other cases are more interesting.

If $U = U_1 \rightarrow U_2$, then, by the inversion lemma, $S = S_1 \rightarrow S_2$ and $T = T_1 \rightarrow T_2$, with $U_1 <: S_1, U_1 <: T_1, S_2 <: U_2$, and $T_2 <: U_2$. By the induction hypothesis, the meet M_1 of S_1 and T_1 lies above U_1, while the join J_2 of S_2 and T_2 lies below U_2. By S-ARROW, $M_1 \rightarrow J_2 <: U_1 \rightarrow U_2$.

If U is a record type, then, by the inversion lemma, so are S and T. Moreover, the labels of S and T are supersets of the labels of U, and the type of every field in U is a supertype of the corresponding fields in S and T. Thus, the join of S and T will contain at least the labels of U, and (by the induction hypothesis) the fields of the join will be subtypes of the corresponding fields of U. By S-RCD, $J <: U$.

For part (2), we again proceed by cases on the forms of S and T. If either is Top, then the meet is the other, and the result is immediate. The cases where S and T have different (non-Top) shapes cannot occur, as we saw in the proof of A.10. If both are Bool, then the result is again immediate. The remaining cases (S and T both arrows or both records) are more interesting.

If $S = S_1 \rightarrow S_2$ and $T = T_1 \rightarrow T_2$, then by the inversion lemma we must have $L = L_1 \rightarrow L_2$, with $S_1 <: L_1, T_1 <: L_1, L_2 <: S_2$, and $L_2 <: T_2$. By the induction hypothesis, the join J_1 of S_1 and T_1 lies below L_1, while the meet M_2 of S_2 and T_2 lies above L_2. By S-ARROW, $L_1 \rightarrow L_2 <: J_1 \rightarrow M_2$.

If S and T are record types, then, by the inversion lemma, so is L. Furthermore, L must have all the labels of S and T (and perhaps more), and the corresponding fields must be in the subtype relation. Now, for each label m_l in the meet M of S and T, there are three possibilities. If m_l occurs in both S and T, then its type in M is the meet of its types in S and T, and the corresponding type in L is a subtype of the one in M by the induction hypothesis. On the other hand, if m_l occurs only in S, then the corresponding type in M is the same as in S, and we already know that the type in L is smaller. The case where m_l occurs only in T is similar. □

16.3.3 SOLUTION: The minimal type of this term is Top—the join of Bool and {}. However, the fact that this term is typable should probably be viewed as a weakness in our language, since it is hard to imagine that the programmer really intended to write this expression—after all, no operations can be performed on a value of type Top, so there is little point in computing it in the first place! There are two possible responses to this weakness. One is simply to remove Top from the system and make ∨ a partial operation. The other is to keep Top, but make the typechecker generate a warning whenever it encounters a term whose minimal type is Top.

16.3.4 SOLUTION: Handling Ref types is straightforward. We simply add one clause to the meet and join algorithms:

$$
S \vee T = \begin{cases} \cdots & \cdots \\ \text{Ref}(T_1) & \text{if } S = \text{Ref}(S_1), T = \text{Ref}(T_1), S_1 <: T_1, \text{ and } T_1 <: S_1 \\ \cdots & \cdots \end{cases}
$$

$$
S \wedge T = \begin{cases} \cdots & \cdots \\ \text{Ref}(T_1) & \text{if } S = \text{Ref}(S_1), T = \text{Ref}(T_1), S_1 <: T_1, \text{ and } T_1 <: S_1 \\ \cdots & \cdots \end{cases}
$$

When we refine Ref with Source and Sink constructors, however, we encounter a major difficulty: the subtype relation no longer has joins (or meets)! For example, the types Ref{a:Nat,b:Bool} and Ref{a:Nat} are subtypes of both Source{a:Nat} and Sink{a:Nat,b:Bool}, but these types have no common lower bound.

There are various ways to address this difficulty. Perhaps the simplest is to add *either* Source or Sink, but not both, to the system. For many application domains, this will suffice. For example, for the refined implementation of classes in §18.12, we need just Source. In a concurrent language with channel types (§15.5), on the other hand, we might prefer to have just Sink, since this will give us the ability to define a server process and pass around just the "send capability" on its access channel (the receive capability is needed only by the server process itself).

With just Source types, the join algorithm remains complete when refined as follows (we also need the Ref clause from above; analogous clauses are added to the meet algorithm):

$$
S \vee T = \begin{cases}
\cdots & \cdots \\
\mathsf{Source}(J_1) & \text{if } S = \mathsf{Ref}(S_1) \quad T = \mathsf{Ref}(T_1) \\
& S_1 \vee T_1 = J_1 \\
\mathsf{Source}(J_1) & \text{if } S = \mathsf{Source}(S_1) \quad T = \mathsf{Source}(T_1) \\
& S_1 \vee T_1 = J_1 \\
\mathsf{Source}(J_1) & \text{if } S = \mathsf{Ref}(S_1) \quad T = \mathsf{Source}(T_1) \\
& S_1 \vee T_1 = J_1 \\
\mathsf{Source}(J_1) & \text{if } S = \mathsf{Source}(S_1) \quad T = \mathsf{Ref}(T_1) \\
& S_1 \vee T_1 = J_1 \\
\cdots & \cdots
\end{cases}
$$

A different solution (suggested by Hennessy and Riely, 1998) is to refine the Ref type constructor so that, instead of one argument, it takes two: the elements of Ref S T are reference cells that can be used to *store* elements of type S and *retrieve* elements of type T. The new Ref is contravariant in its first parameter and covariant in its second. Now Sink S can be defined as an abbreviation for Ref S Top, and Source T can be defined as Ref Bot T.

16.4.1   SOLUTION: Yes:

$$
\frac{\Gamma \vdash t_1 : T_1 \quad T_1 = \mathsf{Bot} \qquad \Gamma \vdash t_2 : T_2 \quad \Gamma \vdash t_3 : T_3 \quad T_2 \vee T_3 = T}{\Gamma \vdash \mathtt{if}\ t_1\ \mathtt{then}\ t_2\ \mathtt{else}\ t_3 : T} \tag{TA-IF}
$$

The alternative rule

$$
\frac{\Gamma \vdash t_1 : T_1 \quad T_1 = \mathsf{Bot} \qquad \Gamma \vdash t_2 : T_2 \quad \Gamma \vdash t_3 : T_3}{\Gamma \vdash \mathtt{if}\ t_1\ \mathtt{then}\ t_2\ \mathtt{else}\ t_3 : \mathsf{Bot}} \tag{TA-IF}
$$

is appealing, and would be safe (since Bot is empty, the evaluation of t_1 can never yield a regular result), but this rule would assign some types to terms that cannot be assigned by the declarative typing rules; choosing it would break Theorem 16.2.4.

17.3.1   SOLUTION: The solution just requires transcribing the algorithms from Exercise 16.3.2.

```
let rec join tyS tyT =
  match (tyS,tyT) with
```

```
        (TyArr(tyS1,tyS2),TyArr(tyT1,tyT2)) →
          (try TyArr(meet tyS1 tyT1, join tyS2 tyT2)
            with Not_found → TyTop)
    | (TyBool,TyBool) →
        TyBool
    | (TyRecord(fS), TyRecord(fT)) →
        let labelsS = List.map (fun (li,_) → li) fS in
        let labelsT = List.map (fun (li,_) → li) fT in
        let commonLabels =
          List.find_all (fun l → List.mem l labelsT) labelsS in
        let commonFields =
          List.map (fun li →
                      let tySi = List.assoc li fS in
                      let tyTi = List.assoc li fT in
                      (li, join tySi tyTi))
                    commonLabels in
        TyRecord(commonFields)
    | _ →
        TyTop

and meet tyS tyT =
  match (tyS,tyT) with
    (TyArr(tyS1,tyS2),TyArr(tyT1,tyT2)) →
      TyArr(join tyS1 tyT1, meet tyS2 tyT2)
  | (TyBool,TyBool) →
      TyBool
  | (TyRecord(fS), TyRecord(fT)) →
      let labelsS = List.map (fun (li,_) → li) fS in
      let labelsT = List.map (fun (li,_) → li) fT in
      let allLabels =
        List.append
          labelsS
          (List.find_all
            (fun l → not (List.mem l labelsS)) labelsT) in
      let allFields =
        List.map (fun li →
                    if List.mem li allLabels then
                      let tySi = List.assoc li fS in
                      let tyTi = List.assoc li fT in
                      (li, meet tySi tyTi)
                    else if List.mem li labelsS then
                      (li, List.assoc li fS)
                    else
                      (li, List.assoc li fT))
```

```
                    allLabels in
              TyRecord(allFields)
        | _ →
              raise Not_found

    let rec typeof ctx t =
      match t with
        ...
      | TmTrue(fi) →
          TyBool
      | TmFalse(fi) →
          TyBool
      | TmIf(fi,t1,t2,t3) →
            if subtype (typeof ctx t1) TyBool then
              join (typeof ctx t2) (typeof ctx t3)
            else error fi "guard of conditional not a boolean"
```

17.3.2   SOLUTION: See the rcssubbot implementation.

18.6.1   SOLUTION:

```
        DecCounter = {get:Unit→Nat, inc:Unit→Unit, reset:Unit→Unit,
                      dec:Unit→Unit};

        decCounterClass =
          λr:CounterRep.
            let super = resetCounterClass r in
              {get   = super.get,
               inc   = super.inc,
               reset = super.reset,
               dec   = λ_:Unit. r.x:=pred(!(r.x))}};
```

18.7.1   SOLUTION:

```
        BackupCounter2 = {get:Unit→Nat, inc:Unit→Unit,
                          reset:Unit→Unit, backup: Unit→Unit,
                          reset2:Unit→Unit, backup2: Unit→Unit};
        BackupCounterRep2 = {x: Ref Nat, b: Ref Nat, b2: Ref Nat};

        backupCounterClass2 =
          λr:BackupCounterRep2.
            let super = backupCounterClass r in
              {get = super.get, inc = super.inc,
               reset = super.reset, backup = super.backup,
               reset2 = λ_:Unit. r.x:=!(r.b2),
               backup2 = λ_:Unit. r.b2:=!(r.x)}};
```

18.11.1   SOLUTION:

```
    instrCounterClass =
      λr:InstrCounterRep.
        λself: Unit→InstrCounter.
          λ_:Unit.
            let super = setCounterClass r self unit in
                {get = λ_:Unit. (r.a:=succ(!(r.a)); super.get unit),
                 set = λi:Nat. (r.a:=succ(!(r.a)); super.set i),
                 inc = super.inc,
                 accesses = λ_:Unit. !(r.a)};

    ResetInstrCounter = {get:Unit→Nat, set:Nat→Unit,
                         inc:Unit→Unit, accesses:Unit→Nat,
                         reset:Unit→Unit};

    resetInstrCounterClass =
      λr:InstrCounterRep.
        λself: Unit→ResetInstrCounter.
          λ_:Unit.
            let super = instrCounterClass r self unit in
                {get = super.get,
                 set = super.set,
                 inc = super.inc,
                 accesses = super.accesses,
                 reset = λ_:Unit. r.x:=0};

    BackupInstrCounter = {get:Unit→Nat, set:Nat→Unit,
                          inc:Unit→Unit, accesses:Unit→Nat,
                          backup:Unit→Unit, reset:Unit→Unit};

    BackupInstrCounterRep = {x: Ref Nat, a: Ref Nat, b: Ref Nat};

    backupInstrCounterClass =
      λr:BackupInstrCounterRep.
        λself: Unit→BackupInstrCounter.
          λ_:Unit.
            let super = resetInstrCounterClass r self unit in
                {get = super.get,
                 set = super.set,
                 inc = super.inc,
                 accesses = super.accesses,
                 reset = λ_:Unit. r.x:=!(r.b),
                 backup = λ_:Unit. r.b:=!(r.x)};
```

```
newBackupInstrCounter =
  λ_:Unit. let r = {x=ref 1, a=ref 0, b=ref 0} in
               fix (backupInstrCounterClass r) unit;
```

18.13.1   SOLUTION: One way to test for identity is using reference cells. We extend the internal representation of our objects with an instance variable `id` of type `Ref Nat`

```
IdCounterRep = {x: Ref Nat, id: Ref (Ref Nat)};
```

and an `id` method that just returns the `id` field:

```
IdCounter = {get:Unit→Nat, inc:Unit→Unit, id:Unit→(Ref Nat)};
idCounterClass =
  λr:IdCounterRep.
    {get = λ_:Unit. !(r.x),
     inc = λ_:Unit. r.x:=succ(!(r.x)),
     id  = λ_:Unit. !(r.id)};
```

Now, the `sameObject` function takes two objects with `id` methods and checks whether the references returned by the `id` methods are the same.

```
sameObject =
  λa:{id:Unit→(Ref Nat)}. λb:{id:Unit→(Ref Nat)}.
    ((b.id unit) := 1;
     (a.id unit) := 0;
     iszero (!(b.id unit)));
```

The trick here is using aliasing to test whether two reference cells are the same: we make sure the second is non-zero, assign zero to the first, and test the second to see whether it has become zero.

19.4.1   SOLUTION: Since every class declaration must include an **extends** clause, and since these clauses are not allowed to be cyclic, the chain of **extends** clauses from every class must eventually end with `Object`.

19.4.2   SOLUTION: One obvious improvements would be to combine the three typing rules for casting into one

$$\frac{\Gamma \vdash t_0 : D}{\Gamma \vdash (C)t_0 : C} \qquad \text{(T-CAST)}$$

and drop the concept of stupid casts. Another would be to omit constructors, since they do nothing anyway.

19.4.6   SOLUTION:

1. The formulation of interfaces for FJ is routine.

2. Suppose we declare the following interfaces:

```
interface A {}
interface B {}
interface C extends A,B {}
interface D extends A,B {}
```

Then C and D have both A and B as common upper bounds, but no least upper bound.

3. Instead of the standard algorithmic rule for conditional expressions,

$$\frac{\Gamma \vdash t_1 : \text{boolean} \qquad \Gamma \vdash t_2 : E_2 \qquad \Gamma \vdash t_3 : E_3}{\Gamma \vdash t_1 ? t_2 : t_3 : E_2 \vee E_3}$$

Java uses the following restricted rules:

$$\frac{\Gamma \vdash t_1 : \text{boolean} \qquad \Gamma \vdash t_2 : E_2 \qquad \Gamma \vdash t_3 : E_3 \qquad \Gamma \vdash E_2 <: E_3}{\Gamma \vdash t_1 ? t_2 : t_3 : E_3}$$

$$\frac{\Gamma \vdash t_1 : \text{boolean} \qquad \Gamma \vdash t_2 : E_2 \qquad \Gamma \vdash t_3 : E_3 \qquad \Gamma \vdash E_3 <: E_2}{\Gamma \vdash t_1 ? t_2 : t_3 : E_2}$$

These are intuitively sound, but they interact poorly with the small-step style of operational semantics used for FJ—the type preservation property is actually false! (It is easy to construct an example that shows this.)

19.4.7   SOLUTION: Surprisingly, handling super is harder than handling self, since we need some way of remembering what class the "currently executing method body" came from. There are at least two ways to accomplish this:

1. Annotate terms with some indication of where super references should be looked up.

2. Add a preprocessing step in which the whole class table is rewritten, transforming references to super into references to this with "mangled" names indicating which class they come from.

19.5.1   SOLUTION: Before giving the main proof, we develop some required lemmas. As always, the critical one (A.14) relates typing and substitution.

A.13   LEMMA: If $mtype(m, D) = \overline{C} \rightarrow C_0$, then $mtype(m, C) = \overline{C} \rightarrow C_0$ for all C <: D.   □

Proof: Straightforward induction on the derivation of C <: D. Note that, whether m is defined in $CT(C)$ or not, $mtype(m, C)$ should be the same as $mtype(m, E)$ where $CT(C) = \text{class C extends E } \{...\}$.   □

A.14   LEMMA [TERM SUBSTITUTION PRESERVES TYPING]: If $\Gamma, \bar{x} : \bar{B} \vdash t : D$ and $\Gamma \vdash \bar{s} : \bar{A}$, where $\bar{A} <: \bar{B}$, then $\Gamma \vdash [\bar{x} \mapsto \bar{s}]t : C$ for some $C <: D$.   □

Proof: By induction on the derivation of $\Gamma, \bar{x} : \bar{B} \vdash t : D$. The intuitions are exactly the same as for the lambda-calculus with subtyping; details vary a little, of course. The most interesting cases are the last two.

Case T-VAR: $t = x$ $x : D \in \Gamma$

If $x \notin \bar{x}$, then the result is trivial since $[\bar{x} \mapsto \bar{s}]x = x$. On the other hand, if $x = x_i$ and $D = B_i$, then, since $[\bar{x} \mapsto \bar{s}]x = s_i$, letting $C = A_i$ finishes the case.

Case T-FIELD: $t = t_0.f_i$ $\Gamma, \bar{x} : \bar{B} \vdash t_0 : D_0$ *fields*$(D_0) = \bar{C}\,\bar{f}$ $D = C_i$

By the induction hypothesis, there is some C_0 such that $\Gamma \vdash [\bar{x} \mapsto \bar{s}]t_0 : C_0$ and $C_0 <: D_0$. It is easy to check that *fields*$(C_0) = ($*fields*$(D_0), \bar{D}\,\bar{g})$ for some $\bar{D}\,\bar{g}$. Therefore, by T-FIELD, $\Gamma \vdash ([\bar{x} \mapsto \bar{s}]t_0).f_i : C_i$.

Case T-INVK: $t = t_0.m(\bar{t})$ $\Gamma, \bar{x} : \bar{B} \vdash t_0 : D_0$ *mtype*$(m, D_0) = \bar{E} \rightarrow D$
$\Gamma, \bar{x} : \bar{B} \vdash \bar{t} : \bar{D}$ $\bar{D} <: \bar{E}$

By the induction hypothesis, there are some C_0 and $\bar{C}$ such that:

$$\Gamma \vdash [\bar{x} \mapsto \bar{s}]t_0 : C_0 \qquad C_0 <: D_0 \qquad \Gamma \vdash [\bar{x} \mapsto \bar{s}]\bar{t} : \bar{C} \qquad \bar{C} <: \bar{D}.$$

By Lemma A.13, *mtype*$(m, C_0) = \bar{E} \rightarrow D$. Moreover, $\bar{C} <: \bar{E}$ by the transitivity of $<:$. Therefore, by T-INVK, $\Gamma \vdash [\bar{x} \mapsto \bar{s}]t_0.m([\bar{x} \mapsto \bar{s}]\bar{t}) : D$.

Case T-NEW: $t = \text{new } D(\bar{t})$ *fields*$(D) = \bar{D}\,\bar{f}$ $\Gamma, \bar{x} : \bar{B} \vdash \bar{t} : \bar{C}$ $\bar{C} <: \bar{D}$

By the induction hypothesis, $\Gamma \vdash [\bar{x} \mapsto \bar{s}]\bar{t} : \bar{E}$ for some $\bar{E}$ with $\bar{E} <: \bar{C}$. We have $\bar{E} <: \bar{D}$ by the transitivity of $<:$. Therefore, by T-NEW, $\Gamma \vdash \text{new } D([\bar{x} \mapsto \bar{s}]\bar{t}) : D$.

Case T-UCAST: $t = (D)t_0$ $\Gamma, \bar{x} : \bar{B} \vdash t_0 : C$ $C <: D$

By the induction hypothesis, there is some E such that $\Gamma \vdash [\bar{x} \mapsto \bar{s}]t_0 : E$ and $E <: C$. We have $E <: D$ by the transitivity of $<:$, which yields $\Gamma \vdash (D)([\bar{x} \mapsto \bar{s}]t_0) : D$ by T-UCAST.

Case T-DCAST: $t = (D)t_0$ $\Gamma, \bar{x} : \bar{B} \vdash t_0 : C$ $D <: C$ $D \neq C$

By the induction hypothesis, there is some E such that $\Gamma \vdash [\bar{x} \mapsto \bar{s}]t_0 : E$ and $E <: C$. If $E <: D$ or $D <: E$, then $\Gamma \vdash (D)([\bar{x} \mapsto \bar{s}]t_0) : D$ by T-UCAST or T-DCAST, respectively. On the other hand, if both $D \not<: E$ and $E \not<: D$, then $\Gamma \vdash (D)([\bar{x} \mapsto \bar{s}]t_0) : D$ (with a *stupid warning*) by T-SCAST.

Case T-SCAST: $t = (D)t_0$ $\Gamma, \bar{x} : \bar{B} \vdash t_0 : C$ $D \not<: C$ $C \not<: D$

By the induction hypothesis, there is some E such that $\Gamma \vdash [\bar{x} \mapsto \bar{s}]t_0 : E$ and $E <: C$. This means that $E \not<: D$. (To see this, note that each class in FJ has just one super class. It follows that, if both $E <: C$ and $E <: D$, then either $C <: D$ or $D <: C$.) So $\Gamma \vdash (D)([\bar{x} \mapsto \bar{s}]t_0) : D$ (with a *stupid warning*), by T-SCAST.   □

A.15   LEMMA [WEAKENING]: If $\Gamma \vdash t : C$, then $\Gamma, x : D \vdash t : C$.   □

Proof: Straightforward induction.   □

A.16   LEMMA: If $mtype(m, C_0) = \overline{D}{\rightarrow}D$, and $mbody(m, C_0) = (\overline{x}, t)$, then for some D_0
and some C <: D we have C_0 <: D_0 and $\overline{x} : \overline{D}$, this : $D_0 \vdash t : C$.   □

Proof: By induction on the derivation of $mbody(m, C_0)$. The base case (where
m is defined in C_0) is easy since m is defined in $CT(C_0)$ and the well-formedness
of the class table implies that we must have derived $\overline{x} : \overline{D}$, this : $C_0 \vdash t : C$
by T-METHOD. The induction step is also straightforward.   □

We are now ready to give the proof of the type safety theorem.

Proof of Theorem 19.5.1: By induction on a derivation of $t \longrightarrow t'$, with a case
analysis on the final rule. Note how stupid warnings are generated in the
T-DCAST subcase, second from the end.

Case E-PROJNEW: $t = $ new $C_0(\overline{v}).f_i$ $t' = v_i$ $fields(C_0) = \overline{D}\ \overline{f}$

From the shape of t, we see that the final rule in the derivation of $\Gamma \vdash t : C$
must be T-FIELD, with premise $\Gamma \vdash$ new $C_0(\overline{v}) : D_0$, for some D_0, and that
$C = D_i$. Similarly, the last rule in the derivation of $\Gamma \vdash$ new $C_0(\overline{v}) : D_0$ must
be T-NEW, with premises $\Gamma \vdash \overline{v} : \overline{C}$ and $\overline{C}$ <: $\overline{D}$, and with $D_0 = C_0$. In particular,
$\Gamma \vdash v_i : C_i$, which finishes the case, since C_i <: D_i.

Case E-INVKNEW: $t = ($new $C_0(\overline{v})).m(\overline{u})$ $t' = [\overline{u}/\overline{x},$ new $C_0(\overline{v})/$this$]t_0$
                     $mbody(m, C_0) = (\overline{x}, t_0)$

The final rules in the derivation of $\Gamma \vdash t : C$ must be T-INVK and T-NEW, with
premises

$$\Gamma \vdash \text{new } C_0(\overline{v}) : C_0 \qquad \Gamma \vdash \overline{u} : \overline{C} \qquad \overline{C} <: \overline{D} \qquad mtype(m, C_0) = \overline{D}{\rightarrow}C.$$

By Lemma A.16, we have $\overline{x} : \overline{D}$, this : $D_0 \vdash t_0 : B$ for some D_0 and B, with
C_0 <: D_0 and B <: C. By Lemma A.15, $\Gamma, \overline{x} : \overline{D}$, this : $D_0 \vdash t_0 : B$. Then,
by Lemma A.14, $\Gamma \vdash [\overline{x} \mapsto \overline{u}, $this$ \mapsto$ new $C_0(\overline{v})]t_0 : E$ for some E <: B. By
transitivity of <:, we obtain E <: C. Letting $C' = E$ completes the case.

Case E-CASTNEW: $t = (D)($new $C_0(\overline{v}))$ C_0 <: D $t' = $ new $C_0(\overline{v})$

The proof of $\Gamma \vdash (D)($new $C_0(\overline{v})) : C$ must end with T-UCAST since ending with T-SCAST or T-DCAST would contradict the assumption C_0 <: D. The
premises of T-UCAST, give us $\Gamma \vdash$ new $C_0(\overline{v}) : C_0$ and D = C, finishing the
case.

The cases for the congruence rules are easy. We show just one:

Case RC-CAST: $t = (D)t_0$ $t' = (D)t_0'$ $t_0 \longrightarrow t_0'$

There are three subcases according to the last typing rule used.

Subcase T-UCAST: $\Gamma \vdash t_0 : C_0$ $C_0 <: D$ $D = C$

By the induction hypothesis, $\Gamma \vdash t_0' : C_0'$ for some $C_0' <: C_0$. By transitivity of $<:$, $C_0' <: C$. Therefore, by T-UCAST, $\Gamma \vdash (C)t_0' : C$ (with no additional *stupid warning*).

Subcase T-DCAST: $\Gamma \vdash t_0 : C_0$ $D <: C_0$ $D = C$

By the induction hypothesis, $\Gamma \vdash t_0' : C_0'$ for some $C_0' <: C_0$. If $C_0' <: C$ or $C <: C_0'$, then $\Gamma \vdash (C)t_0' : C$ by T-UCAST or T-DCAST (without any additional *stupid warning*). On the other hand, if both $C_0' \not<: C$ and $C \not<: C_0'$, then, $\Gamma \vdash (C)t_0' : C$ with a *stupid warning* by T-SCAST.

Subcase T-SCAST: $\Gamma \vdash t_0 : C_0$ $D \not<: C_0$ $C_0 \not<: D$ $D = C$

By the induction hypothesis, $\Gamma \vdash t_0' : C_0'$ for some $C_0' <: C_0$. Then, both $C_0' \not<: C$ and $C \not<: C_0'$ also hold. Therefore $\Gamma \vdash (C)t_0' : C$ with a *stupid warning*.   □

20.1.1   SOLUTION:

```
Tree = µX. <leaf:Unit, node:{Nat,X,X}>;
leaf = <leaf=unit> as Tree;
```

▸ leaf : Tree

```
node = λn:Nat. λt₁:Tree. λt₂:Tree. <node={n,t₁,t₂}> as Tree;
```

▸ node : Nat → Tree → Tree → Tree

```
isleaf = λl:Tree. case l of <leaf=u> ⇒ true | <node=p> ⇒ false;
```

▸ isleaf : Tree → Bool

```
label = λl:Tree. case l of <leaf=u> ⇒ 0 | <node=p> ⇒ p.1;
```

▸ label : Tree → Nat

```
left = λl:Tree. case l of <leaf=u> ⇒ leaf | <node=p> ⇒ p.2;
```

▸ left : Tree → Tree

```
right = λl:Tree. case l of <leaf=u> ⇒ leaf | <node=p> ⇒ p.3;
```

▸ right : Tree → Tree

```
append = fix (λf:NatList→NatList→NatList.
              λl1:NatList. λl2:NatList.
              if isnil l1 then l2 else
              cons (hd l1) (f (tl l1) l2));
```

▸ append : NatList → NatList → NatList

   preorder = fix (λf:Tree→NatList. λt:Tree.
                     if isleaf t then nil else
                     cons (label t)
                         (append (f (left t)) (f (right t))));

▸ preorder : Tree → NatList

  t1 = node 1 leaf leaf;
  t2 = node 2 leaf leaf;
  t3 = node 3 t1 t2;
  t4 = node 4 t3 t3;
  l = preorder t4;
  hd l;

▸ 4 : Nat

  hd (tl l);

▸ 3 : Nat

  hd (tl (tl l));

▸ 1 : Nat

20.1.2 SOLUTION:

   fib = fix (λf: Nat→Nat→Stream. λm:Nat. λn:Nat. λ_:Unit.
         {n, f n (plus m n)}) 0 1;

▸ fib : Stream

20.1.3 SOLUTION:

   Counter = μC. {get:Nat, inc:Unit→C, dec:Unit→C,
             reset:Unit→C, backup:Unit→C};
  c = let create =
     fix (λcr: {x:Nat,b:Nat}→Counter. λs: {x:Nat,b:Nat}.
         {get   = s.x,
         inc   = λ_:Unit. cr {x=succ(s.x),b=s.b},
         dec   = λ_:Unit. cr {x=pred(s.x),b=s.b},
         backup = λ_:Unit. cr {x=s.x,b=s.x},
         reset = λ_:Unit. cr {x=s.b,b=s.b}   })
    in create {x=0,b=0};

▸ c : Counter

20.1.4   SOLUTION:

```
D = μX. <nat:Nat, bool:Bool, fn:X→X>;

lam = λf:D→D. <fn=f> as D;
ap = λf:D. λa:D.
        case f of
          <nat=n> ⇒ divergeᴅ unit
        | <bool=b> ⇒ divergeᴅ unit
        | <fn=f> ⇒ f a;
ifd = λb:D. λt:D. λe:D.
        case b of
          <nat=n> ⇒ divergeᴅ unit
        | <bool=b> ⇒ (if b then t else e)
        | <fn=f> ⇒ divergeᴅ unit;
tru = <bool=true> as D;
fls = <bool=false> as D;
ifd fls one zro;
```

▶ `<nat=0> as D : D`

```
ifd fls one fls;
```

▶ `<bool=false> as D : D`

Readers who feel concerned about the fact that we can code ill-typed terms in this system should note that what we've done is to construct a *data structure* for representing the object language of untyped terms in the metalanguage of the simply typed lambda-calculus with recursive types. The fact that we can do this is no more surprising than the fact (which we've been using in the implementation chapters throughout the book) that we can represent terms of various typed and untyped lambda-calculi as data structures in ML.

20.1.5   SOLUTION:

```
lam = λf:D→D. <fn=f> as D;
ap = λf:D. λa:D. case f of
                    <nat=n> ⇒ divergeᴅ unit
                  | <fn=f> ⇒ f a
                  | <rcd=r> ⇒ divergeᴅ unit;
rcd = λfields:Nat→D. <rcd=fields> as D;
prj = λf:D. λn:Nat. case f of
                    <nat=n> ⇒ divergeᴅ unit
                  | <fn=f> ⇒ divergeᴅ unit
                  | <rcd=r> ⇒ r n;
myrcd = rcd (λn:Nat. if iszero 0 then zro
                    else if iszero (pred n) then one
                    else divergeᴅ unit);
```

20.2.1   SOLUTION: Here are some of the more interesting examples in iso-recursive form:

```
Hungry = μA. Nat → A;
f = fix (λf: Nat→Hungry. λn:Nat. fold [Hungry] f);
ff = fold [Hungry] f;
ff1 = (unfold [Hungry] ff) 0;
ff2 = (unfold [Hungry] ff1) 2;

fix_T =
  λf:T→T.
    (λx:(μA.A→T). f ((unfold [μA.A→T] x) x))
    (fold [μA.A→T] (λx:(μA.A→T). f ((unfold [μA.A→T] x) x)));

D = μX. X→X;
lam = λf:D→D. fold [D] f;
ap = λf:D. λa:D. (unfold [D] f) a;

Counter = μC. {get:Nat, inc:Unit→C};
c = let create = fix (λcr: {x:Nat}→Counter. λs: {x:Nat}.
                      fold [Counter]
                        {get = s.x,
                         inc = λ_:Unit. cr {x=succ(s.x)}})
      in create {x=0};
c1 = (unfold [Counter] c).inc unit;
(unfold [Counter] c1).get;
```

21.1.7   SOLUTION:

$$
\begin{array}{llll}
E_2(\varnothing) & = & \{a\} & \quad E_2(\{a,b\}) & = & \{a,c\} \\
E_2(\{a\}) & = & \{a\} & \quad E_2(\{a,c\}) & = & \{a,b\} \\
E_2(\{b\}) & = & \{a\} & \quad E_2(\{b,c\}) & = & \{a,b\} \\
E_2(\{c\}) & = & \{a,b\} & \quad E_2(\{a,b,c\}) & = & \{a,b,c\}
\end{array}
$$

The E_2-closed sets are $\{a\}$ and $\{a,b,c\}$. The E_2-consistent sets are $\varnothing$, $\{a\}$, and $\{a,b,c\}$. The least fixed point of E_2 is $\{a\}$. The greatest fixed point is $\{a,b,c\}$.

21.1.9   SOLUTION: To prove the principle of ordinary induction on natural numbers, we proceed as follows. Define the generating function $F \in \mathcal{P}(\mathbb{N}) \to \mathcal{P}(\mathbb{N})$ by

$$F(X) \;=\; \{0\} \cup \{i+1 \mid i \in X\}.$$

Now, suppose we have a predicate (i.e., a set of numbers) P such that $P(0)$ and such that $P(i)$ implies $P(i+1)$. Then, from the definition of F, it is easy to see that $F(P) \subseteq P$, i.e., P is F-closed. By the induction principle, $\mu F \subseteq P$. But μF is the whole set of natural numbers (indeed, this can be taken as the *definition* of the set of natural numbers), so $P(n)$ holds for all $n \in \mathbb{N}$.

For lexicographic induction, define $F \in \mathcal{P}(\mathbb{N} \times \mathbb{N}) \to \mathcal{P}(\mathbb{N} \times \mathbb{N})$ to be

$$F(X) \;=\; \{(m, n) \mid \forall (m', n') < (m, n), \; (m', n') \in X\}.$$

Now, suppose we have a predicate (i.e., a set of pairs of numbers) P such that, whenever $P(m', n')$ for all $(m', n') < (m, n)$, we also have $P(m, n)$. As before, from the definition of F, it is easy to see that $F(P) \subseteq P$, i.e., P is F-closed. By the induction principle, $\mu F \subseteq P$. To finish, we must check that μF is indeed the set of all pairs of numbers (this is the only subtle bit of the argument). This can be argued in two steps. First, we remark that $\mathbb{N} \times \mathbb{N}$ is F-closed (this is immediate from the definition of F). Second, we show that no proper subset of $\mathbb{N} \times \mathbb{N}$ is F-closed—i.e., $\mathbb{N} \times \mathbb{N}$ is the smallest F-closed set. To see this, suppose there were a smaller F-closed set Y, and let (m, n) be the smallest pair that does *not* belong to Y; by the definition of F, we see that $F(Y) \nsubseteq Y$, i.e., Y is not closed—a contradiction.

21.2.2   SOLUTION: Define a *tree* to be a partial function $T \in \{1, 2\}^* \rightharpoonup \{\rightarrow, \times, \mathsf{Top}\}$ satisfying the following constraints:

- $T(\bullet)$ is defined;

- if $T(\pi, \sigma)$ is defined then $T(\pi)$ is defined.

Note that occurrences of the symbols $\rightarrow, \times, \mathsf{Top}$ in the nodes of a tree are completely unconstrained, e.g. a node with Top can have non-trivial children, etc. As in §21.2, we overload the symbols $\rightarrow$, $\times$, and Top to be also operators on trees.

The set of all trees is taken as the universe $\mathcal{U}$. The generating function F is based on the familiar grammar for types:

$$\begin{aligned}
F(X) \;&=\; \{\mathsf{Top}\} \\
&\cup\; \{T_1 \times T_2 \mid T_1, T_2 \in X\} \\
&\cup\; \{T_1 \rightarrow T_2 \mid T_1, T_2 \in X\}.
\end{aligned}$$

It can be seen from the definitions of $\mathcal{T}$ and $\mathcal{U}$ that $\mathcal{T} \subseteq \mathcal{U}$, so it makes sense to compare the sets in the equations of interest, $\mathcal{T} = \nu F$ and $\mathcal{T}_f = \mu F$. It remains to check that the equations are true.

$\mathcal{T} \subseteq \nu F$ follows by the principle of coinduction from the fact that $\mathcal{T}$ is F-consistent. To obtain $\nu F \subseteq \mathcal{T}$, we need to check, for any $T \in \nu F$, the two last conditions from Definition 21.2.1. This can be done by induction on the length of π.

$\mu F \subseteq \mathcal{T}_f$ follows by the principle of induction from the fact that $\mathcal{T}_f$ is F-closed. To obtain $\mathcal{T}_f \subseteq \mu F$, we argue, by induction on the size of T, that $T \in \mathcal{T}_f$ implies $T \in \mu F$. (The size of $T \in \mathcal{T}_f$ can be defined as the length of the longest sequence $\pi \in \{1,2\}^*$ such that $T(\pi)$ is defined.)

21.3.3   SOLUTION: The pair (Top, Top $\times$ Top) is not in νS. To see this, just observe from the definition of S that this pair is not in $S(X)$ for any X. So there is no S-consistent set containing this pair, and in particular νS (which is S-consistent) does not contain it.

21.3.4   SOLUTION: For an example of a pair of tree types that are related by νS but not by μS, we can take the pair (T, T) for any infinite type T. Consider the set pairs $R = \{(T(\pi), T(\pi)) \mid \pi \in \{1,2\}^*\}$. An examination of the definition of S easily gives $R \subseteq S(R)$, and applying the principle of coinduction gives $R \subseteq \nu S$. Then $(T, T) \in \nu S$ because $(T, T) \in R$. On the other hand, $(T, T) \notin \mu S$ because μS relates only finite types—this can be established by taking R' to be the set of all pairs of finite types and obtaining $\mu S \subseteq R'$ by the principle of induction.

There are no pairs (S, T) of finite types that are related by νS_f, but not by μS_f, because the two fixed points coincide. This follows from the fact that, for any $S, T \in \mathcal{T}_f$, $(S, T) \in \nu S_f$ implies $(S, T) \in \mu S_f$. (Since T is a finite tree, the latter statement follows, in turn, be obtained by induction on T. One needs to consider the cases of T being Top, $T_1 \times T_2$, $T_1 \rightarrow T_2$, inspect the definition of S_f, and use the equalities $S_f(\nu S_f) = \nu S_f$ and $S_f(\mu S_f) = \mu S_f$.)

21.3.8   SOLUTION: Begin by defining the identity relation on tree types: $I = \{(T, T) \mid T \in \mathcal{T}\}$. If we can show that I is S-consistent, then the coinduction principle will tell us that $I \subseteq \nu S$—that is, νS is reflexive. To show the S-consistency of I, consider an element $(T, T) \in I$, and proceed by cases on the form of T. First, suppose $T = \mathsf{Top}$. Then $(T, T) = (\mathsf{Top}, \mathsf{Top})$, which is in $S(I)$ by definition. Suppose, next, that $T = T_1 \times T_2$. Then, since $(T_1, T_1), (T_2, T_2) \in I$, the definition of S gives $(T_1 \times T_2, T_1 \times T_2) \in S(I)$. Similarly for $T = T_1 \rightarrow T_2$.

21.4.2   SOLUTION: By the coinduction principle, it is enough to show that $\mathcal{U} \times \mathcal{U}$ is F^{TR}-consistent, i.e., $\mathcal{U} \times \mathcal{U} \subseteq F^{TR}(\mathcal{U} \times \mathcal{U})$. Suppose $(x, y) \in \mathcal{U} \times \mathcal{U}$. Pick any $z \in \mathcal{U}$. Then $(x, z), (z, y) \in \mathcal{U} \times \mathcal{U}$, and so, by the definition of F^{TR}, also $(x, y) \in F^{TR}(\mathcal{U} \times \mathcal{U})$.

21.5.2   SOLUTION: To check invertability, we just inspect the definitions of S_f and S and make sure that each set $G_{(S,T)}$ contains at most one element.

In the definitions of S_f and S each clause explicitly specifies the form of a supportable element and the contents of its support set, so writing down

$support_{S_f}$ and $support_S$ is easy. (Compare with the support function for S_m in Definition 21.8.4.)

21.5.4   SOLUTION:

$$
\begin{array}{c|ccccccccc}
i & a & b & c & b & d & e & f & g & g & \\
\hline
  & h &   & a &   & d & e & b &   & c & f & g
\end{array}
$$

21.5.6   SOLUTION: No, an $x \in \nu F \setminus \mu F$ does not have to lead to a cycle in the support graph: it can also lead to an infinite chain. For example, consider $F \in \mathcal{P}(\mathbb{N}) \to \mathcal{P}(\mathbb{N})$ defined by $F(X) = \{0\} \cup \{n \mid n + 1 \in X\}$. Then $\mu F = \{0\}$ and $\nu F = \mathbb{N}$. Also, for any $n \in \nu F \setminus \mu F$, that is for any $n > 0$, $support(n) = \{n + 1\}$, generating an infinite chain.

21.5.13   SOLUTION: First, consider partial correctness. The proof for each part proceeds by induction on the recursive structure of a run of the algorithm:

1. From the definition of *lfp*, it is easy to see that there are two cases where $lfp(X)$ can return *true*. If $lfp(X) = true$ because $X = \varnothing$, we have $X \subseteq \mu F$ trivially. On the other hand, if $lfp(X) = true$ because $lfp(support(X)) = true$, then, by the induction hypothesis, $support(X) \subseteq \mu F$, from which Lemma 21.5.8 yields $X \subseteq \mu F$.

2. If $lfp(X) = false$ because $support(X) \uparrow$, then $X \not\subseteq \mu F$ by Lemma 21.5.8. Otherwise, $lfp(X) = false$ because $lfp(support(X)) = false$, and, by the induction hypothesis, $support(X) \not\subseteq \mu F$. By Lemma 21.5.8, $X \not\subseteq \mu F$.

Next, we want to characterize the generating functions F for which *lfp* is guaranteed to terminate on all finite inputs. For this, some new terminology is helpful. Given a finite-state generating function $F \in \mathcal{P}(\mathcal{U}) \to \mathcal{P}(\mathcal{U})$, the partial function $height_F \in \mathcal{U} \rightharpoonup \mathbb{N}$ (or just *height*) is the least partial function satisfying the following condition:[2]

$$
height(x) = \begin{cases}
0 & \text{if } support(x) = \varnothing \\
0 & \text{if } support(x) \uparrow \\
1 + max\{height(y) \mid y \in support(x)\} & \text{if } support(x) \neq \varnothing
\end{cases}
$$

(Note that $height(x)$ is undefined if x either participates in a reachability cycle itself or depends on an element from a cycle.) A generating function F is said to be *finite height* if $height_F$ is a total function. It is easy to check that, if $y \in support(x)$ and both $height(x)$ and $height(y)$ are defined, then $height(y) < height(x)$.

---

2. Observe that this way of phrasing the definition of *height* can easily be rephrased as the least fixed point of a monotone function on relations representing partial functions.

Now, if F is finite state and finite height, then $lfp(X)$ terminates for any finite input set $X \subseteq \mathcal{U}$. To see this, observe that, since F is finite state, for every recursive call $lfp(Y)$ descended from the original call $lfp(X)$, the set Y is finite. Since F is finite height, $h(Y) = max\{height(y) \mid y \in Y\}$ is well defined. Since $h(Y)$ decreases with each recursive call and is always non-negative, it serves as a termination measure for lfp.

21.8.5   SOLUTION: The definition of S_d is the same as that of S_m, except that the last clause does not contain the conditions $\mathsf{T} \neq \mu\mathsf{X}.\mathsf{T}_1$ and $\mathsf{T} \neq \mathsf{Top}$. To see that S_d is not invertible, observe that the set $G_{(\mu\mathsf{X}.\mathsf{Top},\mu\mathsf{Y}.\mathsf{Top})}$ contains two generating sets, $\{(\mathsf{Top},\mu\mathsf{Y}.\mathsf{Top})\}$ and $\{(\mu\mathsf{X}.\mathsf{Top},\mathsf{Top})\}$ (compare the contents of this set for the function S_m).

Because all the clauses of S_d and S_m are the same, except the last, and the last clause of S_m is a restriction of the last clause of S_d, the inclusion $\nu S_m \subseteq \nu S_d$ is obvious. The other inclusion, $\nu S_d \subseteq \nu S_m$, can be proved using the principle of coinduction together with the following lemma, which establishes that νS_d is S_m-consistent.

A.17   LEMMA: For any two μ-types S, T, if $(\mathsf{S},\mathsf{T}) \in \nu S_d$, then $(\mathsf{S},\mathsf{T}) \in S_m(\nu S_d)$.   □

Proof sketch: By lexicographic induction on (n,k), where $k = \mu\text{-}height(\mathsf{S})$ and $n = \mu\text{-}height(\mathsf{T})$. This induction verifies the informal idea that any derivation of $(\mathsf{S},\mathsf{T}) \in \nu S_d$ can be transformed into another derivation of the same fact, that also happens to be a derivation of $(\mathsf{S},\mathsf{T}) \in \nu S_m$. The restrictions in the rule of left μ-folding dictate that the transformed derivation has the property that every sequence of applications of μ-folding rules starts with a sequence of left μ-foldings, which are then followed by a sequence of right μ-foldings. □

21.9.2   SOLUTION:

$$\frac{}{\mathsf{T} \sqsubseteq \mathsf{T}} \qquad \frac{\mathsf{S} \sqsubseteq \mathsf{T}_1}{\mathsf{S} \sqsubseteq \mathsf{T}_1 \times \mathsf{T}_2} \qquad \frac{\mathsf{S} \sqsubseteq \mathsf{T}_2}{\mathsf{S} \sqsubseteq \mathsf{T}_1 \times \mathsf{T}_2}$$

$$\frac{\mathsf{S} \sqsubseteq \mathsf{T}_1}{\mathsf{S} \sqsubseteq \mathsf{T}_1 {\rightarrow} \mathsf{T}_2} \qquad \frac{\mathsf{S} \sqsubseteq \mathsf{T}_2}{\mathsf{S} \sqsubseteq \mathsf{T}_1 {\rightarrow} \mathsf{T}_2} \qquad \frac{\mathsf{S} \sqsubseteq [\mathsf{X} \mapsto \mu\mathsf{X}.\mathsf{T}]\mathsf{T}}{\mathsf{S} \sqsubseteq \mu\mathsf{X}.\mathsf{T}}$$

(Note, as a point of interest, that the generating function TD differs from the generating functions we have considered throughout this chapter: it is not invertible. For example, $\mathsf{B} \sqsubseteq \mathsf{A} \times \mathsf{B} {\rightarrow} \mathsf{B} \times \mathsf{C}$ is supported by the two sets $\{\mathsf{B} \sqsubseteq \mathsf{A} \times \mathsf{B}\}$ and $\{\mathsf{B} \sqsubseteq \mathsf{B} \times \mathsf{C}\}$, neither of which is a subset of the other.)

21.9.7   SOLUTION: All the rules for BU are the same as the rules for TD given in the solution of Exercise 21.9.2, except the rule for types starting with a μ binder:

$$\frac{\mathsf{S} \preceq \mathsf{T}}{[\mathsf{X} \mapsto \mu\mathsf{X}.\mathsf{T}]\mathsf{S} \preceq \mu\mathsf{X}.\mathsf{T}}$$

21.11.1   SOLUTION: There are lots. A trivial example is μX.T and $[X \mapsto \mu X.T]T$ for just about any T. A more interesting one is μX. Nat $\times$ (Nat $\times$ X) and μX. Nat $\times$ X.

22.3.9   SOLUTION: Here are the main algorithmic constraint generation rules:

$$\frac{\Gamma(x) = T}{\Gamma \vdash_F x : T \;\mid_F \{\}} \qquad \text{(CT-VAR)}$$

$$\frac{\Gamma, x{:}T_1 \vdash_F t_2 : T_2 \;\mid_{F'} C \qquad x \notin dom(\Gamma)}{\Gamma \vdash_F \lambda x{:}T_1.t_2 : T_1 {\to} T_2 \;\mid_{F'} C} \qquad \text{(CT-ABS)}$$

$$\frac{\Gamma \vdash_F t_1 : T_1 \;\mid_{F'} C_1 \qquad \Gamma \vdash_{F'} t_2 : T_2 \;\mid_{F''} C_2 \qquad F'' = X, F'''}{\Gamma \vdash_F t_1\, t_2 : X \;\mid_{F'''} C_1 \cup C_2 \cup \{T_1 = T_2 {\to} X\}} \qquad \text{(CT-APP)}$$

The remaining rules are similar. The equivalence of the original rules and the algorithmic presentation can be stated as follows:

1. (SOUNDNESS) If $\Gamma \vdash_F t : T \;\mid_{F'} C$ and the variables mentioned in Γ and t do not appear in F, then $\Gamma \vdash t : T \;\mid_{F \backslash F'} C$.

2. (COMPLETENESS) If $\Gamma \vdash t : T \;\mid_X C$, then there is some permutation F of the names in X such that $\Gamma \vdash_F t : T \;\mid_\varnothing C$.

Both parts are proved by straightforward induction on derivations. For the application case in part 1, the following lemma is useful:

> If the type variables mentioned in Γ and t do not appear in F and if $\Gamma \vdash_F t : T \;\mid_{F'} C$, then the type variables mentioned in T and C do not appear in $F \backslash F'$.

For the corresponding case in part 2, the following lemma is used:

> If $\Gamma \vdash_F t : T \;\mid_{F'} C$, then $\Gamma \vdash_{F,G} t : T \;\mid_{F',G} C$, where G is any sequence of fresh variable names.

22.3.10   SOLUTION: Representing constraint sets as lists of pairs of types, the constraint generation algorithm is a direct transcription of the inference rules given in the solution to 22.3.9.

```
let rec recon ctx nextuvar t = match t with
      TmVar(fi,i,_) →
        let tyT = getTypeFromContext fi ctx i in
        (tyT, nextuvar, [])
    | TmAbs(fi, x, tyT1, t2) →
        let ctx' = addbinding ctx x (VarBind(tyT1)) in
        let (tyT2,nextuvar2,constr2) = recon ctx' nextuvar t2 in
        (TyArr(tyT1, tyT2), nextuvar2, constr2)
```

```
            | TmApp(fi,t1,t2) →
                let (tyT1,nextuvar1,constr1) = recon ctx nextuvar t1 in
                let (tyT2,nextuvar2,constr2) = recon ctx nextuvar1 t2 in
                let NextUVar(tyX,nextuvar') = nextuvar2() in
                let newconstr = [(tyT1,TyArr(tyT2,TyId(tyX)))] in
                ((TyId(tyX)), nextuvar',
                 List.concat [newconstr; constr1; constr2])
            | TmZero(fi) → (TyNat, nextuvar, [])
            | TmSucc(fi,t1) →
                let (tyT1,nextuvar1,constr1) = recon ctx nextuvar t1 in
                (TyNat, nextuvar1, (tyT1,TyNat)::constr1)
            | TmPred(fi,t1) →
                let (tyT1,nextuvar1,constr1) = recon ctx nextuvar t1 in
                (TyNat, nextuvar1, (tyT1,TyNat)::constr1)
            | TmIsZero(fi,t1) →
                let (tyT1,nextuvar1,constr1) = recon ctx nextuvar t1 in
                (TyBool, nextuvar1, (tyT1,TyNat)::constr1)
            | TmTrue(fi) → (TyBool, nextuvar, [])
            | TmFalse(fi) → (TyBool, nextuvar, [])
            | TmIf(fi,t1,t2,t3) →
                let (tyT1,nextuvar1,constr1) = recon ctx nextuvar t1 in
                let (tyT2,nextuvar2,constr2) = recon ctx nextuvar1 t2 in
                let (tyT3,nextuvar3,constr3) = recon ctx nextuvar2 t3 in
                let newconstr = [(tyT1,TyBool); (tyT2,tyT3)] in
                (tyT3, nextuvar3,
                 List.concat [newconstr; constr1; constr2; constr3])
```

22.3.11   SOLUTION: A constraint generation rule for `fix` expressions can be derived straightforwardly from the typing rule T-FIX in Figure 11-12.

$$\frac{\Gamma \vdash t_1 : T_1 \;\;|_{X_1}\; C_1 \qquad X \text{ not mentioned in } X_1, \Gamma, \text{ or } t_1}{\Gamma \vdash \text{fix } t_1 : X \;\;|_{X_1 \cup \{X\}}\; C_1\{T_1 = X{\to}X\}} \qquad \text{(CT-FIX)}$$

This rule reconstructs t_1's type (calling it T_1), makes sure that T_1 has the form $X{\to}X$ for some fresh X, and yields X as the type of `fix` t_1.

A constraint generation rule for `letrec` expressions can in turn be derived from this one, together with the definition of `letrec` as a derived form.

22.4.3   SOLUTION:

$\{X = \text{Nat}, Y = X{\to}X\}$	$[X \mapsto \text{Nat}, Y \mapsto \text{Nat}{\to}\text{Nat}]$
$\{\text{Nat}{\to}\text{Nat} = X{\to}Y\}$	$[X \mapsto \text{Nat}, Y \mapsto \text{Nat}]$
$\{X{\to}Y = Y{\to}Z, Z = U{\to}W\}$	$[X \mapsto U{\to}W, Y \mapsto U{\to}W, Z \mapsto U{\to}W]$
$\{\text{Nat} = \text{Nat}{\to}Y\}$	Not unifiable
$\{Y = \text{Nat}{\to}Y\}$	Not unifiable
$\{\}$	$[\,]$

22.4.6   SOLUTION: The main data structure needed for this exercise is a representation of substitutions. There are many alternatives; a simple one is to reuse the
`constr` datatype from Exercise 22.3.10: a substitution is just a constraint set,
all of whose left-hand sides are unification variables. If we define a function
`substinty` that performs substitution of a type for a single type variable

```
let substinty tyX tyT tyS =
  let rec f tyS = match tyS with
      TyArr(tyS1,tyS2) → TyArr(f tyS1, f tyS2)
    | TyNat → TyNat
    | TyBool → TyBool
    | TyId(s) → if s=tyX then tyT else TyId(s)
  in f tyS
```

then application of a whole substitution to a type can be defined as follows:

```
let applysubst constr tyT =
  List.fold_left
    (fun tyS (TyId(tyX),tyC2) → substinty tyX tyC2 tyS)
    tyT (List.rev constr)
```

The unification function also needs to be able to apply a substitution to all
the types in some constraint set:

```
let substinconstr tyX tyT constr =
  List.map
    (fun (tyS1,tyS2) →
       (substinty tyX tyT tyS1, substinty tyX tyT tyS2))
    constr
```

Also crucial is the "occur-check" that detects circular dependencies:

```
let occursin tyX tyT =
  let rec o tyT = match tyT with
      TyArr(tyT1,tyT2) → o tyT1 || o tyT2
    | TyNat → false
    | TyBool → false
    | TyId(s) → (s=tyX)
  in o tyT
```

The unification function is now a direct transcription of the pseudocode given
in Figure 22-2. As usual, it takes a file position and string as extra arguments
to be used in printing error messages when unification fails.

```
let unify fi ctx msg constr =
  let rec u constr = match constr with
      [] → []
```

```
  | (tyS,TyId(tyX)) :: rest →
     if tyS = TyId(tyX) then u rest
     else if occursin tyX tyS then
       error fi (msg ∧ ": circular constraints")
     else
       List.append (u (substinconstr tyX tyS rest))
                   [(TyId(tyX),tyS)]
  | (TyId(tyX),tyT) :: rest →
     if tyT = TyId(tyX) then u rest
     else if occursin tyX tyT then
       error fi (msg ∧ ": circular constraints")
     else
       List.append (u (substinconstr tyX tyT rest))
                   [(TyId(tyX),tyT)]
  | (TyNat,TyNat) :: rest → u rest
  | (TyBool,TyBool) :: rest → u rest
  | (TyArr(tyS1,tyS2),TyArr(tyT1,tyT2)) :: rest →
     u ((tyS1,tyT1) :: (tyS2,tyT2) :: rest)
  | (tyS,tyT)::rest →
     error fi "Unsolvable constraints"
in
  u constr
```

This pedagogical version of the unifier does not work very hard to print useful error messages. In practice, "explaining" type errors can be one of the hardest parts of engineering a production compiler for a language with type reconstruction. See Wand (1986).

22.5.6   SOLUTION: Extending the type reconstruction algorithm to handle records is not straightforward, though it can be done. The main difficulty is that it is not clear what constraints should be generated for a record projection. A naive first attempt would be

$$\frac{\Gamma \vdash t : T \mid_X C}{\Gamma \vdash t.l_i : X \mid_{X \cup \{X\}} C \cup \{T = \{l_i : X\}\}}$$

but this is not satisfactory, since this rule says, in effect, that the field l_i can be projected only from a record containing *just* the field l_i and no others.

An elegant solution was proposed by Wand (1987) and further developed by Wand (1988, 1989b), Remy (1989, 1990), and others. We introduce a new kind of variable, called a *row variable,* ranging not over types but over "rows" of field labels and associated types. Using row variables, the constraint generation rule for field projection can be written

$$\frac{\Gamma \vdash t_0 : T \mid_X C}{\Gamma \vdash t_0.l_i : X \mid_{X \cup \{X,\sigma,\rho\}} C \cup \{T = \{\rho\}, \rho = l_i : X \oplus \sigma\}} \qquad \text{(CT-PROJ)}$$

where σ and ρ are row variables and the operator $\oplus$ combines two rows (assuming that their fields are disjoint). That is, the term $t.l_i$ has type X if t has a record type with fields ρ, where ρ contains the field l_i:X and some other fields σ.

The constraints generated by this refined algorithm are more complicated than the simple sets of equations between types with unification variables of the original reconstruction algorithm, since the new constraint sets also involve the associative and commutative operator $\oplus$. A simple form of *equational unification* is needed to find solutions to such constraint sets.

23.4.3   SOLUTION: Here is the standard solution using an auxiliary append

```
append = λX. (fix (λapp:(List X) → (List X) → (List X).
                λl1:List X. λl2:List X.
                 if isnil [X] l1 then l2
                 else cons [X] (head [X] l1)
                               (app (tail [X] l1) l2)));
```

▸ append : ∀X. List X → List X → List X

```
reverse =
  λX.
    (fix (λrev:(List X) → (List X).
            λl: (List X).
             if isnil [X] l
             then nil [X]
             else append [X] (rev (tail [X] l))
                             (cons [X] (head [X] l) (nil [X])))));
```

▸ reverse : ∀X. List X → List X

23.4.5   SOLUTION:

```
and = λb:CBool. λc:CBool.
        λX. λt:X. λf:X. b [X] (c [X] t f) f;
```

23.4.6   SOLUTION:

```
iszro = λn:CNat. n [Bool] (λb:Bool. false) true;
```

23.4.8   SOLUTION:

```
pairNat = λn1:CNat. λn2:CNat.
            λX. λf:CNat→CNat→X. f n1 n2;
fstNat = λp:PairNat. p [CNat] (λn1:CNat. λn2:CNat. n1);
sndNat = λp:PairNat. p [CNat] (λn1:CNat. λn2:CNat. n2);
```

23.4.9   SOLUTION:

```
zz = pairNat c₀ c₀;
f = λp:PairNat. pairNat (sndNat p) (cplus c₁ (sndNat p));
prd = λm:CNat. fstNat (m [PairNat] f zz);
```

23.4.10   SOLUTION:

```
vpred = λn:CNat. λX. λs:X→X.
              λz:X.
                (n [(X→X)→X]
                   (λp:(X→X)→X. λq:(X→X). q (p s))
                   (λx:X→X. z))
                (λx:X. x);
```

▶ vpred : CNat → CNat

I'm grateful to Michael Levin for making me aware of this example.

23.4.11   SOLUTION:

```
head = λX. λdefault:X. λl:List X.
          l [X] (λhd:X. λtl:X. hd) default;
```

23.4.12   SOLUTION: The insertion function is the trickiest part of this exercise. This solution works by applying the given list l to a function that constructs *two* new lists, one identical to the original and the other including e. For each element hd of l (working from right to left), this function is passed hd and the pair of lists already constructed for the elements to the right of hd. The new pair of lists is built by comparing e with hd: if it is smaller or equal, then it belongs at the beginning of the second resulting list; we therefore build the second resulting list by adding e to the front of the *first* list we were passed (the one that does not yet contain e). On the other hand, if e is greater than hd, then it belongs somewhere in the middle of the second list, and we construct a new second list by simply appending hd to the already-constructed second list that we were passed.

```
insert =
  λX. λleq:X→X→Bool. λl:List X. λe:X.
    let res =
      l [Pair (List X) (List X)]
        (λhd:X. λacc: Pair (List X) (List X).
           let rest = fst [List X] [List X] acc in
           let newrest = cons [X] hd rest in
           let restwithe = snd [List X] [List X] acc in
           let newrestwithe =
```

```
            if leq e hd
              then cons [X] e (cons [X] hd rest)
              else cons [X] hd restwithe in
          pair [List X] [List X] newrest newrestwithe)
      (pair [List X] [List X] (nil [X]) (cons [X] e (nil [X])))
    in snd [List X] [List X] res;
```

▸ insert : ∀X. (X→X→Bool) → List X → X → List X

Next we need a comparison function for numbers. Since we're using primitive numbers, we need to use fix to write it. (We could avoid fix altogether by using CNat here instead of Nat.)

```
leqnat =
  fix (λf:Nat→Nat→Bool. λm:Nat. λn:Nat.
        if iszero m then true
        else if iszero n then false
        else f (pred m) (pred n));
```

▸ leqnat : Nat → Nat → Bool

Finally, we construct a sorting function by inserting each element of the list, in turn, into a new list:

```
sort = λX. λleq:X→X→Bool. λl:List X.
          l [List X]
            (λhd:X. λrest:List X. insert [X] leq rest hd)
            (nil [X]);
```

▸ sort : ∀X. (X→X→Bool) → List X → List X

To test that sort is working correctly, we construct an out-of-order list,

```
l = cons [Nat] 9
      (cons [Nat] 2 (cons [Nat] 6 (cons [Nat] 4 (nil [Nat]))));
```

sort it,

```
l = sort [Nat] leqnat l;
```

and read out the contents:

```
nth =
  λX. λdefault:X.
    fix (λf:(List X)→Nat→X. λl:List X. λn:Nat.
          if iszero n
            then head [X] default l
            else f (tail [X] l) (pred n));
```

▶ nth : ∀X. X → List X → Nat → X

  nth [Nat] 0 1 0;

▶ 2 : Nat

  nth [Nat] 0 1 1;

▶ 4 : Nat

  nth [Nat] 0 1 2;

▶ 6 : Nat

  nth [Nat] 0 1 3;

▶ 9 : Nat

  nth [Nat] 0 1 4;

▶ 0 : Nat

The demonstration that a well-typed sorting algorithm could be implemented in System F was a *tour de force* by Reynolds (1985). His algorithm was a little different from the one presented here.

23.5.1   SOLUTION: The structure of the proof is almost exactly the same as for 9.3.9 (see page 107). For the type application rule E-TAPPTABS, we need one additional substitution lemma, paralleling Lemma 9.3.8 (see page 106).

If $\Gamma, X, \Delta \vdash t : T$, then $\Gamma, [X \mapsto S]\Delta \vdash [X \mapsto S]t : [X \mapsto S]T$.

The extra context Δ here is needed to obtain a strong enough induction hypothesis; if it is omitted, the T-ABS case will fail.

23.5.2   SOLUTION: Again, the structure of this proof is very similar to the proof of progress for $\lambda_\rightarrow$, Theorem 9.3.5. The canonical forms lemma (9.3.4) is extended with one additional case

If v is a value of type $\forall X.T_{12}$, then $v = \lambda X.t_{12}$.

which is used in the type application case of the main proof.

23.6.3   SOLUTION: All of the parts are relatively straightforward inductive and/or calculational arguments, except the last, where a bit more insight is needed to see how to piece things together and obtain a contradiction. Pawel Urzyczyn suggested the structure of this argument.

(1) Straightforward induction on t, using the inversion lemma for typing.

(2) We show, by induction on the number of outer type abstractions and applications, that

> If t has the form $\lambda \overline{Y}.\ (r\ [\overline{B}])$ for some $\overline{Y}$, $\overline{B}$, and r (where r is not necessarily exposed), and if $erase(t) = m$ and $\Gamma \vdash t : T$, then there is some type s of the form $s = \lambda \overline{X}.\ (u\ [\overline{A}])$, with $erase(s) = m$ and $\Gamma \vdash s : T$, where furthermore u is exposed.

In the base case, there are no outer type abstractions or applications—i.e., r itself is exposed and we are finished.

In the induction case, the outer constructor of r is either a type abstraction or a type application. If it is a type application, say $r_1\ [R]$, we add R to the sequence $\overline{B}$ and apply the induction hypothesis. If it is a type abstraction, say $\lambda Z.\ r_1$, then there are two subcases to consider:

(a) If the sequence of applications $\overline{B}$ is empty, then we can add Z to the sequence of abstractions $\overline{Y}$ and apply the induction hypothesis.

(b) If $\overline{B}$ is nonempty, then we may write t as

$$t = \lambda \overline{Y}.\ ((\lambda Z.\ r_1)\ [B_0]\ [\overline{B}'])$$

where $\overline{B} = B_0 \overline{B}'$. But this term contains an R-BETA2 redex; reducing this redex leaves us with the term

$$t' = \lambda \overline{Y}.\ ([B_0 \mapsto Z]r_1\ [\overline{B}'])$$

where $[B_0 \mapsto Z]r_1$ contains strictly fewer outer type abstractions and applications than r. Furthermore, the subject reduction theorem tells us that t' has the same type as t. The desired result now follows by applying the induction hypothesis.

(3) Immediate from the inversion lemma.

(4) Straightforward calculation from parts (1), (3), and (2) [twice].

(5) Immediate from part (2) and the inversion lemma.

(6) By induction on the size of T_1. In the base case, where T_1 is a variable, this variable must come from $\overline{X}_1 \overline{X}_2$, since otherwise we would have

$$[\overline{X}_1 \overline{X}_2 \mapsto \overline{A}](\forall \overline{Y}.T_1) \quad = \quad \forall \overline{Y}.W \quad = \quad \forall \overline{Z}.(\forall \overline{Y}.W) \to ([\overline{X}_1 \mapsto \overline{B}]T_2),$$

which cannot be the case (there are no arrows on the left and at least one on the right). The other cases follow directly from the induction hypothesis.

(7) Suppose, for a contradiction, that omega is typable. Then, by parts (1) and (3), there is some exposed term $o = s\ u$ where

$$erase(s) = \lambda x.\ x\ x \qquad erase(u) = \lambda y.\ y\ y$$
$$\Gamma \vdash s : U{\to}V \qquad\qquad \Gamma \vdash u : U.$$

By part (2), there exist terms $s' = \lambda \overline{R}.\ (s_0\ [\overline{E}])$ and $u' = \lambda \overline{V}.\ (u_0\ [\overline{F}])$ with s_0 and u_0 exposed and

$$erase(s_0) = \lambda x.\ x\ x \quad erase(u_0) = \lambda y.\ y\ y$$
$$\Gamma \vdash s' : U{\to}V \qquad\quad \Gamma \vdash u' : U.$$

Since s' has an arrow type, $\overline{R}$ must be empty. Similarly, since s_0 and u_0 are exposed, they must both begin with abstractions, so $\overline{E}$ and $\overline{F}$ are also empty, and we have

$$
\begin{aligned}
o' &= s'\ u' \\
   &= s_0\ (\lambda \overline{V}.\ u_0) \\
   &= (\lambda x{:}T_x.\ w)\ (\lambda \overline{V}.\ \lambda y{:}T_y.\ v),
\end{aligned}
$$

where $erase(w) = x\ x$ and $erase(v) = y\ y$. By the inversion lemma, $U = T_x$ and

$$\Gamma, x{:}T_x \vdash w : W \qquad \Gamma, \overline{V}, y{:}T_y \vdash v : P.$$

Applying part (4) to the first of these, either

(a) $T_x = \forall \overline{X}.X_i$, or

(b) $T_x = \forall \overline{X}_1 \overline{X}_2 . T_1 {\to} T_2$, and, for some $\overline{A}$ and $\overline{B}$,

$$[\overline{X}_1 \overline{X}_2 \mapsto A]T_1 = [\overline{X}_1 \mapsto B](\forall \overline{Z}.T_1 {\to} T_2).$$

By part (5), T_x must have the second form, so, by part (6), the leftmost leaf of T_1 is $X_i \in \overline{X}_1 \overline{X}_2$.

Now, applying part (4) to the typing $\Gamma, \overline{V}, y{:}T_y \vdash v : P$, we have either

(a) $T_y = \forall \overline{Y}.Y_i$, or

(b) $T_y = \forall \overline{Y}_1 \overline{Y}_2 . S_1 {\to} S_2$, and, for some $\overline{C}$ and $\overline{C}$,

$$[\overline{Y}_1 \overline{Y}_2 \mapsto C]S_1 = [\overline{Y}_1 \mapsto D](\forall \overline{Z}'.S_1 {\to} S_2).$$

In the former case, we have immediately that the leftmost leaf of T_y is $Y_i \in \overline{Y}$. In the latter case, we can use (6) to see that that, again, the leftmost leaf of T_y is $Y_i \in \overline{Y}_1\overline{Y}_2$.

But, from the shape of o' and the inversion lemma, we have

$$
\begin{aligned}
\forall \overline{V}.T_y \rightarrow V &= T_x \\
&= \forall \overline{X}_1\overline{X}_2 . T_1 \rightarrow T_2,
\end{aligned}
$$

so, in particular, $T_y = T_1$. In other words, the leftmost leaf of T_1 is the same as that of T_y. In summary, then, we have $T_x = \forall \overline{X}_1\overline{X}_2 . (\forall \overline{Y}.S) \rightarrow T_2$, with both *leftmost-leaf*(S) $= X_i \in \overline{X}_1\overline{X}_2$ and *leftmost-leaf*(S) $= Y_i \in \overline{Y}$. Since the variables $\overline{X}_1\overline{X}_2$ and $\overline{Y}$ are bound at different places, we have derived a contradiction: our original assumption that omega is typable must be false.

23.7.1   SOLUTION:

```
let r = λX. ref (λx:X. x) in
(r[Nat] := (λx:Nat. succ x);
(!(r[Bool])) true);
```

24.1.1   SOLUTION: The package p6 provides a constant a and a function f, but the only operation permitted by the types of these components is applying f to a some number of times and then throwing away the result. The package p7 allows us to use f to create values of type X, but we can't do anything with these values. In p8, both components can be used, but now there is nothing hidden—we might as well drop the existential packaging altogether.

24.2.1   SOLUTION:

```
stackADT =
  {*List Nat,
   {new = nil [Nat],
    push = λn:Nat. λs:List Nat. cons [Nat] n s,
    top = λs:List Nat. head [Nat] s,
    pop = λs:List Nat. tail [Nat] s,
    isempty = isnil [Nat]}}
  as {∃Stack, {new: Stack, push: Nat→Stack→Stack, top: Stack→Nat,
             pop: Stack→Stack, isempty: Stack→Bool}};
▶ stackADT : {∃Stack,
             {new:Stack,push:Nat→Stack→Stack,top:Stack→Nat,
              pop:Stack→Stack,isempty:Stack→Bool}}

let {Stack,stack} = stackADT in
stack.top (stack.push 5 (stack.push 3 stack.new));
```

▸ 5 : Nat

24.2.2   SOLUTION:

```
counterADT =
  {*Ref Nat,
   {new = λ_:Unit. ref 1,
    get = λr:Ref Nat. !r,
    inc = λr:Ref Nat. r := succ(!r)}}
  as {∃Counter,
       {new: Unit→Counter, get: Counter→Nat, inc: Counter→Unit}};
▸ counterADT : {∃Counter,
                  {new:Unit→Counter,get:Counter→Nat,
                   inc:Counter→Unit}}
```

24.2.3   SOLUTION:

```
FlipFlop = {∃X, {state:X, methods: {read: X→Bool, toggle: X→X,
                                             reset: X→X}}};
f = {*Counter,
     {state = zeroCounter,
      methods = {read = λs:Counter. iseven (sendget s),
                 toggle = λs:Counter. sendinc s,
                 reset = λs:Counter. zeroCounter}}}
    as FlipFlop;
▸ f : FlipFlop
```

24.2.4   SOLUTION:

```
c = {*Ref Nat,
     {state = ref 5,
      methods = {get = λx:Ref Nat. !x,
                 inc = λx:Ref Nat. (x := succ(!x); x)}}}
    as Counter;
```

24.2.5   SOLUTION: This type would allow us to *implement* set objects with union methods, but it would prevent us from *using* them. To invoke the union method of such an object, we need to pass it two values of the very same representation type X. But these cannot come from two different set objects, since to obtain the two states we would need to open each object, and this would bind two distinct type variables; the state of the second set could not be passed to the union operation of the first. (This is not just stubbornness on the part of the typechecker: it is easy to see that it would be unsound to pass the concrete representation of one set to the union operation of another, since the representation of the second set may in general be arbitrarily different from the first.) So this version of the NatSet type only allows us to take the union of a set with itself!

24.3.2   SOLUTION: At a minimum, we need to show that the typing and computation rules of existentials are preserved by the translation—i.e., that if we write $[\![-]\!]$ for the function that performs all of these translations, then $\Gamma \vdash t : T$ implies $[\![\Gamma]\!] \vdash [\![t]\!] : [\![T]\!]$ and $t \longrightarrow^* t'$ implies $[\![t]\!] \longrightarrow^* [\![t']\!]$. These properties are easy to check. We might also hope to find that the converses are true—i.e., that an *ill*-typed term in the language with existentials is always mapped to an ill-typed term by the translation, and a stuck term to a stuck term; these properties, unfortunately, fail: for example, the translation maps the ill-typed (and stuck) term $(\{*Nat, 0\}$ as $\{\exists X.X\})$ [Bool] to a well-typed (and not stuck) one.

24.3.3   SOLUTION: I am not aware of any place where this is written out. It seems that it should be possible, but that the transformation will not be local syntactic sugar—it will need to be applied to a whole program all at once.

25.2.1   SOLUTION: The d-place shift of a type T above cutoff c, written $\uparrow^d_c (T)$, is defined as follows:

$$
\begin{aligned}
\uparrow^d_c (\mathsf{k}) &= \begin{cases} \mathsf{k} & \text{if } k < c \\ \mathsf{k}+d & \text{if } k \geq c \end{cases} \\
\uparrow^d_c (\mathsf{T}_1 {\rightarrow} \mathsf{T}_2) &= \uparrow^d_c (\mathsf{T}_1) {\rightarrow} \uparrow^d_c (\mathsf{T}_2) \\
\uparrow^d_c (\forall . \mathsf{T}_1) &= \forall . \uparrow^d_{c+1} (\mathsf{t}_1) \\
\uparrow^d_c (\{\exists, \mathsf{T}_1\}) &= \{\exists, \uparrow^d_{c+1} (\mathsf{T}_1\})
\end{aligned}
$$

Write $\uparrow^d_0 (T)$ for the d-place shift of all the variables in a type T, i.e., $\uparrow^d (T)$.

25.4.1   SOLUTION: It makes space for the type variable X. The result of substituting v_{12} into t_2 is supposed to be well-scoped in a context of the form Γ, X, whereas the original v_{12} is defined relative to just Γ.

26.2.3   SOLUTION: One place where the full $F_{<:}$ rule is required is in the object encoding of Abadi, Cardelli, and Viswanathan (1996), also described in Abadi and Cardelli (1996).

26.3.4   SOLUTION:

```
spluszz = λn:SZero. λm:SZero.
            λX. λS<:X. λZ<:X. λs:X→S. λz:Z.
              n [X] [S] [Z] s (m [X] [S] [Z] s z);
spluspn = λn:SPos. λm:SNat.
            λX. λS<:X. λZ<:X. λs:X→S. λz:Z.
              n [X] [S] [X] s (m [X] [S] [Z] s z);
```

▸ spluspn : SPos → SNat → SPos

26.3.5   SOLUTION:

```
SBool  = ∀X. ∀T<:X. ∀F<:X. T→F→X;
STrue  = ∀X. ∀T<:X. ∀F<:X. T→F→T;
SFalse = ∀X. ∀T<:X. ∀F<:X. T→F→F;
tru = λX. λT<:X. λF<:X. λt:T. λf:F. t;
```

▸ tru : STrue

```
fls = λX. λT<:X. λF<:X. λt:T. λf:F. f;
```

▸ fls : SFalse

```
notft = λb:SFalse. λX. λT<:X. λF<:X. λt:T. λf:F. b[X][F][T] f t;
```

▸ notft : SFalse → STrue

```
nottf = λb:STrue. λX. λT<:X. λF<:X. λt:T. λf:F. b[X][F][T] f t;
```

▸ nottf : STrue → SFalse

26.4.3   SOLUTION: In the abstraction and type abstraction cases in parts (1) and (2), and the quantifier case in (3) and (4).

26.4.5   SOLUTION: Part (1) proceeds induction on subtyping derivations. All of the cases are either immediate (S-REFL, S-TOP) or straightforward applications of the induction hypothesis (S-TRANS, S-ARROW, S-ALL) except S-TVAR, which is more interesting. Suppose the final rule of the derivation of Γ, X<:Q, Δ ⊢ S <: T is an instance of S-TVAR, i.e., S is some variable Y and T is the upper bound of Y in the context. There are two possibilities to consider. If X and Y are different variables, then the assumption Y<:T can also be found in the context Γ, X<:P, Δ, and the result is immediate. On the other hand, if X = Y, then T = Q; to complete the argument, we need to show that Γ, X<:P, Δ ⊢ X <: Q. We have by S-TVAR that Γ, X<:P, Δ ⊢ X <: P. Moreover, by assumption, Γ ⊢ P <: Q, so by weakening (Lemma 26.4.2), Γ, X<:P, Δ ⊢ P <: Q. Pasting these two new derivations together with S-TRANS yields the desired result.

Part (2) is a routine induction on typing derivations, using part (1) for the subtyping premise of the type application case.

26.4.11   SOLUTION: All the proofs are by straightforward induction on subtyping derivations. We show just the first, proceeding by case analysis on the final rule in the derivation. The cases for S-REFL and S-TOP are immediate. S-TVAR cannot happen (the left-hand side of the conclusion of S-TVAR can only be a variable, not an arrow); similarly, S-ALL cannot happen. If the final rule is an instance of S-ARROW, the subderivations are the desired results. Finally, suppose the last rule is an instance of S-TRANS—i.e., we have $\Gamma \vdash S_1 \rightarrow S_2 <: U$ and $\Gamma \vdash U <: T$ for some U. By the induction hypothesis, either U is Top (in which case T is also Top by part (4) of the exercise and we are done) or else U has the form $U_1 \rightarrow U_2$ with $\Gamma \vdash U_1 <: S_1$ and $\Gamma \vdash S_2 <: U_2$. In the latter case, we apply the induction hypothesis again to the second subderivation of the original S-TRANS to learn that either $T = $ Top (and we are done) or else T has the form $T_1 \rightarrow T_2$ with $\Gamma \vdash T_1 <: U_1$ and $\Gamma \vdash U_2 <: T_2$. Two uses of transitivity tell us that $\Gamma \vdash T_1 <: S_1$ and $\Gamma \vdash S_2 <: T_2$, from which the desired result follows by S-ARROW.

26.5.1   SOLUTION:

$$\frac{\Gamma \vdash S_1 <: T_1 \qquad \Gamma, X<:S_1 \vdash S_2 <: T_2}{\Gamma \vdash \{\exists X<:S_1, S_2\} <: \{\exists X<:T_1, T_2\}} \tag{S-SOME}$$

26.5.2   SOLUTION: Without subtyping, there are just four:

```
{*Nat, {a=5,b=7}} as {∃X, {a:Nat,b:Nat}};
{*Nat, {a=5,b=7}} as {∃X, {a:X,b:Nat}};
{*Nat, {a=5,b=7}} as {∃X, {a:Nat,b:X}};
{*Nat, {a=5,b=7}} as {∃X, {a:X,b:X}};
```

With subtyping and bounded quantification, there are quite a few more—for example:

```
{*Nat, {a=5,b=7}} as {∃X, {a:Nat}};
{*Nat, {a=5,b=7}} as {∃X, {b:X}};
{*Nat, {a=5,b=7}} as {∃X, {a:Top,b:X}};
{*Nat, {a=5,b=7}} as {∃X, Top};
{*Nat, {a=5,b=7}} as {∃X<:Nat, {a:X,b:X}};
{*Nat, {a=5,b=7}} as {∃X<:Nat, {a:Top,b:X}};
```

26.5.3   SOLUTION: One way to accomplish this is to nest the reset counter ADT *inside of* the counter ADT:

```
counterADT =
  {*Nat,
   {new = 1, get = λi:Nat. i, inc = λi:Nat. succ(i),
    rcADT =
      {*Nat,
       {new = 1, get = λi:Nat. i, inc = λi:Nat. succ(i),
        reset = λi:Nat. 1}}
      as {∃ResetCounter<:Nat,
           {new: ResetCounter, get: ResetCounter→Nat,
            inc: ResetCounter→ResetCounter,
            reset: ResetCounter→ResetCounter}} }}
```

```
        as {∃Counter,
            {new: Counter, get: Counter→Nat, inc: Counter→Counter,
            rcADT:
              {∃ResetCounter<:Counter,
               {new: ResetCounter, get: ResetCounter→Nat,
                inc: ResetCounter→ResetCounter,
                reset: ResetCounter→ResetCounter}}}};
```

▸ counterADT : {∃Counter,
                   {new:Counter,get:Counter→Nat,inc:Counter→Counter,
                    rcADT:{∃ResetCounter<:Counter,
                           {new:ResetCounter,get:ResetCounter→Nat,
                            inc:ResetCounter→ResetCounter,
                            reset:ResetCounter→ResetCounter}}}}

When these packages are opened, the result is that the context in which the remainder of the program is checked will contain type variable bindings of the form Counter<:Top, counter:{...}, ResetCounter<:Counter, resetCounter:{...}:

```
let {Counter,counter} = counterADT in
let {ResetCounter,resetCounter} = counter.rcADT in
counter.get
  (counter.inc
    (resetCounter.reset (resetCounter.inc resetCounter.new)));
```

▸ 2 : Nat

26.5.4   SOLUTION: All we need to do is to add bounds in the obvious places to the encoding from §24.3. At the level of types, we get:

$$\{∃X<:S,T\} \overset{\text{def}}{=} ∀Y. \ (∀X<:S. \ T→Y) → Y.$$

The changes at the level of terms follow directly from this.

27.1   SOLUTION: Here is one way:

```
setCounterClass =
  λM<:SetCounter. λR<:CounterRep.
  λself: Ref(R→M).
    λr: R.
      {get = λ_:Unit. !(r.x),
       set = λi:Nat.  r.x:=i,
       inc = λ_:Unit. (!self r).set (succ((!self r).get unit))};
```

▸ setCounterClass : ∀M<:SetCounter.
                       ∀R<:CounterRep.
                         (Ref (R→M)) → R → SetCounter

```
instrCounterClass =
  λM<:InstrCounter.
  λR<:InstrCounterRep.
  λself: Ref(R→M).
    λr: R.
      let super = setCounterClass [M] [R] self in
        {get = (super r).get,
         set = λi:Nat. (r.a:=succ(!(r.a)); (super r).set i),
         inc = (super r).inc,
         accesses = λ_:Unit. !(r.a)};
```

▸ `instrCounterClass : ∀M<:InstrCounter.`
                               `∀R<:InstrCounterRep.`
                                   `(Ref (R→M)) → R → InstrCounter`

```
newInstrCounter =
  let m = ref (λr:InstrCounterRep. error as InstrCounter) in
  let m' =
    instrCounterClass [InstrCounter] [InstrCounterRep] m in
  (m := m';
   λ_:Unit. let r = {x=ref 1, a=ref 0} in m' r);
```

▸ `newInstrCounter : Unit → InstrCounter`

28.2.3   SOLUTION: In the T-TABS case, we add a trivial use of S-REFL to supply the extra premise for S-ALL. In the T-TAPP case, the subtype inversion lemma (for full $F_{<:}$) tells us that $N_1 = \forall X<:N_{11}.N_{12}$, with $\Gamma \vdash T_{11} <: N_{11}$ and $\Gamma, X<:T_{11} \vdash N_{12} <: T_{12}$. Using transitivity, we see that $\Gamma \vdash T_2 <: T_{11}$, which justifies using TA-TAPP to obtain $\Gamma \vdash t_1 [T_2] : [X \mapsto T_2]N_{12}$. We finish, as before, using the preservation of subtyping under substitution (Lemma 26.4.8) to obtain $\Gamma \vdash [X \mapsto T_2]N_{12} <: [X \mapsto T_2]T_{12} = T$.

28.5.1   SOLUTION: Theorem 28.3.5 (in particular, the case for S-ALL) fails for full $F_{<:}$.

28.5.6   SOLUTION: Note, first, that bounded and unbounded quantifiers should not be allowed to mix: there should be a subtyping rule for comparing two bounded quantifiers and another for two unbounded quantifiers, but no rule for comparing a bounded to an unbounded quantifier. Otherwise we'd be right back where we started!

   For parts (1) and (2), see Katiyar and Sankar (1992) for details. For part (3), the answer is no: adding record types with width subtyping to the restricted system makes it undecidable again. The problem is that the empty record type is a kind of maximal type (among record types), and it can be used to cause divergence in the subtype checker using a modified version of Ghelli's example. If $T = \forall X <: \{\}.\ \neg\{a: \forall Y <: X.\ \neg Y\}$, then the input $X_0 <: \{a:T\} \vdash X_0 <: \{a: \forall X_1 <: X_0.\ \neg X_1\}$ will cause the subtype checker to diverge.

Martin Hofmann helped me work out this example. The same observation was made by Katiyar and Sankar (1992).

28.6.3   SOLUTION:

1. I count 9 common subtypes:

$$\forall X <: Y' \to Z.\ Y \to Z' \qquad \forall X <: Y' \to Z.\ \text{Top} \to Z' \qquad \forall X <: Y' \to Z.\ X$$
$$\forall X <: Y' \to \text{Top}.\ Y \to Z' \qquad \forall X <: Y' \to \text{Top}.\ \text{Top} \to Z' \qquad \forall X <: Y' \to \text{Top}.\ X$$
$$\forall X <: \text{Top}.\ Y \to Z' \qquad \forall X <: \text{Top}.\ \text{Top} \to Z' \qquad \forall X <: \text{Top}.\ X.$$

2. Both $\forall X <: Y' \to Z.\ Y \to Z'$ and $\forall X <: Y' \to Z.\ X$ are lower bounds for S and T, but these two types have no common supertype that is also a subtype of S and T.

3. Consider $S \to \text{Top}$ and $T \to \text{Top}$. (Or $\forall X <: Y' \to Z.\ Y \to Z'$ and $\forall X <: Y' \to Z.\ X$.)

28.7.1   SOLUTION: The functions $R_{X,\Gamma}$ and $L_{X,\Gamma}$, mapping types to their least X-free supertype and their largest X-free subtype, respectively, are defined in Figure A-2. (To avoid clutter, we elide the subscripts X and Γ.) The two definitions have different side-conditions, since, whenever L appears, we have to check whether it is defined (written $L(T) \neq fail$), while R is always defined, thanks to the presence of the Top type. The correctness of these definitions is proved in Ghelli and Pierce (1998).

28.7.2   SOLUTION: One easy way to show the undecidability of full bounded existentials (due to Ghelli and Pierce, 1998) is to give a translation $[\![-]\!]$ from subtyping problems in full $F_{<:}$ into subtyping problems in the system with only existentials such that $\Gamma \vdash S <: T$ is provable in $F_{<:}$ iff $[\![\Gamma \vdash S <: T]\!]$ is provable in the system with existentials. This encoding can be defined on types by

$$\begin{array}{llll}
[\![X]\!] & = X & [\![\text{Top}]\!] & = \text{Top} \\
[\![\forall X <: T_1.T_2]\!] & = \neg\{\exists X <: T_1, \neg[\![T_2]\!]\} & [\![T_1 \to T_2]\!] & = [\![T_1]\!] \to [\![T_2]\!]
\end{array}$$

where $\neg S = \forall X <: S.X$. We extend it to contexts by $[\![X_1 <: T_1,\ ,\ldots, X_n <: T_n]\!] = X_1 <: [\![T_1]\!],\ \ldots,\ X_n <: [\![T_n]\!]$, and to subtyping statements by $[\![\Gamma \vdash S <: T]\!] = [\![\Gamma]\!] \vdash [\![S]\!] <: [\![T]\!]$.

29.1.1   SOLUTION: $\forall X.X \to X$ is a proper type, with elements like $\lambda X.\lambda x:X.x$. These terms are polymorphic functions that, when instantiated with a type T, yield a function from T to T. By contrast, $\lambda X.X \to X$ is a type operator—a function

$$R(\forall Y<:S.T) \;=\; \begin{cases} \forall Y<:S.\; R(T) \\ \quad \text{if } X \notin FVS \\ \text{Top} \\ \quad \text{if } X \in FV(S) \end{cases} \qquad L(\forall Y<:S.T) \;=\; \begin{cases} \forall Y<:S.\; L(T) \\ \quad \text{if } L(T) \neq \textit{fail} \\ \quad \text{and } X \notin FV(S) \\ \textit{fail} \text{ otherwise} \end{cases}$$

$$R(\{\exists Y<:S.T\}) \;=\; \begin{cases} \{\exists Y<:S, R(T)\} \\ \quad \text{if } X \notin FV(S) \\ \text{Top} \\ \quad \text{if } X \in FV(S) \end{cases} \qquad L(\{\exists Y<:S.T\}) \;=\; \begin{cases} \{\exists Y<:S.\; L(T)\} \\ \quad \text{if } L(T) \neq \textit{fail} \\ \quad \text{and } X \notin FV(S) \\ \textit{fail} \text{ otherwise} \end{cases}$$

$$R(S{\to}T) \;=\; \begin{cases} L(S){\to}R(T) \\ \quad \text{if } L(S) \neq \textit{fail} \\ \text{Top} \\ \quad \text{if } L(S) = \textit{fail} \end{cases} \qquad L(S{\to}T) \;=\; \begin{cases} R(S) \to L(T) \\ \quad \text{if } L(T) \neq \textit{fail} \\ \textit{fail} \\ \quad \text{if } L(T) = \textit{fail} \end{cases}$$

$$R(X) \;=\; T \quad \text{where } X<:T \in \Gamma \qquad\qquad L(X) \;=\; \textit{fail}$$

$$R(Y) \;=\; Y \quad \text{when } Y \neq X \qquad\qquad L(Y) \;=\; Y \quad \text{when } Y \neq X$$

$$R(\text{Top}) \;=\; \text{Top} \qquad\qquad L(\text{Top}) \;=\; \text{Top}$$

Figure A-2: Minimal X-free supertype and maximal X-free subtype of a given type

that, when applied to a type T, yields the proper type T→T of functions from T to T.

In other words, $\forall X.X{\to}X$ is a type whose *elements* are term-level functions from types to terms; instantiating one of these (by applying it to a type, written t [T]) yields an *element* of the arrow type T→T. On the other hand, $\lambda X.X{\to}X$ is *itself* a function (from types to types); instantiating it with a type T (written $(\lambda X.X{\to}X)$ T) yields the type T→T *itself*, not one of its elements.

For example, if fn has type $\forall X.X{\to}X$ and Op = $\lambda X.X{\to}X$, then fn [T] : T→T = Op T.

29.1.2   SOLUTION: Nat→Nat is a (proper) type of functions, not a function at the level of types.

30.3   SOLUTION: Lemma 30.3.1 is used in the T-ABS, T-TAPP, and T-EQ cases. Lemma 30.3.2 is used in the T-VAR case.

30.3.8   SOLUTION: By induction on the total sizes of the given derivations, with a case analysis on the final rules of both. If either derivation ends with QR-REFL, then the other derivation is the desired result. If either derivation ends with QR-ABS, QR-ARROW, or QR-ALL, then by the form of the rules, both derivations must end with the same rule, and the result follows by straightforward use of the induction hypothesis. If both derivations end with QR-APP, then the result again follows by straightforward use of the induction hypothesis. The remaining cases are more interesting.

If both derivations end with QR-APPABS, then we have

$$S = (\lambda X :: K_{11} . S_{12})\ S_2 \qquad T = [X \mapsto T_2]T_{12} \qquad U = [X \mapsto U_2]U_{12},$$

with

$$S_{12} \Rrightarrow T_{12} \qquad S_2 \Rrightarrow T_2 \qquad S_{12} \Rrightarrow U_{12} \qquad S_2 \Rrightarrow U_2.$$

By the induction hypothesis, there are V_{12} and V_2 such that

$$T_{12} \Rrightarrow V_{12} \qquad T_2 \Rrightarrow V_2 \qquad U_{12} \Rrightarrow V_{12} \qquad U_2 \Rrightarrow V_2.$$

Applying Lemma 30.3.7 twice, we obtain $[X \mapsto T_2]T_{12} \Rrightarrow [X \mapsto V_2]V_{12}$ and $[X \mapsto U_2]U_{12} \Rrightarrow [X \mapsto V_2]V_{12}$—that is, $T \Rrightarrow V$ and $U \Rrightarrow V$.

Finally, suppose one derivation (say, the first one) ends with QR-APP and the other with QR-APPABS. In this case, we have

$$S = (\lambda X :: K_{11} . S_{12})\ S_2 \qquad T = (\lambda X :: K_{11} . T'_{12})\ T'_2 \qquad U = [X \mapsto U_2]U_{12},$$

where again $S_{12} \Rrightarrow T_{12}$, $S_2 \Rrightarrow T_2$, $S_{12} \Rrightarrow U_{12}$, and $S_2 \Rrightarrow U_2$. Again, by the induction hypothesis, there are V_{12} and V_2 such that $T_{12} \Rrightarrow V_{12}$, $T_2 \Rrightarrow V_2$, $U_{12} \Rrightarrow V_{12}$, and $U_2 \Rrightarrow V_2$. Applying rule QR-APPABS to the first and second of these and Lemma 30.3.7 to the third and fourth gives us $T \Rrightarrow V$ and $U \Rrightarrow V$.

30.3.10   SOLUTION: We first observe that we can reorganize any derivation of $S \Leftrightarrow^* T$ so that neither symmetry nor transitivity is used in a subderivation of an instance of the symmetry rule—that is, we can get from S to T by a sequence of steps pasted together with QR-TRANS, where each step consists of a single-step reduction optionally followed by a single instance of symmetry. This sequence can be visualized as follows.

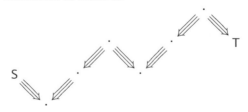

(arrows pointing from right to left are reductions ending with symmetry, while left to right arrows are un-symmetrized reductions). We now use Lemma 30.3.8 repeatedly to add small diamonds to the bottom of this picture until we reach a common reduct of S and T.

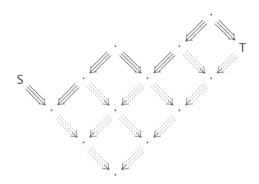

The same argument can also be presented in a standard inductive form, without appealing to pictures, but this will probably just make it harder to understand without making it any more convincing.

30.3.17   SOLUTION: If we add the first weird rule, the progress property will fail; preservation, though, is fine. If we add the second rule, both progress and preservation will fail.

30.3.20   SOLUTION: Compare your solution with the sources for the fomega checker.

30.5.1   SOLUTION: Instead of the type family FloatList n, we now have the *parametric* type family List T n, with the following operations:

```
nil   :  ∀X. FloatList X 0
cons  :  ∀X. Πn:Nat. X → FloatList X (succ n)
hd    :  ∀X. Πn:Nat. List X (succ n) → X
tl    :  ∀X. Πn:Nat. List X (succ n) → List X n
```

31.2.1   SOLUTION:

Γ	⊢	A	<:	Id B	*Yes*
Γ	⊢	Id A	<:	B	*Yes*
Γ	⊢	λX.X	<:	λX.Top	*Yes*
Γ	⊢	λX. ∀Y<:X. Y	<:	λX. ∀Y<:Top. Y	*No*
Γ	⊢	λX. ∀Y<:X. Y	<:	λX. ∀Y<:X. X	*Yes*
Γ	⊢	F B	<:	B	*Yes*
Γ	⊢	B	<:	F B	*No*
Γ	⊢	F B	<:	F B	*Yes*
Γ	⊢	∀F<:(λY.Top→Y). F A	<:	∀F<:(λY.Top→Y). Top→B	*Yes*
Γ	⊢	∀F<:(λY.Top→Y). F A	<:	∀F<:(λY.Top→Y). F B	*No*
Γ	⊢	Top[*⇒*]	<:	Top[*⇒*⇒*]	*No*

32.5.1 SOLUTION: The key observation is that `Object M` *is* an existential type: `Object` is an abbreviation for the operator

$$\lambda M::*\Rightarrow*. \ \{\exists X, \{state:X, methods:M\,X\}\}$$

When we apply this to M we obtain a redex, which reduces to the existential type

$$\{\exists X, \{state:X, methods:M\,X\}\}.$$

Note that no subsumption—hence no information loss—is involved in this transformation.

32.7.2 SOLUTION: The minimal typing property fails for the calculus the way we have defined it. Consider the term

$$\{\#x=\{a=5,b=7\}\}.$$

This can be given both of the types `{#x:{a:Nat}}` and `{#x:{a:Nat,b:Nat}}`, but these types are incomparable. One reasonable fix for this is to explicitly annotate each invariant field in a record term with its intended type. This effectively gives the programmer the responsibility of choosing between the two types above.

32.5.2 SOLUTION:

```
sendget =
  λM<:CounterM. λo:Object M.
    let {X, b} = o in b.methods.get(b.state);

sendreset =
  λM<:ResetCounterM. λo:Object M.
    let {X, b} = o in
      {*X,
        {state = b.methods.reset(b.state),
         methods = b.methods}}  as Object M;
```

32.9.1 SOLUTION:

```
MyCounterM =
  λR. {get: R→Nat, set:R→Nat→R, inc:R→R, accesses:R→Nat,
            backup:R→R, reset:R→R};

MyCounterR = {#x:Nat,#count:Nat,#old:Nat};

myCounterClass =
  λR<:MyCounterR.
```

```
      λself: Unit→MyCounterM R.
      λ_:Unit.
        let super = instrCounterClass [R] self unit in
        {get = super.get,
         set = super.set,
         inc = super.inc,
         accesses = super.accesses,
         reset = λs:R. s←x=s.old,
         backup = λs:R. s←old=s.x}
      as MyCounterM R;

 mc = {*MyCounterR,
         {state = {#x=0,#count=0,#old=0},
          methods = fix (myCounterClass [MyCounterR]) unit}}
         as Object MyCounterM;

 sendget [MyCounterM]
   (sendreset [MyCounterM] (sendinc [MyCounterM] mc));
```

"My dear Watson, try a little analysis yourself," said he, with a touch of im-patience. "You know my methods. Apply them, and it will be instructive to compare results."   —*A. Conan Doyle,* The Sign of the Four *(1890)*

How to put it impeccably may be left as an exercise for the reader. I avail myself here of a favorite ploy by which mathematicians spare themselves sticky patches of exposition.   —*W. v. O. Quine (1987)*

B *Notational Conventions*

B.1 Metavariable Names

IN TEXT	IN ML CODE	USAGE
p, q, r, s, t, u	s, t	terms
x, y, z	x, y	term variables
v, w	v, w	values
nv	nv	numeric values
l, j, k	l	record/variant field labels
μ	store	stores
M, N, P, Q, S, T, U, V	tyS, tyT	types
A, B, C	tyA, tyB	base types
Σ		store typings
X, Y, Z	tyX, tyY	type variables
K, L	kK, kL	kinds
σ		substitutions
Γ, Δ	ctx	contexts
$\mathcal{J}$		arbitrary statements
$\mathcal{D}$		typing derivations
$\mathcal{C}$		subtyping derivations
	fi	file position information
i, j, k, l		numeric subscripts

B.2 Rule Naming Conventions

PREFIX	USAGE
B-	big-step evaluation
CT-	constraint typing
E-	evaluation

PREFIX	USAGE
K-	kinding
M-	matching
P-	pattern typing
Q-	type equivalence
QR-	parallel reduction of types
S-	subtyping
SA-	algorithmic subtyping
T-	typing
TA-	algorithmic typing
XA-	exposure

B.3   Naming and Subscripting Conventions

The choice of metavariable names, numeric subscripts, and primes is guided throughout the book by the following principles:

1. In syntax definitions, the bare metavariable t is used for all terms, T for types, v for values, etc.

2. In typing rules, the main term (the one whose type is being calculated) is always called t, and its subterms are named t_1, t_2, etc. (Occasionally—e.g., in reduction rules—we need names for subterms of subterms; for these we use t_{11}, t_{12}, etc.)

3. In evaluation rules, the whole term being reduced is called t and the term it reduces to is t'.

4. The type of a term t is called T. (Similarly, the type of a subterm t_1 is T_1, etc.)

5. The same conventions are used when stating and proving theorems, except that t is sometimes replaced by s (and T by S or R, etc.) to avoid name clashes between definitions and theorems.

There are a few cases where these rules cannot all be satisfied at the same time. In such cases, the earlier ones are given priority. (For example, in the rule T-PROJ1 in Figure 11-5, rule 4 is relaxed: the type of the subterm t_1 is $T_1 \times T_2$.) The rules are ignored completely in a very small number of cases (for example, the record projection rule T-PROJ in Figure 11-7) where following them would yield unacceptably ugly or unreadable results.

References

Abadi, Martín. Secrecy by typing in security protocols. *Journal of the ACM*, 46(5): 749–786, September 1999. Summary in *Theoretical Aspects of Computer Software (TACS), Sendai, Japan*, 1997; volume 1281 of Springer LNCS.

Abadi, Martín, Anindya Banerjee, Nevin Heintze, and Jon G. Riecke. A core calculus of dependency. In *ACM Symposium on Principles of Programming Languages (POPL), San Antonio, Texas*, pages 147–160, 1999.

Abadi, Martín and Luca Cardelli. On subtyping and matching. In *European Conference on Object-Oriented Programming (ECOOP)*, pages 145–167, 1995.

Abadi, Martín and Luca Cardelli. *A Theory of Objects*. Springer-Verlag, 1996.

Abadi, Martín, Luca Cardelli, and Pierre-Louis Curien. Formal parametric polymorphism. *Theoretical Computer Science*, 121(1–2):9–58, 6 December 1993. Summary in *ACM Symposium on Principles of Programming Languages (POPL), Charleston, South Carolina*, 1993.

Abadi, Martín, Luca Cardelli, Pierre-Louis Curien, and Jean-Jacques Lévy. Explicit substitutions. *Journal of Functional Programming*, 1(4):375–416, 1991a. Summary in *ACM Symposium on Principles of Programming Languages (POPL), San Francisco, California*, 1990.

Abadi, Martín, Luca Cardelli, Benjamin Pierce, and Gordon Plotkin. Dynamic typing in a statically typed language. *ACM Transactions on Programming Languages and Systems*, 13(2):237–268, April 1991b. Summary in *ACM Symposium on Principles of Programming Languages (POPL), Austin, Texas*, 1989.

Abadi, Martín, Luca Cardelli, Benjamin Pierce, and Didier Rémy. Dynamic typing in polymorphic languages. *Journal of Functional Programming*, 5(1):111–130, January 1995. Summary in *ACM SIGPLAN Workshop on ML and its Applications*, June 1992.

Abadi, Martín, Luca Cardelli, and Ramesh Viswanathan. An interpretation of objects and object types. In *ACM Symposium on Principles of Programming Languages (POPL), St. Petersburg Beach, Florida*, pages 396–409, 1996.

Abadi, Martín and Marcelo P. Fiore. Syntactic considerations on recursive types. In *Proceedings of the 11th Annual IEEE Symposium on Logic in Computer Science, LICS '96*, pages 242–252. IEEE Computer Society Press, Los Alamitos, CA, July 1996.

Abelson, Harold and Gerald Sussman. *Structure and Interpretation of Computer Programs*. MIT Press, New York, 1985. Second edition, 1996.

Abramsky, Samson, Radha Jagadeesan, and Pasquale Malacaria. Full abstraction for pcf. *Information and Computation*, 163(2):409–470, December 2000.

Aczel, Peter. An introduction to inductive definitions. In Jon Barwise, editor, *Handbook of Mathematical Logic*, number 90 in Studies in Logic and the Foundations of Mathematics, pages 739–782. North Holland, 1977.

Aczel, Peter. *Non-Well-Founded Sets*. Stanford Center for the Study of Language and Information, 1988. CSLI Lecture Notes number 14.

Agesen, Ole, Stephen N. Freund, and John C. Mitchell. Adding type parameterization to the Java language. In *ACM Symposium on Object Oriented Programming: Systems, Languages, and Applications (OOPSLA)*, pages 49–65, Atlanta, GA, October 1997.

Aho, Alfred V., Ravi Sethi, and Jeffrey D. Ullman. *Compilers: Principles, Techniques, and Tools*. Addison-Wesley, Reading, MA, USA, 1986.

Aiken, Alexander and Edward L. Wimmers. Type inclusion constraints and type inference. In *ACM Symposium on Functional Programming Languages and Computer Architecture (FPCA)*, pages 31–41, 1993.

Amadio, Roberto M. and Luca Cardelli. Subtyping recursive types. *ACM Transactions on Programming Languages and Systems*, 15(4):575–631, 1993. Summary in *ACM Symposium on Principles of Programming Languages (POPL), Orlando, Florida*, pp. 104–118; also DEC/Compaq Systems Research Center Research Report number 62, August 1990.

Appel, Andrew W. *Modern Compiler Implementation in ML*. Cambridge University Press, 1998.

Appel, Andrew W. and Marcelo J. R. Gonçalves. Hash-consing garbage collection. Technical Report CS-TR-412-93, Princeton University, Computer Science Department, 1993.

Arbib, Michael and Ernest Manes. *Arrows, Structures, and Functors: The Categorical Imperative*. Academic Press, 1975.

Ariola, Zena M., Matthias Felleisen, John Maraist, Martin Odersky, and Philip Wadler. A call-by-need lambda calculus. In *ACM Symposium on Principles of Programming Languages (POPL), San Francisco, California*, pages 233–246, January 1995.

Arnold, Ken and James Gosling. *The Java Programming Language*. Addison Wesley, 1996.

Arnold, Ken, Ann Wollrath, Bryan O'Sullivan, Robert Scheifler, and Jim Waldo. *The Jini specification*. Addison-Wesley, Reading, MA, USA, 1999.

Asperti, Andrea and Giuseppe Longo. *Categories, Types, and Structures: An Introduction to Category Theory for the Working Computer Scientist.* MIT Press, 1991.

Aspinall, David. Subtyping with singleton types. In *Computer Science Logic (CSL), Kazimierz, Poland*, pages 1–15. Springer-Verlag, 1994.

Aspinall, David and Adriana Compagnoni. Subtyping dependent types. *Information and Computation*, 266(1–2):273–309, September 2001. Preliminary version in *IEEE Symposium on Logic in Computer Science (LICS)*, 1996.

Astesiano, Egidio. Inductive and operational semantics. In E. J. Neuhold and M. Paul, editors, *Formal Description of Programming Concepts*, IFIP State-of-the-Art Reports, pages 51–136. Springer-Verlag, 1991.

Augustsson, Lennart. A compiler for Lazy ML. In *ACM Symposium on Lisp and Functional Programming (LFP), Austin, Texas*, pages 218–227, August 1984.

Augustsson, Lennart. Cayenne — a language with dependent types. In *International Conference on Functional Programming (ICFP), Baltimore, Maryland, USA*, pages 239–250, 1998.

Baader, Franz and Tobias Nipkow. *Term Rewriting and All That.* Cambridge University Press, 1998.

Baader, Franz and Jörg Siekmann. Unification theory. In D. M. Gabbay, C. J. Hogger, and J. A. Robinson, editors, *Handbook of Logic in Artificial Intelligence and Logic Programming*, volume 2, Deduction Methodologies, pages 41–125. Oxford University Press, Oxford, UK, 1994.

Backus, John. Can programming be liberated from the von Neumann style? A functional style and its algebra of programs. *Communications of the ACM*, 21(8):613–641, August 1978. Reproduced in *Selected Reprints on Dataflow and Reduction Architectures*, ed. S. S. Thakkar, IEEE, 1987, pp. 215–243, and in *ACM Turing Award Lectures: The First Twenty Years*, ACM Press, 1987, pp. 63–130.

Backus, John. The history of Fortran I, II, and III. In Wexelblat, editor, *History of Programming Languages*, pages 25–45. Academic Press, 1981.

Bainbridge, E. Stewart, Peter J. Freyd, Andre Scedrov, and Philip J. Scott. Functorial polymorphism. *Theoretical Computer Science*, 70(1):35–64, 1990. Corrigendum in *TCS* 71(3), 431.

Baldan, Paolo, Giorgio Ghelli, and Alessandra Raffaetà. Basic theory of F-bounded quantification. *Information and Computation*, 153(1):173–237, 1999.

Barendregt, Henk P. *The Lambda Calculus.* North Holland, revised edition, 1984.

Barendregt, Henk P. Functional programming and lambda calculus. In Jan van Leeuwen, editor, *Handbook of Theoretical Computer Science, Volume B*, chapter 7, pages 321–364. Elsevier / MIT Press, 1990.

Barendregt, Henk P. Introduction to generalized type systems. *Journal of Functional Programming*, 1(2):125–154, 1991.

Barendregt, Henk P. Lambda calculi with types. In Abramsky, Gabbay, and Maibaum, editors, *Handbook of Logic in Computer Science*, volume II. Oxford University Press, 1992.

Barras, Bruno, Samuel Boutin, Cristina Cornes, Judicael Courant, Jean-Christophe Filliatre, Eduardo Gimenez, Hugo Herbelin, Gerard Huet, Cesar Munoz, Chetan Murthy, Catherine Parent, Christine Paulin-Mohring, Amokrane Saibi, and Benjamin Werner. The Coq proof assistant reference manual : Version 6.1. Technical Report RT-0203, Inria (Institut National de Recherche en Informatique et en Automatique), France, 1997.

Barwise, Jon and Lawrence Moss. *Vicious Circles: On the Mathematics of Non-wellfounded Phenomena.* Cambridge University Press, 1996.

Berardi, Stefano. Towards a mathematical analysis of the Coquand-Huet calculus of constructions and the other systems in Barendregt's cube. Technical report, Department of Computer Science, CMU, and Dipartimento Matematica, Universita di Torino, 1988.

Berger, Ulrich. Program extraction from normalization proofs. In Marc Bezem and Jan Friso Groote, editors, *Typed Lambda Calculi and Applications*, number 664 in Lecture Notes in Computer Science, pages 91–106, Utrecht, The Netherlands, March 1993. Springer-Verlag.

Berger, Ulrich and Helmut Schwichtenberg. An inverse of the evaluation functional for typed λ-calculus. In Gilles Kahn, editor, *IEEE Symposium on Logic in Computer Science (LICS)*, pages 203–211, Amsterdam, The Netherlands, July 1991. IEEE Computer Society Press.

Birtwistle, Graham M., Ole-Johan Dahl, Bjorn Myhrhaug, and Kristen Nygaard. *Simula Begin.* Studentlitteratur (Lund, Sweden), Bratt Institut fuer neues Lernen (Goch, FRG), Chartwell-Bratt Ltd (Kent, England), 1979.

Bobrow, Daniel G., Linda G. DeMichiel, Richard P. Gabriel, Sonya E. Keene, Gregor Kiczales, and David A. Moon. Common Lisp Object System specification X3J13 document 88-002R. *SIGPLAN Notices*, 23, 1988.

Boehm, Hans-J. Partial polymorphic type inference is undecidable. In *26th Annual Symposium on Foundations of Computer Science*, pages 339–345. IEEE, October 1985.

Boehm, Hans-J. Type inference in the presence of type abstraction. In *ACM SIGPLAN Conference on Programming Language Design and Implementation (PLDI), Portland, Oregon*, pages 192–206, June 1989.

Böhm, Corrado and Alessandro Berarducci. Automatic synthesis of typed Λ-programs on term algebras. *Theoretical Computer Science*, 39(2–3):135–154, August 1985.

Bono, Viviana and Kathleen Fisher. An imperative first-order calculus with object extension. In *European Conference on Object-Oriented Programming (ECOOP)*, 1998.

Bono, Viviana, Amit J. Patel, and Vitaly Shmatikov. A core calculus of classes and mixins. In *European Conference on Object-Oriented Programming (ECOOP)*, volume

1628 of *Lecture Notes in Computer Science*, pages 43–66. Springer-Verlag, June 1999a.

Bono, Viviana, Amit J. Patel, Vitaly Shmatikov, and John C. Mitchell. A core calculus of classes and objects. In *Fifteenth Conference on the Mathematical Foundations of Programming Semantics*, April 1999b.

Bracha, Gilad, Martin Odersky, David Stoutamire, and Philip Wadler. Making the future safe for the past: Adding genericity to the Java programming language. In Craig Chambers, editor, *ACM Symposium on Object Oriented Programming: Systems, Languages, and Applications (OOPSLA)*, ACM SIGPLAN Notices volume 33 number 10, pages 183–200, Vancouver, BC, October 1998.

Braithwaite, Richard B. *The Foundations of Mathematics: Collected Papers of Frank P. Ramsey*. Routledge and Kegan Paul, London, 1931.

Brandt, Michael and Fritz Henglein. Coinductive axiomatization of recursive type equality and subtyping. In Roger Hindley, editor, *Proc. 3d Int'l Conf. on Typed Lambda Calculi and Applications (TLCA), Nancy, France, April 2-4, 1997*, volume 1210 of *Lecture Notes in Computer Science (LNCS)*, pages 63–81. Springer-Verlag, April 1997. Full version in Fundamenta Informaticae, Vol. 33, pp. 309-338, 1998.

Breazu-Tannen, Val, Thierry Coquand, Carl Gunter, and Andre Scedrov. Inheritance as implicit coercion. *Information and Computation*, 93:172–221, 1991. Also in Carl A. Gunter and John C. Mitchell, editors, *Theoretical Aspects of Object-Oriented Programming: Types, Semantics, and Language Design* (MIT Press, 1994).

Bruce, Kim B. The equivalence of two semantic definitions for inheritance in object-oriented languages. In *Proceedings of Mathematical Foundations of Programming Semantics*, Pittsburgh, PA, March 1991.

Bruce, Kim B. A paradigmatic object-oriented programming language: Design, static typing and semantics. *Journal of Functional Programming*, 4(2), April 1994. Summary in *ACM Symposium on Principles of Programming Languages (POPL), Charleston, South Carolina*, under the title "Safe type checking in a statically typed object-oriented programming language".

Bruce, Kim B. *Foundations of Object-Oriented Languages: Types and Semantics*. MIT Press, 2002.

Bruce, Kim B., Luca Cardelli, Giuseppe Castagna, the Hopkins Objects Group (Jonathan Eifrig, Scott Smith, Valery Trifonov), Gary T. Leavens, and Benjamin Pierce. On binary methods. *Theory and Practice of Object Systems*, 1(3):221–242, 1996.

Bruce, Kim B., Luca Cardelli, and Benjamin C. Pierce. Comparing object encodings. *Information and Computation*, 155(1/2):108-133, November 1999. Special issue of papers from *Theoretical Aspects of Computer Software (TACS 1997)*. An earlier version appeared as an invited lecture in the Third International Workshop on Foundations of Object Oriented Languages (FOOL 3), July 1996.

Bruce, Kim B. and Giuseppe Longo. A modest model of records, inheritance, and bounded quantification. *Information and Computation*, 87:196–240, 1990. Also in Carl A. Gunter and John C. Mitchell, editors, *Theoretical Aspects of Object-Oriented Programming: Types, Semantics, and Language Design* (MIT Press, 1994). An earlier version appeared in the proceedings of the IEEE Symposium on Logic in Computer Science, 1988.

Bruce, Kim B. and John Mitchell. PER models of subtyping, recursive types and higher-order polymorphism. In *ACM Symposium on Principles of Programming Languages (POPL), Albuquerque, New Mexico*, January 1992.

Bruce, Kim B., Leaf Petersen, and Adrian Fiech. Subtyping is not a good "match" for object-oriented languages. In *European Conference on Object-Oriented Programming (ECOOP)*, volume 1241 of *Lecture Notes in Computer Science*, pages 104–127. Springer-Verlag, 1997.

Buneman, Peter and Benjamin Pierce. Union types for semistructured data. In *Internet Programming Languages*. Springer-Verlag, September 1998. Proceedings of the International Database Programming Languages Workshop. LNCS 1686.

Burstall, Rod and Butler Lampson. A kernel language for abstract data types and modules. In G. Kahn, D. MacQueen, and G. Plotkin, editors, *Semantics of Data Types*, volume 173 of *Lecture Notes in Computer Science*, pages 1–50. Springer-Verlag, 1984.

Burstall, Rod M. Proving properties of programs by structural induction. *The Computer Journal*, 12(1):41–48, 1969.

Canning, Peter, William Cook, Walt Hill, and Walter Olthoff. Interfaces for strongly-typed object-oriented programming. In *ACM Symposium on Object Oriented Programming: Systems, Languages, and Applications (OOPSLA)*, pages 457–467, 1989a.

Canning, Peter, William Cook, Walter Hill, Walter Olthoff, and John Mitchell. F-bounded quantification for object-oriented programming. In *ACM Symposium on Functional Programming Languages and Computer Architecture (FPCA)*, pages 273–280, September 1989b.

Canning, Peter, Walt Hill, and Walter Olthoff. A kernel language for object-oriented programming. Technical Report STL-88-21, Hewlett-Packard Labs, 1988.

Cardelli, Luca. A semantics of multiple inheritance. In G. Kahn, D. MacQueen, and G. Plotkin, editors, *Semantics of Data Types*, volume 173 of *Lecture Notes in Computer Science*, pages 51–67. Springer-Verlag, 1984. Full version in *Information and Computation*, 76(2/3):138–164, 1988.

Cardelli, Luca. Amber. In Guy Cousineau, Pierre-Louis Curien, and Bernard Robinet, editors, *Combinators and Functional Programming Languages*, pages 21–47. Springer-Verlag, 1986. Lecture Notes in Computer Science No. 242.

Cardelli, Luca. Basic polymorphic typechecking. *Science of Computer Programming*, 8 (2):147–172, April 1987. An earlier version appeared in the *Polymorphism Newsletter*, January, 1985.

Cardelli, Luca. Structural subtyping and the notion of power type. In *ACM Symposium on Principles of Programming Languages (POPL), San Diego, California*, pages 70–79, January 1988a.

Cardelli, Luca. Typechecking dependent types and subtypes. In M. Boscarol, L. Carlucci Aiello, and G. Levi, editors, *Foundations of Logic and Functional Programming, Workshop Proceedings, Trento, Italy, (Dec. 1986)*, volume 306 of *Lecture Notes in Computer Science*, pages 45–57. Springer-Verlag, 1988b.

Cardelli, Luca. Notes about $F_{<:}^{\omega}$. Unpublished manuscript, October 1990.

Cardelli, Luca. Typeful programming. In E. J. Neuhold and M. Paul, editors, *Formal Description of Programming Concepts*. Springer-Verlag, 1991. An earlier version appeared as DEC/Compaq Systems Research Center Research Report #45, February 1989.

Cardelli, Luca. Extensible records in a pure calculus of subtyping. Research report 81, DEC/Compaq Systems Research Center, January 1992. Also in Carl A. Gunter and John C. Mitchell, editors, *Theoretical Aspects of Object-Oriented Programming: Types, Semantics, and Language Design* (MIT Press, 1994).

Cardelli, Luca. An implementation of $F_{<:}$. Research report 97, DEC/Compaq Systems Research Center, February 1993.

Cardelli, Luca. Type systems. In Allen B. Tucker, editor, *Handbook of Computer Science and Engineering*. CRC Press, 1996.

Cardelli, Luca, James Donahue, Lucille Glassman, Mick Jordan, Bill Kalsow, and Greg Nelson. Modula-3 report (revised). Research report 52, DEC/Compaq Systems Research Center, November 1989.

Cardelli, Luca and Xavier Leroy. Abstract types and the dot notation. In *Proceedings of the IFIP TC2 Working Conference on Programming Concepts and Methods*. North Holland, 1990. Also appeared as DEC/Compaq SRC technical report 56.

Cardelli, Luca and Giuseppe Longo. A semantic basis for Quest. *Journal of Functional Programming*, 1(4):417–458, October 1991. Summary in ACM Conference on Lisp and Functional Programming, June 1990. Also available as DEC/Compaq SRC Research Report 55, Feb. 1990.

Cardelli, Luca, Simone Martini, John C. Mitchell, and Andre Scedrov. An extension of System F with subtyping. *Information and Computation*, 109(1–2):4–56, 1994. Summary in TACS '91 (Sendai, Japan, pp. 750–770).

Cardelli, Luca and John Mitchell. Operations on records. *Mathematical Structures in Computer Science*, 1:3–48, 1991. Also in Carl A. Gunter and John C. Mitchell, editors, *Theoretical Aspects of Object-Oriented Programming: Types, Semantics, and Language Design* (MIT Press, 1994); available as DEC/Compaq Systems Research Center Research Report #48, August, 1989, and in the proceedings of MFPS '89, Springer LNCS volume 442.

Cardelli, Luca and Peter Wegner. On understanding types, data abstraction, and polymorphism. *Computing Surveys*, 17(4):471–522, December 1985.

Cardone, Felice. Relational semantics for recursive types and bounded quantification. In *Proceedings of the Sixteenth International Colloquium on Automata, Languages, and Programming*, volume 372 of *Lecture Notes in Computer Science*, pages 164–178, Stresa, Italy, July 1989. Springer-Verlag.

Cardone, Felice and Mario Coppo. Type inference with recursive types: Syntax and semantics. *Information and Computation*, 92(1):48–80, 1991.

Cartwright, Robert and Guy L. Steele, Jr. Compatible genericity with run-time types for the Java programming language. In Craig Chambers, editor, *ACM Symposium on Object Oriented Programming: Systems, Languages, and Applications (OOPSLA), Vancouver, British Columbia*, SIGPLAN Notices 33(10), pages 201–215. ACM, October 1998.

Castagna, Giuseppe. *Object-Oriented Programming: A Unified Foundation*. Springer-Verlag, 1997.

Castagna, Giuseppe, Giorgio Ghelli, and Giuseppe Longo. A calculus for overloaded functions with subtyping. *Information and Computation*, 117(1):115–135, 15 February 1995. preliminary version in LISP and Functional Programming, July 1992 (pp. 182–192), and as Rapport de Recherche LIENS-92-4, Ecole Normale Supérieure, Paris.

Chambers, Craig. Object-oriented multi-methods in Cecil. In *European Conference on Object-Oriented Programming (ECOOP)*, pages 33–56, 1992.

Chambers, Craig. The Cecil language: Specification and rationale. Technical report, University of Washington, March 1993.

Chambers, Craig and Gary Leavens. Type-checking and modules for multi-methods. In *ACM Symposium on Object Oriented Programming: Systems, Languages, and Applications (OOPSLA)*, October 1994. SIGPLAN Notices 29(10).

Chen, Gang and Giuseppe Longo. Subtyping parametric and dependent types. In Kamareddine et al., editor, *Type Theory and Term Rewriting*, September 1996. Invited lecture.

Chirimar, Jawahar, Carl A. Gunter, and Jon G. Riecke. Reference counting as a computational interpretation of linear logic. *Journal of Functional Programming*, 6(2):195–244, March 1996.

Church, Alonzo. An unsolvable problem of elementary number theory. *American Journal of Mathematics*, 58:354–363, 1936.

Church, Alonzo. A formulation of the simple theory of types. *Journal of Symbolic Logic*, 5:56–68, 1940.

Church, Alonzo. *The Calculi of Lambda Conversion*. Princeton University Press, 1941.

Clement, Dominique, Joelle Despeyroux, Thierry Despeyroux, and Gilles Kahn. A simple applicative language: Mini-ML. In *ACM Conference on LISP and Functional Programming*, pages 13–27, 1986.

Clinger, William, Daniel P. Friedman, and Mitchell Wand. A scheme for a higher-level semantic algebra. In John Reynolds and Maurice Nivat, editors, *Algebraic Methods in Semantics*, pages 237–250. Cambridge University Press, 1985.

Colazzo, Dario and Giorgio Ghelli. Subtyping recursive types in Kernel Fun. In *14th Symposium on Logic in Computer Science (LICS'99)*, pages 137–146. IEEE, July 1999.

Compagnoni, Adriana and Healfdene Goguen. Decidability of higher-order subtyping via logical relations, December 1997a. Manuscript, available at `ftp://www.dcs.ed.ac.uk/pub/hhg/hosdec.ps.gz`.

Compagnoni, Adriana and Healfdene Goguen. Typed operational semantics for higher order subtyping. Technical Report ECS-LFCS-97-361, University of Edinburgh, July 1997b.

Compagnoni, Adriana B. Decidability of higher-order subtyping with intersection types. In *Computer Science Logic*, September 1994. Kazimierz, Poland. Springer *Lecture Notes in Computer Science* 933, June 1995. Also available as University of Edinburgh, LFCS technical report ECS-LFCS-94-281, titled "Subtyping in $F_\wedge^\omega$ is decidable".

Compagnoni, Adriana B. and Benjamin C. Pierce. Intersection types and multiple inheritance. *Mathematical Structures in Computer Science*, 6(5):469–501, October 1996. Preliminary version available as University of Edinburgh technical report ECS-LFCS-93-275 and Catholic University Nijmegen computer science technical report 93-18, Aug. 1993, under the title "Multiple Inheritance via Intersection Types".

Constable, Robert L. Types in computer science, philosophy, and logic. In Samuel R. Buss, editor, *Handbook of Proof Theory*, volume 137 of *Studies in logic and the foundations of mathematics*, pages 683–786. Elsevier, 1998.

Constable et al., Robert L. *Implementing Mathematics with the NuPRL Proof Development System*. Prentice–Hall, Englewood Cliffs, NJ, 1986.

Cook, William. Object-oriented programming versus abstract data types. In J. W. de Bakker et al., editors, *Foundations of Object-Oriented Languages*, volume 489 of *Lecture Notes in Computer Science*, pages 151–178. Springer-Verlag, 1991.

Cook, William and Jens Palsberg. A denotational semantics of inheritance and its correctness. In *ACM Symposium on Object Oriented Programming: Systems, Languages, and Applications (OOPSLA)*, pages 433–444, 1989.

Cook, William R. *A Denotational Semantics of Inheritance*. PhD thesis, Brown University, 1989.

Cook, William R., Walter L. Hill, and Peter S. Canning. Inheritance is not subtyping. In *ACM Symposium on Principles of Programming Languages (POPL), San Francisco, California*, pages 125–135, January 1990. Also in Carl A. Gunter and John C. Mitchell, editors, *Theoretical Aspects of Object-Oriented Programming: Types, Semantics, and Language Design* (MIT Press, 1994).

Coppo, Mario and Mariangiola Dezani-Ciancaglini. A new type-assignment for λ-terms. *Archiv Math. Logik*, 19:139–156, 1978.

Coppo, Mario, Mariangiola Dezani-Ciancaglini, and Patrick Sallé. Functional characterization of some semantic equalities inside λ-calculus. In Hermann A. Maurer, editor, *Proceedings of the 6th Colloquium on Automata, Languages and Programming*, volume 71 of *LNCS*, pages 133–146, Graz, Austria, July 1979. Springer.

Coquand, Thierry. *Une Théorie des Constructions*. PhD thesis, University Paris VII, January 1985.

Coquand, Thierry and Gérard Huet. The Calculus of Constructions. *Information and Computation*, 76(2/3):95–120, February/March 1988.

Courcelle, Bruno. Fundamental properties of infinite trees. *Theoretical Computer Science*, 25:95–169, 1983.

Cousineau, Guy and Michel Mauny. *The Functional Approach to Programming*. Cambridge University Press, 1998.

Crary, Karl. Sound and complete elimination of singleton kinds. Technical Report CMU-CS-00-104, Carnegie Mellon University, School of Computer Science, January 2000.

Crary, Karl, Robert Harper, and Derek Dreyer. A type system for higher-order modules. In *ACM Symposium on Principles of Programming Languages (POPL), Portland, Oregon*, 2002.

Crary, Karl, Robert Harper, and Sidd Puri. What is a recursive module? In *ACM SIGPLAN Conference on Programming Language Design and Implementation (PLDI)*, pages 50–63, May 1999.

Crary, Karl, Stephanie Weirich, and J. Gregory Morrisett. Intensional polymorphism in type-erasure semantics. In *International Conference on Functional Programming (ICFP), Baltimore, Maryland, USA*, pages 301–312, 1998.

Crole, Roy. *Categories for Types*. Cambridge University Press, 1994.

Curien, Pierre-Louis and Giorgio Ghelli. Subtyping + extensionality: Confluence of $\beta\eta$-reductions in $F_\le$. In T. Ito and A. R. Meyer, editors, *Theoretical Aspects of Computer Software (Sendai, Japan)*, number 526 in Lecture Notes in Computer Science, pages 731–749. Springer-Verlag, September 1991.

Curien, Pierre-Louis and Giorgio Ghelli. Coherence of subsumption: Minimum typing and type-checking in $F_\le$. *Mathematical Structures in Computer Science*, 2:55–91, 1992. Also in Carl A. Gunter and John C. Mitchell, editors, *Theoretical Aspects of Object-Oriented Programming: Types, Semantics, and Language Design* (MIT Press, 1994).

Curry, Haskell B. and Robert Feys. *Combinatory Logic*, volume 1. North Holland, 1958. Second edition, 1968.

Damas, Luis and Robin Milner. Principal type schemes for functional programs. In *ACM Symposium on Principles of Programming Languages (POPL), Albuquerque, New Mexico*, pages 207–212, 1982.

Danvy, Olivier. Type-directed partial evaluation. In John Hatcliff, Torben Æ. Mogensen, and Peter Thiemann, editors, *Partial Evaluation – Practice and Theory; Proceedings of the 1998 DIKU Summer School*, number 1706 in Lecture Notes in Computer Science, pages 367–411, Copenhagen, Denmark, July 1998. Springer-Verlag.

Davey, Brian A. and Hilary A. Priestley. *Introduction to Lattices and Order.* Cambridge University Press, 1990.

Davies, Rowan. A refinement-type checker for Standard ML. In *International Conference on Algebraic Methodology and Software Technology*, volume 1349 of *Lecture Notes in Computer Science.* Springer-Verlag, 1997.

Davies, Rowan and Frank Pfenning. A modal analysis of staged computation. In *ACM Symposium on Principles of Programming Languages (POPL), St. Petersburg Beach, Florida*, pages 258–270, 1996.

de Bruijn, Nicolas G. Lambda-calculus notation with nameless dummies: a tool for automatic formula manipulation with application to the Church-Rosser theorem. *Indag. Math.*, 34(5):381–392, 1972.

de Bruijn, Nicolas G. A survey of the project AUTOMATH. In J. P. Seldin and J. R. Hindley, editors, *To H. B. Curry: Essays in Combinatory Logic, Lambda Calculus, and Formalism*, pages 589–606. Academic Press, 1980.

De Millo, Richard A., Richard J. Lipton, and Alan J. Perlis. Social processes and proofs of theorems and programs. *Communications of the ACM*, 22(5):271–280, May 1979. An earlier version appeared in *ACM Symposium on Principles of Programming Languages (POPL), Los Angeles, California*, 1977 pp. 206–214.

Detlefs, David L., K. Rustan M. Leino, Greg Nelson, and James B. Saxe. Extended static checking. Technical Report 159, Compaq Systems Research Center (SRC), 1998. Also see `http://research.compaq.com/SRC/esc/overview.html`.

Donahue, James and Alan Demers. Data types are values. *ACM Transactions on Programming Languages and Systems*, 7(3):426–445, July 1985.

Dowek, Gilles, Thérèse Hardin, Claude Kirchner, and Frank Pfenning. Unification via explicit substitutions: The case of higher-order patterns. In M. Maher, editor, *Proceedings of the Joint International Conference and Symposium on Logic Programming*, pages 259–273, Bonn, Germany, September 1996. MIT Press.

Drossopoulou, Sophia, Susan Eisenbach, and Sarfraz Khurshid. Is the Java Type System Sound? *Theory and Practice of Object Systems*, 7(1):3–24, 1999. Summary in European Conference on Object-Oriented Programming (ECOOP), 1997.

Duggan, Dominic and Adriana Compagnoni. Subtyping for object type constructors. In *Workshop on Foundations of Object-Oriented Languages (FOOL), informal proceedings*, January 1999.

Dybvig, R. Kent. *The Scheme Programming Language.* Prentice-Hall, Inc., Englewood Cliffs, New Jersey, second edition, 1996. Available electronically at `http://www.scheme.com/tspl2d/`.

Eidorff, Peter, Fritz Henglein, Christian Mossin, Henning Niss, Morten Heine B. Sørensen, and Mads Tofte. AnnoDomini in practice: A type-theoretic approach to the Year 2000 problem. In Jean-Yves Girard, editor, *Proc. Symposium on Typed Lambda Calculus and Applications (TLCA)*, volume 1581 of *Lecture Notes in Computer Science*, pages 6–13, L'Aquila, Italy, April 1999. Springer-Verlag.

Eifrig, Jonathan, Scott Smith, and Valery Trifonov. Type inference for recursively constrained types and its application to OOP. In *Proceedings of the 1995 Mathematical Foundations of Programming Semantics Conference*, volume 1 of *Electronic Notes in Theoretical Computer Science*. Elsevier, 1995.

Feinberg, Neal, Sonya E. Keene, Robert O. Mathews, and P. Tucker Withington. *The Dylan Programming Book*. Addison-Wesley Longman, Reading, Mass., 1997.

Felleisen, Matthias and Daniel P. Friedman. *A Little Java, A Few Patterns*. MIT Press, Cambridge, Massachusetts, 1998.

Felty, Amy, Elsa Gunter, John Hannan, Dale Miller, Gopalan Nadathur, and Andre Scedrov. Lambda prolog: An extended logic programming language. In E. Lusk; R. Overbeek, editor, *Proceedings on the 9th International Conference on Automated Deduction*, volume 310 of *LNCS*, pages 754–755, Berlin, May 1988. Springer.

Filinski, Andrzej. A semantic account of type-directed partial evaluation. In Gopalan Nadathur, editor, *Proceedings of the International Conference on Principles and Practice of Declarative Programming*, number 1702 in Lecture Notes in Computer Science, pages 378–395, Paris, France, September 1999. Springer-Verlag. Extended version available as technical report BRICS RS-99-17.

Filinski, Andrzej. Normalization by evaluation for the computational lambda-calculus. In Samson Abramsky, editor, *Typed Lambda Calculi and Applications, 5th International Conference, TLCA 2001*, number 2044 in Lecture Notes in Computer Science, pages 151–165, Kraków, Poland, May 2001. Springer-Verlag.

Fisher, Kathleen. Classes = objects + data abstraction. In Kim Bruce and Giuseppe Longo, editors, *Workshop on Foundations of Object-Oriented Languages (FOOL), informal proceedings*, July 1996a. Invited talk. Also available as Stanford University Technical Note STAN-CS-TN-96-31.

Fisher, Kathleen. *Type Systems for object-oriented programming languages*. PhD thesis, Stanford University, 1996b. STAN-CS-TR-98-1602.

Fisher, Kathleen, Furio Honsell, and John C. Mitchell. A lambda calculus of objects and method specialization. *Nordic J. Computing (formerly BIT)*, 1:3–37, 1994. Summary in *Proc. IEEE Symp. on Logic in Computer Science,* 1993, 26–38.

Fisher, Kathleen and John Mitchell. The development of type systems for object-oriented languages. *Theory and Practice of Object Systems*, 1(3):189–220, 1996.

Fisher, Kathleen and John C. Mitchell. On the relationship between classes, objects, and data abstraction. *Theory and Practice of Object Systems*, 4(1):3–25, 1998.

Fisher, Kathleen and John H. Reppy. The design of a class mechanism for Moby. In *SIGPLAN Conference on Programming Language Design and Implementation (PDLI)*, pages 37–49, 1999.

Flanagan, Cormac and Matthias Felleisen. Componential set-based analysis. *ACM SIGPLAN Notices*, 32(5):235–248, May 1997.

Flatt, Matthew and Matthias Felleisen. Units: Cool modules for HOT languages. In *ACM SIGPLAN Conference on Programming Language Design and Implementation (PLDI), Montreal, Canada*, pages 236–248, 1998.

Flatt, Matthew, Shriram Krishnamurthi, and Matthias Felleisen. Classes and mixins. In *ACM Symposium on Principles of Programming Languages (POPL), San Diego, California*, January 1998a.

Flatt, Matthew, Shriram Krishnamurthi, and Matthias Felleisen. A programmer's reduction semantics for classes and mixins. Technical Report TR97-293, Computer Science Department, Rice University, February 1998b. Corrected June, 1999.

Freeman, Tim and Frank Pfenning. Refinement types for ML. In *ACM SIGPLAN Conference on Programming Language Design and Implementation (PLDI), Toronto, Ontario*, June 1991.

Frege, Gottlob. *Begriffschrift, eine der arithmetischen nachgebildete Formelsprache des reinen Denkens*. Halle: L. Nebert, 1879. Available in several translations.

Friedman, Daniel P. and Matthias Felleisen. *The Little Schemer*. MIT Press, 1996.

Friedman, Daniel P., Mitchell Wand, and Christopher T. Haynes. *Essentials of Programming Languages*. McGraw-Hill Book Co., New York, N.Y., second edition, 2001.

Friedman, Harvey. Equality between functionals. In Rohit Parikh, editor, *Logic Colloquium*, volume 453 of *Lecture Notes in Mathematics*, pages 22–37, Berlin, 1975. Springer-Verlag.

Gallier, Jean. On Girard's "Candidats de reductibilité". In Piergiorgio Odifreddi, editor, *Logic and Computer Science*, number 31 in APIC Studies in Data Processing, pages 123–203. Academic Press, 1990.

Gallier, Jean. Constructive logics. Part I: A tutorial on proof systems and typed λ-calculi. *Theoretical Computer Science*, 110(2):249–339, March 1993.

Gandy, Robin O. The simple theory of types. In *Logic Colloquium 76*, volume 87 of *Studies in Logic and the Foundations of Mathematics*, pages 173–181. North Holland, 1976.

Gapeyev, Vladimir, Michael Levin, and Benjamin Pierce. Recursive subtyping revealed. In *International Conference on Functional Programming (ICFP), Montreal, Canada*, 2000. To appear in *Journal of Functional Programming*.

Garrigue, Jaques and Hassan Aït-Kaci. The typed polymorphic label-selective lambda-calculus. In *ACM Symposium on Principles of Programming Languages (POPL), Portland, Oregon*, pages 35–47, 1994.

Garrigue, Jaques and Didier Rémy. Extending ML with semi-explicit polymorphism. In Martín Abadi and Takayasu Ito, editors, *International Symposium on Theoretical Aspects of Computer Software (TACS), Sendai, Japan*, pages 20–46. Springer-Verlag, September 1997.

Ghelli, Giorgio. *Proof Theoretic Studies about a Minimal Type System Integrating Inclusion and Parametric Polymorphism*. PhD thesis, Università di Pisa, March 1990. Technical report TD–6/90, Dipartimento di Informatica, Università di Pisa.

Ghelli, Giorgio. Recursive types are not conservative over $F_\leq$. In M. Bezen and J.F. Groote, editors, *Typed Lambda Calculi and Applications (TLCA), Utrecht, The Netherlands*, number 664 in Lecture Notes in Computer Science, pages 146–162, Berlin, March 1993. Springer-Verlag.

Ghelli, Giorgio. Divergence of $F_\leq$ type checking. *Theoretical Computer Science*, 139 (1,2):131–162, 1995.

Ghelli, Giorgio. Termination of system F-bounded: A complete proof. *Information and Computation*, 139(1):39–56, 1997.

Ghelli, Giorgio and Benjamin Pierce. Bounded existentials and minimal typing. *Theoretical Computer Science*, 193:75–96, 1998.

Gifford, David, Pierre Jouvelot, John Lucassen, and Mark Sheldon. FX-87 Reference Manual. Technical Report MIT/LCS/TR-407, Massachusetts Institute of Technology, Laboratory for Computer Science, September 1987.

Girard, Jean-Yves. *Interprétation fonctionnelle et élimination des coupures de l'arithmétique d'ordre supérieur*. Thèse d'état, Université Paris VII, 1972. Summary in *Proceedings of the Second Scandinavian Logic Symposium* (J.E. Fenstad, editor), North-Holland, 1971 (pp. 63–92).

Girard, Jean-Yves. Linear logic. *Theoretical Computer Science*, 50:1–102, 1987.

Girard, Jean-Yves, Yves Lafont, and Paul Taylor. *Proofs and Types*, volume 7 of *Cambridge Tracts in Theoretical Computer Science*. Cambridge University Press, 1989.

Glew, Neal. Type dispatch for named hierarchical types. In *International Conference on Functional Programming (ICFP), Paris, France*, pages 172–182, 1999.

Gordon, Andrew. A tutorial on co-induction and functional programming. In *Functional Programming, Glasgow 1994*, pages 78–95. Springer Workshops in Computing, 1995.

Gordon, Michael J. Adding eval to ML. Manuscript, circa 1980.

Gordon, Michael J., Robin Milner, and Christopher P. Wadsworth. *Edinburgh LCF*. Springer-Verlag LNCS 78, 1979.

Goto, Eiichi. Monocopy and associative algorithms in extended Lisp. Technical Report TR 74-03, University of Tokyo, May 1974.

Goubault-Larrecq, Jean and Ian Mackie. *Proof Theory and Automated Deduction (Applied Logic Series, V. 6)*. Kluwer, 1997.

Grattan-Guinness, Ivor. *The search for mathematical roots, 1870–1940: Logics, set theories and the foundations of mathematics from Cantor through Russell to Gödel*. Princeton University Press, 2001.

Gries, David, editor. *Programming Methodology*. Springer-Verlag, New York, 1978.

Gunter, Carl A. *Semantics of Programming Languages: Structures and Techniques.* MIT Press, 1992.

Gunter, Carl A. and John C. Mitchell. *Theoretical Aspects of Object-Oriented Programming: Types, Semantics, and Language Design.* MIT Press, 1994.

Hall, Cordelia V., Kevin Hammond, Simon L. Peyton Jones, and Philip L. Wadler. Type classes in Haskell. *ACM Transactions on Programming Languages and Systems,* 18 (2):109–138, March 1996.

Halmos, Paul R. *Naive Set Theory.* Springer, New York, 1987.

Harper, Robert. A simplified account of polymorphic references. *Information Processing Letters,* 51(4):201–206, August 1994. See also (Harper, 1996).

Harper, Robert. A note on: "A simplified account of polymorphic references" [Inform. Process. Lett. **51** (1994), no. 4, 201–206; MR 95f:68142]. *Information Processing Letters,* 57(1):15–16, January 1996. See (Harper, 1994).

Harper, Robert, Bruce Duba, and David MacQueen. First-class continuations in ML. *Journal of Functional Programming,* 3(4), October 1993. Short version in POPL '91.

Harper, Robert, Furio Honsell, and Gordon Plotkin. A framework for defining logics. *Journal of the ACM,* 40(1):143–184, 1992. Summary in LICS'87.

Harper, Robert and Mark Lillibridge. A type-theoretic approach to higher-order modules with sharing. In *ACM Symposium on Principles of Programming Languages (POPL), Portland, Oregon,* pages 123–137, January 1994.

Harper, Robert, John C. Mitchell, and Eugenio Moggi. Higher-order modules and the phase distinction. In *ACM Symposium on Principles of Programming Languages (POPL), San Francisco, California,* pages 341–354, January 1990.

Harper, Robert and Greg Morrisett. Compiling polymorphism using intensional type analysis. In *ACM Symposium on Principles of Programming Languages (POPL), San Francisco, California,* pages 130–141, 1995.

Harper, Robert and Benjamin Pierce. A record calculus based on symmetric concatenation. In *ACM Symposium on Principles of Programming Languages (POPL), Orlando, Florida,* pages 131–142, January 1991. Extended version available as Carnegie Mellon Technical Report CMU-CS-90-157.

Harper, Robert and Christopher Stone. A type-theoretic interpretation of Standard ML. In Gordon Plotkin, Colin Stirling, and Mads Tofte, editors, *Proof, Language and Interaction: Essays in Honour of Robin Milner.* MIT Press, 2000.

Hasegawa, Ryu. Parametricity of extensionally collapsed term models of polymorphism and their categorical properties. In Takayasu Ito and Albert Meyer, editors, *Theoretical Aspects of Computer Software (TACS), Sendai, Japan,* 1991.

Hayashi, Susumu. Singleton, union and intersection types for program extraction. In T. Ito and A. R. Meyer, editors, *Theoretical Aspects of Computer Software (Sendai, Japan),* number 526 in Lecture Notes in Computer Science, pages 701–730. Springer-Verlag, September 1991. Full version in *Information and Computation,* 109(1/2):174–210, 1994.

Henglein, Fritz. Type inference with polymorphic recursion. *ACM Transactions on Programming Languages and Systems*, 15(2):253–289, 1993.

Henglein, Fritz. Dynamic typing: syntax and proof theory. *Science of Computer Programming*, 22(3):197–230, June 1994. Selected papers of the Fourth European Symposium on Programming (Rennes, 1992).

Henglein, Fritz and Harry G. Mairson. The complexity of type inference for higher-order typed lambda-calculi. In *ACM Symposium on Principles of Programming Languages (POPL), Orlando, Florida*, pages 119–130, January 1991.

Hennessy, Matthew. *A Semantics of Programming Languages: An Elementary Introduction Using Operational Semantics.* John Wiley and Sons, 1990. Currently out of print; available from `http://www.cogs.susx.ac.uk/users/matthewh/semnotes.ps.gz`.

Hennessy, Matthew and James Riely. Resource access control in systems of mobile agents. In Uwe Nestmann and Benjamin C. Pierce, editors, *HLCL '98: High-Level Concurrent Languages (Nice, France, September 12, 1998)*, volume 16.3 of *ENTCS*, pages 3–17. Elsevier Science Publishers, 1998. Full version available as CogSci Report 2/98, University of Sussex, Brighton.

Hindley, J. Roger. The principal type-scheme of an object in combinatory logic. *Transactions of the American Mathematical Society*, 146:29–60, 1969.

Hindley, J. Roger. Types with intersection, an introduction. *Formal Aspects of Computing*, 4:470–486, 1992.

Hindley, J. Roger. *Basic Simple Type Theory*, volume 42 of *Cambridge Tracts in Theoretical Computer Science*. Cambridge University Press, Cambridge, 1997.

Hindley, J. Roger and Jonathan P. Seldin. *Introduction to Combinators and λ-Calculus*, volume 1 of *London Mathematical Society Student Texts*. Cambridge University Press, 1986.

Hoang, My, John Mitchell, and Ramesh Viswanathan. Standard ML-NJ weak polymorphism and imperative constructs. In *Proceedings, Eighth Annual IEEE Symposium on Logic in Computer Science*, pages 15–25. IEEE Computer Society Press, 1993.

Hodas, J. S. Lolli: An extension of λProlog with linear context management. In D. Miller, editor, *Workshop on the λProlog Programming Language*, pages 159–168, Philadelphia, Pennsylvania, August 1992.

Hofmann, Martin. Syntax and semantics of dependent types. In *Semantics and Logic of Computation*. Cambridge University Press, 1997.

Hofmann, Martin and Benjamin Pierce. Positive subtyping. In *ACM Symposium on Principles of Programming Languages (POPL), San Francisco, California*, pages 186–197, January 1995a. Full version in *Information and Computation*, volume 126, number 1, April 1996. Also available as University of Edinburgh technical report ECS-LFCS-94-303, September 1994.

Hofmann, Martin and Benjamin Pierce. A unifying type-theoretic framework for objects. *Journal of Functional Programming*, 5(4):593–635, October 1995b. Previous versions appeared in the Symposium on Theoretical Aspects of Computer Science, 1994, (pages 251–262) and, under the title "An Abstract View of Objects and Subtyping (Preliminary Report)," as University of Edinburgh, LFCS technical report ECS-LFCS-92-226, 1992.

Hofmann, Martin and Benjamin C. Pierce. Type destructors. In Didier Rémy, editor, *Informal proceedings of the Fourth International Workshop on Foundations of Object-Oriented Languages (FOOL)*, January 1998. Full version to appear in *Information and Computation*.

Hook, J.G. Understanding Russell – a first attempt. In *Proc. Int. Symp. on Semantics of Data Types, Sophia-Antipolis (France), Springer LNCS 173*, pages 69–85. Springer-Verlag, 1984.

Hopcroft, John E. and Jeffrey D. Ullman. *Introduction to Automata Theory, Languages, and Computation.* Addison-Wesley, 1979.

Hosoya, Haruo and Benjamin Pierce. Regular expression pattern matching. In *ACM Symposium on Principles of Programming Languages (POPL), London, England*, 2001.

Hosoya, Haruo and Benjamin C. Pierce. How good is local type inference? Technical Report MS-CIS-99-17, University of Pennsylvania, June 1999.

Hosoya, Haruo and Benjamin C. Pierce. XDuce: A typed XML processing language (preliminary report). In *International Workshop on the Web and Databases (WebDB)*, May 2000.

Hosoya, Haruo, Jérôme Vouillon, and Benjamin C. Pierce. Regular expression types for XML. *ACM Transactions on Programming Languages and Systems (TOPLAS)*, 2001. To appear; short version in ICFP 2000.

Howard, William A. Hereditarily majorizable functionals of finite type. In Anne Sjerp Troelstra, editor, *Metamathematical Investigation of Intuitionistic Arithmetic and Analysis*, volume 344 of *Lecture Notes in Mathematics*, pages 454–461. Springer-Verlag, Berlin, 1973. Appendix.

Howard, William A. The formulas-as-types notion of construction. In J. P. Seldin and J. R. Hindley, editors, *To H. B. Curry: Essays on Combinatory Logic, Lambda Calculus, and Formalism*, pages 479–490. Academic Press, New York, 1980. Reprint of 1969 article.

Howe, Douglas. *Automating Reasoning in an Implementation of Constructive Type Theory.* PhD thesis, Cornell University, 1988.

Hudak, Paul, S. Peyton Jones, P. Wadler, B. Boutel, J. Fairbairn, J. Fasel, M. M. Guzman, K. Hammond, J. Hughes, T. Johnsson, D. Kieburtz, R. Nikhil, W. Partain, and J. Peterson. Report on the programming language Haskell, version 1.2. *SIGPLAN Notices*, 27(5), May 1992.

Huet, Gérard. A unification algorithm for typed λ-calculus. *Theoretical Computer Science*, 1:27–57, 1975.

Huet, Gérard. *Résolution d'equations dans les langages d'ordre 1,2, ...,ω.* Thèse de Doctorat d'Etat, Université de Paris 7 (France), 1976.

Huet, Gérard, editor. *Logical Foundations of Functional Programming.* University of Texas at Austin Year of Programming Series. Addison-Wesley, 1990.

Hyland, J. Martin E. and C.-H. Luke Ong. On full abstraction for PCF: I, II, and III. *Information and Computation*, 163(2):285–408, December 2000.

Igarashi, Atsushi, Benjamin Pierce, and Philip Wadler. Featherweight Java: A minimal core calculus for Java and GJ. In *ACM Symposium on Object Oriented Programming: Systems, Languages, and Applications (OOPSLA)*, October 1999. Full version to appear in ACM Transactions on Programming Languages and Systems (TOPLAS), 2001.

Igarashi, Atsushi and Benjamin C. Pierce. On inner classes. In *European Conference on Object-Oriented Programming (ECOOP)*, 2000. Also in informal proceedings of the Seventh International Workshop on Foundations of Object-Oriented Languages (FOOL). To appear in *Information and Computation*.

Igarashi, Atsushi, Benjamin C. Pierce, and Philip Wadler. A recipe for raw types. In *Workshop on Foundations of Object-Oriented Languages (FOOL)*, 2001.

Ishtiaq, Samin and Peter O'Hearn. Bi as an assertion language for mutable data structures. In *ACM Symposium on Principles of Programming Languages (POPL), London, England*, 2001.

Jacobs, Bart. *Categorical Logic and Type Theory.* Number 141 in Studies in Logic and the Foundations of Mathematics. North Holland, Elsevier, 1999.

Jagannathan, Suresh and Andrew Wright. Effective flow analysis for avoiding runtime checks. In *Proceedings of the Second International Static Analysis Symposium*, volume 983 of *LNCS*, pages 207–224. Springer-Verlag, 1995.

Jay, C. Barry and Milan Sekanina. Shape checking of array programs. In *Computing: The Australasian Theory Seminar (Proceedings)*, volume 19 of *Australian Computer Science Communications*, pages 113–121, 1997.

Jim, Trevor. Rank-2 type systems and recursive definitions. Technical Report MIT/LCS/TM-531, Massachusetts Institute of Technology, Laboratory for Computer Science, November 1995.

Jim, Trevor. What are principal typings and what are they good for? In ACM, editor, *ACM Symposium on Principles of Programming Languages (POPL), St. Petersburg Beach, Florida*, pages 42–53, 1996.

Jim, Trevor and Jens Palsberg. Type inference in systems of recursive types with subtyping. Manuscript, 1999.

Jones, Mark P. ML typing, explicit polymorphism, and qualified types, 1994a.

Jones, Mark P. *Qualified Types: Theory and Practice*. Cambridge University Press, 1994b.

Jones, Richard and Rafael D. Lins. *Garbage Collection: Algorithms for Automatic Dynamic Memory Management*. Wiley, 1996.

Jouvelot, Pierre and David Gifford. Algebraic reconstruction of types and effects. In *ACM Symposium on Principles of Programming Languages (POPL), Orlando, Florida*, pages 303–310, January 1991.

Jutting, L.S. van Benthem, James McKinna, and Robert Pollack. Checking algorithms for Pure Type Systems. In Henk Barendregt and Tobias Nipkow, editors, *Proceedings of the International Workshop on Types for Proofs and Programs*, pages 19–61, Nijmegen, The Netherlands, May 1994. Springer-Verlag LNCS 806.

Kaes, Stefan. Parametric overloading in polymorphic programming languages. In H. Ganzinger, editor, *Proceedings of the European Symposium on Programming*, volume 300 of *Lecture Notes in Computer Science*, pages 131–144. Springer-Verlag, 1988.

Kahn, Gilles. Natural semantics. In *Proceedings of the Symposium on Theoretical Aspects of Computer Science (STACS)*, volume 247 of *Lecture Notes in Computer Science*, pages 22–39. Springer-Verlag, 1987.

Kamin, Samuel N. Inheritance in Smalltalk-80: A denotational definition. In *ACM Symposium on Principles of Programming Languages (POPL), San Diego, California*, pages 80–87, January 1988.

Kamin, Samuel N. and Uday S. Reddy. Two semantic models of object-oriented languages. In Carl A. Gunter and John C. Mitchell, editors, *Theoretical Aspects of Object-Oriented Programming: Types, Semantics, and Language Design*, pages 464–495. MIT Press, 1994.

Katiyar, Dinesh, David Luckham, and John Mitchell. A type system for prototyping languages. In *ACM Symposium on Principles of Programming Languages (POPL), Portland, Oregon*, pages 138–150, January 1994.

Katiyar, Dinesh and Sriram Sankar. Completely bounded quantification is decidable. In *Proceedings of the ACM SIGPLAN Workshop on ML and its Applications*, June 1992.

Kelsey, Richard, William Clinger, and Jonathan Rees. Revised[5] report on the algorithmic language Scheme. *Higher-Order and Symbolic Computation*, 11(1):7–105, 1998. Also appears in ACM SIGPLAN Notices 33(9), September 1998.

Kennedy, Andrew. Dimension types. In Donald Sannella, editor, *Programming Languages and Systems—ESOP'94, 5th European Symposium on Programming*, volume 788 of *Lecture Notes in Computer Science*, pages 348–362, Edinburgh, U.K., 11–13 April 1994. Springer.

Kernighan, Brian W. and Dennis M. Ritchie. *The C Programming Language*. Prentice Hall, Englewood Cliffs, second edition, 1988.

Kfoury, Assaf J., Harry Mairson, Franklyn Turbak, and Joe B. Wells. Relating typability and expressiveness in finite-rank intersection type systems. In *International Conference on Functional Programming (ICFP), Paris, France*, volume 34.9 of *ACM Sigplan Notices*, pages 90–101, N.Y., September 27–29 1999. ACM Press.

Kfoury, Assaf J. and Jerzy Tiuryn. Type reconstruction in finite-rank fragments of the polymorphic λ-calculus. In *Fifth Annual IEEE Symposium on Logic in Computer Science*, pages 2–11, Philadelphia, PA, June 1990. Full version in *Information and Computation*, 98(2), 228–257, 1992.

Kfoury, Assaf J., Jerzy Tiuryn, and Pawel Urzyczyn. ML typability is DEXPTIME-complete. In *Proc. 15th Colloq. on Trees in Algebra and Programming*, pages 206–220. Springer LNCS 431, 1990.

Kfoury, Assaf J., Jerzy Tiuryn, and Pawel Urzyczyn. Type reconstruction in the presence of polymorphic recursion. *ACM Transactions on Programming Languages and Systems*, 15(2):290–311, April 1993a.

Kfoury, Assaf J., Jerzy Tiuryn, and Pawel Urzyczyn. The undecidability of the semi-unification problem. *Information and Computation*, 102(1):83–101, January 1993b. Summary in *STOC 1990*.

Kfoury, Assaf J., Jerzy Tiuryn, and Pawel Urzyczyn. An analysis of ML typability. *Journal of the ACM*, 41(2):368–398, March 1994.

Kfoury, Assaf J. and Joe B. Wells. Principality and decidable type inference for finite-rank intersection types. In *ACM Symposium on Principles of Programming Languages (POPL), San Antonio, Texas*, pages 161–174, New York, NY, January 1999. ACM.

Kiczales, Gregor, Jim des Rivières, and Daniel G. Bobrow. *The Art of the Metaobject Protocol*. MIT Press, Cambridge, MA, 1991.

Kirchner, Claude and Jean-Pierre Jouannaud. Solving equations in abstract algebras: a rule-based survey of unification. Research Report 561, Université de Paris Sud, Orsay, France, April 1990.

Klop, Jan W. *Combinatory Reduction Systems*. Mathematical Centre Tracts 127. Mathematisch Centrum, Amsterdam, 1980.

Kobayashi, Naoki, Benjamin C. Pierce, and David N. Turner. Linearity and the pi-calculus. In *ACM Symposium on Principles of Programming Languages (POPL), St. Petersburg Beach, Florida*, 1996. Full version in *ACM Transactions on Programming Languages and Systems*, 21(5), pp. 914–947, September 1999.

Kozen, Dexter, Jens Palsberg, and Michael I. Schwartzbach. Efficient recursive subtyping. In *ACM Symposium on Principles of Programming Languages (POPL), Charleston, South Carolina*, pages 419–428, 1993.

Laan, Twan Dismas Laurens. *The Evolution of Type Theory in Logic and Mathematics*. PhD thesis, Techn. Univ. Eindhoven, 1997.

Landin, Peter J. The mechanical evaluation of expressions. *Computer Journal*, 6: 308–320, January 1964.

Landin, Peter J. A correspondence between ALGOL 60 and Church's lambda-notation: Parts I and II. *Communications of the ACM*, 8(2,3):89–101, 158–165, February and March 1965.

Landin, Peter J. The next 700 programming languages. *Communications of the ACM*, 9(3):157–166, March 1966.

Lassez, Jean-Louis and Gordin Plotkin, editors. *Computational Logic, Essays in Honor of Alan Robinson*. MIT Press, 1991.

Läufer, Konstantin. *Polymorphic Type Inference and Abstract Data Types*. PhD thesis, New York University, 1992.

Läufer, Konstantin and Martin Odersky. Polymorphic type inference and abstract data types. *ACM Transactions on Programming Languages and Systems (TOPLAS)*, 16(5):1411–1430, September 1994. Summary in *Phoenix Seminar and Workshop on Declarative Programming*, Nov. 1991.

League, Christopher, Zhong Shao, and Valery Trifonov. Representing Java classes in a typed intermediate language. In *International Conference on Functional Programming (ICFP), Paris, France*, September 1999.

League, Christopher, Valery Trifonov, and Zhong Shao. Type-preserving compilation of Featherweight Java. In *Foundations of Object-Oriented Languages (FOOL8)*, London, January 2001.

Lee, Oukseh and Kwangkeun Yi. Proofs about a folklore let-polymorphic type inference algorithm. *ACM Transactions on Programming Languages and Systems*, 20 (4):707–723, July 1998.

Leivant, Daniel. Polymorphic type inference. In *Proceedings of the 10th Annual ACM Symposium on Principles of Programming Languages*. ACM, 1983.

Lemmon, E. John, Carew A. Meredith, David Meredith, Arthur N. Prior, and Ivo Thomas. Calculi of pure strict implication, 1957. Mimeographed version, 1957; published in *Philosophical Logic*, ed. Davis, Hockney, and Wilson, D. Reidel Co., Netherlands, 1969, pp. 215–250.

Leroy, Xavier. Manifest types, modules and separate compilation. In *ACM Symposium on Principles of Programming Languages (POPL), Portland, Oregon*, pages 109–122, Portland, OR, January 1994.

Leroy, Xavier. The Objective Caml system: Documentation and user's manual, 2000. With Damien Doligez, Jacques Garrigue, Didier Rémy, and Jérôme Vouillon. Available from `http://caml.inria.fr`.

Leroy, Xavier and Michel Mauny. Dynamics in ML. In John Hughes, editor, *ACM Symposium on Functional Programming Languages and Computer Architecture (FPCA) 1991*, volume 523 of *Lecture Notes in Computer Science*, pages 406–426. Springer-Verlag, 1991.

Leroy, Xavier and François Pessaux. Type-based analysis of uncaught exceptions. *ACM Transactions on Programming Languages and Systems*, 22(2):340–377, March 2000. Summary in *ACM Symposium on Principles of Programming Languages (POPL), San Antonio, Texas*, 1999.

Leroy, Xavier and François Rouaix. Security properties of typed applets. In *ACM Symposium on Principles of Programming Languages (POPL), San Diego, California*, pages 391–403, January 1998.

Leroy, Xavier and Pierre Weis. Polymorphic type inference and assignment. In *ACM Symposium on Principles of Programming Languages (POPL), Orlando, Florida*, pages 291–302, 1991.

Lescanne, Pierre and Jocelyn Rouyer-Degli. Explicit substitutions with de Bruijn's levels. In J. Hsiang, editor, *Proceedings of the 6th Conference on Rewriting Techniques and Applications (RTA), Kaiserslautern (Germany)*, volume 914, pages 294–308, 1995.

Levin, Michael Y. and Benjamin C. Pierce. Tinkertype: A language for playing with formal systems. *Journal of Functional Programming*, 2001. To appear. A preliminary version appeared as an invited talk at the *Logical Frameworks and Metalanguages Workshop (LFM)*, June 2000.

Lillibridge, Mark. *Translucent Sums: A Foundation for Higher-Order Module Systems*. PhD thesis, School of Computer Science, Carnegie Mellon University, Pittsburgh, PA, May 1997.

Liskov, Barbara, Russell Atkinson, Toby Bloom, Elliott Moss, J. Craig Schaffert, Robert Scheifler, and Alan Snyder. *CLU Reference Manual*. Springer-Verlag, 1981.

Liskov, Barbara, Alan Snyder, Russell Atkinson, and J. Craig Schaffert. Abstraction mechanisms in CLU. *Communications of the ACM*, 20(8):564–576, August 1977. Also in S. Zdonik and D. Maier, eds., *Readings in Object-Oriented Database Systems*.

Luo, Zhaohui. *Computation and Reasoning: A Type Theory for Computer Science*. Number 11 in International Series of Monographs on Computer Science. Oxford University Press, 1994.

Luo, Zhaohui and Robert Pollack. The LEGO proof development system: A user's manual. Technical Report ECS-LFCS-92-211, University of Edinburgh, May 1992.

Ma, QingMing. Parametricity as subtyping. In *ACM Symposium on Principles of Programming Languages (POPL), Albuquerque, New Mexico*, January 1992.

Mackie, Ian. Lilac: A functional programming language based on linear logic. *Journal of Functional Programming*, 4(4):395–433, October 1994.

MacQueen, David. Using dependent types to express modular structure. In *ACM Symposium on Principles of Programming Languages (POPL), St. Petersburg Beach, Florida*, pages 277–286, January 1986.

MacQueen, David, Gordon Plotkin, and Ravi Sethi. An ideal model for recursive polymorphic types. *Information and Control*, 71:95–130, 1986.

MacQueen, David B. Using dependent types to express modular structure. In *ACM Symposium on Principles of Programming Languages (POPL), St. Petersburg Beach, Florida*, 1986.

Magnusson, Lena and Bengt Nordström. The ALF proof editor and its proof engine. In Henk Barendregt and Tobias Nipkow, editors, *Types for Proofs and Programs*, pages 213–237. Springer-Verlag LNCS 806, 1994.

Mairson, Harry G. Deciding ML typability is complete for deterministic exponential time. In *ACM Symposium on Principles of Programming Languages (POPL), San Francisco, California*, pages 382–401. ACM Press, New York, 1990.

Martin-Löf, Per. An intuitionistic theory of types: predicative part. In H. E. Rose and J. C. Shepherdson, editors, *Logic Colloquium, '73*, pages 73–118. North-Holland, Amsterdam, 1973.

Martin-Löf, Per. Constructive mathematics and computer programming. In *Logic, Methodology and Philosophy of Science, VI*. North Holland, Amsterdam, 1982.

Martin-Lof, Per. *Intuitionistic Type Theory*. Bibliopolis, 1984.

Martini, Simone. Bounded quantifiers have interval models. In *Proceedings of the ACM Conference on Lisp and Functional Programming*, pages 174–183, Snowbird, Utah, July 1988. ACM.

McCarthy, John. History of LISP. In R. L. Wexelblatt, editor, *History of Programming Languages*, pages 173–197. Academic Press, New York, 1981.

McCarthy, John, S. R. Russell, D. Edwards, et al. *LISP Programmer's Manual*. Massachusetts Institute of Technology, A.I. Lab., Cambridge, Massachusetts, November 1959. Handwritten Draft + Machine Typed.

McKinna, James and Robert Pollack. Pure Type Sytems formalized. In M. Bezem and J. F. Groote, editors, *Proceedings of the International Conference on Typed Lambda Calculi and Applications*, pages 289–305. Springer-Verlag LNCS 664, March 1993.

Meertens, Lambert. Incremental polymorphic type checking in B. In *ACM Symposium on Principles of Programming Languages (POPL), Austin, Texas*, 1983.

Milner, Robin. A theory of type polymorphism in programming. *Journal of Computer and System Sciences*, 17:348–375, August 1978.

Milner, Robin. *A Calculus of Communicating Systems*, volume 92 of *Lecture Notes in Computer Science*. Springer-Verlag, 1980.

Milner, Robin. *Communication and Concurrency*. Prentice Hall, 1989.

Milner, Robin. The polyadic π-calculus: a tutorial. Technical Report ECS–LFCS–91–180, Laboratory for Foundations of Computer Science, Department of Computer Science, University of Edinburgh, UK, October 1991. Appeared in *Proceedings of the International Summer School on Logic and Algebra of Specification*, Marktoberdorf, August 1991. Reprinted in *Logic and Algebra of Specification*, ed. F. L. Bauer, W. Brauer, and H. Schwichtenberg, Springer-Verlag, 1993.

Milner, Robin. *Communicating and Mobile Systems: the Pi-Calculus*. Cambridge University Press, 1999.

Milner, Robin, Joachim Parrow, and David Walker. A calculus of mobile processes (Parts I and II). *Information and Computation*, 100:1–77, 1992.

Milner, Robin and Mads Tofte. Co-induction in relational semantics. *Theoretical Computer Science*, 87:209–220, 1991a.

Milner, Robin and Mads Tofte. *Commentary on Standard ML*. MIT Press, Cambridge, Massachusetts, 1991b.

Milner, Robin, Mads Tofte, and Robert Harper. *The Definition of Standard ML*. MIT Press, 1990.

Milner, Robin, Mads Tofte, Robert Harper, and David MacQueen. *The Definition of Standard ML (Revised)*. MIT Press, 1997.

Mitchell, John C. Coercion and type inference (summary). In *ACM Symposium on Principles of Programming Languages (POPL), Salt Lake City, Utah*, pages 175–185, January 1984a.

Mitchell, John C. Type inference and type containment. In *Proc. Int. Symp. on Semantics of Data Types, Sophia-Antipolis (France)*, pages 257–278, Berlin, June 1984b. Springer LNCS 173. Full version in *Information and Computation*, vol. 76, no. 2/3, 1988, pp. 211–249. Reprinted in *Logical Foundations of Functional Programming*, ed. G. Huet, Addison-Wesley (1990) 153-194.

Mitchell, John C. Representation independence and data abstraction (preliminary version). In *ACM Symposium on Principles of Programming Languages (POPL), St. Petersburg Beach, Florida*, pages 263–276, 1986.

Mitchell, John C. Toward a typed foundation for method specialization and inheritance. In *ACM Symposium on Principles of Programming Languages (POPL), San Francisco, California*, pages 109–124, January 1990a. Also in Carl A. Gunter and John C. Mitchell, editors, *Theoretical Aspects of Object-Oriented Programming: Types, Semantics, and Language Design* (MIT Press, 1994).

Mitchell, John C. Type systems for programming languages. In J. van Leeuwen, editor, *Handbook of Theoretical Computer Science, Volume B*, pages 365–458. North-Holland, Amsterdam, 1990b.

Mitchell, John C. *Foundations for Programming Languages*. MIT Press, Cambridge, Massachusetts, 1996.

Mitchell, John C. and Robert Harper. The essence of ML. In *ACM Symposium on Principles of Programming Languages (POPL), San Diego, California*, January 1988. Full version in *ACM Transactions on Programming Languages and Systems*, vol. 15, no. 2, 1993, pp. 211–252, under the title "On the type structure of Standard ML".

Mitchell, John C. and Albert R. Meyer. Second-order logical relations (extended abstract). In Rohit Parikh, editor, *Logic of Programs*, volume 193 of *Lecture Notes in Computer Science*, pages 225–236, Berlin, 1985. Springer-Verlag.

Mitchell, John C. and Gordon D. Plotkin. Abstract types have existential types. *ACM Trans. on Programming Languages and Systems*, 10(3):470–502, 1988. Summary in *ACM Symposium on Principles of Programming Languages (POPL), New Orleans, Louisiana*, 1985.

Morris, James H. Lambda calculus models of programming languages. Technical Report MIT-LCS//MIT/LCS/TR-57, Massachusetts Institute of Technology, Laboratory for Computer Science, December 1968.

Morrisett, Greg, Matthias Felleisen, and Robert Harper. Abstract models of memory management. In *Proceedings of the Seventh International Conference on Functional Programming Languages and Computer Architecture (FPCA'95)*, pages 66–77, La Jolla, California, June 25-28, 1995. ACM SIGPLAN/SIGARCH and IFIP WG2.8, ACM Press.

Morrisett, Greg, David Walker, Karl Crary, and Neal Glew. From System F to Typed Assembly Language. In *ACM Symposium on Principles of Programming Languages (POPL), San Diego, California*, pages 85–97, January 1998.

Mugridge, Warwick B., John Hamer, and John G. Hosking. Multi-methods in a statically-typed programming language. In Pierre America, editor, *ECOOP '91: European Conference on Object-Oriented Programming*, volume 512 of *Lecture Notes in Computer Science*, pages 307–324. Springer-Verlag, 1991.

Mycroft, Alan. Dynamic types in ML. Manuscript, 1983.

Mycroft, Alan. Polymorphic type schemes and recursive definitions. In M. Paul and B. Robinet, editors, *Proceedings of the International Symposium on Programming*, volume 167 of *LNCS*, pages 217–228, Toulouse, France, April 1984. Springer.

Myers, Andrew C., Joseph A. Bank, and Barbara Liskov. Parameterized types for Java. In *ACM Symposium on Principles of Programming Languages (POPL), Paris, France*, pages 132–145, January 1997.

Nadathur, Gopalan and Dale Miller. An overview of λProlog. In Robert A. Kowalski and Kenneth A. Bowen, editors, *Logic Programming: Proceedings of the Fifth International Conference and Symposium, Volume 1*, pages 810–827, MIT Press, Cambridge, Massachusetts, August 1988.

Naur, Peter et al. Revised report on the algorithmic language Algol 60. *Communications of the ACM*, 6:1-17, January 1963.

Necula, George C. Proof-carrying code. In *ACM Symposium on Principles of Programming Languages (POPL), Paris, France*, pages 106–119, 15-17 January 1997.

Necula, George C. and Peter Lee. Safe kernel extensions without run-time checking. In *2nd Symposium on Operating Systems Design and Implementation (OSDI '96), October 28-31, 1996, Seattle, WA*, pages 229-243, Berkeley, CA, USA, October 1996. USENIX press.

Necula, George C. and Peter Lee. Safe, untrusted agents using proof-carrying code. In G. Vigna, editor, *Mobile Agents and Security*, volume 1419 of *Lecture Notes in Computer Science*, pages 61–91. Springer-Verlag, 1998.

Nelson, Greg, editor. *Systems Programming with Modula-3*. Prentice-Hall, 1991.

Nipkow, Tobias and David von Oheimb. Java$_{light}$ is type-safe — definitely. In *ACM Symposium on Principles of Programming Languages (POPL), San Diego, California*, pages 161–170, January 1998.

O'Callahan, Robert and Daniel Jackson. Lackwit: A program understanding tool based on type inference. In *Proceedings of the 1997 International Conference on Software Engineering*, pages 338–348. ACM Press, 1997.

Odersky, Martin. Functional nets. In *Proc. European Symposium on Programming (ESOP)*, pages 1–25. Springer-Verlag, 2000. Lecture Notes in Computer Science 1782.

Odersky, Martin and Konstantin Läufer. Putting type annotations to work. In *ACM Symposium on Principles of Programming Languages (POPL), St. Petersburg Beach, Florida*, pages 54–67, St. Petersburg, Florida, January 21–24, 1996. ACM Press.

Odersky, Martin, Martin Sulzmann, and Martin Wehr. Type inference with constrained types. *Theory and Practice of Object Systems*, 5(1):35–55, 1999. Summary in *Workshop on Foundations of Object-Oriented Languages (FOOL), informal proceedings*, 1997.

Odersky, Martin and Philip Wadler. Pizza into Java: Translating theory into practice. In *ACM Symposium on Principles of Programming Languages (POPL), Paris, France*, pages 146–159, January 1997.

Odersky, Martin and Christoph Zenger. Nested types. In *Workshop on Foundations of Object-Oriented Languages (FOOL 8)*, January 2001.

Odersky, Martin, Christoph Zenger, and Matthias Zenger. Colored local type inference. *ACM SIGPLAN Notices*, 36(3):41–53, March 2001.

O'Hearn, Peter W., Makoto Takeyama, A. John Power, and Robert D. Tennent. Syntactic control of interference revisited. In *MFPS XI, conference on Mathematical Foundations of Program Semantics*, volume 1 of *Electronic Notes in Theoretical Computer Science*. Elsevier, March 1995.

O'Toole, James W. and David K. Gifford. Type reconstruction with first-class polymorphic values. In *ACM SIGPLAN Conference on Programming Language Design and Implementation (PLDI), Portland, Oregon*, pages 207–217, June 1989.

Palsberg, Jens and Christina Pavlopoulou. From polyvariant flow information to intersection and union types. In *ACM Symposium on Principles of Programming Languages (POPL), San Diego, California*, pages 197–208, 1998.

Palsberg, Jens and Michael I. Schwartzbach. *Object-Oriented Type Systems*. Wiley, 1994.

Park, David. Concurrency and automata on infinite sequences. In P. Deussen, editor, *Proceedings of the 5th GI-Conference on Theoretical Computer Science*, volume 104 of *Lecture Notes in Computer Science*, pages 167–183. Springer-Verlag, Berlin, 1981.

Paulin-Mohring, Christine. Extracting F_ω's programs from proofs in the calculus of constructions. In *ACM Symposium on Principles of Programming Languages (POPL), Austin, Texas*, pages 89–104, January 1989.

Paulson, Laurence C. *ML for the Working Programmer*. Cambridge University Press, New York, NY, second edition, 1996.

Perry, Nigel. *The Implementation of Practical Functional Programming Languages.* PhD thesis, Imperial College, 1990.

Peyton Jones, Simon L. and David R. Lester. *Implementing Functional Languages.* Prentice Hall, 1992.

Pfenning, Frank. Partial polymorphic type inference and higher-order unification. In *ACM Symposium on Lisp and Functional Programming (LFP), Snowbird, Utah,* pages 153–163, July 1988. Also available as Ergo Report 88-048, School of Computer Science, Carnegie Mellon University, Pittsburgh.

Pfenning, Frank. Elf: A language for logic definition and verified meta-programming. In *Fourth Annual Symposium on Logic in Computer Science,* pages 313–322, Pacific Grove, California, June 1989. IEEE Computer Society Press.

Pfenning, Frank. On the undecidability of partial polymorphic type reconstruction. *Fundamenta Informaticae,* 19(1,2):185–199, 1993a. Preliminary version available as Technical Report CMU-CS-92-105, School of Computer Science, Carnegie Mellon University, January 1992.

Pfenning, Frank. Refinement types for logical frameworks. In Herman Geuvers, editor, *Informal Proceedings of the Workshop on Types for Proofs and Programs,* pages 285–299, Nijmegen, The Netherlands, May 1993b.

Pfenning, Frank. Elf: A meta-language for deductive systems. In A. Bundy, editor, *Proceedings of the 12th International Conference on Automated Deduction,* pages 811–815, Nancy, France, June 1994. Springer-Verlag LNAI 814.

Pfenning, Frank. The practice of logical frameworks. In Hélène Kirchner, editor, *Proceedings of the Colloquium on Trees in Algebra and Programming,* pages 119–134, Linköping, Sweden, April 1996. Springer-Verlag LNCS 1059. Invited talk.

Pfenning, Frank. Logical frameworks. In Alan Robinson and Andrei Voronkov, editors, *Handbook of Automated Reasoning.* Elsevier, 1999.

Pfenning, Frank. *Computation and Deduction.* Cambridge University Press, 2001.

Pfenning, Frank and Peter Lee. Metacircularity in the polymorphic λ-calculus. *Theoretical Computer Science,* 89(1):137–159, 21 October 1991. Summary in *TAPSOFT '89, Proceedings of the International Joint Conference on Theory and Practice in Software Development, Barcelona, Spain,* pages 345–359, Springer-Verlag LNCS 352, March 1989.

Pierce, Benjamin C. *Basic Category Theory for Computer Scientists.* MIT Press, 1991a.

Pierce, Benjamin C. *Programming with Intersection Types and Bounded Polymorphism.* PhD thesis, Carnegie Mellon University, December 1991b. Available as School of Computer Science technical report CMU-CS-91-205.

Pierce, Benjamin C. Bounded quantification is undecidable. *Information and Computation,* 112(1):131–165, July 1994. Also in Carl A. Gunter and John C. Mitchell, editors, *Theoretical Aspects of Object-Oriented Programming: Types, Semantics, and Language Design* (MIT Press, 1994). Summary in *ACM Symposium on Principles of Programming Languages (POPL), Albuquerque, New Mexico.*

Pierce, Benjamin C. Even simpler type-theoretic foundations for OOP. Manuscript (circulated electronically), March 1996.

Pierce, Benjamin C. Bounded quantification with bottom. Technical Report 492, Computer Science Department, Indiana University, 1997a.

Pierce, Benjamin C. Intersection types and bounded polymorphism. *Mathematical Structures in Computer Science*, 7(2):129–193, April 1997b. Summary in *Typed Lambda Calculi and Applications*, March 1993, pp. 346–360.

Pierce, Benjamin C. and Davide Sangiorgi. Typing and subtyping for mobile processes. In *Logic in Computer Science*, 1993. Full version in *Mathematical Structures in Computer Science* , Vol. 6, No. 5, 1996.

Pierce, Benjamin C. and Martin Steffen. Higher-order subtyping. In *IFIP Working Conference on Programming Concepts, Methods and Calculi (PROCOMET)*, 1994. Full version in *Theoretical Computer Science*, vol. 176, no. 1-2, pp. 235–282, 1997 (corrigendum in TCS vol. 184 (1997), p. 247).

Pierce, Benjamin C. and David N. Turner. Statically typed friendly functions via partially abstract types. Technical Report ECS-LFCS-93-256, University of Edinburgh, LFCS, April 1993. Also available as INRIA-Rocquencourt Rapport de Recherche No. 1899.

Pierce, Benjamin C. and David N. Turner. Simple type-theoretic foundations for object-oriented programming. *Journal of Functional Programming*, 4(2):207–247, April 1994. Summary in *ACM Symposium on Principles of Programming Languages (POPL), Charleston, South Carolina*, 1993.

Pierce, Benjamin C. and David N. Turner. Local type argument synthesis with bounded quantification. Technical Report 495, Computer Science Department, Indiana University, January 1997.

Pierce, Benjamin C. and David N. Turner. Local type inference. In *ACM Symposium on Principles of Programming Languages (POPL), San Diego, California*, 1998. Full version in *ACM Transactions on Programming Languages and Systems (TOPLAS)*, 22(1), January 2000, pp. 1–44.

Pierce, Benjamin C. and David N. Turner. Pict: A programming language based on the pi-calculus. In Gordon Plotkin, Colin Stirling, and Mads Tofte, editors, *Proof, Language and Interaction: Essays in Honour of Robin Milner*, pages 455–494. MIT Press, 2000.

Pitts, Andrew M. Polymorphism is set theoretic, constructively. In Pitt, Poigné, and Rydeheard, editors, *Category Theory and Computer Science, Edinburgh*, pages 12–39. Springer-Verlag, 1987. LNCS volume 283.

Pitts, Andrew M. Non-trivial power types can't be subtypes of polymorphic types. In *Fourth Annual Symposium on Logic in Computer Science, Pacific Grove, California*, pages 6–13. IEEE, June 1989.

Pitts, Andrew M. Parametric polymorphism and operational equivalence. *Mathematical Structures in Computer Science*, 10:321–359, 2000.

Plasmeijer, Marinus J. CLEAN: a programming environment based on term graph rewriting. *Theoretical Computer Science*, 194(1–2), March 1998.

Plotkin, Gordon. Call-by-name, call-by-value, and the λ-calculus. *Theoretical Computer Science*, 1:125–159, 1975.

Plotkin, Gordon and Martín Abadi. A logic for parametric polymorphism. In M. Bezem and J. F. Groote, editors, *Typed Lambda Calculi and Applications (TLCA), Utrecht, The Netherlands*, number 664 in Lecture Notes in Computer Science, pages 361–375. Springer-Verlag, March 1993.

Plotkin, Gordon, Martín Abadi, and Luca Cardelli. Subtyping and parametricity. In *Proceedings of the Ninth IEEE Symposium on Logic in Computer Science*, pages 310–319, 1994.

Plotkin, Gordon D. Lambda-definability and logical relations. Memorandum SAI-RM-4, University of Edinburgh, Edinburgh, Scotland, October 1973.

Plotkin, Gordon D. LCF considered as a programming language. *Theoretical Computer Science*, 5:223–255, 1977.

Plotkin, Gordon D. Lambda-definability in the full type hierarchy. In Jonathan P. Seldin and J. Roger Hindley, editors, *To H. B. Curry: Essays on Combinatory Logic, Lambda Calculus and Formalism*, pages 363–373. Academic Press, London, 1980.

Plotkin, Gordon D. A structural approach to operational semantics. Technical Report DAIMI FN-19, Computer Science Department, Aarhus University, Aarhus, Denmark, 1981.

Poll, Erik. Width-subtyping and polymorphic record update. Manuscript, June 1996.

Pollack, Robert. Implicit syntax. Informal Proceedings of First Workshop on Logical Frameworks, Antibes, May 1990.

Pollack, Robert. *The Theory of LEGO: A Proof Checker for the Extended Calculus of Constructions*. PhD thesis, University of Edinburgh, 1994.

Pottier, François. Simplifying subtyping constraints. In *International Conference on Functional Programming (ICFP), Amsterdam, The Netherlands*, 1997.

Pottinger, Garrell. A type assignment for the strongly normalizable λ-terms. In *To H. B. Curry: Essays on Combinatory Logic, Lambda Calculus, and Formalism*, pages 561–577. Academic Press, New York, 1980.

Quine, Willard V. *Quiddities: An Intermittently Philosophical Dictionary*. Harvard University Press, Cambridge, MA, 1987.

Ramsey, Frank P. The foundations of mathematics. *Proceedings of the London Mathematical Society, Series 2*, 25(5):338–384, 1925. Reprinted in (Braithwaite, 1931).

Ranta, Aarne. *Type-Theoretical Grammar*. Clarendon Press, Oxford, 1995.

Reade, Chris. *Elements of Functional Programming*. International Computer Science Series. Addison-Wesley, Wokingham, England, 1989.

Reddy, Uday S. Objects as closures: Abstract semantics of object oriented languages. In *ACM Symposium on Lisp and Functional Programming (LFP), Snowbird, Utah*, pages 289–297, Snowbird, Utah, July 1988.

Relax. Document Description and Processing Languages — Regular Language Description for XML (RELAX) — Part 1: RELAX Core. Technical Report DTR 22250-1, ISO/IEC, October 2000.

Rémy, Didier. Typechecking records and variants in a natural extension of ML. In *ACM Symposium on Principles of Programming Languages (POPL), Austin, Texas*, pages 242–249, January 1989. Long version in Carl A. Gunter and John C. Mitchell, editors, *Theoretical Aspects of Object-Oriented Programming: Types, Semantics, and Language Design* (MIT Press, 1994).

Rémy, Didier. *Algèbres Touffues. Application au Typage Polymorphe des Objets Enregistrements dans les Langages Fonctionnels.* PhD thesis, Université Paris VII, 1990.

Rémy, Didier. Extending ML type system with a sorted equational theory. Research Report 1766, Institut National de Recherche en Informatique et Automatisme, Rocquencourt, BP 105, 78 153 Le Chesnay Cedex, France, 1992a.

Rémy, Didier. Projective ML. In *ACM Symposium on Lisp and Functional Programming (LFP)*, pages 66–75, 1992b.

Rémy, Didier. Typing record concatenation for free. In *ACM Symposium on Principles of Programming Languages (POPL), Albuquerque, New Mexico*, January 1992. Also in Carl A. Gunter and John C. Mitchell, editors, *Theoretical Aspects of Object-Oriented Programming: Types, Semantics, and Language Design* (MIT Press, 1994).

Rémy, Didier. Programming objects with ML-ART: An extension to ML with abstract and record types. In Masami Hagiya and John C. Mitchell, editors, *International Symposium on Theoretical Aspects of Computer Software (TACS)*, pages 321–346, Sendai, Japan, April 1994. Springer-Verlag.

Rémy, Didier. *Des enregistrements aux objets.* Mémoire d'habilitation à diriger des recherches, Université de Paris 7, 1998. In English, except for introductory chapter; includes (Rémy, 1989) and (Rémy, 1992b).

Rémy, Didier and Jérôme Vouillon. Objective ML: An effective object-oriented extension to ML. *Theory And Practice of Object Systems*, 4(1):27–50, 1998. Summary in *ACM Symposium on Principles of Programming Languages (POPL), Paris, France*, 1997.

Reynolds, John. Three approaches to type structure. In *Mathematical Foundations of Software Development*. Springer-Verlag, 1985. Lecture Notes in Computer Science No. 185.

Reynolds, John C. Towards a theory of type structure. In *Proc. Colloque sur la Programmation*, pages 408–425, New York, 1974. Springer-Verlag LNCS 19.

Reynolds, John C. User-defined types and procedural data structures as complementary approaches to data abstraction. In Stephen A. Schuman, editor, *New Directions in Algorithmic Languages 1975*, pages 157–168, Rocquencourt, France, 1975. IFIP

Working Group 2.1 on Algol, INRIA. Reprinted in (Gries, 1978, pages 309–317) and (Gunter and Mitchell, 1994, pages 13–23).

Reynolds, John C. Syntactic control of interference. In *ACM Symposium on Principles of Programming Languages (POPL), Tucson, Arizona*, pages 39–46, 1978. Reprinted in O'Hearn and Tennent, *ALGOL-like Languages*, vol. 1, pages 273–286, Birkhäuser, 1997.

Reynolds, John C. Using category theory to design implicit conversions and generic operators. In N. D. Jones, editor, *Proceedings of the Aarhus Workshop on Semantics-Directed Compiler Generation*, number 94 in Lecture Notes in Computer Science. Springer-Verlag, January 1980. Also in Carl A. Gunter and John C. Mitchell, editors, *Theoretical Aspects of Object-Oriented Programming: Types, Semantics, and Language Design* (MIT Press, 1994).

Reynolds, John C. *The Craft of Programming*. Prentice-Hall International, London, 1981.

Reynolds, John C. Types, abstraction, and parametric polymorphism. In R. E. A. Mason, editor, *Information Processing 83*, pages 513–523, Amsterdam, 1983. Elsevier Science Publishers B. V. (North-Holland).

Reynolds, John C. Polymorphism is not set-theoretic. In G. Kahn, D. B. MacQueen, and G. D. Plotkin, editors, *Semantics of Data Types*, volume 173 of *Lecture Notes in Computer Science*, pages 145–156, Berlin, 1984. Springer-Verlag.

Reynolds, John C. Preliminary design of the programming language Forsythe. Technical Report CMU-CS-88-159, Carnegie Mellon University, June 1988. Reprinted in O'Hearn and Tennent, *ALGOL-like Languages*, vol. 1, pages 173–233, Birkhäuser, 1997.

Reynolds, John C. Syntactic control of interference, part 2. Report CMU-CS-89-130, Carnegie Mellon University, April 1989.

Reynolds, John C. Introduction to part II, polymorphic lambda calculus. In Gérard Huet, editor, *Logical Foundations of Functional Programming*, pages 77–86. Addison-Wesley, Reading, Massachusetts, 1990.

Reynolds, John C. The coherence of languages with intersection types. In T. Ito and A. R. Meyer, editors, *Theoretical Aspects of Computer Software (Sendai, Japan)*, number 526 in Lecture Notes in Computer Science, pages 675–700. Springer-Verlag, September 1991.

Reynolds, John C. Normalization and functor categories. In Olivier Danvy and Peter Dybjer, editors, *Preliminary Proceedings of the 1998 APPSEM Workshop on Normalization by Evaluation, NBE '98,* (Chalmers, Sweden, May 8–9, 1998), number NS-98-1 in BRICS Note Series, Department of Computer Science, University of Aarhus, May 1998a.

Reynolds, John C. *Theories of Programming Languages*. Cambridge University Press, 1998b.

Reynolds, John C. and Gordon Plotkin. On functors expressible in the polymorphic typed lambda calculus. *Information and Computation*, 105(1):1–29, 1993. Summary in (Huet, 1990).

Robinson, Edmund and Robert Tennent. Bounded quantification and record-update problems. Message to Types electronic mail list, October 1988.

Robinson, J. Alan. Computational logic: The unification computation. *Machine Intelligence*, 6:63–72, 1971.

Russell, Bertrand. Letter to Frege, 1902. Reprinted (in English) in J. van Heijenort, editor, *From Frege to Gödel: A Source Book in Mathematical Logic, 1879–1931*; Harvard University Press, Cambridge, MA, 1967; pages 124–125.

Schaffert, Justin Craig. A formal definition of CLU. Master's thesis, MIT, January 1978. MIT/LCS/TR-193.

Scheifler, Robert William. A denotational semantics of CLU. Master's thesis, MIT, May 1978. MIT/LCS/TR-201.

Schmidt, David A. *Denotational Semantics: A Methodology for Language Development*. Allyn and Bacon, 1986.

Schmidt, David A. *The Structure of Typed Programming Languages*. MIT Press, 1994.

Schönfinkel, Moses. Über die Bausteine der mathematischen Logik. *Mathematische Annalen*, 92:305–316, 1924. Translated into English and republished as "On the building blocks of mathematical logic" in (van Heijenoort, 1967, pp. 355–366).

Scott, Michael L. *Programming Language Pragmatics*. Morgan Kaufmann, 1999.

Severi, Paula and Erik Poll. Pure type systems with definitions. In *Proceedings of Logical Foundations of Computer Science (LFCS)*, pages 316–328. Springer-Verlag, 1994. LNCS volume 813.

Shalit, Andrew. *The Dylan Reference Manual: The Definitive Guide to the New Object-Oriented Dynamic Language*. Addison-Wesley, Reading, Mass., 1997.

Shields, Mark. *Static Types for Dynamic Documents*. PhD thesis, Department of Computer Science, Oregon Graduate Institute, February 2001.

Simmons, Harold. *Derivation and Computation : Taking the Curry-Howard Correspondence Seriously*. Number 51 in Cambridge Tracts in Theoretical Computer Science. Cambridge University Press, 2000.

Smith, Frederick, David Walker, and Greg Morrisett. Alias types. In Gert Smolka, editor, *Ninth European Symposium on Programming*, volume 1782 of *Lecture Notes in Computer Science*, pages 366–381. Springer-Verlag, April 2000.

Smith, Jan, Bengt Nordström, and Kent Petersson. *Programming in Martin-Löf's Type Theory. An Introduction*. Oxford University Press, 1990.

Solomon, Marvin. Type definitions with parameters. In *ACM Symposium on Principles of Programming Languages (POPL), Tucson, Arizona*, pages 31–38, January 23–25, 1978.

Sommaruga, Giovanni. *History and Philosophy of Constructive Type Theory*, volume 290 of *Synthese Library*. Kluwer Academic Pub., 2000.

Somogyi, Zoltan, Fergus Henderson, and Thomas Conway. The execution algorithm of Mercury, an efficient purely declarative logic programming language. *Journal of Logic Programming*, 29(1-3):17-64, October–November 1996.

Sørensen, Morten Heine and Paweł Urzyczyn. Lectures on the Curry-Howard isomorphism. Technical Report 98/14 (= TOPPS note D-368), DIKU, Copenhagen, 1998.

Statman, Richard. Completeness, invariance and λ-definability. *Journal of Symbolic Logic*, 47(1):17-26, 1982.

Statman, Richard. Equality between functionals, revisited. In *Harvey Friedman's Research on the Foundations of Mathematics*, pages 331-338. North-Holland, Amsterdam, 1985a.

Statman, Richard. Logical relations and the typed λ-calculus. *Information and Control*, 65(2-3):85-97, May–June 1985b.

Steffen, Martin. *Polarized Higher-Order Subtyping*. PhD thesis, Universität Erlangen-Nürnberg, 1998.

Stone, Christopher A. and Robert Harper. Deciding type equivalence in a language with singleton kinds. In *ACM Symposium on Principles of Programming Languages (POPL), Boston, Massachusetts*, pages 214-227, January 19-21, 2000.

Strachey, Christopher. Fundamental concepts in programming languages. Lecture Notes, International Summer School in Computer Programming, Copenhagen, August 1967. Reprinted in *Higher-Order and Symbolic Computation*, 13(1/2), pp. 1-49, 2000.

Stroustrup, Bjarne. *The C++ Programming Language*. Addison Wesley Longman, Reading, MA, third edition, 1997.

Studer, Thomas. Constructive foundations for featherweight java. In R. Kahle, P. Schroeder-Heister, and R. Stärk, editors, *Proof Theory in Computer Science*. Springer-Verlag, 2001. Lecture Notes in Computer Science, volume 2183.

Sumii, Eijiro and Benjamin C. Pierce. Logical relations for encryption. In *Computer Security Foundations Workshop*, June 2001. Submitted (by invitation) to *Journal of Computer Security*.

Sussman, Gerald Jay and Guy Lewis Steele, Jr. Scheme: an interpreter for extended lambda calculus. MIT AI Memo 349, Massachusetts Institute of Technology, December 1975. Reprinted, with a foreword, in *Higher-Order and Symbolic Computation*, 11(4), pp. 405-439, 1998.

Syme, Don. Proving Java type soundness. Technical Report 427, Computer Laboratory, University of Cambridge, June 1997.

Tait, William W. Intensional interpretations of functionals of finite type I. *Journal of Symbolic Logic*, 32(2):198-212, June 1967.

Tait, William W. A realizability interpretation of the theory of species. In R. Parikh, editor, *Logic Colloquium*, volume 453 of *Lecture Notes in Mathematics*, pages 240–251, Boston, 1975. Springer-Verlag.

Talpin, Jean-Pierre and Pierre Jouvelot. The type and effects discipline. In *Proc. IEEE Symp. on Logic in Computer Science*, pages 162–173, 1992.

Tarditi, David, Greg Morrisett, Perry Cheng, Christopher Stone, Robert Harper, and Peter Lee. TIL : A type-directed optimizing compiler for ML. In *ACM SIGPLAN Conference on Programming Language Design and Implementation (PLDI), Philadephia, Pennsylvania*, pages 181–192, May 21–24 1996.

Tarski, Alfred. A lattice-theoretical fixpoint theorem and its applications. *Pacific Journal of Mathematics*, 5:285–309, 1955.

Tennent, Robert D. *Principles of Programming Languages*. Prentice-Hall, 1981.

Terlouw, J. Een nadere bewijstheoretische analyse van GSTTs. Manuscript, University of Nijmegen, Netherlands, 1989.

Thatte, Satish R. Quasi-static typing (preliminary report). In *ACM Symposium on Principles of Programming Languages (POPL), San Francisco, California*, pages 367–381, 1990.

Thompson, Simon. *Type Theory and Functional Programming*. Addison Wesley, 1991.

Thompson, Simon. *Haskell: The Craft of Functional Programming*. Addison Wesley, 1999.

Tiuryn, Jerzy. Type inference problems: A survey. In B. Rovan, editor, *Mathematical Foundations of Computer Science 1990, Banskà Bystrica, Czechoslovakia*, volume 452 of *Lecture Notes in Computer Science*, pages 105–120. Springer-Verlag, New York, NY, 1990.

Tofte and Birkedal. A region inference algorithm. *ACMTOPLAS: ACM Transactions on Programming Languages and Systems*, 20, 1998.

Tofte, Mads. Type inference for polymorphic references. *Information and Computation*, 89(1), November 1990.

Tofte, Mads and Jean-Pierre Talpin. Implementing the call-by-value lambda-calculus using a stack of regions. In *ACM Symposium on Principles of Programming Languages (POPL), Portland, Oregon*, January 1994.

Tofte, Mads and Jean-Pierre Talpin. Region-based memory management. *Information and Computation*, 132(2):109–176, 1 February 1997.

Trifonov, Valery and Scott Smith. Subtyping constrained types. In *Proceedings of the Third International Static Analysis Symposium*, volume 1145 of *LNCS*, pages 349–365. Springer-Verlag, September 1996.

Turner, David N., Philip Wadler, and Christian Mossin. Once upon a type. In *ACM Symposium on Functional Programming Languages and Computer Architecture (FPCA), San Diego, California*, 1995.

Turner, Raymond. *Constructive Foundations for Functional Languages*. McGraw Hill, 1991.

Ullman, Jeffrey D. *Elements of ML Programming*. Prentice-Hall, ML97 edition, 1997.

Ungar, David and Randall B. Smith. Self: The power of simplicity. In *ACM Symposium on Object Oriented Programming: Systems, Languages, and Applications (OOPSLA)*, pages 227–241, 1987.

U.S. Dept. of Defense. *Reference Manual for the Ada Programming Language*. GPO 008-000-00354-8, 1980.

van Benthem, Johan. *Language in Action: Categories, Lambdas, and Dynamic Logic*. MIT Press, 1995.

van Benthem, Johan F. A. K. and Alice Ter Meulen, editors. *Handbook of Logic and Language*. MIT Press, 1997.

van Heijenoort, Jan, editor. *From Frege to Gödel*. Harvard University Press, Cambridge, Massachusetts, 1967.

van Wijngaarden, Adriaan, B. J. Mailloux, J. E. L. Peck, C. H. A. Koster, M. Sintzoff, C. H. Lindsey, L. G. L. T. Meertens, and R. G. Fisker. Revised report on the algorithmic language ALGOL 68. *Acta Informatica*, 5(1–3):1–236, 1975.

Vouillon, Jérôme. *Conception et réalisation d'une extension du langage ML avec des objets*. PhD thesis, Université Paris 7, October 2000.

Vouillon, Jérôme. Combining subsumption and binary methods: An object calculus with views. In *ACM Symposium on Principles of Programming Languages (POPL), London, England*, 2001.

Wadler, Philip. Theorems for free! In *Functional Programming Languages and Computer Architecture*, pages 347–359. ACM Press, September 1989. Imperial College, London.

Wadler, Philip. Linear types can change the world. In *TC 2 Working Conference on Programming Concepts and Methods (Preprint)*, pages 546–566, 1990.

Wadler, Philip. Is there a use for linear logic? In *Proceedings of ACM Symposium on Partial Evaluation and Semantics-Based Program Manipulation*, pages 255–273, 1991.

Wadler, Philip. New languages, old logic. *Dr. Dobbs Journal*, December 2000.

Wadler, Philip. The Girard-Reynolds isomorphism. In Naoki Kobayashi and Benjamin Pierce, editors, *Theoretical Aspects of Computer Software (TACS), Sendai, Japan*, Lecture Notes in Computer Science. Springer-Verlag, 2001.

Wadler, Philip and Stephen Blott. How to make *ad-hoc* polymorphism less *ad hoc*. In *ACM Symposium on Principles of Programming Languages (POPL), Austin, Texas*, pages 60–76, 1989.

Wadsworth, Christopher P. *Semantics and pragmatics of the lambda-calculus*. PhD thesis, Programming Research Group, Oxford University, 1971.

Wand, Mitchell. Finding the source of type errors. *13th ACM SIGACT-SIGPLAN Symposium on Principles of Programming Languages (POPL)*, pages 38–43, 1986.

Wand, Mitchell. Complete type inference for simple objects. In *Proceedings of the IEEE Symposium on Logic in Computer Science*, Ithaca, NY, June 1987.

Wand, Mitchell. Corrigendum: Complete type inference for simple objects. In *Proceedings of the IEEE Symposium on Logic in Computer Science*, 1988.

Wand, Mitchell. Type inference for objects with instance variables and inheritance. Technical Report NU-CCS-89-2, College of Computer Science, Northeastern University, February 1989a. Also in Carl A. Gunter and John C. Mitchell, editors, *Theoretical Aspects of Object-Oriented Programming: Types, Semantics, and Language Design* (MIT Press, 1994).

Wand, Mitchell. Type inference for record concatenation and multiple inheritance. In *Fourth Annual IEEE Symposium on Logic in Computer Science*, pages 92–97, Pacific Grove, CA, June 1989b.

Weis, Pierre, María-Virginia Aponte, Alain Laville, Michel Mauny, and Ascánder Suárez. The CAML reference manual, Version 2.6. Technical report, Projet Formel, INRIA-ENS, 1989.

Wells, Joe B. Typability and type checking in the second-order λ-calculus are equivalent and undecidable. In *Proceedings of the Ninth Annual IEEE Symposium on Logic in Computer Science (LICS)*, pages 176–185, 1994.

Whitehead, Alfred North and Bertrand Russell. *Principia Mathematica*. Cambridge University Press, Cambridge, 1910. Three volumes (1910; 1912; 1913).

Wickline, Philip, Peter Lee, Frank Pfenning, and Rowan Davies. Modal types as staging specifications for run-time code generation. *ACM Computing Surveys*, 30(3es), September 1998. Article 8.

Wille, Christoph. *Presenting C#*. SAMS Publishing, 2000.

Winskel, Glynn. *The Formal Semantics of Programming Languages: An Introduction*. MIT Press, 1993.

Wirth, Niklaus. The programming language Pascal. *Acta Informatica*, 1(1):35–63, 1971.

Wright, Andrew K. Typing references by effect inference. In Bernd Krieg-Bruckner, editor, *ESOP '92, 4th European Symposium on Programming, Rennes, France*, volume 582 of *Lecture Notes in Computer Science*, pages 473–491. Springer-Verlag, New York, N.Y., 1992.

Wright, Andrew K. Simple imperative polymorphism. *Lisp and Symbolic Computation*, 8(4):343–355, 1995.

Wright, Andrew K. and Matthias Felleisen. A syntactic approach to type soundness. *Information and Computation*, 115(1):38–94, 15 November 1994.

Xi, Hongwei and Robert Harper. A dependently typed assembly language. In *International Conference on Functional Programming (ICFP), Firenze, Italy*, 2001.

Xi, Hongwei and Frank Pfenning. Eliminating array bound checking through dependent types. In *ACM SIGPLAN Conference on Programming Language Design and Implementation (PLDI), Montreal, Canada*, pages 249–257, 1998.

Xi, Hongwei and Frank Pfenning. Dependent types in practical programming. In *ACM Symposium on Principles of Programming Languages (POPL), San Antonio, Texas*, ACM SIGPLAN Notices, pages 214–227, 1999.

XML 1998. Extensible markup language (XML™), February 1998. XML 1.0, W3C Recommendation, `http://www.w3.org/XML/`.

XS 2000. XML Schema Part 0: Primer, W3C Working Draft. `http://www.w3.org/TR/xmlschema-0/`, 2000.

Yelick, Kathy, Luigi Semenzato, Geoff Pike, Carleton Miyamoto, Ben Liblit, Arvind Krishnamurthy, Paul Hilfinger, Susan Graham, David Gay, Phil Colella, and Alex Aiken. Titanium: a high-performance Java dialect. *Concurrency: Practice and Experience*, 10(11–13):825–836, September 1998. Special Issue: Java for High-performance Network Computing.

Zwanenburg, Jan. Pure type systems with subtyping. In J.-Y. Girard, editor, *Typed Lambda Calculus and Applications (TLCA)*, pages 381–396. Springer-Verlag, 1999. Lecture Notes in Computer Science, volume 1581.

The secret to creativity is knowing how to hide your sources. —Albert Einstein

Index